Allen Dennie

A MANUAL OF
PRONUNCIATION

MORRISS H. NEEDLEMAN

CO-AUTHOR OF *A Survey-History of English Literature, An Outline-History of American Literature*

New York

BARNES & NOBLE, INC.

COLLEGE OUTLINE SERIES

Barnes & Noble, Inc., Publishers, 105 Fifth Ave., New York 3, N.Y.

ACCOUNTING, Elementary
ACCOUNTING PROBLEMS with Answers
ALGEBRA, College
AMERICAN Colonial and Revolutionary History
AMERICAN LITERATURE
ANCIENT History
ANCIENT, Medieval, and Modern History
ANTHROPOLOGY, General

BACTERIOLOGY: Principles and Practice
BIOLOGY, General
BOTANY, General
BUSINESS AND GOVERNMENT
BUSINESS LAW

CALCULUS
CHEMISTRY, First-Year College
CHEMISTRY, Mathematics for General
CHEMISTRY, Organic
CORPORATION FINANCE

DOCUMENTED PAPERS, Writing

ECONOMICS: Dictionary
ECONOMICS: Principles
ECONOMICS: Readings
EDUCATION: History
ENGLAND: History
ENGLISH GRAMMAR
ENGLISH LITERATURE: Dictionary
ENGLISH LITERATURE: History, to Dryden
ENGLISH LITERATURE: History, since Milton
EUROPE, 1500–1848: History
EUROPE since 1815: History
EXAMINATIONS, How to Write Better

FRENCH GRAMMAR

GEOLOGY: Principles
GEOMETRY, Analytic
GEOMETRY, Plane: Problems
GERMAN GRAMMAR
GERMAN LITERATURE
GOVERNMENT, American

HYDRAULICS for Firemen

INTERNATIONAL RELATIONS

JOURNALISM: Survey

LABOR PROBLEMS and Trade Unionism
LATIN AMERICA: History
LATIN AMERICA in Maps
LATIN AMERICAN Civilization: Readings
LATIN AMERICAN Economic Development
LOGARITHMIC and Trigonometric Tables

MARKETING
MIDDLE AGES: History
MONEY AND BANKING
MUSIC: History

PHILOSOPHY: Introduction
PHILOSOPHY: Readings
PHYSICS, First-Year College
PHYSICS without Mathematics
PLAY PRODUCTION
POLITICAL SCIENCE
POLITICS, Dictionary of American
PRONUNCIATION: Manual
PSYCHOLOGY, Educational
PSYCHOLOGY, General
PUNCTUATION

RESEARCH AND REPORT WRITING
RUSSIA: History

SHAKESPEAREAN NAMES: Dictionary
SHAKESPEARE'S PLAYS: Outlines
SLIDE RULE, Practical Use of
SOCIOLOGY: Principles
SOCIOLOGY: Readings
SPANISH GRAMMAR
STATISTICAL METHODS
STATISTICIANS, Tables for
STUDY: Best Methods

TRIGONOMETRY
TUDOR AND STUART PLAYS: Outlines

UNITED STATES to 1865: History
UNITED STATES since 1865: History
UNITED STATES in the Second World War

WORLD since 1914: History

ZOOLOGY, General

PREFACE

This *Manual of Pronunciation* differs from similar handbooks in several particulars:

1. The introductory GUIDE TO PRONUNCIATION is intended not as an original contribution to speech study, but as an orderly synthesis of what has been stated in more specialized publications. In discussing the approximately 44 sounds represented by about 250 common spellings in the English language, and in analyzing other characteristics of our tongue, the introductory part of this manual has heeded certain principles.

The GUIDE has aimed to present its material simply and completely: taking little for granted, it repeats explanations several times whenever such repetition appears desirable. Condensing the material is not enough, for such reduction often results in abstract statements that the student has difficulty in understanding or in unclear generalizations which he memorizes. To save lines of type at the expense of the consultant's understanding is false economy.

Throughout, the GUIDE has subscribed in the main to the descriptive rather than to the prescriptive school. Suggestions are meant primarily as helps, not as rules; and if any part of the introduction seems dogmatic, it is unintentional.

2. Most lists—perhaps all lists—of words often mispronounced give no consideration to the differences between vocabularies in oral and written materials. Often selected for analysis are "literary" words or "elegant" words or "hard" words. This *Manual of Pronunciation* has, however, weighted frequency of use as the first principle in the selection of entries. Many authorities were consulted for their individual compilations of words most often mispronounced; and those words that showed up most frequently in a master list are entered in this reference book. With few exceptions the list of about 5800 words selected as commonly mispronounced are everyday (or spoken) rather than "literary" (or written) or "elegant" or "hard" words. For example, one expert recommended *chalice* and *chartreuse* for entry. But since no other authority had included *chalice*, that word is excluded from this compilation. As for *chartreuse*, one other consultant did make the recommendation; but since the word was low on the compiled frequency list of words that are likely to be spoken and was also absent from the Thorndike list, that word is also

omitted. It may be noted that about ninety-nine per cent of the words in this *Manual* appears in Edward L. Thorndike's *A Teacher's Word Book of the Twenty Thousand Words* ... (1932).

3. The method of presenting each pronunciation is eclectic yet unique and practical, appealing as it does to the layman, the student, the teacher, and the phonetician. It is common knowledge that many dictionary users do not interpret diacritical marks correctly and fully. For such consultants we recommend the SIMPLIFIED column, which is easier to use not only because it allows only *one* symbol for *one* sound[1] but also because it takes advantage of the fact that the user knows both the values of the letters in the English alphabet and the normal sound of certain combinations of letters. For the student and the teacher familiar with the diacritical marks we recommend the DIACRITICAL column; yet even for them the SIMPLIFIED column might be consulted profitably when there is any doubt as to alternative interpretations of a diacritical symbol. (See SPECIAL NOTES, III, b: page xxi.) Finally, for the student of phonetics, we recommend the PHONETIC column, which lends itself to many obvious uses.

4. No manual or dictionary founded on the methods of modern scholarship can legislate any pronunciation; it can only endeavor to record what usage at any time actually is, including wherever practical any regional variations. Since every language spoken by a living people is normally undergoing constant change, modern language study recognizes not only that it can not provide a body of fixed dogma about pronunciation but also that dictionaries, like grammars, become out of date as time passes. For example, one of our best unabridged dictionaries has not revised its pronunciations since 1934, and consequently its later editions do not as yet record that *grimace* (page 141) is also pronounced acceptably as grĭm′ĭs (*simplified system*, GRIM is; *phonetic system*, ′grɪm ɪs), *program* (page 241) as prō′grăm (*simplified system*, PROH gruhm or PROH gr'm; *phonetic system*, ′pro grəm), and *tourniquet* (page 294) as tûr′nĭ kā (*simplified system*, TUHR ni kay; *phonetic system*, ′tɝ nɪ ke). In this *Manual* the pronunciations are up-to-date, recording what is the prevailing usage or usages among the best speakers of our language. Every pronunciation in the SIMPLIFIED and the DIACRITICAL columns is backed by authority.

5. As a rule, dictionaries record the more formal type of speech and avoid the colloquial kind. This *Manual* recognizes the two types as educated American English, and has endeavored to record both

---

[1] The ideal system for representing sounds is that there should be one symbol for one sound, and one sound for one symbol; or, to be more scientific, one symbol for each phoneme, or family of sounds. Insofar as it has been possible, the SIMPLIFIED column employs one value for each symbol and one symbol for each sound-type.

cultivated formal English and cultivated colloquial English. The standard is General American, with indications in the Phonetic column of the Eastern and the Southern varieties.

6. No single dictionary, not even an Unabridged selling at many times the price of this manual, presents so many pronunciations in good usage for the selected words. No longer need you consult dictionary after dictionary to determine whether you or others are pronouncing a word acceptably. By having the variants this one *Manual of Pronunciation* does the task for you—at a saving of time and expense.[1]

7. Where only one pronunciation is given for a word, the student should not allow himself the privilege of deviating from it. Where more than one pronunciation is given, the student is advised to check off an acceptable pronunciation he is already using; as a rule he should not substitute an alternate pronunciation except for special reasons. Just as a student does not study the spelling of a word he can already spell, so a student should not study the pronunciation of a word he is already pronouncing acceptably—except for comparative or research purposes. Every pronunciation in the Simplified and Diacritical columns is a good pronunciation unless labeled otherwise.

8. The *Manual of Pronunciation* is practical. Within a relatively short time, for example, the layman to whom diacritical marks and phonetic symbols are confusing or unknown can use the Simplified column; and with a little practice he can teach himself to interpret either or both the Diacritical and the Phonetic columns. From years of familiarity with diacritical marks the student or the teacher may prefer the Diacritical column; but both can use not only the Phonetic column but also the Simplified column. For example, *laugh* (page 182) is marked in the Diacritical column as "läf; låf; §§ 20(5), 26(2)." Unless the consultant refers to the sections indicated, he may conclude that the word *laugh* is pronounced with some type of "broad a." But a glance to the left (the Simplified column) shows at once that not only is a kind of "broad a" used but also (and this is a much more frequent sound in that word) the sound of ă as in *at*. Finally, the Phonetic column has more than one practical use: it may be used to habituate transcriptions in IPA (International Phonetic Alphabet) symbols of such pronunciations as are given in the Diacritical column; it may be used to recognize other varieties of speech; and the like.

9. Every pronunciation in the Simplified and the Diacritical columns is in cultivated use unless labeled otherwise. (See point 7

---

[1] It is not claimed that this handbook lists every acceptable pronunciation; it is claimed that this handbook lists *more* acceptable pronunciations than any other dictionary.

above.) On the assumption, however, that a student of phonetics will understand the reason for other variants that are not without warrant, additional pronunciations are given in the PHONETIC column.[1]

10. Phonetic dictionaries do not usually divide the pronunciation into syllables, but we have done so because such division is of help to students. (See, especially, §37.2, page xci, final paragraph.)

Nor are the foregoing ten departures the only particulars in which this *Manual of Pronunciation* deviates from the conventional plan of similar compilations. Consultants, we are confident, will run across many other instances. Tersely, in this one manual will be found the answers to questions for which a number of books are usually required.

All criticisms are welcome. Suggestions that may improve the usefulness of this manual will be incorporated, if possible, in succeeding editions. Kindly address the author in care of Barnes and Noble, Inc., Fifth Avenue at Eighteenth Street, New York 3, N. Y.

MORRISS H. NEEDLEMAN

ACKNOWLEDGMENTS

In preparing the *Manual of Pronunciation* I have fallen under heavy obligation to numerous scholars and teachers whose advice I sought and whose recommendations have materially improved the text. Although it is impossible to indicate adequately the sources of all the ideas contained in a book such as this, it is possible, fortunately, to express the debt I owe to a number of authorities, both associates and strangers.

Sincere thanks go to Oscar James Campbell of Columbia University, H. F. Harding of Ohio State University, H. L. Mencken of Baltimore, and E. Turner Stump of Kent State University, through whose courtesies I was first able to correspond respectively with E. V. K. Dobbie, Bert Emsley, Raven I. McDavid, Jr., and Eleanor L. Gray.

It is a pleasure to acknowledge the valuable criticism made by Henry Alexander of Queen's University (Kingston, Ontario), Elliott V. K. Dobbie of Columbia University, A. H. Monroe of Purdue University, Esther K. Sheldon of Queens College, Clarence D. Thorpe of

---

[1] We recognize that the PHONETIC column is more accurate because it gives more acceptable variants, and that the SIMPLIFIED and the DIACRITICAL columns are precisely the ones which need the broader picture, since phoneticians are already more aware of the facts of language and it is the layman who is confused and badgered. Nor is it our purpose to set up phoneticians as a privileged group who alone can understand that there are other variants.

the University of Michigan, Karl W. Wallace of the University of Virginia, and René Wellek of Yale University.

To each of these I express my appreciation for a variety of positive and encouraging opinions, and for a willing response to the questions put to them while the manual was being written: Harlen M. Adams of Chico State College, Giuliano Bonfante of Princeton University, Edward K. Brown of the University of Chicago, Henry I. Christ of Andrew Jackson High School (St. Albans, New York), Thomas L. Doyle of Bushwick High School (Brooklyn, New York), Joseph Gallant of Theodore Roosevelt High School (New York City), Robert M. Gorrell of the University of Nevada, W. Wilbur Hatfield of Chicago, George R. Havens of Ohio State University, Rudolf Kirk of Rutgers University, Raymond W. Pence of De Pauw University, J. C. Seegers of Temple University, Robert L. Sheppard of John Adams High School (Ozone Park, New York), and Newman I. White of Duke University.

Following is a group to whom I am particularly grateful for many advisory opinions, for careful study of drafts, for ideas concerning the material itself, and the like: Virgil A. Anderson of Stanford University, Theodore Andersson of Yale University, Sculley Bradley of the University of Pennsylvania, W. Norwood Brigance of Wabash College, Lionel Crocker of Denison University, Seth A. Fessenden of Cornell College, Eleanor L. Gray of Kent State University, Ward H. Green of the Tulsa Public Schools (Tulsa, Oklahoma), Frederick Hard of Scripps College, Irving Lorge of Columbia University, Roy P. Ludke of New York City, George S. McCue of Colorado College, Kemp Malone of The Johns Hopkins University, Albert H. Marckwardt of the University of Michigan, Robert T. Oliver of The Korean Commission (Washington, D. C.), Arthur Secord of Brooklyn College, Richard H. Thornton of Ginn and Company, Russell H. Wagner of the University of Virginia, Andrew T. Weaver of the University of Wisconsin, and Helen C. White of the University of Wisconsin.

To W. Cabell Greet of Barnard College, Columbia University, and to his publishers I am thankful for permission to quote from his *World Words: Recommended Pronunciations* (1948). To Bert Emsley of the Ohio State University I am especially indebted for a careful reading of the GUIDE TO PRONUNCIATION and for stimulating suggestions. To Louise Pound of the University of Nebraska I owe much for her prompt encouragement and high praise of the *Manual*. To Charles K. Thomas of Cornell University I am under obligation not only for recent courtesies but also for making available a valuable preliminary report on the teaching of phonetics and the use of the phonetic alphabet.[1] To G. and C. Merriam Company I am deeply

---

[1] Subsequently revised and adapted for publication, the report was published by C. K. Thomas under the title of "A Symposium on Phonetics and Standards of Pronunciation," *The Quarterly Journal of Speech,* XXI (October, 1945), pp. 318–327.

appreciative of the permission to make free use of the famous Merriam-Webster diacritical symbols and especially of "A Guide to Pronunciation" by Paul W. Carhart and John S. Kenyon. (G. and C. Merriam Company's *Webster's Collegiate Dictionary, Fifth Edition,* is the best handy-size dictionary, and also is the largest abridgment of *Webster's New International Dictionary, Second Edition.*)

I thank Louise B. Hinds of Barnes and Noble, Inc., for acting as liaison between author and printer. I take a special pleasure in voicing my appreciation of the scholarly aid and editorial supervision that Roger R. Walterhouse of Barnes and Noble, Inc., gave to these pages.

Finally, for invaluable assistance at all stages I owe a debt which this mention can not pay to my wife Jeanette.

In all these acknowledgments I wish to make clear that mine must be the responsibility for all shortcomings.

Morriss H. Needleman

TABLE OF CONTENTS

HOW TO USE THIS MANUAL

1. Choose Only One System. Three systems of notation are used—the SIMPLIFIED, the DIACRITICAL, and the PHONETIC. Choose only one system, and it will present the acceptable pronunciation or pronunciations.

2. Which System Should You Select? If you are familiar with the Merriam-Webster dictionaries, it may be advisable to choose the DIACRITICAL SYSTEM. Many, however, will prefer the SIMPLIFIED SYSTEM. Teachers and students of voice and speech, who are interested in an alphabet of *sounds*, will favor the PHONETIC SYSTEM. No matter which one you select, it will give the information you seek.

3. Use of Key Words. At the extreme left is the column called "KEY WORDS," in which the *sounds* of spoken English have been arranged according to the *letters* of the alphabet. Thus, since the "a" has about nine different sounds, it is *italicized* in nine different key words: h*a*t, *a*pe, *a*lways, b*a*r (and f*a*ther), d*a*re, *a*sk, w*a*tch, *a*ttack, Chin*a*. After the letter "a" and all its sounds comes the letter "b" and its only sound, as in *b*it. In the same way the alphabetization continues down through the letter "z."

Note that two letters are missing: "c" and "x." The letter "c" spells three "soft" sounds and one "hard" sound; the letter "x" spells six sounds in English. For a discussion about any and all sounds in the English language, consult the GUIDE TO PRONUNCIATION (pages xxvi–cxxiii); for example, for the sounds spelled by the letters "c" and "x," see §§ 22(1, 2, 3), 43, 43(1), 52.

4. Certain Combinations and Definite Speech Sounds. The GUIDE (pages xxvi–cxxiii) explains the specific combinations of vowels and consonants that are frequently pronounced in the same way. For a quick summary, see § 52.

5. Foreign Sounds. Symbols for the sounds in words taken from foreign languages are given in SPECIAL NOTES, VII, "Foreign Sounds" (pages xxii–xxiii).

KEY WORDS	SIMPLIFIED SYSTEM	
	Symbol	*Spoken Form* (Pronunciation)
(*Italicized part* means sound to be transcribed.)	(* means having the usual English value)	
h*a*t	a	hat
*a*pe	ay	ayp
*alway*s	ay i uh	AWL wayz AWL wiz AWL wuhz
b*ar* f*a*ther	ah	bahr FAH t̶h̶uhr
d*are*	ehr	dehr
*a*sk	a ah	ask ahsk
(The sound ranges from a in *hat* to ah in *father*.)		
w*a*tch	ah aw	wahtch wawtch
(American English has no key word that will indicate sound to be transcribed. See *odd*, page xiv.)	(Sounded between ah in *father* and aw in *ball*. This historical "short o" is usually pronounced either with ä or with ô.)	
*a*ttack	uh (unaccented)	uh TAK
Chin*a*	uh (unaccented)	CHAI͡ nuh
*b*it	*b	bit
*ch*in wit*ch*	ch	chin wich
*d*o wis*d*om	*d̶	doo WIZ duhm
ver*dure*	juhr jo͞or dyuhr dyo͞or	VUHR juhr VUHR jo͞or VUHR dyuhr VUHR dyo͞or
g*e*t	e	get
*e*ve	ee	eev
h*ere*	ĭer ir eer	hĭer hir heer
*e*vent	i	i VENT

SYMBOLS

DIACRITICAL MARKS		PHONETIC ALPHABET	
Symbol	*Spoken Form* (Pronunciation)	*Symbol*	*Spoken Form* (Pronunciation)
(* means having the usual English value)		(* means having the usual English value)	
ă	hăt	æ	hæt
ā	āp	e	ep
â	ôl′wâz	⎧ e ⎨ ɪ ⎩ ə	′ɔl wez ′ɔl wɪz ′ɔl wəz
ä	⎧ bär ⎨ ⎩ fä′thēr	ɑ	⎧ bɑr ⎨ ⎩ ′fɑ ðɚ
âr	dâr	ɛr	der (*also:* dær)
à	àsk	a	ask
(The sound is about midway between ă and ä.)		([a] is sounded between [æ] in [hæt] and [ɑ] in [′fɑ ðɚ]. General American sounds the *ask*-words as [æ]; *E also* as [ask] and [ɑsk].)	
ŏ	wŏch	ɒ	wɒtʃ (*also:* wɑtʃ, wɔtʃ)
(Although sounded between ä in *father* and ô in *ball*, this rounded or intermediate ŏ sound may represent either the historical "short o" or the open unrounded ä.)		(The vowel [ɒ] lies acoustically between [ɑ] and [ɔ].)	
ă (unaccented)	ă tăk′	ə	ə ′tæk
à (unaccented)	chī′nà	ə	′tʃaɪ nə
*b	bĭt	*b	bɪt
ch	⎧ chĭn ⎨ ⎩ wĭch	tʃ	⎧ tʃɪn ⎨ ⎩ wɪtʃ
*d	⎧ dōo ⎨ ⎩ wĭz′dŭm	*d	⎧ du ⎨ ⎩ ′wɪz dəm
dū	vûr′dūr	⎧ dʒɚ dʒʊr djɚ djʊr	′vɚ dʒɚ ′vɚ dʒʊr ′vɚ djɚ ′vɚ djʊr
ĕ	gĕt	ɛ	get
ē	ēv	i	iv
⎧ ẽr ⎨ ⎩ ēr	⎧ hẽr ⎨ ⎩ hēr	⎧ ɪər ɪr ir	⎧ hɪər hɪr hir
ĕ	ĕ vĕnt′	ɪ	ɪ ′vɛnt

KEY WORDS	SIMPLIFIED SYSTEM	
	Symbol	*Spoken Form* (Pronunciation)
taken	uh (unaccented)	TAYK uhn
maker	uhr	MAYK uhr
foot	*f	fŏŏt
get	*g	get
hush	*h	huhsh
ill chin city	i (accented or unaccented)	il chin SIT i
ice aisle whine	aî	aîs aîl hwaîn
charity	uh (unaccented)	CHAR uh ti
joy wedge	j	joi wej
key cow (noun)	*k	kee kow
lake ball	*l	layk bawl
me wisdom	*m	mee WIZ duhm
no chin	*n	noh chin
sing England	ng	sing ING gluhnd
odd (See watch, listed under the letter "A," page xii.)	o	od
open no	oh	OH puhn noh
obedience	oh uh	oh BEE di uhns uh BEE di uhns
orb ball raw	aw	awrb bawl raw
soft	aw o	sawft soft

DIACRITICAL MARKS		PHONETIC ALPHABET	
Symbol	*Spoken Form* (Pronunciation)	*Symbol*	*Spoken Form* (Pronunciation)
ĕ (unaccented)	tāk′ĕn	ə	'tek ən
ẽr	māk′ẽr	ɚ	'mek ɚ
*f	fŏŏt	*f	fʊt
*g	gĕt	*g	gɛt
*h	hŭsh	*h	hʌʃ
ĭ (accented or unaccented)	ĭl chĭn sĭt′ĭ	ɪ (accented or unaccented)	ɪl tʃɪn 'sɪt ɪ
ī	īs īl hwīn	aɪ	aɪs aɪl hwaɪn
ĭ (unaccented)	chăr′ĭ tĭ	ə	'tʃær ə tɪ
j	joi wĕj	dʒ	dʒɔɪ wɛdʒ
*k	kē kou	*k	ki kaʊ
*l	lāk bôl	*l	lek bɔl
*m	mē wĭz′dŭm	*m	mi 'wɪz dəm
*n	nō chĭn	*n	no tʃɪn
ng	sĭng ĭng′glănd	ŋ	sɪŋ 'ɪŋ glənd
ŏ	ŏd	ɑ	ɑd (*also:* ɒd)
ō	ō′pĕn nō	o	'o pən no
ŏ	ŏ bē′dĭ ĕns	o ə	o 'bi dɪ əns ə 'bi dɪ əns
ô	ôrb bôl rô	ɔ	ɔrb bɔl rɔ
ŏ	sŏft	ɔ ɒ	sɔft sɒft

KEY WORDS	SIMPLIFIED SYSTEM	
	Symbol	*Spoken Form* (Pronunciation)
connect	uh (unaccented)	kuh NEKT
wisdom		WIZ duhm
oil	oi	oil
joy		joi
foot	ŏŏ	fŏŏt
bull		bŏŏl
too	oo	too
cow (noun)	ow	kow
about		uh BOWT
pit	*p	pit
quick	*kw	kwik
rose		rohz
very	*r	VER i
bar		bahr
sing	*s	sing
shame		shaym
hush	sh	*huhsh*
wish		wish
toil		toil
	*t	
pit		pit
tooth	th	tooth
then		then
	t̶h̶	
further		FUHR t̶h̶uhr
	chuhr	NAY chuhr
nature	chŏŏr	NAY chŏŏr
	tyuhr	NAY tyuhr
	tyŏŏr	NAY tyŏŏr
up	uh (accented: always *italicized* or CAPITALIZED)	uhp
use (verb)	yoo	yooz
fuse		fyooz
unite (verb)	yŏŏ	yŏŏ NAIT
further	*uhr*, UHR (accented: always *italicized* or CAPITALIZED)	FUHR t̶h̶uhr

DIACRITICAL MARKS		PHONETIC ALPHABET	
Symbol	*Spoken Form* (Pronunciation)	*Symbol*	*Spoken Form* (Pronunciation)
ŏ (unaccented)	kŏ nĕkt′ / wĭz′dŭm	ə	kə 'nɛkt / 'wɪz dəm
oi	oil / joi	ɔɪ	ɔɪl / dʒɔɪ
o͝o	fo͝ot / bo͝ol	ʊ	fʊt / bʊl
o͞o	to͞o	u	tu
ou	kou / *a* bout′	aʊ	kaʊ / ə 'baʊt
*p	pĭt	*p	pɪt
*kw	kwĭk	*kw	kwɪk
*r	rōz / vĕr′ĭ / bär	*r	roz / 'vɛr ɪ / bɑr
*s	sĭng	*s	sɪŋ
sh	shām / hŭsh / wĭsh	ʃ	ʃem / hʌʃ / wɪʃ
*t	toil / pĭt	*t	tɔɪl / pɪt
th	to͞oth	θ	tuθ
th	thĕn / fûr′thĕr	ð	ðɛn / 'fɝ ðɚ
tû̬	nā′tû̬r	tʃɚ / tjɚ	'ne tʃɚ / 'ne tjɚ
ŭ (accented)	ŭp	ʌ (accented)	ʌp
ū	ūz / fūz	ju	juz / fjuz
û	û nĭt′	jʊ	jʊ 'naɪt
ûr	fûr′thĕr	ɝ (accented syllable only : **r** sounded)	'fɝ ðɚ
		ɜ (accented syllable only : **r** silent or "dropped")	'fɜ ðə

KEY WORDS	SIMPLIFIED SYSTEM	
	Symbol	Spoken Form (Pronunciation)
further (Same sound as in *maker*, listed under the letter "E," page xiv.)	uhr (unaccented: always in roman type; never italicized or capitalized)	FUHR ~~thuhr~~
circ*us*	uh (unaccented)	SUHR kuhs
*v*ision	*v	VIZH uhn
*w*itch	*w	wich
*wh*ine	hw	hwain
*y*es	y	yes
⌈zero		⌈ZĬER oh
⎨	*z	⎨ZIR oh
⎪		⎪ZEER oh
⌊use (verb)		⌊yooz
vision	zh	VIZH uhn

DIACRITICAL MARKS		PHONETIC ALPHABET	
Symbol	*Spoken Form* (Pronunciation)	*Symbol*	*Spoken Form* (Pronunciation)
ẽr	fûr′thẽr	ɚ (unaccented syllable only: r sounded)	′fɜ ðɚ
		ə (unaccented syllable only: r silent or "dropped")	′fɜ ðə
ŭ (unaccented)	sûr′kŭs	ə (unaccented syllable or "neutral vowel," called *schwa*)	′sɝ kəs
*v	vĭzh′ŭn	*v	′vɪʒ ən
*w	wĭch	*w	wɪtʃ
hw	hwīn	hw	hwaɪn
y	yĕs	j	jɛs
*z	⎧ zẽr′ō ⎨ zēr′ō ⎩ ūz	*z	⎧ ′zɪər o ⎪ ′zɪr o ⎨ ′zir o ⎩ juz
zh	vĭzh′ŭn	ʒ	′vɪʒ ən

SPECIAL NOTES

I

uh (unaccented). In the key to DIACRITICAL MARKS observe that each italicized symbol *a* or *e* or *i* or *o* or *u* (no matter what diacritical mark appears above each) is an indeterminate sound used for unstressed vowels, and each is sounded "uh" [IPA:ə], as in *abound* (*ȧ* bound′), *taken* (tāk′ĕn), *charity* (chăr′*ĭ* tĭ), *observe* (ŏb zûrv′), *focus* (fō′kŭs). Do not confuse such unaccented vowels with those in roman type, such as ă, ȧ, ĕ, ĭ, ŏ, ŭ.

This unaccented, neutral vowel sound, called *schwa*, is represented by "uh" in the SIMPLIFIED SYSTEM column. It will help to remember that an apostrophe in place of "uh" might be used to represent the neutral sound of a vowel in an unaccented syllable. For example, although this book transcribes *England, fluent, handsome, malignant,* and *sepulcher* in the SIMPLIFIED column as ING gluhnd, FLOO uhnt, HAN suhm, muh LIG nuhnt, and SEP uhl kuhr, it could just as well have transcribed each respectively as ING gl'nd, FLOO 'nt, HAN s'm, muh LIG n'nt, and SEP 'l kuhr or SEP 'l k'r. When "uh" (roman type) appears in the SIMPLIFIED column, it is unstressed. (An apostrophe ['] before l, m, or n—or between two consonants—indicates either no vowel whatever in the syllable, or a very slight vowel sound. See "V," page xxii.)

II

uh (accented). Although "uh" is used to represent the unaccented vowel sound in such words as *a*bound, tak*e*n, char*i*ty, *o*bserve, and foc*u*s, it is also used to represent the accented vowel as in *u*p. To distinguish between the indeterminate "uh" or *schwa* and the stressed *"uh,"* the latter is always *italicized* or CAPITALIZED in the SIMPLIFIED SYSTEM column. (Note, too, that any syllable italicized in the SIMPLIFIED SYSTEM column is to receive a secondary stress: see "VIII. Accent" below.) Observe the distinctions made in the second syllable of *chestnut:*

SIMPLIFIED SYSTEM	DIACRITICAL MARKS	PHONETIC ALPHABET
CHES *nuht*	chĕs′nŭt	ˈtʃes nʌt
CHEST *nuht*	chĕst′nŭt	ˈtʃest nʌt
CHEST nuht	chĕst′nŭt	ˈtʃest nət

III

Variant Pronunciations. When variant pronunciations are given, it must not be assumed that the first has greater frequency and validity than the second, that the second has greater frequency and validity than the third, and so on. No matter in which order a pronunciation is listed, each is good usage unless specifically labeled otherwise (see "IX," page xxiv).

a) In other words, when two or more alternate pronunciations are given, the order of listing, while it *may* indicate the order of current preference, often does not do so. Two examples may suffice:

1. Long e (ē as in *eve*) + r, when followed by e in the same syllable (as in *here* and *sincere*) may be transcribed diacritically by ẹ̄r or ēr. But in General American the sound is closer to that of short i (ĭ as in *city*) + r, as in *spirit*. In the DIACRITICAL column the vowel sound is transcribed first as ẹ̄ and then as ē; in the SIMPLIFIED column the vowel sound is transcribed first as ĭer (= ẹ̄r), then as ir (= ĭr), and finally as eer (= ēr). Yet, although given second in the SIMPLIFIED column, the ir pronunciation is most likely the most frequent one. We reiterate that each of the three pronunciations is employed by equally cultivated speakers, and that the one listed first is not necessarily "preferred." See § 24(2).

2. In such words as *authority, corridor, foreign, forest, horrid,* and *orange,* short o (ŏ as in *odd*) + r, when accented and followed by a vowel or a second r in the succeeding syllable, is a sound ranging from ô (= aw) + r to ä (= ah) + r. Although the prevailing vowel in General American speech may be ô (= aw), we give the ä (= ah) sound first and the ô (= aw) sound second. (In the PHONETIC column we include also the vowel [ɒ], as in *watch*.) Again we urge you to remember that the order in which the pronunciations are shown does not indicate that the first is preferable to the second, or the second to the third— and so on. See § 34(6.1).

b) Nor are the same number of variant pronunciations given in each column. For example, the SIMPLIFIED column may have more variants because it often interprets the marks of the DIACRITICAL column:

1. Thus, *oral* is transcribed in the DIACRITICAL column as ō′răl, but interpreted in the SIMPLIFIED column as tantamount to both OH ruhl and AW ruhl. In addition, a reference to § 34(3) makes available more information about the variants.

2. In the same way *tube* is transcribed in the DIACRITICAL column as tūb and interpreted in the SIMPLIFIED column as tyoob and toob, with specific references to §§ 40(4), 48(2), and 50(32) for fuller details.

3. Again, the sound of ŏ as in *obey* (ŏ bā′) may be either the long ō as in *open* or the unaccented, neutral vowel sound "uh" or schwa. As a rule the vowel in an unstressed syllable tends to become weakened or obscure, the distinctness with which it is pronounced varying according to style or to familiarity of the word, or according to the habit or intent of the speaker. However, where there seems to be a preponderance of opinion, we have indicated only one sound in the SIMPLIFIED column; where there is no such preponderance, we have interpreted the sound as both a long ō as in *open* and an unstressed *o* as in *dissolute*. In the SIMPLIFIED column, accordingly, *docility* is interpreted as doh SIL uh ti; *dominion* as duh MIN yuhn; and *sporadic* as spoh RAD ik, spaw RAD ik, spuh RAD ik. Cross-references are given whenever necessary or desirable; for example, consulting the reference to *sporadic* will reveal the reason for the pronunciation spaw RAD ik. See § 34(12.1, 2).

4. In the unaccented ending -ture, most good American speakers sound the syllable in one or more of several ways—colloquially, as "chuhr"; carefully, as "chōōr"; or even precisely, as "tyōōr" or "tyuhr." In words of two syllables the unstressed ending -ture is generally "chuhr," as in *nature;* in words of more than two syllables not accented on the penult the -ture is most often "chuhr" or "chōōr." However, although in our key word *nature* the unaccented ending -ture is interpretable as tantamount to "chuhr," "chōōr," "tyuhr," "tyōōr," yet in its dictionary place (on page 207), *nature* has only two of the four interpretations in the SIMPLIFIED column (and only two General American interpretations in the PHONETIC column). The point is that although the unaccented ending -ture may be interpreted in several ways, each word ending in unstressed -ture (or, incidentally, in unstressed -dure, as in *verdure*) is transcribed according to its own use by good American speakers. See § 50(31.c, d, e).

IV

Pronouncing the "r." All r's are marked in the respelling for pronunciation as being pronounced. Final r and r before a consonant are frequently omitted in

Eastern American and in some types of Southern American, although the r is pronounced if a vowel follows. In General American r is pronounced wherever written. See §§ 37(1.3), 37(4).

Those speakers who believe that the r sound should be pronounced only before a vowel or who regard r as a silent letter before a consonant or a pause may be guided by the spelling of the word. Perhaps some day a major American dictionary will initiate the practice of enclosing in parentheses the r of a respelled word, thereby indicating that the r may or may not be pronounced.

V

Syllabic l, m, n. When l or m or n forms a syllable by itself, it is syllabic. In both the SIMPLIFIED and DIACRITICAL columns the transcription for each is respectively 'l, 'm, 'n; in the PHONETIC column, ḷ, m̩, n̩. Examples: *saddle* (săd′'l), ['sæd ḷ]; *prism* (prĭz'm̩), [prɪzm̩]; *reason* (rē′z'n), ['ri zn̩]. See "I," page xx; also §§ 9, 31(1.2, 3), 32(2.1, 2, 3), 33(2).

VI

Two Dots [:]. Two dots or a colon [:] after a vowel means that the vowel is pronounced long. The sign [:], which indicates time length, or duration, is used primarily whenever speakers in the East and South "drop" the r after [ɑ] or [a], thereby lengthening the vowel sound.

VII

Foreign Sounds. The pronunciation of many words or names of foreign origin may be indicated in most instances by English phonetics (in the SIMPLIFIED and DIACRITICAL columns). However, certain foreign sounds have no exact equivalent in English speech. Below is a selective listing of such sounds, common in other languages:

β   Voiced bilabial fricative occurring mostly in Spanish words. The sound of *v* as in *vision* is made by biting the lower lip with the upper teeth and making a voiced sound. To achieve the Spanish *bv* sound, open lips slightly, let the lower lip protrude, and sound the b without touching the lips together completely.

ǥ   Fricative *g* sound pronounced like x (see below), but pronounced with voiced breath.

N   Indicates that the symbol N has no sound of its own and is not pronounced, but that the preceding vowel or vowel-sound is nasalized.

ɲ   Palatal n may be approximated by pressing the tongue against the backs of the lower teeth while trying to sound n.

ø   To approximate the mid-front rounded vowel of French *peu* or German *schön*, sound ā as in *ape* with the lips rounded as for ō in *open*. The German *o umlaut* resembles the English sound û as in *hurt*, but differs from it by being pronounced with the lips rounded and with the tongue nearer the teeth than in û.

ü   To produce the sound of ü as in French *menu* and German *Müller*, round the lips as though to sound o͞o in *too* and then, with the lips still in that position, sound ē as in *eve*. (When the consonantal y precedes the French ü, cut the sound off sharply and clearly. See y below.)

x The small-capital ᴋ [IPA:x] is pronounced as in German *ich* or *ach* and in Scotch *loch*. Approximately like that of English k in *look* and *pick*, the sound is made without full contact between the back of the tongue and the roof of the mouth. In German the combination *ch* has the sound of k immediately followed by an h sound. To make that sound, have the tongue in position to pronounce the word *yes* and then expel the breath voicelessly between the back of the tongue and the roof of the mouth. Although the back of the tongue approaches the velum, it does not cut off the breath. (See ç below.)

y Sound ɪ as in *city* or ē as in *eve* with lips rounded as for ōō in *too*. The resulting sound is y, the high-front rounded vowel of French *menu* [mə 'ny] or German *kühn* [ky:n]. See ü above.

ʎ Try to sound l while holding the tongue pressed against the backs of the lower teeth. Such procedure results in the palatal l, or palatal lateral.

ɔ Round the lips as for ô in *orb* but sound ŭ as in *but*. The pronunciation approximates the sound of French "short o" as in *Somme* [F., söm].

æ̃ (or ɛ̃), ã, õ (or ɔ̃), œ̃. When pronounced like a nasal American pronunciation of *bong*, *bang*, and *burn* (with the r silent in the East and South), the vowel sounds æ, ɑ, o, œ become respectively the French nasalized vowels æ̃ (or ɛ̃), ã, õ (or ɔ̃), œ̃. Nasalization is indicated by a tilde (˜) placed over a vowel or diphthong.

Φ bi-labial *f*, the "candle-blowing" sound

ç The more forward variety of the sound of *ch* in German *ich*. This book uses x (see above) to represent both the sound of *ch* not only in German *ach* and Scotch *loch*, but also the sound of *ch* in German *ich*.

ɬ the Welsh fricative *l*

ḷ voiceless *l* (also in English)

ɱ labio-dental nasal

œ the sound of *eu* in French *neuf*. This low-front or lower mid-front rounded vowel appears also in German, as in *können*.

ṛ voiceless *r* (also in English)

ɥ the sound of u in French *nuit* and *nuance*

ʍ inverted w (hw)

ʔ glottal stop (also in English)

VIII

Accent. Accent or stress is indicated differently and in the following manner in each column:

a) SIMPLIFIED COLUMN. In the SIMPLIFIED column the primary or strong accent is shown by CAPITAL letters, and the secondary or somewhat weaker accent by *italicized* letters.

b) DIACRITICAL COLUMN. In the DIACRITICAL column the primary or heavier accent is shown by a heavy oblique mark (ʹ), and the secondary accent by a lighter oblique mark (ʹ), at the *end* of the syllable.

c) PHONETIC COLUMN. In the PHONETIC column the primary or more distinct accent is shown by a vertical stress-mark (ʹ) above the line *before* a syllable, and the secondary accent by a vertical stress mark (ˌ) below the line *before* a syllable.

WORD	SIMPLIFIED	DIACRITICAL	PHONETIC
dissect	di SEKT	dĭ sĕktʹ	dɪ 'sɛkt
panacea	*pan* uh SEE uh	pănʹá sēʹá	ˌpæn ə 'si ə

IX

Restriction of Pronunciation. Section 51 (pages cxviii–cxx) gives additional details about specific variations of usage as indicated by limiting words. Following is an explanation of the more important abbreviations or designations used:

Abbreviation	*Meaning*
arch.	archaic. Generally unacceptable except in special context or for special uses.
B.	Acceptable in American speech, but especially British.
colloq.	colloquial. Acceptable in everyday speech.
com.	commonly. A pronunciation approaching the colloquial or familiar.
dial.	dialectal. As a general rule, unacceptable. Used only by a certain class or in a certain district.
emph.	emphatic. Used sparingly for emphasis.
esp.	especially
freq.	frequently and acceptable
gaining ground	Pronunciation recorded as acceptable by at least one major American authority.
gen.	generally
humor.	humorous
infreq.	infrequently, but acceptable
loosely	A pronunciation approaching the colloquial or familiar, but perhaps better avoided.
occas.	occasionally
pop.	popularly. A pronunciation approaching the colloquial or familiar.

X

Abbreviations. In addition to the abbreviations listed and explained in "IX. Restriction of Pronunciation," the following shortened forms are also used:

Abbreviation	*Meaning*	*Abbreviation*	*Meaning*
adj.	adjective	GA	General American
adv.	adverb	gram.	grammar
anat.	anatomy	Haw.	Hawaiian
Angl.	Anglicized	her.	heraldry
AS	Anglo-Saxon	hist.	historical, historical pronunciation
Calif.	California		
cap.	capitalized	hum.	humorous, humorously
chem.	chemistry	Hung.	Hungarian
comp.	compound, compounds	Ind.	Indiana
contr.	contraction	inf.	informal
demons.	demonstrative pronoun	interj.	interjection
E	Eastern	It.	Italian
E.	English (Anglicized)	Jap.	Japanese
engin.	engineering	joc.	jocularly
exc.	except	L., Lat.	Latin
F.	French	masc.	masculine
fem.	feminine	ME	Middle English
G.	German	MW	Middle Western

Abbreviation	Meaning	Abbreviation	Meaning
n.	noun	*rhet.*	rhetorical, rhetorically
N	Northern	*Russ.*	Russian
naut., Naut.	nautical, Nautical	*S*	Southern
NE	New England	*Sc.*	Scottish
N. Y.	New York	*sing.*	singular
N. Y. C.	New York City	*Sp.*	Spanish
Pg.	Portuguese	*tech.*	technical
pl., plur.	plural	*U. S.*	United States
poet.	poetic, poetry	*v.*	verb, both transitive and
p. p.	past participle		intransitive
pref.	preferably	*v. i.*	intransitive verb
pres. t.	present tense	*v. t.*	transitive verb
pro.	pronoun	*var.*	variant
p. t.	past tense	*W*	Western
rel.	relative pronoun	*zool.*	zoology

XI

References to Sections. Numbers following the pronunciations in the SIMPLI-
FIED or DIACRITICAL column refer to section (§) or sections (§§) in the GUIDE
TO PRONUNCIATION on pages xxvi–cxxiii.

GUIDE TO PRONUNCIATION[1]

When the English tongue we speak,
Why is *break* not rhymed with *freak*?
Will you tell me why it's true
We say *sew*, but likewise *few*?
And the maker of the verse
Can not cap his *horse* with *worse*?
Beard sounds not the same as *heard*,
Cord is different from the *word*.
Cow is *cow*, but *low* is low;
Shoe is never rhymed with *foe*.
Think of *hose* and *dose* and *lose*,
And of *goose* and yet of *choose*.
Think of *comb* and *tomb* and *bomb*,
Doll and *roll*, and *home* and *some*,
And since *pay* is rhymed with *say*,
Why not *paid* with *said*, I pray?
We have *blood* and *food* and *good*;
Mould is not pronounced like *could*.
Wherefore *done*, but *gone*, and *lone*?
Is there any reason known?
And, in short, it seems to me
Sounds and Letters disagree.

STANDARDS OF PRONUNCIATION

§ 1. SPELLING AND PRONUNCIATION

Spelling is not an adequate guide to current pronunciation. If it were, we should sound the b in *doubt*,* the c in *victuals*,* the g in *sign** and *gnaw*,* the h in *honor*,* the k in *know*,* the l in *calf** and *palm*,* the n in *solemn*,* the p in *receipt*,* the t in *mortgage** and *soften*,* and the w in *wrap*.* If our spelling were phonetic, many words that are spelled alike would not be pronounced differently, as the ough in *cough*,* *bough*,* *through*,* *rough* (rŭf), *though* (thō), *hiccough* (hĭk′ŭp); and many words that are spelled differently would not be pronounced alike, as *complement** and *compliment*,* *desert** and *dessert*,* *stationary** and *stationery*.* If we were to follow spelling as an infallible guide to present-day pronunciation, we should soon become hopelessly confused.

---

[1] a) For the three separate keys used in this manual, see pages xii–xix.

b) In the present GUIDE symbols enclosed in parentheses ( ) are usually sounds in the Webster-Merriam diacritical system; symbols enclosed in brackets [ ] are sounds in the IPA phonetic transcription. The brackets are used to distinguish the sounds from letters and spelling forms.

c) The asterisk (*) after a word means that the word and its pronunciation will be found in its alphabetical place in the manual on pages 1–319.

However, although on the whole we do not spell as we pronounce, we sometimes pronounce as we spell. For example, the influence of spelling has made us sound initial h in *heretic,** *hospital,** and *human,** although not in *honest** and *hour.** The l sounded in *fault** and *vault,** and the th sounded in *authority,** *catholic*, *mathematics*, and *theater** are "spelling-pronunciations," by which term is meant the altering of an established traditional pronunciation to one that more nearly conforms to the spelling. As stated by J. S. Kenyon,[1] "an underlying principle of spelling-pronunciation" is that the "words that have resisted spelling-pronunciation (*hour*, *Thomas*) are more common words, and therefore more likely to be thoroughly learned by children before they learn to read and write. On the other hand, if we first learn words from books, or if we see them in print oftener than we use them, we are more apt to guess at the pronunciation from the spelling." As a result, such familiar words as *come,** *comfort,** and *company,** since they were learned by ear and not acquired by eye, still retain a "short" u sound despite the spelling with *o*. But the less common words such as *combat** and *constable** have also a spelling-pronunciation with a "short" o sound. When a spelling-pronunciation becomes established, it is as acceptable as the older traditional pronunciation; in fact, spelling-pronunciation has often superseded phonetically natural pronunciation. See also §§ 27(1.5, 6), 39(7.1, 2), 42(3).

§ 2. PRONUNCIATION AND WRITING

There is more than one difference between speaking and writing. We speak long before we write; and long before we learn to use periods, or commas, or colons, or question marks, or exclamation points we are able to convey different meanings by a nod of the head, a frown on the face, a shake of the fist, a lifting of the eyebrow. Or, by slightly modifying inflection (change in the pitch or tone), we may suggest many shades of meaning. For example, *no* may be spoken as a simple negative answer, or as a question, or as a statement of strong feeling, or as an expression of surprise, or as a bantering reply. Also, say aloud four times the following sentence, putting the stress on a different word:

I have found money.
I *have* found money.
I have *found* money.
I have found *money*.

Observe how a different meaning is given each reading.

§ 3. AMERICAN REGIONAL PRONUNCIATIONS

Although we Americans spell each of the four words in that illustrative sentence the same way, and pronounce each in about the same way, yet many of us continue asking what is the correct pronunciation of this word or that word.

Before we can answer that question, we must recognize that American regional pronunciations are frequently divided into three main types, the New England (NE) or Eastern (E), the Southern (S), and finally the General American (GA), the last-named of which is also often designated as Northern (N), or Western (W), or Middle Western (MW).

1) Eastern (E) pronunciation is that prevailing in New England east of the Connecticut River, in the maritime provinces of Canada, and in New York City and environs.[2] This is the speech of some 14,000,000 people in parts of Canada,

---

[1] *American Pronunciation: A Textbook of Phonetics for Students of English*, p. 114 (Ann Arbor, Michigan: George Wahr, 1943). See especially pages 110–117 (§§ 142–150).

[2] Whether New York City speech is actually Eastern, or perhaps Southern, or even in a class by itself is still a matter of active controversy. For example, Professor Charles K. Thomas divides the country into seven major speech areas

in most parts of New England, and in the City of New York. In this manual Eastern (E) pronunciation is indicated only in the PHONETIC column.

2) Southern (S) pronunciation is that heard in Virginia, North Carolina, South Carolina, Tennessee, Florida, Georgia, Alabama, Mississippi, Arkansas, Louisiana, Texas, and sections of Maryland, West Virginia, Kentucky, and Oklahoma. More specifically, it prevails south of Chesapeake Bay and the Potomac River, south of West Virginia and the Ohio, in lowland Arkansas, in most of Louisiana, and in southeastern Texas over an area including Beaumont, Galveston, Houston, and the surrounding country. Altogether it is spoken by about 28,000,000 people. Only in the PHONETIC column does this manual indicate Southern (S) pronunciation.

3) We have just stated that Eastern speech prevails in the six New England states, in the maritime provinces of Canada, and in the City of New York; and that Southern speech prevails in most of what is commonly called the South. General American (GA) or Northern (N) pronunciation is that spoken by the rest of the United States; or, more accurately, by all of the country outside the East and the South, including Canada from Montreal westward. It is the speech of about 98,000,000 people. General American (GA) is the standard presented in this manual in all three columns, the SIMPLIFIED, the DIACRITICAL and the PHONETIC.

§ 4. "CORRECT" PRONUNCIATION

While three main types of speech are distinguishable, yet most Americans say most words, perhaps eighty or ninety per cent of all words, in about the same way. To the question "Which is the correct pronunciation for the remaining words?" the answer is, "Each of the three main regional pronunciations is acceptable." Not one is the only "correct" pronunciation, for the "correctness" of each depends on the *appropriateness* of a given set of circumstances—the nature of the audience, the formality of the occasion, the social circle one is part of, the region one lives in. For example, even the style of speech will often determine the kind of pronunciation: the more formal speaker will pronounce *seated* as sēt'ĕd while the less formal speaker will say sēt'ĭd or even sēt'ĭd [§ 24(5)].

If we are asked to define "correct" pronunciation, we may define it

> . . . as the pronunciation of the educated, careful speakers of the general region in which one happens to have formed his speech habits. This definition allows for the differences in pronunciation which we hear in different regions of the English-speaking world. If one has grown up, for example, in the southern part of the United States, he is entirely justified in using the speech of the educated, cultured speakers of the South, which we call "southern speech." One whose linguistic background lies along the northern Atlantic coast may reasonably be expected to use the type of speech characteristic of that section, which we call "eastern speech." And one reared in any part of the remaining area of the United States may properly use the speech of his educated and cultured fellows, which we call "general American speech." [1]

In brief, the pronunciation of any word in America is acceptable or "correct" if it is a pronunciation used by a majority of educated speakers under a similar set of circumstances in a given American major speech area.

(New York City is one) instead of the traditional three. See C. K. Thomas, *An Introduction to the Phonetics of American English* (1947), p. 144.

[1] G. W. Gray and C. M. Wise, *The Bases of Speech*, p. 35 (New York: Harper and Brothers, 1934).

§ 5. STYLES OF SPEECH AND THE DICTIONARY

We have already noted that the principle of pronouncing words as they are spelled is a poor guide (§ 1). Another popular misconception is that of taking the dictionary to be the infallible guide for determining what pronunciation is acceptable at any given time.

No dictionary makes such a claim for itself. For example, *Webster's New International Dictionary of the English Language, Second Edition* (Introduction, p. xii) says that one of the two limitations imposed upon the pronunciation editor

> . . . consists in the necessity for making a choice among the different styles of speech suitable for different occasions. In this edition, the style adopted for representation is that of formal platform speech—and this must be clearly remembered by consultants of the pronunciations here given. The omission of less precise pronunciations of familiar words does not, of course, indicate either that those pronunciations do not exist or that the editors of the dictionary refuse to recognize them. They do exist, and very naturally so when the occasion suits. In familiar casual conversation consonants are often dropped or slurred, vowels of unaccented syllables become indistinct, syllables are often dropped out of the pronunciation of words. The recording of all such colloquial pronunciations of every separate word is not, however, possible in such a Dictionary as the NEW INTERNATIONAL.[1]

The foregoing passage has several implications. One is that when a dictionary sometimes marks a pronunciation as *colloquial*, it means that the pronunciation is spoken by cultured people on less formal occasions, and that the pronunciation is acceptable. A second is that the dictionary is less reliable in guiding our pronunciation of the everyday words than of the less common words. Rarely do we use *Caliban* * and *machination* * in our speech; and therefore the pronunciation of such words changes slowly if at all. But since we do use *absorb,* * *citizen,* * *data,* * *government,* * *suite,* * and other words more often, their pronunciation is likely to change more rapidly. Finally, to quote G. W. Gray and C. M. Wise again:[2]

> Many, perhaps most, words in English have only one correct pronunciation. Granting normal variations in the use of the members of a phoneme, there is only one correct way to pronounce *just* [dʒʌst], *being* ['biiŋ], *district* ['dɪstrɪkt], *adult* [ə'dʌlt].[3] Such pronunciations may be found in the dictionary, and may be depended upon. . . . Any deviation from the dictionary pronunciation of these words . . . can indicate only carelessness or ignorance.
>
> But there is another type of word in respect to which opinions as to variant pronunciation cannot be ascribed to ignorance and cannot be reconciled by the dictionary. This is the type of word whose pronunciation varies as the result of *difference of locality*. In many instances of this type, the dictionary, instead of being an ever-present help, as with the first type, becomes a potential hindrance, in that it seems to substantiate equally well two diametrically opposite opinions. The *Standard*

---

[1] Published by G. and C. Merriam Company: Springfield, Massachusetts, 1934, *et. seq.*

[2] *The Bases of Speech* (1934), p. 195 *f.*

[3] While G. W. Gray and C. M. Wise state a concept with which this handbook is in agreement, their choice of *just* * and *adult* * as illustrative words is a mistake. See *just* and *adult* in their vocabulary place in this manual.

Dictionary, for example, spells out a sort of phonetic pronunciation of the word *secular,* thus: sec′yu-lar. Southerners, Easterners and Englishmen would instantly interpret this explanatory spelling as [sɛkjʊlɑ]; but speakers from the general American speech area would as instantly and positively interpret it as [sɛkjʊlɑr]. In addition to the controversy thus set up between sections, controversies between slow speakers and rapid speakers might readily arise as to the pronunciation of the [ɑ] in the last syllable, some contending that it should be [ə], producing [′sɛkjʊlə] or [′sɛkjʊlər]. . . . It thus becomes evident that in respect to this second type of word, where locality figures in producing variants, the question as to how to pronounce a word is not easy to answer at once.

§ 6. CONNECTED SPEECH AND THE DICTIONARY

A little while ago (§ 5) we indicated one of the two limitations self-imposed by the pronunciation editor of the Merriam-Webster Unabridged. Another limitation is that dictionaries make no attempt to record the pronunciation of words as they occur in connected speech. The dictionary isolates each word, and indicates the pronunciation of each from the point of view of

> . . . an unrelated entity. . . . It would be impossible, even were it desirable, to attempt to record the pronunciation of "running speech," that is, of words as elements in connected spoken discourse, to attempt to indicate rising or falling pitch, syllabic emphasis or lack of emphasis, contraction or prolongation of sounds—in short, the countless minor variations to which the pronunciation of a word is susceptible under the influence of other words with which it is temporarily associated.[1]

§ 7. USAGE AND PRONUNCIATION

No matter what a dictionary records, you will do well to observe extensively the current usage of the best speakers, and to remember that many a word—especially the more familiar ones—may have several equally acceptable pronunciations instead of just one "correct" one. The only over-all principle is that in spoken language, as in written language, *usage is the determining factor.*

If there is a standard of pronunciation, it is the usage that prevails currently among the educated Americans throughout the United States or in any of the three main regions (§ 3). For each of the approximately 5800 words selected, this handbook endeavors to record as many as possible of the pronunciations in the best present usage. In addition to the practice of every major American dictionary of presenting General American pronunciation, this manual also indicates in the PHONETIC column the most general Eastern (E) and the most general Southern (S) varieties.

§ 8. VOWEL IN UNACCENTED SYLLABLE

Good English does not require that every syllable be pronounced distinctly. In fact, obscuration of unaccented vowels occurs not only in informal speech but also in formal speech, although unstressed vowels are more likely to occur in the former. One general rule affecting the pronunciation of our words is that in talk the vowel in an unaccented syllable tends to become weakened or obscure, the vowels a, o, and u approaching the neutral vowel uh [ə], and the vowels e and i approaching ĭ [ɪ] or uh [ə].

---

[1] *Webster's New International Dictionary of the English Language, Second Edition,* p. xii (Springfield, Massachusetts: G. and C. Merriam Company, 1934, *et seq.*)

1) In the DIACRITICAL column the italicized symbols ă, ĕ, ŏ, ŭ represent either the obscured form of the full vowel ă, ĕ, ŏ, ŭ or, especially in formal speech, a vowel sound that indicates more or less the quality of the full vowel.

2) In the DIACRITICAL column the symbol ĭ represents a sound ranging from that of y in *sanity* to that of i in *sanity*. The y in *very* and the ie in *collie* is a sound just a bit more relaxed than the ĭ [ɪ] in *bill*. In narrow transcription it may be shown with a tongue modifier [ɪ⊤]. But for our purposes the y in *sanity* and the i in the same word are each represented by the symbol ĭ [ɪ]. See also §§ 28(4.5), 28(5.4, 5).

3) In similar fashion the symbols ā, ē, ō, ū are used to express more or less obscured forms of the vowels ā, ē, ō, ū. Often the ā and ĕ are sounded as ĭ, ō as ŏ [ə], and ū as ŭ [ə]. See also §§ 20(8), 24(11.1, 2), 34(12.2, 3), 40(12).

PRELIMINARY ASPECTS

§ 9. SYLLABLES, VOWELS, AND CONSONANTS

Later we shall discuss the sounds of spoken English as arranged alphabetically according to the spelling (§§ 20–46), but before we do that there may be an advantage in considering other aspects now (§§ 9–19).

1) A syllable may consist of one vowel (a, e′dict) or a diphthong (*oi* in oil), or of a vowel with one or more consonants (me, sylph, lus′ter), or of one or more consonants without a vowel, as in *battle* (băt′ ′l) and *button* (bŭt′ ′n). Of course a syllable may form either a whole word (sun) or a commonly recognized division of a word (sun′set′).

2) A vowel may be said to be syllabic when it forms a syllable alone, as a in a mount′, e in e′qual.

A consonant is said to be syllabic when it forms a syllable without a vowel, either alone as the l in *saddle* (săd′ ′l) or the n in *lesson* (lĕs′ ′n), or with a group of consonants, as in *handled* (hăn′d′ld) and *thousand* (thou′zănd; but also syllabic as in thou′z′nd).

3) A vowel is said to be nonsyllabic when, instead of forming a syllable, it constitutes the unstressed, or subordinate, part of a diphthong, as i in oi (*oil*) or u in ou (*out*). The unstressed part may be the first part of a rising diphthong or the last part of a falling diphthong.

A consonant is said to be nonsyllabic when it is in the same syllable with a vowel (*am, ban, black, rend*), or with a syllabic consonant (*saddled*, pronounced săd′ ′ld).

4) l, m, n, sometimes ng, and certain forms of r may be syllabic. When each is, it takes on many of the qualities of a true vowel, and is often classified as a true vowel or as a vowel-like consonant. See *angle*,* *considerable*,* *disconsolate*,* *preferable*,* *tassel*,* *valuable**; *prism*,* *rhythm**; *bison*,* *blazon*,* *elusion*,* *poison*.* Also see § 5.

a) Pronounce *rattle* (răt′ ′l) and *saddle* (săd′ ′l). Observe that in sounding [t] + [l], or [d] + [l], the tip of the tongue stays in contact with the gum ridge and the plosives [t] and [d] are exploded around the sides of the tongue and into the [l] instead of over the tip of the tongue. When each plosive is exploded into the [l], no vowel sound intervenes when the tongue moves from the preceding [t] or [d] to the [l] position. In such instances the [l] is said to be syllabic, for it forms a syllable by itself without the aid of another vowel sound. Note: To indicate in phonetic transcription that the sound represented is syllabic, place a short vertical line [ˌ] under the letter: *rattle* (răt′ ′l; IPA ˈræt ḷ), *saddle* (săd′ ′l; IPA ˈsæd ḷ).

b) In similar manner the consonant [m] and, more often, the consonant [n] may form syllables alone without the aid of a vowel. In such cases they are said to be syllabic. Examples: *prism* (prĭz′m; IPA ˈprɪzm̩), *blossom* (blŏs′ŭm:

IPA 'blɑs əm; also frequently blŏs′ 'm; IPA 'blɑs m̩), *brighten* (brīt′ 'n; IPA 'braɪt n̩), *reason* (rē′z'n; IPA 'ri zn̩), *taken* (tāk′ĕn; IPA 'tek ən; also frequently tāk′ 'n; IPA 'tek n̩).

     c) In word groups the ng may be syllabic: *look and go* may become lŏŏk 'ng gō. Syllabic ng [ŋ] is found only in substandard speech.

     d) r may also occur syllabically, as in *better*, usually pronounced bĕt′ĕr but also bĕt′ 'r (the r being trilled or fricative).

     5) l, r, or n in an unaccented syllable often decides whether the vowel preceding each should be sounded; or whether the l, r, or n is syllabic or nonsyllabic. The shorter the form, the more colloquial the style of pronunciation. In the PHONETIC column see *battery,* beverage,* boisterous,* boundary,* cadaverous,* delivery,* factory,* family,* heterodox,* literature,* mackeral,* memories,* Niagara,* olfactory,* opera,* quandary,* satisfactory,* temperament.** See §§ 20(10.3), 24(14), 28(5.6), 31(1.2), 32(2.1, 2, 3), 33(2), 34(14.2), 40(13.4).

     6) (a) A vowel is a speech sound uttered with voice or whisper and allowed to pass out of the mouth with relative freedom or very little obstruction, thereby being distinguished from a consonant, a speech sound in which the breath stream is obstructed by the lips, tongue, teeth, or the like. The vowel is identified by the resonance form of the vocal cavities; the consonant, by constriction in the breath channel.

     b) When two vowel sounds unite in one syllable to form one speech sound, the resulting sound is called a diphthong, as oi in *oil*, ou in *out*, i in *ice*.

Diphthongs must be carefully distinguished from digraphs, which are two vowel letters or two consonants spelling a single sound, as ea in *break*, eo in *leopard*, th in *with*, aw in *lawn*, oa in *soap*, oe in *toe*, ui in *suit*.

     c) When three vowel sounds join to form one syllable, the resulting sound is called a triphthong. Examples are īr in *fire* (fīr) or IPA [faɪr; *ES* faɪ ə(r)], our in *sour* (sour) or IPA [saʊr; *ES* saʊ ə(r)], and ūr or ûr in *pure* (pūr) or IPA [pjʊr; *ES* pjʊ ə(r)]. The triphthong īr begins with the diphthong ī [aɪ] and ends with the middle vowel ĕr [ɚ; *ES* ə(r)]: see the next paragraph; the triphthong our is made up of the diphthong ou [aʊ] and the middle vowel ĕr [ɚ; *ES* ə(r)]; the triphthong ūr or ûr is composed of yŏŏ [jʊ] and ĕr [ɚ; *ES* ə(r)].

Although the three vowel sounds are united into one continuous glide, each group sound tends to become dissyllabic or two-syllabled. That accounts for the phonetic transcription of the triphthong īr as [aɪɚ; *ES* aɪ ə(r)], for our as [aʊ ɚ; *ES* aʊ ə(r)], and for ūr or ûr as [jʊɚ; *ES* jʊ ə(r)]. True triphthongs are rare. In words like *liar*, *nigher*, *ire*, *power*, and *shower*, the ĕr is more or less often pronounced as a second syllable. Observe that each of the three triphthongs ends in [r]. Triphthongs are not to be confused with trigraphs, which are three letters spelling a single consonant, vowel, or diphthong, as the eau in *beauty*, the gue in *tongue*.

§ 10. STRESS AND ACCENT

     1) By the term *stress* is meant the intensity, force, or prominence of a sound, syllable, or word. Stress (force) may be produced by one element such as pitch or duration of sound, or by a combination of such elements.

     2) Although *stress* (or force of utterance that increases the relative loudness of a speech sound, syllable, or word) is usually the chief element of *accent* in English, and therefore the terms *stress* and *accent* are often used interchangeably (*primary stress* and *primary accent* are synonymous, as are *secondary stress* and *secondary accent*), yet by the term *accent* is often meant the prominence of one syllable over another or over others in any word of more than one syllable. In this sense only a plurisyllable has accent.

     3) The term *even accent* (also called *even stress* or *level stress*) means equal or nearly equal accent on two syllables, or level stress occurring especially in compound or group words. See § 10(7.e, f, i).

4) By the term *shifting accent* or *shifting stress* is meant that the accents (whether primary or secondary) may change places as a consequence of such factors as emphasis, contrast, position among other words, varying usage, meaning (see *sentence stress* immediately below), and various syntactical relations. See § 11.

5) *Sense stress* (also called *sentence accent* or *sentence stress*) refers to the prominence or degrees of prominence given to particular words in a phrase, clause, sentence, or any successive words of a sense group. Whereas *word stress* or *word accent* distinguishes syllables within a word, *sentence stress* is the normal variation in the degrees of prominence given to any part of a sense group.

6) As a rule a monosyllable is said to have no accent, although it may have sense stress (see § 2). However, a monosyllable may be marked first with primary accent and then with secondary accent in order to show varying sense stress that depends upon connected speech. For example, in phonetic transcription *was* may be marked ['wɑz, ˌwɑz, 'wɒz, ˌwɒz (*stressed*); wəz (unstressed)]. See *there.**

7) As a rule, "even" accent occurs in compound words or word groups. Normally it is found

    a) In proper names, as Hen′ry Jones′, North′ Cape′, Elev′enth Av′enue.

    b) In titles with names, as Cap′tain Har′vey, Miss′ Hen′ry, M′r. Walt′.

    c) In the numerals thir′teen′ to nine′teen′, twen′ty-one′ to twen′ty-nine′, thir′ty-one′ to thir′ty-nine′, and so on.

    d) In the ordinals thir′teenth′ to nine′teenth′, twen′ty-first′ to twen′ty-ninth′, thir′ty-first′ to thir′ty-ninth′, and so on.

    e) In many compound adjectives, as half′-mast′, ill′-starred′, lop′sid′ed, made′-up′, mat′ter-of-course′, Mo bile′ *but* Mo′bile Bay′ (see *a* above), nam′by-pam′by, pres′ent-day′, right′-an′gled, six′ty-fourth′ (see *d* above), up′side-down′.

    f) In many adverbs, as up′stairs′, well′-nigh′.

    g) In certain compound verbs where the "even" accent distinguishes the verb from its corresponding noun, as set′up′ (v.), set′up′ (n). (See § 12.)

    h) In words given emphasis, as *almost,** *primarily.**

    i) In certain words often written separately, but resembling compounds, as base′ hit′, cast′ steel′, half′ truth′. See § 11.

§ 11. SHIFTING ACCENT

Shifting accent occurs in a number of situations and is attributable to one or more of several forces. A reference to this section means that the word in question may be subject to variation of accent even if a fixed accentuation is shown in the vocabulary entry.

Among the reasons for shift of accent are the following:

1) Compounds in the predicate position (His fortune is ill′-starred′), or compounds succeeded by an unaccented word (an ill′-starred′ and hurt life), or compounds succeeded by a pause (a life, ill′-starred′ and miserable) retain their "even" accent (§ 10). The accentuation shifts, however, when the compound is attributive (or whenever a strong stress follows), as an ill′-starred′ fortune. Note that *–starred* is now weaker than *ill–*, whereas originally *–starred* was either equally accented or even a bit more heavily accented than *ill–*. Thus "The beaver is brown′-tailed′," but "a brown′-tailed′ beaver"; "The action is slow′-mo′tion," but "a slow′-mo′tion action."

2) Likewise, under similar conditions, the accents sometimes change places in certain adjectives, as "My friend is bul′let head′ed," but "a bul′let head′ed friend." See *abject,** *expert.**

3) Similarly nouns, noun phrases, and compound verbs may have movable word accent or stress.

4) Often, for the sake of contrast or emphasis, certain words have a variable accent; for example, *export,* necessarily.**

Additional examples (pages 1–319): *archangel,* cockatoo,* decade,* direct,* electrician,* employee,* finance,* first-class,* first-rate,* forbear,* gasolene,* heirloom,* Javanese,* Jugoslav,* kerosene,* light-hearted,* limousine,* long-headed,* long-lived,* lopsided,* macaroon,* Milan,* open-minded,* opportune,* ornate,* premature,* pretense,* research,* second-hand,* suicidal,* thereof,* whippoorwill.** See also § 12.

§ 12. ACCENTS AND PARTS OF SPEECH

Although no exceptionless rules can be given for the position of word accent in our language, yet accent often distinguishes verbs from nouns, adjectives from nouns, nouns from adjectives, and so on.

1) For illustrations of the tendency to distinguish verbs from nouns of the same spelling by a different accent, see *accent,* addict,* ally,* attribute,* camouflage,* combat,* contrast,* decrease,* discount,* extract,* ferment,* guillotine,* increase,* object,* perfume,* quarantine,* record,* sojourn,* upset.**

2) Adjectives distinguished from verbs by accent (see in vocabulary): *absent,* abstract,* afternoon,* frequent,* subject.**

3) Verbs distinguished from adjectives and nouns (see in vocabulary): *converse,* intimate,* inverse,* occult,* offset,* reflex,* retail,* transfer.**

4) Also, a noun may be distinguished from its adjective and verb (*compact**), or an adjective distinguished from its noun and verb (*concave**), or a noun distinguished from its adjective (*ingrate**), or a compound noun distinguished from a corresponding verb [see § 10(7.g)].

5) Finally, some words do not shift the primary accent, but the noun is distinguished from the verb by a reduced vowel. See *augment,* doctorate,* intimate,* separate.**

§ 13. BRITISH AND AMERICAN PRACTICE

In certain classes or groups of words the accentuation is not always identical in both British and American practice. As a rule American usage tends to both a primary and a secondary accent and fuller vowel where British usage tends to only a primary accent and obscure vowel.

1) In British usage words ending in –ary (*secretary**), –ery (*cemetery**), –ory (*amatory*) have only a main or primary accent; in American usage such words have both a primary and a secondary accent. However, although in the –ary words (*dictionary,* necessary,* secretary**) most Americans pronounce the a as ĕ (gĕt), American usage accepts also the usual British pronunciation with only one primary accent; and the designation *B*, before an entry means just that. See §§ 24(9.2), 34(5.4), 51(4). In the vocabulary see *adversary,* aviary,* epistolary,* February,* formulary,* fragmentary,* honorary,* itinerary,* January,* judiciary,* legendary,* literary,* luminary,* military,* momentary,* pecuniary,* pulmonary,* residuary,* revolutionary,* salivary,* salutary,* sanctuary,* secondary,* secretary,* voluntary.**

2) In some words ending in –mony (*ceremony*) British usage has only one accent while American usage has usually two accents.

3) Words ending in –ative (*nominative**) follow no set rule either in English or American usage. When the secondary accent is lost, or when the primary accent is followed immediately by the syllable in which the a occurs, the a in –ative is often obscured or the syllable is often reduced. See § 50(3).

4) In British practice the vowel of the next to last syllable of words ending in –burgh (*burgh,* Edinburgh**), –borough (*Marlborough*), –bury (*Canterbury*), –berry (*Queensberry*), is either obscured or dropped. In compound words ending with –berry (*raspberry**), similar obscuration occurs not only in British but also in American speech.

5) Numerous other words show that American speech tends to retain two accents and fuller vowel.

§ 14. STRONG AND WEAK FORMS

In the sentence, "She is going to make him ham and eggs," the dictionary would transcribe each word as follows:

WORD	DICTIONARY TRANSCRIPTION
She	shē
is	ĭz
going	gō′ĭng
to	tōō
make	māk
him	hĭm
ham	hăm
and	ănd
eggs	ĕgz

But when you speak, you normally say, "shēz gō′ĭng tōō māk′ ĭm hăm ănd ĕgz," or "shēz gō′ĭng tŭ māk′ ĭm hăm ăn ĕgz."

The dictionary form of the word is called the "strong" form; the forms shēz, tōō, tŭ, ĭm, ănd, ăn are called "weak" forms. A knowledge of weak forms and their proper use to subordinate the unessential makes it possible to emphasize the important words and preserve the rhythm of English speech. Placing too much stress on words that should be weak makes understanding of the meaning as difficult as does the invariable use of the strong form. See §§ 15, 16.

§ 15. SENSE STRESS

Sense stress [§ 10(5)] depends largely on meaning, on the relation of ideas in a phrase, clause, or sentence. Fundamental to good oral reading is the emphasis on main points and the subordination of minor ones; and such differentiation can be achieved only by careful use of "strong" and "weak" forms. As a rule the pronunciation as given in a dictionary is the "strong" form.

Among the general tendencies of sense stress in English are the following:

1) Nouns, verbs, adjectives, and adverbs are usually "strong" forms; articles, auxiliary verbs, pronouns, prepositions, conjunctions, and other connective words are usually "weak" forms. See § 16.

2) "Even" accent or "even" stress [§ 10(3, 7)] is expected in several situations.

    a) "Even" stress is likely to occur when a subject word that is a noun is followed by its verb (The man′ struck′).

    b) "Even" stress is likely to occur when a subject word that is a noun is followed by a verb phrase, the "even" stress being put on the subject word and on that part of the verb phrase that is not auxiliary in nature (The man′ has been struck′).

    c) "Even" stress occurs when a verb is followed by an object (She struck′ gold′).

    d) "Even" stress occurs when an adverb is followed by a verb, or when a verb is followed by an adverb (She soon′ tired′; She tired′ soon′).

    e) Adverb plus adverb take "even" stress (She tired ver′y soon′).

    f) Adverb plus adjective take "even" stress (She is too′ tired′).

    g) When an adjective is followed by a noun (fine′ per′son; great′er love′) the stress may be "even," but usually the adjective is somewhat weaker than the noun.

    h) When a noun is followed attributively by an adjective, the stress may be "even" (winds′ be calmed′, ad dress′ un known′), but usually the noun is somewhat weaker than the adjective.

i) Interrogative *who* is usually stronger than relative *who*. Demonstrative *that* is usually stronger than relative *that* or conjunction *that*; and therefore the "strong" form is used when *that* is a demonstrative pronoun. See § 16: "Other Connectives."

§ 16. GRADATION

1) As J. S. Kenyon states,

> It is a characteristic of English . . . that the vowels of unaccented syllables have gradually become obscured to a sound quite different in resonance, or quality, from what they had formerly been, and from the present-day vowels that have preserved their full quality under accent. This fact escapes the attention of many because the same spelling is kept for the obscured vowel that was used to spell it before it became obscured in course of time, and the same spelling that is also used for the accented vowel that takes its place when its syllable is accented.[1]

The change from one vowel to another that accompanies a change in the degree of stress is called *gradation*. Examples: the vowel of *day* to the second vowel of *Monday* (mŭn′dĭ); *manly* (măn′lĭ), *postman* (pōst′măn); *folk* (fōk), *Norfolk* (nôr′fŭk).

2) Gradation, or the variation of vowel quality accompanying variation of stress, may occur not only in a syllable of a word but in the whole word itself, such a word usually being a monosyllable. Recall that monosyllables are also subject to variable sense stress (§ 10.6). As a result of gradation of vowels that goes with variation of stress, monosyllables may have not only a "strong" form but also one or more "weak" forms. Of course the dictionary gives the stressed form; and connected speech alone allows the unstressed form.

Strong (Stressed) and Weak (Unstressed) Form

Note: When identical transcriptions are given for both the "strong" and the "weak" form, sound the unstressed form with a slightly weaker vowel. For example, the strong form of the pronoun *he* is hē′ ['hi] and one weak form is also given as hĕ [hi]. See also § 8(3).

Incidentally, narrow transcription would reveal the distinction by placing two dots [:] after a letter to indicate that the sound represented is long: *strong (stressed) form*, ['hi:]; *weak (unstressed)*, [hi].

ARTICLES

WORD	STRONG (STRESSED) FORM	WEAK (UNSTRESSED) FORM
a*	ā′ ['e]	*a* [ə]
an	ăn′ ['æn]	*ăn* [ən]
the	thē′ ['ði]	*before consonants*, thĕ [ðə]
		before vowels, thĭ [ði], thĕ [ði]

AUXILIARY VERBS

WORD	STRONG (STRESSED) FORM	WEAK (UNSTRESSED) FORM
am	ăm′ ['æm]	*ăm* [əm]
'm (*in* I'm)		'm [m]
are	är′ ['ɑr; *ES* 'ɑ:(r)]	ĕr [ɚ; *ES* ə(r)]
're (*in* we're, *etc.*)		r [r; *ES* ə(r)]
be	bē′ ['bi]	bĕ [bi], bĭ [bɪ]

[1] J. S. Kenyon, *American Pronunciation: A Textbook of Phonetics for Students of English*, p. 90 (Ann Arbor, Michigan: George Wahr, 1943). See pages 90–101 (§§ 130–136).

WORD	STRONG (STRESSED) FORM	WEAK (UNSTRESSED) FORM
can	kăn′ ['kæn]	kăn [kən, kn̩]
could	kŏŏd′ ['kʊd]	kŭd [kəd]
do	dōō′ ['du]	dōō [*before vowels*, dʊ; *before consonants*, də]
does	dŭz′ ['dʌz]	dŭz [dəz, dz]
had	hăd′ ['hæd]	hăd [həd, əd]
'd (*in* I'd, *etc.*)		d [d]
has	hăz′ ['hæz]	hăz [həz, əz]
's (*in* he's, Herbert's, *etc.*)		z [*after voiced sounds*, z] s [*after voiceless sounds*, s]
have	hăv′ ['hæv]	hăv [həv], ăv [əv]
've (*in* I've, *etc.*)		v [v]
is	ĭz′ ['ɪz]	ĭz [ˌɪz]
's (*in* she's, Robert's, *etc.*)		z [*after voiced sounds*, z] s [*after voiceless sounds*, s]
may	mā′ ['me]	mä [me], mĭ [mɪ], *ma* [mə]
must	mŭst′ ['mʌst]	mŭst [məst; *before consonants also* məs]
shall	shăl′ ['ʃæl]	shăl [ʃəl], sh'l [ʃl̩]
should	shŏŏd′ ['ʃʊd]	shŭd [ʃəd, ʃd]
was	wŏz′ ['wɑz, 'wɒz, 'wʌz]	wŭz [wəz, wz]
were	wûr′ ['wɝ; *ES also* 'wɜ(r)]; *B.*, wâr′ ['wɛr, 'wær; *ES* 'wɛə(r), 'wæə(r)]	wĕr [wɚ; *ES* wə(r)]
will	wĭl′ ['wɪl]	wĭl [wəl]
'll (*in* who'll, Fred'll, *etc.*)		'l [l̩]; *also, after vowels*, əl, l]
would	wŏŏd′ ['wʊd]	wŭd [wəd]
'd (*in* she'd, it'd, *etc.*)		ŭd [əd], d [d]

PRONOUNS

WORD	STRONG (STRESSED) FORM	WEAK (UNSTRESSED) FORM
he	hē′ ['hi]	hĕ [hi], ĕ [i], hĭ [hɪ], ĭ [ɪ]
her	hûr′ ['hɝ; *ES also* 'hɜ(r)]	hĕr [hɚ, ɚ; *ES* hər, ə(r)]
him	hĭm′ ['hɪm]	ĭm [ɪm, hɪm]
his	hĭz′ ['hɪz]	ĭz [ɪz, hɪz]
me	mē′ ['mi]	mĕ [mi], mĭ [mɪ]
my	mī′ ['maɪ]	mī [maɪ, məɪ; *unstressed before vowels*, məɪ; *unstressed before consonants*, mə]
one	wŭn′ ['wʌn]	wŭn [wən]
she	shē′ ['ʃi]	shĕ [ʃi], shĭ [ʃɪ]
some	sŭm′ ['sʌm]	sŭm [səm, sm̩]
them	ᵺĕm′ ['ðɛm]	ᵺĕm [ðəm], ᵺ'm [ðm̩]
us	ŭs′ ['ʌs]	ŭs [əs]; *also*, ŭz [əz]
's (*in* let's)		's [s]
we	wē′ ['wi]	wĕ [wi], wĭ [wɪ]
you	yōō′ ['ju]	yŏŏ [jʊ, jə]
your	yŏŏr′ ['jʊr; *ES* 'jʊə(r), 'jɔə(r), *E also* 'jɔə(r)]	yŏŏr, yĕr [jʊr, jɚ; *ES* jʊə(r), jɔə(r), jə(r), *E also* jɔə(r)]

PREPOSITIONS

WORD	STRONG (STRESSED) FORM	WEAK (UNSTRESSED) FORM
at	ăt′ ['æt]	ăt [ət, ɪt]
by	bī′ ['baɪ]	bī [baɪ, bəɪ], bå [bə]
for	fôr′ ['fɔr; ES 'fɔə(r)]	fẽr [fɚ; ES fə(r)]
from	frŏm′ ['fram, 'frɒm]	frŏm [frəm]
into	ĭn′tōō ['ɪn tu]	before vowel, usually ĭn′tōō ['ɪn tʊ]; before consonant, usually ĭn′tŭ ['ɪn tə]
of	ŏv′ ['av, 'ɒv]	ŏv [əv]; before consonants, often ŭ [ə]; after vowels, often v [v]
on	ŏn′ ['an, 'ɒn]	ŏn [an, ɒn]; also, especially in S and W, ŏn [ən]
till	tĭl′ ['tɪl]	tĭl [tɪl], t'l [tl̩]
to	tōō′ ['tu]	before vowel, tōō [tʊ], tŭ [tə]; before consonant, tŭ [tə]
upon	ŭ pŏn′ [ə 'pan, ə 'pɒn]	infrequently, ŭ pŭn [ə pən]

CONJUNCTIONS

WORD	STRONG (STRESSED) FORM	WEAK (UNSTRESSED) FORM
and	ănd′ ['ænd]; before consonants, often ăn′ ['æn]	before vowels, usually ănd [ənd], 'nd [n̩d]; before consonants and often before vowels, ăn [ən], 'n [n̩]
nor	nôr′ ['nɔr; ES 'nɔə(r)]	nôr [nɔr; ES nɔə(r)], nẽr [nɚ; ES nə(r)]
or	ôr′ ['ɔr; ES 'ɔə(r)]	ôr [ɔr; ES ɔə(r)], ẽr [ɚ; ES ə(r)]
than	thăn′ ['ðæn]	thăn [ðən], th'n [ðn̩], 'n [n̩], n [n]
that		~~that~~ [ðət]

OTHER CONNECTIVES

WORD	STRONG (STRESSED) FORM	WEAK (UNSTRESSED) FORM
as	ăz′ ['æz]	ăz [əz], z [z]
but	bŭt′ ['bʌt]	bŭt [bət]
so	sŏ′ ['so]	sŏ [so], sŭ [sə, sʊ]
that (demons.)	thăt′ ['ðæt]	
that (rel.)		~~that~~ [ðət]
what	hwŏt′ ['hwat, 'hwɒt]	hwŏt [hwət], wŏt [wət]

§ 17. INTONATION

When a German speaks German, when a Frenchman speaks French, or when a Russian speaks Russian, you can recognize a difference in the rise and fall in pitch of the voice. Let a German or a Frenchman or a Russian begin to learn English, and each will speak it to the tune, or melody, of his mother tongue. This characteristic rise and fall in pitch, or tune or melody of speech, is called intonation; and no language is entirely mastered until its characteristic intonation is mastered. It must be remembered, however, that these pitch patterns and tunes of speech are different in different regions, varying even from section to section within the region.

Professor Hermann Klinghardt, a German linguistic scholar, evolved the following system by means of which you can study the intonation of a language:

A horizontal line, known as a *measuring line*, is used to indicate the normal pitch of the voice.

A heavy dot ⬤ indicates a stressed syllable.
A light dot ⏤ marks an unstressed syllable.

A dot with an up-glide indicates a rising inflection.

A dot with a down-glide ⌐ marks a falling inflection.

Finally, observe that a dot is used for every syllable, and that a down-glide is always characteristic of the last *stressed* syllable.

EXAMPLES

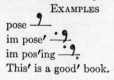

pose

im pose'

im pos'ing

This' is a good' book.

At least two main tendencies characterize English intonation:

First, a complete thought ends with a falling inflection or down-glide. When a question begins with a question word (*who, which, where, when, what*), the same principle holds.

EXAMPLES

She is there'.

She is a good' girl'.

I shall walk'.

Where' shall I walk'?

When' did she go'?

Second, an incomplete thought or a question that does not begin with a question word is spoken with a rising inflection or up-glide.

EXAMPLES

Pos'ing for a mo'ment

Ex press'ing the thought

Shall you walk'?

Is she here'?

Is she walk'ing?

Note 1: In the examples just given, observe that the first stressed syllable in an intonation group, or phrase, is the highest in pitch in the group, or phrase. Therefore, the heavy dot indicating this syllable that is higher in pitch than any other syllable in the group is placed well above the measuring line. One or more unstressed syllables preceding the first stressed syllable are placed in a line just above the measuring line; and an unstressed syllable succeeding the last stressed syllable is placed just below the measuring line (except where the second rule applies). An unstressed syllable placed just below the measuring line is spoken in a pitch either lower than or as low as the normal pitch of the voice.

Note 2: As a rule the stressed syllable is usually higher in pitch than an unstressed one.

§ 18. ANALYSIS OF VOWELS AND DIPHTHONGS

"Of course I know the vowels in our language. They are a, e, i, o, and u."

"Go on."

xxxix

"But there are only five, aren't there?"

The answer is that there are more than three times that number common in American speech.

1) Vowels, or resonant speech sounds produced by relatively open and unobstructed throat and mouth passageways [see § 9(6)], may be classified in two ways: (a) according to the part of the tongue used in producing the vowel; and (b) according to the position of the tongue.

In forming each vowel the tongue is bunched or arched in the mouth. A *front* vowel is one made with the *front* of the tongue at the *front* of the mouth; a *middle* or *mid-* vowel is one made with the *middle* of the tongue arched at the *middle* of the mouth, and a *back* vowel is one made with the *back* of the tongue arched at the *back* of the mouth.

The position of the tongue in producing a vowel determines whether a vowel is called *high* (high in tongue placement, not in pitch), *half-high, half-low,* or *low.* The closer the tongue is bunched or arched near the roof of the mouth, the higher the vowel.

2) Since you are probably more acquainted with the Webster diacritical marks than with either the simplified or the phonetic system (full keys appear on pages xii–xix), we shall first use the Webster diacritical symbols for our discussion.

DIACRITICAL SYSTEM

Front Vowels	Middle Vowels	Back Vowels
ē — ēve		ōō — tōō
ĭ — bĭt		ŏŏ — fŏŏt
ā¹ — āpe	ûr — fûr′ther	ō — ō′pen, nō
ĕ — gĕt	ẽr — mak′ẽr, fur′thẽr	ô — ôrb, ball, raw
ă — hăt	ă, ȧ, ĕ, ĭ, ŏ, ŭ (neutral vowel or	ŏ — ŏdd, watch
	schwa), as in ăt tack′, Chi′nȧ,	[see page xxi]
	tak′ĕn, char′ĭ ty, cŏn nect′, cir′cŭs	
ȧ — ȧsk	ŭ — ŭp, ŭn′der	ä — bär, fä′ther

3) In the cardinal vowel diagram below is shown the approximate position in the mouth at which the bunching, or chief point of tension, occurs. While not representing actual tongue placement, the chart does indicate both the relative positions of the tongue and the direction of movement and change in the formation of the various sounds.

CHART OF ENGLISH VOWELS
(Diacritical System)

Tongue Placement	Front Vowels	Middle Vowels	Back Vowels	Tongue Placement
High	ē		ōō	High
	ĭ		ŏŏ	
Half-High	ā	ûr	ō	Half-High
Half-Low	ĕ	ẽr	ô	Half-Low
	ă	ə²	ŏ	
Low	ȧ	ŭ	ä	Low

¹ In actual speech the vowel ā as in āpe becomes a diphthong when it occurs in a syllable which is accented or stressed. See also § 20(1).

² The symbol [ə] is called the schwa. It is the neutral sound represented in the diacritical system by the italicized ă in ăt tack′, ȧ in Chi′nȧ, ĕ in tak′ĕn, ĭ in char′ĭ ty, ŏ in cŏn nect′, ŭ in cir′cŭs.

The left of the figure represents the front of the mouth; the right of the figure represents the back of the mouth. The bottom of the figure represents the floor of the mouth.

4) The chart given above shows the relative positions of the English vowels on the vowel scale, and the relative position of the lower jaw and tongue in producing vowels. While looking in a mirror, say the front vowels ē, ĭ, ā, ĕ, ă, à. Observe that in forming the sound ē, the tongue is raised high in front toward the hard palate (the palate just behind the gum ridge); in forming the sound ĭ, the tongue is bunched a little lower and a little farther back; in forming ā, the tongue is arched lower than it is for ĭ, the preceding sound; and so through progressive steps the tongue is lowered from a position high in the mouth to a position in which it lies more or less flat. Observe also the shape and the position of the lips in the formation of the front vowels. For ē the lower jaw is dropped very slightly so that there is not much space between the teeth, and the lips are spread; for ĭ the jaw is dropped a bit from the position for ē, and the lips are kept spread; for ā the jaw is dropped a little more, and the lips are kept spread; and so on. Briefly, the lips are unrounded in making the front vowels, and both the tongue and the jaw are progressively lowered a little farther as you go down the scale.

The back vowels are o͞o, o͝o, ō, ô, ŏ, ä. In producing o͞o, the back of the tongue is arched or bunched toward the soft palate (see § 19.3a, "Linguavelar, or Tongue-and-Soft-Palate, Sounds); for o͝o, the back of the tongue is arched a little lower; and so on, proceeding downward through the series of back vowels. Now sound the same vowels, contrasting the lip positions with those that characterize the front vowels ē, ĭ, ā, ĕ, ă, à. Instead of being spread more or less and somewhat retracted at the corners, as for the front vowels, the lips are markedly protruded and closely rounded in the production of o͞o; the lips are less closely rounded and the mouth is more widely open for o͝o; the lips are markedly protruded and closely rounded for ō; the lips are less closely rounded for ô (although in Eastern speech the sound is a half-low, rounded, tense back vowel, made with the jaw dropped considerably and the lips protruded and rounded); the lips are slightly rounded for ŏ; and the lips are neutral for ä.

For the middle vowels ûr, ẽr, ə, ŭ, the tongue is arched highest for ûr and lowest for ŭ; the lips are spread slightly for ûr and most for ŭ.

Now, still using a mirror, practice the scale consecutively, beginning with ē and descending through the front series (ĭ, ā, ĕ, ă, à). Observe that the jaw, which is only slightly open for ē, is dropped a little for ĭ, a little more for ā, still more for ĕ, still farther for ă, and a little farther yet for à. The jaw, only slightly open for ē, has been lowered so far by the time it has reached à that the mouth is now quite wide open.

From this wide-open position for à, proceed upward through the back series of vowels (ä, ŏ, ô, ō, o͝o, o͞o) toward the back of the mouth. Observe that the jaw is raised slightly for each succeeding vowel.

Now say the middle vowels ûr, ẽr, ə, ŭ. Observe that the lips are unrounded, although the vowels require a somewhat open mouth.

5) Given directly below is exactly the same information about vowels explained immediately above in § 18(3), the only difference being that the identical material is presented in two different keys, the phonetic and the simplified (for fuller details, see pages xii–xix).

PHONETIC ALPHABET

Note: For the key words, see under DIACRITICAL SYSTEM (page xl).

FRONT VOWELS	MIDDLE VOWELS	BACK VOWELS
i — iv		u — tu
ɪ — bɪt		ʊ — fʊt
e — ep	ɝ — 'fɝ ðɝ	o — 'o pən, no
ɛ — get	ɚ — 'mek ɚ, 'fɝ ðɚ	ɔ — ɔrb, bɔl, rɔ
æ — hæt	ə — ə'tæk, 't∫aɪ nə, 'tek ən,	ɒ — ɑd (also: ɒd), wɒt∫ (also:
	't∫ær ə ɪ, kə 'nɛkt,	wɑt∫, wɒt∫)
	'sɝ kəs	
a — ask	ʌ — ʌp, 'ʌn dɚ	ɑ — bɑr, 'fɑ ðɚ

CHART OF ENGLISH VOWELS
(Phonetic System)

Tongue Placement	Front Vowels	Middle Vowels	Back Vowels	Tongue Placement

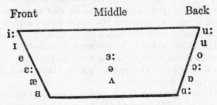

High	i		u	High
Half-High	ɪ	ɝ	ʊ	Half-High
Half-Low	e ɛ	ɚ	o	Half-Low
Low	æ a[1]	ə ʌ	ɒ ɑ	Low

The left of the figure represents the front of the mouth; the right of the figure represents the back of the mouth. The bottom of the figure represents the floor of the mouth.

---

[1] The student should not be confused by any different listing of the vowels in a chart of English vowels. For example, a number of phoneticians, chiefly those who speak or recommend Eastern and Southern speech (§ 3), present the chart as follows:

Front	Middle	Back
i:		u:
ɪ		u
e	ɜ:	o
ɛ:	ə	ɔ:
æ	ʌ	ɒ
ɑ		ɑ:

a) The [:] indicates prolongation or lengthening of the sound which it follows.

b) The symbol [e] represents the sound ĕ as in *get*. In the chart used by this manual the symbol [e] is the sound ā as in *ape*.

c) [ɛ:] is a sound represented in the diacritical marks by â. It is almost always used as the first element of a diphthong in such words as *air* and *there*. It is seldom or never used in English apart from the diphthong. The vowel in *air* occurs only before r in stressed syllables.

d) The symbol [ɑ] is indicated diacritically by à. When [a] is used in the chart, the preference is that it be sounded neither as ă [æ] nor as ä [ɑ:], but as a pure vowel in syllables ending in the sounds of [f], [o], [s], and [sk].

e) The sound û [ɜ:] is regarded as the highest mid-vowel, although in a relative position it is a half-high mid-vowel. In making the sound, the tip of

SIMPLIFIED SYSTEM

Note: For the key words, see under DIACRITICAL SYSTEM (page xl).

FRONT VOWELS	MIDDLE VOWELS	BACK VOWELS
ee — eev		oo — too
i — bit		o͞o — fo͝ot
ay — ayp	uhr, UHR [stressed: always *italicized* or CAPITALIZED] — FUHR t͟huhr	oh — OH puhn, noh
e — get	uhr [unstressed: always in roman type] — MAYK uhr, FUHR t͟huhr	aw — awrb, bawl, raw
a — hat	uh [unstressed: always in Roman type] — uh TAK, CHAI͡ nuh, TAYK uhn, CHAR uh ti, kuh NEKT, SUHR kuhs	o — ´odd
a, ah [*sounded between* a *and* ah] ask, ahsk	uh, UH [stressed: always *italicized* or CAPITALIZED] — *uhp,* UHN duhr	ah — bahr, FAH t͟huhr

CHART OF ENGLISH VOWELS

(Simplified System)

Tongue Placement	Front Vowels	Middle Vowels	Back Vowels	Tongue Placement
High	ee		o͞o	High
Half-High	i ay	*uhr,* UHR	o͝o oh	Half-High
Half-Low	e	uhr	aw	Half-Low
Low	a *ranges from* a *to* ah	uh *uh,* UH	o ah	Low

The left of the figure represents the front of the mouth; the right of the figure represents the back of the mouth. The bottom of the figure represents the floor of the mouth.

6) When two vowels are pronounced in the same syllable, a diphthong is produced [see § 9(6.b)]. Each diphthong begins with one vowel sound and ends with another; and each of its two component parts is called an *element* of the diphthong. The first element is normally stronger than the second; and to show a lack of stress, narrow transcription uses a small curved line over the second element. See also § 16(2, Note).

---

the tongue is to be placed on the back of the lower front teeth. Such phoneticians regard as a fault any tendency to curl the tip of the tongue backward, for such rising of the tongue tip causes a sound called "inversion," regarded by them as a mispronunciation [§ 37(2.2)]. In prŏducing [ɜː] the front of the tongue is held lower and further forward than for [ɝ], and there is no retroflexion.

f) [ɔː] is classified as a half-low, rounded, tense back vowel. This group of phoneticians objects if the sound is made with the arch of the tongue too far back in the mouth; or if the sound is made with the lips unrounded, thereby making the ô [ɔː] tend to be pronounced like the ä [ɑː] in *father.*

DIPHTHONGS ENDING IN UNSTRESSED [ɪ]

WORD	BROAD TRANSCRIPTION (Used in This Manual)	NARROW TRANSCRIPTION (Not Used in This Manual)
ape	e [ep]	eɪ [eɪp]
ice	aɪ [aɪs]	aɪ̆ [aɪ̆s]
oil	ɔɪ [ɔɪl]	ɔɪ̆ [ɔɪ̆l]

DIPHTHONGS ENDING IN UNSTRESSED [ŭ]

WORD	BROAD TRANSCRIPTION (Used in This Manual)	NARROW TRANSCRIPTION (Not Used in This Manual)
open	o ['o pən]	oŭ ['oŭ pən]
cow (n.)	aʊ [kaʊ]	aŭ [kaŭ]

DIPHTHONGS ENDING IN UNSTRESSED [ɔ̆]

WORD	BROAD TRANSCRIPTION (Used in This Manual)	NARROW TRANSCRIPTION (Not Used in This Manual)
here	ɪ [hɪr]	ɪɔ̆ [hɪɔ̆(r)]
there	ɛ [ðer]	ɛɔ̆ [ðɛɔ̆(r)]
poor	ʊ [pʊr]	ʊɔ̆ [pʊɔ̆(r)]
door	ɔ [dɔr]	ɔɔ̆ [dɔɔ̆(r)]

7) In General American speech, however, we usually recognize not nine but only six diphthongs—ā [e, eɪ], ī [aɪ], oi [ɔɪ], o [o, oʊ], ow [aʊ], and (not given in foregoing listings) "long" ū [ju] as in *view*. (We are not using the small curved line over the second element of the diphthong.)

When two symbols are used for one blended sound, each symbol indicates a different position of the articulatory mechanism. Thus, in the diphthong ā [eɪ], as pronounced in *day* [see § 20(1.1)], the mouth is set for the vowel ā [e], begins to sound the vowel, but shifts to a position approximately that for the vowel ĭ [ɪ]. To sound ō as in ō'pen, the lips are rounded, the back of the tongue starts to say ŏ as in ŏ bey', and then glides quickly to ŏŏ [ʊ] as in *fŏŏt*. The combination of these two vowel sounds makes the diphthong ō. For ou [aʊ] as in a bout', the tongue begins in the position for ä [ɑ] as in *bar* and then glides to ŏŏ [ʊ] as in *foot*; and the two vowels blend into the diphthong ou [aʊ]. In "long" u in *view*, the tongue and lips are in the position for ĭ as in *is*, but quickly change to that for ōō in *too*. A diphthong, as you see, may now be defined as a continuous glide (see § 19) in which the articulatory organs move from the position of one vowel sound to that of another within the same syllable.

8) We still have to consider how to make the falling (centering) diphthongs, those ending in [ə].

a) Watch your tongue in the mirror as you say *here*. In Eastern and Southern speech (see § 3) the front part of the tongue begins in the position for ĭ [ɪ] as in *is* and quickly glides to the position for the off-glide represented by ȧ [ə] as in *China*. Since the Easterner and the Southerner sound this diphthong as an ĭ [ɪ] followed by the off-glide ȧ [ə], it is transcribed as [ɪɔ̆]. For others the diphthong begins with the ĭ as in *is*, is lengthened, and is finished with the tip of the tongue curled back for r as in *rebel*.

b) Watch your tongue in the mirror as you say â as in *air*. In Eastern and Southern speech the tongue tip stays behind the lower front teeth, the front part of the tongue lifts to a position halfway between the vowel position ĕ as in *get* and ă as in *at*, and then glides to the position for ȧ as in *China*. Since the symbol for â in Eastern and Southern speech is [ɛ:], the sound of â in *air* and *there* is transcribed as [ɛɔ̆]. In General American speech, however, the tip of the tongue may be curled back for r as the second tongue position in producing this diphthong.

c) Say *poor*. Even if you should try to watch your tongue in the mirror, you would not be able to see your tongue because the lips are rounded for ŏŏ as in *foot*. But the tongue does glide quickly from ŏŏ [ʊ] to *à* [ə], resulting in the diphthong ŏŏr. Easterners and Southerners pronounce it [ʊə̆]. For other Americans the second tongue position is that for r with the tongue tip curled back.

d) Watch your tongue as you say *door*. Does it begin in the position for ô [ɔ] as in *raw* and then glide to *à* as in *China?* For Easterners and Southerners the first element is [ʊ] and the second is the neutral vowel (unstressed) [ə]—or [ʊə̆]. In such words as *orb* and *wore* (o + r), the diacritical mark is usually ōr [ɔə̆], but the pure vowel ô [ɔ:] is often used in acceptable American speech. Many Americans say *door* as dô [dɔ], not dôê [dɔə̆]. In acceptable American speech the first sound may be either ō or ô, and the second sound either ê or r. In General American the diphthong is said with the final tongue position for r.

§ 19. ANALYSIS OF CONSONANTS

Now that you have had a brief analysis of vowels and diphthongs (§ 18), you should also have a short introduction to English consonants.

1) As indicated earlier [§ 9(6.a)], a consonant is a speech sound characterized by constriction in the breath channel. When the consonant sound being produced causes a vibration in the vocal cords (feeling your larynx or Adam's apple will help determine whether or not the enunciation is causing a vibration), the consonant is said to be *voiced;* and when the consonant sound being produced causes no vibration in the vocal cords, the consonant is said to be *voiceless*.

2) A voiced sound often has a counterpart that is voiceless. Some phoneticians call the voiced sound a *cognate*. Thus, [b] is the cognate of [p], [d] of [t], [g] of [k], [v] of [f]. It is also possible to recognize that cognates are sounds formed with the same place of articulation, such as [b], [p], [m]. (By a *cognate substitution* is meant a mispronunciation resulting from the substitution of a voiced sound for its unvoiced cognate or companion sound, or the substitution of an unvoiced sound for its voiced sound.)

3) Consonants may be classified (a) according to the organs by which the sounds are articulated (place of articulation), (b) according to the manner of articulation, and (c) according to the presence or absence of vibration in the vocal cords (voiced or voiceless).

a) According to Place of Articulation

Labial, or Lip, Sounds. Labial, or lip, sounds are usually divided into *bilabial consonants* because the two lips articulate against each other [p, b, m, w], and into *labiodental consonants* because the lower lip is held against the cutting edge of the upper teeth [f, v]. Also correct is the use of the single word *labiodental* to mean a sound formed with the lips, or one lip, and the teeth.

Linguadental, or Tongue-Teeth, Sounds. A linguadental, or tongue-teeth, sound is one made with the tip of the tongue against the teeth. The two linguadental consonants are th [θ] in *tooth* and th [ð] in *then*.

Lingua-Alveolar, or Tongue–Gum-ridge, Sounds. Some sounds are formed with the tongue touching the ridge just above and behind the upper front teeth or with the tongue being near the ridge, or alveolus. Whether made with the tip of the tongue on the upper gum ridge, as in [t] and [d], [n], [l], or with the tip of the tongue retracted a bit from the position for [t], and with the sides of the tongue making tight contact with the upper teeth and gums, the consonants are called lingua-alveolar (or tongue-gum, or postdental, or superdental, or gum-ridge) sounds.

In making [s] some speakers do not form a narrow groove between the tongue

tip and the upper gum ridge (the front of the hard palate). One speaker will
make the sounds [s] and [z] with the tip of the tongue free but pointing toward
the gums; another will keep the tongue tip back of the lower teeth and bunch
the middle front of the tongue toward the gum ridge to make the narrow groove
through which to blow a fine stream of air.

Linguapalatal, or Tongue-and-Hard-Palate, Sounds. Linguapalatal sounds
are produced with the front of the tongue, behind the tip, near or touching
the hard palate. In making such sounds the tip of the tongue is somewhat retracted and lowered from its position for [s]. English has only one front palatal
sound, the nonfricative y [j] as in *yard, yes, your.*

Linguavelar, or Tongue-and-Soft-Palate, Sounds. As you know, the palate
is the roof of the mouth, composed of the structures that separate the mouth
from the nasal cavity. The bony part in front is called the *hard palate*, and the
fleshy part in back is called the *soft palate*, or *velum*. In English the velar consonantal sounds are k [k], g [g], and ng [ŋ], each of which is produced with
the back of the tongue raised against or near the velum, or soft palate. (The
vowels ä [ɑ], ô [ɔ], ō [o], ōō [u] are also velar sounds.)

Glottal Sounds. The glottis is an opening at the upper part of the windpipe,
between the vocal cords; and glottal sounds are those produced in the glottis.
An example of a glottal sound in English is h [h], also called a glottal fricative
or a glottal aspirate.[1]

b) According to Manner of Articulation

Stop-Plosives, or Plosives. In English the stop-plosives, or plosives (variously called stops, explosives, occlusives, mutes, checks, shut consonants, stopped
consonants, momentaneous consonants) are [p] and [b], [t] and [d], [k] and
[g], the first of each pair being voiceless and the second voiced. The production
of a stop-plosive (a) involves full stoppage of the breath passage, and (b) is
characterized by a release or explosion of impounded breath. For the production
of [p] and [b], the lips stop or block the mouth; for the production of [t] and
[d], the tip of the tongue forms a blockage against the gums; for the production
of [k] and [g], the back of the tongue by being raised against the soft palate
blocks or stops the passage of air in the back of the mouth. Complete stoppage
of air in the mouth occurs, since for each sound the velum is raised, thereby
cutting off the nasal passages and not allowing air to pass through them.

The sounds ch [tʃ] and dg [dʒ] may also be included; but are usually classed
as *affricates* (see below). The glottal stop is produced by complete stoppage of
the breath passage by the closed glottis.

The voiceless stop-plosives [p, t, k] may be said in two ways. (a) When
[p], [t], or [k] is followed by a vowel or a diphthong, or is followed by a pause,
each is puffed out quite strongly, or *aspirated*. (b) When [p], [t], or [k] is followed by a consonant, each is puffed out not so strongly, and is said to be
unaspirated.

Continuants. Opposed to the abrupt sounds called stop-plosives are the continuants, or consonant sounds that may be continued or prolonged during one
breath. Continuants may be further classified according to manner of emission
as *nasals, laterals*, or *fricatives.*

a) Nasals. Nasal continuants, or sonorants, are produced by stopping the
air in the mouth and emitting the air solely through the nostrils. The soft palate
is lowered. Each nasal continuant is emitted through the nose only. The nasal
continuants are m [m] (mouth closed at the lips), n [n] (at the tongue point),

---

[1] Some phoneticians recognize [h] as "the only legitimate [glottal] sound in
English," and regard another glottal sound called a glottal stop [?] as an undesirable sound in English. But the glottal stop (called also glottal plosive,
glottal catch) is frequently used in standard American English.

and ng [ŋ] (at the tongue back). There is a nasal consonant for each pair of stop-plosives: [m] is the nasal equivalent of the oral sound [b], [n] of [d], and [ŋ] of [g]. The members of each pair of nasals and stop-plosives are formed similarly, except that the nasals do not open suddenly and are emitted nasally. Remember also that [m], [n], and [ŋ] are the only sounds in English that are resonated primarily in the nasal cavities.

b) Laterals. The only lateral in English is l [l]. The lateral l [l] is produced by placing the tongue tip against the upper gum ridge (that is, against the gums of the upper front teeth) and sending air over the sides of the tongue. The tongue tip touches the upper teeth or the palate but is free at one or both sides. There are various l [l] sounds, of which the two general types are observed in the words *leaf* and *gull*. For l in *leaf* the body of the tongue is a bit convex; and this "brighter" l is usually used before a vowel. For the l in *gull* the tongue is more concave in shape. The lateral l [l] may also be classed with the glides (see below).

c) Fricatives. A fricative sound is one made by forcing the breath through a narrow opening formed by placing the tongue or lips near the palate, the teeth, and the like. Since the oral passage is greatly narrowed but not shut, each fricative sound is accompanied by audible friction or frictional rustling of the breath. The greater the blockage of the breath stream, the greater the consonantal character. Fricatives are voiced or voiceless: v [v] and f [f], th [ð] and th [θ], z [z] and s [s], zh [ʒ] and sh [ʃ], r [r], h [h]. The fricatives may also be divided as simple fricatives (nonhissing sounds, resembling the escape of gas or steam) as [f, ð, θ, r, h] and as sibilant fricatives (strong hisses) as [z, s, ʒ, ʃ].

Affricates. An affricate is a sound made when a stop is closely followed by any consonant uttered with a perceptible expulsion of decided friction of breath. A diphthong, we have seen, is produced by a blend of two *vowel* sounds in such a way that they lose their individual identity and are spoken in one syllable. An affricate is also the result of a blending together—but a blending together of two *consonant* sounds that lose their individual identity and are said in one syllable.

In English the two affricates commonly treated as regular speech sounds are ch [tʃ] and j [dʒ], each of which is usually described as a combination of a plosive and a fricative. In fact, the pronunciation of the two affricates illustrates a phonetic law that when a plosive is followed by a fricative, the explosion is made through the narrow opening of the fricative, and the two pairs of sounds t [t] and sh [ʃ], and d [d] and zh [ʒ], are so closely blended respectively into tsh [tʃ] and dzh [dʒ] that each is a unit.

Other consonant groups in English, such as th in *eighth* and tr in *trip*, are not usually treated as affricates.

Glides. A glide is a transitional or indefinite sound made in passing from a definite speech sound to another, as the sounds of w [w], wh [hw], the initial sound y [j] in *yes*. The lateral l [l] and the consonant r [r] may also be classed with the glides. In the production of such a sound, we begin with one sound and then glide smoothly off it—that is, each glide is the result of a movement or gliding of either the tongue or the lips or both tongue and lips during the formation of the sound. A glide that precedes a definite speech sound is called a *fore-glide*, or *on-glide;* a glide that follows a definite speech sound is called an *afterglide*, or *off-glide*. Glides may be voiced or voiceless.

Vowel-like Consonants. Consonants that have many of the characteristics of vowels are called *vowel-like:* l [l], m [m], n [n], ng [ŋ], r [r], w [w], and the initial sound y [j] as in *yeast,** your,** youth.** For example, such consonants resemble vowels in that they are produced through a relatively open passageway. See §§ 20(10.3), 24(14), 31(1), 32(2), 33(2), 34(14.2).

Syllabic Consonants. A consonant forming a syllable by itself or with one or more consonants is said to be syllabic. See §§ 9, 31(4), 32(2), 33(2).

c) According to the Presence or Absence of Vibration (Voiced or Voiceless)

Place your fingers on your larynx (Adam's apple). Observe carefully which consonant sounds in each pair make you feel a vibration as you say the following:

$$b - p$$
$$v - f$$
$$d - t$$
$$z - s$$

Such consonants as b, v, d, and z made you feel a distinct vibration, required you to use your vocal cords, and therefore are called *voiced consonants*. On the other hand, such consonants as p, f, t, and s are made only with the breath stream, and therefore, because of the absence of vibration, are called *voiceless consonants*.

Instead of classifying consonants in the suggested threefold way [§ 19(3)], it may even be desirable to classify consonants in one way—either as voiced or voiceless. Such simplification would regard each separate adjustment of the articulators as forming two sounds, one being produced by forcing the breath out, as in the formation of [p], the other being produced by emitting the vocalized breath, as in the formation of [b]. But not every voiced consonant has its counterpart.

d) Comments on the Articulation of Consonants

It remains only to add that intelligibility of speech depends heavily on the articulation of consonants.[1]

Stop-Plosives followed by Consonants. When a voiceless stop-plosive occurs initially, it is always aspirated—that is, with the release of the sound there is a noticeable puff or explosion of air. But this aspiration should not be permitted to become so extreme that it arouses adverse criticism. (1) When one plosive follows another, either in the same word, as in "ke*pt*," or as the final and initial sounds of adjacent words, as in "hea*d g*arment," the first one is not altogether released but is held for joining with the second. (2) When a stop-plosive is followed by a nasal, as in "figh*t n*ews," the plosive is exploded over the soft palate through the nasal chambers. (3) When a stop-plosive is followed by a fricative, as in "bough*t sh*ells," the explosion is so closely blended or integrated with the following sound that it is barely heard as an explosion. (4) When a stop-plosive is followed by a glide, as in "ru*b w*ell," the tongue or the lips of the tongue (depending on the sound to be made) are placed approximately as they would be for the glide before the plosive is exploded. When [t] or [d] is followed by [l], the tip of the tongue remains in contact with the gumridge, and the explosion takes place over or around the sides of the tongue instead of over the tip.

Nasals followed by Consonants. Like the plosives, the nasal consonants are often weakened or omitted. (1) When nasals are followed by stop-plosives, note that in a syllable containing the letter combination *nk*, as in "ri*nk*," the *n* is pronounced *ng* [ŋ]; and that in such words as "li*nger*" and "stro*nger*," the *ng* is pronounced ng + g [ŋg]: see § 33.4,5. (2) When a nasal is followed by a nasal, note the following: first, an *m* or *n* doubled in the spelling is usually pronounced as only one sound; second, two nasals occurring in separate syllables are pronounced separately: see §§ 32.3, 33.1,5.

---

[1] See W. N. Brigance and F. M. Henderson, *A Drill Manual for Improving Speech* (1939), pp. 88–123; V. A. Anderson, *Training the Speaking Voice* (1942), pp. 253–284; C. K. Thomas, *An Introduction to the Phonetics of American English* (1947), pp. 115–119.

CHART OF ENGLISH CONSONANTS
Place of Articulation (Vertical Columns)

Manner of Articulation (Horizontal Rows)	Bilabial (Lip-Lip) Voiceless	Bilabial (Lip-Lip) Voiced	Labiodental (Lip-Teeth) Voiceless	Labiodental (Lip-Teeth) Voiced	Linguadental (Tongue-Teeth) Voiceless	Linguadental (Tongue-Teeth) Voiced	Lingua-Alveolar (Tongue-Gum-ridge) Voiceless	Lingua-Alveolar (Tongue-Gum-ridge) Voiced	Lingua-palatal (Tongue-Hard Palate) Voiceless	Lingua-palatal (Tongue-Hard Palate) Voiced	Linguavelar (Tongue-Soft Palate) Voiceless	Linguavelar (Tongue-Soft Palate) Voiced	Glottal (Vocal Cords) Voiceless	Glottal (Vocal Cords) Voiced
Stop-Plosives	p	b					t	d			k	g		
Continuants { Nasal		m						n				ng[ŋ]		
Continuants { Lateral								l						
Continuants { Fricative			f	v	th[θ]	th[ð]	s	z	sh[ʃ]	zh[ʒ]			h	
Affricates							ch[tʃ]	dz[dʒ]						
Glides	hw	w												
Vowel-like Consonants		m w						l r n		r y	y[j]	ng[ŋ]		
Syllabic Consonants		m						n̩ l̩						

Note: a) A consonant may be classified more than once on the chart. For explanation, read § 19.

b) Some phoneticians would make variations in or additions to the chart as given above. They may classify sh [ʃ] and zh [ʒ] as lingua-alveolar sounds because, like s and z, each may be made with the tip of the tongue free, but pointing toward the gums. Other phoneticians would add to chart j, l, and r (the modifier [ˌ] indicates unvoicing). They would also explain that at the beginning and end of a breath group the consonants b [b], d [d], g [g], v [v], z [z], th [ð], and zh [ʒ] are partially unvoiced in English; and that when the consonants w [w], y [j], l [l], and r [r] follow p [p], t [t], or k [k] in the same syllable, each in the former group is partially unvoiced. Also, some phoneticians would explain that h [h] is often voiced between voiced sounds; and to denote this voiced sound, they use the phonetic symbol [ɦ]—thus, *Ohio* [oˈɦaɪ o].
See §§ 29(1.5), 31(3.1), 32(2.4), 33(1.8), 37(1.5), 42(1.2).

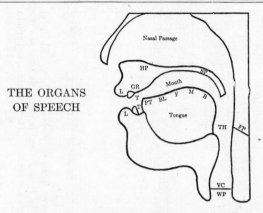

THE ORGANS
OF SPEECH

DIAGRAM OF THE SPEECH ORGANS

LL — Lips. Essential to certain articulations. Help shape the resonators of the mouth in the formation of the vowel sounds; help in the production of the labial consonants.

TT — Teeth.

GR — Gum ridge, or Teeth ridge. The upper, front alveolar process or ridge, right behind the sockets of the upper front teeth.

HP — Hard Palate. The front, bony part of the roof of the mouth.

SP — Soft Palate, or Velum. The fleshy back part of the roof of the mouth.

PT — Tongue Point.

BL — Blade of Tongue. Flat part of tongue just behind the tip, or point. Usually refers to the small part that can protrude from the mouth.

F — Front of Tongue. The part that lies directly under the hard palate.

M — Middle of Tongue.

B — Back of Tongue. The part that lies under the soft palate, or velum.

NP — Nasal Passage. It is closed by raising the soft palate, or velum.

TH — Throat, or Pharynx. The passage, for outgoing air, from the lungs to the mouth. One of the chief resonators.

VC — Vocal Cords. Two pairs of mucous membrane. The upper one, called *superior vocal cords* or *false vocal cords*, has no direct connection with the production of voice. The lower one, called *inferior vocal cords* or *true vocal cords*, can be tightened or loosened to help make the sounds of the voice.

WP — Windpipe, or Trachea. The passage for the breath from the throat (or pharynx) to the lungs.

FP — The Food Passage.

Mouth, or Oral Cavity — The nearly oval-shaped cavity, containing the tongue and the teeth, between the lips and the throat. The most important single resonator of the voice, especially in the formation of the vowel tones.

Tongue — The protrusible and freely movable organ or piece of flesh of the floor of the mouth. The most important single organ of articulation in the mouth, for upon some adjustment of tongue position depend the majority of the sounds, both vowels and consonants.

Nasal Cavity — One of the three principal resonators of the voice, the other two being the mouth cavity and the throat cavity. In English, since vowels are never nasalized, all vowels are expected to be produced with the nasal cavity closed by the velum; but it is likely that most speakers do sound their vowels with some degree of nasal resonance.

l

THE SOUNDS OF SPOKEN ENGLISH

(Arranged Alphabetically According to the Spelling)

§ 20. A

We have already introduced the important vowels and consonants of the English language. Now we shall examine the sounds in greater detail. For example, instead of a short consideration of the sound of ā as in āpe, we shall present a discussion of the many sounds the letter a represents in our language. Thus, § 20 will expand the following bird's-eye view of the dozen or so sounds for which the letter a stands:

Accented

ā as in āpe, § 20(1)	ȧ as in ȧsk, § 20(5)
â as in dâre, § 20(2)	a as in ball, §§ 20(6), 34(4)
ă as in hăt, § 20(3)	a as in watch, §§ 20(4.2), 20(7), 34(6)
ä as in bär, fä′ther, § 20(4)	

Unaccented

ȧ as in al′wȧys, § 20(8)	à as in Chi′nà, § 20(11)
a as in vil′lage, § 20(9)	a as in li′ar, § 22(3)
ŏ as in ăt tack′, ăt tack′, § 20(10)	"Silent a": § 20(10.3)

1. ā as in āpe. (Simplified Symbol: ay. Phonetic Symbol: e.)

1) Say *day*. Observe that the tip of the tongue is behind the lower front teeth, the front is raised toward the hard palate, and the lips are spread. In unstressed syllables and in its shortened form, the sound may be simple, but generally tends to become a diphthong, being made up of the half-high front vowel ā as in āpe and the high, lax front vowel ĭ as in *bit*.

2) The sound ā, as in *ape, day, date, lay, able, eight, faith*, is usually a diphthong, made, as diphthongs are, of a combination of a strongly accented vowel and an unaccented vowel. For example, if you pronounce the word *day* slowly, you will hear a sound that starts with the so-called "long" a and glides toward or ends in a sound resembling ĭ as in *bit*.

Although usually a diphthong, in America the vanishing ĭ sound is either not prominent or not present before voiceless consonants, as in *gate* and *lace*, and the sound becomes a pure vowel. The two sound elements in ā are [e] and [ɪ], and may be written phonetically as [eɪ], as in *day* [deɪ] and *lace* [leɪs]; but since for practical purposes it does not matter whether it is a diphthong or a single vowel, the one symbol [e] is often used, as in this *Manual of Pronunciation*, to represent this sound, as in *day* [de] and *lace* [les].

2. â, âr as in dâre. (Simplified symbol: ehr. Phonetic symbol: ɛr.)

1) Raise front of tongue toward the roof of mouth and then lower tongue slightly. In Eastern American and Southern American speech, the tongue tip stays behind the lower front teeth, the front part lifts to a position intermediate between the vowel position ĕ as in *end* and ă as in *hat*, and then glides quickly to the position for à as in à bout′; but in General American the tongue tip may be curled back for r as the second tongue position in sounding this diphthong. The neutral vowel [ə] almost always follows âr; and the sound may be either bisyllabic or diphthongal.

2) As a rule, "long" a (ā) + r + e (*dare, de clare′**) in the same syllable is pronounced very much like the sound of "short" e (ĕ as in *get*) + r, as in ber′ry, A mer′i ca.*

3) â occurs in *air, dare, malaria, Mary,* pear, where,* various.** The â sound, intermediate between ă in *hat* and ĕ in *get* and occurring only before r in stressed syllables, is a blend of the half-low front vowel ĕ [ɛ] and the neutral vowel ĕ [ə]. When the diphthong starts nearer the vowel sound ĕ [ɛ], it is called the [ɛə] type; when the diphthong starts nearer the vowel sound ă [æ], it is called the [æə] type. Of the two chief varieties, the [ɛə] type is the more frequent, except perhaps in New England.

4) The â sound appears usually in stressed or accented syllables once identical with or containing the ā sound before r. Although today a clear ā vowel only occasionally occurs before r, it is sometimes used in formal speech to distinguish such words as *vary* (văr′ĭ) from *very* (vĕr′ĭ), *Mary** (mār′ĭ) from *merry* (mĕr′ĭ), *hairy** from *Harry, chary** from *cherry, wary** from *wherry.* Such instances veer away from the tendency in America to lower the ā sound in the more common longer words toward the short ĕ (ĕ as in *get*) where the vowel is followed by r and another vowel.

5) Identical in the 1600's with the "long" a (ā), the comparatively "long" vowel sound â may still be heard in such words as *barbarian,* malaria,** and *vary.* Although such words may be pronounced either with ā or â, the tendency is to lower the ā before r to a more open front sound. Cf. "long" e + r lowered to ę̄ in *here:* § 24(2); ō + r lowered to ôr: § 34(3); o͞o + r lowered to o͝o: § 34(21.3).

6) When the â has a weak stress in longer words ending in –ary (*dictionary,* necessary,* visionary*) the ā sound is made a little shorter and lighter. See § 13(1).

7) In summary, observe that a + r + a vowel is not always shortened to the vowel ĕ as in *end,* for there is a group of words in which a + r + a vowel is pronounced ă as in *hat,* as in *comparison,* Harry,* and *tariff.* Note, also, such pairs as *barbârian** and *barbăric,* declâre** and *declărative.* Briefly, the only guide to the pronunciation of such words is actual cultivated usage.

3. ă as in hăt. (Simplified Symbol: a. Phonetic Symbol: æ.)

1) The sound ă is the first sound in *at* and *apple.* In making the sound of ă as in *hat* the front of the tongue is slightly raised toward the roof of the mouth and is a little farther back than for â in *air* or *dare.* The tip of the tongue is behind the lower front teeth. For this low, tense front vowel the soft palate is raised. Open mouth a little more for ă than for â.

2) The ā in *ape* and *day* is commonly called "long" a; the ă in *at, fat, hat, lack, dandy, cap, bag, Sam, Mather,* and *plaid,** is commonly called "short" a. Avoid raising the tongue too high toward the hard palate. Be careful not to nasalize the sound; be careful not to substitute the low back vowel ä as in *arm* for ă.

3) In such words as char′i ty and par′rot observe that "short" a (ă) + r accented is followed either by a vowel or by a second r in the following syllable. The general rule is to pronounce the combination as ăr.

4) In General American there is a strong tendency to use ă [æ] instead of ä [ɑ] in proper names and book-words like *Alabama,* lava,** and *strata.**

4. ä as in bär, fä′ther. (Simplified Symbol: ah. Phonetic Symbol: ɑ.)

1) Tongue should lie flat or almost flat in mouth, lips and jaws should be released, as you say ä as in *ah,* the sound the doctor asks you to make when he wishes to see your throat easily, for the sound puts the back of the tongue low in the mouth and the tip of the tongue behind the lower teeth. This is the lowest back vowel; it is the only back vowel made without rounding the lips, which are not only unrounded but also wider open than in any other vowel sound.

2) ä, as in *ah, arm, bar, father,* and *tar,* while classifiable as a mid-back vowel sound, is generally described as a low-back vowel sound. In General American, as well as in Southern American, speech, the ä sound appears in words spelled with o, as in *doll, lot, rock, top,* and in words where the letter a follows an ini-

tial w, as in *wash* and *watch*. Except in those words spelled with o, as in *rock*, *hot*, and *not*,* the accented ä is today a comparatively long sound.

3) In unstressed syllables, as in *ar cha'ic** and *ar te'ri al*,* or in partly stressed syllables, as in *ar'bi tra'tion* and *ar'gu men'ta tive*,* the letter a receives a shorter sound. This shorter a appears frequently in those words where the a is spelled o, as in *document* and *octagon*, and where the word begins with wa, as in *wallet* and *wash*.* See §§ 34(6), 34(7.3).

5. á as in ásk. (Simplified Symbols: a, ah. Phonetic Symbol: a.)

1) The vowel á [a] as in *ask*, a sound midway between the ă in *hat* and the ä in *bar*, is the lowest of the front vowels. á [a] is made with the front of the tongue low in the mouth, the jaw dropped considerably, and the lips slightly spread. The sound, not widely used in America, is present in fewer than two hundred words, typical of which are *ask*,* *basket*,* *broadcast*,* *chance*,* *dance*,* *example*, *path*, *task*,* *vast*.* Those who recommend the sound say that there is an observable tendency for Americans to accept á [a] as a pure vowel in syllables ending in the sounds of f [f], th [θ], s [s], sk [sk]. It may be noted that the true á [a] generally appears before ff (*chaff*,* *distaff*,* *giraffe*,* *phonograph*,* *quaff**), ft (*aft*, *after*,* *craft*, *daft*, *draft*,* *shaft**), ns or nc (*answer*,* *chance*,* *dance*,* *enhance*,* *France*,* *Lancelot*,* *trance**), nt (*aunt*,* *chant*, *enchant*,* *plant*,* *shan't**), sk (*ask*,* *bask*, *cask*,* *flask*,* *masque**), sp (*aspect*,* *clasp*,* *gasp*,* *raspberry**), ss (*brass*,* *class*,* *grass*,* *pass**), st (*aghast*,* *alabaster*,* *blast*,* *broadcast*,* *disaster*,* *fast*,* *past**), voiceless th (*bath*,* *lath*,* *path*,* *wrath**). But most Americans sound the á as ă in *hat*.

2) Some Americans pronounce the so-called "*ask* words" with the vowel sound intermediate between the vowel in *hat* and the vowel in *bar*, obtaining the medial sound partly by having the tongue slightly lower than it is in *hat* and slightly higher than it is in *bar*. Such is the sound heard especially on the stage and in Eastern United States and England; but the sound is heard much less frequently in the moving pictures and on the radio, where the "stage diction" is modified considerably so that the definite localisms of either Eastern or Southern speech (similar to but not identical with Southern English speech) are eliminated and the pronunciation becomes identifiable with no particular section, the purpose being to use speech that sounds cultured all over America.

A larger number of Americans pronounce the *ask* words with the ä in *bar* and *palm*,* but the majority pronounce them with the ă in *hat* and *fan*.

3) The important point to remember is that, whether you use the ă in *hat*, the ä in *bar*, or the medial á, you must be consistent in the use of this sound. Do not, for example, say "äsk" and "äunt," using the "Italian" or "broad" a, and then say "chănce"* and "clăss,"* using the ă as in *hat*.

Avoid also the error of giving the sound of ä or of á to such words as *back*, *cabin*, *had*, and *man*,* which properly take the vowel ă in all of America. Note, too, that before *sh* the sound is always ă, as in *dash*, *fashion*,* and *national*.* Finally, for the many who use ă as in *hat* for all the *ask* type of words, remember to permit neither undue flatness nor nasalization.

4) The soundest advice in regard to the vowel sound in the *ask* type of words is to make no attempt to acquire the medial sound á if it is not already in your speech or if it is not characteristic of the community in which you live. Most Americans use the ă as in *hat;* and if the intermediate á attracts undue attention, it will label your speech artificial or affected or pedantic or even offensive.

6. a as in ball = ô, § 34(4). (Simplified Symbol: aw. Phonetic Symbol: ɔ.)

1) In such words as *ball*, *law*,* *raw*, *land*, *balk*,* and *warm*, the vowel sound is tantamount to ô as in *orb* [§ 34(4)]. Lips are closely rounded, the mouth assuming an elliptical form with the widest part running vertically; the back

of the tongue is raised toward the soft palate; the tongue tip assumes a slightly lower position. This half-low, rounded, tense back vowel should not be placed too far back in the throat.

2) The symbol ô is used to represent both the briefer sound [ɔ] as in *although** and *audacity** and the longer sound [ɔ:] as in *Arkansas,** *draw, salt,** *walnut,** and *wharf.** The sound is long in stressed syllables before a voiced consonant or a pause; half-long before a voiceless consonant; and usually short in unstressed syllables.

3) The short ô [ɔ] is not identical with the ŏ [ɒ] in *odd, fog, not,** and *stop.* See § 34(6).

4) Generally the ô sound is indicated in spelling by au, as in *audacity** and *austere,* and, when final, by aw, as in *gnaw** and *saw.** An interesting survival is *water,** pronounced either wô′tĕr, wŏt′ĕr, or wä′tĕr. [See also § 34(7).]

5) Just as the word *water** is often pronounced with ŏ, or a short ä, [ŏ, § 34(6)], so one sound or the other is occasionally introduced by Americans into such au and ou words as *autumn,** *daughter,** *bought,* and *thought.**

7. a as in wan = ŏ, **§ 34(6).** A w preceding the a in words like *wan** and *quality* and *what** rounds the a sound into ŏ.

8. å as in al′wåys. (Simplified Symbols: ay, i, uh. Phonetic Symbols: e, ɪ, ə.)

1) The sound called "half-long" a ("half-long" not in duration but in quality), which appears in *always,** *chaotic,** *impresario,** and *vacation,** and adjectives or nouns in -åte, such as *aggregate** and *licentiate,** occurs in syllables having no marked primary or secondary accent but yet sufficiently stressed to retain the ā-like quality of the vowel.

The symbol å often varies in range from ā to ĭ. Thus the dictionary gives the pronunciation of *always* as ôl′wåz, ôl′wĭz; *chaotic* as kå ŏt′ĭk; *impresario* as ĭm′prå sä′rĭ ō, ĭm′prĭ sä′rĭ ō; *vacation** as vå kā′shŭn, và kā′shŭn; *aggregate** as ăg′grē gåt (adj. and n.), ăg′grē gāt (v.); *licentiate** as lĭ sĕn′shĭ ăt (n.), lĭ sĕn′shĭ āt (v.t.).

2) Frequently the symbol å is used to distinguish an adjective or a noun from its corresponding verb, which is given the full ā sound. (Observe and compare such words as *appropriate,** *consummate,** *delegate,** *duplicate,** *intimate,** *terminate.**) In informal speech the å in such adjectives and nouns is often pronounced ĭ, as in ă prō′prĭ ĭt, kŏn sŭm′ĭt, and so on; or even with the schwa. See § 50(2).

9. a as in village = ĭ. (Simplified Symbol: i. Phonetic Symbol: ɪ.)

1) In numerous words the unaccented a is pronounced ĭ, as in *climate,** *furnace, village.* So, also, are ai and ay in terminating syllables, as in *always,** *Calais* (kăl′ā; kăl′ĭs), *Thursday,** *yesterday.**

2) Sometimes the -day is pronounced -då [§ 20(8)]. However, when -day has a secondary accent, especially in compound-like words, it is sounded dā.

3) For the a = ĭ sound that differentiates a verb from its noun or adjective, see § 20(8).

4) For the a = ĕ as in *necessary,** see § 13(1).

10. ă as in ăt tack′. (Simplified Symbol: uh. Phonetic Symbol: ə.)

1) In deliberate, formal, or emphatic speech the symbol ă [ə], as given in *attack* (ă tăk′), *abrupt* (ăb rŭpt′), and *adjourn** (ă jûrn′), may be given the full sound of ă as in *hat.* But most sounds indicated by the symbol ă [ə] tend to the neutral vowel à [ə: § 20(11)] as in the first and last syllables of *America,** *companion, Dakota;* as in the intermediate syllables of *lovable** and *sympathetic;* and as in the last syllables of *April, erosion,** *fireman, importance, servant,** *troublesome,* and *vacant.* Tersely, in most instances the diacritical marking ă [ə]

tends to be or is one of several dictionary notations for the same sound—the neutral vowel or schwa (also called the obscure vowel, the indeterminate vowel, the indefinite vowel, the voice murmur). This neutral vowel or schwa [ə] never occurs in a stressed syllable. See §§ 20(11), 24(4), 28(5.5), 34(12.2,3), 34(13.1,2, 3), 40(12).

2) Also the ă [ə] may be pronounced as a sound showing a range between the limits of á [ə: § 20(11)] in Chi′nà and ă [æ] in ăg′gre gate.*

3) In some words, where the ă [ə] sound occurs between two consonants, that sound may disappear. Thus, such words are often pronounced both with and without the intervening vowel—*certain** (sûr′tĭn, sûr′t'n), *fatal* (fā′tăl, fā′t'l), *journal* (jûr′năl, jûr′n'l). [For syllabic consonants, see §§ 9(1-5), 24(14), 28(5.6), 31(1.2), 31(4), 32(2.1,2,3), 33(2), 34(14.2), 40(13.4).

11. á as in Chi′nà. (Simplified Symbol: uh. Phonetic Symbol: ə.)

1) The sound ă as in *attack* [§ 20(10)] appears in unaccented initial syllables, generally terminating in a consonant in the spelling; it occurs also in terminating closed syllables, as in *loy′al* and *dis′tant*. On the other hand, á as in *about,** *alone, around,** *boa,** *idea,** *sofa*, or like the ē in *father* pronounced without the r, appears in unaccented open syllables. The á, unlike the ă, always has the sound of the neutral vowel or schwa, the most frequently used vowel sound in English and the sound toward which vowel sounds in unaccented syllables and diphthongs (and certain unstressed words) tend. When the sound is made, the tongue is relaxed and the lips are in a neutral position.

2) Of perhaps a half dozen general rules that are used consciously or unconsciously in English conversation, there is one that has the fewest departures. In talk the vowel in an unaccented syllable tends to become weakened or obscure. Each of the so-called five vowels (§ 18) approaches the sound of the neutral vowel or schwa uh [ə]—that is, in an unaccented syllable the vowels a, e, i, o, u tend to be pronounced as uh [ə], as in *a*ttack, t*a*ken, ch*a*rity, c*o*nnect, wisd*o*m, circ*u*s. In addition, for the vowels e and i in an unstressed syllable the tendency is to weaken each in the direction of ĭ as in *bit*, and not to go as far as the obscure or neutral vowel uh [ə], as in ang*e*l,* mom*e*nt, tak*e*n, circum-stance,* circ*u*s. See §§ 20(10), 24(4), 28(5.5), 34(12.2,3), 34(13.1,2,3), 40(12).

12. ae, æ.

1) In words of Greek origin usually spelled ae, as in *Æschylus, aesthetic** (also *esthetic*), and *aestival* (also *estival*), the ae is often pronounced in America as the ĕ in *ĕnd* and *gĕt*. In England the usual pronunciation is as the ē in *bee, eve*, and *equal*.

2) In common English words the tendency is to change the symbol æ (or digraph ae) to ē as in *eve;* thus, *mediaeval* (also *medieval**).

13. Digraph ai. The digraph ai may have such sounds as the following:

ā as in āpe—*ai*m, c*ai*sson, d*ai*ly, f*ai*l, g*ai*t, k*ai*lyard, m*ai*ze, qu*ai*l, r*ai*sin,* w*ai*f

â as in dâre—*air,** f*ai*ry,* h*ai*r, l*ai*r

ĕ as in gĕt—s*ai*d*

ī as in īce—*ai*sle,* B*ai*ram, d*ai*mon, H*ai*duk, J*ai*n, k*ai*ser, P*ai*ute, T*ai*no, T*ai*ping

Special Note: When a͡i or A͡I (note the curved line or ligature) is used in the SIMPLIFIED column, it is always to be pronounced "long" i (ī) as in *ice*. See §§ 28(2), 28(3).

14. aN.

1) When French words are marked ăN or äN or ôN, the n sound is not pro-

nounced. Nasalize the vowel before the N, making the nasal äN between a nasalized ä of *ah* and a nasalized ô of *born;* and the nasal ôN between a nasalized ô of *born* and a nasalized ō of *old.*

2) Nasalized i is pronounced like a nasal American pronunciation of ă as in *sang.* A double nasal, such as mm, represents a single consonant sound which is pronounced, not silent [see § 32(3.1,2)]; therefore, the vowel preceding the double nasal is not nasalized. Remember that the symbol N (small capital) means that the preceding vowel is nasalized.

15. au; aw; ay.

1) In words from the Anglo-Saxon, Old French, Latin, and Greek, the digraph au is pronounced ô as in *ôrb* [§ 34(4), 34(24.2)]. Examples: *aught,* caucus,* daub,* fault,* Gaul, gauze, haunch** (but see 2 below), *nausea,* paucity, raucous, sauce.*

2) The digraph au + n may be sounded not only as ô (ôrb) but also as ä (ah, bär). Examples: *daunt** (dônt; dänt), *gaunt,* haunch,* haunt,* jaunty,* launch,* launder,* maunder, paunch,* saunter.**

3) In words from the German the au is pronounced ou as in *about: Faust, gauss, Hausa, kauri, Mauser, sauerkraut.** Comparatively recent words from the French, however, often have the sound ō (ōpen): *hautboy, mauve,* sauté,* sauterne, vaudeville.**

4) The digraph aw + k, aw + l, aw + n, or final aw is pronounced ô as in *ôrb: gawky, awl, fawn, jaw, hawk, lawn, mawkish.*

5) ay as a digraph most often has the sound of ā (āpe), as in *say;* but also has the sound ĭ in *Friday* [§ 20(9.1)]. ay may have other sounds: e.g., å in *foray,** ä in *Maya,* ī in *Cayuse* and *kayak.*

§ 21. B

1. English b. (Simplified Symbol: b. Phonetic Symbol: b.)

1) By putting your lips lightly together for an instant and blowing them apart suddenly as you make a voiced sound (voiced because the vocal cords are vibrating), you sound the bilabial stop-plosive b as in *be, ball, bay, dab, abrupt, sobs.* b is the voiced cognate of p [§ 35(1)].

2) b is not pronounced before t, as in *debt* and *doubt,* or initially before any consonants except l and r: not pronounced in *bdelium;* pronounced in *block* and *brush.*

3) After m, as in *bomb,* comb,* lamb,** and *lambkin,* the b is usually not sounded.

4) When between m and l (the combination -mbl-), the b is always pronounced, as in *humble** and *tremble.**

5) When b is between m and e (m + b + a vowel), the b usually is pronounced as part of the second syllable, as in *num'ber* and *tim'ber.*

6) bb is usually pronounced single, as in *jobber* (jŏb'ẽr)—except in compounds, as in *job-breaking* (jŏb'brāk'ĭng).

In English one general rule is that doubled consonants are usually pronounced as a single sound, except in compounds. When a doubled consonant approximates a single sound, as in *jobber,* the single sound goes with the accented syllable (jŏb'ẽr). See also §§ 23(1.10), 25(1.4), 26(1.3), 30(2.2), 31(5.1), 32(3.1,2), 33(5.1), 35(5), 37(6), 38(13.2,3,4), 39(9.1), 45(4.1,2).

2. Spanish b; German b.

1) To make the Spanish b, sound the English v not with the lower lip and the upper teeth but with both lips. In fact, v is in Spanish an alternative spelling for b; and the form most familiar in English is generally used, as *Cordova*

rather than *Cordoba.* The sound is identical with that of modern Greek b, as in *beta;* the IPA symbol for the voiced bilabial spirant or fricative is [β].

2) German-born students tend to use an aspiration that makes the [b] sound like [p]—see § 35(1); they tend to devoice final [b], pronouncing it as [p]. Spanish students must be cautioned to speak the sound with firm lip closure when the [b] occurs between vowels, or intervocalically.

In the English pronunciation of words from the Sanskrit and numerous recent East Indian words beginning with bh (*bhang*), the h may be omitted. However, East Indian natives sound bh as b + h, as pronounced separately in *cob'head'*. See, also, §§ 22(11.1), 23(3), 29(3), 30(2.1), 35(4.5), 39(7.4).

§ 22. C

1. "Soft" c. The letter c spells three "soft" sounds [for "hard" c = k, see § 22(2)]:

1) c before e, i, or y is the voiceless s sound, as in *celery, citizen,* cycle,* acidity,* dance,* sacrifice.** When c closes a syllable, that general rule (which comes from the French) still applies: thus, pac'i fy. When c does not appear before e, i, or y, and yet is to be given the sound of s, a cedilla (a mark like a comma) is put under c to show that the c has the s sound even when preceding a, o, or u; e.g., *façade.**

2) When the c is combined with the i or e [§ 38(12.4)], as in *delicious** and *ocean,** the c is the voiceless sh [ʃ] sound.

3) Rarely does c spell the voiced z sound [z], as in one pronunciation of *sacrifice** and *suffice.**

2. "Hard" c = k. The letter c spells one "hard" sound.

1) When final, c = k, as in arc, mu'sic.

2) Almost always before any letter except e, i, y, or h, the c = k, as in *account,* catch,* collapse,* culture.** The rule is also applicable when c closes a syllable, as in sac'ri fice.* Exception: scep'tic.

3) Before e or i, cc is pronounced ks, as in suc cess', suc cinct'.*

4) Before any letter except e, i, y, or h, the cc = k, as in *accede,* accost,* occident.*

3. Silent c; cz = ch.

1) In *czar** and its derivatives (*czarevitch, czarevna, czarina*), c is as silent as it is in such words as *corpuscle,* indict,* muscle,** and *victuals.**

2) In *Czech** and its derivatives cz is pronounced ch [tʃ].

4. Spanish c. Castilian Spaniards pronounce c before e and i like the th in *then;* other Spaniards, including those in Spanish America, pronounce the c before e and i as the s in *sing.* Thus: *cedula* (sĕd'û lȧ; *Castilian*, thä'thōō lä), *ceibo* (sā'ĕ bō; thā'ĕ bō).

5. ch = tsh; ch = j. Of the four sounds that the digraph ch has, two are the following [for the other two, see § 22(6,7,8)]:

1) In such words as *chafe,* chimney,** and *church,** ch has a pronunciation like tsh (t + sh). To make this affricate, raise the tip of the tongue as though you were going to say t [§§ 19, 39(1.2)], and then hurry into the sound of sh [§§ 19, 38(11)] as in *shame.* Whether ch is one sound or two sounds, it functions as a single speech sound resulting from the two voiceless or breathed sounds t [t] and sh [ʃ] made in quick succession and becoming the voiceless tsh [tʃ].

2) Combined with h, c has a second pronunciation. In some unstressed syllables ch [tʃ] is voiced to j [dʒ], as in *Greenwich** (England). Such words as *cabbage** and *knowledge** were once spelled with ch.

6. ch = sh.

1) In addition to the two sounds in English already described [§ 22(5)], ch has the sound of sh [ʃ] commonly given by Englishmen in such words as *belch,* *branch,** *haunch,** *launch,** *luncheon,** *pinch, truncheon,** *wrench.** As a rule Americans do not omit the t element of ch [tʃ] as in *children,** although such omission is made frequently by Britishers in words where ch [tʃ] follows l and n. See also §§ 22(7), 23(1.3), 25(4.3).

7. ch (in French words) = sh. Combined with h, c has the sound of sh in words of French origin, as *chagrin,** *chalet,** *chamois,** *chaperon,** *chanson,** *chivalry,** *chute,** *machine,** *mustache.** Cf. § 25(4.2).

8. ch = k.

1) The digraph ch is also sounded "hard" like k, especially in words of Greek origin, as in *architect,** *character,** *chrysanthemum,** *echo,** *epoch.**
2) This "hard" k is given in words from the Hebrew, as in *Chaldean.* For the pronunciation of arch-, see *arch-.**
3) In words from the Italian, k is the sound when ch precedes e and i, as in *scherzo* (skĕr'tsō).

9. Silent ch. In some words (*fuchsia,** *schism,** *yacht**) the *ch* is silent.

10. English and Foreign ch.

1) Several observations may be made about the digraph ch [§ 22(5–9)]:
   a) ch [tʃ] is an affricate [§ 19] when it has the sound of approximately tsh (t + sh). The sound ch [tʃ] is made by joining the voiceless plosive t [t] to the voiceless sibilant fricative sh [ʃ].
   b) In certain unaccented syllables the digraph ch is voiced to j [dʒ], the voiced correlative of voiceless ch [tʃ]. The sound j [dʒ] results from joining the voiced plosive d [d] to the voiced sibilant fricative zh [ʒ].
   c) After *l* and *n*, the t element of ch [tʃ] is sometimes omitted, less frequently by Americans than by Englishmen.
   d) In post-Chaucerian (modern) French loan words the ch has the sh sound. In pre-Chaucerian (older) French loan words the t and d elements in French ch [tʃ] and j [dʒ] are retained.
   e) ch has the sound of k in most words from the Greek (directly or indirectly) and from the Hebrew.
2) In addition to these several sounds in English, ch is also used to represent a front (palatal) or back (velar) voiceless fricative in partially Anglicized words from Scotch, Celtic, Dutch, German, Modern Greek, and other languages. Occurring initially, and also after consonants and front vowels, is the palatal voiceless fricative sounded as ch in German *ich* (called the "Ich-laut" [ç]); occurring in German also after back vowels is the velar voiceless fricative (called the "Ach-laut" [x]).
Both sounds occur in Scotch, the palatal fricative sound [ç] after front vowels and the velar fricative sound [x] after back vowels.
Whether the ch sound is palatal (front) or velar (back), it is sounded approximately like that of English k in *took* and in *Dick,* but is made without full contact between the back of the tongue and the roof of the mouth. The pronunciation is indicated by a small capital ᴋ (IPA:x). Compare gh [§ 26(2.2)].

11. Foreign ch, chh; English ck.

1) In words from the Sanskrit and modern East Indian languages, ch and chh (chhatri—chŭt'rĕ—"funerary monument; resthouse") are each pronounced like English ch in child. However, many prefer to sound chh as ch + h, as

pronounced separately in *patchhead* (păch'hĕd'). See §§ 21(3), 23(3), 29(3), 30(2.1), 35(4.5), 39(7.4).

2) Usually occurring after short vowels in English, ck is pronounced as a single k sound, as in *luck* and *cockatoo*.* See § 30(2.2).

§ 23. D

1. English d.

1) The sound of d, as in *dairy*,* *dance*,* *deaf*,* *do*, is a voiced stop-plosive made by having the tip of the tongue touching the roof of the mouth just behind the upper front teeth and then by blowing the tongue down with a voiced breath.

2) [d] is the voiced cognate of [t]. Make neither sound on the teeth, for letting the tongue touch the teeth in the production of d or t results in *dentalization*. It should be noted that [d] and [t] are more or less frequently classed as *dental* sounds, as are th [θ], th [ð], n, l, r, s, z, sh, zh, ch, j [dʒ].

3) When [d] is followed by [l], no vowel sound intervenes—and the [l] is said to be syllabic, as in *saddle* (săd' 'l). But avoid eliding the [d] when found in the medial position. A poor speaker may "swallow" the [d], pronouncing *saddle* as să' 'l ['sæ l̩] or să''l ['sæ əl], or may substitute the glottal stop for the [d], as ['sæ ?l]. See also §§ 9, 31(1.2,3), 39(1.3).

4) The sound of the letter d is always silent in *handkerchief*,* *handsome*,* and *Wednesday*.*

5) Often or regularly the letter d is silent in ordinary conversation in pronouncing such words as *grandfather, grandsire, grandstand*, as it also is in unstressed "and" before the same consonant, as in *deaf-and-dumb* (dĕf' 'n dŭm': see § 16).

6) The letter d is also silent in familiar speech when it is final before a consonant in the next word, as in gran(d) *tour*, Ol(d) *Testament*, gran(d) *joke*. See *grand*.*

7) n + d + a consonant, or l + d + a consonant, is often silent in familiar speech, as in *frien(d)s, fiel(d)s*. The d may be silent only when flanked on the right by b, c, f, g, j, k, m, n, p, q, s, t, or v.

8) An excrescent sound in a word is a sound not rightfully part of the word, but growing out of the action of the vocal organs in forming neighboring sounds, especially the sounds preceding and following. In *alder*,* *astound, dwindle, kindred*, and *thunder*, for example, the d is excrescent.

9) [d], as we know [§§ 19, 23(1.1)], is an alveolar sound, with the tip of the tongue placed lightly against the upper gum ridge and then voiced by the vibrating breath stream released over the tongue tip. But [d], an alveolar sound, is palatalized before i, as in *soldier*—that is, the utterance of the [d] is modified to dj [dʒ] by having the tongue tip brought simultaneously to or near the hard palate.

The sound [d] is likewise palatalized before ū (yōō [ju]), as in *verdure*.* As with *soldier*,* so with *verdure** the d approaches or becomes a j [dʒ] sound. Undoubtedly current are the pronunciations VUHR juhr ['vɝ dʒɚ] and, perhaps less frequently, VUHR dyuhr ['vɝ djɚ]. Also heard are VUHR jŏŏr ['vɝ dʒʊr] and VUHR dyŏŏr ['vɝ djʊr], regarded by more than one authority as artificial or perhaps even obsolete. See §§ 39(9.2), 40(11.9), 50(31,33), and the SPECIAL NOTES, III, b.4 (page xxi).

10) Like most of the double letters in our language, dd is pronounced single except in compounds. For an important rule, see § 21(1.6). Consult also §§ 25(1.4), 26(1.3), 30(2.2), 31(5.1), 32(3.1,2), 33(5.1), 35(5), 37(6), 38(13.2,3,4), 39(9.1), 45(4.1,2).

11) Only one d is sounded in dg, as in *hedgerow,** and dj (d + dzh), as in *adjective*. But the rule does not follow for combinations, where the d and g, or the d and j (dzh), are sounded separately, as in *red jar, mad jaunt*.

12) For dg and dge, see § 25(3.2,3).

13) Such words as *bulge, change,* and *sounds* are pronounced either bŭlj or bŭldgj, chănj or chăndj, soundz or sounz. For the loss of the d, see § 25(4.3).

14) There are three important general rules for the sounding of –ed as a past-tense suffix [see also § 24(16.4,5)]:

    a) –ed as a past tense of a verb is sounded as d [d] after voiced sounds, and as t [t] after voiceless sounds. Examples: *rib, ribbed* [d]; *rip, ripped* [t]; *live, lived* [d]; *knife, knifed* [t]. See the chart of English consonants, § 19 (p. xlix).

    b) When [d] or [t] is followed by the –ed ending, pronounce the –ed as a separate syllable formally as –ĕd and more naturally as –ĭd or ĭd. Examples: *need, needed; wait, waited*.

    c) If the original verb ends with the sound ch (*patch, patched*), f (*hoof, hoofed*), k (*pick, picked*), p (*hop, hopped*), s (*yes, yessed*), sh (*push, pushed*), the e is silent and the [d] is pronounced [t].

15) The characteristic feature of regular verbs is that they have one form for the present tense and one form (or a common form) for both the past tense and the past participle. Thus we have *talk, talked, talked; bleed, bled, bled; strike, struck, struck*. There are, however, a number of other verbs that have two ways of forming the past tense and the past participle. Such verbs have not only one form for both the past tense and the past participle, but actually two such common forms.

The past and the past participle of *burn** are *burned* (bûrnd) and *burnt* (bûrnt); of *dream* are *dreamed* and *dreamt;* of *dwell* are *dwelled* and *dwelt*. Likewise, we have *leaned* and *leant, learned* and *learnt, smelled* and *smelt, spelled* and *spelt, spoiled* and *spoilt*. Note the substitution of the t for the regular –ed ending.

Most writers will spell the d pronunciation with - ed; but will write *burned, dreamed, dwelled, leaned, smelled, spelled,* and *spoiled* while they may pronounce the words as *burnt, dreamt, dwelt, leant, smelt, spelt,* and *spoilt,* or will read *burnt* for *burned, dreamt* for *dreamed,* and so on.

Observe, first, that the d pronunciations are spelled –ed, and the t pronunciations are spelled either –ed or –t. Recall, also, that the –ed and –d endings of the past and the past participle are pronounced –t after voiceless consonants except t. Again, note that –ed, when a separate syllable, is pronounced either ĕd, ĭd, or ĭd [§ 24(5)]; when combined with a preceding sonant (voiced sound), is pronounced d; and when pronounced with a preceding surd (voiceless sound), is pronounced t.

Finally, the past participle of a verb is pronounced with the shortened or contracted form of –ed (d or t, as in *blessed*) except where the final consonant of the root word requires pronunciation as a separate syllable, as in *deed′ed, fat′ed, gait′ed, seed′ed, wait′ed*. Except after t or d, the e in –ed of the past and the past participle of a verb is silent. However, the past participle when used as an adjective may also be pronounced with the full form of –ed, as in *bless′ed,** *curs′ed*.

See also § 24(16.4,5)

    a) In archaic, poetic, or ecclesiastical style, –ed is often preserved as a separate syllable. Styles of speaking that are rhetorical, poetic, or solemn often give *beloved** (bĕ lŭvd′) as bĕ lŭv′ĕd, bĕ lŭv′ĭd; *enthroned* (ĕn thrōnd′) as ĕn thrōn′ĕd, ĕn thrōn′ĭd; *horned* (hôrnd) as hôr′nĕd, hôr′nĭd.

    b) When adverbs are formed by the addition of –ly to an adjective ending in –ed, the –ed is generally retained as a distinct syllable. Thus, *confessed* (kŏn fĕst′) + –ly becomes *confessedly* (kŏn fĕs′ĕd lĭ, kŏn fĕs′ĭd lĭ) and *designed* (dĕ zīnd′) + –ly becomes *designedly* (dĕ zīn′ĕd lĭ, dĕ zīn′ĭd lĭ). See § 24(5.1,2).

2. Foreign d.

1) Initially, Spanish d is softer and less explosive than English d; medially or finally, Spanish d is like ~~th~~ in *then*. In everyday Spanish, final d is often silent or almost silent. Examples of medial d: *"caudillo"* (kou ~~thēl'~~yō; *Sp.*, kou ~~thē'~~yō); *escudo* (ĕs kōō'dō; *Sp.*, ĕs kōō'~~th~~ō; *Pg.*, ĕs kōō'~~th~~ōō).

2) Spanish –nd is like English –nd.

3) In intervocalic positions, Spanish-Americans must take care not to pronounce [d] as ~~th~~ [ð].

4) German-born students must not pronounce [d] as [t] in final positions.

3. Foreign dh. In Sanskrit, Hindustani, and derived East Indian languages, dh is sounded as d + h, as in *dhai* (d'hä'ē); but in English is acceptably pronounced as d, as in *dhak* (däk; dôk), *"dhan"* (dŭn), *dhyana* (dyä'nä). See §§ 21(3), 22(11.1), 29(3), 30(2.1), 35(4.5), 39(7.4).

§ 24. E

The letter e has eight accented and three unaccented sounds:

Accented

ē in ēve, bee, ē'qual, § 24(1)   e in sergeant = ä, §§ 24(8), 20(4)
ę̄ in hęre, § 24(2)   e in where = â, §§ 24(9), 20(2)
ĕ in gĕt, § 24(3)   e in English = ĭ, §§ 24(10), 28(4)
ę in herd = û, §§ 24(6), 40(7)   e in eh = ā, §§ 24(10), 20(1)

Unaccented

ĕ in ĕ vent', § 24(11)   ĕ in tak'ĕn, § 24(14,16)
ē in mak'ēr, §§ 24(7,11)   Note: For consonant e, see § 24(15);
                                       for silent e, see § 24(14,16).

1. e as in ēve, bee, ē'qual. (Simplified Symbol: ee. Phonetic Symbol: i.)

1) ē as in ēve is the highest front vowel, its pure sound being formed with lips tense and spread (the smile position) and the teeth almost together. Place the tongue tip behind or on the back of the lower front teeth and hold the front of the tongue high toward the hard palate. Keep throat relaxed.

2) The "long" e as in *e'qual* and *re-do'* appears only in syllables having some stress.

3) Avoid introducing an off-glide when pronouncing such words as *deal* and *heal*. Each ē is pronounced as one sound—dēl [dil], hēl [hil]—and preferably not as two—dē'ăl ['di əl], hē'ăl ['hi əl].

2. ę̄ as in hęre. (Simplified Symbols: ĭe, i, ee. Phonetic Symbols: ɪə, ɪ, i.)

1) The diphthong ę̄ as in hęre is made up of the high, lax vowel ĭ [ɪ] as in *bit, is, chin, ill* and of the neutral vowel uh [ə], which is an off-glide for the first element ĭ [ɪ]. We have seen how r affects or distinctly alters its preceding "long" a sound, lowering that sound to â [ɛə] as in *dâre* [§ 20(2)]. In like manner "long" e + r is lowered to ę̄ [ɪə], the cause being again the fore-glide of the r. The two chief varieties of â are indicated by [ɛə] and [æə]; similarly, since the first element of the diphthong ę̄ is ĭ [ɪ] and the second glides off into unstressed uh [ə], the ę̄ may be written [ɪə].

For words with "long" e (ē) + r + a vowel, as in *dreary* and *weary*, one speaker will use the higher ē [i], another will use an intermediate vowel that is much closer to ē [i] than to ĭ [ɪ], and most speakers will tend to lower the ē [i] so that it approaches ĭ [ɪ]. Also, for words ending with "long" e (ē) + final r, as in *fear, hear, year*, or ending with "long" e̸ (ē) + r + a consonant (*beard*), the sound will most often be closer to ĭ [ɪ] and less often be sounded as ē [i].

2) In pronouncing *here*, many speakers in America use the fore-glide of the r; and therefore in the SIMPLIFIED column we show such pronunciation by the symbol ĭe, and in the PHONETIC column by the transcription [ɪə]. Professor Charles K. Thomas believes that "the first pronunciation of *here* (with the schwa) seems to emphasize a drawling pronunciation unnecessarily." [1] However, we are retaining the glide because it is still more or less conspicuous in America.

For our second pronunciation in the SIMPLIFIED column we are using the symbol i as in *bit, is, chin, ill*. It is generally agreed that for most Americans "long" e (ē) + r, when followed by e in the same syllable, is farther from the sound of "long" e (ē) and very much closer to the sound of "short" i (ĭ) + r as in *spirit*. Observe that before r in the same syllable (*dear, leer, mere, pierce*) we have reduced the ē [i] of earlier English to ĭ [ɪ].

Finally, we should recognize that, since the vowel in *here* is but a lengthened ĭ as in *bring*, most dictionaries indicate the ę̄ as ē. The prolongation of the ĭ [ɪ] sound can be indicated as [ɪ:]. Briefly, we give a third pronunciation: in the SIMPLIFIED column it is indicated by ee (equivalent to the ē of most dictionaries), and in the PHONETIC column we indicate it by [i]. As said a moment ago, a more desirable symbol of the sound is [ɪ:], but in the interest of simplicity and for the sake of not confusing the student, we are using (quite compromisingly) [i], which is, at best, a spelling-pronunciation (§ 1). See also SPECIAL NOTES, III, a.1 (page xx).

3) In *hero**** and *zero**** syllabic division (he ro, ze ro) makes the "long" e possible. In such words the [r] may be pronounced either at the end of one syllable or at the beginning of the next. If we use [r] in the same syllable (her o, zer o), we tend to say [ɪ]; if we use [r] in the next syllable (he ro, ze ro), we tend to say [i]. Even those who object to showing "heer" [hir] as a third pronunciation for *here* do recognize HEE roh ['hi ro] and ZEE roh ['zi ro], but still consider undesirable the pronunciation ZĬE roh ['zɪə ro]. Yet there is agreement on ē'rá̇,* although the dictionary using ę̄ will list ę̄'rá̇ as a second pronunciation.

4) A few words having an ē sound are pronounced not infrequently as if the ē is followed by an r sound. In *idea,* museum,* real,** and some other words the ē is lowered to ę̄.

Some speech experts urge that we should avoid substituting ē [i] in a word like *real*. But the evidence appears that REE uhl ['ri əl] and even the one-syllabled REEL [ril] is more frequent than RI uhl ['rɪ əl].

3. ě as in gět. (Simplified Symbol: e. Phonetic Symbol: ɛ.)

To make the sound of ě as in gět, lower the front of the tongue and drop the jaw much farther than for ĭ [ɪ], as explained in §§ 18, 28(4.1,4). Keep the lips spread as for ē [i] and ĭ [ɪ]. Not only is the arch of the tongue high but it also is well forward.

4. Unaccented ě (Initial and Medial). Unstressed or unaccented e in initial syllables and in medial syllables ranges from an ě sound (as in gět) to an ĭ (as in bĭt, ĭs, and ĭll) to the ě sound (as in tak'ĕn). The acceptable variation from a distinct ě [ɛ] sound to ĭ [ɪ] or even ě [ə] depends upon the everydayness of the word or the formality of the style of speech. The use of ě [ə] is especially frequent before l.

Briefly, in familiar talk the vowel in an unaccented syllable tends to become weakened or obscure. Just as the vowel ă in *attack** and á̇ in *China* approach the neutral vowel [ə], so the vowel ě approaches ĭ [ɪ] or ĭ [ə] as in concentrate,* decide,* entire,* envelope,* piety,* variety.* To be noted, also, is that when unstressed before a consonant sound, ex– is not only ěks but also ĭks, as in *excess.** See also § 49(6). For the neutral vowel [ə], see §§ 20(10), 20(11), 28(5.5), 34(12.2,3), 34(13.1,2,3), 40(12).

---

[1] In a letter to the author.

5. Unaccented ĕ (Final).

1) As in initial and medial syllables [§ 24(4)], so in final syllables an unstressed or unaccented ĕ may range from ĕ to ĭ, according to how formal or colloquial the words are. Some speakers consistently use ĭ both in deliberate and familiar speech.

The following will exemplify short ĕ in unaccented syllables: *bayonet,* brethren,* congress,* dogged,* forest,* light-hearted,* object,* regardless.** The sound is frequent in the third singular present of verbs, as *urges* and *rushes;* in the plural or the genitive of nouns terminating in a sibilant, as *breeches** and *George's;* in adjectives and verbs like *located,* long-headed,* unprecedented,* wanted.** See §§ 38(5.3), 48(3.c).

2) When the short ĕ occurs in unaccented final syllables, obscuration in the direction of ĕ [ə] is common; thus, *kitchen** is pronounced acceptably as kĭch'ĕn, kĭch'ĭn, kĭch'ĕn. See § 24(13.2).

6. e as in herd = û, § 40(7). In American speech the sound of e as in *herd, fern,* and (in an accented syllable when followed by a consonant) *per'son** may be pronounced in at least two ways, but in each the jaw is lowered midway, the lips are unrounded, and the tongue is arched in the middle. The difference between the two pronunciations of ûr [§ 40(7)] is that in General American speech the [ɝ] is formed by slightly retracting the tongue and elevating or bunching the middle part of it higher toward the hard palate than it is in producing the sound [ɜ] commonly heard in certain sections of the East and South. Easterners and Southerners, when producing the sound [ɜ], keep the lips straight, the tongue tip behind the lower teeth, and the arch lifted slightly in the middle. See § 18, page xlii *f.,* footnote, part e; and § 40(7).

7. ẽr as in mak'ẽr.

1) In words like *baker, cavern, maker, never,* and *perform,* the sound ĕ in the unstressed syllables is the unstressed vowel corresponding to û [§§ 24(6), 40(7)]. The vowel ẽr is always unaccented, and is always shorter, weaker, and more relaxed than ûr. In General American speech the sound [ɚ] is produced by arching the tongue a bit higher and farther forward than it is in producing the sound [ə] characteristic of Eastern and Southern American speech. Briefly, the sound [ɝ] when unaccented in a word or syllable takes the form of [ɚ]; and the speaker who would use [ɜ] in the accented syllable would use [ə] in the unaccented syllable.

2) Avoid spelling-pronunciations wrongly implied by such various unaccented endings as –ar (*liar, sugar*), –er (*father*), –ir (*elixir,* nadir*), –or (*honor**), –our (*honour**), –ur (*augur*), –ure (*pleasure*). In each instance the final unstressed syllable is pronounced ẽr [ɚ *or* ə(r)].

3) In day-to-day speech the r element has dropped out from the sound (but not from the spelling) ẽr, leaving behind ĕ [ə]. The loss of the r element is called *dissimilation* [see § 48(1)]. Examples are *caterpillar** (kăt'ẽr pĭl'ẽr; kăt'ĕ pĭl'ẽr); *governor** (gŭv'ẽr nẽr; gŭv'ĕ nẽr); *surprise** (sẽr prīz'; sĕ prīz'); *thermometer** (thẽr mŏm'ĕ tẽr; thĕ mŏm'ĕ tẽr). See also § 37(2).

4) When the r appears in an unaccented syllable in such words as *flattery, history,** and *mystery,** the loss of ĕ before r may take place. Thus (flăt'ẽr ĭ; flăt'rĭ), (hĭs'tŏ rĭ; hĭs'trĭ), (mĭs'tẽr ĭ; mĭs'trĭ).

5) When ẽr is spelled out to indicate momentary hesitation or doubt, it should be read without any r sound—as û, ĕ.

8. e as in sergeant = ä, § 20(4).

1) Whether spelled *sergeant* or *serjeant,* the pronunciation in both England and America is sär'jĕnt.

2) However, in other words retaining the old spelling er (ĕ before r final or

followed by a consonant), the ä sound in such words as *Berkeley,* clerk,** and *Derby* has yielded in America to a spelling-pronunciation of the e in *herd* [§ 24(6)] = ûr [§ 40(7)]. Americans pronounce *Berkeley* as bûrk′lǐ; Englishmen pronounce it bärk′lǐ, and only rarely bûrk′lǐ. In America *clerk* is klûrk, except in local dialect, as in Kentucky, where klärk, as throughout England, is usual. For *Derby*, meaning any prominent race or contest, Americans say dûr′bǐ or där′bǐ; but when meaning the annual race for three-year-old-horses run at Epsom (near London), they say där′bǐ, the pronunciation given by Englishmen, although in dialectal speech Englishmen also say dûr′bǐ.

9. e as in where = â, § 20(2).

1) The sound of e in *where,* there,** and any similar word occurs only before r and is pronounced â as in dâre. Other spellings for e = â are seen in *e'er,* heir,* pear, their.* See § 20(2).

2) For additional information about references in the dictionary (pages 1–319) marked § 24(9), consult § 13(1), where words with –ary are discussed: e.g., *arbitrary,* beneficiary,* capillary,* dictionary,* judiciary,* epistolary,* fragmentary,* luminary,* military,* necessary,* obituary,* pecuniary,* salutary,* temporary,* voluntary.**

10. e = ǐ.

1) *England,* English,* linger,* link,* wing,* and other words were once sounded with the vowel ĕ [ɛ]. Today the sound is ǐ [ɪ].

2) The interjection *eh* may be pronounced either ā or ĕ.

3) In not a few words e (that is, ĕ) may be sounded as a syllabic vowel, or either as a syllabic vowel or as a diphthong with a consonant y [j] sound. See *gaseous,* hideous,* piteous.**

11. ĕ as in ĕ vent′.

1) Briefer than ē in *eve* and *bee* is unstressed ĕ in ĕ vent′, dĕ fend′, Ė li′jah. In formal or platform delivery the ĕ sound may be a short ē [i]; in familiar and even in formal style, the ĕ becomes identical in common words with the slurred vowel ǐ [ə], as in *illuminate.**

2) Just as the ā and â sounds are used to distinguish adjectives from the corresponding verbs [§ 20(8,9)], in similar manner the ē [i] and ĕ [ɪ] sounds are used to distinguish meanings in some words. Thus: *re-cede* (rē sēd′), "cede back or grant again," and *recede* (rĕ sēd′), "move back or withdraw"; *re-count* (rē kount′), "count again," *recount* (rē′kount or rē kount′), "a second count," and *recount** (rĕ kount′), "tell in detail."

3) In several foreign languages including the Italian the Merriam-Webster diacritical symbol ĕ indicates a very brief ē sound.

12. ē as in mak′ēr.

1) For the sound of ē in *mak′ēr,* see § 24(7.1).

2) Perhaps no other unstressed vowel is more common than ē [ə]. Observe its occurrence in id*e*a,* tak*e*n, penc*i*l, lem*o*n, circ*u*s, and also in carr*i*age,* fam*o*us, for*ei*gn,* waistcoat* (wĕs′kŭt, the phonetically regular pronunciation).

3) In de (dē) and other French words, ē represents the unstressed, neutral vowel [ə].

13. ĕ as in tak′ĕn.

1) In everyday speech, unstressed ĕ as in tak′en and mo′ment is obscured. The symbol ĕ may indicate a sound ranging from a recognizable ĕ as in *get* to ǐ as in *bit,* but most often represents the neutral vowel [ə].

2) Except for a handful of words in which final –en is pronounced ǐn (*linen,* lǐn′ǐn; *woolen,* wōol′ǐn), or is quite silent [*garden,* gär′d'n: see § 33(2)], words in final –en are usually sounded with the neutral vowel [ə]—thus, gold*e*n, oak*e*n, flax*e*n. See § 24(5.2).

14. Unaccented e before n or l.

1) When we say *vessels*, we are not certain whether or not the second syllable contains a vowel. However, in pronouncing the group of sounds we pass directly from the [s] to the [l] and from that to the [z] without opening the mouth sufficiently for the production of a vowel. The unaccented e before l has disappeared, leaving l to form a syllable with another consonant. In pronouncing *vessels* there is no vowel whatever in the second syllable.

What is true of unaccented e before l is likewise true of unaccented e before n. In each instance the unaccented e often disappears completely, and l or n is left to form a syllable alone or with another consonant. That happens in *cancel** (kăn'sĕl, kăn's'l), *evanescent*,* (ĕv'à nĕs'ĕnt, ĕv'à nĕs' 'nt), *kindergarten** (kĭn'dēr gär't'n), and other words. In such instances the l or n is the most important element of the syllable, and each is called "syllabic." Where a pronunciation is acceptable with or without the vowel, its inclusion or omission depends usually on the style of speech. See *eleven*,* *garden*,* *latent*,* *patent*,* *potent*,* *present*,* *student*,* *subsistence*.*

2) Consult also §§ 9, 20(10.3), 28(5.6), 31(1.2), 31(4), 32(2.1,2,3), 33(2), 34(14.2), 40(13.4), and SPECIAL NOTES, V, "Syllabic l, m, n" (page xxii).

15. e as a Consonant.

1) In such words as *extraneous** and *piteous*,* unaccented e soon succeeded by another vowel having a bit more stress helps form a rising diphthong having as its first element a "consonantal" i or consonant y [j] sound. y is a consonant only before a vowel.

2) Particularly in familiar words where the t, d, s, or z sound precedes unaccented e, the sound preceding unaccented e is frequently palatalized by the y [j] element to ch [tʃ], j [dʒ], or sh [ʃ]. See *grandeur*,* *ocean*,* *righteous*.*

16. Silent e.

1) Recall that unaccented e before n or l often disappears completely [§ 24(14)], so that in such words as *cancel** and *kindergarten** there is no vowel in the second (last) syllable of can'cel and the fourth (last) syllable of kin'der gar'ten. In those pronunciations e is as silent as it is at the end of many words, as in *fame*, *knife*, and *knave*.*

2) Final e (a) may show the vowel long, as in māne, fēte, fīne, lōpe, rūbe (compare măn, fĭn, lŏp, rŭb); (b) may show a "soft" c = s, as in dāce,* fāce, lāce, māce, pāce, rāce (compare lāce and lăc); (c) may show a "soft" g = j, as in gāge, sāge (compare găg, săg); may show l syllabic after consonants, as in *battle* (băt' 'l).

3) Only after sibilants (s, z, sh, zh, ch, j [dʒ]), is the e in –es of nouns and verbs sounded [§ 24(5.1)]. Elsewhere in the –es of nouns and verbs it is silent.

4) Only after t or d, or occasionally in rhetorical style, is the e in –ed of the past and the past participles of verbs sounded. Elsewhere it is silent. [See § 23(1.14,15).]

5) When –ed forms the past tense of verbs, it is pronounced as [d] after voiced sounds (ba*th*ed, lea*n*ed) and as [t] after voiceless sounds (anne*x*ed, fi*sh*ed, hissed); and as a separate syllable –ed if it follows either t or d (li*ft*ed, re*st*ed, fa*d*ed, befrie*nd*ed). Put another way, the –ed ending when preceded by either [t] or [d] is sounded as a separate syllable, and the d remains [d]. See § 23(1.14,15).

17. ea.

1) The digraph ea has at least eight sounds:

> ē as in ēve and bee—b*ea*d, fr*ea*k, l*ea*k, r*ea*ch, s*ea*m, wr*ea*the
> ẹ as in hẹre—b*ea*rd, dr*ea*ry, f*ea*r, n*ea*r, r*ea*r, w*ea*ry
> â as in dâre—p*ea*r, w*ea*r

û as in fûr′ther—*earn*, y*earn*
ä as in bär—h*earth*, h*earken*
ĕ as in gĕt—br*ead*, d*eath*
ĭ as in bĭt, pĭt′y—guin*ea* (unaccented)
ā as in āpe—*great*, Y*eats*

2) In *ideal** (ī dē′ăl; ī dḙ′ăl), *create* (krḙ āt′), and other words in which ea is not a digraph, the letters ea represent different sounds in separate syllables.

18. eau. All words in which the letter-combination eau occurs have come from the French. In some words eau is pronounced ū [ju], as in *beauteous,** *beauty*;* in others, ō [o], as in *beau,** *Beaumont;* and, rather exceptionally, ē [i], as in the English name *Beaucham* (bē′chăm).

19. ee.

1) Another spelling for ē as in ēve is ee, as in *bee, deep, feet, heel, peek, teem, redeem.*

2) An r following ee lowers the ē sound to ḙ as in hḙre—thus, *beer* (bḙr), *jeer* (jḙr), *peer* (pḙr). See § 24(2.1,2).

3) Americans pronounce *been** usually as bĭn, less frequently as bēn, and often (unstressed) as bĕn. Englishmen sound *been* usually as bēn, although some speakers use bĭn only when unstressed and others as both a "weak" and a "strong" form. See §§ 15, 16.

4) Spelling-pronunciation (§ 1) tends to lengthen to ē as in ēve the ĭ sound as in words still spelled with ee. See, for example *breech,** *breeches,** *creek,** *steelyard.**

5) Although spelling-pronunciation shows a tendency to restore ē in words still spelled ee (see 4 above), it can not so operate in any word formerly spelled with ee but now with i. In such a word, ee has been shortened to ĭ—thus, *sick* (formerly spelled *seek*), and likewise *livelong,** *nickname, riddle,* and *silly.*

20. ei, ey. The digraph ei (usually spelled ey when final, as in *hey, obey*) represents several sounds:

ei spells ā (āpe) as in *neigh, vein;* also in Anglicized French words (but not French words), as in *beige, Seine.**

ei spells ē (ēve), as in *ceiling, receive;* and also in *deil* (dēl) and other Scottish spellings.

When unaccented, ei and ey are each sounded ĭ (bĭt) as in *forfeiture** and *money.**

When r succeeds ei, ei spells â (dâre), as in *their.*

In *eidetic* (ī dĕt′ĭk), *Leibnitzianism* (līp nĭt′sĭ ăn ĭz′m, līb nĭt′sĭ ăn ĭz′m) *geyser** (gī′zĕr, gī′sĕr; in England, also gā′zĕr and gē′zĕr), or in other such words of Greek or Latin or Teutonic origin, ei has the sound of ī (īce).

21. eo. The digraph eo spells ē (ēve), ĕ (gĕt), ō (ōpen), and ou (about), as in *people* (pē′p'l), *jeopardize,** *yeomanry,** *MacLeod* (măk loud′), *feoffment* (fĕf′mĕnt, fēf′mĕnt).

22. eu, ew.

1) eu (also spelled ew as in *dew, ewe, few, newt*) spells the sound of ū (yōō) as in *fuse.* Examples: *Deuteronomy* (dū′tĕr ŏn′ŏ mĭ), *feudatory.**

2) eu + r, or eu in an unaccented syllable, is usually sounded û (yōō), as in *European,** *eugenics.* See § 40(4.9).

3) n + ew, or s + ew, is often pronounced also as ōō, as in *new, sewage.* See §§ 40(4.4,10), 50(32.b).

4) *Sew* and *shew** (archaic in the United States), once pronounced sū and shū, are now pronounced sō and shō. *Ewe** is sounded not only as ū, but also (dialectally) as yō.

5) In *chauffeur,** "feuilleton," "jeune fille,"* and other words from the French, eu may represent either the sound [ø] or [œ]; but, when respelled, both sounds are indicated by û as in *fûr′ther*. See § 34(15) and SPECIAL NOTES, VII, "Foreign Sounds" (page xxii *f*.).

§ 25. F, G

1. f.

1) Like v, f is made by placing the lower lip lightly against the edges of the upper front teeth and then blowing the air out through the crevices between lip and teeth. F, as in *flee, fed, after,** *duffel, photographer,** *Pharaoh,** *chafe,** *telephone,** *leaf,** *cuff*, is the voiceless, labiodental fricative consonant corresponding to voiced v (§ 41(1, 2)].

2) This voiceless correlative of v is also spelled gh, as in *laugh,** *tough*, and *ph*, as in *diphtheria,** *philanthropy.**

3) The especially British (and acceptably American) pronunciation nĕv′ū for *nephew** (nĕf′ū; nĕv′ū) preserves the older ME *neveu, nevou, nevu*, from OF *neveu, nevou*, and also from F *neffewe*. The ph in *nephew* merely copies the ph spelling in Greek derivatives.

4) Pronounce ff as a single f sound (*buff,** *buffalo, different**) except in combinations, when the sound is doubled (*calf-footed, self-fed*). See §§ 21(1.6), 23(1.10), 26(1.3), 30(2.2), 31(5.1), 32(3.1,2), 33(5.1), 35(5), 37(6), 38(13.2,3,4), 39(9.1), 45(4.1,2).

5) Nouns ending in f (*loaf, wife*) usually have the corresponding voiced sound v in the plural (*loaves, wives**).

6) A few languages have a bilabial f [Φ], called the "candle-blowing" sound. See SPECIAL NOTES, VII, "Foreign Sounds," page xxii.

2. "Hard" g as in get.

1) To make "hard" g, as in *get,** *go, bag, bog,** *bogy, graduate,** *egg,** raise the back of the tongue to the soft palate and then lower the tongue quickly or blow it down with a voiced breath. It is the sudden release of air that makes a slight explosive sound. (See also b, d, p, t, and especially k, which, like g, is a stopplosive, back-tongue velar sound, but, unlike g, is voiceless. g is the voiced cognate of k.)

2) When final, g is always "hard," as in *bag, drug, leg, rug*. It is also "hard" in derivatives from such words, as in *baggy, druggist, ragged*, and where g is doubled for differentiating such words as *ragged* and *raged*.

3) "Hard" g occurs before a, o, u, l, r, or a consonant in the same syllable: *bagatelle, got, linguist, daguerreotype, gaberdine,** *goad, gondola,** *guarantee,** *guardian,** *guide,** *guess,** *guinea,** *language,** *glad*.

4) In *beget, geyser,** *give*, and other words of Germanic origin, g before e and i is "hard." This means that g before e and i is most often "soft" (= j [dʒ]).

5) "Hard" g occurs also in some other words, such as *Gideon* and *ger* from the Hebrew; *gerefa* and *gesith* from the Anglo-Saxon; and usually when the g is doubled, as in *baggy, jagged* [§ 26(1.3)].

6) Other spellings for "hard" g are gh [*ghetto, ghoul**—§ 26(2.1), gu [*guardian,** *guess,** *guide,** *guernsey**—§ 26(5)], and –gue [*rogue*—§ 26(6)].

7) For x when pronounced gz and gzh, see §§ 43(1), 52.

3. "Soft" g = j as in joy, § 29(1.2).

1) In native words "soft" g = j is never initial. See § 29(1.2). The simple rule is that g before e or i or y is sounded j [dʒ]—*gelatin,** *genealogy,** *gibbet,** *engine,** *cage, exaggerate.** The rule is derived from the French, as is the rule that c before e or i or y is sounded s [§ 22(1.1)].

2) At the end of a syllable, "soft" g is also spelled dg (*budge,** *budging, dodger*). dg appears after short vowels (*ledge*).

3) At the end of a word, "soft" g is as a rule spelled –ge, –dge (*cage, edge,** *fudge, nudge*).

4. g = zh as in massage.

1) In *camouflage,** *garage,** *gendarme,** *massage,** *mirage,** *prestige,** *rouge,** and some other French loan words only partly Anglicized, the g sound is pronounced zh.

2) The zh sound occurs only medially in English words (*decision,** *elision*), and never initially or finally. As the French loan words with g become more and more Anglicized (§ 46), the tendency to change the zh [ʒ] to the j [dʒ] sound becomes stronger and stronger. [Cf. § 22(7).] In England one acceptable pronunciation of *garage** is gằr′ĭj; in America there is already manifest a tendency to gá räj′, a loose pronunciation verging on acceptability or already acceptable.

3) The spelling g after l or n (*bulge, flange,** *grange,** *manager,** *sponge**) may sometimes be given a zh sound. In such words the d element of "soft" g [dʒ] is occasionally omitted. See §§ 23(1.13), 33(5.1).

5. Silent g.

1) The letter g spells three sounds, "hard" g, "soft" g, and zh. But g is not sounded before final m or n, as in *diaphragm,** *phlegm,** *benign,** *impugn,** *sign.** g remains silent when such words are inflected, as in *diaphragmed* and *signed*. However, in such derivatives as *diaphragmatic, phlegmatic,** *benignant,** and *signature,** g is sounded.

2) g is not only silent when followed by n in the same syllable, but initial g before n is also silent, as in *gnash,** *gneiss,** *gnome.** See §§ 30(1.5), 37(1.4).

3) For g in the digraph ng, see § 33(4.1,2,3).

6. Foreign g.

1) Dutch g, except occasionally when initial, is very much like German ch in *ach* [§ 22(10.2)], and is indicated in most dictionaries by ᴋ or kh.

2) At the end of a word or syllable, German g, when single, is sounded nearly like k or ᴋ [§ 22(10.2)]. In all other positions, German g is pronounced by English speakers as g in *get*.

3) Spanish g has several sounds. Pronounce g as in *gay* except before e and i. Before e and i, Castilians make the g a voiceless fricative like German ch in *ach* or like Scotch ch in *loch* [§ 22(10.2)], while American Spaniards sound it like h in *had*. See *Los Angeles.** The g is occasionally silent when preceded by a vowel and followed by u; and in such words with gu, the u is sounded as w, especially after la, as in "*agua*" (ä′gwä; ä′wä), *la guacharo* (lä gwä′chä rō; lä wä′chä rō), *guayroto* (gwī rō′tō; wī rō′tō). What really happens in such words is that the spirant g in gu between vowels is so soft that it has vanished.

§ 26

1. ge; gg.

1) The letter j does not occur often at the end of words, where –ge frequently spells j (*barge, forge*). –ge = j appears in such words as *corsage** and *prestige.** See also § 25(3).

2) In some recent French loan words yet to be fully Anglicized, –ge spells the zh sound of g, as in *rouge,** *ménage* (må näzh′) and *menage* (mĕ näzh′), *menagerie.** See §§ 25(4.1), 46.

3) Just as ff spells a single f sound except in combinations, so gg generally spells a single g sound, as in *eggshell*. The sound is also single when doubled before a suffix, as in *bagging*. gg before e is occasionally sounded gj or j, as in *suggest,** or j, as in *exaggerate.** See §§ 21(1.6), 23(1.10), 25(1.4), 26(1.3), 30(2.2), 31(5.1), 32(3.1,2), 33(5.1), 35(5), 37(6), 38(13.2,3,4), 39(9.1), 45(4.1,2).

2. gh.

1) "Hard" g [§ 25(2)] is also spelled gh, as in *aghast*,* *ghost*,* *ghoul*.* The spelling gh for "hard" g (as in *get*) appears also in words of Dutch origin (*Ghent*,* *gherkin*), of Italian origin (*ghetto*), and of Hindu origin (*ghat, ghee*).

2) In most English words the gh no longer has the sound of German ch and of Scottish ch in *loch* (lŏk) or *hough* (hŏk; *Scottish* hŏк). See § 22(10.2). Today the gh within a syllable is either silent, as in *caught, delight,* *freight, nigh, right, sought,* *through,* *weigh*, or is sounded f, as in *cough,* *draught,* *enough, laugh.** In some words, such as *delight,* *haughty,* and *sleigh,** gh has never been pronounced, in each being an example of reverse (or inverse) spelling.

3. gli. Italian words containing gli are frequently sounded like lli [lj] as in *billion** (bĭl'yŭn), very much like that of the Italian palatal l [ʎ], as in *seraglio.** Where gli is final in words from Italian, it is sounded ly [lj] + ē [i].

4. Foreign gn.

1) French or Italian words containing gn are sounded so that gn is nearly like French or Italian palatal n [ɲ]. In such loan words the gn is pronounced like ni in *bunion* (bŭn'yŭn) and *mignonette* (mĭn'yŭn ĕt').

2) For initial g before n, or for final –gn, see § 25(5).

5. gu.

1) gu followed by a or e or i in the same accented syllable represents usually the "hard" g, as in *guardian,* *guest,* *guide*;* but if appearing in unaccented syllables is occasionally pronounced "hard" g + w, as in *anguiform* (ăng'gwĭ fôrm), *language,* *languid,* *linguist* (lĭng'gwĭst). See also qu, § 36.

2) In a few words of foreign origin the gu is pronounced as gw, as in *guaco* (gwä'kō), *guano* (gwä'nō), *Guelph* (gwĕlf).

6. gue. Where –gue is final, as in *catalogue, monologue, plague,** and *rogue*, it is sounded "hard" g as in *get.** See also §§ 25(2.6), 36.

§ 27. H

1. English h.

1) If you just open your mouth and sigh, you will have produced the consonant sound h, as in *half, hush, behold*. This is a pure aspirate, made by sending a puff of breath through the glottis when the vocal cords are close enough to cause friction but not voice. The position of the aspirate h depends upon the position of the vowel that follows it, and also takes on the quality of the vowel that follows it.

Pronounce slowly and hold for a moment the vowel ä [a]. Then pronounce hä [ha]. Observe that no change or practically no change takes place in the position of the jaw, lips, and tongue. The difference is that ä [a] begins with voice, while hä [ha] begins with breath. In other words, when you are about to sound a syllable or a word beginning with h [h], the articulators get set for the sound which is to follow the h [h]. Briefly, the sound h is only breath, modified by the shape of the mouth resonator for the following vowel.

2) The consonant h [h] is not only a way of beginning vowel sounds, but is also a method of approaching the glides w [w] and y [j], as found in the words *whining** and *hue.** Many careful speakers prefer to begin such words with h [h] in order to distinguish *whine* (hwīn) from *wine* (wīn), and *hue** (hū = hyoō) from *you* (yoō). See § 42(4).

3) The h sound is not pronounced when it sometimes appears at the end of a syllable or a word (*eh, high*). The sound occurs only initially, or before vowels, or w, as in *when** (hwĕn), or y, as in *human** (hū'măn = hyoō'măn). h is silent in rh words, as in *rhapsody,* *rhubarb,* *rhythm.** See §§ 27(2.1), 37(5).

4) h is sounded whenever it is spelled initially in accented syllables (not merely in syllables having primary accent) of all native English words.

5) English words of Old French origin, while retaining the h in their spelling, as in *heir*,* *honest*,* *honor*,* *hour*,* are pronounced with no aspirate h in them. For a century and a half, however, there has been a gradual restoration of the Latin h sound, which had disappeared in the French derivatives; but the restoration of the h sound has been occurring in those words still being spelled with h. The more familiar words (*heir*,* *honest*,* *hour*,* and the like) are still sounded without h. A different group is being pronounced with and without h, as *herb*,* *homage*,* *humble*,* *humor*,* *vehement*,* *vehicle*.* (In the United States we sound the h in *hotel* [hō'tĕl']; in England some prefer ō tĕl' consistently, while others use it sometimes when the word is not initial.) Such words as *able* [OF. *hable* (F. *habile*); L. *habilis*] and *arbor* lost h in their spelling, and are therefore no longer pronounced with the h sound. See also *exhaust*,* *exhilarate*,* *exhort*,* *forehead*,* *hospital*.* Read also § 1.

6) Initial h in syllables having little or no stress is often dropped; e.g., *annihilate*,* *forehead*,* *shepherd*,* *vehicle*.* It should be emphasized that this is true of unstressed medial h. In a large number of words, spelling-pronunciation (§ 1) has led to a wavering restoration of the h sound (see *vehemence*,* *vehicle*.

7) The h is not sounded in the unstressed forms of pronouns in familiar speech, as in "We told (h)er to go"; "They saw (h)er." See § 16. However, such pronouns, particularly when initial in sentences and clauses, or after a pause, are accented slightly and retain a more or less audible h sound. Also, while h is usually pronounced when initial in longer words (see pages 143–153), either "a" or "an" may precede such words, especially when the stress is not on the first syllable, as "an historical novel," "a historical novel." In words beginning with h but not accented on the first syllable, the h was formerly not pronounced, so that "an" was used. Whenever the h is pronounced, some speakers continue to say "an," but perhaps a larger number prefer "a" before such words.

2. Other Aspects of h.

1) h following a vowel in the same syllable (*ah*, *eh*, *oh*, *Sarah*), or h preceded by r in the same syllable (*myrrh*, *rhubarb*) is silent. See §§ 27(1.3), 37(5).

2) When h ends an accented syllable, the vowel is generally long.

3) The phonetic letter [ɦ] is used to denote the voicing of [h] between voiced sounds, as in *behind*, *Ohio*. Although the vocal cords do separate a little, the separation is so slight that they do not stop vibrating. (See § 19, "Chart of English Consonants," Note b, page xlix.)

4) h is part of the digraphs ch [§ 22(5–9)], gh [§ 26(2)], kh [§ 30(2.1)], rh [§ 37(5)], sh [§ 38(11,12), th [§ 39(4–7)].

5) wh is discussed in § 42(4).

§ 28. I

The letter i spells four accented and five unaccented sounds:

Accented

ī as in īce, aisle, whīne, § 28(2)	i in fir = û, §§ 24(6), 28(8), 40(7)
ĭ as in bĭt, pĭt'y, § 28(4)	i in pique = ē, §§ 24(1), 28(6)

Unaccented

ĭ in cred'ĭt, § 28(5)	"Silent" i, § 28(5)
ĭ in par'ĭ ty, § 28(5)	"Consonant" i, § 28(9)
i in na'dir = ē, § 28(8)	

1. Principal Sounds of i. Although the chart given immediately above indicates that the letter i has nine sounds, it is just as useful to recognize that in English the letter i has five different pronunciations of varying value:

1) "Long" i—in both accented and unaccented syllables.

2) "Short" i—in both accented and unaccented syllables. The "short" i may not only become obscured in unstressed open syllables, but may often be lost before l or n.

3) i before r, when accented and followed by a consonant, is pronounced like the u in *further* and *hurt*, as in *fir*. But i before r, when unstressed and followed by a consonant, is sounded as the e before r in *lover*, as in *nadir*.

4) In such words as *oil* and *void*, the i appears at the end of a diphthong and is sounded as y. i may represent also a y sound before a vowel, as in *opinion*.*

5) In such words as *police** and *chic* (shēk; *also* shĭk), the Continental (European) value of i is preserved; and is sounded as the ē in *eve*.

2. ī ("Long" i) as in īce. (Simplified Symbol: a͡i, A͡I. Phonetic Symbol: aɪ.)

1) "Long" i, the diphthong in *ice, whine, aisle,** also heard in *five,** *lime, sigh, flighty,* begins with the low front vowel à [a] as in *ask** and glides toward the high, lax front vowel ĭ [ɪ] as in *bit, is, ill, chin, pity,* and *city.** Keeping the tongue up a little will help produce the sound. In blending both elements into one, sound the first on the back of the tongue, stressing this first element à [a] more than the second element ĭ [ɪ].

Special Note: When you use the SIMPLIFIED column remember that the symbol a͡i or A͡I (with a ligature or tie over the top of a͡i or A͡I) is always sounded as "long" i (ī) as in *ice*. For the digraph ai, see § 20(13).

2) Other spellings of "long" i (ī) appear in *aisle,** *aye** ("yes"), *buy,** *by, choir,** *dye, eyelet, geyser,** *guy, height,** *I, lie, tie.* Observe that in the short and familiar words ie is pronounced ī. (When followed by a consonant in an accented syllable, ie is usually pronounced as "long" e [ē], as in *niece, relieve.*)

3) A triphthong is the result of three vowel sounds united into one continuous glide. "Long" i + the neutral vowel [ə] + silent r give us a triphthong, as in *fire*. (Two other triphthongs are *sour* and *pure*.) See §§ 9(6.b,c), 34(24.4).

3. ī ("Long" i: Secondary or No Stress). (Simplified Symbol: a͡i, A͡I. Phonetic Symbol: aɪ.)

1) In dī am′e ter,* ī den′ti ty, trī um′phal, and other words in which "long" ī does not receive the primary accent, the ī [aɪ] is still a diphthong, but shorter than the ī when fully stressed.

2) When ī has no accent, as in fast everyday talk, it is obscured to the neutral vowel [ə]—thus, "Bring my hat" = Brĭng mȧ hăt [brɪŋ mə hæt]. See § 16.

Special Note: Observe that a͡i or A͡I in the SIMPLIFIED column is always pronounced ī as in *ice*. For the digraph ai, see § 20(13).

4. Accented i as in bĭt, pĭt′y. (Simplified Symbol: i. Phonetic Symbol: ɪ.)

1) Accented i, as in *bĭt, is, ill, pity, city,** *remit, if, admit,** *picture,** is a high front vowel made by lowering the tongue only slightly from the position for ē [i], dropping the jaw a small bit, and keeping the lips spread. Although the tongue is in the position for ē [i], its front is relaxed to a slightly lower position than for ē [i].

2) When accented and followed by a vowel or by a second r in the next syllable, ĭr (that is, short ĭ [ɪ] + r + a vowel or a second r in the succeeding syllable) is pronounced ĭr, a sound close to ēr. Examples: mir′acle, spir′it,* ir′rigate, mir′ror, stir′rup.*

3) The same sound (accented and unaccented) is spelled in other ways, as in *always,** *breeches,** *built, business,** *carriage,** *foreign,** *forfeit,** *honey,** *guinea,** *marriage,** *mythology,** *sieve,** *syrup,** *women.** In *mirror, spirit,** and other words the unaccented i appears before r and a vowel. See § 28(5).

4) Avoid (a) dropping the tongue too far back and (b) making the vowel too tense in unstressed prefixes and in unstressed suffixes. Remember that such affixes are usually unstressed, and that this lack of stress tends to make the vowels in them weak. The prefixes be– (*believe**), de– (*deceive*), se– (*select*), pre– (*predict*), re– (*relieve*), and others are often pronounced ĭ [ɪ] rather than ē [i] or uh [ə], as well as such unstressed suffixes –ed (*lifted*), –et (*market*), –est (*smallest*), –it (*credit*), –less (*needless*), –ness (*slimness*). See §§ 49, 50.

5) Words ending in –y (*city,** *very**), –ly (*lovely,** *sincerely*), and –ie (*Auntie*) are usually transcribed as ĭ [ɪ]. In the speech of many it is sounded as a bit more relaxed than ĭ [ɪ]—that is, as a kind of "short" ē [i]. Although most Americans sound the unaccented terminal –y (*city,** *candy**) and the plurals (*candies*) and participles (*candied*), as "short" i [ɪ], yet in some sections, as in the midwest and especially in the New England states, the sound resembles "long" e (ē). See especially §§ 8(2), 28(5.4).

5. Unaccented i.

1) Unaccented i occurs in many words, as in *practice, rabbit, illicit,** *implacable,** *tedium.**

2) When final, unaccented i is changed in spelling to –y or –ey, as in *choppy* and *money.**

3) The same sound is spelled in other ways, as in *cabbage,** *climate,** *palace** [§ 20(9)], *college,** *heedless, hostess, knowledge,** *noted, rushes, smallest* [§ 24(5)], *character, circuit,** *pigeon* [§ 28(4)].

4) Accented ĭ [§ 28(4)] and unaccented ĭ are not always the same in sound. Many Americans sound final unaccented ĭ like accented ĭ; others sound it as a kind of dull ē [i] or ĕ [ɪ]. Since this handbook is presenting only broad transcription, it uses the symbol ĭ [ɪ] for both accented and unaccented ĭ—as do many phoneticians. See §§ 8(2), 28(4.5).

5) Unaccented short ĭ either before or after an accented syllable in any but the short word is frequently obscured in ordinary speech, becoming almost or quite the same as the *a* in Chi′ná ['tʃaɪ nə]. Words such as *citizen** and *artificial** may accordingly be pronounced sĭt′ĭ zĕn, sĭt ĭ zĕn, sĭt′i z'n, and är′tĭ fĭsh′ăl, är′tĭ fĭsh′ăl. That is the reason for marking many such words separately with both the symbol ĭ [uh; IPA ə] and ĭ [i; IPA ɪ]. Both pronunciations are acceptable. See §§ 20(10), 20(11), 24(4), 34(12.2,3), 34(13.1,2,3), 40(12).

Also, where only the symbol ĭ [ɪ] is given, many good speakers may be using ĭ [ə]. Both are acceptable; but as a rule this handbook marks the less common words only with ĭ [ɪ], it being understood that in longer words and also in more familiar words an unaccented short ĭ before or after an accented syllable may be retracted further toward the neutral vowel. Tersely, unstressed ĭ is frequently pronounced [ə]; and when not pronounced [ə], becomes [ɪ].

6) When l or n (or even m) comes at the end of a word and forms a syllable by itself, it is called syllabic—that is, the l or n (or even m) has taken the place of a vowel in a syllable. Only in unstressed syllables do syllabics occur, as in *little** (lĭt′ 'l; IPA 'lɪt l̩), *garden** (gär′d'n; IPA 'gɑr dn̩].

When following ĭ in unaccented syllables, particularly in everyday speech, l or n may become a syllabic consonant, as in *council** (koun′sĭl; koun's'l), *pupil* (pū′p'l; pū′pĭl), *Latin** (lăt′ĭn; lăt′ 'n). In certain words, whether in formal or colloquial speech, ĭ always becomes silent, as in *basin** (bā′s'n) and *cousin** (kŭz′ 'n).

When an ĭ sound is spelled other than by the letter i, the n may become syllabic, as in *curtain** (kûr′tĭn; kûr′t'n) and *sudden* (sŭd′ 'n; sŭd′ĭn). The change may also take place not only in medial syllables but also, even if less frequently, in initial syllables. In such words this manual is conservative, in many instances not showing the syllabic consonants unless there appears to be a preponderance of evidence that the ĭ has become silent before l or n. See §§ 9(1–5), 20(10.3), 24(14), 31(1.2), 31(4), 32(2.1,2,3), 33(2), 34(14.2), 40(13.4).

7) In words from Latin or French that terminate in –ile, as *contractile,* * *domicile,* * *ductile,* * *facile,* * *projectile,* * the tendency is to pronounce such as ĭl. In England, however, the tendency is toward īl, as in *docile,* * *fertile,* * *hostile,* * *puerile,* * *servile,* * *sterile,* * *virile.* * Some words have both ĭl and īl in their pronunciation. Another group, especially the more common words, may lose the ĭ sound. See also *agile,* * *fertile,* * *imbecile,* * *immobile,* * *juvenile,* * *mobile,* * *versatile,* * *volatile.* *

6. –ine. There is no fairly exceptionless rule for the pronunciation of the suffix –ine of adjectives and nouns, the ending being pronounced usually in any one or more of three ways: ĭn, īn, or ēn. Some are pronounced prevailingly alike in both America and England, although perhaps the tendency in the latter is toward īn and in the former toward ĭn. See *Alexandrine,* * *crystalline,* * *Levantine,* * *libertine,* * *morphine,* * *Palestine,* * *Philistine,* * *pristine,* * *turbine,* * *vaseline.* *

7. –ine; –ide. For the terminations –ine and –ide, Americans favor ēn and īd, although ĭn and ĭd are likewise acceptable. See *chloride,* * *chlorine,* * *iodide,* * *iodine,* * *oxide,* * *strychnine.* *

8. i as in irk = û, § 40(7); **i as in na′dir** = ẽ, § 24(12); **i as in fire** = ī, § 28(2).

1) In *irk, bird, circus, virgin,* accented i before r final, or accented i before r final followed by another consonant, is identical with the sound of e in *herd* (û) and û in *fûr′ther.* See §§ 24(6), 40(7).

2) Unaccented i before r final, as in *elixir* * and *nadir,* is sounded as ẽ in *baker.* See §§ 24(7.1), 24(12.1).

3) For traces that remain of the û sound for ir + a vowel, where i is now customary, see § 40(7).

4) ir + e in the same syllable is pronounced as "long" i (ī) + r, as in *fire, dire, mire, rehire* (re hire′). See § 28(2.3).

9. i as a Consonant. Speed of utterance usually determines whether such words as *alien* * and *tedious* * should be pronounced as āl′yĕn or ā′lĭ ĕn, tēd′yŭs or tē′dĭ ŭs. No rule without many exceptions can be formulated to indicate when the consonant y [j] sound, as in *yes,* should be pronounced as an unaccented ĭ or ĕ sound gliding rapidly into a following vowel. American English shows a tendency to converting the vowel ĭ into the nonsyllabic y.

See *ameliorate,* * *audience,* * *bilious,* * *civilian,* * *collier,* * *Columbia,* * *Episcopalian,* * *filial,* * *genial,* * *Indian,* * *ingenious,* * *leniency,* * *magnolia,* * *mania,* * *opinion,* * *perennial,* * *pneumonia,* * *salient,* * *venial.* *

10. Foreign il; ill.

1) For French initial il–, French initial ill–, and French medial –il–, pronounce the i normally and the l approximately as in English.

2) French medial –ill– is sounded like English ē (ēve) + consonant y (strong vanish). So is French final –il, as a general rule in all words but monosyllables.

3) A vowel sound + –il or –ill results in a y sound for the –il or –ill, as in *travail* meaning "frame" (trȧ′vä′y′; trȧ vāl′).

§ 29. J

1. English j. (Simplified Symbol: j. Phonetic Symbol: dʒ.)

1) The sound of the affricate j [dʒ] as in *January,* * *jewel,* * *jut, logic,* * is a digraph made by joining the voiced plosive d [d] to the voiced sibilant fricative zh [ʒ]. Raise your tongue as you did for d [d] [see § 23(1.1)] and then go quickly into the sound of zh [ʒ], as in *vision.* * In other words, you get the first sound in

joy by making the two voiced sounds d [d] and zh [ʒ] in rapid succession. [dʒ] is the voiced cognate of [tʃ].

2) Other spellings for the sound j [dʒ] are g (*Magellan, regimen,* clergy*), ge (*George, sage*), dg (*dodging*), dge (*edge**), ch (*Greenwich,* Harwich*), di (*soldier**), dj (*Hadjemi* and other Oriental words), du (*verdure**).

3) In English words spelled with the letter j (*hallelujah* is an exception), the j sound is thus pronounced because it is retained from the French sound j [dʒ], as seen in *gentle, regiment*. This Old French [dʒ] sound later lost its first element [d], thus giving j [dʒ] its modern French sound zh [ʒ].

In French modern loan words not fully Anglicized, j has the zh [ʒ] sound, as in *bijou* (bē′zhōō; bē′zhōō′), "*déjà vu*" (dȧ′zhȧ′vü′), "*déjeuner*" (dȧ′zhŭ′nā′; *English*, dȧ′zhē nä), "déjeuné" (dȧ′zhŭ′nā′); but *dejeune* is pronounced dĕ jōōn′. See *garage,* mirage,* regime.** See § 46.

4) In some words there is a choice between sounding d [d] and j [dʒ]; for example, *educate** may be pronounced in at least two ways. See § 23(1.9).

5) In *huge** the sound j [dʒ] is voiceless at the beginning and voiced at the end. To show that it has been devoiced at the beginning of its sound, a small circle is put below its symbol: j̥. See §§ 31(3.1), 32(2.4), 33(1.8), 37(1.5), 42(1.2); also, § 19, "Chart of English Consonants," Note b (page xlix).

2. Spanish j; German j. In "*agujón*" (ȧ′gōō hōn′), *marijuana* (mä′rĕ hwä′nä: also spelled *marihuana*), and other Spanish words, the j is sounded as an h strongly aspirated. Spanish j resembles ch in German *ach* and Scottish *loch* [§ 22(10.2)]. Spaniards will have to guard against substituting [x] for [dʒ], and Germans will have to guard against substituting y [j] for [dʒ].

3. Foreign jh. In *jheel* (jēl), *jhool* (jōōl), *jhow* (jou), *Jhuria* (jōō′rĭȧ), jh may be pronounced j, although in many East Indian words jh = j + h, as pronounced separately in *ledgeholder* (lĕj′hōl′dẽr). See §§ 21(3), 22(11.1), 23(3), 30(2.1), 35(4.5), 39(7.4).

§ 30. K

1. English k.

1) Like "hard" g [§ 25(2)] and ng [ŋ: § 33(4)], k in *kit, kilometer,* skillet,* basket,* lark, silk, oak*, is a back-tongue velar sound. The k sound is made by raising the back of the tongue to the soft palate and then blowing it down with the breath. k is a voiceless stop-plosive, its voiced correlative being "hard" g [§ 25(2)].

2) The k sound is otherwise spelled as in *cat, accused,* stucco, tack, biscuit,* bookcase, clique, chitin, click, baccarat, acquaint,* liquor,* quadrille,* ache, khaki,* character, six.**

3) In *lax, box, exit,* luxury,** and similar combinations, k is part of the sound x, the full sound being ks. See § 43(1), 52.

4) k, like p and t, is puffed out quite strongly or aspirated when its sound is followed either by a vowel or a diphthong, or by a pause. When k is followed by a w (*quick*:* § 36), it is also aspirated.

When k (or p or t) is followed by a consonant in the same breath group, it is said to be unaspirated because it is not puffed out so strongly. See §§ 35(1.2), 39(1.4).

5) Initial k, like initial g [§ 25(5.2)], is now silent before n in the same syllable, as in *knack,* knead,* knoll,* knuckle.** Except when preceded by a vowel with which it makes a syllable, k is short—thus *knowledge,* acknowledge* (in the latter of which the k sound still remains). Cf. § 37(1.4).

6) Between certain consonants and ng [ŋ], a k sound may be excrescent, as in *length** [lĕngkth: § 33(4.4)].

7) For к, see § 22(10.2).

2. kh.

1) *kh* in *khaki,* khan,* khedive, Khufu, Khyber Pass*, and most English words from Arabic, Turkish, Persian, East Indian, and other languages may be pronounced k even if marked ᴋ [§ 22(10.2)]. See §§ 21(3), 22(11.1), 23(3), 29(3), 35(4.5), 39(7.4).

2) The combination kk [most often spelled ck: § 22(11.2)] in English words almost always spells a single k sound, unless the word is compound, when the sound is doubled. Examples: *Bokkeveld* (bŏk'ĕ vĕlt); *bookkeeping* (book'kēp'ĭng). See also §§ 21(1), 23(1.10), 25(1.4), 26(1.3), 31(5.1), 32(3.1,2), 33(5.1), 35(5), 37(6), 38(13.2,3,4), 39(9.1), 45(4.1,2).

§ 31. L

1. English l.

1) l, the first sound in *leap* and *low*, and appearing elsewhere, as in *flay, sly, blast,* clip, holy, realm, all*, is our only lateral sound. To form this voiced oral continuant, follow these steps: Raise front of tongue to roof of mouth, making the underpart touch the upper front teeth. Spread tongue so that its sides touch the side teeth; or flatten the front of the tongue against the upper gum. Now make a voiced sound over both sides of the raised tongue (bilateral l). If the voiced breath passes out on one side of the tongue, the sound is said to be unilateral.

2) When l follows t or d, the tip of the tongue, instead of dropping to complete the stop, stays in contact with the gum ridge. The sides of the tongue are drawn in, resulting in a lateral space through which the plosive is exploded into the l around the sides of the tongue. No vowel sound intervenes; and the l is said to be syllabic. Briefly, when l occurs in an unstressed syllable, it often takes the place of the vowel in forming the syllable; and the tongue tip must be held firmly in position until the l is completed. Allow no vowel sound between t or d and l, nor substitute the neutral vowel for it. Also, when syllabic l follows consonants other than t or d, permit no vowel to occur between l and the preceding consonant. Examples: *saddle* (săd' 'l); *cattle* (kăt' 'l). See §§ 9(1–5), 20(10.3), 24(14), 28(5.6), 31(4), 32(2.1,2,3), 33(2), 34(14.2), 40(13.4).

3) Note the following: a) Only the sonorant consonants l, m, n, ng [ŋ] can be syllabic; (b) Only in unaccented syllable may these sonorants be syllabic; and (c) Each sonorant can be syllabic only after certain consonants.

2. "Clear" l; "Dark" l.

1) It is both the shape and position of the body of the tongue and the shape of the lips that determine the particular resonance or quality of an l sound. By "clear" l is meant an l sound having the resonance of a front vowel (ē, ĭ, ā, ĕ, ȧ, ă); by "dark" l, an l having the resonance often of a back vowel (ä, ô, ō, ŏŏ, ōō) or also of a mid-vowel (û, ē, ŭ). (See § 18.) A "clear" or "light" l is more likely to occur when l precedes a vowel, especially a high front vowel, for then the elevated point of the tongue is more likely to be farther forward in the mouth and the lip opening somewhat wider than when l is found in the final position as in *bawl*, or when it precedes a consonant as in *pulp*, or when it is used syllabically as in *cattle* (kăt' 'l). Put another way, "clear" l, which is an l sound formed with the tongue tip in the l position on the teeth ridge while the rest of the tongue has a position very much like that of a front vowel, is usually heard before vowels in the same syllable, while "dark" l, made with the tongue tip in the l position of a back vowel, is usually heard before consonants, and when final or syllabic.

2) Many Americans tend to make the l far back in the mouth and with very little movement of the front of the tongue. The resulting "dark" l is a blurred sound, not infrequently labeled as "dialectal." Do not allow the tongue to drop

too far back. In other words, make the l sound well forward in the mouth—except where "dark" l is normal.

3) Initial l among Americans, while at times noticeably "dark," is generally "clearer" than final l. Colloquial speech does not always show the difference of sound between such words as *real** (rē′ăl) and *reel* (rēl), for *real* is also pronounced rēl. *Dial,** a two-syllable word (dī′ăl), is more and more being sounded acceptably as a one-syllable word (dīl).

4) The letter l is silent in *should, would,* and *could;* and in some other words, as *almond, folk, half, salmon, walk, yolk.*

5) In *altar, fault,* vault,* Walter,* and other words in which l had been silent from their very introduction into English until the eighteenth century or later, the sound has since been restored and in each today is a spelling-pronunciation. See § 1.

3. Devoiced l; Voiceless l.

1) While usually voiced, the l sound becomes partially unvoiced when it follows a voiceless consonant. The first part of the l when it is preceded by a voiceless consonant is devoiced, as in *plant,* club, flip, slant.** (A small circle below a consonant shows that the consonant usually voiced has been devoiced, as ḷ, m̥.) See §§ 29(1.5), 32(2.4), 33(1.8), 37(1.5), 42(1.2); also § 19, "Chart of English Consonants," Note b (page xlix).

2) In French words, voice final l only when soon followed by another word.

3) Welsh ll [l with looped crossbar: ɬ] is a voiceless l. Its strongly fricative sound may be approximated by forcing out the voiceless breath at one side of the tongue near the back teeth while the tongue touches the teeth ridge in front and at the other side. In such words as *Lleu* (hlĕ′ü; lĕ′ü) and *Llewellyn* (hlĭ wĕl′ĭn; lōō ĕl′ĭn), narrow the aperture at one side of the tongue while sounding h and l simultaneously without voice. When a Welsh name is Anglicized (§ 46), the f is sometimes substituted for the Welsh voiceless fricative, as in *Fluellen* (*fluellen, fluellin,* from Welsh, *llysiau Llewelyn,* literally meaning "Llewelyn's herbs"). Sometimes, also, such Anglicized pronunciations are replaced by English thl [θl], as in *Llanelly* (lä nĕth′lĭ; lä nĕl′ĭ; thlä nĕth′lĭ; [*Welsh* la ′neɬ i]).

4. Syllabic l.
l, like m and n, is also vowel-like and may be syllabic. For examples wherein l either forms a syllable by itself without the help of another vowel sound or forms a syllable with other consonants, see *Babel,* battle,* cancel,* castle,* colonel,* desultory,* facile,* futile,* penalty,* ribald,* sibyl,* wistful.** See also §§ 9(1–5), 20(10.3), 24(14), 28(5.6), 31(1.2), 32(2.1,2,3), 33(2), 34(14.2), 40(13.4).

5. ll.

1) When ll occurs in English, it usually spells a single l sound, as in *bellows,* knoll,* yelled* (yĕld). But that is not true in compounds (e.g., *bell-like* = bĕl′līk) and before suffixes (e.g., *solely* = sōl′lĭ; *fully* = fŏŏl′ĭ and also fŏŏl′lĭ). See §§ 21(1.6), 23(1.10), 25(1.4), 26(1.3), 30(2.2), 32(3.1,2), 33(5.1), 35(5), 37(6), 38(13.2,3,4), 39(9.1), 45(4.1,2).

2) ll in Castilian Spanish is like lli in *billion* (bĭl′yŭn), as in *"caballero"* (kä′văl yä′rō, kä′bäl yä′rō). See § 21(2). In American Spanish, and in many parts of Spain, ll is pronounced as y, as in *Villahermosa* (vē′yär ĕr mō′sä; vēl′yär ĕr mō′sä), *"caudillo"* (kou thĕl′yō; kou thē′yō; *also* kou dē′lyō; kou dē′yō).

3) In Welsh words, ll represents a voiceless fricative l: see § 31(3.3).

§ 32. M

1. English m.

1) m, as in *me, men, smite, lamb,* fame, human,* solemn,* ram, stamp, drama,* phlegm,* palm,* wisdom,** is produced by keeping the lips closed and allowing or

forcing the vibrating breath stream out gradually through the nose. The soft palate is lowered or down. m is a continuant, nasal, voiced lip sound.

2) m, like p and b, is a labial; for in forming each, the lips are closed. p is made by blowing the lips apart with the breath; b, by blowing them apart with a voiced sound; m, by making a voiced sound through the nose. See §§ 21(1.1), 35(1.1).

3) m (also p) followed by f frequently becomes labiodental (see § 19); e.g.; *comfort** (kŭm'fĕrt) may be heard as (kŭmp'fĕrt).

2. Syllabic m.

1) m occasionally forms a syllable alone without the aid of a vowel, as in the everyday expression "Hit 'em" (hit' 'm) or, especially after the hormoganic p, as in *cup and spoon** (frequently pronounced kŭp' 'm spōōn). It may also form a syllable with other consonants, as in *rhythmed* (rĭth̶' 'md; rĭth' 'md). See § 31(4).

2) Syllabic m is not as frequent as syllabic l [§ 31(4)] or n [§ 33(2)]. Though the spelling of many words appears to suggest syllabic m, as in *cataclysm,** *catechism,** *chasm,** *feudalism,** *macrocosm,* *prism,** *schism,** yet in such words the neutral vowel [ə] often is inserted into the pronunciation. Thus, for example, *cataclysm** is pronounced not only kăt'à klĭz'm but also (as indicated in the SIMPLIFIED and PHONETIC columns) as kăt'à klĭz ăm. However, only one form is given in the DIACRITICAL column because it is generally agreed that, although m is a vowel-like consonant and may be syllabic, yet m is not too frequently pronounced as a true syllabic. See (3) below.

3) m may once have been syllabic after t or d, but today, although the neutral vowel [ə] may appear quickly, m is no longer recognized as syllabic after t or d, as in *bottom* (bŏt'ŭm), *Adam* (ăd'ăm). Words such as *blossom* and *bosom** are in the category in which m was perhaps once syllabic but today spells out the vowel. See §§ 9(1–5), 20(10.3), 24(14), 28(5.6), 31(1.2), 31(4), 33(2), 34(14.2), 40(13.4).

4) "Yes," "no," and other meanings are often communicated by *voiceless* m [m̥]. (The small circle marks a devoiced consonant that is usually voiced.) m may also be devoiced when its sound is initiated; thus, in *small* (smôl), the preceding voiceless consonant s devocalizes m at the beginning, but at the end the m is voiced. See §§ 29(1.5), 31(3.1), 33(1.8), 37(1.5), 42(2.1); also, § 19, "Chart of English Consonants," Note b (page xlix).

3. mm; mn.

1) Like kk and ll, each of which usually spells a single sound, mm is as a rule pronounced as a single m sound, as in *rammer* (răm'ĕr), except in combinations, where it has two sounds, as in *boom-making* (bōōm'māk'ĭng). See §§ 21(1.6), 23(1.10), 25(1.4), 26(1.3), 30(2.2), 31(5.1), 33(5.1), 35(5), 37(6), 38(13.2,3,4), 39(9.1), 45(4.1,2).

2) In such words as *immatchable* (ĭm măch'à b'l) and *immemorable* (ĭm mĕm'ŏ rà b'l), im is followed by m in the next syllable, and in formal speech is pronounced very much like that of a "double" m, achieved by sounding the two m's as a prolonged m. This is true especially when the im–, an assimilated form of in– ("not"), is negative in force. However, two pronunciations are acceptable, and are often indicated. In colloquial speech, only one m is ordinarily pronounced. See § 49(8).

3) In *mneme* (nē'mĕ), *mnemonic* (nĕ mŏn'ĭk), *Mnium* (nī'ŭm), and other words from the Greek, initial m before n is usually (but not always) silent. *Mnason* (Biblical) may be pronounced nā'sŏn or m'nā'sŏn.

§ 33. N

1. English n.

1) In *no, none, bone, demesne,* knave,* gnash,* income, annual, Danny, handsome,* snout, Wednesday,* onus, inn, champagne, when, learn, winner, pneumatic,* comptroller,* mnemonic,* the sound of n is formed by placing the tip of the tongue on the upper gum or gum ridge, in the same position as for d and t; and by holding the tongue tip on the gum ridge while you make a voiced sound through the nose. Like m [§ 32(1)], n is a voiced nasal continuant. Be careful not to make this voiced, tongue-back velar nasal on your teeth.

2) m + final n in the same syllable makes the n silent, as in *autumn,* condemn,* damn,* hymn, limn, solemn.** But n after m keeps its normal sound when placed in the next syllable; thus, au tum'nal,* dam na'tion, sol'em nize.* See (3) below.

3) Final n after m is usually sounded before a suffix when the suffix begins with a vowel (*damned,* damning,* hymnal, limner,* solemnize**). But it is not sounded in *hymned.*

4) Although final n after m before a vowel in derivatives is ordinarily pronounced, the n of mn before a consonant is always silent (*hymns, condemns, solemnly*).

5) The participles *damned,* damning,** and *limning** are generally pronounced without n; but the n is often sounded for certain purposes or in certain senses. Other examples wherein the n may or may not be pronounced are *condemner* and *contemner.*

6) Pronunciations for *kiln** and *limekiln* either retain the n (spelling-pronunciation) or omit the n (historical pronunciation). When the n is not retained in the spelling, the n is not pronounced, as in *mill* (formerly *myln, miln*) and *ell* (formerly *elne, eln*).

7) The word *open* (ō'pĕn) is often pronounced ō'p'm. The n is assimilated to p; that is, the lip sound p has helped change the tongue-point alveolar nasal into the lip nasal. In individual words and in phrases, n in colloquial speech often becomes m by assimilation to lip consonants.

8) n may also be devoiced or devocalized at the beginning of its sound when preceded by a voiceless consonant; e.g., in *snow* (snō), n is voiceless at the beginning and voiceless at the end. The small circle indicates unvoicing—thus ṇ. See §§ 29(1.5), 31(3.1), 32(2.4), 37(1.5), 42(1.2); and § 19, "Chart of English Consonants," Note b (page xlix).

2. Syllabic n. (Simplified Symbol: 'n. Phonetic Symbol: ṇ.)

1) It has been seen that l or m may form a syllable by itself. n also may be syllabic, as in *basin** (bā's'n), *christen** (krĭs' 'n). Pronouncing such words as *didn't** (dĭd' 'nt) and *wouldn't* (wo͝od' 'nt) as ['dɪd ənt] and ['wʊd ənt] is perhaps substandard, although recognized as correct by at least one modern dictionary. See § 51(2.7).

In addition to forming a syllable by itself, n may form a syllable with other consonants, as in *garden** (gär'd'n), *venal** (vē'năl, vē'n'l). n in initial syllables is less frequently syllabic, as in *fanatic** (fȧ năt'ĭk; f'n ăt'ĭk).

See also *blazon,* certain,* chasten,* Christendom,* coalescence,* complacence,* conversant,* credence,* decadence,* decedent,* diapason,* excrescence,* personal,* resin,* satin.**

2) For other syllabic consonants, see §§ 9(1–5), 20(10.3), 24(14), 28(5.6), 31(1.2), 31(4), 32(2.1,2,3), 40(13.4).

3. ñ. Spanish ñ is like ni in *bunion* (bŭn'yŭn), where the ni = n + y. See *canyon.**

4. ng. (Simplified Symbol: ng. Phonetic Symbol: ŋ.)

1) Raise the back of the tongue to the soft palate. Hold the back of the tongue gently but firmly against the lowered soft palate while you make a voiced sound through your nose. The sound emitted through the nose is the voiced nasal continuant *ng* [ŋ] as in *sing*.

This simple nasal consonant ng [ŋ] (two other nasal consonants are m and n) is neither n nor g nor a combination of n and g, but a separate sound related to neither n nor g. ng [ŋ] is one consonant: it is a single sound formed by a single position of the articulatory mechanisms; but indicated, as digraphs are, by two letters. See § 9(6.b).

2) Historically, the digraph ng as in *sing* represented the sound ng plus a g sound, as still found in *finger** (fĭng′gēr) and other words. But for more than two centuries the stop or explosive g sound, when final, has not been sounded. All that is left in the *sing* type of words is the ng [ŋ]; but the simple nasal sound [ŋ] is still represented by the two letters ng.

3) Observe that the loss of g more than two hundred years ago left the single ng [ŋ] sound (see 2 above). When such a word as *singing** (sĭng′ĭng) is pronounced "sĭng′ĭn," the g is dropped only in the spelling sense, for no g is being dropped out of the simple consonant sound ng [ŋ] usually represented by the two letters ng.

One or two authorities have stated that in Southern American speech it is not incorrect to say *comin'*, although many good speakers say *coming*.* Interesting, too, the tendency to sound ng [ŋ] for final n in such a word as *singing** is due to the spelling ng (§ 1). This does not mean that we should say [ɪn] for [ɪŋ].

In summary, remember that in such words as *sing** and *singing** there is no g sound. When a speaker says *singin'* or *comin'*, it is a misconception to believe that he has "dropped the *g*," for in the continuous, simple voiced sound ng [ŋ] there is no g sound. What the speaker has done is to substitute [n] for [ŋ]. The mistaken impression that we are omitting a sound is enforced by the apostrophe (*singin'*, *comin'*); but, instead of "dropping a *g*," we are shaping our tongue for the alveolar n instead of the velar ng [ŋ].

4) Rules for a k or g sound:
   a) When before a k (or "hard" c) or g sound in the same syllable, the letter n always is sounded ng [ŋ] as in *ink*, *thank*,* *sanc′tion*,* *young*.* However, when before the k or g sound in the following syllable, the letter n may represent either the n or ng [ŋ] sound, or even both. Despite its many exceptions, a rule that has been helpful is to sound ng [ŋ] when its syllable is stressed.
   b) In *anger* (ăng′gēr), *blink* (blĭngk), *carbuncle* (kär′bŭng k′l), and other words where ng [ŋ] is followed by a g or k sound, the ng [ŋ] is also spelled with n.
   c) A k or g sound may or may not be sounded between ng [ŋ] and certain other consonants, as in *anxious** (ăngk′shŭs; ăng′shŭs) *length** (lĕngth; lĕngkth), *strength** (strĕngth; strĕngkth). The statement applies also to the derivatives of *length* and *strength*. See § 30(1.6). For examples (4.a–c) in the vocabulary (pp. 1–319), see *anxious*,* *punctilious*,* *punctual*,* *sanction*,* *sanctuary*,* *unction*,* *bronchitis*,* *concave** (adj.), *concord*,* *concourse*,* *nightingale*;* *conquest*,* *jonquil*,* *tranquil**; *cincture*,* *extinct*,* *extinguish**; *length*,* *lengthen*,* *strength**, *strengthen**; *elongate*,* *elongation*.* Other examples are *anxiety*,* *banquet*,* *clangor*,* *congratulate*,* *congress* (v.i.), *congruent*,* *delinquent*,* *dinghy*,* *distinct*,* *ensanguine*,* *hangar*.* In the SIMPLIFIED and DIACRITICAL columns are recorded acceptable pronunciations; in the PHONETIC column are recorded not only the acceptable pronunciations but also variants not without warrant (see, for example, *concubine*,* *idiosyncrasy*,* *incongruity**).

5) Four general rules for the pronunciation of *ng* as in *sing,* * ng + g as in *linger,* * and nj as in *plunge* are these:

    a) A root word ending in ng has the pronunciation ng [ŋ]. In other words, g is not to be pronounced when the letters ng occur at the end of a word or syllable.

        Examples: *bring,* * *clang, fling, hang, thong, rung, wrong;* also *harangue,* * *meringue, tongue* (in each of which the ue is silent, thereby making ng [ŋ] the final sound). But note *dengue* (dĕng′gā; dĕng′gĕ).

    b) Our first rule states that when a word ends in the letters ng, the sound is ng [ŋ] alone. A second rule is that a root word ending in ng [ŋ] and adding a suffix retains the pronunciation ng [ŋ], as *sing,* * *singer.* * Put another way, the g is silent when a suffix is added to a word ending in ng. Observe that a word still remains when the suffix is cut off, as the –er in *singer.*

        Examples: *hanging,* * *ringer, youngster.*

        Exceptions: Pronounce ng + g [ŋg] in the following words: (1) the comparative and superlative degrees of the adjectives *long,* * *strong,* * and *young* *; (2) words ending in ng [ŋ] and adding a suffix –al, as *diphthongal;* and (3) compounds of *long* in which one or more syllables are added to the word *long,* as *elongate* * and *elongation.* * In *hangar* * either ng [ŋ] or ng + g [ŋg] may be used.

ng [ŋ]	ng + g [ŋg]	ng + g [ŋg]
long*	longer*	longest*
strong*	stronger*	strongest*
young*	younger*	youngest*
diphthong*	diphthongal	
	elongate*	
	elongation*	
	prolongate	
	prolongation	

    c) Rule b, for example, means that when the suffix –er, meaning "the doer," is added to a word ending in ng, the word is sounded ng [ŋ]. However, some words appear to have a suffix; but if you drop off what appears to be a suffix, you will see that the syllable remaining has no meaning as a word by itself. Memorize the rule: a root word that has ng within it requires ng + g [ŋg]. In other words, ng found medially (within a word) is pronounced [ŋg] unless the syllable ending in ng is the root of the word.

        Examples: *anger, bungle, England,* * *English,* * *language,* * *linger,* * *mangle, single.* *

        Exceptions: Pronounce ng [ŋ] in *gingham,* * *tungsten,* and words like *Bingham, Nottingham,* and *Washington.* Also, when words end in –ngue (*harangue,* * *meringue, tongue*), or in –ngth (*length* *), or in –ngthen (*lengthen* *), the pronunciation is ng [ŋ].

    d) When words end in the letters –nge, the ng is pronounced nj [n + dʒ = ndʒ]. The ng is also pronounced [nʒ].

        Examples: *change, cringe, flange,* * *fringe, lounge, lunge, mange, orange,* * *plunge, range, revenge, singe, sponge,* * *strange, tinge.*

        Note these spellings; *change,* but *changing; cringe,* but *cringing;* and so on. Rule d still applies.

5. nge; nn.

1) Words ending in –nge have the pronunciation nj [ndʒ], as in *hinge* [§ 33(4.5d)]. Also, the combination in –nge in different syllables is occasionally sounded nj [ndʒ], as in *danger* (dan′ger) and *sponges* (spon′ges). See also § 25(4.3).

2) nn is sounded as a single n sound, as in *Fanny* (făn′ĭ), *inn* (ĭn), *dinned* (dĭnd) ; but not in combinations, for in such instances nn has a doubled sound, as in *unneighborly* (ŭn nā′bēr lĭ), *leanness* (lēn′nĕss; lēn′nĭs), *innoxious* (ĭ nŏk′shŭs; ĭn nŏk′shŭs). See §§ 21(1.6), 23(1.10), 25(1.4), 26(1.3), 30(2.2), 31(5.1), 32(3.1, 2), 35(5), 37(6), 38(13.2,3,4), 39(9.1), 45(4.1,2), 49(9).

§ 34. O

The letter o has nine accented and five unaccented sounds:

Accented

ō as in ō′pen, nō, § 34(2)	o as in move = ōō, § 34(8)
ō as in fōrd, ō′ral, § 34(3)	o as in wolf = ŏŏ, § 34(9)
ô as in ôrb, § 34(4)	o as in shove = ŭ, § 34(10)
ŏ as in ŏdd, § 34(6)	o as in word = û, § 34(11)
ŏ as in sŏft, § 34(7)	

Unaccented

ŏ as in ŏ be′di ence, § 34(12)	o as in for sooth′; also as in sail′or = ē,
ŏ as in cŏn form′, § 34(13)	§§ 24(7), 24(12), 34(6), 34(13,14)
ŏ as in cŏn nect′, wis′dŏm, § 34(14)	o (silent) as in but′ton, § 34(14)

1. Principal Sounds of o. The chart presented immediately above indicates that the letter o has fourteen sounds. In essence, however, there are four general types of o:

1) "Long" o—as in *open* and *no*. The "long" o becomes somewhat modified before an r. Also, the "long" o is a bit shorter in unaccented syllables and rapidly spoken words.

2) "Short" o—as in *odd* and *not*.

3) "Intermediate" o—as in *born, ford, pork:* very much like the *aw* sound in *law*.

4) "Obscure" o—as in *connect* and *button*.

2. ō as in ō′pen, nō. (Simplified Symbol: oh. Phonetic Symbol: o.)

1) ō is the "long" o sound in *o′pen,* no, go, old,** and *vote*. In American speech the "long" o is often sounded as a diphthong when it occurs in a stressed syllable. ō tends to be (but is not always) a pure vowel when it is used in an unstressed syllable, as in *opinion** (ō pĭn′yŭn), or when it is in a stressed syllable succeeded by an unstressed syllable beginning with a weak vowel, as in *boa** (bō′á).

Even though spelled by the one letter o, the sound is a blend of two sounds. The first element of the diphthong ō is stressed [o] and the second is lightly touched [ʊ]. That is why the "long" o is often represented phonetically as [oʊ] in a stressed position, and as [o] in an unstressed position. But since in American speech the "long" o is not only a diphthong but also a single vowel, and since for practical purposes it does not matter whether it is one or the other, the one symbol [o] is used for the sake of simplicity. See § 18(7).

2) "Long" o is a blend of the half-high, rounded back vowel ō and the high, lax back vowel ŏŏ (see 1 above). To produce an ō of good quality keep the lips round. Although not prominent in America, pronouncing accented ō [oʊ] as a diphthong is usually recommended.

3) ō or "long" o is also spelled variously, as in *beaux,* bowl,* bureau,* brooch,* chauffeur,* foam, folk,* know,* oath,* ohm,* owe, roe, sew, shoulder, show, though, trousseau,* yeomanry.**

3. ōr (ō + r). See also § 34(5). (Simplified Symbols: ohr, awr. Phonetic Symbols: or, ɔr.)

1) The combination ōr ("long" o + r) as in *more,** *floor,** and *four** may start in one of two ways. Not too many Americans begin the sound with the tongue in position for ô as in *orb* and then have it glide to *á* as in Chi'na. Other speakers, perhaps a majority, say the diphthong with the final tongue position of r. The first sound, then, may be ō or ô; the second *á* (= ĕ) or r. Another way of describing the diphthong ōr is by saying that it begins with either ō or ô and ends with [r]; that is, "long" o occurring before r has as its vanish the neutral vowel ĕ [ə], representing slightingly or weakly the fore-glide of the r. In other words, in General American speech ōr is pronounced either [or] or [ɔr]. See §§ 34(5.1, 2).

2) The combination ōr is frequently described as a diphthong made up of the half-low back vowel ô [ɔ] + the neutral vowel [ə]. Those who do not pronounce r except before a vowel often substitute the pure vowel ô [ɔ] for the diphthong ōr [ɔə].

3) Many Americans (J. S. Kenyon says a majority of Americans) use the [or] and the [ɔr] to distinguish between such pairs of words as *boarder* ['bor dər] and *border* ['bɔr dər], *hoarse** [hors] and *horse** [hɔrs], *oar** [or] and *or* [ɔr], *wore* [wor] and *war* [wɔr]. In J. S. Kenyon's opinion, such distinction of vowel is prevailing American pronunciation. (This manual, however, is not using the vowel symbol [ɚ] to express a monosyllabic vowel forming a diphthong with the preceding vowel.)

4) For most general speech purposes the following rules are helpful:
a) "Long" o (ō) + r in a monosyllable (a word of one syllable), or "long" o (ō) + r + a consonant in a monosyllable is usually pronounced aw + r [ɔr]. Examples: *for, nor; cord, lord, fort**; *horse.**
b) "Long" o (ō) + r in an accented syllable when followed by a consonant is usually pronounced aw + r [ɔr]. Examples: ap por'tion,* for'te,* or'der.
c) A workable general rule is that a vowel is given its "long" sound (ā, ē, ī, ō, ū) whenever that vowel is followed by any single consonant (except r) + final silent e in the same syllable. However, "long" o (ō) + any consonant (*including* r) + final silent e in the same syllable is pronounced ōr [or]. Examples: a dore',* chore,* en core',* ig nore',* more,* ore,* pore,* soph'o more,* store,* syc'a more.* See also § 34(16.2).
d) "Short" o (ŏ) + r in an accented syllable + either a second r or any vowel in the very next syllable is usually pronounced ŏr, which in American speech is a sound varying from aw + r (ôr) to ah + r (är). Examples: bor'row, im mor'al [§ 34(5.2)].
e) -or in an unaccented syllable is sounded as ẽr (= uhr). See § 34(13.4); also SPECIAL NOTES, III, "Variant Pronunciations," a.2 (page xxi).

5) For the diacritical symbol ōr this handbook uses ohr and awr in the SIMPLIFIED column, and [or] and [ɔr] in the PHONETIC column. But it must be remembered that there are regional variations between both sounds.

4. ô as in ôrb. (Simplified Symbol: aw. Phonetic Symbol: ɔ.)

1) ô as in *orb, lord,* and *born** is otherwise spelled with a, or au, or aw, or ou, or oa, or ag, or i, as in *ball, chalk; caught, maul; awe, jaw, spawn, lawgiver**; *bought, trough**; *broad; Magdalen**; *memoir.**

2) ô is a half-low, rounded back vowel. Round your lips well as though to say ōō in *moon.** Dropping the jaw, pull down your lips, making sure to protrude your lips and keep them round. Say ô as in *all* and *orb.* Observe that the lips are rounded decidedly in the form of an ellipse and, like the back of your tongue, are tense. See also § 20(6).

3) Avoid sounding ô too far back in the mouth. Avoid pronouncing ô like ä, a tendency in midwestern speech. Avoid pronouncing ô with an r-colored offglide, which makes such a word as *saw** [sɔ] resemble "sawr" or *sore* [sɔr], or such an expression as *saw it* ['sɔ ɪt] resemble *sawr it* ['sɔr ɪt]. Each is an example

of *intrusive r*, which strictly, however, is an r sound that has been added to a word ending in a vowel when followed by a vowel, as in "sawr it." See § 37(3).

5. ōr, ōrr. See also §34(3). (Simplified Symbols: ohr, awr. Phonetic Symbols: or, ɔr.)

1) When "long" o occurs before r, its sound may be ō [oə] as in *afford** (ă fōrd*'*). When not so pronounced, ō + final r, or ō + r + a consonant, is sounded ô, as in *for* (fôr), *horse** (hôrs), *forte** (*Music*, fôr*'*tā), *portend** (pōr tĕnd*'*; pôr tĕnd*'*). See § 34(3); also, SPECIAL NOTES, III, "Variant Pronunciations," a.2 (page xxi).

2) "Long" o + r (or rr) + a vowel is often sounded ō as in *story* (stō*'*rĭ). However, in other words o + r (or rr) + a vowel is pronounced ŏ, as in *borrow* (bŏr*'*ō) and *immoral* (ĭm mŏr*'*ăl; ĭ mŏr*'*ăl). See § 34(3,6). But derivatives from words that have o + the r sound (spelled r or rr) + a vowel, while they are occasionally pronounced with ŏ, generally keep the ô of the stem (see *abhor,* abhorrent**). In America the tendency is to sound ô before r [§ 34(7)]. In most parts of New England and among the good speakers in New York, o is pronounced ô when o, oa, ou, and like combinations appear before r—although the r is not sounded when final. See §§ 34(3), 34(16).

3) When final in an unaccented syllable, the combination –or is almost always obscured, as in *sailor* (sāl*'*ĕr), *ancestor,* bachelor, neighbor*. See § 34(13.4).

4) In such words as *amatory,* deprecatory,* feudatory,* imprecatory,* judicatory,* predatory,** and *repertory,** the pronunciation may be either –tō*'*rĭ or (acceptable American but especially British) –tĕr ĭ. This secondary accent in American English is today a noticeable difference from British English. See § 13.

6. ŏ as in ŏdd. (Simplified Symbol: o. Phonetic Symbols: ɑ, *also* ɒ.)

1) To produce the sound of ŏ, commonly called "short" o, as in *odd, not,* hot, rock, stop, property,* watch,** round your lips as you did for ô [§ 34(4.2)] and pull your lips down but not so far, for the mouth is opened wider for ŏ than for ô. The back of the tongue is slightly raised. Since the sound ŏ as in *odd* and *watch* [wɒtʃ] is medial between ô and ä, and must be pronounced with slight lip-rounding, it may help if you put your mouth in position for ô and then say ä as in *father*. In fact, the rounded sound as in *watch* is commonly pronounced in Southern and General American speech like the ä in *father*, and usually in Eastern American as a medial sound [ɒ] between the vowels ô and ä. In brief, "short" o has regional variations, ranging from ä to ô; and therefore the ŏ sound may indicate either the "short" o [ɒ] or the unrounded ä [ɑ].

2) The ŏ sound follows the general rule in English that a vowel in an unaccented syllable tends to become weakened or obscure. Occasionally, however, the ŏ sound appears in a syllable not without some stress, as in *carbon.**

7. ŏ̄ as in sŏ̄ft. (Simplified Symbols: aw, o. Phonetic Symbols: ɔ, ɒ.)

1) The symbol ŏ̄ as in sŏ̄ft indicates either a choice between ŏ [ɒ: § 34(6)] and ô [ɔ: § 34(4)], or a sound intermediate between them. In General American the sound ŏ̄ in sŏ̄ft has regional variations ranging from ä to ô, but many teachers of speech urge the avoidance of the sound ä [ɑ: § 20(4)].

2) In one-syllable words labeled ŏ̄, perhaps the ô [ɔ] sound is more frequent; in other than a one-syllable word, perhaps the unrounded ŏ (= ä) sound.

Examples (note that each vowel is followed by a voiceless fricative, either f or th [θ] or s): *boss, broth,* cloth,* cost, cough,* cross,* doff, frost,* froth,* gloss, loft,* moss, moths,* off,* scoff, soft,* troth.** But observe, also, that some plurisyllables are pronounced ô [ɔ] even in General American: *Boston,* coffee,* offer,* office.**

3) The pronunciation is ô often in words where the r is final (*for, war*), where the r + a consonant is final (*form, warm*), where the r is intervocal (*quarrel,**

warrior*), or where certain words begin with w (*want,* wash,* wander**): it is the w that often rounds the vowel to [ɒ] or [ɔ]. See § 20(4.3).

4) o + ng as in *long,* song,* strong,* throng, wrong* is most often pronounced aw [ɔ], and sometimes ŏ [ɒ]. (It is the w that may round the [ɔ] to [ɒ].)

5) When the medial sound [ɒ] is used in such words as *dog* and *not*, the pronunciation represents Eastern American Speech.

6) See *authoritative,* authority,* chorister,* corollary,* corridor,* Doric,* Florentine,* florid,* forecastle,* horoscope,* horrid,* incorrigible,* minority,* moral,* orange,* orator,* quarantine,* Warwick.**

8. o as in move = ōō. In *do,* lose, move, tomb,* who*, and similar words, the o is an infrequent spelling for the ōō sound as in *tooth*. See § 34(21.2).

9. o as in wolf = ŏŏ. An occasional spelling for the ŏŏ sound as in *foot* is the o in such words as *wolf* and *woman.** See § 34(22.2).

10. o as in shove = ŭ.

1) In certain words o = ŭ as in *up*. Many such words were sounded as a "short" u (= ŏŏ) during the Middle English period; and most of them were spelled in Anglo-Saxon with u or in Old French with o (= ŏŏ). o = ŭ appears in *above* (*AS* abufan), *come** (*AS* cuman), *honey** (*ME* honi, huni, from *AS* hunig), *love* (*ME* love, luve, from *AS* lufu), *monk* (*AS* munuc), *shove** (*ME* shouven, from *AS* scūfan), *some* (*ME* som, sum, from *AS* sum), *tongue* (*ME* tunge, tonge, from *AS* tunge), *won* (*ME* wonen, wunen, wonien, from *AS* wunian), *wonder** (*AS* wundrian), *wont* (adj.—*ME* wunt, woned, from *AS* wunian). In such words as *comfort,* company,* cover, dozen,** and *govern*, the Old French spelling had the o. Observe that we pronounce o = ŭ in the everyday words, because we speak those words long before we learn to spell them. But we show a tendency to pronounce such words as *combat, constable,** and *wont** with [ɑ] or [ɒ] or [o] chiefly because we acquire such words not by ear but by eye. Spelling-pronunciation (§ 1) has left its mark on such words.

2) Another group of words with o = ŭ changed gradually from the Middle English sound ō to the modern sound ŭ, passing from ō to ōō to ŏŏ to ŭ. Examples: *blood, brother,* flood,* month*.

3) In a fourth group of words, including *none** and *nothing,** a dialect pronunciation of ŭ substituted for the normal ō.

11. o as in word = û. Especially in words derived from the Anglo-Saxon and beginning most often with wor as in *word,* world,* worth*, the r in o + r transformed the Middle English ŏŏ sound into û. See §§ 24(6,7), 34(10).

12. ŏ as in ŏ be′di ence.

1) ŏ as in ŏ be′di ence,* ŏ bey′ is the half-high back vowel. The sound, usually the first element of the diphthong ō [§ 34(2)], appears in comparatively few words and always in an unaccented syllable. In such unstressed syllables ŏ is used to represent a shorter variety of "long" o as in *November* (Nŏ vĕm′bēr), *opinion** (ŏ pĭn′yŭn), *potato** (pŏ tā′tō), *violet** (vī′ŏ lĕt, vī′ŏ lĭt).

2) The ŏ symbol may also represent, especially in familiar speech, not only a weakened ō but also a sound that approaches or even becomes the neutral vowel ŭ [ə]. The marking ŏ in the DIACRITICAL column is interpreted in the SIMPLIFIED column as either ō [o] or uh [ə], or both, depending upon the apparent preponderance of evidence. See SPECIAL NOTES, III, "Variant Pronunciations," b.3, page xxi); and also §§ 20(10), 20(11), 24(4), 28(5.5), 34(13.1,2,3), 40(12).

3) In an unstressed syllable as in hĭs′tŏ ry,* the ŏ may be obscured to the neutral vowel ŭ [ə] or even omitted. The consonant may become syllabic (hĭs′t′rĭ) or nonsyllabic (hĭs′trĭ). Such is especially true of words containing l, r, or n in an unaccented syllable. See also § 9(1-5).

4) ŏ is also used in this manual as the symbol for "short" o in French, German, Italian, and Dutch words.

13. ŏ as in cŏn form′; or as in sail′or.

1) When o is unaccented, the sound may vary from ŏ [ɒ] in *odd, not,** and *hot* to the obscure neutral vowel *o* [ə], in *connect* (kŏ nĕkt′). The degree to which the vowel in an unstressed syllable tends to be weakened depends on several factors; e.g., the more familiar the talk the closer the sound is usually to [ə], the more deliberate the speech the closer the sound is usually to ŏ [ɒ]. See §§ 20(10), 20(11), 24(4), 28(5.5), 34(12.2,3), 40(12).

2) When such words as *commensurate,** *commode,** *console** (verb), *consume,** *contain,** and *information** are marked with ŏ, it indicates that the ŏ [ɒ] sound has been weakened or obscured. See also *crayon,** *obnoxious** (PHONETIC column), *obscenity.**

3) The formality or the informality of your speech often determines your pronunciation. Accordingly the symbol ŏ is sometimes used to show that a word may be pronounced either ô or ē; thus, *forsooth** is transcribed fŏr sōōth′, but is pronounced fôr sōōth′ in deliberate speech and fēr sōōth′ in colloquial speech.

4) Final –or, like final –er (*lawyer, fighter, down-and-outer*), is usually pronounced –ēr in the common words (*sailor, labor**). However, in technical or learned words, the combination –or, even when final in an unaccented syllable, is not obscured but rather pronounced –ôr (*donor**). See §§ 24(7,12), 34(3.4e).

5) For the American –or (*favor,** *humor**) spelled –our (*favour,** *humour**) in British use, see § 34(24.5).

14. ŏ as in connect = ŭ, § 40(12); o as in button = Silent o.

1) The sound of the neutral vowel [ə] is given to o in the final unstressed syllable of *atom, elation,* and other words. When the o is not given the usual or normal ŏ sound, the symbol ŭ marks the obscuration. Thus, *atom* (ăt′ŭm), *elation* (ē lā′shŭn). See § 40(12).

2) In those words where the o becomes silent, the o is replaced by a syllabic consonant, as in *mutton* (mŭt′ 'n), or may lose a syllable, as in *beckoning* (bĕk′ŭn ĭng; bĕk′nĭng). See §§ 9(1–5), 20(10.3), 24(14), 28(5.6), 31(1.2), 31(4), 32(2.1,2, 3), 33(2), 40(13.4).

3) For o in *sailor* and *benefactor,* see §§ 24(7,12), 34(13.4).

15. Foreign ö; oe.

1) In German words ö (also written oe) is the mid-front rounded vowel [ø] of German *schön.* (The French spelling for the same sound is eu, as in *peu*—also spelled œu as in *œuvre.*) The symbol û is used to respell the sound, approximated by attempting to sound ā as in *ape* with lips rounded as for ō in *go.* See §§ 24(22), 34(18); also, SPECIAL NOTES, VII, "Foreign Sounds" (pages xxii f.).

2) For the English digraph oe, see § 34(17).

16. oa; oar; oor.

1) About three centuries ago the digraph oa was used to indicate the sound ô as in *orb* [§ 34(4)]. Today oa most commonly spells the "long" o (ō) as in *load, loathe,** *soak,* and *broach.*

2) oar as in *board, hoard, hoarse,** ore as in *adore,** *more,** *stevedore,** [see § 34(3.4,c)], and oor as in *door** and *floor** are usually pronounced ōr (= ohr, awr). In American speech the sounds oar, ore, and oor are often not distinguished from that in such words as *nor, horse,** and *apportion.** See [§ 34(3.4, a and b)].

In the SIMPLIFIED column we show the sound usually by ohr and awr; in the DIACRITICAL column by ōr; and in the PHONETIC column by [or] and [ɔr]. See §§ 34(3,5).

17. English œ.

1) The digraph oe may spell three sounds: ō as in *foe, goes;* ōō as in *canoe,* shoe;* and ŭ as in *does.* Most common is the sound of ō.

2) For German oe = ö, see § 34(15).

18. oeu = œu = eu. French oeu or œu (*boeuf, oeuwre*) and French eu (*deux, peu*), have the same vowel sounds. See §§ 24(22), 34(15).

19. oi as in oil. (Simplified Symbol: oy. Phonetic Symbol: ɔɪ.)

1) oi as in *oil** is a combination of the half-low, rounded back vowel of ô [ɔ] in *orb* and the high, lax front vowel ĭ [ɪ] as in *bit.* In producing that diphthong make sure not to substitute the û [ɜ] or [ə] for the ô. Round the lips when making the sound oi.

2) The sound oi is found also in *joy* and *royal.* See § 34(26).

20. oo.

1) The letters oo usually spell the sounds ōō [u] in *too* and ŏŏ [ʊ] in *foot.** See §§ 34(21,22).

2) In *blood* and *flood** the original sound ōō [u] was shortened to ŏŏ [ʊ] and finally to ŭ [ʌ] as in *up.* In such words as *foot** and *took** the ōō was lowered only to the intermediate ŏŏ. Many words [See § 34(22.5)] still vary in pronunciation between "long" u [u] as in *too* and the "shortened" or "lowered" u [ʊ] as in *foot.**

3) The letters oo are pronounced ō in *door** (dōr) and *floor** (flōr). [But see §§ 34(3), 34(16).] The word *brooch** is historically the same word as *broach,* and therefore is pronounced *brōch* or (spelling-pronunciation) *brōōch.* See § 1.

21. ōō as in tōō. (Simplified Symbol: oo. Phonetic Symbol: u.)

1) The sound ōō as in *too* is the highest and roundest and tensest back vowel. Raise the back of the tongue high, until it nearly touches the soft palate. Open the mouth slightly and round as well as protrude your lips into a small circle. Both the lips and the back of the tongue are tense. Make the voiced sound ōō as in *too.*

2) ōō as in *cool, food,* loon, soon, woof* is also spelled as in *amour,* blue,* bruise,* canoe,* do,* flute,* fruit, grew, lose, prude,* ragout,* rendezvous,* rude, souvenir,* true,* you.* See § 40(4).

3) r following an ōō sound, as in *poor,** tends to lower or succeeds in lowering the ōō sound to that of ŏŏ (pŏŏr). This sound of ŏŏr as in *poor* is a combination of the high back vowel ŏŏ [ʊ] + the neutral vowel [ə]. Its various spellings include *assure,* boor, plural,* sure,* tour.** See also §§ 18(7), 18(8.c,d), 40(4.9).

4) For the lowering of the ōō element of the ū sound before r, as in *bureau,* endure,* European,* and *mature,** see § 40(4.9).

5) Standard Scottish English retains the oo sound before r; and such words as *poor** and *sure** are pronounced pōōr and shōōr.

22. ŏŏ as in fŏŏt. (Simplified Symbol: ŏŏ. Phonetic Symbol: ʊ.)

1) Round your lips and raise the back of your tongue as if you were going to sound ōō in *too.* Now lower the back of the tongue just slightly, relax the jaw and lips, and, keeping the lips rounded, sound the high, back lax vowel ŏŏ as in *foot.**

2) ŏŏ, as in *book,* cook,* foot,* good,** is the same sound as in *couldn't, full,* put,* wolf, worsted.**

3) Almost all authorities agree on the sounding of ōō in the following words:

behoove	fool	proof	stool
bloom	gloom	roost	stoop
boom	goose	school*	swoon

boon	groove	scoop	swoop
boot	hoot	scoot	too
booty	loom	shoo	tool
booth*	loon	shoot	toot
brood	loop	sloop	tooth
choose	loose*	smooth*	troop
coo	loot	snoop	woo
croon	mood	snooze	woof
doom	moon*	spook	
droop	pool	spool	

4) Most authorities recommend the sound ŏŏ in these words:

book*	foot*	look	stood
brook	good*	nook*	took*
cook*	hood*	rook	wood*
crook	hook*	shook	wool

5) About other words the authorities disagree, some recommending ōō and others recommending ŏŏ. The words in dispute include the following:

broom*	hoof*	room*	soot*
coop	hoop*	root*	spoon*
groom	roof*	soon	whoop*

23. ōō Lowered to ŏŏ. Such varied causes as the use of phrases spoken like compounds, or of words in compounds, or of sense stress, or of sentence rhythm have in certain words changed the ōō to ŏŏ. This ōō sound is also frequently reduced or lowered to ŏŏ in unaccented syllables and in words not stressed in the sentence (§§ 14, 16). The very speaker who says grōōm will also say bride′grŏŏm′; he will say *value** (văl′ū ['væl ju]) and the next moment (văl′û ['væl jʊ]); "I′ give′ it′ to′ you′" (all stressed: ī gĭv ĭt tōō yōō) and also "Give all′ you want" (gĭv ôl′ yŏŏ wänt). See §§ 15, 16.

24. ou as in cow, a bout′; –our as in sour. (Simplified Symbol: ow. Phonetic Symbol aʊ.)

1) Combining the low back vowel ä [ɑ] as in *bar* and the high, rounded back vowel ŏŏ [ʊ] as in *foot** gives the diphthong ou [aʊ] as in *cow, bout, about,* *our,* *oust.** Avoid allowing the tongue to rise too far in front as the diphthong is begun, for that will make the initial element approximate the sound of ă [æ] instead of making that first element tantamount to ä [ɑ]. Or, placing the first element too forward in the mouth may well make the first sound an à [ɒ] instead of an ä [ɑ]. Also avoid stressing the ŏŏ [ʊ] sound. See § 18(7).

2) au today usually spells ô [§§ 20(15.1), 34(4)]. au = ou no longer appears except in words other than those from native English, as in *"Sauerbraten"* (zou′ĕr brä′tĕn); *sauerkraut**; *Saura* (sou′rȧ).

3) ou is also a spelling for the following sounds:

> ō in *dough**
> ōō in *boudoir,** *couger, dour, foulard**
> ŏŏ in *gourmand, would**
> ô in *cough**
> ŭ in *couple*
> ŏ in *houghband*
> û in *courtesy**
> ŭ in *egregious**
> ð in *borough**
> ē̆ in *glamour**

4) –our and –ower each is a combination sounded as a triphthong, as in *sour*, *power*, *hour*,* *tower*, *cower*. See § 9(6.c).

5) In such words as *favor*,* *honor*,* *humor*,* *labor*, the –ẽr sound spelled by –or is spelled by the British –our, as in *favour*, *honour*,* *humour*,* *labour*.* The –our spelling is acceptable American.

25. ow.

1) In *cow*, *how*,* *now*,* *vow*, ow is the customary spelling for the diphthong ou [aʊ] when it is final.

2) When medial, as in *cowl*, *fowl*,* *howl**, *scowl*, the diphthong au [aʊ] is occasionally spelled ow.

3) When pronounced ō (*open*) as in *dough*,* ou is occasionally spelled –ow– medially, as in *bowl*,* and more often spelled –ow finally, as in *know*,* *row*.

4) Final unaccented –ow is usually sounded ō, as in *arrow*,* *fellow*,* *gallows*,* *marshmallow*,* *widow*,* *window*,* *yellow*.* Good speakers often pronounce the ow as ŏŏ [ʊ], but seldom reduce the ow to the neutral vowel *ŭ* [ə]. See *borough*.* Consult § 50(26).

26. oy as in joy. (Simplified Symbol: oy. Phonetic Symbol: ɔɪ.)

oy is always pronounced oi as *oil*,* *soil*, *toil* [§ 34(19)]. Occasionally oy = oi occurs medially, as in *royal*, *goyim*, but usually occurs finally, as in *boy*, *enjoy*. See § 34(19.2).

§ 35. P

1. English p.

1) Like b, p is a bilabial plosive sound produced by closing the lips firmly but lightly, building up pressure in the mouth, and separating the two lips quickly and simultaneously by the force of the breath. The two sounds p and b are alike except that p is voiceless (breathed) and b is voiced. See § 21(1.1).

2) When p occurs initially, it is puffed out or aspirated, as are all the voiceless plosives. Like k or t, also, p is aspirated when followed by a vowel or a diphthong, or when followed by a pause, or when final in a phrase. When p, like k and t, is followed by a consonant, the puff of breath is slight and so the plosive is said to be unaspirated. As a general rule, p is puffed out or aspirated when followed by an accented syllable, and puffed out less or unaspirated when the p is unstressed. (Some foreigners omit the aspiration initially. As a result, the sound seems like [b] to us.) See §§ 30(1.4), 39(1.4).

3) p is often silent. See *clapboard*,* *corps*,* *cupboard*,* *raspberry*,* *receipt*.*

4) In the more generally known Greek derivatives, p is usually silent, as in *pneumatic*,* *pneumonia*,* *psalm*ₙ* *Ptolemaic* (tŏļ′ē mā′ĭk). But see *psychology*,* a common word.

5) In less common words the p is occasionally pronounced. See *pseudonym*,* *Psyche*,* *psychiatric*,* *psittacosis* (sĭt′á kō′sĭs; psĭt′á kō′sĭs). Thus, *ptarmigan* is tär′mĭ găn, whereas *ptarmic* is both tär′mĭk and p′tär′mĭk.

2. Excrescent p.

1) In such words as *Sampson*, *Thompson*, *glimpse*, the regular spelling with p represents the excrescent sound. Formerly the spellings were *Samson*, *Thomson*, and *glimse*.

2) The p sound may appear as an excrescent even when unspelled in a word. Examples are *comfort** (kŭm′fẽrt, kŭmp′fẽrt); *dreamt* (drĕmt, drĕmpt); *warmth* (wôrmth, wôrmpth). Another group includes ph– sounded-as-f [see § 35(4)]: *Humphrey* (hŭm′frĭ, hŭmp′frĭ); *lymph* (lĭmf, lĭmpf); *triumph* (trī′ŭmf, trī′umpf). See *nymph*,* *something*.*

3. pf.

1) When pf occurs initially, it has the sound of p + f.

2) In English pf occurs initially only in the interjection *pfui* (pfoo̅′ĭ; foo̅′ĭ).

3) pf often occurs initially in German, as in *pfennig* (pfĕn′ĭg) and *pfund* (pfoont).

4) Initial pf is sounded first as a bilabial p and then as a labiodental f; but the p may be assimilated to f. See §§ 19, 35(2.2).

4. ph.

1) ph is sounded as f in *phenomenon, philanthropist,* * *Philistine,* * *philosophic,* * *phlegm,* * *phonograph,* * *photographer,* * *physic,* * and other Greek derivatives.

2) Initial ph is often silent when followed immediately by th: thus, *phthalic* (thăl′ĭk; fthăl′ĭk), *phthisis* (thī′sĭs; fthī′sĭs). Interesting is the pronunciation of *phthisic* (tĭz′ĭk).

3) ph is preponderantly sounded f, but occasionally p, in such words as *diphtheria,* * *diphthong,* * *naphtha.* *

4) ph is occasionally pronounced v, as in *Stephen* (stē′vĕn), *nephew.* *

5) In *Phagun* (pä′goon; fä′goon), *Phalgun* (päl′goon; fäl′goon), *phansigar* (pän′sĕ gär′; fän′sĕ gär′), *phulkari* (pool′kä rē; p'hool′kä rē), *phulwara* (pool wä′ rä; p'hool wä′rä), ph may be sounded as p (and sometimes f) instead of p + h, as properly required by words from the Sanskrit and derived East Indian languages. See §§ 21(3), 22(11.1), 23(3), 29(3), 30(2.1), 39(7.4).

5. pp. Except in combinations, as *dampproof* (dămp′proof′; dămp′proof′), pp is pronounced as single p (*dapple, apparent* *). See §§ 21(1.6), 23(1.10), 25(1.4), 26(1.3), 30(2.2), 31(5.1), 32(3.1,2), 33(5.1), 37(6), 38(13.2,3,4), 39(9.1), 45(4.1,2).

§ 36. Q

English q.

1) In English q is always followed by u.

2) qu ordinarily represents the sound kw (*quadruple,* * *quaff,* * *quarrel,* * *quick,* * *quorum* *). In a few words the French value k is retained (*coquette,* * *quatorze, quay* *).

3) In the terminal –que, as *antique,* * *burlesque,* * *oblique,* * *toque, unique,* u and e are silent and q is sounded k. Cf. § 26(6).

§ 37. R

1. English r.

1) In the formation of r, as in *bar, farce,* * *neared, rage, very,* * the soft palate is raised, the lips are slightly protruded, and the sides of the tongue are against the upper side teeth. Sometimes it is the tip of the tongue that is lifted to the gum ridge; sometimes the middle that is raised toward the hard palate. No matter which part of the tongue is used for producing any given sound with r, the breath stream is gradually sent out over the raised part. Like the glide consonants [l] and [j], the glide consonant [r] depends chiefly upon the movement of the tongue.

2) r may stand for a consonant or for a vowel. When initial, or between two vowels, the sound r is classified as a consonant. Whenever r is final or precedes a consonant, it has the value of a vowel. In some sections of the country r is "dropped" whenever it is final or before a consonant. See §§ 37(1.5), 37(3).

3) For our purposes it may not be necessary to know the distinctions among the chief kinds of r: (a) the tongue-point trill r or trilled r; (b) the uvular r or

velar r (sometimes called guttural r); (c) the fricative r; (d) the frictionless continuant r; and (e) the retroflex r [§ 37(2)].

Your r should be sounded as it is by the best speakers of the section in which you live. For example, the sound r in Eastern Speech when it is not omitted is made by raising or pointing the tongue tip toward the roof of the mouth, curling the tongue tip slightly back toward the throat, and making a voiced sound—the voiced fricative r. [But see § 37(2.2).]

4) Just as n may be preceded by g or k in the spelling without having the g or n pronounced, so r may be preceded by the letter w in the spelling without having the w pronounced (*wrap,* wreck, wriggle,* wrong, wry**). See §§ 25(5), 30(1.5).

5) When r is voiceless at the beginning and voiced at the end, as in *tree, trial, try*, the glide r is said to be devocalized. r is a vowel-like consonant (§ 19), and its first part is partially unvoiced when it follows an unaspirated p, t, or k in the same syllable. [j], [w], and [l] may also be partially unvoiced when they follow voiceless consonants. See §§ 29(1.5), 31(3.1), 32(2.4), 33(1.8), 42(1.2); also, § 19, "Chart of English Consonants," page xlix.

2. Other Aspects of r.

1) Retroflex r, made by having the tongue tip raised and curled back, or "retroflexed," is a tongue-point consonant. (Other tongue-point consonants are t, d, n, l. See § 19.)

2) When the tip of the tongue is turned upward and backward, the process is known as *inversion*. Inversion often affects the vowel sound before r. Easterners and Southerners, however, keep the tongue tip behind the lower teeth while making the vowel sound preceding r. See § 40(7); and also § 18, footnote, part e, page xlii *f*.

3) Except in Southern speech, r before a vowel in the same or a closely following word is always pronounced.

4) When the r follows a vowel (*bar, farce**), the sound is either softened or omitted in Eastern and Southern American speech, with the result that *bar* [*General American* bär] becomes [*Eastern and Southern American* bä:], and *farce* [*GA* färs] becomes [*ES* fä:s; *E also* fä:s].

5) By a "linking" r is meant a final r sound retained before a vowel of the next word (their *own*; over *and* over; far *away*) by a speaker who generally omits the r before a consonant or a pause. Such usage is called either "linking" r or "r-glide." See "intrusive" r, §§ 37(3), 40(7.4); also, § 24(7).

6) Speakers who do not usually "drop" their r's may do so in certain words (by dissimilation): see *governor,* surprise,* thermometer.** See also §§ 24(7.3,4), 48(1).

3. "Intrusive" r.

1) An r sound is often added to a word ending in a vowel (*idea**) when followed by a word beginning with a vowel (*idea of*, pronounced "idear of"). Whenever a word ending in ĕ [ə] takes on an r sound when a vowel follows, the r is called "intrusive" r. Prefer *saw it* (sô′ĭt) to *saw rit* (sô rĭt). See § 34(4.3).

2) Another variety of "intrusive" r occurs when the sound of r is inserted between two vowels of the same word even though the letter r does not appear in the spelling. Prefer *sawing* (sô′ĭng) to "*sawring*" (sô′rĭng).

4. Sounding the r. See also § 37(2).

1) In General American, r is pronounced when it appears before a consonant and when it is a final sound; but in Eastern and Southern American, r is not pronounced when it appears before a consonant (*first,* serve, park*) or as a final sound (*jar*). As a rule, most Americans sound r between vowels in a word, or whenever a vowel follows immediately in the same word. Differences in pronunciation occur when r comes at the end of a word, or before a consonant. See § 3.

2) Some authorities urge that r be not sounded when it precedes a consonant

in the same word or another word, or when it precedes a pause, or when it is a final, or when it follows a vowel in the same syllable; and they urge that the r be pronounced when it is the initial sound, or before a vowel in a syllable, or when a word ending in r is followed by one beginning with a vowel. One contention is that retroflexion [§ 37(2)] when a vowel is followed by an r impairs quality. Most authorities, however, accept the sounding of r in such instances. But phoneticians do generally caution that the final r (as in *poor, their, pour, hear*) be not "burred" or inverted or made too prominent.

3) In this handbook all r's are shown to be pronounced in all three columns, SIMPLIFIED, DIACRITICAL, and PHONETIC.

It is to be understood that those who sound r only before a vowel in the syllable will naturally omit r before a consonant or when r follows a vowel in the same syllable, even though the vocabulary (pages 1–319) marks all r's in the respelling for pronunciation as being pronounced.

For those who use the PHONETIC column, this manual indicates also when the r is not sounded in the East and the South (or, occasionally, elsewhere). See also SPECIAL NOTES, IV, "Pronouncing the 'r,' " page xxi *f.*

Finally, the symbol r is used in the way explained by J. S. Kenyon and T. A. Knott in their impartial, scholarly, tolerant, and pioneering achievement, *A Pronouncing Dictionary of American English*.[1] The present manual, also, (a) uses the symbol r for the consonant where it is a semivowel or a glide consonant before a vowel in the same syllable; (b) uses the symbol [ɚ] to represent a syllable either by itself or with a consonant—in other words, to represent the *syllabic* vowel; and (c) uses the symbol [ɚ] in a few words "to represent the speech of those who 'drop their r's' . . . where all speakers would normally sound the *r* before a vowel." Fourthly:

> The symbol r is also used between ə and a vowel in such a position as in *flattery* 'flætərɪ, which might (less conveniently) be regarded as *flatter* 'flætɚ plus –*y* –ɪ, or by those who "drop their *r*'s" as 'flætə plus –ri. The slight difference in sound between 'flætɚ·ɪ and 'flætə·rɪ depends on where the last syllable begins, and is here disregarded.[2]

Despite the fact that this manual in all three columns shows the division of words into syllables, it was concluded that the Kenyon-Knott approach is the most desirable from the point of view of simplicity. After all, the mechanical division of syllables in the printed word is partly conventional, and does not always correspond to the actual division made in the spoken word. Not only is the boundary line between syllables frequently uncertain, but the division of words into syllables in actual speech may vary in the same word according to the degree of audibility of speech sounds, the fall or the rise of breath pressure, and other conditions of speech. It is generally agreed, for example, that in phonetics a word should be divided into syllables according to *sound;* and that it is usually better to end a syllable on a vowel whenever that is possible. Put another way, it means that in phonetic syllabication each syllable, wherever possible, begins with a consonant; and when a single consonant comes between two vowels, it is placed with the second. But in the interest of simplicity it was decided to follow the general rule of syllabicating words identically in all three columns. It was felt that such parallel syllabication would be best. Therefore, this manual shows *city* as SIT i (in the SIMPLIFIED column), as sĭt′ĭ (in the DIACRITICAL column), and as ['sɪt ɪ] in the PHONETIC column, instead of (respectively) SI ti, sĭ′ti, and ['sɪ tɪ].

---

[1] Introduction, p. xxi *f.* (pp. xv–xlix). Published by G. and C. Merriam Company: Springfield, Massachusetts (1944).

[2] For a fuller discussion, consult J. S. Kenyon, *American Pronunciation: A Textbook of Phonetics for Students of English*, pp. 230–235 (§ 377 *ff.*) (Ann Arbor, Michigan: George Wahr, 1943.)

It seems advisable to explain briefly that the [-r] as used in Kenyon-Knott and in this manual stands for a postvocalic sound which may always contain some schwa before it. The problem is essentially that of distinguishing between postvocalic [r] and prevocalic [r]. Postvocalic, as you know, means immediately following a vowel; prevocalic means occurring immediately before a vowel; and intervocalic means situated between vowels. Students are sometimes able to understand the distinctions by remembering three points:

 a) Postvocalic [r] is an *uh*r sound—[ər], [ɚ]
 b) Prevocalic [r] is a *r*uh sound—[rə]
 c) Intervocalic [r] tends to follow the prevocalic pattern.
  Examples:
   here—[hɪər], not [hɪr]
   rat—[ræt], not [ɚæt]
   carry—['kærɪ], not ['kæɚɪ]
   There is [*General American,* ðɛr] or [ðɛər ɪz]; (*Eastern American,* ðɛr ɪz
   (*liaison*) [1]

5. rh. rh is sounded r whenever rh appears in the same syllable, as *rhapsody,** *rheum,** *rhubarb,** *rhythm.** See § 27(2.1).

6. rr.

1) In *berry* (bĕr′ĭ), *lorry* (lŏr′ĭ), *narrow* (năr′ō), and like words, rr is pronounced as a single r. See §§ 21(1.6), 23(1.10), 25(1.4), 26(1.3), 30(2.2), 31(5.1), 32(3.1,2), 33(5.1), 35(5), 38(13.2,3,4), 39(9.1), 45(4.1,2).

2) In such combinations as *earreach* (ēr′rēch′; ēr′rēch′), *far-ranging* (fär′rän′jĭng), and *gear-rolling* (gēr′rōl′ĭng; gēr′rōl′ĭng), rr is pronounced double.

3) In such combinations as *irrational,** *irrelevant,** *irreligious,** in which the ir is followed by r in the next syllable, deliberate speakers often prolong the r, particularly in those words where the ir is negative in force. This prolongation gives the r the effect of a double r. But often speakers pronounce a single r. (See *irresolute.**) Consult § 49(10).

§ 38. S

The letter s has the following four sounds:

Voiceless

s as in *sing,* § 38(2)	sh as in *shame,* § 38(11)

Voiced

z as in *zero,* § 38(3)	zh as in *vision,* §§ 38(8,10), 45(2)

1. Principal Sounds of s. The letter s represents chiefly only two sounds, the sibilant, voiceless fricative s, as in *sing;* and its voiced cognate z, as in *zero.* In a few words (as the chart given immediately above indicates), the s may represent the voiceless palatalized sibilant sh, as in *nauseous,** *scansion,* *sugar,* and *sure.** In some words, the s may represent the voiced palatalized sibilant zh, as in *derision,** *leisure,** and *measure.**

2. s as in sing. (Simplified Symbol: s. Phonetic Symbol: s.)

1) Raise the tip of your tongue to the roof of the mouth just behind the upper front teeth (without permitting the tongue tip to rest against the teeth). Send a fine stream of air gently through the narrow groove formed between the tongue tip and the front of the hard palate, directing the stream of breath in a thin, straight line along the groove in the tongue so that it strikes the cutting edges of

---

[1] I am indebted directly to Dr. Bert Emsley for this simple explanation.

your front teeth (incisors). The resulting sound, sharp and hissing (but not whistling), should be the voiceless sibilant fricative, sometimes also made by keeping the tongue tip back of the lower teeth and arching the middle front of the tongue upward toward the gum ridge. The tongue tip should not be visible in the production of s (or of z).

2) Initial s spells voiceless s, as in *sad*,* *scalp*,* *season*,* *sign*,* *sing*,* *sloth*,* *snout*,* *soften*,* *sphere*.* Voiceless s is also heard in *hips, racks, yes*.* Other spellings occur in *lass*,* *whisker*,* *lace, cement, facile*,* *psalm*,* *psychology*,* *scenic*,* *quartz*,* *lax*. In such words as *aisle*,* *apropos*,* *chamois*,* *corps** (sing.), *debris*,* *island*,* *rendezvous*,* *viscount*,* the s is silent. See also *Arkansas*,* *Illinois*,* *Saint Louis*.*

3) There are many varieties of defective s [and also z, § 45(1.1,4)]. The breath stream sent over the sides of the tongue and over the bicuspids or over the canine teeth results in a "lateral" s, or lateral lisp. A "whistling" s may be caused by making the tongue tip too tense; and a "hissing" s by prolonging the sound or by not controlling the breath stream. Another common incorrect form of [s] is the substitution of voiceless th [θ] for s [s] by placing the tongue tip too close to the teeth.

4) Producing a satisfactory s depends upon several factors, including the following:

  a) Avoid building up and using too much breath pressure.

  b) Avoid prolonging the s. Stress the sound following it without "swallowing" the s.

  c) The edges of the upper and lower front teeth should be brought almost together, so that the edges of the upper and lower teeth just about meet. At all times the sides of the tongue should be pressed against the upper side teeth and gum ridge.

  d) Lower the tip of the tongue behind either the upper or lower front teeth, never allowing the tongue tip to fall so low that it covers the cutting edges of the upper and lower incisors.

  e) The tongue blade should be grooved down the center just beneath the gum ridge.

  f) Send the small stream of air straight out so that it strikes the sharp, cutting edges of the upper and lower incisors. Spread the lips sufficiently to keep the edges of the teeth free. It is the edges of the incisors that should intercept the breath stream as it is forced out gradually.

3. Voiced s = [z]. Voiced s [z] is heard in *easy, as*,* *bosom*,* *has*,* *observe, pigs*. Although s is a voiceless sound (see chart, § 19), it has followed the rule that voiceless sounds in unaccented positions often become voiced.

4. Sources of Voiced s = [z]. See also § 38(5).

1) In words often unstressed ("He's *as* good *as* I"; "Tell *his* mother about it") or lacking stress (John′ny's; gush′es; church′es), the s is voiced [= z]. Formerly *as*,* *his*,* and the like were pronounced with the voiceless s as in *sing*.*

2) Another chief source of voiced s [= z] is voice assimilation between voiced sounds, as in *easy*.

3) A third important source of voiced s [= z] is in such words as *lose* and *rise*,* where s appeared between two vowels (that is, final e was once sounded).

4) Occasionally the verb has z [z] and the noun or adjective has s [s]. See *abuse*,* *advice*,* *advise*,* *diffuse*,* *excuse*,* *grease*,* *house*,* *rise*,* *use*.*

5. Adding the Sound [s] or [z] to Stem. See also § 48(3).

1) When the stem of the noun or verb ends in any of the voiceless consonant sounds p, t, k, f, th [θ], add the sound s. Thus: *lips, cats, books, cliffs* (plural of

nouns); *Philip's, Herbert's, Isaac's, Joseph's, Ruth's* (possessive in –'s); *peeps, bets, looks, strafes, froths* (third singular present indicative). See § 19.

2) When the stem of the noun or verb ends in any of the voiced consonant sounds b, d, g, v, t͟h [ð], m, n, ng [ŋ], l, or in any vowel sound, add the sound z [z]. The rule applies to plural of nouns (*almonds, catalogues, stones, abdomens, rings*), to possessives in –'s (*Job's, Olive's, Rhoda's*), and to the third singular present indicative (*dims, sings, calls*).

3) Rule 1 has stated that after voiceless sounds except sibilants the ending –s or –es in the plural of nouns, or in the possessive with –'s, or in the third singular present indicative is pronounced s [s]. Rule 2 has stated that after voiced sounds except sibilants the ending –s or –es is pronounced z [z].

Finally, another rule is that after sibilants, whether voiced or voiceless, the ending –s or –es is pronounced ĕz, ĭz [§ 24(5.1)], as in *edges, leases, lurches, poses, Rose's, rushes, tosses.*

4) A summary-rule is that the final consonant (such as s) is probably voiceless if it is preceded by a voiceless sound in the same syllable; the final consonant is voiced if it is preceded by a voiced sound in the same syllable. See § 48(3).

6. dis–; –ese.

1) The prefix dis– is occasionally pronounced dĭz, but most often dĭs. See pages 92–95 for examples. Consult § 49(3).

2) In such words as *Chinese,* Javanese,* manganese,** and *Portuguese,** present usage shows a tendency for the z [z] sound.

7. Palatalized s as in censure. When s is palatalized by a following ĭ or y sound, regardless of the spelling of the sound, the s [s] is sounded as sh [ʃ] as in *censure* (sĕn′shĕr) and *scansion* (skăn′shŭn). See also *nausea,* nauseous,* nauseate.** See § 38(12).

8. Voiced s (= z) in vision. Voiced s [= z], when palatalized by a following ĭ or y sound, has the zh [ʒ] sound, as in *fusion* (fū′zhŭn), *leisure,* measure,* vision.** See § 38(12).

9. sc.

1) Generally sound sc before e, i, and y as voiceless s, as in *ascend,* discipline,* scenic,* science,* scythe,* viscid.* Exception: *sceptic* (skĕp′tĭk.) See § 22(1,2).

2) Although sc is usually pronounced as voiceless s wherever c would be sounded as voiceless s, sc is pronounced sk where c would be sounded k, as in *escape,* scalp,* scope,* scourge,* scratch,* sclerosis,* viscous.** Briefly, sc has the sound of sk before a, o, u, r, l.

3) In some words sc is palatalized to sh [ʃ], as in *conscience**; in a few words sc is sometimes voiced to z [z], as in *discern.** See § 38(12).

10. sch. sch in the same syllable may be pronounced in three different ways:

1) Like sk, as in *schedule,* school,* scheme* (skēm), *scholar* (skŏl′ĕr), *schooner* (skōōn′ĕr).

2) Like sh, as in *Schleswig-Holstein,* Schick test* (shĭk tĕst), *schilling* (shĭl′ĭng), *schist* (shĭst), *schnorrer* (shnōr′ĕr).

3) Like s, as in *scepter,* schism.**

11. sh. (Simplified Symbol: sh. Phonetic Symbol: ʃ.)

1) sh is a sound distinctly different from either s or h. In the same syllable, sh is one sound [ʃ], and not a blend of s and h. Although sh [ʃ] is most commonly spelled as in *cash, rush, ship,** the sound sh [ʃ] is also found in *anxious,* chandelier,* chauffeur,* Chicago,* conscience,* issue,* machine, mission, notion, ocean,* social,* spacious,* sugar, sure,* tension, tissue.**

2) Say s [s] as in *sing.** Now say sh [ʃ] as in *shame.* If made properly the

sh [ʃ] will be formed with the tongue point a bit retracted and lowered from its position for [s], and the middle of the tongue raised higher toward the hard palate. The groove in the tongue is wider; the tongue is relaxed; the lips are slightly protruded. The unvoiced sibilant fricative is sh [ʃ]. sh can also be produced by rapid s [s] + y [j]. For the voiced sibilant fricative s [s], see § 45(2).

3) In a name such as *Sheepshead Bay*, the second s and h are in separate syllables and therefore each is given its own sound, being pronounced shēps′hĕd′bā.

4) Improper division in a few names has led to a pronunciation now generally acceptable. Thus, in *Lewisham* (= Lewis + ham), the pronunciation lū′ĭsh ăm may be even more frequent than the historical pronunciation lū′ĭs ăm. See *Waltham*, § 39(7.3).

5) In a number of words the pronunciation is either sh [ʃ] or zh [ʒ], or varies between them. See *Asia*,* *luxurious*,* *sumach*.*

12. Other Aspects of s.

1) s + a consonant y sound + a lightly stressed or an unstressed vowel palatalize s to sh [ʃ]. In the vocabulary see *anxious*,* *issue*,* *luxury*,* *nauseous*.* See also §§ 38(7,8,11).

2) In familiar speech, when final s makes contact with initial y, palatalization of s [s] to sh [ʃ] may occur, as in *this yacht* (thĭsh yät′; thĭsh ät′).

3) In familiar speech, when final z [z] makes contact with initial y, the same palatalization may occur, as in *these years* (thēzh yẽrz′; thēzh ẽrz′).

4) In such words as *conscience** and *nauseous*,* the y sound described in number 1 (above) was once an unaccented ĭ or ĕ sound. Lack of stress converted this earlier unaccented sound to a y [j] sound. However, in a number of words such influences as the spelling, or of analogy, or of speech rhythm have sometimes brought back the ĭ or ĕ sound. As a result, variations in pronunciation occur in such words as *Asia*,* *Asiatic*,* *ambrosia*,* *annunciation*,* *associate*,* *appreciate*,* *appreciation*,* *association*,* *nausea*,* *nauseate*.*

5) See such sections as 23(1), 38(12), and 40(11) for palatalization of d to j, and of t to ch, in the same word (*question*,* *soldier**).

13. ss.

1) ss may be pronounced in the following ways:

> z, as in *dissolve**
> zh, as in *abscission* (ăb sĭzh′ŭn)
> s, as in *glossary*.*

2) ss may be pronounced as single s, as in *access*,* *message*,* *Missouri*,* except in combinations, as in *misshape* (mĭs shāp′) and *misspell* (mĭs spĕl′). See §§ 21(1.6), 23(1.10), 25(1.4), 26(1.3), 30(2.2), 31(5.1), 32(3.1,2), 33(5.1), 35(5), 37(6), 39(9.1), 45(4.1,2).

3) In some words two s sounds are shortened to one, as in *dissect** and *dissonance*.*

4) Two s sounds may in certain words be shortened to one or pronounced separately, as in *dissimilitude* (dĭs′ĭ mĭl′ĭ tūd; dĭs′sĭ mĭl′ĭ tūd), *dissyllabic* (dĭs′ĭ lăb′ĭk; dĭs′sĭ lăb′ĭk). But see § 49(3).

§ 39. T

1. Sounded t.

1) The sound t occurs in *tiny*,* *trip*, *twin*, *stop*, *stroll*, *note*, *bet*, *vote*, *cant*, *latter*, *fast*,* *chart*, *next*. It appears also in *Thomas*, *chalked*, *debt*,* *indict*,* *receipt*,* *yacht*.*

2) Like [d], the sound [t] is a postdental, or lingua-alveolar, plosive. After touching the tip of the tongue to the roof of the mouth just behind the upper

teeth, blow the tongue down quickly with the breath. Both [d] and [t] are made exactly alike: for each, point the tip of the tongue against the upper gum ridge (or on the middle of the upper gum) and then release the tongue tip suddenly. The resulting sound will be either t (breathed) or d (voiced).

3) Common is the fault of making the [t] or [d] on the teeth, or "swallowing" or eliding the [t] or [d] when found in the medial position. Habituate the use of the tongue tip firmly but lightly, keeping the tongue tip in tight contact with the gum ridge just above the upper teeth. In poor speech the [t] may be elided, or the glottal stop may be substituted for it; thus, *little** [lɪl] or [lɪʔl].

4) When followed by a vowel or diphthong, or when followed by a pause, t, like p or k [§§ 30(1.4), 35(1.2)], is puffed out strongly. This puff of breath, or aspiration, is strongest when t is followed by an accented vowel or by w; it is not so strong when the t follows s or is in an unstressed position. Before a consonant in the same breath group, t is unaspirated.

5) Germans, Spaniards, Frenchmen, and Italians often omit the aspiration, thereby confusing [t] with [d]. Make sure that the tongue is not placed against the teeth, but approximately one-fifth or one-fourth inch back of the teeth. In other words, t is not dental in English.

6) For palatalization of t to ch [tʃ] in *question,** or of d to j [dʒ] in *soldier,** see §§ 23(1.9), 38(12), 40(11.8,9,10).

2. Silent t.

1) t may be silent, as it is in *chasten,** *glisten,** *mortgage,** *often,** *waistcoat,** *wristband.** See also § 1.

2) t is usually silent in combinations, as in "nex*t* day." The tendency for t to be silent is especially strong when it appears between two consonants, as in "mus*t* go," "pas*t* perfect." Before another t, the sound is held, as in "las*t* time."

3. Excrescent t.

1) In such words as *against** and *amidst,** the t, though excrescent, is pronounced. An excrescent t, however, is unacceptable today in the pronunciation of *across** (mispronounced *á krŏst*), *once** (corrupted into wŭnst), *twice* (its dialectal variant being twīst), and *orphan* (its erroneous or dialectal variant being *orphant*).

2) Frequently, excrescent t is pronounced (between n and s, n and sh [ʃ], n and th [θ]) in words in which it is not part of the spelling, as in *answer,** *chance,** *ensconce,** *ninth, once,** *patience,** *rinse,** *since,** *wince*.

3) For tch, see ch [§ 22(5.1)].

4. th as in tooth; t̶h̶ as in then. (Simplified Symbols: th as in *tooth*; t̶h̶ as in *then*. Phonetic Symbols: θ as in *tooth;* ð as in *then*.)

1) Voiceless th [θ] is the first sound in *theater** and *thin*, and the last sound in *tooth, hath,* and *myth;* voiced t̶h̶ [ð] is the first sound in *then* and the last sound in *smooth.**
Press the tip of the tongue or the front of the tongue lightly against the lower edge of your upper front teeth. Blow out, and the sound is that of th [θ] in *thin*. Now, instead of allowing a stream of breath to flow through the highly constricted space between the teeth and the tongue, thereby resulting in the voiceless, fricative tongue-teeth sound th [θ], allow a stream of voiced air to flow through, and the resulting sound is the voiced fricative t̶h̶ [ð] as in *then* and *this*. It is the outrush of air through the narrow slit between the tongue tip and the upper teeth that causes the th [θ] or t̶h̶ [ð]. The tongue tip is usually not protruded; it is barely visible between the teeth.

2) Final th is usually voiceless, as in *cloth, health, mouth** (noun), *north, south, tenth, youth.** Among the exceptions are *bequeath,** *mouth** (verb), and *smooth,** each of which has lost a final –e.

3) When –th is final and voiced [ð], it is generally spelled –the, as in *lathe*,*
rathe (obsolete, dialectal, archaic, or poetic). See also § 39(6).

4) Although not without exceptions, a general rule is that such important
words as nouns, adjectives, and adverbs are likely to begin with the voiceless
th [θ], whereas such unimportant words as pronouns and connectives are likely
to begin with th [ð], the voiced cognate of th [θ]. In all the pronominals (pronouns, pronominal adjectives, pronominal adverbs) is again seen the tendency
of voiceless consonants to become voiced either by loss of stress [see § 38(3)] or
by lack of stress; and lack of stress in the sentence has vocalized th [θ] to th [ð]
in such pronominal words as *than*,* *that*,* *the*,* *their*, *them*,* *then*, *there*,* *they*,
this,* *thither*,* *though*,* *thus*.*

5. Pluralizing th, th. Three general rules may be helpful for pronouncing th
when it is pluralized.

1) In singular nouns such as *bath*,* *mouth*,* *oath*,* *sheath*,* and *wreath*,* the
final th is pronounced th [θ] as in *tooth*. But in the plural such nouns are pronounced thz [ðz]. See the starred words.

2) In other nouns, the plural may be pronounced either thz [ðz] or ths [θs],
as in *truths** and *youths*.*

3) Where the singular has th [ð], the plural ends in thz [ðz].

4) See also *clothes*,* *cloths*,* *fifths*,* *forthwith*,* *therewith*,* *thither*,* *wherewith*,*
with,* *withdraw*,* *withstand*,* *wraith*.*

6. Distinguishing Parts of Speech. Voiced th [ð] often distinguishes between
nouns or adjectives and verbs, as in *bath*,* *bathe**; *breath*, *breathe*; *cloth*,* *clothe**;
loath,* *loathe**; *sheath*,* *sheathe**; *sooth*,* *soothe**; *teeth*, *teethe*. In such words the
final –e was formerly pronounced. Voiced th [ð] is also used in the verbs *be-
queath*,* *mouth*,* and *smooth*,* although the final –e has disappeared. See also
§ 39(4.2,3). Briefly, the spelling –th at the end of a word often indicates the
voiceless consonant th [θ], whereas the spelling –the indicates the voiced consonant th [ð].

⌐. Other Aspects of t.

1) Just as th is pronounced t in *Esther** and *Thomas*, so it is pronounced t in
such words Greek in origin as *Anthony*,* *phthisic* (tĭz′ĭk), and *thyme*.* This th
spelling of the t sound is derived from Latin, in which th was sounded t.

2) th, once pronounced t in such words as *authority*,* *theater*,* *Arthur*, *Eliza-
beth*, and *Nathan*, is through the influence of spelling-pronunciation now sounded
th. See § 1.

3) Sound separately t and h when each is in a different syllable, as in *nuthook*
(nŭt′hŏŏk′) and *Chatham* (Chăt′ăm; *U. S. also*, Chăt′hăm′). But in certain place
names the traditional pronunciation has given way to the spelling-pronunciation
(§ 1). For example, the name *Waltham* is made up of *Walt* + *ham*; and in England the t and the h each once had its own sound, being pronounced wôlt′ăm.
[Remember that in England the sound of h is usually that of an aspiration or
breathing. Also, recall the general rule that h is usually dropped at the beginning
of an unaccented syllable: see § 27(1.6).]
A considerable time ago the h sound was lost, and the letters th were mis-
takenly taken to represent th as in *tooth*. As a result, the British are now pronouncing the t and h not only as a single t sound, but also as a single th sound
(wôl′tăm; wôl′thăm). In America, of course, the original individuality of t and
h has been merged into the one sound th, and *Waltham* is pronounced wôl′thăm.
Gotham, however, remains gŏt′ăm in England, although it is gŏth′ăm or gō′thăm
in the United States. See § 38(11.4).

4) In words from the Sanskrit and derived East Indian languages th may be
sounded in English as t, as in *Bathala* (bä tä′lä). But in those languages them-

selves th is properly sounded as t + h, as in the English word *pothole* (pŏt′hōl′).
See §§ 21(3), 22(11.1), 23(3), 29(3), 30(2.1), 35(4.5).

5) For yᵉ and yᵗ, in which the y spells th, see § 44(4.5).

8. ti; tt.

1) ti has the sound of sh in such words as *cautious, mention, national,* * *quotient,* * *partiality.* *

2) After s, t retains its own sound and alsc combines with the following ĭ into a ch sound, as in *bestial* * and *question.* *

9. tt; ture; tz.

1) Pronounce tt as a single t sound, as in *battery* * (bǎt′ĕr ĭ), *putt* (pŭt), *rotten* (rŏt′ 'n). In combinations, tt is given a double sound, as in *outtaste* (out tāst′), *out-Tory* (out Tō′rĭ). See §§ 21(1.6), 23(1.10), 25(1.4), 26(1.3), 30(2.2), 31(5.1), 32(3.1,2), 33(5.1), 35(5), 37(6), 38(13.2,3,4), 45(4.1,2).

2) In dissyllables (words of two syllables) the unaccented ending –ture is most usually sounded –chuhr [-tʃɚ], although other pronunciations are indicated in the vocabulary. [-tʃɚ] is doubtlessly the most natural in *adventure,* * *agriculture,* * *capture,* * *discomfiture,* * *feature,* * *futurism,* * *mixture,* * *nature,* * *signature,* * *texture,* * *vulture,* * and numerous other words in the vocabulary.

If the syllable preceding –ture (in a word of more than two syllables) is accented, then the pronunciation in the less common words tends to be sounded with a light accent –chŏŏr [ˌtʃʊr], but also –chuhr [-tʃɚ]. Although for such words as *amateur* * (note the ending), *ligature,* * and *literature,* * the pronunciation –chŏŏr [ˌtʃʊr] appears to be frequent, yet that is probably not true of such words as *armature,* * *expenditure,* * and *overture,* * in each of which –chuhr [-tʃɚ] appears preponderant.

For more details, see § 23(1.9), 40(11.9), 50(31,33).

3) In *quartz* * (kwôrts), *waltz* * (wôltz; *B.,* wôls), and similar words from the German, -tz is pronounced ts. –tz– may appear elsewhere than at the end, as in *howitzer* (hou′ĭt sĕr).

§ 40. U

The letter u spells eight accented and two unaccented sounds [for silent u, see § 40(13); for consonant u, see § 40(14)]:

Accented

ū as in ūse, fūse, §§ 40(2), 40(4.5)   ŭ as in ŭp, ŭn′der, § 40(6)
u in chew, June; rule, true,   û as in fûr′ther, hûrt, §§ 40(7), 24(6)
    § 40(4.6,8)   ü as in (French) menü, (German)
ū as in cūre, fū′ry, § 40(4.9)   Müller, § 40(9)
u as in full, put = ŏŏ, §§ 40(5),   u = ĕ as in bur′i al; u = ĭ as in build,
    34(22)   § 40(10)

Unaccented

û as in û nite′, § 40(11)   ŭ as in cir′cŭs, § 40(12)

1. Principal Sounds of u. The letter u is variously pronounced, as the chart immediately preceding this section indicates. However, the four principal sounds of u are two "long" u sounds and two "short" u sounds.

Section 40(2–10) will discuss all the sounds that the letter u represents.

2. ū as in ūse. (Simplified Symbol: yoo. Phonetic Symbol: ju.)

1) "Long" u as in *use,* * *fuse, presumable,* * *lunatic,* * *cube, duty,* * and otherwise

spelled as in *beauty,* Hugh, few,* suit,* view,* yew,** and *you,* is made up of the consonant y [j] as in *yes* and the vowel o͞o [u] as in *too*.

To form the sound ū as in *use* and *fuse,* raise the middle of the tongue until it touches the hard palate lightly (thereby producing the first element y [j]), and then move the tongue to the position for o͞o as in *too* [§ 34(21.1)]. Or, produce the sound of the consonant [j] by raising the front of the tongue until it almost touches the hard palate. Once the voiced sound is made, the tongue glides to the position for o͞o [u].

Frequently, instead of [ju] the diphthong [ɪu] or [ɪʉ] is used. When so used, [ɪ] is usually made with tongue drawn back a bit followed by [ʉ] with tongue pushed forward. See item 2 below.

2) In the words listed above [§ 40(2.1)], the spellings u, eau, ugh, ew, ie, and the like are pronounced not only as though an invisible y [j] preceded each, but also as though an invisible ɪ [ɪ] often preceded each. Thus *fuse** [fjuz, fɪuz], *presume* [prɪ 'zum, prɪ 'zɪum, prɪ 'zjum], *lunatic** ['lu nə tɪk, 'lɪu nə tɪk], *cube* [kjub, kɪub], *duty* ['dju tɪ, 'dɪu tɪ, 'du tɪ], *beauty* ['bju tɪ, 'bɪu tɪ], *Hugh* [hju, hɪu], *few* [fju, fɪu], *suit** [sjut, sɪut, sut], *view* [vju, vɪu], *yew** [ju, jɪu], *you* [*stressed* ju; *unstressed* jʊ, jə]. The DIACRITICAL column marks such words as ū; the SIMPLIFIED column usually marks such words as yo͞o and also often as o͞o; the PHONETIC column marks such words as [ju] or [u]. The diphthong ɪ̆o͞o [ɪu] is also used, especially in General American; but this manual does not indicate the variation, although its prevalence among the best speakers testifies that ɪ̆o͞o [ɪu] in many words is cultivated American English. For our purposes yo͞o [ju] and o͞o [u] are sufficient; but it should be remembered that the variant ɪ̆o͞o [ɪu *or* ɪʉ] is often acceptable. See §§ 40(3,4), 48(2).

3) "Long" u or ū appears in syllables having either a primary or strong accent (dū'ty,* dū'te ous*) or a secondary or weaker accent, regardless of whether or not a subordinate stress is indicated by a secondary accent mark (res'i due,* cur'few, per'fume*).

4) In unstressed syllables the symbol u̇ is used to show a modification of ū. See § 40(11).

3. ɪ̆ + o͞o; y + o͞o. Although the sound of u is less frequently equal to the diphthong composed of ɪ̆ + o͞o [ɪu *or* ɪʉ] than it is to y + o͞o [ju], we know that a speaker may use [ju] at one time and [ɪu] at another time, and often for the same words. In producing ɪ̆ + o͞o [ɪu *or* ɪʉ], each element may have equal stress, or one more than the other; but when the first element ɪ̆ [ɪ] receives less stress, it approaches the consonantal y [j], and accordingly the [ɪu *or* ɪʉ] may more readily change into [ju]. In most "long" u words the ɪ̆ [ɪ] has shaded off into consonant y [j]; and that is another reason that this manual uses [ju] rather than [ɪu *or* ɪʉ]. Of course both could be utilized; but for our purposes the distinction may not be necessary. Remember that the difference between [ju] and [ɪu] is not phonemic. See also §§ 40(2,4), 48(2).

4. Sounding the "Long" u. The phonetic nature of the sound preceding the accented u affects the "long" u sound, as the phonetic nature of the preceding sound affects the unaccented u̇ [§ 40(11)].

1) Sound y in initial ū (accented) or initial u̇ (unaccented), as in (accented) *use,* usage,* unify, ewer,* Euclid* or as in (unaccented) *euphonious,* university,* uranium,* urea** [see § 40(11)].

2) "Long" u is never sounded o͞o [u] but always either or both ɪ̆o͞o [ɪu *or* ɪʉ] or yo͞o [ju] after the sounds b [b] as in *beautiful** ['bju–, 'bɪu–], c [= k] as in *cue* [kju, kɪu], f [f] as in *feud** [fjud, fɪud], and *futile** ['fju–, 'fɪu–], g [g] as in *gew-gawry* ['gju–, 'gɪu–], h [h] as in *huge** [hjudʒ, hɪudʒ; *also* jʊdʒ], k [k] as in *kewpie* ['kju–, 'kɪu–], m [m] as in *music* ['mju–, 'mɪu–], p [p] as in *pugilist* ['pju–, 'pɪu–], v [v] as in *view** [vju, vɪu]. See § 50(32).

Likewise, after b, c = k, f, g, h, k, m, p, v, preceding unaccented û, the varieties [ɪu] and [ju] are regular [§ 40(11)].

3) After tongue-point fricatives s [s], th [θ], and z [z], the "long" u is pronounced not only either ĭoo [ɪu *or* ɪʉ] or yoo [ju], as explained immediately above [§ 40(3,4)], but also often oo [u]. Remember, then, that the first element, either ĭ [ɪ] or y [j], is omitted or suppressed. Such pronunciations are acceptable: accordingly, *consume** [kən ˈsjum, –ˈsɪum, –ˈsum], *presume* [prɪ ˈzjum, –ˈzɪum, –ˈzum], *enthusiasm** [–ˈθju–, –ˈθɪu–, –ˈθu–].

In unaccented û the first element of the û is also often omitted. See § 40(11.4).

4) After nasal n [n] and tongue-point stops d [d] and t [t], the "long" u is perhaps more frequently sounded either ĭoo [ɪu *or* ɪʉ] or yoo [ju] than oo [u]. There are speech experts who disapprove the omission of the initial element, and urge that no substitution of oo [u] be made for ĭoo [ɪu *or* ɪʉ] or for yoo [ju]. But all three pronunciations are heard; for example, *new-fashioned* [ˈnju ˈfæʃ ənd, ˈnɪu–, ˈnu–], *duteous** [ˈdju tɪ əs, ˈdɪu–, ˈdu–], *tunic** [ˈtju nɪk, ˈtɪu–, ˈtu–]. See §§ 24(22.3), 40(4.10), 49(32.b).

5) After l the sound of ū may be either ĭoo [ɪu *or* ɪʉ], yoo [ju], or oo [u]. In America the tendency is perhaps toward oo [u]. Examples: *lunacy** [ˈlu nə sɪ, ˈlɪu–; *also* ˈlju–], *lure** [lʊr, lɪʊr; *also* ljʊr], *lute** [lut, lɪut; *also* ljut]. Since this manual omits the sound [ɪu *or* ɪʉ], that pronunciation is to be assumed by the user of this manual.

But the oo [u] is the commonly used sound when another consonant precedes the l in the same syllable, as in *blue** [blu; *also* blɪu], *blueprint* [ˈblu prɪnt; ˈblɪu–], *clue** [klu; *also* klɪu], *plume** [plum; *also* plɪum], and *preclude** [prɪ ˈklud; *also* prɪ ˈklɪud]. However, if the consonant is in the preceding syllable (that is, if the consonant precedes the l in a different syllable), then the ū may be sounded either [ɪu *or* ɪʉ], or [ju], or [u].

6) y [j], the first element of ū, is generally omitted after ch [tʃ] and j [dʒ], except after the palatalization of ch = tsh [tʃ] and j = dzh [dʒ], in which instances there may be an ĭ glide to the following vowel. Thus *chew** [tʃu; *also* tʃɪu], *juice** [dʒus; *also* dʒɪus], *junior** [ˈdʒun jɚ; *also*, ˈdʒɪun jɚ].

Likewise in unaccented û, similar variations occur: see § 40(11). Although this manual does not show the ĭ glide, it is to be understood as being possible in pertinent words.

7) When s or z is palatalized to sh [ʃ] or zh [ʒ], the y element usually disappears. See § 38(12). But yoo [ju] or ĭoo [ɪu *or* ɪʉ] is also heard. Examples: *cashew* [ˈkə ʃu, ˈkə ʃɪu; *also* ˈkæʃ u], *issue** [ˈɪʃ u, ˈɪʃ ju], *usurious** [ju ˈʒʊr ɪ əs; *but also* [ju ˈʒɪu rɪ əs, ju ˈʒju rɪ əs].

8) We have seen that ū is not used after l combined with another consonant in the same syllable, nor is ū used after sh [ʃ], zh [ʒ], ch = tsh [tʃ], or j = dzh [dʒ]. The y element is also silent after r, as in *rude* [rud; *also* rɪud], *fruit* [frut; *also* frɪut], *grew* [gru; *also* grɪu], *true** [tru; *also* trɪu].

In some words after r, ch, j, l (after a consonant in the same syllable), and also after sh and zh, we often show a distinction in meaning by sounding ū as ĭoo [ɪu *or* ɪʉ]. Dictionaries, for example, show the pronunciation of *rude* (rōōd) and *rood* (rōōd) as being identical in sound; but in the speech of many there is a distinction, one being pronounced as ŏŏ [u] and the other as ĭoo [ɪu *or* ɪʉ]: thus *rude* [rud, rɪud] and *rood* [rud], *chews* [tʃuz, tʃɪuz] and *choose* [tʃuz]. See also § 40(11).

9) When ū ([ju], [ɪu *or* ɪʉ], or [u]) is followed by r, the oo element of the ū sound is usually lowered to ŏŏ [ʊ]. Such is similarly true both of the oo sound [§ 34(21)] and the unaccented û [§ 40(11)]. In brief, when ū is followed by r, its sound is less like oo and more like ŏŏ. ûr is pronounced like ûr, the first occurring in accented or partly-accented syllables, and the second occurring only in unaccented syllables. See §§ 24(22.2), 40(11).

Examples: *bureau,* * *cure,* * *curious,* * *demure,* * *during,* * *endure,* * *European,* * *fury,* * *jury,* * *mature,* * *urea.* *

10) r + "long" u is always sounded as rōō (*rule, rumor*). j + "long" u is sounded as jōō (*Judy, June, junior*). A growing tendency in American speech is toward ōō when d or n or s or t is followed by "long" u (*duty,* * *nutriment,* * *suit,* * *tune* *), although precise speakers still use the "long" u (ū). Also, d or s or t followed by "long" u is pronounced ōō perhaps even more often than ū, as in *due,* * *sue, Tuesday.* * Finally, "long" u + r + e in the same syllable (*cure,* * *pure*) is pronounced ūr or yōōr (but see 9 above), as are the derivatives in which another vowel may replace the final e (*curative, purify*).

5. u in full = ŏŏ as in foot. u has the sound of ōō in such words as *full* * and *push*. This sound of u = ŏŏ as in *foot* * and *good* [§ 34(22)] is otherwise spelled in *wolf, wood,* * *woman,* * and so on. See also § 34(9).

6. ŭ as in ŭp, ŭn′der. (Simplified Symbol: *uh* or UH. Phonetic Symbol: ʌ.)

1) ŭ as in *up, un′der, rub, gush′er, blun′der, un com′mon* is a low mid-vowel having almost the same sound as *ȧ* [ə] as in *China*, except that ŭ is used generally in a stressed syllable while *ȧ*, the neutral vowel, is used only in unstressed syllables. (See item 2.) This "short" u sound is found also in *blood, come,* * *does, dove, frontier,* * *hiccough, troublous,* * *twopence* (tŭp′ĕns; as two words in England, tōō pĕns or tōō pĕns), *won*.

ŭ is formed by dropping the middle of the tongue and lowering the jaw moderately from the position for *ȧ* as in *China*. See § 20(11). When the sound ŭ is made, the lips are relaxed and unrounded. (Phoneticians are not agreed as to the exact position of this sound, whose formation differs a bit in various parts of the country.)

2) As said before, the ŭ sound occurs only when accented, though the accent may be light, as in *uncommon* (ŭn kŏm′ŭn), *unconscious,* * *uproot* * (ŭp rōōt′). When ŭ is not even slightly stressed, it becomes *ȧ* [ə], as in *unless* (ŭn lĕs′; ŭn lĕs′) and *submerse* (sŭb mûrs′). See item 1 above; also § 40(12).

3) Substituting ä [ɑ] for ŭ [ʌ] in the first syllable of such words as *comfort,* * *coming*, and *company* * is a foreignism. Make sure that you pronounce the letter o as ŭ [ʌ]. See § 1.

7. û as in hûrt, fûr′ther. (Simplified Symbol: *uhr* or UHR. Phonetic Symbol: ɝ.)

1) û as in *hurt, further, churl,* * *churn, hurdle* is a sound otherwise spelled as in *err,* * *fir, learn,* * *term, earth, colonel,* * *journey, worse, refer,* * *myrrh, concert.* * The sound ûr occurs only in stressed or semistressed syllables.

2) In General American speech the r is pronounced; in Eastern and Southern American speech, it is not. Accordingly, the sound is made in two ways; but in each the jaw is lowered midway, the lips are unrounded, and the tongue is arched in the middle. See § 24(6).

a) In General American speech the sound [ɝ] is made by moderately retracting the tongue and elevating its middle portion upward toward the hard palate. When the tip of the tongue is raised toward the roof of the mouth and curled backward and upward, we speak of the r as a "retroflex" r, or of the sound produced as a "retroflex" variety of [ɝ]. See § 37(2).

b) In Eastern and Southern American speech the sound [ɜ] is formed by raising the middle of the tongue to a half-high position, touching the tongue tip lightly to the back of the lower front teeth, and making the sound û [ɜ] as in *hurt* and *further*. The lips are spread slightly; they are not rounded. The difference between the General American sound [ɝ] and the Eastern and Southern American sound [ɜ] is that in producing the latter [ɜ] the tip of the tongue is not drawn so far back as for [ɝ] and the arching or bunching is not so high. Put affirmatively, the front of the tongue is held lower and farther forward in producing the Eastern and Southern American sound [ɜ].

3) The degree of retroflexion, or raising the tongue and curling it backward and upward toward the palate, must not be excessive. When it is, the sound issuing is called an inversion [§ 37(2)] and is considered either less pleasant or less desirable than the one made by raising the middle of the tongue to a half-high position. Also, a mispronunciation characteristic of New York City is a dialect form that diphthongizes the sound, making the vowel [ɜ] into the nonstandard diphthong [ɜɪ].

4) In General American, Eastern American, and Southern American the "linking" r [§ 37(2.5)] is as a rule pronounced when a final r in one word is followed by a vowel in the same word group or phrase, as in "It did occur *in* that room."

5) Whenever u appears in a syllable having a slight stress, rapidity of discourse or informal usage may so reduce this light accent that the û may also be pronounced ē [ə].

6) When û, as in *hurt* and *further*, or the same sound as otherwise spelled [§ 40(7.1)] is followed by an r sound, the sound of the vowel before r is usually pronounced û [ɝ] in General American; but not only [ɜ] in Eastern and Southern American, but also [ʌ]. See *courage,* *hurricane.*

7) The û sound remains also in words such as *squirrel* and *stirrup.*

8. û as in jeu, jeune, schön. The sound in French words having either the rounded mid-front vowel [ø] or the rounded low-front vowel [œ] or the sound in German words having either the mid-front-round [ø] or the low-front-round [œ] may be indicated by the symbol û. See also SPECIAL NOTES, VII, "Foreign Sounds," page xxii *f.*

9. ü as in menü, Müller. The sound in French words having the rounded high-front vowel [y] as in *menu* or in German words having a similar vowel as in *Müller* is indicated by the symbol ü. See also SPECIAL NOTES, VII, "Foreign Sounds," page xxii *f.*

10. u as in burial = ĕ; u as in busy = ĭ. Unusual is the u as a spelling for the sound of ĕ as in *get* and of ĭ in *bit:* for example, *burial* (bĕr′ĭ ăl), *burier* (bĕr′ĭ ēr), *bury* (bĕr′ĭ); *busily* (bĭz′ĭ lĭ), *business,* *busy* (bĭz′ĭ). [For the sound of ĭ as in *build,* see § 40(15.1)].

11. û as in û nite′. (Simplified Symbol: yo͞o. Phonetic Symbol: jʊ.)

1) û as in *unite, tremulous, tumultuous,* *supreme, unanimous,* occurs only in unstressed syllables. Such varying factors as sense stress or sentence rhythm determine whether in unaccented syllables the sound û is pronounced either as o͝o [ʊ] or as a shorter form of o͞o [u], but as a rule the diacritical symbol û indicates a sound more like o͝o [ʊ] than o͞o [u].

2) Unaccented û is very much like that of accented ū with respect to the use of the first element ĭ [ɪ] or y [j], which depends upon the preceding consonant. Like initial ū, initial û is always pronounced with y [j], as in *uranium, usurp,* *utensil,* *euphonious,* *eugenics, eupeptic, urea* (û rē′à; ū′rē à).

3) y is occasionally suppressed or even lost after the tongue-point fricative s. Moreover, in colloquial speech, the vowel may be reduced to ŭ [ə]. See *superior.*

4) Just as ū = yo͞o is not used after ch = tsh [tʃ], j = dzh [dʒ], sh [ʃ], zh [ʒ] [see § 40(4.16)], so the y in û = yo͝o may frequently be lost after ch = tsh [tʃ], j = dzh [dʒ], sh [ʃ], and zh [ʒ]. See *asexual,* *judicatory,* *virtuous,* *visual.*

5) After r in the same syllable, the y is completely silent; thus in *prudence* (pro͞o′dĕns) and *prude,* the y is lost. See §§ 40(4.8), 50(32.b).

6) When a consonant is followed by l, the y is consistently lost [§ 40(4.5)]. However, in such words as *evaluate* (ĕ văl′û āt) and *salutary,** observe that the û appears in an unaccented syllable, but that the l preceding û belongs to the syllable preceding û. As a result, the û, being phonetically initial, is pronounced y [j]. See § 50(32.b).

7) The û after r in a preceding syllable may also take a y sound, as in *erudition,** garrulous,** querulous,** virulent.**

8) In words like *censure* (sĕn′shēr) and *treasure,** the s sound and the z sound before u are palatalized respectively to sh [ʃ] and zh [ʒ]. See § 38(12). Just as the sound û when entirely unaccented may be reduced to the sound ē [ə: § 24(7)], so in familiar speech the u may change to ē before r. See *measure,** treasury,** sensuous,** usually,** visual.**

However, the s sound is palatalized neither when it is initial, as in *supremacy*, (sû prēm′a̤ sĭ; sŏŏ prēm′a̤ sĭ, sŭ prēm′a̤ sĭ), nor sometimes when it is medial, as in *insular** and *peninsular.** Sometimes the first element of u may be not only weakened but even lost: see *succumb.**

9) The tie bar ‿ under tû in such a word as *nature* or under the dû in such a word as *verdure** indicates palatalization. This means that the off-glide of the t in *nature* has blended with the first element of û to produce a sound ranging from ty [tj] to a wholly palatalized ch [tʃ]. In similar fashion the off-glide of the d in *verdure* has combined with the first element of û to form a sound varying from dy [dj] to a wholly palatalized j [dʒ]. In the ordinary words having tû or dû, the natural pronunciation is the completely palatalized ch [tʃ], or j [dʒ]. See also SPECIAL NOTES, III, "Variant Pronunciations," b.4 (page xxi); §§ 23(1.9), 50(31,33).

10) When ū is slightly accented, the same palatalization (see number 9 above) also occurs; when wholly accented, such palatalization takes place as a rule only in substandard or occasionally in colloquial speech. Of course this palatalization does occur in everyday talk in such expressions as "I greet you" [aɪ ′grit ʃu]. "We lead you" [wi ′lid ʒu].

12. ŭ as in cir′cŭs. (Simplified Symbol: uh. Phonetic Symbol: ə.)

1) Like the italicized symbols ă, a̤, ĕ, ĭ, and ŏ that are used to represent more or less the obscured vowel sound [ə], the italicized ŭ indicates the neutral vowel [ə] in the unaccented syllables of such words as *circus** (sûr′kŭs), *circumspect,** stratum,** succumb.** See §§ 20(10), 20(11), 24(4), 28(5.5), 34(12.2,3), 34(13.1,2,3).

2) The ŭ [ə] is also used to show the obscuration of sound in such words as *bottom* (bŏt′ŭm), *circuitous,** circulation* (sûr′kŭ lā′shŭn), *dungeon,** gammon* (găm′ŭn), *gladsome* (glăd′sŭm), *porpoise,** righteous** [also note the completely palatalized ch: § 40(11.9)], *tortoise,** truncheon.** See § 8.

13. gu–; qu–; –ful.

1) After g the u may be silent, as in *guard,** guess,** guide,** catalogue, plague,** tongue, vogue*. See §§ 26(5.1), 26(6).

2) u preceded by g in the same syllable before a, e, or i (that is, gu + a, e, or i in the same syllable) indicates "hard" g. See § 26(5).

3) u regularly follows q, the qu most often being sounded as kw. See § 36.

4) In the unstressed ending –ful used to form adjectives such as *cheerful* and *graceful*, and also in the half-stressed ending –ful of compound nouns such as *spoonful* and *glassful*, the –ful is pronounced fŏŏl. However, when the –ful is used as an adjective suffix, it may also be pronounced f′l.

In fact, when –ful is used to form adjectives, the ending is less frequently sounded fŏŏl [fʊl] than it is pronounced fŭl [fəl] or the l is made syllabic, being sounded f′l [fļ]. Only in deliberate speech is the pronunciation fŏŏl [fʊl] heard. More frequently the u is obscured to the neutral vowel ŭ [ə]; or, in familiar speech, the u is silent, the l always being syllabic [fļ]. See §§ 31(4), 50(11).

On the other hand, the noun suffix –ful has a more or less subordinate accent and is pronounced fŏŏl (spŏŏn′fŏŏl; glås′fŏŏl). Its u is not silent even in familiar speech, whereas the u in the common adjective ending –ful is consistently silent. See § 50(11).

5) For other sounds that may disappear entirely, see §§ 20(10.3), 24(14), 28(5.5,6), 34(14.1,2).

14. u as a Consonant = w. After g (*languid**) and after q = k (see pages 247–249), the letter u may spell w. Sometimes, too, the letter u may be equivalent to w even when not following g or q (= k), as in *cuirassier*,* *persuasive*,* *suavity*,* *suite*.* See §§ 24(15), 28(9), 44(4).

15. ui; uy.

1) When ui is a digraph, it may spell the sound of ĭ as in *build* (bĭld), *guild*,* *guinea*,* or the sound of ōō as in *juice*,* or the sound of ū as in *nuisance*,* *pursuit* (pĕr sūt′), and *suit*.* But ui is not always a digraph [see §§ 26(5.1), 36].

2) Although the French ui may be pronounced as a consonantal ü (see SPECIAL NOTES, VII, "Foreign Sounds," page xxii) + ē, it is usually pronounced in English like the pronoun *we* (wē). Examples: *cuisine* (kwĕ zēn′), *Ouija* (wē′jȧ), *suite*,* *tuille* (twēl).

3) In *buy* the uy is sounded ī as in *ice*.

4) In *guy* and *plaguy* the u indicates the "hard" g. In such words uy is no more a digraph than ui is in *genuine*,* *quiet*,* and *quite*.

5) ui and uy in *colloquial*,* *soliloquy*, and the like, have the sound of wĭ (kŏ lō′kwĭ ăl; sŏ lĭl′ŏ kwĭ).

§ 41. V

English v; Spanish v.

1) v as in *veil, Vivian, even*,* *give, verve*, or as otherwise spelled f as in *of* (ŏv; ov) or ph as in *nephew** and *Stephen* (stē′vĕn), is the voiced cognate or correlative of f [§ 25(1.1)].

2) To produce the sound of f, we bite the lower lip lightly with our upper teeth and blow out through the small space or crevices between the teeth and the lip. f is voiceless. To form the sound of v, we place our lower lip lightly against the upper teeth as we do for f, but this time we either allow the air to flow through the small space or blow the air out quickly, thereby making the voiced fricative v.

3) Spaniards must be cautioned not to pronounce v as [b] when it is initial, or at any time as the bilabial spirant [β], the latter of which sounds to our ears like a w. Germans may tend to pronounce initial v as [f].

§ 42. W

1. w as in witch. (Simplified Symbol: w. Phonetic Symbol: w.)

1) Push out your lips and round them. Now let voiced air flow through the small opening. The resulting sound is the voiced, bilabial, glide consonant w [w] as in *war, dwell, swim, twenty, awhile*, and otherwise spelled o as in *one, choir*,* and *memoir*,* u as in *anguish, persuasive*,* and qu = kw (§ 36.)

Compare [w] with [b] or [m]. Observe that in saying w as in *witch*, you bring your lips together, round them a little, and send a voiced sound out through the little opening between. In making [w] there is much less interruption of tone by the lips than in making either [b] or [m]. The friction is so slight that [w] may be classed as a vowel-like consonant or a semivowel. See also § 9(6.a).

2) The glide w, like the glides l and r and like the nasal continuants m and n, may be unvoiced (devoiced, devocalized) when preceded by certain voiceless consonants. Like l and r, w may be voiceless at the beginning and voiced at the end; e.g., in *twine*. [̥] at the bottom indicates unvoicing; thus, w̥. See also §§ 29(1.5), 31(3.1), 32(2.4), 33(1.8), 37(1.5); and also § 19, "Chart of English Consonants," page xlix.

2. Silent w; Consonant w; ow. See also § 42(3).

1) w is silent before r, as in *wrack, wrap,* and so on (see page 316 *f.*).

2) Like y [j] [§ 44(4)], consonant w [w] is sounded only before a vowel sound, as in *want,* well,* widow,* work** (page 312 *ff.*). Unlike y, w by itself can not spell a vowel or a diphthong.

3) The letter w is often final, as in *bow* (bō—"a weapon"), *know.** In such words as *cow,* and *now,** the w in final position is the second element in the diphthong ou as in *about.** See § 34(25).

3. Silent w. The sound w has disappeared in three classes of instances:

1) Although w is spelled before r, the w is silent: see § 42(2.1).

2) When initial, w retains its sound before o͞o, as in *womb* (wo͞om), *woo* (wo͞o), *woof,* (wo͞of), *woozi* (*Slang,* wo͞oz′ĭ; wo͞oz′ĭ), *wound** (wo͞ond; wound). But when not initial, w may or may not be silent.

3) w tends to become silent or to disappear altogether before the vowels of unstressed syllables or unstressed words, as *answer,* boatswain* (bō′s'n; bŏt′swän′), *coxswain* (kŏk′s'n; kŏk′swän), *toward,* He'd fight* (from *He would fight*).

4) The tendency for w to become silent in unaccented syllables is especially strong in place names ending in –wich and –wick, as in *Greenwich** and *Warwick.** In some names the w has disappeared even in the spelling (formerly *Edwinesburch;* now *Edinburgh*); in other names spelling-pronunciation (§ 1) has restored the lost w sound (as in *Sandwich*).

4. wh as in whine. (Simplified Symbol: hw. Phonetic Symbol: hw.)

As you know, the voiced glide w as in *war* is made by rounding the lips, raising the back of the tongue, and then separating the lips quickly [§ 42(1)]. Its voiceless cognate is wh as in *wharf,* wheat, whiff,* why.** To make the sound wh, push out your lips and make a small circle as you did for w [§ 42(1)], and blow through the little opening.

wh represents either a voiceless w sound [ʍ] or h + w [hw], both of which are very much alike in sound. A large number of speakers pronounce all words beginning with wh as if each began with w alone, pronouncing *whet** as *wet, when** as *wen, whit* as *wit, which** as *witch.** By such use of the plain w, no discrimination is made between the voiceless wh in *where** and the voiced w in *wear.* Most careful speakers observe the distinctions between wh [hw] and w [w]. See § 27(1.2).

§ 43. X

The letter x spells a half dozen sounds in English:

> gz as in *exaggerate,* exempt,* exert**
> ks as in *exceed,* excuse,* exodus,* fox* (fŏks)
> gzh as in *luxuriance**
> ksh as in *anxious,* luxury**
> sh as in *anxious**
> z as in *anxiety,** and initially in *Xerxes**
> (zûrk′sēz), *xylophone,** and other Greek
> derivatives

1. English x.

1) x tends to be voiced (gz, gzh, z) when it is immediately preceded by an unaccented vowel; x tends to be voiceless (ks, ksh, sh) when it is immediately preceded by an accented vowel or by a consonant sound. Cf. §§ 38(4), 39(5).

2) When the letter x spells the sound ksh or gzh or sh, the i, or the y element of ū or ŭ [§ 38(12)], palatalizes the s or z element of x.

2. Spanish x.

1) In Spanish, x is in familiar speech like English s—especially when x precedes another consonant.

2) Usually, Spanish x is sounded as ks; occasionally, like gs.

3) x in Spanish may sometimes represent k, which is respelled with h [§ 29(2)].

§ 44. Y

1. y as in yes. (Simplified Symbol: y. Phonetic Symbol: j.)

1) y [j], the first sound in *yes*, is a semivowel, or vowel-like consonant, made by raising the front of the tongue toward the hard palate and then blowing it down with a voiced breath. The sound is also classified as a voiced, fricative, tongue, front-palate glide.

2) The sound y [j] is inserted before o͞o [u] in certain words; and the combination yo͞o [ju] is often described as one sound. See §§ 40(2,3,4).

2. y = ī, or ĭ, or û, or ĕ.

1) In addition to the one consonant (semivowel or vowel-like consonant), the letter y spells these four vowels:

> ī (*ice*) as in *my*
> ĭ (*bit*) as in *nymph**
> û (*hurt*) as in *myrtle*
> ĕ as in *zephyr**

2) Unless followed by a vowel, the consonant y [j] can not be used. In such words as *day* and *copy*, the letter y stands for a vowel sound.

3. Final y, Final ey.

1) For the variation between unaccented final y (*cop′y, chop′py*) and accented ĭ, or between unaccented ey (*hon′ey,* * *mon′ey**) and accented ĭ, see §§ 8(2), 28(4,5), 28(5.4,5).

2) For the pronunciation not only of final y (= ĭ) and final ey, but also of medial y (*paralysis*), see § 28(5).

4. Consonant y; y^e, y^t.

1) The consonantal sound of the letter y is [j] as in *yes,* * *you, vineyard*. To form the glide consonant y [j], the tongue begins in a position very much like that for the vowel ē [i], and then shifts quickly to the position for the vowel that follows. This rapid shift during continuous voicing produces the sound of y [j].

2) English y is spelled not only y in such words as *yes,* * *you, year, young,* * and *vineyard*, but also i, as in *onion**; e, as in *feud**; j, as in *hallelujah* (hăl′ĕ lo͞o′yä); g, as in *vignette* (vĭn yĕt′).

3) The y sound is heard in many words, although it is not spelled by a separate letter in such words: see § 40(4).

4) The consonant y sound occurs only before vowels. Therefore, when y appears terminally, it may be one of several vowel sounds: (a) a vowel (*heavy*); (b) a diphthong (*wry**); (c) the second element of a diphthong oi (*joy*); or (d) the second element, or vanish, of the ā sound [eɪ] (*ray*).

5) In Old English th of *the* was represented by the thorn letter (þ). Later, in Middle English manuscripts, the y, because it resembled the thorn letter most, was not infrequently used for th, particularly in abbreviations y^e and y^t, for *the** and *that.**

To impart an air of antiquity, a sign is made to read *Ye Olde Tea Shoppe;* but in such pseudo-archaic spelling the y is still properly pronounced th, not y— thus, *The Olde Tea Shoppe*.

§ 45. Z

1. z as in zero.

1) To form the sound of z as in *zero*, place the teeth in the same position as for s [§ 38(2.1)], raise the tongue tip, and send a stream of voiced air gently through the groove down the middle of the tongue and through the front teeth. The result will be the fricative z [z], the voiced cognate of s [s]. As in voiceless s, the upper and lower front teeth are brought fairly close together but not tightly closed; the tongue is held immediately in back of the top of the upper teeth without allowing the tongue tip to touch the teeth; and the voiced air [z] or the breath stream [s] is sent down the tiny groove formed between the tongue tip and the front of the hard palate. Whereas voiceless s has a hissing quality, the voiced z has a buzzing quality.

2) z as in *zany, lazy, dozen, fuzz, amazed,* is also spelled with s as in *gears, possess, jobs, rises, music, busy, is, girls* [§ 38(3,4,5)]. Other spellings include c as in *sacrifice,** cz as in *czar,** sc as in *discern** [§ 38(9.3)], and x as in *xylophone.**

3) For examples of pairs in which the verb has z [z] and a different part of speech has s [s], see § 38(4.4).

4) The interdental lisp is the substitution of the voiceless th [θ] for the [s], as explained in § 38(1.3). Likewise, one variety of defective z is the substitution of the voiced th [ð] for the [z].

2. Other Aspects of z.

1) z has the sound of zh [ʒ] as in *seizure.** zh [ʒ] is the voiced cognate of sh [ʃ].

2) The sound zh [ʒ] is also spelled by s, as in *decision.**

3) zh [ʒ] is also indicated by j as in *bijou* (bē′zhōō; bē′zhōō′) and by g as in *corsage** and *massage.** The spellings j and g for the sound zh appear in French derivatives.

4) zh [ʒ] is also the second element of j [dʒ].

3. Spanish z.

1) As pronounced in Castilian Spanish, z is sounded like th in *tooth.* Thus: *"cenizo"* (sä nē′sō; *Castilian,* thä nē′thō).

2) In American Spanish, z is like s in *sing.* Thus: *erizo* (ä rē′sō).

4. zz—Italian z.

1) zz is sounded as a single z, as in *buzzard* (bŭz′ērd), *huzza* (hŭ zä′; hŏŏ zä′), *hussy,** *whizzer* (hwĭz′ēr). See especially § 21(6); also, §§ 23(1.10), 25(1.4), 26(1.3), 30(2.2), 31(5.1), 32(3.1,2), 33(5.1), 35(5), 37(6), 38(13.2,3,4), 39(9.1).

2) In combinations the z may spell either a long or a double z sound, as in *That is zinc* (thăt ĭz-zĭngk).

3) Italian z, whether voiced, or voiceless, or doubled, is in English usually pronounced ts and dz. In Italian, however, the z may have not only the sound of ts and dz, but also, when doubled, the sound of t-ts and d-dz. In English the pronunciation for *bezzo* is bĕt′sō and for *mezzo* is mĕd′zō, mĕt′sō (*also,* mĕz′ō).

FINAL ASPECTS

§ 46. ENGLISH PRONUNCIATION OF FOREIGN WORDS

English pronunciations are usually preferred for foreign names and other foreign words when used in English contexts, especially when such foreign names and words have become completely English in meaning and usage. But, as with written language, so with spoken language, the use of either the Anglicized pronunciation of a foreign word or the foreign pronunciation of a foreign word depends on "levels of usage," on "appropriateness" (see §§ 4, 51). Thus, for example, on the most formal musical programs the nuance of foreign pronunciation may be desirable even when the dictionary records also an established Anglicized pronunciation (§ 51.1).

Somewhere between the styles appropriate for the preacher and the after-dinner speaker, between the styles appropriate for Supreme Court decisions and familiar talks, lies the style appropriate for the broadcaster; and for many purposes it is helpful to remember the sane advice that Professor W. Cabell Greet[1] gives radio speakers:

> When faced with the necessity of choosing between English and foreign pronunciations, broadcasters should of course use the pronunciations commonly employed in the comfortable English of educated people acquainted with the place and the subject. Names that are not Anglicized in English dictionaries probably have no English pronunciation, and they should be pronounced in foreign style.

Professor Greet then points out that there seems to be a tendency to rebuke our public speakers and editors "if they freely Anglicize foreign names. For one reason or another there is a new and somewhat foreign standard of correctness or appropriateness of pronunciation."

> Whatever the causes, there is established today a learned standard of handling newly arrived foreign names. We may well call it a new kind of Anglicizing: the rule, or the aspiration, is to adopt the foreign pronunciation insofar as it can be rendered by customary English sounds in the phrasing and rhythm of an English sentence. It is not good taste to introduce sounds that are foreign to English.

> But a word of caution must be added. Absurd foreignisms will be labeled pretentious and asinine, fine as the line is between what seems absurd and what seems "correct." The pronunciations must conform to the customs of idiomatic English. The "Parisian" r, for instance, is not welcomed.

Briefly, this *Manual of Pronunciation* recommends the general approach as stated in Section 51(1). As H. W. Fowler[2] puts it:

> To say a French word in the middle of an English sentence exactly as it would be said by a Frenchman in a French sentence is a feat demanding an acrobatic mouth; the muscles have to be suddenly adjusted to a performance of a different nature, & after it as suddenly recalled to the normal state; it is a feat that should not be attempted; the greater its success as a *tour de force*, the greater its failure as a step in the conversational progress; for your collocutor, aware that he could not have done it himself, has his attention distracted whether he admires or is humiliated.

---

[1] W. Cabell Greet, *World Words: Recommended Pronunciations*, pages xiv, xv, xvi (New York: Columbia University Press, 1948).

[2] H. W. Fowler, *A Dictionary of Modern English Usage*, page 194 (London: Oxford: At the Clarendon Press, 1927).

§ 47. DEBATABLE PRONUNCIATIONS

1) Section 277 of *Webster's New International Dictionary of the English Language*[1] presents a list of about 1100 words whose current pronunciation is debatable. In tabular form is listed the pronunciation of each of these words as given by four English and by four American dictionaries. A reference to § 47(1) means that the word also appears in the famous Merriam-Webster "Synopsis of Words Differently Pronounced by Different Orthoepists," better known as "Section 277." The section has not been revised since 1934.

2) A reference to § 47(2) means that the word appears in "Appendix I: Disputed Pronunciations" of the *New Standard Dictionary of the English Language.*[2] By a letter-and-key device are registered the preferences of seven dictionaries, four of which were not canvassed by the Merriam-Webster [see § 47(1)], and the opinion of each of twenty-five consultants for the individual word. "Appendix I: Disputed Pronunciations" has not been revised since 1913.

3) If you are referred to § 47(3), it means that the word in question appears both in Section 277 of the Merriam-Webster and in the section called "Disputed Pronunciations" in the Funk and Wagnalls. See § 47(1,2).

§ 48. DISSIMILATION; LONG U = ̶I̶U̶; PLURALS OF NOUNS

1) *Dissimilation* is said to have occurred when one of two identical sounds near each other in a word is lost or dropped. By *R*– dissimilation is meant the loss of an r sound in one syllable when there is another r sound in the same word. When this dissimilative tendency in a particular word functions widely in the speech of educated people, the pronunciation is good usage. [For the addition of an r sound, see § 37(3)]. Examples of dissimilation [see also § 24(7)]: *caterpillar,** *enterprise,** *February,** *governor,** *government,** *library,** *particularly,** *paraphernalia,** *reservoir,** *secretary,** *surprise,** *thermometer.**

2) For "long" u, only two pronunciations are shown in this manual. But in addition to yo͞o [ju] and o͞o [u], "long" u is often sounded as the diphthong ĭ + o͞o, or ĭo͞o [ɪu *or, preferably,* ɪ̶u̶]. For an explanation, see §§ 40(2.2), 40(3,4).

When you are referred to this section, it is to remind you that an additional pronunciation for the word in question is possible. For example, the only pronunciation shown for *beauty** (page 31) is ['bju tɪ], but the reference to § 48(2) means that also acceptable is ['bɪu tɪ], or (more accurately) ['bɪ̶u̶ tɪ]. Even the rule [§ 50(32.b)] that "long" u is sounded o͞o [u] when the l is preceded in the same syllable by b becomes modified by a reference to this section. On page 35 the pronunciation for *blue* is [blu]; but since you are referred to § 48(2), you are to understand that another pronunciation is [blɪu] or [blɪ̶u̶].

3) To pronounce the plural of nouns, the possessive singular of nouns, and the third singular present indicative of verbs, three general rules are helpful:

   a) When the stem of the noun or the verb ends in the *sound* of p, t, k, f, or th (as in *tooth:* [θ]), add the *sound* s.

     1) Plural of nouns: *chip, chips; yacht, yachts**; *risk, risks**; *cuff, cuffs; fifth, fifths.** Exceptions: Some nouns ending in f change the f to v and add –es to form the plural. The sound changes from s to z: *calf, calves**; *elf, elves**; *half, halves; leaf, leaves; shelf, shelves; wife, wives.** Other nouns such as *oath,** *width,** and *wreath* change from the sound th [θ] in the singular to th̶z̶ [ðz] in the plural: see § 39(5).

     2) Possessive singular in 's: *Rudolph, Rudolph's; Annette, Annette's; Frederick, Frederick's; Jeff, Jeff's; Edith, Edith's.*

---

[1] Second Edition, Unabridged, pages lix–lxxviii (Springfield, Massachusetts: G. and C. Merriam Company, 1934, *et seq.*)

[2] Pages 2762–2779 (New York: Funk and Wagnalls Company, 1946).

　　3) Third singular present indicative: *help, helps; respect, respects*; cook, cooks; laugh, laughs; froth, froths.* See also §§ 24(5), 39(5).

b) Rule (a) states that the *sound* s is added when the stem of the noun or the verb ends in the voiceless consonant *sound* p, t, k, f, or th [θ] (as in *tooth*). The second rule is to add the *sound* z when the stem of the noun or the verb ends in any vowel *sound* or in any of the voiced consonant *sounds* b, d, g, v, th [ð] (as in *then*), m, n, ng [ŋ], l.

　　1) Plural of nouns: (a) Vowel sounds—*pea, peas;* (from *memory*) *memori-es; bay, bays; myrrh, myrrhs; maker, makers; idea, ideas; view, views; book, books; doe, does; jaw, jaws; corps** (singular), *corps** (plural); *baa, baas; eye, eyes; cow, cows; hue, hues.* (b) Consonant sounds—*rib, ribs; gibe, gibes*; hood, hoods; bag, bags; archive, archives*; lathe, lathes; room, rooms; alms*; fern, ferns; song, songs; doings*; bill, bills; victuals.**

　　2) Possessive singular in 's: (a) Vowel sounds—*Jesse, Jesse's; Gregory, Gregory's; Fay, Fay's; Saire, Saire's; Burr, Burr's; Seymour, Seymour's; Peter, Peter's; Elihu, Elihu's; Hugh, Hugh's; Mayo, Mayo's; Alma, Alma's; Alvah, Alvah's; Esau, Esau's; Rye, Rye's; Joy, Joy's;* (b) Consonant sounds: *Caleb, Caleb's; Conrad, Conrad's; Hedwig, Hedwig's; Eve, Eve's; Emil, Emil's; Hiram, Hiram's; Bertram, Bertram's; Evelyn, Evelyn's; Fielding, Fielding's; Carl, Carl's.*

　　3) Third singular present indicative: (a) Vowel sounds—*see, sees;* (from *bury*) *buri-es; pay, pays; batter, batters; stir, stirs; subpoena, subpoenas; boo, boos; mew, mews; row, rows; gnaw, gnaws; buy, buys; allow, allows; enjoy, enjoys.* (b) Consonant sounds: *rob, robs; bed, beds; say, says; dive, dives; wreathe, wreathes; fume, fumes; win, wins; ring, rings; kneel, kneels.*

c) In *spelling*, as you know, nouns ending in the *letter* or letters s, sh, ch, z, x, add es to form the plural. The es is pronounced ĕz [εz], or ĭz [ɪz], or ĭz [əz], depending on the formality or informality of speech. [See § 24(5).] In spelling, also, only s is added to nouns ending in se, ze, ce, or dge with silent e, and such words are pronounced ĕz [εz], ĭz [ɪz], or ĭz [əz].

In pronunciation, where we are concerned only with *sound*, the rule is easier to state and has wider application. Rule *a* disposed of the voiceless consonant sounds p, t, k, f, th [θ]; rule *b* disposed of any vowel sound (each vowel sound is voiced) and the voiced consonant sounds b, d, g, v, th [ð] m, n, ng [ŋ], l. The third rule now accounts for other sounds:

To form the plural of nouns, or the possessive in 's, or the third singular present indicative of verbs in a word ending in any of the sibilants s, sh [ʃ], ch [tʃ], z, zh [ʒ], or j [dʒ], add the syllable ĕz [εz], ĭz [ɪz], or ĭz [əz].

　　1) Plural of nouns: *face, faces; circumstance, circumstances*; lash, lashes; torch, torches; tease, teases; buzz, buzzes; orange, oranges*; box, boxes* (x = ks).

　　2) Possessive singular in 's: *Bruce, Bruce's; Ashe, Ashe's; Beach, Beach's; Barnes, Barnes's; Lorge, Lorge's: Rex, Rexes.*

　　3) Third singular present indicative: *race, races; crush, crushes; match, matches; rise,* rises; buzz, buzzes; camouflage, camouflages; wedge, wedges.*

§ 49. PREFIXES

Note: Where only one pronunciation is given for each of the prefixes in this manual (pages 1–319), it is to be understood that the variants may also be appropriate, depending upon such factors as style of speaking, rapidity of utterance, familiarity of the word, sense stress, and the like.

1) be–. bĕ [bi], bĭ [bɪ]; also bŭ [bə]. be + l is often pronounced b'l [bl̩].
Examples: *bedizen,** *believe,** *belike,** *besought,** *betroth.** See § 28(4.4).

2) de–. dĕ [di], dĭ [dɪ]; also dŭ [də]. Examples: *debar,** *decry,** *deduce,** *denounce,** *desist.** See § 28(4.4).

3) dis–. Usually dĭs [dɪs], but in a few words dĭz [dɪz]. (Latin dis– appears as di– before b, d, g, l, m, n, r, v, and occasionally j; as dif– before f; and sometimes as dir– before vowels but usually as dis–.) Examples: *disable,** *disarm,** *disaster,** *disband,** *discard,** *discern,** *discomfiture,** *discrepancy,** *disdain,** *disease,** *dishonest.** See §§ 38(6.1), 38(13.3,4).

4) e–. (a) When used as an unstressed word initial, the sound may be ē [i], ĭ [ɪ], ĕ [ɛ], or (often before l) ĕ [ə]. (b) Takes the place of ex– (see number 6 below) before b, d, g, h, l, m, n, r, and v. Examples: *eccentric,** *Ecclesiastes,*¹ *effect** (see number 6 below), *effete,** *effrontery,** *elect,** *emaciate,** *enigma,** *episcopate,** *erect,** *eventually.**

5) en–. ĕn [ɛn]; less formal, especially when not even lightly stressed, ĭn [ɪn]; occasionally, ĭn [ən]. Usually becomes em– (ĕm; when wholly unstressed, ĭm; least often, ĭm) before p, b, and m. Examples: *embitter,** *employ,** *enabling,** *enchant,** *enslave,** *envelope.**

6) ex–. (a) ĕks [ɛks]; when wholly unstressed, ĭks [ɪks]; in familiar speech or rapid talk, sometimes ŭks [əks]. (b) As a general rule, sounded ĕks, ĭks, or ĭks before a consonant; and ĕgz, ĭgz, or ĭgz before a vowel, unless the prefix before the vowel is accented, in which circumstance either the ĕks-group or ĕgz-group is possible. The less common words often violate the general rule that ĕgz, ĭgz, or ĭgz is sounded when the prefix is unaccented before an accented vowel or silent h. (c) ex– may appear as e–: see (4) above. (d) ex– occasionally appears as es–. Examples of ex–: *exert,** *exorbitant,** *extract,** *exult.** See also § 24(4).

7) il–. ĭl– [ɪl–]. When il– means "not," and is followed by l in the next syllable, the two l's are usually pronounced as a single lengthened l sound, and this prolonged or "double" l may be shown in a pronunciation key by being respelled with two l's. In less formal, less emphatic or unemphatic, or more rapid speech, only one l sound is usual. Since il– is an assimilated form of in–, meaning "not," see (9) below. Examples: *illicit,** *illimitable,** *illuminate,** *illusion.**

8) im–. ĭm [ɪm]. Like il– (see [7]), im– meaning "not" is an assimilated form of in– (see [9]). When im– is definitely negative in force, and is followed by m in the next syllable, the two m's are pronounced by many careful speakers as a prolonged m. To show this double m sound, the word is respelled with two m's. The more colloquial or rapid the utterance, the greater the tendency to sound only one m. Remember that words compounded with im– meaning "not" may have shifting accent or contrasting stress: See § 11; also § 32(3.2). Examples: *immobile,** *immortal,** *immunize.**

9) in–. (a) Prefix meaning "not," "non–," "un–" is pronounced ĭn [ɪn]. When a word with in– followed by n in the next syllable is respelled for pronunciation with two n's, sound both n's as a prolonged n, except in colloquial or rapid utterance. (b) in– becomes il– before l, im– before a labial (see chart, § 19, page xlix), and ir– before r. See (7) and (8) above, and (9) below. (c) When only the normal stress is given for words beginning with un–, it is to be understood that a contrasting stress or a shifting accent is possible. See § 11. Examples: *imbue,** *immaculate,** *inalienability,** *inapplicable,** *incarnate,** *incompatible,** *incompetent,** *incredulity,** *indecisive,** *indubitable,** *innate,** *intractable.**

10) ir–. ĭr [ɪr]. An assimilated form of in– (see [9]). Pronounce as a prolonged r the prefix ir– when it is followed by r in the next syllable. Words such as *irrational,** *irreconcilable,** *irrelevant,** *irremediable,** and *irretrievable,** in which ir– is clearly negative in force, are usually respelled with two r's to represent the more careful pronunciation. Other examples in which r is pronounced either as a single r or as a kind of lengthened or "double" r are *irradiate,** *irreligious,** *irrepressible,** *irresolute,** *irresponsible.** See § 37(6.3).

11) out–. out [aʊt]. (a) In nouns, primary accent is usually on the combining form of the adverb out–, as in outcast (out′cȧst′). (b) With verbs, primary accent is usually on the verbal element (but see § 11), as in outcast* (out cȧst′). In such words the prefix is separable, as it is in outhurl, outjest. (c) Primary accent is usually on verbal element (of verbs, or adjectives, or nouns), where the prefix out– is inseparable, as in outargue (out är′gū), outfish, outlabor, outwallop, outzany.

12) over–. ō′vĕr ['o vɚ]. Words formed with over– vary in accent, even in the same word, according to meaning, accent, rhythm, sense, stress, and emphasis. See §§ 10, 11. Examples: overbalance,* overflow,* overlook,* overseer.*

13) pre–. Stressed: prē [pri], prĕ [pri, prɪ]. Unstressed: prĭ [prɪ], prĕ [pri] prĭ [prə]. There is also a tendency to say pĕr [pɚ], although many careful speakers avoid that pronunciation. This transposition of letters, syllables, or sounds is called metathesis; and such reversal of the order of sounds should be remembered because of its substandard use in prefixes that include r. Examples: preamble,* precede,* prefer,* prefix,* premature,* preponderate,* preventive.* See § 28(4.4).

14) pro–. Latin prefix. Stressed: prō [pro]; occasionally, prŏ [prə]. Unstressed: prō [pro]; especially in the common words, prŏ [prə]. Examples: procedure,* production,* progress* (verb), project* (verb), projectile,* prologue,* propose,* protect.*

15) re–. Stressed: rē [ri]. Unstressed: rĭ [rɪ], rĕ [ri], rĭ [rə]. In deliberate speech, whether stressed or unstressed, rē [ri] is usual, as it is frequently when the prefix is followed by a vowel. Examples: rebound,* recline,* refer,* reinforce,* relaxation,* reorganize,* repose, residuum,* resume.* See § 28(4.4).

16) se–. Unstressed word initial: sĭ [sɪ], sĭ [sə], sĕ [si]. When followed by l, s'l [sl] is a not infrequent variant. Examples: sebaceous,* secrete,* secretive,* secure,* seduce,* semester,* seraphic,* selectivity, selector,* See § 28(4.4).

17) sub–. Stressed: sŭb [sʌb]. Unstressed: sŭb [səb]. Compounds beginning with sub–, especially nouns, often shift their accent, the variability depending on position, contrast, emphasis, and the like: see § 11. Examples: subsidiary,* subsist,* substantial,* suburb,* subdivision,* subside.*

18) th–. Initial th– as in the, this, then, and other pronominal words [see § 39(5)] is now voiced = ŧħ [ð]. In the word with,* usage is variable; and its th or ŧħ sound has affected the pronunciation of compounds. See that,* them,* there,* therewith,* thither,* wherewith,* with,* withdraw,* withstand.*

19) trans–. trăns [træns]; if followed by a voiced sound, often trănz [trænz]. Examples with [træns]: transference,* transparent,* transport.* Both [træns] and [trænz]: transact,* transgress,* transition,* transmissible.

20) un–. Meaning "not." ŭn [ʌn]. Compounds formed with un– often shift their accent: see § 11. The ŭ [ʌ] is usually accented, even if slightly. Examples: unconscious,* unduly,* unequivocal,* unfrequent,* unlearned,* until,* unwary.*

21) under–. ŭn′dĕr ['ʌn dɚ]. Meaning, rhythm, and sense stress cause variable accent: see § 11. Examples: underfoot, underhand, undersigned, understudy.*

22) up–. ŭp [ʌp]. The accent in compounds beginning with this prefix often varies according to rhythm and meaning: see § 11. Examples: upgrade, uphill, uplift,* uproot,* upset,* upstream.

23) wh– (not properly a prefix). For initial wh spelled in a word like whine or nowhere* this manual uses the symbol hw, which possibly is still the preponderant pronunciation in America. But many Americans and Englishmen pronounce words beginning with wh as if each begins with w. See § 42(4). Examples: whack,* whale,* wharf,* wheedle,* whimper,* whither, why.*

24) GENERAL CAUTION. As a rule, prefixes as well as suffixes (§ 50) are unstressed. Such lack of stress makes the vowels in those affixes weak. Good speakers, even precise speakers, do not stress these weak syllables, for they know that so doing will tend to equalize the stress incorrectly.

§ 50. SUFFIXES

Note: In this manual (pages 1–319) when only one pronunciation is indi-cated for each of the suffixes, it is to be understood that the others are possible variants. See § 49, Note.

1) –age. Unstressed: usually ĭj [ɪdӡ]; often ĭj [ədӡ]. When only one pro-nunciation is indicated, the other may also be understood as a possible variant, especially in colloquial speech. Examples: *beverage,* homage,* luggage,* voyage.** See § 20(8).

2) –ate. (a) Unstressed: ăt [et], ĭt [ɪt]; often ĭt [ət]. Examples: *climate,* indeterminate,* prelate,* testate.** (b) Stressed (even if no accent mark is shown): āt [et]. Especially true of verbs formed by Anglicizing Latin verbs of the first conjugation. Examples: *accelerate,* extricate,* liberate,* perambulate.**

3) –ative. ā′tĭv [ˌe tɪv], ȧ tĭv [ə tɪv]. When only the former pronunciation is given, the latter may also be assumed as possible, especially in ordinary con-versation. Observe that the ā′tive occurs as a rule in a word of more than three syllables, in which the primary accent is frequently on the second syllable before –ative. See § 13(3). Examples: *authoritative,* combative,* quantitative,* seda-tive,* vibrative.**

4) –ed, –d. To form past tense of verbs and past participle. (a) As a separate syllable: ĕd [ɛd], ĭd [ɪd], as in *doubled,* started.** (b) When combined with a preceding voiced sound: d [d], as in *estranged,* opined.** (c) When combined with a preceding voiceless sound: t [t], as in *bivouacked,* traversed.** See §§ 23(1.14,15), 24(16.4,5), 28(4.4).

5) –ed. In adjectives: ĕd [ɛd], ĭd [ɪd]. The formal sound is ĕd [ɛd]. The more natural sound ĭd [ɪd] may even become ĭd [əd]. See § 24(5). Examples: *disinterested,* dogged,* learned.** Note how the –ed may be pronounced as a sep-arate syllable.

6) –es, –s. Used to form the third person singular indicative, the plural of nouns, the possessive of nouns. (a) Pronounced s after voiceless consonant sounds f [f], k [k], p [p], t [t], th [θ]. Not so pronounced after s [s], sh [ʃ], ch [tʃ]. (b) Pronounced z [z] after all vowel sounds, and after the voiced consonant sounds b [b], d [d], g [g], l [l], m [m], n [n], ng [ŋ], r [r], th [ð], v [v], w [w]. Not so pronounced after z [z], zh [ӡ], dz [dӡ]. Compare these exceptions with the exceptions in (a). (c) Pronounced ĭz [ɪz] and often ĭz [əz] after ch [tʃ], j [dӡ], s [s], sh [ʃ], z [z], zh [ӡ]. See § 48(3).

7) –ese. ēz [iz], ēs [is]. Tendency in American English is toward ēz [iz]. Examples: *Chinese,* Japanese,* manganese,* Portuguese.** See § 38(6.2).

8) –ess. Used to form feminine nouns: ĕs [ɛs], ĭs [ɪs]; ĭs [əs] is a frequent variant. When lightly accented (with or without accent mark), is sounded ĕs [ɛs], especially in poetry. Examples: *marchioness,* patroness,* princess,* seam-stress.**

9) –est. Used to form the superlative of adjectives: ĕst [ɛst], ĭst [ɪst]; also possible, ĭst [əst]. When lightly stressed in poetry, especially ĕst [ɛst]. Ex-amples: *farthest,* latest,* longest,* strongest,* youngest.** See § 28(4.4).

10) –et. ĕt [ɛt], ĭt [ɪt]; also ĭt [ət]. Examples: *bonnet,* cornet,* faucet,* pamphlet.** See §§ 24(5), 28(4.4).

11) –ful. (a) As an adjective suffix: fŏŏl [ˈfʊl], f'l [fḷ]; also fŭl [fəl]. Ex-amples: *beautiful,* wistful.** (b) As a noun suffix: fŏŏl [fʊl]. Examples: *hand-ful, spoonful.* See § 40(13.4).

12) –ical. ĭ kăl [ɪ kəl]. Examples: *apostolical, ethical, musical.* When adverb is formed by adding –ly, the pronunciation for –ically is either ĭ kăl ĭ [ɪ kəl ɪ] or ĭ k′l ĭ [ɪ kḷ ɪ]. Examples: *apostolically, ethically, musically.*

13) –ile. Suffix in adjectives: ĭl [ɪl]; less frequently, īl [aɪl]. See § 28(5). Examples: *contractile,* fragile,* mercantile,* versatile.**

14) –ing. Sounded ĭng [ɪŋ̣]. In actual connected speech often sounded ng [ŋ], ĭn [ɪn], ĭn [ən], 'n [n̩]. Following a k [k] or g [g] sound, ĭng [ɪŋ] is often replaced by syllabic ng [ŋ]. See § 33(4).

15) –ism. ĭz'm [ɪz m̩]. Most dictionaries make the m syllabic in such words as *aphorism,** *baptism,** *idealism,** *Judaism,** *plebianism,** *prism,** *sophism.** But the vowel, though brief, does appear; and there is evidence that [ɪz əm] is more frequent than [ɪz m̩].

16) –ity. ĭ tĭ [ə tɪ], but ĭ tĭ [ɪ tɪ] is also heard. Examples: *equality,** *felicity,** *ingenuity,** *quiddity,** *senility.**

17) –ive. ĭv [ɪv]. Examples: *decorative,** *evasive,** *lucrative,** *restorative.**

18) –less. (a) lĕs [les], lĭs [lɪs]. The lĭs form is more natural: see § 24(5). The form lŭs [ləs] also occurs often. Examples: *fathomless,** *meaningless, regardless, ruthless.** (b) Sound two l's whenever this unstressed suffix is added to a word ending in l [l] or 'l [l̩], as in *jowlless* (joul'lĕss, joul'lĭs; jōl'lĕs, jōl'lĭs) and *saddleless* (săd' 'l lĕs, săd' 'l lĭs). See § 28(4.4).

19) –like. (a) līk [laɪk]. Examples: *clocklike, trapezelike.* (b) When –like is added to words ending in l or in an l sound, two l sounds are pronounced; thus, *ball, ball-like; bridle, bridlelike.*

20. –ly. lĭ [lɪ]. (a) A suffix forming adjectives; a suffix forming adverbs. Although indicated as lĭ [lɪ], the sound often tends to ē [i]: see §§ 8(2), 28(4.5), 28(5.4,5). Although only lĭ [lɪ] is given, it is to be recognized that many speakers make the sound closer to lē [li] than to lĭ [lɪ]. Examples: *abstractly,** *cleanly,** *grievously,** *minutely,** *really.** (b) When a head word ends in an l or an l sound, and –ly is added, usage varies as to whether a single l sound or two l sounds should be sounded; and sometimes both are acceptable.

21) –man, –men. Singular: măn [mæn], in formal speech or for definite purpose; măn [mən], for all other purposes. Plural: in compounds usually mĕn [men]. Examples: *Dutchman,** *gentleman,** *policeman,** *talisman.**

22) –ment. (a) Unstressed: mĕnt [mənt], as in *argument,** *disparagement,** *indictment,** *preferment.** (b) Stressed: mĕnt [ment] as in *augment,** *compliment** (verb), *ferment, fragment** (verb), *frequent** (verb), *torment.**

23) –ness. (a) Seldom nĕs [nes], more often nĭs [nɪs], and frequently nŭs [nəs]. See §§ 24(5), 28(4.4). Examples: *cleanliness,** *greatness, kindliness, worldliness.* (b) Sound two n's when –ness is added to a word ending in n [n] or 'n [n̩], as in *green, greenness; sudden* (sŭd' 'n; sŭd' ĭn), *suddenness.*

24) –ng. See § 33(4).

25) ous. ŭs [əs]. Examples: *analogous,** *contiguous,** *egregious,** *nefarious,** *specious,** *viscous.**

26) –ow. ō [o], as in *arrow,** *marshmallow,** *widow.** See § 34(25.4). In connected discourse, however, the full –ō [-o] sounds prissy; it is, as Professor Kemp Malone has said, a pseudo-refined spelling pronunciation (§ 1). Many Americans sound it either as ȧ [ə] or, as described by J. S. Kenyon, as an advanced or fronted [ö].

27) –sia. In *magnesia,** *Persia,** and like words, the –sia is pronounced not only as indicated but also as [ʃjə, ʒjə, sɪ ə, sjə].

28) –sion. Sometimes shŭn [ʃən], as in *capitation,** *oppression.* At other times zhŭn [ʒən], as in *cohesion,** *evasion,** *perversion.** Both pronunciations are given in some other words, as in *animadversion,** *conversion,** *dispersion,** *excursion,** *reversion,** *version,** with a tendency to shŭn [ʃən]. Less frequently sh'n [ʃn̩], heard more often in England. See also *inversion.**

29) –tia. shȧ [ʃə], shĭ ȧ [ʃɪ ə]; also often shyȧ [ʃjə]. Examples: *inertia,** *Portia.**

30) –tion. shŭn [ʃən]; less often sh'n [ʃn̩]. Examples: *abolition,** *constitution,** *equation,** *lotion,** *situation.**

31) –tu–, –ture.

    (a) In everyday speech unaccented –tu– as in *congratulate** (kŏn grăt'ṷ lāt) and *century** (sĕn′tū̆ rĭ) is often pronounced chuh: kuhn GRACH uh layt [kən 'græt∫ ə let] and SEN chuh ri ['sɛn t∫ə rɪ]. Acceptable as well are kuhn GRACH o͝o layt [kən 'græt∫ ʊ let] and kuhn GRAT yo͝o layt [kən 'græt jʊ let]; SEN cho͝o ri ['sɛn t∫ʊ rɪ] and SEN tyuh ri ['sɛn tjʊ rɪ]. When this manual does not show the natural pronunciation with chuh, that pronunciation is to be considered equally as acceptable as those shown in the SIMPLIFIED column. (All the pronunciations, however, are usually presented in the PHONETIC column.) See § 50(33).

b) Even in colloquial speech a word such as *estuary** (ĕs′tū̆ ĕr′ĭ), with unaccented –tu– as in *congratulate* and *century* (see a above), tends to be pronounced cho͝o [t∫ʊ] rather than chuh [t∫ə]. This tendency is strongest when –tu– is followed by a vowel, as in *estuary* (ES cho͝o *er* i) ['ɛs t∫ʊ ˌer ɪ]. Other pronunciations are (ES tyo͝o *er* i) → ['ɛs tjʊ ˌer ɪ] and, especially British but acceptable American (ES tyo͝o uhr i)→ ['ɛs tjʊ ər ɪ].

c) Final –ture as an unaccented syllable, as in *nature*,* *fracture*,* *adventure*,* *literature*,* has more than one pronunciation. Although SPECIAL NOTES, "Variant Pronunciations," III, b.4 (page xxi) has a brief explanation, it should be reiterated that authorities are by no means in complete agreement about final –ture [or final –dure, as in *verdure*,* § 23(1.9)].

  1) In *nature*,* *fracture*,* and like two-syllable words (dissyllables), final –ture is always unaccented; and in ordinary conversation is NAY chuhr ['ne t∫ɚ], recognizably the most natural or most colloquial pronunciation, or NAY tyuhr ['ne tjɚ]. Many Americans (some authorities think most) say NAY cho͝or ['ne t∫ʊr]; some speak it precisely as NAY tyo͝or ['ne tjʊr]. It should be noted that NAY cho͝or and NAY tyo͝or are sometimes characterized or stamped either as prissy, old-fashioned, archaic, or even obsolete.

  2) In plurisyllables (words of more than one syllable) not accented on the penult (actually, in words of three or more syllables not accented on the next-to-last syllable), the unaccented final ending –ture is usually pronounced cho͝or [ˌt∫ʊr] or chuhr [t∫ɚ]. The more common the word or the more colloquial the style, the greater the tendency to say chuhr. Otherwise the –ture is not without some accent, and is accordingly pronounced cho͝or [ˌt∫ʊr].

  Therefore a word such as *adven′ture*,* a three-syllable word accented on the penult, is pronounced very much like *nature* (see c above) as chuhr [t∫ɚ] and tyuhr [tjɚ]. On the other hand, a word such as *literature** (lĭt′ẽr *á* tū̆r) is a plurisyllable not accented on the penult (or the next-to-last syllable), and accordingly is usually pronounced cho͝or [ˌt∫ʊr] or chuhr [t∫ɚ]. Equally acceptable are tyo͝or [ˌtjʊr] and tyuhr [tjɚ].

d) If there is one general conclusion to be made about unaccented u in words like *congratulate** and *century*,* and in words like *nature*,* *fracture*,* *adventure*,* and *literature*,* it is that in all everyday words the most or the only natural pronunciation is the sound of ch [t∫] rather than ty [tj]. See §§ 23(1.9), 40(11.9), 50(31,33), and SPECIAL NOTES, III, b.4.

e) For words ending in –ture as many as four pronunciations are likely when the DIACRITICAL column shows the pronunciation as tū̆r. As explained above (a–d), the number of acceptable spoken forms depends on certain factors.

It is possible that for one or two of the words the presentation of so many "acceptable" pronunciations may have an almost intimidating appearance; but it should not have. For example, a consultant should remember the distinctions of levels of usage or extent of usage. Or a consultant, once he finds among the acceptable listings a pronunciation to which he is already habituated, need be concerned about no other possibilities unless for comparative or research purposes.

It should also be remembered that the SIMPLIFIED column interprets the symbols given in the DIACRITICAL column. To many users the dictionary marking of tŭr in a word such as *literature* conveys no more than one pronunciation—and they are not too sure even of that. In other words, the dictionary transcription tŭr indicates all the pronunciations presented in the SIMPLIFIED column—but the average user, even if once aware of that, has forgotten it.

Matters become even more confused when a word ending in unaccented -ture is transcribed in the DIACRITICAL column not only as tŭr but also in additional ways. A formidable example is *premature* (see page 237), which is given four different transcriptions in the DIACRITICAL column. Properly interpreted, as many as nine pronunciations have thereby been specified; but most users do not realize that. When they see so many acceptable pronunciations given in the SIMPLIFIED column, they should no more charge this manual with confusing them than they would charge the dictionary. This description, though apparently confusing, is a true picture of a complicated situation that actually exists. The consultant is free to use any pronunciation that is acceptable.

32) a) Unaccented u (not strictly a suffix). In everyday pronunciation of words like *angular,** *deputy,** *obduracy,** and *peninsula,** unaccented u may be pronounced yo͞o [jʊ] or, most commonly, yuh [jə]. It is least frequently sounded yo͞o [ju].

b) Accented u (not strictly a suffix). Two general rules help to determine when a u is "long," as in *use, fuse:* (1) In an accented syllable ending in u, the vowel is usually "long," as in *assidu'ity, du'al, du'ty, fu'neral, indu'bitable, lu'nacy, nu'trient, pellu'cid, recu'perate, undu'ly.* (2) The combination u + a single consonant (except r) in an accented syllable + final silent e usually means that the u is "long," as in *allude,** *astute,** *consume,** *costume,** *deduce,** *duke,** *inopportune,** *nude,** *obtuse,** *resume,** *tube,** *tune.** For [ɪu] or [ɨu], see §§ 40(2.2), 40(3,4), 48(2).

CHART FOR PRONOUNCING "LONG" U

as yo͞o [ju], o͞o [u], or both yo͞o [ju] and o͞o [u]

When Preceded By	Pronounce "u" As	Examples
b	yo͞o	*attribute,** *beauteous,** *beauty**
bl	o͞o	*blue, bluet, bluing*
c = k	yo͞o	See examples under k.
cl	o͞o	*clue,** *clupeid*
d	yo͞o, o͞o	*adduce,** *dew,** *introduce,** *unduly**
f	yo͞o	*diffuse,** *feudatory,** *funeral, perfume**
fl	o͞o	*flue,** *fluent,** *flute**
g	yo͞o	*angular**
gl	o͞o	*glue,** *glumaceous, gluten**
h	yo͞o	*hue,** *huge,** *human,** *humus*
j	only o͞o	*June,** *jute, **jeweler,** *jewelry**
k	yo͞o	*accumulative,** *cuneiform,** *peculiar,** *recuperate**

l	o͞o, yo͞o. But see bl, cl, fl, gl.	*aluminum,* * *collusion,* * *lucid,* * *pellucid* *
m	yo͞o	*mutual,* * *mucilaginous,* * *Munich* *
n	yo͞o, o͞o	*diminution,* * *knew,* * *new,* * *neutral,* * *pneumatic,* * *revenue* *
p	yo͞o	*dispute,* * *impugn,* * *indisputable,* * *therapeutic* *
r	only o͞o	*rubric,* * *rule,* * *ruse,* * *ruthless* *
s	yo͞o, o͞o	*consume,* * *exude,* * *insular,* * *suicide* *
t	yo͞o, o͞o	*attitude,* * *fatuity,* * *obtuse,* * *tune* *
th	yo͞o, o͞o	*enthusiasm,* * *enthusiast* *
v	yo͞o	*view* *
z	yo͞o, o͞o	*Zeus* *

Summary:

When the sound of "long" u is preceded by bl–, cl–, fl–, or gl–, the pronunciation is always o͞o [u]. See also § 48(2).

When the sound of "long" u is preceded by d, n, s, or t, the pronunciation is yo͞o [ju] or o͞o [u], although many cultured speakers prefer the yo͞o [ju].

When the sound of "long" u is preceded by l, the pronunciation is either yo͞o [ju] or o͞o [u], except that the sound is always o͞o when the l is preceded in the same syllable by b, c, f, or g.

Initial u, when it starts either a word (*university* *) or a syllable (*reg′u late*) is always preceded by the sound y [j] as in *yes*. In an accented syllable, initial u is usually yo͞o [ju]; in an unaccented syllable, either yŏŏ [jʊ] or yuh [jə]. This also means that whenever u ends an unaccented syllable, the u tends to be pronounced either yŏŏ [jʊ] or yuh [jə].

The combination d + ue (–due–), s + ue (–sue–), or t + ue (–tue–) is often given the sound of do͞o [du], so͞o [su], to͞o [tu], although many careful speakers still retain the sound of "long" u, pronouncing such combinations as dyo͞o [dju], syo͞o [sju], tyo͞o [tju]. Examples: *due,* * *subdue,* * *sue,* *Tuesday.* * See § 40(4.10).

For the sound of "long" u + r, see § 40(4.9).

Consult also § 40(2,3,4).

33) –tū̆–, –dū̆– (not strictly a suffix). Unaccented –dū̆– and –tū̆– are most commonly juh [dʒə] and chuh [tʃə], except that when a vowel follows either –dū̆– or –tū̆– the tendency is to lengthen the sound to jŏŏ or jo͞o [dʒʊ or dʒu], chŏŏ or cho͞o [tʃʊ or tʃu]. See §§ 23(1.9), 40(11.9), 50(31). Examples: *adulation,* * *adulatory,* * *assiduous,* * *congratulate,* * *corduroy,* * *credulous,* * *deciduous,* * *educate,* * *fraudulent,* * *gradual,* * *grandeur,* * *individual,* * *pendulum,* * *procedure,* * *residual,* * *schedule,* * *verdure.* * For –tū̆–: *actual,* * *century,* * *constituency,* * *contemptuous,* * *effectual,* * *estuary,* * *fistula,* * *fortune,* * *impetuosity,* * *natural,* * *obituary,* *picturesque,* * *punctual,* * *Septuagint,* * *situate,* * *spiritual,* * *tortuous,* * *virtue.* *

34) Special Note (not strictly a suffix). No matter whether you use the SIMPLIFIED, or the DIACRITICAL, or the PHONETIC column—or two or all three— you must make sure that you understand the key or keys. For example, in the SIMPLIFIED column, remember that âi or A͡I (note the curved line or ligature on top) is always sounded "long" i (ī: IPA aɪ), as in *ice, wine, whine, aisle*. Again, ow is always sounded as in *cow* and *howl*. Thirdly, each single symbol always has the same sound. When the pronunciation of *talc* * (tălk; IPA tælk) is given in the SIMPLIFIED column as talk, pronounce the a so that it has the sound ă as in *hat, bat, rat*. In other words, even though the pronunciation for *talc* is given in the SIMPLIFIED column as talk, you must pronounce it as tălk [tælk], not as tôk (ô as in *orb, lord*), meaning "to speak or converse." One final example: *hyssop* * is shown as HIS uhp; and you must make certain that you sound the s as in *sing*, and not as the z sound in *zero* or *use* just because HIS looks like the pronoun *his*, which is pronounced hĭz. When in doubt, always refer to the keys—or consult the section [§] or sections [§§] listed under each word.

§ 51. RESTRICTION OF PRONUNCIATION

Note: See SPECIAL NOTES, III, "Variant Pronunciations," and IX, "Restriction of Pronunciation," pages xx–xxi, xxiv.

1) Anglicizing. When foreign words such as *chauffeur**** and *garage**** have become English in use, pronunciation, or character, they are said to have been Anglicized. As a rule it is not wise to pronounce a foreign word with its foreign sounds. Instead, look to these three principles: (a) Be guided by the usage in your social group. (b) Avoid tongue-twisting foreign expressions not easy for you. (c) When given a choice between a foreign pronunciation and an Anglicized pronunciation, prefer the latter. Examples: *entente,**** *liason,**** *Molière,**** *Richelieu,**** *Versailles.**** Exception: Musical terms, especially proper names, on the radio. See § 46.

2) Unacceptable Pronunciations. For one reason or another a pronunciation may not be sufficiently supported by educated speakers. Sometimes, one group of expert observers will label a pronunciation as *dialectal* (= unacceptable), while a second group will characterize it as *colloquial* (= acceptable: see item 3 below). For these and similar differences, you will have to use your own judgment, basing your conclusion on certain factors, such as indicated in Sections 4–8.

Not accepted as good English at the present time are the pronunciations labeled as follows:

    a) Archaic. Not used in daily speech; retained for special uses only. Examples: *blessed**** (p.t.), *soot,**** *strew.****

    b) Dialectal. A form of speech peculiar to a district or class, differing distinctively from the standard spoken form. Examples: *column,**** *deaf,**** *Halloween,**** *plague.****

    c) Formerly. In time past; once; heretofore—but not currently. Examples: *donkey,***[1]** *ergo,**** *quoth.****

    d) Loosely. Not closely or exactly enough to be acceptable. Example: *garage.**** See, however, § 25(4.2).

    e) Obsolete. No longer in use at the present time. See *archaic.* Example: *lilac.****

    f) Provincial. Countrified; rural; confined to a definite locality. Example: *idea.****

    g) Substandard. Below the standard of good speech. See §§ 33(2.1), 40(11.10).

3) Informal Spoken English. It would perhaps have been better to use only one term to designate colloquial cultivated English. However, although it is not always possible to draw precise lines of distinction between and among the various spoken forms of everyday talk, this manual has tried to indicate the different styles of colloquial. Every term below means a pronunciation is acceptable usage today. For other subject or usage lables, see (2) above and (11) below.

    a) Colloquial. Appropriate in ordinary conversation, including the intimate speech among educated people. Examples: *creek,**** *diabetes,**** *mademoiselle.****

    b) Familiar. Friendly utterance implying the freedom of continued acquaintance. Examples: *landlord,**** *sandwich.****

    c) Commonly. Generally used by plain people; unpretentiously. Examples: *Honolulu,**** *slake.****

    d) Popularly. Having general currency; used by, suited to, or intended for ordinary people. Examples: *Bologna,**** *kimono,**** *spouse.****

---

[1] The word *donkey* pronounced dŭng′kĭ [ˈdʌŋ kɪ] is generally recognized as older and less frequent. That pronunciation, however, is heard often in New York City, and appears to be predominant in southeastern Pennsylvania and southern New Jersey. In this compiler's opinion, it is a pronunciation in good usage. But the Webster-Merriam does not think so.

e) Established Errors. An "established error" in pronunciation is no longer an error. See §§ 1, 39(7.3). Example: *ye.**

4) British or Especially British. A word marked *B.* (British) or *especially British* is a pronunciation acceptable in American speech. See §§ 13(1), 24(9.2), 34(5.4). See *aesthetic,** *Alexandrine,** *amatory,** *banana,** *circumstance,** *dictionary,** *domicile, laboratory, mustache,** *nephew,** *papa,** *patrimony, saline,** *voluntary.**

5) Gaining Ground. Dictionaries can not always record every acceptable pronunciation. When a word is characterized as "gaining ground," it means that in the opinion of at least one major dictionary or of competent observers the pronunciation so marked may be used in ordinary conversational context. Examples: *absorb,** *aviator,** *citizen,** *immersion,** *program.*

6) Group Preferences or Subject Labels. Special pronunciations are distinguished by such self-explanatory terms or phrases as *among doctors,* or *lawyers,* or *natives; logic, tanning;* and the like. Examples: *alkaline,** *conduit,** *depot,** *donor,** *ensign,** *forceps,** *khaki,** *iodine,** *mainsail,** *recognizance,** *route,** *sumac,** *trio.**

7) Homographs and Homonyms. Homographs are two or more words having the same spelling, but different in derivation and meaning, such as *refuse* meaning "worthless matter; rubbish," and *refuse,* meaning "to say no to; decline." When homographs have different pronunciations, a meaning is given to distinguish each. On the other hand, such words as *bare* and *bear, meat* and *meet, their* and *there* are called homonyms because each pair, though spelled differently and having different meanings, is pronounced exactly alike. Sometimes homonyms are spelled the same way, as *bowl* (noun) meaning a "hollow, rounded dish," and *bowl* (noun) meaning a "wooden ball used in games." But whether spelled exactly alike or spelled differently, homonyms are always pronounced identically.

If you are referred to this section, examine the word in question. If a definition is given, you are to know that the word is to be pronounced as shown only for that meaning, for the word is a homograph—that is, one of two or more words spelled identically, but different in derivation and meaning. If no definition is given, it means that the word is a homonym—that is, one having the same pronunciation as another, but differing from it in origin, meaning, and, frequently, in spelling. Where no definition is given for a homograph, it denotes that the pronunciation is exactly the same for each member of the homograph group. Examples: *brogue,** *freeze,** *leave,** *irony,** *might,** *palmy,** *prayer,** *primer,** *recitative,** *rout,** *salve,** *singer,** *well.**

8) Order of Variant Pronunciations: I. The only purpose of such characterizations as *infrequently, not infrequently, sometimes, rarely,* and the like is to indicate relative familiarity of pronunciation. Every pronunciation so marked is acceptable; none is incorrect or substandard. See §§ 4–8 and also § 51(9). Examples: *baptize,** *bellows,** *compensate,** *ostrich,** *ptomaine,** *squalor,** *tirade.**

9) Order of Variant Pronunciations: II. When the variant pronunciations of a word are of approximately equal frequency and validity, they are printed without any such designations as given in "Order of Variant Pronunciations, I" [§ 51(8)]. For those pronunciations which present sources indicate have greater frequency than those identified in "Order of Variant Pronunciation, I," but less frequency than those not characterized in any way, the designations "often" or "frequently" is used. Again it must be emphasized that unless otherwise stated every pronunciation is valid and in cultivated use. See also SPECIAL NOTES, III, "Variant Pronunciations," pages xx-xxi. Examples: *apron,** *Bordeaux,** *Orpheus,** *syringe,** *thither.**

10) American Usage. The pronunciations given in this manual are those appropriate or in use among educated native-born speakers of the United States.

a) Regional Variants. We are accepting the traditional division into the three main regional speech areas.[1] See § 3.

b) "U.S." or "United States": While we make no attempt to record a pronunciation that prevails in different parts of the English-speaking world (remember that the italicized abbreviation *B.* means a preponderantly British pronunciation but one prevalent as well as acceptable among Americans), yet the occasional designation *U.S.* or *United States* indicates a spoken form distinctive in the United States of America. Example: *cornet.**

11) Miscellaneous Labels. Other self-explanatory terms or phrases show how, when, or where certain pronunciations, or pronunciations for specific meanings, are used. Among such identifications are "contrast," "emphasis," "generic name," "historical pronunciation," "French," "Latin," "among natives," "humorous," "jocular," "literary word," "poetic," "rhetorical," and shifting accent." For other group, subject, or usage distinctions, see number 3 above. Examples: *abstract,** *amen,** *chivalry,** *damned,** *doings,** *forecastle,** *exquisite,** *export,* *octopus, positively,** *Roosevelt,** *schoolman,** *tribune,** *wind.**

§ 52. NORMAL INTERPRETATION OF ENGLISH SPELLING

Certain spelling combinations of vowels and consonants often give in English the same speech sounds. Below is a short list of such combinations and the most common or most frequent interpretation of each. (For the sound values of prefixes and suffixes, see §§ 49 and 50; for the sound values of the spelling combinations that follow, consult the section or sections as indicated.)

SPELLING AND SECTION	NORMAL INTERPRETATION
au § 20(15)	as in *aught, haugh'ty; saw, crawl*
ay § 20(15)	as in *bay, play*
c § 20(1,2)	1) as s before e, i, y, as in *cel'er y, cit'y, cym'bal* 2) as k before any letter but e, i, y, or h (except in the combination ch, given below)
ch § 22(5,7)	a single sound as in *Chi'na, reach;* also for tch as in *catch'ing, stretch;* for te as in *right'eous* (ri'chŭs); for ti as in *Chris'tian, ques'tion.* See also j and k.
d § 23(1)	as in *do, wis'dom;* also for ed as in *burned.* See –ed.
du § 23(1.9)	almost a j sound, as in *ver'dure, grad'u al;* also for deu as in *gran'deur.*
ea § 24(17)	as in *dean, re veal'*
ear § 24(2)	as in *ear, dear, near*
–ed § 24(16.5)	a separate syllable, as in *want'ed;* otherwise as d, as in *burned.* See d above.
ee § 24(1)	as in *feet*
eu § 24(22)	"long" u as in *deuce, eu'lo gy*
f § 25(1)	as in *foot;* also for ph as in *phan'tom, Phil'ip, tel'e phone;* for gh as in *cough, laugh*

---

[1] While the general tendency is to consider the territory in New York State east of the Hudson River as falling within the Eastern zone, more than one phonetician—mindful of the heterogeneous language stocks of New York City and its immediate environs—regards the New York City area as a distinct unit.

SPELLING AND SECTION	NORNAL INTERPRETATION
g §§ 25(2), 26(2,5,8)	1) "hard" before a, o, u, l, and r, and at the end of a syllable, as in *gape, get, golf, gum, glance, gro'cer y, drug, jig;* also for gu in the same syllable before a, e, and i as in *guard, guess, guide;* for final gue as in *cat'a logue, plague, vogue;* for gh as in *ghost.* See gh; see ng.
§§ 25(3), 29(1)	2) "soft" g = j in Latin or Roman derivatives before e, i, or y as in *gen'er al, en'gine, ex ag'ger ate.* See j.
§ 25(5)	3) g is silent before final m or n, as in *sign, benign, diaphragm*
gh § 26(2)	Is sounded at the beginning of a syllable as "hard" g (see above), as in *a ghast', ghost;* also sounded as f as in *laugh.*
gn § 25(5)	When gn begins a word, the g is silent, as in *gnaw, gnome.* See kn.
gz, g-z §§ 25(3), 43(1.a)	for x as in *ex ist', anx i'e ty*
h § 27(2)	silent after a vowel in the same syllable, as in *bah, Mes si'ah, oh, rhu'barb, Sar'ah*
hw § 42(4)	for wh as in *what, wheel, whip*
ie § 28(2)	1) sounded as "long" i in the short and common words, as in *die, lie, pie, tie.* 2) sounded as "long" e when followed by a consonant in an accented syllable, as in *field, liege, re lieve'.*
igh § 28(2)	"long" i as in *high, nigh, sigh*
j § 29(1)	as in *joy;* also for "soft" g as in *gen'tle, venge'ful;* for ge and gi as in *pi'geon, re lig'ion;* for di as in *sol'dier;* for dg(e) as in *edge, lodge, lodg'ment.* See g ("soft").
k §§ 30(1), 20(2), 36	as in *key;* also for "hard" ch as in *char'ac ter, ep'och;* for "hard" c as in *cup;* for ck as in *sack;* for qu as in *con'quer, co quette';* for que as in *an tique'.*
kn § 30(1.5)	When kn begins a word, the k is silent, as in *knave, knew, knock, knucle.* See gn.
к (small capital); § 22(10); also "Foreign Sounds," page xxiii (under x)	for ch as in *ich, ach* (G.), *loch* (Sc.)
ks, k-s §§ 30(1.3), 43(1.b)	for x as in *vex, wax, ex'cel lent, per plex'*
ksh, k-sh § 43(1.d)	for x or xi as in *anx'ious, lux'u ry*
kw § 36	for qu as in *quaff, que'ry, Quin'cy, quo'tient*
mn §§ 32(3.1), 33(1.2)	When mn ends a syllable or a word, the n is silent, as in *col'umn, con demn', hymn, sol'emn.* But when m in one syllable is followed by n in the next syllable, the n is usually sounded— *col um'nar, con dem'na ble, hym'nal, sol'em nize.*
n §§ 33(1.1), 33(4.4)	as in *no, chin;* becomes ng [ŋ] before k (or "hard" c) or "hard" g in the same syllable— that is, give a g sound after n and before k (or "hard" c) or "hard" g, as in *ink, fin'ger, rank, can'ker, anx'ious, sanc'tion, young.* See ng [ŋ].

SPELLING AND SECTION	NORMAL INTERPRETATION
N (small capital) § 20(14); also "Foreign Sounds," page xxii	has no sound of its own, but indicates a nasal tone (as in French or Portuguese) of the preceding vowel, as in *bon* (bôN), *enfant* (än'fäN')
ng § 33(4.5)	a single nasal sound as in *sing, Eng'land;* also for ngue, as in *tongue;* for n before the sound of k (or "hard" c) or "hard" g (see under n) as in *Con'gress, e lon'gate, junc'tion, lin'ger, sin'gle, think, un'cle.* See n. As a rule, however, when n is in one syllable and k (or "hard" c) in the next syllable, or when n is in one syllable and "hard" g in the next syllable, each has its normal sound, as in *un kempt', in clu'sive, en graft', un gra'cious.*
oa § 34(16)	as in *boat, oats, soap*
oar § 34(3)	as in *oar, board, coarse, hoarse, soared*
oe § 34(17)	as in *doe, foe, toe, goes*
ö, oe § 34(15)	represented by û as in *hurt: schön* (shûn), *jeu* (zhû). See u below.
oi, oy §§ 34(19), 34(26)	as in *oil, joy*
oo § 34(20,21,22)	1) as in *tooth;* also as in *rude, ru'mor* 2) as in *foot;* also as in *pull, pul'pit*
ou, ow § 34(24,25)	as in *out, a bout', thou; cow.* See ow.
ow § 34(25)	as in *cow, now, scowl.* See ou.
oy § 34(26)	same as oi in oil: *boy, toy, enjoy, loyal*
ph § 35(4)	as f in *phantom.* See f.
qu § 36	as kw in *quick.*
que § 36	When que ends a word—as in *burlesque, unique* —the u and e are silent and the q is sounded as k.
s (always voiceless, or "sharp") § 38(2,13)	1) as in *sing;* also for "soft" c as in *cell, trace;* for ss as in *miss*
§ 38(3,4,5)	2) for voiced ("soft") s, see z below.
sc §§ 38(2,9), 38(10)	1) as s before e, i, and y (see c), as in *cell, dice, i'cy; scene, science, scythe* 2) as sk before a, o, u, l, and r—in other words, sc is like sk where c would be sounded k, as in *scale, scourge, scur ril'i ty, scle ro'sis, Scrip'ture*
sh § 38(7,11,12)	as in *shame, hush;* also for ch as in *chute, ma chine', chaise;* for ce as in *o'cean, crus ta'cean;* for ci as in *gra'cious, so'cial;* for sci as in *con'scious;* for s as in *sug'ar, sure;* for se as in *nau'seous;* for si as in *ex ten'sion;* for ss as in *is'sue;* for ssi as in *pas'sion;* for ti as in *at ten'tion, na'tion*
t §§ 39(1), 23(1.14)	as in *too;* also for –ed as in *baked, capped;* for th as in *thyme, Thomas, Thames*
tch § 22(5)	as in *batch, Dutch, wretch.* See ch.
th (voiceless) § 39(4)	as in *tooth.* More frequent than the voiced th.
th (voiced) § 39(5)	as in *then.* So pronounced especially when followed by e, as in *both'er, mouthe*

Spelling and Section	Normal Interpretation
ti § 39(8)	sh as in *am bi′tion, na′tion, pa′tience*
u §§ 40(7,8), 34(17), 24(22)	as in *hurt, fur′ther;* as in *her, fern, fir;* for German ö, oe, as in *schön* (shûn), *Goe′the* (gû tĕ); for French eu as in *jeu* (zhû), *seul* (sûl)
u § 40(9)	For German ü as in *für, grün, Sün′de;* for French u as in *du, lune, me nu′*
w § 42(1)	as in *witch;* also for u as in *as suage′* (ȧ swāj′), *per suade′;* for o in *choir* (kwīr)
x	for ks. See ks above.
y § 44(2,4)	as in *yes;* also for i as in *un′ion* (ūn′yŭn), *fa mil′iar* (fȧ mĭl′yẽr)
z §§ 45(1), 38(3,4,5)	as in *ze′ro;* also for voiced ("soft") s, as in *eas′y, is, hives, rouse, mu′sic, nears, whigs;* for x as in *xy′lo phone* or *xyl′o phone*
zh § 45(2)	for z as in *az′ure;* for zi as in *gla′zier;* for s as in *lei′sure, u′su al;* for si as in *de lu′sion, vi′sion;* for ssi as in *ab scis′sion;* for g as in *ga rage′, gen′re, mi rage′, rouge.* See "hard" g.

A MANUAL OF PRONUNCIATION

A

	SIMPLIFIED	DIACRITICAL	PHONETIC
a (indefinite article or adj.)	uh	*ȧ*	ə
	Emph. or hesitating: ay	*Emph. or hesitating:* ā	*Emph. or hesitating:* e

NOTE: The use of *ȧ* (uh; I.P.A.: ə), the unstressed form of the indefinite article "a," is in keeping with the natural or characteristic pattern of spoken English. When used to secure unnecessary emphasis, the stressed form *ā* (ay; I.P.A.: e) often connotes affectation, formalism, or the like.

	SIMPLIFIED	DIACRITICAL	PHONETIC
abandon (v.t.)	uh BAN duhn	*ȧ* băn′dŭn	ə 'bæn dən
—— (n.)	uh BAN duhn	*ȧ* băn′dŭn	ə 'bæn dən
	ah bahN DAWN	*ȧ*′bäN′dôN′ § 20(14)	*F.*, a bᾱ 'dɔ̃ [- 'dõ]
abash	uh BASH	*ȧ* băsh′	ə 'bæʃ
abbé	AB ay	ăb′ā	'æb e
	a BAY	*ȧ*′bā′	æ 'be
	ah BAY		*F.*, a 'be
abbey	AB i	ăb′ɪ	'æb ɪ
abdomen	ab DOH men	ăb dō′mĕn	æb 'do mɛn,
	AB duh muhn	ăb′dŏ mĕn § 47(3)	-mən, 'æb də mən, -mɛn
abdominal	ab DOM uh nuhl	ăb dŏm′ĭ năl	æb 'dam ə nəl,
	ab DOM i nuhl	ăb dŏm′ɪ năl	-ɪ nəl, -n̩, əb-; *ES also* -'dɒm-
Aberdeen	*ab* uhr DEEN	ăb′ĕr dēn′	ˌæb ɚ 'din; *ES* -ə 'din
abeyance	uh BAY uhns	*ȧ* bā′ăns	ə 'be əns
abhor	uhb HAWR	ăb hôr′	əb 'hɔr, æb-; *ES*
	ab HAWR	ăb hôr′ § 34(5)	-'hɔə(r)
abhorrent	uhb HAWR uhnt	ăb hôr′ĕnt	əb 'hɔr ənt,
	ab HAWR uhnt	ăb hôr′ĕnt	-'har-, -'hɒr-,
	uhb HOR uhnt	ăb hŏr′ĕnt	æb 'hɔr-,
	ab HOR uhnt	ăb hŏr′ĕnt § 34(5, 7)	-'har-, -'hɒr-
abject (adj.)	AB jekt	ăb′jĕkt	'æb dʒɛkt
	ab JEKT	ăb jĕkt′ § 11	æb 'dʒɛkt
—— (n.)	AB jekt	ăb′jĕkt	'æb dʒɛkt
abjure	ab JOOR	ăb jŏŏr′	æb 'dʒʊr, əb-;
	ab JOOR	ăb jŏŏr′ §§ 40(4), 48(2)	*ES* -'dʒʊə(r)
ablution	uhb LOO shuhn	ăb lū′shŭn	əb 'lu ʃən
	uhb LYOO shuhn		əb 'lju ʃən
	ab LOO shuhn	ăb lū′shŭn	æb 'lu ʃən
	ab LYOO shuhn	§§ 47(2), 48(2), 50(30, 32)	æb 'lju ʃən

abolition	*ab* uh LISH uhn	ăb′ŏ lĭsh′ŭn § 50(30)	ˌæb ə 'lɪʃ ən
abominably	uh BOM uh nuh bli uh BOM i nuh bli	*a* bŏm′*i* n*a* blĭ *a* bŏm′ĭ n*a* blĭ § 50(20)	ə 'bɑm ə nə blɪ, -'bɑm ɪ-, 'bɑm nə-; *ES* *also* -'bɒm-
aborigines	*ab* uh RIJ uh neez *ab* uh RIJ i neez	ăb′ŏ rĭj′*i* nēz ăb′ŏ rĭj′ĭ nēz	ˌæb ə 'rɪdʒ ə niz ˌæb ə 'rɪdʒ ɪ niz
about	uh BOWT § 50(34)	*a* bout′	ə 'baut
Abraham	AY bruh ham	ā′br*a* hăm	'e brə hæm, -həm
abscess	AB ses AB sis	ăb′sĕs ăb′sĭs § 24(5)	'æb sɛs 'æb sɪs
abscond	ab SKOND	ăb skŏnd′	æb'skɑnd, əb-; *ES also* -'skɒnd
absent (adj.)	AB suhnt AB s'nt	ăb′sĕnt ăb′ s'nt	'æb sənt 'æb sn̩t
—— (v.t.)	ab SENT	ăb sĕnt′	æb 'sɛnt, əb-
absentee	*ab* suhn TEE	ăb′sĕn tē′	ˌæb sən 'ti, -sn̩-
absolute	AB suh loot AB suh lyoot	ăb′sŏ lūt §§ 47(2), 48(2), 50(30, 32)	'æb sə lut, -ljut, -sl̩-
absolutely	AB suh loot li AB suh lyoot li	ăb′sŏ lūt lĭ §§ 48(2), 50(30, 32)	'æb sə lut lɪ, -ljut-, -sl̩-
	Emph. (*pop.*): *ab* suh LOOT li *ab* suh LYOOT li	*Emph.* (*pop.*): ăb′sŏ lūt′lĭ §§ 50(30, 32), 51(3, 11)	*Emph* (*pop.*): ˌæb sə 'lut lɪ ˌæb sə 'ljut lɪ
absolve	uhb SOLV ab SOLV *B.*, uhb ZOLV ab ZOLV	ăb sŏlv′ ăb sŏlv′ *B.*, ăb zŏlv′ ăb zŏlv′ § 47(2)	əb 'salv, æb-, -'sɒlv *B.*, əb 'zɒlv æb 'zɒlv
absorb	uhb SAWRB ab SAWRB *Gaining ground:* uhb ZAWRB ab ZAWRB	ăb sôrb′ ăb sôrb′ *Gaining ground:* ăb zôrb′ ăb zôrb′ § 51(5)	əb 'sɔrb, æb-; *ES* -'sɔəb *Gaining ground:* əb 'zɔrb, æb-; *ES* -'zɔəb
abstain	uhb STAYN ab STAYN	ăb stān′ ăb stān′	əb 'sten æb 'sten
abstemious	ab STEE mi uhs	ăb stē′mĭ ŭs § 50(25)	æb 'sti mɪ əs, əb-
abstinence	AB stuh nuhns AB sti nuhns	ăb′stĭ nĕns ăb′stĭ nĕns	'æb stə nəns 'æb stɪ nəns
abstract (adj.)	AB strakt ab STRAKT	ăb′străkt ăb străkt′ § 11	'æb strækt æb 'strækt
—— (n.)	AB strakt	ăb′străkt § 12	'æb strækt
—— (v.)	ab STRAKT	ăb străkt′	æb 'strækt

	SIMPLIFIED	DIACRITICAL	PHONETIC
—— (v.– also, "abridge"; trace title")	AB strakt	ăb′străkt § 51(11)	′æb strækt
abstractly	AB strakt li ab STRAKT li	ăb′străkt lĭ ăb strakt′lĭ §§ 47(2), 50(20)	′æb strækt lɪ æb ′strækt lɪ
abstruse	ab STROOS	ăb strōōs′ § 48(2)	æb ′strus, əb-
absurd	uhb SUHRD ab SUHRD	ŭb sûrd′ ăb sûrd′ § 20(10)	əb ′sɜd, æb-, -′zɜd; ES -′sɜd, -′zɜd
abuse (v.t.)	uh BYOOZ	ȧ būz′	ə ′bjuz
—— (n.)	uh BYOOS	ȧ būs′ § 38(4)	ə ′bjus
abusive	uh BYOO siv	ȧ bū′sĭv	ə ′bju sɪv
abut	uh BUHT	ȧ bŭt′	ə ′bʌt
abysmal	uh BIZ muhl	ȧ bĭz′măl	ə ′bɪz məl
abyss	uh BIS	ȧ bĭs′	ə ′bɪs
acacia	uh KAY shuh	ȧ kā′shȧ	ə ′ke ʃə
academic	ak uh DEM ik	ăk′ȧ dĕm′ĭk	ˌæk ə ′dɛm ɪk
academician	uh kad uh MISH uhn	ȧ kăd′ĕ mĭsh′ăn § 47(2)	əˌ kæd ə ′mɪʃ ən
academy	uh KAD uh mi	ȧ kăd′ĕ mĭ	ə ′kæd ə mɪ
accede	ak SEED	ăk sēd′	æk ′sid, ək-
accelerate	ak SEL uhr ayt ak SEL uh rayt	ăk sĕl′ĕr āt § 50(2)	æk ′sel ər et æk ′sel ə ret
accelerator	ak SEL uhr ay tuhr ak SEL uh ray tuhr	ăk sĕl′ĕr ā′tēr	æk ′sel ər ˌe tɚ, -ə ˌre-; ES -tə(r)
accent (n.)	AK sent B., AK suhnt	ăk′sĕnt B., ăk′sŭnt	′æk sent; B., ′æk sənt, -sṇt
—— (v.t.)	ak SENT AK sent	ăk sĕnt′ ăk′sĕnt §§ 12, 47(1), 51(4)	æk ′sent ′æk sent
accept	ak SEPT	ăk sĕpt′	æk ′sept, ɪk-, ək-
acceptable	ak SEP tuh b'l	ăk sĕp′tȧ b'l	æk ′sep tə bḷ, ɪk-, ək-
accepter	ak SEP tuhr	ăk sĕp′tēr	æk ′sep tɚ, -ɪk-, ək-; ES -tə(r)
access	AK ses	ăk′sĕs § 47(2)	′æk sɛs
accessary	ak SES uh ri	ăk sĕs′ȧ rĭ § 47(2)	æk ′sɛs ə rɪ, ək-
accessorily	ak SES uh ri li	ăk sĕs′ŏ rĭ lĭ § 50(20)	æk ′sɛs ə rɪ lɪ, ək-
accessory	ak SES uh ri	ăk sĕs′ŏ rĭ § 47(2)	æk ′sɛs ə rɪ, ək-
acclamation	ak luh MAY shuhn ak li MAY shuhn	ăk′lȧ mā′shŭn ăk′lĭ mā′shŭn § 50(20)	ˌæk lə ′me ʃən ˌæk lɪ ′me ʃən

accomplishment	uh KOM plish muhnt	ă kŏm′plĭsh mĕnt § 50(22)	ə ˈkɑm plɪʃ mənt; *ES also* -ˈkɒm-
accost	uh KAWST uh KOST	ă kŏst′ § 34(7)	ə ˈkɔst ə ˈkɒst
account	uh KOWNT § 50(34)	ă kount′	ə ˈkaʊnt
accouter	uh KOO tuhr	ă kōō′tĕr	ə ˈku tɚ; *ES* -tə(r)
accredit	uh KRED it	ă krĕd′ĭt	ə ˈkrɛd ɪt
accrue	uh KROO	ă krōō′ § 22(2)	ə ˈkru, æ-
accumulate (v.)	uh KYOO myŏŏ layt	ă kū′mŭ lāt § 50(32)	ə ˈkju mjʊ let, -mjə-, -mju-
—— (adj.)	uh KYOO myŏŏ lit	ă kū′mŭ lăt § 20(8, 9)	ə ˈkju mjʊ lɪt, -mjə-, -mju-
accuracy	AK yŏŏ ruh si	ăk′û rȧ si § 47(2)	ˈæk jʊ rə sɪ, -jə-, -ju-
accurate	AK yŏŏ rit	ăk′û rĭt	ˈæk jʊ rɪt, -jə-, -ju-
accursed	uh KUHR sed uh KUHR sid uh KUHRST	ă kûr′sĕd ă kûr′sĭd ă kûrst′ §§ 24(5), 47(2)	ə ˈkɝ sed, -sɪd, ə ˈkɝst; *ES also* -ˈkɜ-, -ˈkɜst
accused	uh KYOOZD	ă kūzd′ § 50(4)	ə ˈkjuzd
acetic	uh SEE tik uh SET ik	ă sē′tĭk ă sĕt′ĭk § 47(3)	ə ˈsi tɪk, æ ˈsi-, ə ˈsɛt ɪk, æ ˈsɛt-
acetylene	uh SET uh leen uh SET i leen	ă sĕt′ĭ lēn ă sĕt′ĭ lēn § 47(2)	ə ˈsɛt ə lin, -ɪ lɪn, -ˈsɛt l̩-
achievement	uh CHEEV muhnt	ȧ chēv′mĕnt § 50(22)	ə ˈtʃiv mənt
Achilles	uh KIL eez	ȧ kĭl′ēz	ə ˈkɪl iz
acid	AS id	ăs′ĭd § 22(1)	ˈæs ɪd
acidity	uh SID uh ti uh SID i ti	ă sĭd′ĭ tĭ ă sĭd′ĭ tĭ	ə ˈsɪd ə tɪ, -ˈsɪd ɪ-, æ ˈsɪd-
acme	AK mi AK mee	ăk′mĕ	ˈæk mɪ ˈæk mi
acorn	AY kawrn AY kuhrn	ā′kôrn ā′kĕrn § 47(2)	ˈe kɔrn, -kɚn; *ES* -kɔən, -kən
acquaint	uh KWAYNT	ă kwānt′	ə ˈkwent
acquiesce	*ak* wi ES	ak′wĭ ĕs′	ˌæk wɪ ˈɛs
acquiescence	*ak* wi ES uhns	ăk′wĭ ĕs′ĕns	ˌæk wɪ ˈɛs əns, -n̩s
acrid	AK rid	ăk′rĭd	ˈæk rɪd
acrimony	AK ruh *moh* ni AK ri *moh* ni B., AK ri muhn i	ăk′rĭ mō′nĭ ăk′rĭ mō′nĭ B., ăk′rĭ mŭn ĭ § 51(4)	ˈæk rə ˌmo nɪ ˈæk rɪ ˌmo nɪ B., ˈæk rɪ mən ɪ
across	uh KRAWS uh KROS	ȧ krŏs′ §§ 34(7) 39(3), 47(2)	ə ˈkrɔs ə ˈkrɒs

	SIMPLIFIED	DIACRITICAL	PHONETIC
activity	ak TIV uh ti	ăk tĭv′ĭ tĭ	æk ′tɪv ə tɪ
	ak TIV i ti	ăk tĭv′ĭ tĭ	æk ′tɪv ɪ tɪ
acts	akts	ăkts §§ 48(3), 50(6)	ækts
actual	AK chŏŏ uhl	ăk′tû ăl	′æk tʃʊ əl
	AK tyŏŏ uhl	§§ 47(1) 50(33)	′æk tjʊ əl
actually	AK chŏŏ uhl i	ăk′tû ăl lĭ	′æk tʃʊ əl ɪ
	AK tyŏŏ uhl i	§ 50(20, 33)	′æk tjʊ əl ɪ
acumen	uh KYOO men	ă kū′měn	ə kju mɛn, -mɪn
adage	AD ij	ăd′ĭj	′æd ɪdʒ
adamant	AD uh mant	ăd′á mănt	′æd ə mænt
	B., AD uh muhnt	B., ăd′á mănt	B., ′æd ə mənt
adamantine	ad uh MAN tin	ăd′á măn′tĭn	ˌæd ə ′mæn tɪn
	ad uh MAN tain	ăd′á măn′tīn	ˌæd ə ′mæn taɪn
	ad uh MAN teen § 50(34)	ăd′á măn′tēn	ˌæd ə ′mæn tin
adaptation	ad ap TAY shuhn	ăd′ăp tā′shăn	ˌæd æp ′te ʃən, -əp-
addict (v.)	uh DIKT	ă dĭkt′	ə ′dɪkt
—— (n.)	AD ikt	ăd′ĭkt §§ 12, 47(1)	′æd ɪkt
address (v.)	uh DRES	ă drĕs′ § 12	ə ′drɛs
—— (n.)	uh DRES	ă drĕs′	ə ′drɛs
	AD res	ăd′rĕs	′æd rɛs
—— (n.–also, "written directions on a letter, or "place to which mail is sent," esp.)	AD res	ăd′rĕs §§ 47(1), 51(11)	′æd rɛs
adduce	uh DYOOS	ă dūs′ §§ 48(2), 50(32)	ə ′djus
	uh DOOS		ə ′dus
adept (n.)	AD ept	ăd′ĕpt	′æd ɛpt
	uh DEPT	ă dĕpt′	ə ′dɛpt
—— (adj.)	uh DEPT	ă dĕpt′ § 47(2)	ə ′dɛpt
adequate	AD i kwit	ăd′ĕ kwĭt	′æd ɪ kwɪt, ′æd ə-
adherence	ad HĬER uhns	ăd hĕr′ĕns	æd ′hɪər əns,
	ad HIR uhns	§ 24(2)	-′hɪr-, -′hir-,
	ad HEER uhns	ăd hēr′ĕns	əd-; ES -′hɪər-
adieu	uh DYOO	á dū′	ə ′dju
	uh DOO	F., à dyû′	ə ′du
adipose	AD i pohs	ăd′ĭ pōs § 47(2)	′æd ɪ pos, ′æd ə-
Adirondacks	ad uh RON daks	ăd′ĭ rŏn′dăks	ˌæd ə ′rɑn dæks,
	ad i RON daks	ăd′ĭ rŏn′dăks	ˌæd ɪ-; ES also -′rɒn-
adjacent	uh JAY suhnt	ă jā′sĕnt	ə ′dʒe sənt, -sn̩t
adjoin	uh JOIN	ă join′	ə ′dʒɔɪn
adjourn	uh JUHRN	ă jûrn′	ə ′dʒɜn; ES ə ′dʒɜn
adjudge	uh JUHJ	ă jŭj′	ə ′dʒʌdʒ

	SIMPLIFIED	DIACRITICAL	PHONETIC
adjunct	AJ uhngkt	ăj′ŭngkt	′ædʒ ʌŋkt
adjust	uh JUHST	ă jŭst′	ə ′dʒʌst
adjutant	AJ ŏŏ tuhnt	ăj′ŏŏ tănt	′ædʒ ʊ tənt, ′ædʒ ə-
administrative	uhd MIN is *tray* tiv	ăd mĭn′ĭs trā′tĭv	əd ′mɪn ɪs ˌtre tɪv, æd ′mɪn-, -ɪ ˌstre-, -ə ˌstre-
	uhd MIN i *stray* tiv		
	ad MIN is *tray* tiv	ăd mĭn′ĭs trā′tĭv	
	ad MIN i *stray* tiv	§ 51(4)	
	B., uhd MIN is truh tiv	B., ăd mĭn′ĭs trȧ tĭv	B., əd ′mɪn ɪs trə tɪv
administrator	uhd MIN is *tray* tuhr	ăd mĭn′ĭs trā′tĕr § 47(2)	əd ′mɪn ɪs ˌtre tɚ, -ɪ ˌstre-, -ə ˌstre-, -æd-; ES -tə(r)
	uhd MIN i *stray* tuhr		
admirable	AD muh ruh b′l	ăd′mĭ rȧ b′l	′æd mə rə bl̩
	AD mi ruh b′l	ăd′mĭ rȧ′b′l	′æd mɪ rə bl̩
admiral	AD muh ruhl	ăd′mĭ răl	′æd mə rəl
	AD mi ruhl	ăd′mĭ răl	′æd mɪ rəl
admiralty	AD muh ruhl ti	ăd′mĭ răl tĭ	′æd mə rəl tɪ
	AD mi ruhl ti	ăd′mĭ răl tĭ	′æd mɪ rəl tɪ
admiration	ad muh RAY shuhn	ăd′mĭ rā′shŭn	ˌæd mə ′re ʃən
	ad mi RAY shuhn	ăd′mĭ rā′shŭn § 50(30)	ˌæd mɪ ′re ʃən
admit	uhd MIT	ăd mĭt′	əd ′mɪt
	ad MIT	ăd mĭt′	æd ′mɪt
adobe	uh DOH bi	ȧ dō′bĭ	ə ′do bɪ
adolescent	ad uh LES uhnt	ăd′ŏ lĕs′ĕnt	ˌæd ə ′les ənt, -′lesn̩t, ˌæd l̩′es-
Adonis	uh DOH nis	ȧ dō′nĭs	ə ′do nɪs
	uh DON is	ȧ dŏn′ĭs § 47(1)	′dɑn-, -dɒn-
adoration	ad uh RAY shuhn	ăd′ŏ rā′shŭn	ˌæd ə ′re ʃən
adore	uh DOHR	ȧ dōr′ §§ 34(3),	ə ′dor, ə ′dɔr; ES
	uh DAWR	47(1)	ə ′doə(r), E also ə ′dɔə(r)
Adriatic	ay dri AT ik	ā′drĭ ăt′ĭk	ˌe drɪ ′æt ɪk
	ad ri AT ik	ăd′rĭ ăt′ĭk	ˌæd rɪ ′æt ɪk
adroit	uh DROIT	ȧ droit′	ə ′drɔɪt
adulation	aj ŏŏ LAY shuhn	ăd′ū lā′shŭn	ˌædʒ ʊ ′le ʃən,
	ad yŏŏ LAY shuhn	§50(33)	ˌædʒ ə-, ˌæd jʊ-, -jə-
adulatory	AJ ŏŏ luh *toh* ri	ăd′ū lȧ tō′rĭ	′ædʒ ʊ lə ˌto rɪ,
	AJ ŏŏ luh *taw* ri		-ˌtɔ rɪ, ′ædʒ ə-,
	B., AJ ŏŏ luh tuhr i	B., ăd′û lȧ tĕr ĭ	′æd jʊ-, -jə-; B.,
	AD yŏŏ luh *toh* ri	§§ 34(3),	-tə rɪ
	AD yŏŏ luh *taw* ri	50(33), 51(4)	
	B., AD yŏŏ luh tuhr i		

	SIMPLIFIED	DIACRITICAL	PHONETIC
adult	uh DUHLT AD *uhlt*	*a* dŭlt′ ăd′ŭlt §§ 40(6), 47(3)	ə ′dʌlt ′æd ʌlt
advance	uhd VANS uhd VAHNS ad VANS ad VAHNS	ăd vàns′ ăd vàns′ §§ 20(5), 47(1)	əd ′væns, æd-; *E* *also* -′vans, -′vɑns
advantage	uhd VAN tij uhd VAHN tij ad VAN tij ad VAHN tij	ăd vàn′tĭj ăd vàn′tĭj §§ 20(5), 47(1)	əd ′væn tɪdʒ, æd-; *E also* -′van-, -′vɑn-
advantageous	*ad* vuhn TAY juhs	ăd′văn tā′jŭs	ˌæd vən ′te dʒəs
advent, Advent	AD vent *B.,* AD vuhnt	ăd′vĕnt *B.,* ăd′vĕnt	′æd vent *B.,* ′æd vənt
adventitious	*ad* ven TISH uhs	ăd′vĕn tĭsh′ŭs	ˌæd ven ′tɪ ʃəs
adventure	uhd VEN chuhr uhd VEN tyuhr ad VEN chuhr ad VEN tyuhr	ăd vĕn′tûr ăd vēn′tûr §§ 47(1), 50(31)	əd ′ven tʃɚ, -tjɚ, æd-; *ES* -tʃə(r), -tjə(r)
adversary	AD vuhr *ser* i *B.,* AD vuhr suhr i	ăd′vĕr sĕr′ĭ *B.,* ăd′vĕr sĕr ĭ §§ 13, 20(2), 24(9), 51(4)	′æd vɚ ˌser ɪ; *ES* -və-; *B.,* -sə rɪ
adverse (adj.)	uhd VUHRS ad VUHRS AD *vuhrs*	ăd vûrs′ ăd vûrs′ ăd′vûrs §§ 40(6), 47(2)	əd ′vɝs, æd-, ′æd vɝs; *ES also* -′vɝs, -′vɜs
adversely	uhd VUHRS li ad VUHRS li AD *vuhrs* li	ăd vûrs′lĭ ăd vûrs′lĭ ăd′vûrs lĭ §§ 40(6), 50(20)	əd ′vɝs lɪ, æd-, ′æd vɝs lɪ; *ES* *also* -′vɝs-, -′vɜs-
advertise	AD vuhr t͡aiz *ad* vuhr TAĪZ § 50(34)	ăd′vĕr tīz ăd′vĕr tīz′ § 47(2)	′æd vɚ taɪz, ˌæd vɚ ′taɪz; *ES* -və-
advertisement	*ad* vuhr TAĪZ muhnt uhd VUHR tiz muhnt uhd VUHR tis muhnt *ad* VUHR tis muhnt	ad′vĕr tīz′mĕnt ăd vûr′tĭz mĕnt ăd vûr′tĭs mĕnt ăd′vûr′tĭs mĕnt § 47(3)	ˌæd vɚ ′taɪz mənt, əd ′vɝ tɪz-, -′vɝ tɪs-, ˌæd ′vɝ tɪs-; *ES* ˌæd və-, *also* -′vɝ-
advice	uhd VA͡IS ad VA͡IS	ăd vīs′ ăd vīs′	əd ′vaɪs æd ′vaɪs
advise	uhd VA͡IZ ad VA͡IZ	ăd vīz′ ăd vīz′ § 38(4)	əd ′vaɪz æd ′vaɪz
advocacy	AD vuh kuh si	ăd′vŏ kȧ sĭ	′æd və kə sɪ
Aegean	i JEE uhn ee JEE uhn	ĕ jē′ăn ē jē′ăn	ɪ ′dʒi ən i ′dʒi ən
aegis, egis	EE jis	ē′jĭs § 20(12)	′i dʒɪs

	SIMPLIFIED	DIACRITICAL	PHONETIC
Aeneid (The)	i NEE id ee NEE id EE ni id	ĕ nē′ĭd ē nē′ĭd ē′nĕ ĭd	ɪ 'ni ɪd, i 'ni-, 'i nɪ-, -əd
aeon, eon	EE uhn EE on	ē′ŏn ē′ŏn	'i ən, -ɑn; *ES also* 'i ɒn
aerate, aërate	AY uhr ayt AY uh rayt *B.,* EHR ayt	ā′ĕr āt § 47(1), 51(4) *B.,* âr′āt	'e ər et 'e ə ret *B.,* 'ɛr et, 'ær-; *ES* 'æ ə ret, *E* *also* 'ɛə ret
aerating, **aërating** (See *"aerate."*)	AY uhr *ayt* ing AY uh *rayt* ing *B.,* EHR ayt ing	ā′ĕr āt′ĭng *B.,* âr′āt ĭng	'e ər ˌet ɪŋ 'e ə ˌret ɪŋ *B.,* 'ɛr et ɪŋ, 'ær-; *ES* 'æə ret-, *E* *also* 'ɛə ret-
aerial, **aërial** (n.)	EHR i uhl	âr′ĭ ăl	'ɛr ɪ əl, 'ær-; *ES* 'æə rɪ-, *E also* 'ɛə rɪ-
—— (adj.)	ay ĬER i uhl ay IR i uhl ay EER i uhl EHR i uhl	ā ẽr′ĭ ăl §§ 24(2), 47(1) ā ēr′ĭ ăl âr′ĭ ăl	e 'ɪər ɪ əl, e 'ɪr-, e 'ir-, 'ɛr ɪ əl, 'ær-; *ES* 'æə rɪ-, *E* *also* 'ɛə rɪ-
aeronaut, **aëronaut**	EHR uh nawt AY uhr uh nawt	âr′ŏ nôt § 47(3) ā′ĕr ŏ nôt	'ɛr ə nɔt, 'ær-, 'e ər ə nɔt, 'e ə rə 'nɔt; *ES* æə rə-, *E also* 'ɛə rə-
Aeschylus	ES ki luhs *B.,* EES ki luhs	ĕs′kĭ lŭs *B.,* ēs′kĭ lŭs § 51(4)	'ɛs kɪ ləs, -kə- *B.,* 'is kɪ ləs
Aesop	EE sop	ē′sŏp	'i sɑp, -səp; *ES* *also* -sɒp
aesthetic, **esthetic**	es THET ik *B.,* ees THET ik	ĕs thĕt′ĭk *B.,* ēs thĕt′ĭk §§ 20(12), 51(4)	ɛs 'θɛt ɪk *B.,* is 'θɛt ɪk
affect	uh FEKT	ă fĕkt′	ə 'fɛkt
affiance	uh FAI uhns § 50(34)	ă fī′ăns	ə 'faɪ əns
affidavit	af uh DAY vit af i DAY vit	ăf ĭ dā′vĭt ăf ĭ dā′vĭt	æf ə 'de vɪt æf ɪ 'de vɪt
affix (v.t.)	uh FIKS	ă fĭks′	ə 'fɪks
—— (n.)	AF iks	ăf′ĭks § 12	'æf ɪks
affluence	AF loo uhns AF lyoo uhns	ăf′lû ĕns §§ 40(11), 48(2), 50(32)	'æf lʊ əns, -lu-, -ljʊ-, -lju-
affluent	AF loo uhnt AF lyoo uhnt	ăf′lû ĕnt §§ 40(4), 48(2), 50(32)	'æf lʊ ənt, -lu-, -ljʊ-, -lju-
afford	uh FOHRD uh FAWRD	ă fōrd′ §§ 34(3), 47(1)	ə 'ford, ə 'fɔrd; *ES* ə 'foəd, *E* *also* ə 'fɔəd

	SIMPLIFIED	DIACRITICAL	PHONETIC
Afghanistan	af GAN i stan af *gahn* i STAHN	ăf găn′ĭ stăn ăf găn′ĭ stän′	æf 'gæn ɪ stæn æf ˌgɑn ɪ 'stɑn
after	AF tuhr AHF tuhr	åf′tẽr § 20(5)	'æf tɚ; *ES* -tə(r), *E also* 'af-, 'ɑf-
afternoon (n.)	*af* tuhr NOON *ahf* tuhr NOON	åf′tẽr nōōn′ § 20(5)	ˌæf tɚ 'nun; *ES* -tə-, *E also* ˌaf-, ˌɑf-
—— (adj.)	AF tuhr *noon* AHF tuhr *noon*	åf′tẽr nōōn′ § 11	'æf tɚ ˌnun; *ES* -tə-, *E also* 'af-, 'ɑf-
again	uh GEN B. (*and also poet.*): uh GAYN	å gĕn′ § 47(2) B. (*and also poet.*): å gän′ § 51(4, 11)	ə 'gɛn B. (*and also poet.*): ə 'gen
against	uh GENST B. (*and also poet.*): uh GAYNST	å gĕnst′ § 39(3) B. (*and also poet.*): å gänst′ §51(4,11)	ə 'gɛnst B. (*and also poet.*): ə 'genst
agape ("*gaping*")	uh GAYP uh GAP uh GAHP	å gāp′ å găp′ å gäp′ § 47(3)	ə 'gep ə 'gæp ə 'gɑp
Agassiz (**L. J. R.**)	AG uh si	ăg′å sĕ	'æg ə sɪ
agate	AG it AG uht	ăg′ĭt ăg′åt § 47(1)	'æg ɪt 'æg ət
aged—"*old; well advanced in age*"	AY jed AY jid	ā′jĕd ā′jĭd § 24(5)	'e dʒed 'e dʒɪd
—— " *of the age of; (of an animal) past the age of maturity*"	ayjd	ājd	edʒd
—— in comp.	ayjd	ājd	edʒd
aggrandize	AG ruhn da͡iz uh GRAN da͡iz § 50(34)	ăg′răn dīz ă grăn′dīz	'æg rən daɪz ə 'græn daɪz
aggravate	AG ruh vayt	ăg′rå vāt	'æg rə vet
aggregate (n., adj.)	AG ri git AG ri gayt	ăg′rĕ găt ăg ′rĕ gāt § 20(8)	'æg rɪ gɪt 'æg rɪ get
—— (v.)	AG ri gayt	ăg′rĕ gāt § 20(8, 9)	'æg rɪ get
aghast	uh GAST uh GAHST	å gàst′ §§ 20(5), 26(2)	ə 'gæst; *E also* ə 'gast, ə 'gɑst
agile	AJ il AJ a͡il § 50(34)	ăj′ĭl ăj′ĭl §§ 28(5), 47(1)	'ædʒ ɪl, -əl, -aɪl
agitate	AJ uh tayt AJ i tayt	ăj′ĭ tāt ăj′ĭ tāt	'ædʒ ə tet 'ædʒ ɪ tet
agrarian	uh GREHR i uhn uh GRAY ri uhn	å grâr′ĭ ăn § 20(2)	ə 'grɛr ɪ ən, ə 'gre rɪ-; *ES* *also* ə 'grɛə rɪ-

agriculture	AG ri *kuhl* chuhr AG ri *kuhl* tyuhr	ăg′rĭ kŭl′tûr §§ 47(1), 50(31)	'æg rɪ ˌkʌl tʃɚ, -tjɚ; ES -tʃə(r), -tjə(r)
ague	AY gyoo	ā′gū	'e gju
aide-de-camp, aid-de-camp	AYD duh *kamp* AYD duh KAMP AYD duh KAHN *F.*, ed duh KAHN	ād′dĕ kămp′ ād′dĕ kămp′ ād′dĕ kän′ *F.*, ĕd′dĕ kän′ § 47(1)	'ed də ˌkæmp 'ed də 'kæmp 'ed də 'kɑ̃ *F.*, ɛd də 'kɑ̃
aigrette	ay GRET *ay* GRET AY gret e GRET	ā grĕt′ ā′grĕt′ ā′grĕt å grĕt′ § 47(1)	e 'gret ˌe 'gret 'e gret ɛ 'gret
ailment	AYL muhnt	āl′mĕnt	'el mənt
air	ehr	âr	ɛr, ær; ES æə(r), E also ɛə(r)
aisle	ai͡l § 50(34)	īl § 38(2)	aɪl
Ajaks	AY jaks	ā′jăks	'e dʒæks
Akron	AK ruhn	ăk′rŭn	'æk rən
Alabama	*al* uh BAM uh *al* uh BAH muh	ăl′*å* băm′*å* ăl′*å* bä′m*å*	ˌæl ə 'bæm ə ˌæl ə 'bɑ mə
alabaster	AL uh *bas* tuhr AL uh *bahs* tuhr	ăl′*å* băs′tēr §§ 20(5), 47(2)	'æl ə ˌbæs tɚ; ES -tə(r), E also -ˌbas-, -ˌbɑs-
alarm	uh LAHRM	*å* lärm′	ə 'lɑrm; ES ə 'lɑːm, E also ə 'lɑːm
alas	uh LAS uh LAHS	*å* lås′ § 20(5)	ə 'læs; E also ə 'las, ə 'lɑs
albeit (arch.)	awl BEE it	ôl bē′ĭt	ɔl 'bi ɪt
albino	al BAI͡ noh *B.*, al BEE noh § 50(34)	ăl bī′nō *B.*, ăl bē′nō §§ 47(3), 51(4)	æl 'baɪ no *B.*, æl 'bi no
albumen	al BYOO men	ăl bū′mĕn	æl 'bju mɛn, -mɪn, -mən
albumin	al BYOO min	ăl bū′mĭn	æl 'bju mɪn, -mən
alchemist	AL ki mist	ăl′kĕ mĭst	'æl kɪ mɪst, -kə-
alchemy	AL ki mi	ăl′kĕ mĭ	'æl kɪ mɪ, -kə-
alcove	AL kohv	ăl′kōv	'æl kov
Alden (John)	AWL den AWL duhn AWL din	ôl′dĕn ôl′dĕn ôl′dĭn	'ɔl dɛn 'ɔl dən 'ɔl dɪn
alder	AWL duhr	ôl′dēr	'ɔl dɚ; ES -də(r)
alert	uh LUHRT	*å* lûrt′	ə 'lɝt; ES also ə 'lɜt

Alexandrine
  ("*verse*")
	al eg ZAN drin
	B., *al* eg ZAN
	  drai͡n
	  § 50(34)
		ăl′ĕg zăn′drĭn
		B., ăl′ĕg zăn′drīn
		§§ 28(6), 47(2),
		51(4)
			ˌæl ɛg 'zæn drɪn,
			ˌɛl ɪg-; *B.*,
			-draɪn

algebra	AL ji bruh	ăl′jĕ br*a*	'æl dʒɪ brə
algebraic	*al* ji BRAY ik	al′jĕ brā′ĭk	ˌæl dʒɪ 'bre ɪk
alias	AY li uhs	ā′lĭ *ă*s	'e lɪ əs
alibi	AL uh bai͡	ăl′*i* bī	'æl ə baɪ
	AL i bai͡ § 50(34)	ăl′ĭ bī	'æl ɪ baɪ
alien	AYL yuhn	āl′yĕn	'el jən
	AY li uhn	ā′lĭ ĕn §§ 28(9), 47(2)	'e lɪ ən
alienate	AYL yuhn ayt	āl′yĕn āt	'el jən et
	AY li uhn ayt	ā′lĭ ĕn āt	'e lɪ ən et
aliment (n.)	AL uh muhnt	ăl′*i* mĕnt	'æl ə mənt
	AL i muhnt	ăl′ĭ mĕnt	'æl ɪ mənt
—— (v.)	AL uh ment	ăl′*i* mĕnt	'æl ə mɛnt
	AL i ment	ăl′ĭ mĕnt	'æl ɪ mɛnt
alimentary	*al* uh MEN tuh ri	ăl′*i* mĕn′t*a* rĭ	ˌæl ə 'mɛn tə rɪ,
	al i MEN tuh ri	ăl′ĭ mĕn′t*a* rĭ	ˌæl ɪ-, -trɪ
alkali	AL kuh lai͡	ăl′k*a* lī	'æl kə laɪ
	AL kuh li § 50(34)	ăl′k*a* lĭ § 47(2)	'æl kə lɪ
alkaline	AL kuh lain͡	ăl′k*a* līn	'æl kə laɪn
	AL kuh lin § 50(34)	ăl′k*a* lĭn § 47(3)	'æl kə lɪn
	Among chemists, gen.:	*Among chemists, gen.:*	*Among chemists, gen.:*
	AL kuh lin	ăl′k*a* lĭn § 51(6)	'æl kə lɪn
allege	uh LEJ	*a* lĕj′	ə 'lɛdʒ
alleged	uh LEJD	*a* lĕjd′	ə 'lɛdʒd
allegedly	uh LEJ ed li	*a* lĕj′ĕd lĭ § 50(20)	ə 'lɛdʒ ɛd lɪ, -ɪd lɪ
allegiance	uh LEE juhns	*a* lē′jăns § 47(2)	ə 'li dʒəns
alley	AL i	ăl′ĭ	'æl ɪ
allied	uh LAID͡ § 50(34)	*a* līd′	ə 'laɪd
Allies,	uh LAIZ͡	*a* līz′	ə 'laɪz
allies	AL ai͡z § 50(34)	ăl′ĭz § 50(6)	'æl aɪz
allow	uh LOW § 50(34)	*a* lou′	ə 'laʊ
alloy (n.)	uh LOI	*a* loi′	ə 'lɔɪ
	AL oi	ăl′oi	'æl ɔɪ
—— (v.)	uh LOI	*a* loi′ § 12	ə 'lɔɪ
allude	uh LOOD	*a* lūd′ §§ 48(2), 50(32)	ə 'lud
	uh LYOOD		ə 'ljud
allure	uh LOOR	*a* lūr′ §§ 40(2), 48(2), 50(32)	ə 'lʊr, ə 'ljʊr; *ES*
	uh LYOOR		ə 'lʊə(r), ə 'ljʊə(r)
allusion	uh LOO zhuhn	*a* lū′zhŭn §§ 48(2), 50(28, 32)	ə 'lu ʒən,
	uh LYOO zhuhn		ə 'lju-, æ-
ally (v.)	uh LAI͡ § 50(34)	*a* lī′ § 12	ə 'laɪ

	SIMPLIFIED	DIACRITICAL	PHONETIC
—— (n.)	uh LAI͡	ă lī′	ə 'laɪ
	AL ai͡ § 50(34)	ăl′ī § 47(1)	'æl aɪ
almanac	AWL muh nak	ôl′má năk	'ɔl mə næk
almond	AH muhnd	ä′mănd	'ɑ mənd
	AM uhnd	ăm′ŭnd	'æm ənd
	AL muhnd	ăl′mŏnd § 47(3)	'æl mənd
almost	AWL mohst	ôl′mōst § 11	'ɔl most
	Emph. or alone, also:	*Emph. or alone, also:*	*Emph. or alone, also:*
	awl MOHST	ôl mōst′ § 51(11)	ɔl 'most
alms	ahmz	ämz §§ 48(3), 50(6)	ɑmz
along	uh LAWNG	á lông′ §§ 34(7), 47(2)	ə 'lɔŋ
	uh LONG		ə 'lɒŋ
aloof	uh LOOF	á lōōf′	ə 'luf
aloud	uh LOWD § 50(34)	á loud′	ə 'laʊd
alpaca	al PAK uh	ăl păk′á	æl 'pæk ə
alpine, Alpine	AL pai͡n	ăl′pīn	'æl paɪn
	AL pin § 50(34)	ăl′pĭn § 47(3)	'æl pɪn
already	awl RED i	ôl rĕd′ĭ § 11	ɔl 'red ɪ
altercate	AWL tuhr kayt	ôl′tẽr kāt	'ɔl tɚ ket, 'æl-;
	AL tuhr kayt	ăl′tẽr kāt	ES -tə-
altercation	*awl* tuhr KAY shuhn	ôl′tẽr kā′shŭn	ˌɔl tɚ 'ke ʃən,
	al tuhr KAY shuhn	ăl′tẽr kā′shŭn § 47(3)	ˌæl-; ES -tə-
alternate (v.)	AWL tuhr nayt	ôl′tẽr nāt	'ɔl tɚ net,
	AL tuhr nayt	ăl′tẽr nāt §§ 20(8, 9), 47(2)	'æl-; ES -tə-
—— (n., adj.)	AWL tuhr nit	ôl′tẽr nĭt	'ɔl tɚ nɪt, æl-,
	AL tuhr nit	ăl′tẽr nĭt	ɔl 'tɝ nɪt, æl-;
	awl TUHR nit	ôl tûr′nĭt	ES -tə-, *also*
	al TUHR nit	ăl tûr′nĭt § 47(3)	-'tɝ-
alternating	AWL tuhr *nayt* ing	ôl′tẽr nāt′ĭng	'ɔl tɚ ˌnet ɪŋ,
	AL tuhr *nayt* ing	ăl′tẽr nāt′ĭng	'æl-; ES -tə-
alternative	awl TUHR nuh tiv	ôl tûr′ná tĭv	ɔl 'tɝ nə tɪv, æl-;
	al TUHR nuh tiv	ăl tûr′ná tĭv	ES also -'tɝ-
although	awl ŦHOH	ôl ŧhō′ § 20(6)	ɔl 'ðo
alum	AL uhm	ăl′ŭm	'æl əm
aluminum	uh LOO mi nuhm	á lū′mĭ nŭm §§ 48(2), 50(32)	ə 'lu mɪ nəm,
	uh LYOO mi nuhm		ə 'lju mɪ nəm
alumnae	uh LUHM nee	á lŭm′nē	ə 'lʌm ni
alumni	uh LUHM nai͡ § 50(34)	á lŭm′nī	ə 'lʌm naɪ

	SIMPLIFIED	DIACRITICAL	PHONETIC
always	AWL wiz AWL wayz AWL wuhz	ôl′wĭz ôl′wāz ôl′wŭz §§ 20(8), 42(3)	′ɔl wɪz ′ɔl wez ′ɔl wəz
am	am *Unstressed:* uhm 'm	ăm § 16 *Unstressed:* ŭm 'm	æm *Unstressed:* əm m̦
amanuensis	uh *man* yŏŏ EN sis	ȧ măn′û ĕn′sĭs	ə ˌmæn jʊ ′ɛn sɪs, -ju-
amass	uh MAS	ȧ măs′	ə ′mæs
amateur	AM uh *chŏŏr* AM uh chuhr AM uh *tyŏŏr* AM uh tyuhr *am* uh TUHR *am* uh TYŎŎR *am* uh TYOOR *am* uh TŎŎR *am* uh TOOR	ăm′ȧ tûr ăm′ȧ tûr′ ăm′ȧ tūr′ §§ 40(4), 47(3), 48(2), 50(31)	′æm ə ˌtʃʊr, -tʃɚ, -ˌtjʊr, -tjɚ, -tʊr, ˌæm ə ′tɝ, -′tʊr; *ES* ′æm ə ˌtʃʊə(r), -tʃə(r),-ˌtjʊə(r), -tjə(r), -tʊə(r), ˌæm ə ′tʊə(r), *E also* -′tɜ(r)
amatory	AM uh *toh* ri AM uh *taw* ri *B.,* AM uh tuhr i	ăm′ȧ tō′rĭ §§ 34(3), 51(4) *B.,* ăm′ȧ tēr ĭ	′æm ə ˌto rɪ ′æm ə ˌtɔ rɪ *B.,* ′æm ə tə rɪ
ambassador	am BAS uh duhr	ăm băs′ȧ dẽr	æm ′bæs ə dɚ; *ES* -də(r)
ambergris	AM buhr grees AM buhr gris	ăm′bẽr grēs ăm′bẽr grĭs	′æm bɚ gris, -grɪs; *ES* -bə-
ambiguity	*am* bi GYOO uh ti *am* bi GYOO i ti	ăm′bĭ gū′ĭ tĭ ăm′bĭ gū′Ĭ tĭ	ˌæm bɪ ′gju ə tɪ ˌæm bɪ ′gju ɪ tɪ
ambrosia	am BROH zhi uh am BROH zi uh *B.,* am BROH zhuh	ăm brō′zhĭ ȧ ăm brō′zĭ ȧ *B.,* ăm brō′zhȧ] §§ 38(12), 47(3), 51(4)	æm ′bro ʒɪ ə æm ′bro zɪ ə *B.,* æm ′bro ʒə æm ′bro ʒɪ ə
ambush	AM bŏŏsh	ăm′bŏŏsh	′æm bʊʃ
ameliorate	uh MEEL yuh rayt	ȧ mēl′yŏ rāt §§ 28(9), 47(3)	ə ′mil jə ret
amen (interj.)	AY MEN *Often, usu. in lit- urgy and always in singing:* AH MEN	ā′měn′ § 47(2) *Often, usu. in lit- urgy and always in singing:* ä′měn′ § 51(11)	′e ′mɛn, e- *Often, usu. in lit- urgy and always in singing:* ′ɑ ′mɛn, ɑ-
amenable	uh MEE nuh b'l uh MEN uh b'l	ȧ mē′nȧ b'l ȧ měn′ȧ b'l § 47(1)	ə ′mi nə bl̦ ə ′mɛn ə bl̦
amend	uh MEND	ȧ měnd′	ə ′mɛnd
amenity	uh MEN uh ti uh MEN i ti uh MEE nuh ti uh MEE ni ti	ȧ měn′ĭ tĭ ȧ měn′Ĭ tĭ ȧ mē′nĭ tĭ ȧ mē′nĭ tĭ	ə ′mɛn ə tɪ ə ′mɛn ɪ tɪ ə ′mi nə tɪ ə ′mi nɪ tɪ

	SIMPLIFIED	DIACRITICAL	PHONETIC
America	uh MER i kuh	*ȧ* mĕr′ĭ kȧ	ə ′mɛr ɪ kə, -ə kə
American	uh MER i kuhn	*ȧ* mĕr′ĭ kăn	ə ′mɛr ɪ kən, -ə kən
amiable	AY mi uh b'l	ā′mĭ *ȧ* b'l § 28(9)	′e mɪ ə bl̩
amicable	AM i kuh b'l	ăm′ĭ kȧ b'l	′æm ɪ kə bl̩
ammonia	uh MOH ni uh	ă mō′nĭ *ȧ*	ə ′mo nɪ ə
	uh MOHN yuh	ă mōn′yȧ	ə ′mon jə
among	uh MUHNG	*ȧ* mŭng′	ə ′mʌŋ
amorous	AM uh ruhs	ăm′ŏ rŭs	′æm ə rəs
amour	uh MŌŌR	*ȧ* mŏŏr′	ə ′mur, æ-, ɑ-; *ES*
	uh MOOR	ă mŏŏr′	-muə(r), *E also*
	ah MOOR	*ȧ* mōōr′ §§ 34(21), 40(4)	ɑ:-
ampere	AM pĭer	ăm′pĕr	′æm pɪər, -pɪr,
	AM pir	ăm′pēr	-pir, æm ′per,
	AM peer	§ 24(2)	-′pær; *ES*
	am PEHR	ăm pâr′	-pɪə(r), -′peə(r), -′pæə(r)
amulet	AM yŏŏ let	ăm′ŭ lĕt	′æm ju lɛt, -jə-,
	AM yŏŏ lit	ăm′ŭ lĭt	-ju-, -lɪt
	AM yuh lit		
analogous	uh NAL uh guhs	*ȧ* năl′ŏ gŭs § 50(25)	ə ′næl ə gəs
analogy	uh NAL uh ji	*ȧ* năl′ŏ jĭ	ə ′næl ə dʒɪ
analysis	uh NAL uh sis	*ȧ* năl′ĭ sĭs	ə ′næl ə sɪs
	uh NAL i sis	*ȧ* năl′ĭ sĭs	ə ′næl ɪ sɪs
analytical	*an* uh LIT i kuhl	ăn′*ȧ* lĭt′ĭ kăl	‚æn ə ′lɪt ɪ kəl, -kl̩, ‚æn l̩-
anarchist	AN uhr kist	ăn′ȧr kĭst	′æn ɚ kɪst; *ES* -ə kɪst
anathema	uh NATH i muh	*ȧ* năth′ĕ mȧ	ə ′næθ ɪ mə, -′næθ ə-
anathematize	uh NATH i muh taiz	*ȧ* năth′ĕ mȧ tīz	ə ′næθ ɪ mə taɪz, -′næθ ə-
anatomical	*an* uh TOM i kuhl	ăn′*ȧ* tŏm′ĭ kăl	‚æn ə ′tɑm ɪ kəl, -kl̩; *ES also* -′tɒm-
anatomize	uh NAT uh maiz	*ȧ* năt′ŏ mīz	ə ′næt ə maɪz
anatomy	uh NAT uh mi	*ȧ* năt′ŏ mĭ	ə ′næt ə mi
ancestor	AN *ses* tuhr	ăn′sĕs′tēr	′æn ‚ses tɚ, -ses-; *ES* -tə(r)
	AN ses tuhr	ăn′sĕs tēr	
anchor	ANG kuhr	ăng′kĕr	′æŋ kɚ; *ES* -kə(r)
anchorite	ANG kuh rait § 50(34)	ăng′kŏ rīt	′æŋ kə raɪt
anchovy	an CHOH vi	ăn chō′vĭ	æn ′tʃo vɪ
	AN choh vi	ăn′chō vĭ	′æn tʃo vɪ
	AN chuh vi	§ 47(1)	′æn tʃə vɪ
ancient	AYN shuhnt	ān′shĕnt	′en ʃənt

	SIMPLIFIED	DIACRITICAL	PHONETIC
and	and *Unstressed:* uhn (Before consonants) 'nd 'n'	ănd § 16 *Unstressed:* ăn (Before consonants) 'nd 'n'	ænd *Unstressed:* ən (Before consonants) n̩d n̩
andirons	AND a͡i uhrnz § 50(34)	ănd′ī′ērnz	ˈænd ˌaɪ ɚnz; *ES* -ənz
anemia, anaemia **anemic,** **anaemic**	uh NEE mi uh uh NEE mik a NEE mik uh NEM ik a NEM ik	à nē′mĭ à à nē′mĭk ă nē′mĭk à nĕm′ĭk ă nĕm′ĭk § 47(3)	ə ˈni mɪ ə ə ˈni mɪk æ ˈni mɪk ə ˈnɛm ɪk æ ˈnɛm ɪk
anemone	uh NEM uh ni uh NEM uh nee	à nĕm′ŏ nĕ	ə ˈnɛm ə nɪ ə ˈnɛm ə ni
anesthesia, **anaesthesia**	*an* uhs THEE zhi uh *an* is THEE zhi uh *an* es THEE zhi uh *an* uhs THEE zhuh *an* is THEE zhuh *an* uhs THEE zi uh *ăn* es THEE zi uh	ăn′ĕs thē′zhĭ à ăn′ĕs thē′zhĭ à ăn′ĕs thē′zhĭ à ăn′ĕs thē′zhà ăn′ĕs thē′zhà ăn′ĕs thē′zĭ à ăn′ĕs thē′zĭ à § 47(1)	ˌæn əs ˈθi ʒɪ ə ˌæn ɪs ˈθi ʒɪ ə ˌæn ɛs ˈθi ʒɪ ə ˌæn əs ˈθi ʒə ˌæn ɪs ˈθi ʒə ˌæn əs ˈθi zɪ ə ˌæn ɛs ˈθi zɪ ə
anesthetic, **anaesthetic**	*an* uhs THET ik *an* is THET ik	ăn′ĕs thĕt′ĭk ăn′ĭs thĕt′ĭk	ˌæn əs ˈθɛt ɪk ˌæn ɪs ˈθɛt ɪk
anew	uh NYOO uh NOO	à nū′ §§ 48(2), 51(32)	ə ˈnju ə ˈnu
angel	AYN juhl	ān′jĕl § 9	ˈen dʒəl
angelic	an JEL ik	ăn jĕl′ĭk	æn ˈdʒɛl ɪk
angle	ANG g'l	ăng′g'l	ˈæŋ gl̩
Anglo Saxon	ANG gloh SAK s'n	ăng′glŏ săk′s'n	ˈæŋ glo ˈsæk sn̩
angular	ANG gyo͞o luhr	ăng′gů lēr § 50(32)	ˈæŋ gjʊ lɚ, -gjə-, -gju-; *ES* -lə(r)
animadversion	*an* uh mad VUHR shuhn *an* i mad VUHR shuhn *an* uh mad VUHR zhuhn *an* i mad VUHR zhuhn	ăn′ĭ măd vûr′shŭn ăn′ĭ măd vûr′shŭn ăn′ĭ măd vûr′zhŭn ăn′ĭ măd vûr′zhŭn § 50(28)	ˌæn ə mæd ˈvɝ ʃən, ˌæn ɪ-, -ʒən; *ES* *also* -ˈvɜ-
animadvert	*an* uh mad VUHRT *an* i mad VUHRT	ăn′ĭ măd vûrt′ ăn′ĭ măd vûrt′	ˌæn ə mæd ˈvɝt, ˌæn ɪ-; *ES also* -ˈvɜt
annex (v.)	uh NEKS	ă nĕks′	ə ˈnɛks

	SIMPLIFIED	DIACRITICAL	PHONETIC
—— (n.)	AN eks uh NEKS	ăn′ĕks ă nĕks′ §§ 12, 47(2)	ˈæn ɛks ə ˈnɛks
annihilate	uh NAI uh layt uh NAI i layt uh NAI huh layt § 50(34)	ă nī′ĭ lāt ă nī′ĭ lāt ă nī′hĭ lāt	ə ˈnaɪ ə let ə ˈnaɪ ɪ let ə ˈnaɪ hə let
annoy	uh NOI	ă noi′	ə ˈnɔɪ

annunciation,
  Annunciation
	uh *nun* si AY
	  shuhn
	uh *nun* shi AY
	  shuhn
		ă nŭn′sĭ ā′shŭn
		ă nŭn′shĭ ā′shŭn
		§§ 38(12), 47(3)
			ə ˌnʌn sɪ ˈe ʃən
			ə ˌnʌn ʃɪ ˈe ʃən

anonymous	uh NON uh muhs uh NON i muhs	*ă* nŏn′ĭ mŭs *ă* nŏn′ĭ mŭs	ə ˈnɑn ə məs, -ɪ məs; *ES also* ə ˈnɒn-
another	uh NUHTH uhr	ă nŭth′ĕr	ə ˈnʌð ɚ; *ES* -ə(r)
answer	AN suhr AHN suhr	ăn′sēr §§ 20(5), 39(3), 42(3), 47(1)	ˈæn sɚ; *ES* -sə(r), *E also* ˈan-, ˈɑn-
antarctic (once spelled *antartic*)	ant AHRK tik	ănt ärk′tĭk	ænt ˈark tɪk; *ES* -ˈɑːk-, *E also* -ˈɑːk-

	*Sometimes (and
	  also pop.):*
	ant AHR tik
		*Sometimes (and
		  also pop.):*
		ănt är′tĭk
		§ 51(3, 8)
			*Sometimes (and
			  also pop.): ES*
			ænt ˈar tɪk; *ES*
			-ˈɑ: tɪk, *E also*
			-ˈɑ:-

antelope	AN ti lohp	ăn′tĕ lōp	ˈæn tɪ lop
Anthony (Saint)	AN thuh ni AN tuh ni	ăn′thŏ nĭ ăn′tŏ nĭ §§ 1, 39(7)	ˈæn θə nɪ ˈæn tə nɪ
anthropoid	AN thruh poid AN throh poid	ăn′thrŏ poid ăn′thrō poid §§ 47(2), 51(4)	ˈæn θrə pɔɪd ˈæn θro pɔɪd
anti— (prefix)	AN ti—	ăn′tĭ—	ˈæn tɪ—
antidote	AN ti doht	ăn′tĭ dōt	ˈæn tɪ dot
antipathy	an TIP uh thi	ăn tĭp′*ă* thĭ	æn ˈtɪp ə θɪ
antipode	AN ti pohd	ăn′ tĭ pōd	ˈæn tɪ pod
antipodes	an TIP uh deez	ăn tĭp′ŏ dēz	æn ˈtip ə diz
antique	an TEEK	ăn tēk′ § 11	æn ˈtik
antiquity	an TIK wuh ti an TIK wi ti	ăn tĭk′wĭ tĭ ăn tĭk′wĭ tĭ	æn ˈtɪk wə tɪ æn ˈtɪk wɪ tɪ
antislavery	*an* ti SLAYV uhr i	ăn′tĭ slāv′ĕr ĭ	ˌæn tɪ ˈslev ər ɪ
antithesis	an TITH i sis	ăn tĭth′ĕ sĭs	æn ˈtɪθ ɪ sɪs
Antony (Mark)	AN tuh ni	ăn′tŏ nĭ	ˈæn tə nɪ
anxiety	ang ZAI uh ti § 50(34)	ăng zī′ĕ tĭ § 33(4)	æŋ ˈzaɪ ə tɪ, æŋg-

	SIMPLIFIED	DIACRITICAL	PHONETIC
anxious	ANGK shuhs ANG shuhs	ăngk′shŭs ăng′shŭs §§ 33(4), 38(12)	ˈæŋk ʃəs ˈæŋ ʃəs
any	EN i	ĕn′ĭ § 24(3)	ˈɛn ɪ
apathetic	*ap* uh THET ik	ăp′*ȧ* thĕt′ĭk	ˌæp ə ˈθɛt ɪk
apathy	AP uh thi	ăp′*ȧ* thĭ	ˈæp ə θɪ
aperture	AP uhr chuhr AP uhr tyuhr	ăp′ēr tū̆r § 50(31)	ˈæp ɚ tʃɚ, -tjɚ; *ES* -tʃə(r), -tjə(r)
apex	AY peks	ā′pĕks	ˈe pɛks
aphorism	AF uh riz′m AF uh riz uhm	ăf′ŏ rĭz′m § 50(15)	ˈæf ə rɪzm̩ ˈæf ə rɪz əm
Aphrodite	*af* ruh DAI ti § 50(34)	ăf′rŏ dī′tĕ	ˌæf rə ˈdaɪ tɪ
Apocalypse, **apocalypse**	uh POK uh lips	*ȧ* pŏk′*ȧ* lĭps	ə ˈpak ə lɪps; *ES* *also* -ˈpɒk-
apostle, Apostle	uh POS ′l	*ȧ* pŏs′ ′l	ə ˈpas l̩; *ES also* -ˈpɒs-
apostolic	*ap* uhs TOL ik	ăp′ŏs tŏl′ĭk	ˌæp əs ˈtal ɪk; *ES* *also* -ˈtɒl-
apotheosis	uh *poth* i OH sis *ap* uh THEE uh sis *ap* uh thi OH sis	*ȧ* pŏth′ĕ ō′sĭs ăp′ŏ thē′ŏ sĭs ăp′ŏ thē ō′sĭs § 47(3)	ə ˌpaθ ɪ ˈo sɪs, ˌæp ə θi ˈo-, ˌæp ə ˈθi ə-; *ES* *also* ə ˌpɒθ ɪ ˈo-
Appalachian	*ap* uh LACH i uhn *ap* uh LAY chi uhn	ăp′*ȧ* lăch′ĭ ăn ăp′*ȧ* lā′chĭ ăn § 47(2)	ˌæp ə ˈlætʃ ɪ ən, -ˈle tʃɪ-, -tʃən-, -ˈlætʃ ən
appall	uh PAWL	ă pôl′	ə ˈpɔl
appanage	AP uh nij	ăp′*ȧ* nij	ˈæp ə nɪdʒ
apparatus	*ap* uh RAY tuhs *ap* uh RAT uhs	ăp′*ȧ* rā′tŭs ăp′*ȧ* răt′ŭs § 47(1)	ˌæp ə ˈre təs, -ˈræt əs, -ˈra təs
apparent	uh PAR uhnt uh PEHR uhnt	ă păr′ĕnt ă pâr′ĕnt §§ 20(2), 47(3)	ə ˈpær ənt, -ˈpɛr-; *ES also* -ˈpɛər-
apparition	*ap* uh RISH uhn	ăp′*ȧ* rĭsh′ŭn § 50(30)	ˌæp ə ˈrɪʃ ən
appear	uh PǏER uh PIR uh PEER	ă pē̆r′ § 24(2) ă pēr′	ə ˈpɪər, -ˈpɪr, -ˈpir; *ES* -ˈpɪə(r)
appellate (adj.)	uh PEL it uh PEL ayt a PEL ayt	ă pĕl′ăt ă pĕl′āt ă pĕl′āt	ə ˈpɛl ɪt ə ˈpɛl et æ ˈpɛl et
—— (v.)	AP uh layt	ăp′ĕ lāt § 20(8, 9)	ˈæp ə let
appendicitis	uh *pen* di SAI tis § 50(34)	ă pĕn′dĭ sī′tĭs § 47(1)	ə ˈpen dɪ ˈsaɪ tɪs, -ˈsi-, -də-
Appian Way	AP i uhn WAY	ăp′ĭ ăn wā′	ˈæp ɪ ən ˈwe
applicable	AP li kuh b′l	ăp′lĭ k*ȧ* b′l	ˈæp lɪ kə bl̩

apportion	uh POHR shuhn uh PAWR shuhn	ă pōr′shŭn §§ 34(3), 50(30)	ə ′pɔr ʃən, ə ′pɔr-; *ES* ə ′pɔə-, *E* *also* ə ′pɔə-
apposite	AP uh zit	ăp′ŏ zĭt	′æp ə zɪt
appreciate	uh PREE shi ayt	ă prē′shĭ āt §38(12)	ə ′pri ʃɪ et
appreciation	uh *pree* shi AY shuhn uh *pree* si AY shuhn	ă prē′shĭ ā′shŭn ă prē′sĭ ā′shŭn §38(12)	ə ˌpri ʃɪ ′e ʃən ə ˌpri sɪ ′e ʃən
appreciative	uh PREE shi *ay* tiv uh PREE shi uh tiv	ă prē′shĭ ā′tĭv ă prē′shĭ ă tĭv	ə ′pri ʃɪ ˌe tɪv ə ′pri ʃɪ ə tɪv
apprehend	*ap* ri HEND	ăp′rĕ hĕnd′	ˌæp rɪ ′hɛnd
apprise, apprize	uh PRAIZ § 50(34)	ă prīz′	ə ′praɪz
approbation (n.)	*ap*ruh BAY shuhn	ăp′rŏ bā′shŭn	ˌæp rə ′be ʃən
appropriate (adj.)	uh PROH pri it	ă prō′prĭ ĭt § 20(8, 9)	ə ′pro prɪ ɪt
—— (v.)	uh PROH pri ayt	ă prō′prĭ āt	ə ′pro prɪ et
approximate (n., adj.)	uh PROK suh mit uh PROK si mit	ă prŏk′sŭ mĭt ă prŏk′sĭ mĭt	ə ′prɑk sə mɪt, -sɪ-; *ES also* -′prɒk-
—— (v.)	uh PROK suh mayt uh PROK si mayt	ă prŏk′sŭ māt ă prŏk′sĭ māt § 20(8, 9)	ə ′prɑk sə met, -sɪ-; *ES also* -′prɒk-
appurtenance	uh PUHR ti nuhns	ă pûr′tĕ năns	ə ′pɝ tɪ nəns, -tn̩əns; *ES also* -′pɜ-
apricot	AY pri kot AY pri kuht AP ri kuht AP ri kot	ā′prĭ kŏt ā′prĭ kŏt ăp′rĭ kŏt ăp′rĭ kŏt § 47(3)	′e prɪ kɑt, -kət, ′æp rɪ kət, -kɑt; *ES also* -kɒt
a priori	*ay* pri OH rai͡ *ay* prai͡ OH rai͡ *ah* pri OH ri § 50(34)	ā′prī ō′rī ā′prī ō′rī ä′prĭ ō′rĕ	ˌe prɪ ′o raɪ, ˌe praɪ-, -′ɔ raɪ, ˌɑ prɪ ′o rɪ
apron	AY pruhn *Often:* AY puhrn	ā′prŭn § 47(2) *Often:* ā′pĕrn § 51(9)	′e prən *Often:* ′e pɚn; *ES* ′e pən
apropos	*ap* ruh POH	ăp′rŏ pō′ §§ 38(2), 47(1)	ˌæp rə ′po
aptitude	AP tuh tyood AP ti tyood AP tuh tood AP ti tood	ăp′tĭ tūd ăp′tĭ tūd §§ 48(2), 50(32)	′æp tə tjud ′æp tɪ tjud ′æp tə tud ′æp tɪ tud

	SIMPLIFIED	DIACRITICAL	PHONETIC
aquarium	uh KWEHR i uhm uh KWAY ri uhm	à kwâr′ĭ ŭm § 20(2)	ə ˈkwɛr ɪ əm, ə ˈkwe rɪ-; *ES* ə ˈkweə rɪ-
aquatic	uh KWAT ik uh KWOT ik	à kwăt′ĭk à kwŏt′ĭk	ə ˈkwæt ɪk, ə ˈkwɑt-, ə ˈkwɒt-
aqueduct	AK wi *duhkt*	ăk′wĕ dŭkt § 40(6)	ˈæk wɪ dʌkt
aqueous	AY kwĭ uhs AK wĭ uhs	ā′kwĕ ŭs ăk′wĕ ŭs	ˈe kwɪ əs ˈæk wɪ əs
aquiline	AK wi laîn AK wi lin § 50(34)	ăk′wĭ līn ăk′wĭ lĭn § 47(3)	ˈæk wɪ laɪn ˈæk wɪ lɪn
Arab	AR uhb	ăr′ăb	ˈær əb
Arabic	AR uh bik	ăr′à bĭk	ˈær ə bɪk
arbiter	AHR bi tuhr	är′bĭ tẽr	ˈɑr bɪ tɚ; *ES* ˈɑ: bɪ tə(r), *E* *also* ˈɑ:-
arbitrament	ahr BIT ruh muhnt	är bĭt′rà mĕnt	ɑr ˈbɪt rə mənt; *ES* ɑ: ˈbɪt-, *E* *also* ɑ:-
arbitrary	AHR buh *trer* i *B.,* AHR buh truhr i §§ 20(2), 24(9)	är′bĭ trĕr′ĭ *B.,* är′bĭ trẽr ĭ §§ 20(2), 24(9)	ˈɑr bə ˌtrer ɪ *B.,* ˈɑr bə trə rɪ; *ES* ˈɑ: bə-, *E* *also* ˈɑ:-
arbitrate	AHR buh trayt AHR bi trayt	är′bĭ trāt är′bĭ trāt	ˈɑr bə tret, -bɪ-; *ES* ˈɑ:-, *E also* ˈɑ:-
arbutus	ahr BYOO tuhs *Often (Lat.), esp.* *when cap.:* AHR byoŏ tuhs	är bū′tŭs *Often (Lat.), esp.* *when cap.:* är′bū tŭ §§ 47(3), 51(9, 11)	ɑr ˈbju təs; *ES* ɑ:-, *E also* ɑ:- *Often (Lat.), esp.* *when cap.:* ˈɑr bjʊ təs, -bjə-; *ES* ˈɑ:-, *E also* ˈɑ:-
arch—	ahrch— (*So pronounced* *exc. in "arch-* *angel" and de-* *rivatives)*	ärch— (*So pronounced* *exc. in "arch-* *angel" and de-* *rivatives)*	ɑrtʃ—; *ES* ɑ:tʃ—, *E also* ɑ:tʃ—
archaic	ahr KAY ik	är kā′ĭk	ɑr ˈke ɪk; *ES* ɑ: ˈke-, *E also* ɑ:-
archangel	AHRK AYN juhl AHRK *ayn* juhl	ärk′ān′jĕl ärk′ān′jĕl §§ 11, 22(8)	ˈɑrk en dʒəl, -ˌen-; *ES* ˈɑ:k-, *E also* ˈɑ:k-
archbishop (n.)	AHRCH BISH uhp	ärch′bĭsh′ŭp (*see* ARCH—)	ˈɑrtʃ ˈbɪʃ əp; *ES* ˈɑ:tʃ-, *E also* ˈɑ:tʃ-
—— (v.)	*ahrch* BISH uhp	ärch′bĭsh′ŭp § 22(8)	ˌɑrtʃ ˈbɪʃ əp; *ES* ˌɑ:tʃ-, *E also* ˌɑ:tʃ-

	SIMPLIFIED	DIACRITICAL	PHONETIC
archduke	AHRCH DYOOK AHRCH DOOK	ärch′dūk′ §§ 22(8), 48(2), 50(32)	'ɑrtʃ 'djuk, -'duk; ES 'ɑ:tʃ-, E also 'ɑ:tʃ-
Archimedes	*ahr* ki MEE deez	är′kǐ mē′dēz	ˌɑr kɪ 'mi diz; ES ˌɑ:kɪ-, E also ˌɑ:kɪ-
archipelago	*ahr* ki PEL uh goh	är′kǐ pĕl′*a* gō	ˌɑr kɪ 'pɛl ə go; ES ˌɑ:kɪ-, E also ˌɑ:kɪ-
architect	AHR kuh tekt AHR ki tekt	är′kǐ tĕkt är′kǐ tĕkt § 22(8)	'ɑr kə tɛkt, -kɪ-; ES 'ɑ:-, E also 'ɑ:-
architecture	AHR kuh *tek* chuhr AHR kuh *tek* tyuhr AHR ki *tek* chuhr AHR ki *tek* tyuhr	är′ki tĕk′tûr är′kǐ tek′tûr § 50(31)	'ɑr kə ˌtɛk tʃɚ, -tjɚ, -kɪ-; ES 'ɑ:kə-, 'ɑ:kɪ-, -tʃə(r), -tjə(r), E also 'ɑ:-
archives	AHR kaivz § 50(34)	är′kīvz § 48(3)	'ɑr kaɪvz; ES 'ɑ:- E also 'ɑ:-
arctic (See "*antarctic.*")	AHRK tik	ärk′tǐk	'ɑrk tɪk; ES 'ɑ:k-, E also 'ɑ:k-
	Sometimes (and also pop.): AHR tik	*Sometimes (and also pop.):* är′tǐk § 51(3, 8)	*Sometimes (and also pop.):* 'ɑr tɪk; ES 'ɑ:tɪk, E also 'ɑ:-
arduous	AHR jŏŏ uhs AHR dyŏŏ uhs	är′dû ŭs § 50(33)	'ɑr dʒʊ əs, -djʊ-; ES 'ɑ:-, E also 'ɑ:-
are	ahr	är §§ 16, 47(2)	ɑr; ES ɑ:(r), E also ɑ:(r)
	Unstressed: uhr -r	*Unstressed:* ẽr 're	*Unstressed:* ɚ; ES ə(r) -r; ES ə(r)
area	AY ri uh EHR i uh	ā′rē *a* âr′ĕ *a* § 47(3)	'e rɪ ə 'ɛr ɪ ə; ES 'æə rɪ ə, E also 'ɛə-
arena	uh REE nuh	*a* rē′n*a*	ə 'ri nə
argosy	AHR guh si	är′gŏ sǐ	'ɑr gə sɪ; ES 'ɑ:-, E also 'ɑ:-
argue	AHR gyoo	är′gū	'ɑr gju, -gjʊ
argument	AHR gyŏŏ muhnt	är′gû mĕnt § 50(22)	'ɑr gjʊ mənt, -gjə-, -gju-; ES 'ɑ:-, E also 'ɑ:-
argumentative	*ahr* gyŏŏ MEN tuh tĭv	är′gû mĕn′t*a* tǐv	ˌɑr gjʊ 'mɛn tə tɪv, -gjə-, -gju-; ES ˌɑ:-, E also ˌɑ:-
aria	AH ri uh EHR i uh AY ri uh	ä′rǐ *a* âr′Ǐ *a* ā′rǐ *a* § 47(1)	'ɑ rɪ ə, 'ɛr ɪ ə, 'ær ɪ ə, 'ɛ rɪ ə; ES also 'æə rɪ ə, E also 'ɛə rɪ ə

	SIMPLIFIED	DIACRITICAL	PHONETIC
arid	AR id	ăr′ĭd	′ær ɪd
Ariel	EHR i el	âr′ĭ ĕl	′ɛr ɪ ɛl, ′ær-, ′e rɪ-,
	AY ri el	§ 20(2)	-əl; ES ′æə rɪ-,
			E also ′ɛə-
aristocrat	uh RIS tuh krat	ă rĭs′tŏ krăt	ə ′rɪs tə kræt
	AR is tuh krat	ăr′ĭs tŏ krăt	′ær ɪs tə kræt
		§ 47(3)	
aristocratic	uh *ris* tuh KRAT	ă rĭs′tŏ krăt′ĭk	ˌə rɪs tə ′kræt ɪk
	ik		
	ar is tuh KRAT ik	ăr′ĭs tŏ krăt′ĭk	ˌær ɪs tə ′kræt ɪk
arithmetic (n.)	uh RITH muh tik	ȧ rĭth′mĕ tĭk	ə ′rɪθ mə tɪk
—— (adj.)	*ar* ith MET ik	ăr′ĭth mĕt′ĭk	ˌær ɪθ ′met ɪk
Arkansas	*River and state:*	*River and state:*	*River and state:*
	AHR kuhn saw	är′kăn sô	′ɑr kən sɔ; ES
			′ɑː-, E also ′ɑː-
	River, also:	*River, also:*	*River, also:*
	ahr KAN zuhs	är kăn′zȧs	ɑr ′kæn zəs; ES
		§ 38(2)	ɑː-, E also ɑː-
armada	ahr MAY duh	är mā′dȧ	ɑr ′me də, -′mɑ-;
	ahr MAH duh	är mä′dȧ	ES ɑː ′me-,
		§ 47(1)	ɑː ′mɑ-, E also
			ɑː-
armature	AHR muh chuhr	är′mȧ tŭr	′ɑr mə tʃɚ, -tjɚ,
	AHR muh tyuhr	§ 50(31)	-ˌtʃʊr; ES
			′ɑː mə tʃə(r),
			-tjə(r),-ˌtʃʊə(r).
			E also ′ɑː-
armistice	AHR muh stis	är′mĭ stĭs	′ɑr mə stɪs, -mɪ-;
	AHR mi stis	är′ mĭ stĭs	ES ′ɑː-, E also
			′ɑː-
army	AHR mi	är′mĭ	′ɑr mɪ; ES ′ɑː-, E
			also ′ɑː-
aroma ("*odor*")	uh ROH muh	ȧ rō′mȧ	ə ′ro mə
around	uh ROWND	ȧ round′	ə ′raʊnd
	§ 50(34)		
arraign	uh RAYN	ă rān′	ə ′ren
arras	AR uhs	ăr′ăs	′ær əs
arrest	uh REST	ă rĕst′	ə ′rest
arrow	AR oh	ăr′ō § 34(25)	′ær o, -ə
arsenic (n., v.)	AHR si nik	är′sĕ nĭk	′ɑr sɪ nɪk, -sn̩-;
	AHR s'n ik	är′s'n ĭk	B., ′ɑrs nɪk; ES
	B., AHRS nik	B., ärs′nĭk	′ɑː-, ′ɑːs-, E also
		§§ 47(2), 51(4)	′ɑː-, ′ɑːs-
—— (adj.)	ahr SEN ik	är sĕn′ĭk	ɑr ′sen ɪk; ES ɑː-,
			E also ɑː-
Artemis	AHR ti mis	är′tĕ mĭs	′ɑr tɪ mɪs, -tə-;
			ES ′ɑː-, E also
			′ɑː-

	SIMPLIFIED	DIACRITICAL	PHONETIC
arterial	ahr TĬER i uhl ahr TIR i uhl ahr TEER i uhl	är tẹr′ĭ ăl § 24(2) är tēr′ĭ ăl	ɑr ˈtɪər ɪ əl, -ˈtɪr-, -ˈtir-; ES ɑ: ˈtɪər-, E also ɑ:-
artifice	AHR tuh fis AHR ti fis	är′tĭ fĭs är′tĬ fĭs	ˈɑr tə fɪs, -ti-; ES ˈɑ:-, E also ˈɑ:-
artificer	ahr TIF uh suhr ahr TIF i suhr	är tĬf′ĭ sẽr är tĬf′ĭ sẽr	ɑr ˈtɪf ə sə˞, -ˈtɪf ɪ-; ES ɑ:ˈtɪf ə sə(r), -ˈtɪf ɪ-, E also ɑ:-
artificial	ahr tuh FISH uhl ahr ti FISH uhl	är′tĬ fĬsh′ăl är′tĬ fĬsh′ăl	ˌɑr tə ˈfɪʃ əl, -tɪ-; ES ˌɑ:-, E also ˌɑ:-
artisan, artizan	AHR tuh zuhn AHR ti zuhn	är′tĬ zăn är′tĬ zăn § 47(3)	ˈɑr tə zən, -tɪ-; ES ˈɑ:-, E also ˈɑ:-
artist	AHR tist	är′tĬst	ˈɑr tɪst; ES ˈɑ:-, E also ˈɑ:-
artistic	ahr TIS tik	är tĬs′tĬk § 20(4)	ɑr ˈtɪs tɪk; ES ɑ:-, E also ɑ:-
artistry	AHR tis tri	är′tĬs trĬ	ˈɑr tɪs trɪ; ES ˈɑ:-, E also ˈɑ:-
artists	AHR tists	är′tĬsts § 48(3)	ˈɑr tɪsts; ES ˈɑ:-, E also ˈɑ:-
as (adv.)	az *Unstressed:* uhz	ăz *Unstressed:* ăz § 16	æz *Unstressed:* əz
asafetida	*as* uh FET i duh	ăs′ȧ fĕt′ĭ dȧ	ˌæs ə ˈfɛt ɪ də
asbestos, asbestus	as BES tuhs az BES tuhs	ăs bĕs′tŏs ăz bĕs′tŏs § 47(3)	æs ˈbɛs təs, -tʌs, æz-
ascend	uh SEND	ȧ sĕnd′	ə ˈsɛnd
ascertain	*as* uhr TAYN	ăs′ẽr tān′	ˌæs ɚ ˈten; ES ˌæs ə-
ascetic	uh SET ik	ȧ sĕt′ĭk	ə ˈsɛt ɪk
asexual	ay SEK shoŏ uhl uh SEK shoŏ uhl ay SEKS yoŏ uhl	ā sĕk′shoŏ ăl ā sĕks′ŭ ăl	e ˈsɛk ʃʊ əl, ə ˈsɛk-, æ ˈsɛk-, e ˈsɛks ju əl
Asia	AY zhuh AY shuh	ā′zhȧ ā′shȧ	ˈe ʒə ˈe ʃə
Asiatic	*ay* zhi AT ik *ay* shi AT ik	ā′zhĬ ăt′ĭk ā′shĬ ăt′ĭk §§ 38(12), 47(3)	ˌe ʒɪ ˈæt ɪk ˌe ʃɪ ˈæt ɪk
asinine	AS uh naīn AS i naīn § 50(34)	ăs′ĭ nīn ăs′ĭ nīn § 47(2)	ˈæs ə naɪn ˈæs ɪ naɪn
ask	ask ahsk	ȧsk §§ 20(5), 47(1)	æsk; E also ask, ɑsk
askance	uh SKANS	ȧ skăns′ § 20(5)	ə ˈskæns
askew	uh SKYOO	ȧ skū′	ə ˈskju
asparagus	uhs PAR uh guhs	ăs păr′ȧ gŭs	əs ˈpær ə gəs
aspect (n.)	AS pekt	ăs′pĕkt § 12	ˈæs pɛkt

	SIMPLIFIED	DIACRITICAL	PHONETIC
—— (v.t.)	as PEKT	ăs pĕkt′ § 20 (5)	æs ′pɛkt
asperity	as PER uh ti	ăs pĕr′ĭ tĭ	æs ′pɛr ə tɪ
	as PER i ti	ăs pĕr′ĭ tĭ § 20(5)	æs ′pɛr ɪ tɪ
asphalt	AS fawlt	ăs′fôlt	′æs fɔlt
	AS falt	ăs′fălt	′æs fælt
aspirant	uhs PAIR uhnt	ăs pīr′ănt	əs ′paɪr ənt
	uh SPAIR uhnt	§§ 47(2), 50(34)	ə ′spaɪr ənt
	AS puh ruhnt	ăs′pĭ rănt	′æs pə rənt
	AS pi ruhnt	ăs′pĭ rănt	′æs pɪ rənt
assassin	uh SAS in	ă săs′ĭn	ə ′sæs ɪn
assault	uh SAWLT	ă sôlt′	ə ′sɔlt
assent	uh SENT	ă sĕnt′	ə ′sɛnt
assert	uh SUHRT	ă sûrt′	ə ′sɝt; *ES also* ə ′sɜt
asseveration	uh *sev* uhr AY shuhn	ă sĕv′ĕr ā′shŭn	ə ˌsɛv ər ′e ʃən
	uh *sev* uh RAY shuhn		ə ˌsɛv ə ′re ʃən
assiduity	*as* i DYOO uh ti	ăs′ĭ dū′ĭ tĭ	ˌæs ɪ ′dju ə tɪ
	as i DOO uh ti		ˌæs ɪ ′du ə tɪ
	as i DYOO i ti	ăs′ĭ dū′ĭ tĭ	ˌæs ɪ ′dju ɪ tɪ
	as i DOO i ti	§§ 48(2), 50(32)	ˌæs ɪ ′du ɪ tɪ
assiduous	uh SIJ o͝o uhs	ă sĭd′ů ŭs	ə ′sɪdʒ ʊ əs
	uh SID yo͝o uhs	§ 50(33)	ə ′sɪd ju əs
assign	uh SAIN § 50(34)	ă sīn′	ə ′saɪn
assignee	*as* uh NEE	ăs′ĭ nē′	ˌæs ə ′ni
	as i NEE	as′ĭ nē′	ˌæs ɪ ′ni
assimilate	uh SIM uh layt	ă sĭm′ĭ lāt	ə ′sɪm ə let
	uh SIM i layt	ă sĭm′ĭ lāt	ə ′sɪm ɪ let
associate (v.)	uh SOH shi ayt	ă sō′shĭ āt	ə ′so ʃɪ et
—— (n., adj.)	uh SOH shi it	ă sō′shĭ ăt	ə ′so ʃɪ ɪt
	uh SOH shi ayt	§§ 20(8, 9), 28(9), 47(1)	ə ′so ʃɪ et
association	uh *soh* si AY shuhn	ă sō′sĭ ā′shŭn	ə ˌso sɪ ′e ʃən
	uh *soh* shi AY shuhn	ă sō′shĭ ā′shŭn §§ 38(12), 47(3)	ə ˌso ʃɪ ′e ʃən
assume	uh SYOOM	ă sūm′ §§ 40(4), 48(2)	ə ′sjum
	uh SOOM		ə ′sum
assure	uh SHOOR	ă sho͝or′ § 34(21)	ə ′ʃʊr; *ES* ə ′ʃʊə(r)
ast**h**ma	AZ muh	ăz′ma̍	′æz mə
	AS muh	ăs′ma̍ § 47(2)	′æs mə
	Not infreq.:	*Not infreq.:*	*Not infreq.:*
	ASTH muh	ăsth′ma̍	′æsθ mə
	AST muh	ăst′ma̍ § 51(8)	′æst mə
astronomer	uhs TRON uh muhr	ăs trŏn′ŏ mēr	əs ′trɑn ə mɚ; *ES* -mə(r), *also* -′trɒn-

	SIMPLIFIED	DIACRITICAL	PHONETIC
astute	as TYOOT as TOOT	ăs tūt′ §§ 47(1), 48(2), 50(32)	æs 'tjut, -'tʊt, ə 'stjut, ə 'stut
ate	ayt	āt § 47(2)	et
Athelstan	ATH uhl stan	ăth′ĕl stăn	'æθ əl stæn; (hist.) 'æð-
Athena	uh THEE nuh	ȧ thē′nȧ	ə 'θi nə
athlete	ATH leet	ăth′lēt	'æθ lit
athletic	ath LET ik	ăth lĕt′ĭk	æθ 'lɛt ɪk
atmosphere	AT muhs fï er AT muhs fir AT muhs feer	ăt′mŏs fẹr § 24(2) ăt′mŏs fēr	'æt məs fɪər, -fɪr, -fir; ES -fɪə(r)
atrocious	uh TROH shuhs	ȧ trō′shŭs § 50(25)	ə 'tro ʃəs
atrocity	uh TROS uh ti uh TROS i ti	ȧ trŏs′ĭ tĭ ȧ trŏs′ĭ tĭ	ə 'trɑs ə tɪ, -ɪtɪ; ES also -'trɒs-
atrophy	AT ruh fi	ăt′rŏ fĭ	ˌæt rə fɪ
attaché	at uh SHAY a ta SHAY ah tah SHAY	ăt′ȧ shā′ ă tä shā′ ä′tä′shā′ F., ȧ′tȧ′shā′ § 47(1)	ˌæt ə 'ʃe, æ tæ 'ʃe, ˌɑ ˌtɑ 'ʃe, ə 'tæʒ e; F., a ta 'ʃe
attack	uh TAK	ă tăk′	ə 'tæk
attacked	uh TAKT	ă tăkt′ § 50(4)	ə 'tækt
attitude	AT uh tyood AT uh tood AT i tyood AT i tood	ăt′ĭ tūd ăt′Ĭ tūd §§ 48(2), 50(32)	'æt ə tjud 'æt ə tud 'æt ɪ tjud 'æt ɪ tud
attorney	uh TUHR ni	ă tûr′nĭ	ə 'tɝ nɪ; ES also ə 'tɜ-
attribute (v.t.)	uh TRIB yoot	ă trĭb′ŭt § 12	ə 'trɪb jʊt, -jut
—— (n.)	AT ruh byoot AT ri byoot	ăt′rĭ būt ăt′ rĭ būt § 50(32)	'æt rə bjut 'æt rɪ bjut
auburn	AW buhrn	ô′bẽrn	'ɔ bɚn; ES 'ɔ bən
auction	AWK shuhn	ôk′shŭn	'ɔk ʃən
audacious	aw DAY shuhs	ô dā′shŭs § 50(25)	ɔ 'de ʃəs
audacity	aw DAS uh ti aw DAS i ti	ô dăs′ĭ tĭ ô dăs′ ĭ tĭ § 20(6)	ɔ 'dæs ə tɪ ɔ 'dæs ɪ tɪ
audience	AW di uhns AWD yuhns	ô′dĭ ĕns ôd′yĕns § 28(9)	'ɔ dɪ əns 'ɔd jəns
auditorium	aw duh TOH ri uhm aw duh TAW ri uhm aw di TOH ri uhm aw di TAW ri uhm	ô′dĭ tō′rĭ ŭm ô′dĭ tō′rĭ ŭm § 34(3)	ˌɔ də 'to rɪ əm ˌɔ də 'tɔ rɪ əm ˌɔ dɪ 'to rɪ əm ˌɔ dɪ 'tɔ rɪ əm

	SIMPLIFIED	DIACRITICAL	PHONETIC
auditory	AW duh *toh* ri	ô′dĭ tō′rĭ	′ɔ də ˌto ɪɪ
	AW duh *taw* ri		′ɔ də ˌtɔ ɪɪ
	AW di *toh* ri	ô′dĭ tō′rĭ	′ɔ dɪ ˌto ɪɪ
	AW di *taw* ri	§§ 34(3), 51(4)	′ɔ dɪ ˌtɔ ɪɪ
	B., AW duh tuhr i	*B.*, ô′dĭ tēr ĭ	*B.*, ′ɔ də tə ɪɪ
aught	awt	ôt § 20(15)	ɔt
augment (v.)	awg MENT	ôg mĕnt′	ɔg ′mɛnt
—— (n.)	AWG ment	ôg′mĕnt § 12	′ɔg mɛnt
augury	AW gyŏŏ ri	ô′gû rĭ § 50(32)	′ɔ gjʊ ɪɪ, -gjə-, -gju-
august (adj.)	aw GUHST	ô gŭst′ § 11	ɔ ′gʌst
Augustine	AW guhs teen	ô′gŭs tēn	′ɔ gəs tin
	aw GUHS tin	ô gŭs′tĭn § 47(2)	ɔ ′gʌs tɪn
——in "St. Augustine" (*place*), always	AW guhs *teen*	ô′gŭs tēn′	′ɔ gəs ˌtin
aunt	ahnt	änt	ɑnt, ænt; *E also* ant
	ant	ȧnt §§ 20(5), 34(4)	
aura	AW ruh	ô′rȧ	′ɔ rə
aureole	AW ri ohl	ô′rĕ ōl	′ɔ rɪ ol
auricle	AW ri k'l	ô′rĭ k'l	′ɔ rɪ kḷ
auspices	AWS pi sez	ôs′pĭ sĕz	′ɔs pɪ sɛz
	AWS pi siz	ôs′pĭ sĭz	′ɔs pɪ sɪz
auspicious	aws PISH uhs	ôs pĭsh′ŭs	ɔs ′pɪʃ əs
author	AW thuhr	ô′thĕr § 1	′ɔ θɚ; *ES* ′ɔ θə(r)
authoritative	aw THOR uh *tay* tiv	ô thôr′ĭ tā′tĭv	ɔ ′θɑr ə ˌte tɪv, ɔ ′θɒr-, ɔ ′θɒr-, -ɪ ˌte-
	aw THOR i *tay* tiv	ô thôr′ɪ tā′tĭv	
	aw THAWR uh *tay* tiv	ô thôr′ĭ tā′tĭv	
	aw THAWR i *tay* tiv	ô thôr′ɪ tā′tĭv §§ 1, 34 (5, 7)	
authoritatively	aw THOR uh *tay* tiv li	ô thôr′ĭ tā′tĭv lĭ	ɔ ′θɑr ə ˌte tɪv lɪ, ɔ ′θɒr-, ɔ ′θɒr-, -ɪ ˌte-
	aw THOR i *tay* tiv li	ô thôr′ɪ tā′tĭv lĭ	
	aw THAWR uh *tay* tiv li	ô thôr′ĭ tā′tĭv lĭ	
	aw THAWR i *tay* tiv li	ô thôr′ɪ tā′tĭv lĭ § 34(5, 7)	
authority	aw THOR uh ti	ô thôr′ĭ tĭ	ɔ ′θɑr ə tɪ, ɔ ′θɒr-, ɔ ′θɒr- -ɪ tɪ
	aw THOR i ti	ô thôr′ɪ tĭ	
	aw THAWR uh ti	ô thôr′ĭ tĭ	
	aw THAWR i ti	ô thôr′ɪ tĭ §§ 1, 20(6), 34(5, 7)	

	SIMPLIFIED	DIACRITICAL	PHONETIC
autobiography	*aw* tuh ba͡i OG ruh fi *aw* toh ba͡i OG ruh fi *aw* tuh bi OG ruh fi *aw* toh bi OG ruh fi	ô′tŏ bī ŏg′rȧ fĭ § 50(34) ô′tŏ bĭ ŏg′rȧ fĭ	ˌɔ tə baɪ ˈag rə fɪ, -to-,-tə bɪ-,-to-, ˌ-ˈŋg-
autocracy	aw TOK ruh si	ô tŏk′rȧ sĭ	ɔ ˈtak rə sɪ; *ES* *also* ɔ ˈtɒk-
autocrat	AW tuh krat	ô′tŏ krăt	ˈɔ tə kræt
automaton	aw TOM uh tuhn aw TOM uh ton	ô tŏm′ȧ tŏn ô tŏm′ȧ tŏn	ɔ ˈtam ə tən, -tan; *ES also* ɔˈtɒmətɒn,-tən
automobile (adj.)	*aw* tuh MOH bil *aw* tuh MOH beel	ô′tŏ mō′bĭl ô′tŏ mō′bēl	ˌɔ tə ˈmo bɪl ˌɔ tə ˈmo bil
—— (n., v.i.)	*aw* tuh muh BEEL aw tuh muh BEEL *aw* tuh MOH bil *aw* tuh MOH beel aw tuh MOH beel AW tuh muh *beel*	ô′tŏ mŏ bēl′ ô tô mô bēl′ ô′tŏ mō′bĭl ô′tŏ mō′bēl ô tŏ mō′bēl ô′tŏ mŏ bēl′ § 47(1)	ˌɔ tə mə ˈbil ɔ tə mə ˈbil ˌɔ tə ˈmo bɪl ˌɔ tə ˈmo bil ɔ tə ˈmo bil ˈɔ tə mə ˌbil
autonomy	aw TON uh mi	ô tŏn′ŏ mĭ	ɔ ˈtan ə mɪ; *ES* *also* ɔ ˈtɒn-
autumn	AW tuhm	ô′tŭm	ˈɔ təm
autumnal	aw TUHM nuhl aw TUHM n'l	ô tŭm′năl ô tŭm′n'l § 33(1)	ɔ ˈtʌm nəl ɔ ˈtʌm nl̩
auxiliary	awg ZIL yuh ri	ôg zĭl′yȧ rĭ § 47(1)	ɔg ˈzɪl jə rɪ, -ˈzɪl ɪ e rɪ, -ˈzɪl ə rɪ
avalanche	AV uh lanch AV uh lahnch	ăv′ȧ lȧnch §§ 20(5), 47(3)	ˈæv ə læntʃ, ˈæv ļ-; *E also* -lantʃ, -lɑntʃ
avatar	*av* uh TAHR	ăv′ȧ tär′	ˌæv ə ˈtar; *ES* -ˈtɑ:(r), *E also* -ˈtɑ:(r)
avaunt	uh VAWNT uh VAHNT	ȧ vônt′ ȧ vänt′ § 47(2)	ɔ ˈvɔnt ɔ ˈvant
avenue	AV i nyoo AV i noo	ăv′ê nū § 50(32)	ˈæv ɪ nju ˈæv ɪ nu
aver (v.)	uh VUHR	ȧ vûr′	ə ˈvɝ; *ES also* ə ˈvɜ(r)
average	AV uhr ij	ăv′ēr ĭj	ˈæv ɚ ɪdʒ, ˈæv rɪdʒ
aversion	uh VUHR zhuhn uh VUHR shuhn	ȧ vûr′zhŭn ȧ vûr′shŭn §§ 47(1), 50(28)	ə ˈvɝ ʒən, -ʃən; *ES* *also* -ˈvɜ-

	SIMPLIFIED	DIACRITICAL	PHONETIC
aviary	AY vi *er* i *B.,* AY vi uhr i	ā′vĭ ĕr′ĭ *B.,* ā′vĭ ēr ĭ §§ 13, 20(2), 24(9), 51(4)	′e vɪ ˌɛr ɪ *B.,* ′e vɪ ə rɪ
aviation	*ay* vi AY shuhn	ā′vĭ ā′shŭn § 50(30)	ˌe vɪ ′e ʃən, ˌæv ɪ-
aviator	AY vi *ay* tuhr	ā′vĭ ā′tēr § 47(1)	′e vɪ ˌe tɚ; *ES* -tə(r)
	Gaining ground: AV i *ay* tuhr	*Gaining ground:* ăv′ĭ ā′tēr § 51(5)	*Gaining ground:* ′æv ɪ ˌe tɚ; *ES* -tə(r)
avidity	uh VID uh ti uh VID i ti	*a* vĭd′*i* tĭ *a* vĭd′ĭ tĭ	ə ′vɪd ə ɪt ə ′vɪd ɪ tɪ
avoirdupois	*av* uhr duh POIZ AV uhr duh *poiz*	ăv′ēr dŭ poiz′ ăv′ēr dŭ poiz′	ˌæv ɚ də ′pɔɪz, ′æv ɚ də ˌpɔɪz; *ES* ˌæv ə-, ′æv ə-
Avon (town: Mass.; Conn.)	AY von AV uhn	ā′vŏn ăv′ŭn	′e vɑn, -vɒn ′æv ən
—— (river: England)	AY vuhn AV uhn	ā′vŭn ăv′ŭn	′e vən ′æv ən
avouch	uh VOWCH § 50(34)	*a* vouch′	ə ′vautʃ
awakening	uh WAYK uhn ing	*a* wāk′ĕn ĭng § 50(14)	ə ′wek ən ɪŋ, ə ′wek nɪŋ, -n̩ɪŋ
awful	AW fool AW f'l	ô′fŏol ô′f'l § 40(13)	′ɔ fʊl ′ɔ fl̩
—— "*inspiring reverential fear; impressive*"	AW fool	ô′fŏol	′ɔ fʊl
—— (slang or inf.) "*very bad; very great; ugly*"	AW f'l	ô′f'l § 51(11)	′ɔ fl̩
awkward	AWK wuhrd	ôk′wērd	′ɔk wɚd; *ES* -wəd
awry	uh RAI § 50(34)	*a* rī′	ə ′raɪ
ay (interj.–"*ah! alas!*")	ay	ā	e
aye, ay (adv.–"*all the while*")	ay	ā	e
aye, ay (adv., n.– "*yes*")	ai § 50(34)	ī	aɪ
Ayrshir	EHR shir	âr′shĭr	′ɛr ʃɪr, ′ær-, -ʃɚ; *ES* ′æə ʃɪə(r), -ʃə(r), *E also* ′ɛə-
azalea	uh ZAYL yuh *Cap.:* uh ZAY li uh	*a* zāl′y*a* *Cap.:* *a* zā′lĕ *a*	ə ′zel jə *Cap.:* ə ′ze lɪ ə

	SIMPLIFIED	DIACRITICAL	PHONETIC
Azores	uh ZOHRZ uh ZAWRZ	*ȧ* zōrz′ § 34(3)	ə ˈzorz ə ˈzɔrz; *ES* ə ˈzoəz, *E also* ə ˈzɔəz
azure	AZH uhr AY zhuhr AZH ŏŏr AZH ōōr	ăzh′ēr ā′zhēr ăzh′ŏŏr § 47(3)	ˈæʒ ɚ, ˈe ʒɚ, ˈæʒ ʊr; *ES* -ə(r), -ʒə(r), -ʊə(r)

B

Babel, babel	BAY buhl BAY b'l	bā′bĕl bā′b'l § 31(3)	ˈbe bəl ˈbe bl̩
baboon	ba BOON	bă bōōn′	bæ ˈbun, bə-
baby	BAY bi	bā′bĭ	ˈbe bɪ
bacilli	buh SIL aͥ͡ *ı* § 50(34)	bȧ sĭl′ī	bə ˈsɪl aɪ
bacillus	buh SIL uhs	bȧ sĭl′ŭs	bə ˈsɪl əs
backgammon	BAK *gam* uhn *bak* GAM uhn bak GAM uhn	băk′găm′ŭn băk′găm′ŭn băk găm′ŭn § 47(1)	ˈbæk ˌgæm ən ˌbæk ˈgæm ən bæk ˈgæm ən
backslide (n.) —— (v.i.)	BAK *slaͥ͡d* *bak* SLAͥ͡D BAK *slaͥ͡d* § 50(34)	băk′slīd′ băk′slīd′ băk′slīd′ §§ 12, 47(3)	ˈbæk ˌslaɪd ˌbæk ˈslaɪd ˈbæk ˌslaɪd
bacon	BAY kuhn BAY k'n	bā′kŭn bā′k'n	ˈbe kən ˈbe kn̩
bacteria	bak TĬER i uh bak TIR i uh bak TEER i uh	băk tēr′ĭ *ȧ* § 24(2) băk tēr′ĭ *ȧ*	bæk ˈtɪər ɪ ə, -ˈtɪr-, -ˈtir-; *ES* -ˈtɪər-
bade	bad	băd § 47(2)	bæd
Bahamas	buh HAY muhz *B.,* buh HAH muhz	bȧ hā′mȧz *B.,* bȧ hä′mȧz § 51(4)	bə ˈhe məz *B.,* bə ˈhɑ məz
bairn	behrn bayrn	bârn bärn	bɛrn, bæərn, bern; *ES* bæən, beən, *E also* bɛən
baize	bayz	bāz	bez
balcony	BAL kuh ni	băl′kȯ nĭ § 47(2)	ˈbæl kə nɪ

balk	bawk	bôk	bɔk
Balkan	BAWL kuhn bahl KAHN	bôl′kăn bäl kän′	'bɔl kən bɑl 'kɑn
ballad	BAL uhd	băl′ăd	'bæl əd
balloon	buh LOON	bă lōōn′	bə 'lun, bļ 'un
balm	bahm	bäm	bɑm; *E also* bɑm
balmy	BAHM i	bäm′Ĭ	'bɑm ɪ; *E also* 'bam-
balsam	BAWL suhm	bôl′săm	'bɔl səm
balustrade	*bal* uhs TRAYD *bal* uh STRAYD *bal uhs* TRAYD	băl′ŭs trād′ §§ 40(6), 47(1) băl′ŭs trād′	ˌbæl əs 'tred ˌbæl ə 'stred ˌbæl ʌs 'tred
banana	buh NAN uh *B.*, buh NAH nuh	bȧ năn′ȧ *B.*, bȧ nä′nȧ §§ 47(3), 51(4)	bə 'næn ə *B.*, bə 'nɑ nə
banditti	ban DIT i	băn dĭt′Ĭ	bæn 'dɪt ɪ
bandy	BAN di	băn′dĬ	'bæn dɪ
banquet	BANG kwet BANG kwit	băng′kwĕt băng′kwĬt §§ 24(5), 33(4)	'bæŋ kwɛt 'bæŋ kwɪt
Banquo	BANG kwoh BANG koh	băng′kwō băng′kō	'bæŋ kwo, -ko, 'bæn-
baptism	BAP tiz'm BAP tiz uhm	băp′tĬz'm § 50(15)	'bæp tɪzm̩ 'bæp tɪz əm
Baptist	BAP tist	băp′tĬst	'bæp tɪst
baptize	bap TA͞IZ *Not infreq.:* BAP ta͞iz § 50(34)	băp tīz′ *Not infreq.:* băp′tĬz § 51(8)	bæp 'taɪz *Not infreq.:* 'bæp taɪz
Barbados	bahr BAY dohz	bär bā′dōz	bɑr 'be doz; *ES* bɑ: 'be-, *E also* bɑ:-
barbarian	bahr BEHR i uhn bahr BAY ri uhn	bär bâr′Ĭ ăn § 20(2)	bɑr 'bɛr ɪ ən, -'bær-, -'be rɪ-; *ES* bɑ:-, *E also* bɑ:-
barbaric	bahr BAR ik	bär băr′Ĭk	bɑr 'bær ɪk; *ES* bɑ:-, *E also* bɑ:-
barbarism	BAHR buh riz'm BAHR buh riz uhm	bär′bȧ rĬz'm	'bɑr bə rɪzm̩, -rɪz əm; *ES* 'bɑ:-, *E also* 'bɑ:-
barbarity	bahr BAR uh ti bahr BAR i ti	bär băr′ĭ tĬ bär băr′Ĭ tĬ	bɑr 'bær ə tɪ, -ɪ tɪ; *ES* bɑ:-, *E also* bɑ:-
barbarous	BAHR buh ruhs	bär′bȧ rŭs § 50(25)	'bɑr bə rəs, -brəs; *ES* 'bɑ:-, *E also* 'bɑ:-

	SIMPLIFIED	DIACRITICAL	PHONETIC
barbecue	BAHR bi kyoo BAHR buh kyoo	bär′bĕ kū bär′bĕ kū §§ 48(2), 50(32)	′bɑr bɪ kju, -bə-; *ES* ′bɑ:-, *E also* ′bɑ:-
barberry	BAHR *ber* i BAHR buhr i	bär′bĕr′ĭ bär′bĕr ĭ	′bɑr ˌbɛr ɪ, -bər ɪ; *ES* ′bɑ:-, *E also* ′bɑ:-
bared	behrd	bârd	bɛrd, bæɛrd; *ES* bæəd, *E also* bɛəd
bargain	BAHR gin	bär′gĭn	′bɑr gɪn; *ES* ′bɑ:-, *E also* ′bɑ:-
barium	BEHR i uhm BAY ri uhm	bâr′ĭ ŭm bā′rĭ ŭm § 47(1)	′bɛr ɪ əm, ′bæɛr-, ′be rɪ-; *E also* ′bɛə rɪ-
barrage (*"gunfire; sub- ject to artillery fire"*)	buh RAHZH *B.*, BAR ahzh	bȧ räzh′ *B.*, bär′äzh § 51(4)	bə ′rɑʒ, bɑ- *B.*, ′bær ɑʒ
barrel	BAR uhl	bär′ĕl	′bær əl, -ɪl
barricade	*bar* uh KAYD *bar* i KAYD	bär′ĭ kād′ bär′ĭ kād′	ˌbær ə ′ked ˌbær ɪ ′ked
barrier	BAR i uhr	bär′ĭ ēr	′bær ɪ ɚ; *ES* -ə(r)
Baruch (*Bible*)	BEHR uhk BAY ruhk	bâr′ŭk bā′rŭk	′bɛr ək, ′bær-, ′be rək
basal	BAYS uhl BAYS ′l § 50(34)	bās′ăl bās′ ′l	′bes əl ′bes ḷ
basalt	buh SAWLT BAS awlt	bȧ sôlt′ băs′ôlt § 47(2)	bə ′sɔlt ′bæs ɔlt
bases (pl. of *basis*)	BAY seez	bā′sēz §§ 48(3), 50(6)	′be siz
bases (pl. of *base*)	BAYS ez BAYS iz § 50(34)	bās′ĕz bās′ĭz §§ 24(5), 48(3)	′bes ɛz ′bes ɪz
basil	BAZ uhl BAZ ′l BAZ il	băz′ĭl băz′ ′l băz′ĭl	′bæz əl ′bæz ḷ ′bæz ɪl
basilisk	BAS uh lisk BAS i lisk BAZ uh lisk BAZ i lisk	băs′ĭ lĭsk băs′ĭ lĭsk băz′ĭ lĭsk băz′ĭ lĭsk § 47(3)	′bæs ə lɪsk ′bæs ɪ lɪsk ′bæz ə lɪsk ′bæz ɪ lɪsk
basin	BAY s'n	bā′s'n § 33(2)	′be sṇ
basket	BAS ket BAHS ket BAS kit BAHS kit	băs′kĕt băs′kĭt §§ 20(5), 24(5), 47(2)	′bæs ket, -kɪt; *E also* ′bas-, ′bɑs-
bass (*"tone"*)	bays § 50(34)	bās	bes
bass (*"fish"*)	bas	băs	bæs
bastard	BAS tuhrd	băs′tĕrd § 47(2)	′bæs tɚd; *ES* -təd

	SIMPLIFIED	DIACRITICAL	PHONETIC
bastille, bastile	bas TEEL *F., bas* TEE y' *F., bahs* TEE y'	băs tēl' *F.,* bȧs'tē'y' § 47(2)	bæs 'til *F.,* bas 'ti: j
batch	bach	băch	bætʃ
bath	bath bahth	bȧth §§ 20(5), 39(6), 47(2)	bæθ; *E also* baθ, bɑθ
baths	baŧħz bahŧħz	bȧŧħz §§ 39(5), 47(2), 48(3)	bæðz; *E also* baðz, bɑðz
bathe	bayŧħ	bāŧħ	beð
baton (v.t.)	BAT uhn	băt'ŭn	'bæt ən
—— (n.)	*bah* TAWN ba TAWN BAT uhn ba TON	bȧ'tôn' §§ 12, 47(3) băt'ŭn bă tŏn'	*F.,* ba 'tɔ̃ [-'tō]; bæ-, 'bæt ən, bæ 'tɑn; *ES* *also* -'tɒn
battalion	buh TAL yuhn	bă tăl'yŭn	bə 'tæl jən, bæ-
battery	BAT uhr i	băt'ĕr ɪ § 9	'bæt ər ɪ, 'bæt rɪ
battle	BAT 'l	băt' 'l § 31(3)	'bæt ḷ
bayonet	BAY uh net BAY uh nit	bā'ŏ nĕt bā'ŏ nĭt § 24(5)	'be ə nɛt 'be ə nɪt
bayou	BA͡I oo § 50(34)	bī'o͞o	'baɪ u, -ju
bazaar, bazar	buh ZAHR	bȧ zär'	bə 'zɑr; *ES* -'zɑ:(r), *E also* -'za:(r)
be	bee *Unstressed:* bi	bē *Unstressed:* bĭ § 16	bi *Unstressed:* bɪ
beard	bĭerd bird beerd	bḝrd §§ 24(2), 50(34)	bɪərd, bɪrd, bird; *ES* bɪəd, *S also* bɛəd
beatific	*bee* uh TIF ik	bē'ȧ tĭf'ĭk	ˌbi ə 'tɪf ɪk
beatitude	bi AT uh tyood bi AT uh tood bi AT i tyood bi AT i tood	bē ăt'ĭ tūd bē ăt'ĭ tūd §§ 48(2), 50(32)	bɪ 'æt ə tjud bɪ 'æt ə tud bɪ 'æt ɪ tjud bɪ 'æt ɪ tud
beau	boh	bō	bo
beauteous	BYOO ti uhs	bū'tĕ ŭs §§ 28(9), 47(2), 48(2), 50(32)	'bju tɪ əs
beautiful	BYOO tuh fool BYOO ti fool BYOO tuh f'l	bū'tĭ fo͝ol bū'tĭ fo͝ol bū'tĭ f'l § 48(2)	'bju tə fʊl, -tɪ-, -fəl, -fḷ
beauty	BYOO ti	bū'tĭ §§ 48(2), 50(32)	'bju tɪ
beaux	bohz	bōz	boz
because	bi KAWZ bi KOZ	bē kôz' bē kŏz'	bɪ 'kɔz, bə-, -'kɒz
bedight	bi DA͡IT § 50(34)	bē dīt'	bɪ 'daɪt

	SIMPLIFIED	DIACRITICAL	PHONETIC
bedizen	bi DIZ 'n *B.*, bi DĀI z'n	bĕ dĭz′ 'n *B.*, bĕ dī′z'n §§ 47(3), 49(1), 51(4)	bɪ ′dɪz n̩ *B.*, bɪ ′daɪ zn̩
Bedouin	BED ŏŏ in BED ŏŏ een	bĕd′ŏŏ ĭn bĕd′ŏŏ ēn § 47(2)	′bɛd ʊ ɪn ′bɛd ʊ in
Beelzebub	bi EL zi *buhb*	bĕ ĕl′zĕ bŭb § 40(6)	bɪ ′ɛl zɪ bʌb, bi-
been	bin *B.*, been *Unstressed, often:* ben	bĭn *B.*, bēn § 51(4) *Unstressed, often:* bĕn §§ 16, 47(3)	bɪn *B.*, bin *Unstressed, often:* ben
Beethoven (**Ludwig van**)	BAY toh vuhn BAYT hoh vuhn	bā′tō vĕn bāt′hō vĕn	′be to vən, -vn̩ ′bet ho vən
before	bi FOHR bi FAWR	bĕ fōr′ § 34(3)	bɪ ′for, -′fər, bə-; *ES* -′foə(r), *E* *also* -′fɔə(r)
beguile	bi GĀIL § 50(34)	bĕ gīl′	bɪ ′gaɪl
behemoth	bi HEE muhth BEE hi moth BEE hi mohth	bĕ hē′mŏth bē′hĕ mŏth bē′hĕ mōth	bɪ ′hi məθ, ′bi hɪ maθ, -moθ, -mn̩θ, -məθ, -hə-
being	BEE ing	bē′ĭng § 50(14)	′bi ɪŋ
beldam	BEL duhm	bĕl′dăm	′bɛl dəm
beleaguer	bi LEE guhr	bĕ lē′gẽr	bɪ ′li gɚ; *ES* -gə(r)
Belial	BEE li uhl BEEL yuhl	bē′lĭ ăl bēl′yăl	′bi lɪ əl ′bil jəl
believe	bi LEEV	bĕ lēv′ § 49(1)	bɪ ′liv, bə-, bl̩ ′iv
belike	bi LĀIK § 50(34)	bĕ līk′ § 49(1)	bɪ ′laɪk
belladonna	*bel* uh DON uh	bĕl′*a* dŏn′*a*	ˌbɛl ə ′dɑn ə; *ES* *also* -′dɒn-
bellows	BEL ohz *Sometimes:* BEL uhs	bĕl′ōz *Sometimes:* bĕl′ŭs §§ 47(2), 51(8)	′bɛl oz, -əz *Sometimes:* ′bɛl əs
belong	bi LAWNG bi LONG	bĕ lŏng′ § 34(7)	bɪ ′lɔŋ, -′lɒŋ, bə-
beloved	bi LUHV ed bi LUHV id bi LUHVD	bĕ lŭv′ĕd bĕ lŭv′ĭd bĕ lŭvd′ § 24(5)	bɪ ′lʌv ɛd bɪ ′lʌv ɪd bɪ ′lʌvd
beneath	bi NEETH bi NEEŦH	bĕ nēth′ bĕ neth′ § 47(3)	bɪ ′niθ bɪ ′nið
beneficent	bi NEF uh suhnt bi NEF i suhnt bi NEF i s'nt	bĕ nĕf′*i* sĕnt bĕ nĕf′ĭ sĕnt bĕ nĕf′*i* s'nt	bɪ ′nɛf ə sənt, -′nɛf ɪ-, -sn̩t, bə-
beneficiary	*ben* i FISH i *er* i *ben* i FISH uhr i	bĕn′ĕ fĭsh′ ĭ ĕr′ĭ bĕn′ĕ fĭsh′ẽr ĭ §§ 20(2), 24(9)	ˌben ɪ ′fɪʃ ɪ ˌɛr ɪ, -′fɪʃ ər ɪ, ˌben ə-

	SIMPLIFIED	DIACRITICAL	PHONETIC
benevolence	bi NEV uh luhns	bĕ nĕv′ŏ lĕns	bɪ ˈnɛv ə ləns, bə-
benign	bi NAÎN § 50(34)	bĕ nīn′ § 25(5)	bɪ ˈnaɪn
benignant	bi NIG nuhnt	bĕ nĭg′nănt	bɪ ˈnɪg nənt
benison	BEN i z′n	bĕn′ĭ z′n	ˈbɛn ɪ zn̩, -ɪ sn̩,
	BEN i s′n	bĕn′ĭ s′n § 47(2)	-ə zn̩, -ə sn̩
bequeath	bi KWEETH	bĕ kwēth′	bɪ ˈkwið, bə-
	Occas.:	*Occas.:*	*Occas.:*
	bi KWEETH	bĕ kwēth′	bɪ ˈkwiθ, bə-
		§§ 39(4), 47(1), 51(8)	
bequeathed	bi KWEETHD	bĕ kwēthd′	bɪ ˈkwiðd, bə-
	Occas.:	*Occas.:*	*Occas.:*
	bi KWEETHD	bĕ kwēthd′	bɪ ˈkwiθd
		§ 51(8)	
bequest	bi KWEST	bĕ kwĕst′	bɪ ˈkwɛst
Berkeley (Calif.)	BUHRK li	bûrk′lĭ	ˈbɝk lɪ; *ES also* ˈbɜk-
Berlin (Germany)	*buhr* LIN	bûr lĭn′	bɝ ˈlɪn, bə-; *ES*
	buhr LIN	§ 47(2)	*also* bɜ-, *ES*
	G., ber LEEN	*G.,* bĕr lēn′	bə-; *G.,* ber ˈliːn
Bernard	BUHR nahrd	bûr′närd	ˈbɝ nɑrd, -nɚd,
	BUHR nuhrd	bûr′nĕrd	bɚ ˈnɑrd; *ES*
	buhr NAHRD	bĕr närd′	*also* ˈbɜ-, *ES*
			-nɑːd, -ˈnɑːd,
			-nəd, bə-, *E also*
			-naːd, -ˈnaːd
besought	bi SAWT	bĕ sôt′ § 49 (1)	bɪ ˈsɔt
bestial	BEST yuhl	bĕst′yăl	ˈbɛst jəl
	BES tyuhl	bĕs′tyăl	ˈbɛs tjəl
	BES chuhl	bĕs′chăl	ˈbɛs tʃəl
		§§ 39(8), 47(3)	
Bethlehem	BETH li uhm	bĕth′lĕ ĕm	ˈbɛθ lɪ əm
	BETH li hem	bĕth′lĕ hĕm	ˈbɛθ lɪ hɛm
betroth	bi TRAWTH	bĕ trôth′	bɪ ˈtrɔθ
	bi TROTH	§§ 34(7), 47(3), 49(1)	bɪ ˈtrɒθ
	bi TROHTH	bĕ trōth′	bɪ ˈtroð
betrothal	bi TRAWTH uhl	bĕ trôth′ăl	bɪ ˈtrɔθ əl
	bi TROTH uhl	§§ 34(7), 49(1)	bɪ ˈtrɒθ əl
	bi TROHTH uhl	bĕ trōth′ăl	bɪ ˈtroð əl
between	bi TWEEN	bĕ twēn′	bɪ ˈtwin, bə-
bevel	BEV uhl	bĕv′ĕl	ˈbɛv əl, -l̩
beverage	BEV uhr ij	bĕv′ĕr ĭj	ˈbɛv ər ɪdʒ,
		§§ 9, 50(1)	bɛv rɪdʒ
bey	bay	bā	be
bias	BAÎ uhs § 50(34)	bī′ăs	ˈbaɪ əs
Biblical	BIB li kuhl	bĭb′lĭ kăl	ˈbɪb lɪ kəl, -kl̩
bicycle	BAÎ sik′l § 50(34)	bī′sĭk′l	ˈbaɪ sɪkl̩

bier	bĭer bir beer	bēr § 24(2) bēr	bɪər, bɪr, bir; *ES* bɪə(r), *S also* bɛə(r)
bigamy	BIG uh mi	bĭg′á mĭ	'bɪg ə mɪ
bight	bait § 50(34)	bīt	baɪt
bigoted	BIG uht ed BIG uht id	bĭg′ŭt ĕd bĭg′ŭt ĭd § 24(5)	'bɪg ət ɛd 'bɪg ət ɪd
bilge	bilj	bĭlj	bɪldʒ
bilious	BIL yuhs	bĭl′yŭs § 28(9)	'bɪl jəs
billet-doux	BIL ay DOO *F., bee ye* DOO	bĭl′ā dōō′ *F.,* bē′yĕ′dōō′	'bɪl e 'du, 'bɪl ɪ-; *F.,* bi jɛ 'du
billiards	BIL yuhrdz	bĭl′yērdz	'bɪl jɚdz; *ES* -jədz
billion	BIL yuhn	bĭl′yŭn	'bɪl jən
binocular	bin OK yŏō luhr bi NOK yŏō luhr baī NOK yŏō luhr	bĭn ŏk′û lēr §§ 47(2), 50(34) bī nŏk′û lēr	bɪn 'ak ju lɚ, -jə-, bɪ 'nak-, baɪ-; *ES* -lə(r), *also* -ɒk-, -'nɒk-
biographer	baī OG ruh fuhr bi OG ruh fuhr § 50(34)	bī ŏg′rá fēr bī ŏg′rá fēr	baɪ 'ag rə fɚ, bɪ-, -'ɒg-; *ES* -fə(r)
biographical	baī uh GRAF i kuhl § 50(34)	bī′ŏ grăf′ĭ kŭl	ˌbaɪ ə 'græf ɪ kəl, -kl̩
biography	baī OG ruh fi bi OG ruh fi § 50(34)	bī ŏg′rá fĭ bī ŏg′rá fĭ	baɪ 'ag rə fɪ, bɪ 'ag, baɪ 'ɒg-, bɪ-
biology	baī OL uh ji § 50(34)	bī ŏl′ŏ jĭ § 28(3)	baɪ 'al ə dʒɪ; *ES* *also* -'ɒl-
bird	*buhrd*	bûrd § 40(6)	bɝd; *ES also* bɜd
biscuit	BIS kit	bĭs′kĭt	'bɪs kɪt
Bismarck (Otto von)	BIZ mahrk *G.,* BIS mahrk	bĭz′märk *G.,* bĭs′märk	'bɪz mɑrk; *ES* -mɑːk, *E also* -mɑːk; *G.,* 'bɪs-
bismuth	BIZ muhth BIS muhth	bĭz′mŭth bĭs′mŭth	'bɪz məθ 'bɪs məθ
bison	BAī s'n BAī z'n § 50(34)	bī′s'n bī′ z'n §§ 9, 47(2)	'baɪ sn̩ 'baɪ zn̩
bittern	BIT uhrn	bĭt′ērn	'bɪt ɚn; *ES* -ən
bitumen	bi TYOO muhn bi TOO muhn BIT yŏō muhn BICH ŏō muhn	bĭ tū′měn §§ 47(2), 48(2), 50(32, 33) bĭt′û měn bĭt′û měn	bɪ 'tju mən bɪ 'tu mən 'bɪt ju mən 'bɪtʃ ʊ mən
bituminous	bi TYOO muh nuhs bi TYOO mi nuhs bi TOO muh nuhs	bĭ tū′mĭ nŭs bĭ tū′mĭ nŭs §§ 48(2), 50(32)	bɪ 'tju mə nəs, -'tu-, -mɪ-, baɪ-

bivouack	BIV ŏŏ ak BIV wak	bĭv′ŏŏ ăk bĭv′wăk § 47(3)	'bɪv ʊ æk 'bɪv wæk
bivouacked	BIV ŏŏ akt BIV wakt	bĭv′ŏŏ ăkt bĭv′wăkt §§ 47(1), 50(4)	'bɪv ʊ ækt 'bɪv wækt
bizarre	bi ZAHR	bĭ zär′	bɪ 'zɑr; *ES* -'zɑ:(r), *E also* -'zɑ:(r)
blackguard	BLAG ahrd	blăg′ärd	'blæg ɑrd, -ɚd; *ES* -ɑ:d, -əd, *E* *also* -ɑ:d
blanch	blanch blahnch	blȧnch §§ 20(5), 22(6), 47(2)	blæntʃ; *E also* blɑntʃ, blɑntʃ
blandishment	BLAN dish muhnt	blăn′dĭsh mĕnt § 50(22)	'blæn dɪʃ mənt
blaspheme	blas FEEM	blăs fēm′	blæs 'fim
blasphemy	BLAS fi mi	blăs′fĕ mĭ	'blæs fɪ mɪ
blast	blast blahst	blȧst §§ 20(5), 47(3)	blæst; *E also* blast, blɑst
blatant	BLAY tuhnt	blā′tănt	'ble tənt, -tn̩t
blazon	BLAY z'n	blā′ z'n §§ 9, 33(2)	'ble zn̩
blessed (p.t. of *bless*)	blest	blĕst	blɛst
	Arch.: BLES ed BLES id	*Arch.:* blĕs′ĕd blĕs′ĭd §§ 24(5), 51(2)	*Arch.:* 'blɛs ɛd 'blɛs ɪd
blessed (adj.)	BLES ed BLES id *Sometimes:* blest	blĕs′ĕd blĕs′ĭd § 24(5) *Sometimes:* blĕst § 51(8)	'blɛs ɛd 'blɛs ɪd *Sometimes:* blɛst
blight	blaīt § 50(34)	blīt	blaɪt
blithe	blaīth *Not infreq.:* blaīth	blīth *Not infreq.:* blīth §§ 47(2), 51(8)	blaɪð *Not infreq.:* blaɪθ
blockade	blok AYD blo KAYD	blŏk ād′	blɑk 'ed, blɑ 'ked; *ES also* blɒk-, blɒ-
blouse (n.)	blowz blows *F.*, blooz § 50(34)	blouz blous *F.*, blōōz § 47(1)	blaʊz blaʊs *F.*, bluz
—— (v.i.)	blowz § 50(34)	blouz	blaʊz
bludgeon	BLUHJ uhn	blŭj′ŭn	'blʌdʒ ən
blue	bloo	blōō §§ 40(4), 47(2), 48(2)	blu
boa	BOH uh	bō′ȧ	'bo ə

boatswain	BOH s'n BOHT *swayn*	bō′ s'n bōt′swān′ § 42(3)	′bo sn̩ ′bot ˌswen
Boccaccio (Giovanni)	bohk KAHT choh boh KAH chee oh (joh VAHN ee)	bŏk kät′chŏ bō kä′chē ō (jō vän′ē)	*It.,* bok ′kat tʃo bo ′ka tʃi o (dʒo ′van i)
bodice	BOD is	bŏd′ĭs	′bɑd ɪs; *ES also* ′bɒd-
Boer	boŏr boor *E.,* bohr bawr	bo͞or § 40(4) *E.,* bōr	bʊr, bor, bɔr; *ES* bʊə(r), boə(r), *E also* bɔə(r)
bog	bog	bŏg § 34(6)	bɑg, bɔg, bɒg
boil	boil	boil	bɔɪl
boiler	BOIL uhr	boil′ẽr	′bɔɪl ɚ; *ES* -ə(r)
boisterous	BOIS tuhr uhs	bois′tẽr ŭs §§ 9, 50(25)	′bɔɪs tɚ əs, -trəs
Bologna	boh LOH nyah	bŏ lō′nyä	bo ′lo nja; *It.,* bo ′loɲ ɲa
	Pop.: buh LOHN yuh buh LOH nuh	*Pop.:* bŏ lōn′yŭ bŏ lō′nŭ § 51(3)	*Pop.:* bə ′lon jə bə ′lo nə
Bolshevik, **bolshevik**	BOL shuh vik BOHL shuh vik	bŏl′shĕ vĭk bōl′shĕ vĭk	′bal ʃə vɪk, ′bol-; *ES also* ′bɒl-
Bolsheviki, **bolsheviki**	*bol* shuh VEE ki *bohl* shuh VEE ki *Russ.,* *buhl* shuh vi KEE	bŏl′shĕ vē′kĕ bōl′shĕ vē′kĕ *Russ.,* bŏl′shĕ vē kē′	ˌbal ʃə ′vi kɪ, ˌbol-; *ES also* ˌbɒl-; *Russ.,* ˌbol ʃə vɪ ′ki
bomb	bom *Occas.:* *buhm*	bŏm § 21(1) *Occas.:* bŭm §§ 47(3), 51(8)	bɑm; *ES also* bɒm *Occas.:* bʌm
bombard (v.t.)	bom BAHRD *buhm* BAHRD § 40(6)	bŏm bärd′ bŭm bärd′ § 47(2)	bam ′bɑrd, bʌm-; *ES* -′bɑːd, *also* bɒm-, *E also* -′bɑːd
—— (n.)	BOM bahrd	bŏm′bärd § 47(2)	′bam bard; *ES* -bɑːd, *also* ′bɒm-, *E also* -bɑːd
bonanza	boh NAN zuh	bŏ năn′zà	bo ′næn zə
bonbon	BON *bon*	bŏn′bŏn′ § 20(14)	′ban ˌban; *ES also* ′bɒn ˌbɒn
	F., *bawN* BAWN	*F.,* bôN′bôN′	*F.,* bɔ̃ ′bɔ̃ [bõ ′bõ]
bonnet	BON et BON it	bŏn′ĕt bŏn′ĭt §§ 24(5), 50(10)	′ban ɛt, -ɪt; *ES* *also* ′bɒn-
book	boŏk	boͦok § 34(22)	bʊk

	SIMPLIFIED	DIACRITICAL	PHONETIC
booth	booth B., booth	bōōth B., bōōth §§ 47(1), 51(4)	buθ B., buð
Bordeaux (n.)	bawr DOH bawr DOH	bôr'dō' bôr·dō'	ˌbɔr 'do, bɔr-; ES ˌbɔə 'do, bɔə-
—— (adj.)	bawr DOH Often: BAWR doh	bôr'dō' Often: bôr'dō' § 51(9)	ˌbɔr 'do; ES ˌbɔə- Often: 'bɔr ˌdo; ES 'bɔə ˌdo
born	bawrn	bôrn	bɔrn; ES bɔən
borne (p.p. of bear)	bohrn bawrn	bōrn § 34(3)	born, bɔrn; ES boən, E also bɔən
borough	BUHR oh	bûr'ŏ § 34(25)	'bɝ o, -ə; ES also bɜ ro, bʌ-, -rə
bosom	BOOZ uhm BOO zuhm	bŏŏz'ŭm bŏŏ'zŭm §§ 32(2), 47(3)	'buz əm 'bu zəm
Bosporus	BOS puh ruhs	bŏs'pŏ rŭs	'bɑs pə rəs; ES also 'bɒs-
Boston	BAWS tuhn BOS tuhn	bŏs'tŭn § 34(7)	'bɔs tən, 'bɒs-, -tn̩
bottle	BOT 'l	bŏt' 'l § 31(3)	'bat l̩; ES also 'bɒt-
boudoir	BOO dwahr BOO dwawr	bŏŏ'dwär bŏŏ'dwôr	'bu dwɑr, -dwɔr; ES -dwɑ:(r), -dwɔə(r)
bough	bow § 50(34)	bou	baʊ
bouillon	boo YAWN BOOL yuhn BOOL yuhn bŏŏl YON BOOL yon	bŏŏ'yôn' bŏŏl'yŭn bŏŏl'yŭn bŏŏl yŏn' bŏŏl'yŏn § 47(3)	F., bu 'jɔ̃ [-'jõ], 'bʊl jən, 'bʊl-, -jɑn, -jɒn, bʊl 'jɑn, -'jɒn
boulder	BOHL duhr	bōl'dẽr	'bol dɚ; ES -də(r)
boulevard	BOO luh vahrd BOOL uh vahrd B., BOOL vahr BOOL vahrd	bŏŏ'lĕ värd bŏŏl'ĕ värd §§ 47(2), 51(4) B., bŏŏl'vär bŏŏl'värd	'bu lə vard, 'bʊl ə-; ES -vɑ:d, E also -vɑ:d; B., 'bul var, -vard; ES -vɑ:(r), -vɑ:d, E also -vɑ:(r), -vɑ:d
Boulogne	boo LAWN y' E., bŏŏ LOHN boo LOHN bŏŏ LOIN	bŏŏ'lôn'y' E., bŏŏ lōn' bŏŏ lōn' bŏŏ loin'	F., bu 'lɔɲ E., bʊ 'lon, bu-, bə-, -'lɔɪn
boundary	BOWN duh ri § 50(34)	boun'dȧ rĭ § 9	'baʊn də rɪ, -drɪ
bouquet	boo KAY boh KAY	bŏŏ kā' bō kā' § 47(3)	bu 'ke bo 'ke

	SIMPLIFIED	DIACRITICAL	PHONETIC
—— "*aroma or fragrance*," pref.	boo KAY	bōō kā′	bu ′ke
Bourbon, bourbon	BŎŎR buhn	bŏŏr′bŭn	′bʊr bən; *ES* ′bʊə bən
—— also, (local pronunciation, Kentucky)	BUHR buhn	bûr′bŭn	′bɝ bən; *ES also* ′bɜ-
bourgeois ("*middle class*")	bŏŏr ZHWAH BŎŎR zhwah *F.,* boor ZHWAH	bŏŏr zhwä′ bŏŏr′zhwä *F.,* bōōr′zhwä′	bʊr ′ʒwa, ′bʊr ʒwa; *ES* bʊə-, ′bʊə-; *F.,* bʊr ′ʒwa
bourgeoisie	*bŏŏr zhwa* ZEE *boor zhwa* ZEE *bŏŏr zhwah* ZEE *boor zhwah* ZEE	bŏŏr′zhwȧ′zē′ § 40(4) bŏŏr′zhwä′zē′ *F.,* bōōr′zhwä′zē′	ˌbʊr ˌʒwa ′zi, -ˌʒwa-; *ES* ˌbʊə-; *F.,* bʊr ʒwa ′zi
bourn, bourne ("*brook*")	bohrn bawrn	bōrn bôrn	born, bɔrn; *ES* boən, *E also* bɔən
bowl	bohl	bōl §§ 47(2), 51(7)	bol
bowsprit	BOW sprit BOH sprit § 50(34)	bou′sprĭt bō′sprĭt § 47(3)	′baʊ sprɪt ′bo sprɪt
bracken	BRAK uhn	brăk′ĕn	′bræk ən
brackish	BRAK ish	brăk′ĭsh	′bræk ɪʃ
brae	bray bree	brā brē	bre bri
Brahma	BRAH muh	brä′mȧ	′brɑ mə
—— "*Asiatic chicken*," pop. also	BRAY muh	brā′mȧ	′bre mə
branch	branch brahnch	brȧnch §§ 20(5), 47(2)	bræntʃ; *E also* brantʃ, brɑntʃ
brass	bras brahs	brȧs §§ 20(5), 47(2)	bræs; *E also* bras, brɑs
brassière	bruh ZĬER bruh ZIR bruh ZEER *bras* i EHR *brahs* i EHR	brȧ zêr′ § 24(2) brȧ zēr′ brȧs′ĭ âr′	brə ′zɪər, -′zɪr, -′zir, ˌbræs ɪ ′ɛr, ˌbras-; *ES* brə ′zɪə(r), ˌbræs ɪ ′eə(r), ˌbrɒs-
bravado	bruh VAH doh bruh VAY doh	brȧ vä′dō brȧ vā′dō § 47(1)	brə ′va do brə ′ve do
bravo (n.– "*villain*")	BRAH voh BRAY voh	brä′vō brä′vō § 47(1)	′brɑ vo ′bre vo
—— (interj.)	BRAH voh	brä′vō § 47(2)	′brɑ vo
brazier	BRAY zhuhr	brā′zhēr §§ 28(9), 51(7)	′bre ʒɝ; *ES* -ʒə(r)

	SIMPLIFIED	DIACRITICAL	PHONETIC
bread	bred	brĕd	brɛd
breadth	bredth	brĕdth	brɛdθ, brɛtθ
breadths	bredths	brĕdths	brɛdθs, brɛtθs
		§§ 39(5), 50(6)	
breech (n.)	breech	brēch	britʃ
—— (v.t.)	breech	brēch	britʃ
	Not infreq.:	*Not infreq.:*	*Not infreq..*
	brich	brĭch § 51(8)	brɪtʃ
breeches	BRICH ez	brĭch′ĕz	′brɪtʃ ɛz
	BRICH iz	brĭch′ĭz	′brɪtʃ ɪz
		§§ 24(5), 47(2)	
Bremen (U.S.)	BREE muhn	brē′mĕn	′bri mən
—— (Germany)	BRAY muhn	brā′mĕn	′bre mən
	BREM uhn	brĕm′ĕn	′brɛm ən
brethren	BRETH ren	brĕth′rĕn	′brɛð rɛn, -rɪn,
	BRETH rin	brĕth′rĭn §24(5)	-rən
Breton	BRET uhn	brĕt′ŭn	′brɛt ən, -n̩; *F.,*
	F., bruh TAWN	*F.,* brē tôn′	brə ′tɔ̃ [-′tõ]
		§§20(14), 47(2)	
breviary	BREE vi *er* i	brē′vĭ ĕr′ĭ	′bri vɪ ˌɛr ɪ
	BREV i *er* i	brĕv′ĭ ĕr′ĭ	′brɛv ɪ ˌɛr ɪ
	B., BREV i uhr i	*B.,*brĕv′ĭ ēr ĭ	*B.,* ′brɛv ɪ ər ɪ
	BREE vi uhr i	brē′vĭ ēr ĭ	′bri vɪ ər ɪ
		§§20(2), 24(9),	
		47(3), 51(4)	
brew	broo	brōō §§ 40(4),	bru
		48(2)	
brigade (n., v.t.)	bri GAYD	brĭ gād′	brɪ ′ged
	In post-	*In post-*	*In post-*
	Elizabethan	*Elizabethan*	*Elizabethan*
	poetry (noun	*poetry (noun*	*poetry (noun*
	only), often:	*only), often:*	*only), often:*
	BRIG ayd	brĭg′ād § 51(11)	′brɪg ed
brigadier	*brig* uh DĬER	brĭg′*ȧ* dẽr′	ˌbrɪg ə ′dɪər,
	brig uh DIR	§ 24(2)	-′dɪr, -′dir;
	brig uh DEER	brĭg′*ȧ* dēr′	*ES* -′dɪə(r),
			S also -′dɛə(r)
brigand	BRIG uhnd	brĭg′*ȧ*nd	′brɪg ənd
brigantine	BRIG uhn teen	brĭg′*ȧ*n tēn	′brɪg ən tin
	BRIG uhn tain	brĭg′*ȧ*n tīn § 47(2)	′brɪg ən taɪn
brightened	BRAIT 'nd	brīt′ 'nd	′braɪt n̩d
	§ 50(34)		
brilliant	BRIL yuhnt	brĭl′yănt	′brɪl jənt
brilliantine	*bril* yuhn TEEN	brĭl′yăn tēn′	ˌbrɪl jən ′tin
	BRIL yuhn *teen*	brĭl′yăn tēn′	′brɪl jən ˌtin
bring	bring	brĭng § 50(14)	brɪŋ
bringer	BRING uhr	brĭng′ẽr § 50(14)	′brɪŋ ɚ; *ES* -ə(r)
bristle	BRIS 'l	brĭs′ 'l § 31(3)	′brɪs l̩

Britannia	bri TAN i uh bri TAN yuh	brĭ tăn′ĭ ȧ brĭ tăn′yȧ § 47(1)	brɪ ˈtæn ɪ ə brɪ ˈtæn jə
Briton	BRIT uhn BRIT ′n	brĭt′ŭn brĭt′ ′n	ˈbrɪt ən ˈbrɪt n̩
Brittany	BRIT uh ni	brĭt′ȧ nĭ	ˈbrɪt ə nɪ, ˈbrɪt n̩ɪ
broadcast	BRAWD *kast* BRAWD *kahst*	brôd′kȧst′ § 20(5)	ˈbrɔd ˌkæst; E also -ˌkast, -ˌkast
Broadway	BRAWD *way*	brôd′wā′	ˈbrɔd ˌwe
brocade	broh KAYD	brŏ kād′	bro ˈked
brogue	brohg	brōg § 51(7)	brog
bromide	BROH mai͡d BROH mid § 50(34)	brō′mīd brō′mĭd § 47(3)	ˈbro maɪd ˈbro mɪd
bronchial	BRONG ki uhl	brŏng′kĭ ȧl	ˈbraŋ kɪ əl; ES ˈbrɒŋ-
bronchitis	bron KAI͡ tis brong KAI͡ tis § 50(34)	brŏn kī′tĭs brŏng kī′tĭs § 33(4)	bran ˈkaɪ tɪs, braŋ-; ES also brɒn-, brɒŋ-
bronco, broncho	BRONG koh	brŏng′kō	ˈbraŋ ko; ES also ˈbrɒŋ-
brooch	brohch brooch	brōch brōōch §§ 34(20), 47(3)	brotʃ brutʃ
broom	broom bro͝om	brōōm brŏŏm §§ 34(22), 47(1)	brum brʊm
broth	brawth broth	brŏth §§ 34(7), 47(2)	brɔθ brɒθ
brother	BRUHTH uhr	brŭth′ĕr § 34(10)	ˈbrʌð ɚ; ES -ə(r)
brougham	broom BROO uhm BROH uhm	brōōm brōō′ŭm brō′ŭm § 47(3)	brum ˈbru əm ˈbro əm
bruise	brooz	brōōz § 48(2)	bruz
brunet, brunette	broo NET	brōō nĕt′	bru ˈnɛt
brusque	bruhsk bro͝osk F., broosk	brŭsk brŏŏsk F., brüsk § 47(1)	brʌsk brʊsk F., brysk
buccaneer	*buhk* uh NI͡ER *buhk* uh NIR *buhk* uh NEER	bŭk′ȧ nēr′ § 24(2) bŭk′ȧ nēr′	ˌbʌk ə ˈnɪər, -ˈnɪr, -ˈnir; ES -ˈnɪə(r)
Buddha	BO͝OD uh	bŏŏd′ȧ	ˈbʊd ə
budge	*buhj* § 40(6)	bŭj	bʌdʒ
budget	BUHJ et BUHJ it	bŭj′ĕt bŭj′ĭt § 24(5)	ˈbʌdʒ ɛt ˈbʌdʒ ɪt

	SIMPLIFIED	DIACRITICAL	PHONETIC
Buenos Aires	BWAY nohs A͡I rays	bwā′nōs ī′räs	'bwe nos 'aɪ res,
	BOH nuhs EHR iz	bō′nŏs âr′ĕz	'bo nəs 'ɛr ɪz, -'ær ɪz, -'er ɪz, -'iz; *ES*
	BOH nuhs EHR eez	bō′nŏs âr′ēz	'bo nəs 'ɛə rɪz
buff	*buhf* § 40(6)	bŭf	bʌf
—— v., interj.– also,	bŏͦf	bŏͦf	bʊf
buffet (n.–"*blow of hand*"; v.– "*strike*")	BUHF et	bŭf′ĕt	'bʌf ɛt
	BUHF it	bŭf′ĭt § 24(5)	'bʌf ɪt
buffet (n.–"*set of shelves; cupboard; sideboard*")	bŏͦ FAY	bŏͦ fā′	bʊ 'fe, bʌ-, bə-
	B., BUHF et	B., bŭf′ĕt	B., 'bʌf ɛt
	BUHF it	bŭf′ĭt	'bʌf ɪt
	F., *boo* FE	F., bü′fĕ′ §§ 47(1), 51(4)	F., by 'fɛ
—— "*counter for refreshments; restaurant*"	bŏͦ FAY	bŏͦ fā′	bʊ 'fe
	BOOF ay	bŏͦf′ā	'bʊf e
	F., *boo* FE	F., bü′fĕ′ § 47(1)	F., by 'fɛ
bulk	*buhlk* § 40(6)	bŭlk	bʌlk
bullet	BOOL et	bŏͦl′ĕt	bʊl ɛt
	BOOL it	bŏͦl′ĭt § 24(5)	bʊl ɪt
bulletin	BOOL uh tin	bŏͦl′ĕ tĭn	'bʊl ə tɪn
	BOOL uh t'n	bŏͦl′ĕ t'n § 47(2)	'bʊl ə tn̩
bulwark	BOOL wuhrk	bŏͦl′wĕrk	'bʊl wɚk; *ES* -wək
buoy	boi	boi	bɔɪ
	BOO i	bŏͦ′ĭ § 47(3)	'bu ɪ
buoyant	BOI uhnt	boi′ănt	'bɔɪ ənt
	BOO yuhnt	bŏͦ′yănt § 47(3)	'bu jənt
bureau	BYOO roh	bū′rō	'bjʊ ro, 'bjʊ rə
	BYOO roh	§§ 34(2, 25), 40(4), 47(3), 48(2)	
bureaucracy	byŏͦ ROK ruh si	bū rŏk′ra sĭ	bjʊ 'rak rə sɪ,
	byoo ROK ruh si	bū rŏk′ra sĭ	bju-, -'ro krə-;
	byŏͦ ROH kruh si	bū rō′kra sĭ	*ES also* -'rɒk-
	byoo ROH kruh si	bū rō′kra sĭ §47(3)	
burgh	*buhrg*	bûrg	bɝg; *ES also* bɜg;
	Sc., BUHR oh	*Sc.*, bŭr′ŏ	*Sc.*, 'bʌr o,
	BUHR uh § 40(6)	bŭr′ŭ	'bʌr ə
burgher	BUHR guhr	bûr′gĕr	'bɝ gɚ; *ES* -gə(r), *also* 'bɜ-
burglar	BUHR gluhr	bûr′glĕr	'bɝ glɚ; *ES* -glə(r), *also* 'bɜ-
burial	BER i uhl	bĕr′ĭ ăl	'ber ɪ əl

burlesque	*buhr* LESK	bûr lĕsk′ § 40(6, 7)	bɝ ˈlɛsk, bə-; *ES also* bɜ-, *ES* bə-
burn	*buhrn* § 40(6)	bûrn	bɝn; *ES also* bɜn
burro	BUHR oh BŌŌR oh	bûr′ō bŏŏr′ō § 47(1)	ˈbɝ o, ˈbʊr o, -ə; *ES also* bɜ-, bʌr-
burst	*buhrst* § 40(6)	bûrst	bɝst; *ES also* bɜst
bury	BER i	bĕr′ĭ	ˈbɛr ɪ
bushel	BŌŌSH uhl BŌŌSH ′l	bŏŏsh′ĕl bŏŏsh′ ′l	ˈbʊʃ əl ˈbʊʃ l̩
business ("*employment*")	BIZ nes BIZ nis	bĭz′nĕs bĭz′nĭs § 24(5)	ˈbɪz nɛs ˈbɪz nɪs
bustle	BUHS ′l	bŭs′ ′l	ˈbʌs l̩
butcher	BŌŌCH uhr	bŏŏch′ēr	ˈbʊtʃ ɚ; *ES* -ə(r)
butter	BUHT uhr	bŭt′ēr	ˈbʌt ɚ; *ES* -ə(r)
button	BUHT ′n	bŭt′ ′n	ˈbʌt n̩
buy	bai § 50(34)	bī	baɪ
Byzantine	bi ZAN tin bi ZAN tain bai ZAN tain BIZ uhn tin BIZ uhn tain BIZ uhn teen bi ZAN teen § 50(34)	bĭ zăn′tĭn bĭ zăn′tīn bī zăn′tīn bĭz′ăn tĭn bĭz′ăn tīn bĭz′ăn tēn bĭ zăn′tēn § 47(3)	bɪ ˈzæn tɪn, -taɪn, -tɪn, -tin, baɪ ˈzæn taɪn, ˈbɪz ən tɪn, -taɪn, -tin, ˈbɪz n̩-

C

cabal	kuh BAL	ká băl′ § 47(2)	kə ˈbæl
cabbage	KAB ij	kăb′ĭj §§ 22(5), 50(1)	ˈkæb ɪdʒ
cacao	kuh KAH oh kuh KAY oh	ká kä′ō ká kā′ō § 47(2)	kə ˈkɑ o, kɑ- kə ˈke o
cache	kash	kăsh	kæʃ
cadaverous	kuh DAV uhr uhs	ká dăv′ēr ŭs §§ 9, 50(25)	kə ˈdæv ər əs, -ˈdæv rəs
cadet	kuh DET	ká dĕt′	kə ˈdɛt

	SIMPLIFIED	DIACRITICAL	PHONETIC
caesura, cesura	si ZYOO ruh	sĕ zū′rȧ	sɪ ˈzjʊ rə
	si ZOO ruh		sɪ ˈzu rə
	si ZYOO ruh		
	si ZOO ruh	§§ 40(4), 50(32)	
	si SYOO ruh	sĕ sū′rȧ	sɪ ˈsjʊ rə
	si SOO ruh		sɪ ˈsu rə
	si SYOO ruh		
	si SOO ruh	§§ 40(4), 50(32)	
	si ZHOO ruh	sĕ zhoō′rȧ	sɪ ˈʒʊ rə
	si ZHOO ruh	§ 40(4)	
café–"coffee"	ka FAY	kȧ′fā′	ˌkæ ˈfe; *E also*
	kah FAY		ˌkɑ-, ˌkɑ-
café –"*restaurant*"	ka FAY	kă fā′	kæ ˈfe
	kah FAY	kä′fā′	ˌkɑ ˈfe
	B., KAF ay	B., kăf′ā § 51(4)	B., ˈkæf e
cafeteria	*kaf* uh TĬER i uh	kăf′ĕ tẽr′ĭ ȧ	ˌkæf ə ˈtɪər ɪ ə,
	kaf uh TIR i uh	§ 24(2)	-ˈtɪr-, -ˈtir-,
	kaf uh TEER i uh	kăf′ĕ tēr′ĭ ȧ	ˌkæf ɪ-; *ES*
			-ˈtɪər-
caffeine	KAF ee in	kăf′ĕ ĭn	ˈkæf i ɪn, -i in,
	KAF ee een	kăf′ĕ ēn	-i aɪn, ˈkæf ɪ-
	KAF ee ain	kăf′ĕ īn	
	Pop.:	*Pop.:*	*Pop.:*
	KAF een	kăf′ēn	ˈkæf in
	KAF ain § 50(34)	kăf′īn §§ 47(1),	ˈkæf aɪn
		57(3)	
cairn	kehrn	kârn	kɛrn, kærn; *ES*
			kæən, *E also*
			kɛən
Cairo (Egypt)	KAI roh §50(34)	kī′rō	ˈkaɪ ro
Cairo (Illinois;	KAY roh	kā′rō	ˈke ro
Georgia)	KEHR oh	kâr′ō	ˈkɛr o; *ES* ˈkɛə ro
caitiff	KAY tif	kā′tĭf	ˈke tɪf
cajole	kuh JOHL	kȧ jōl′	kə ˈdʒol
calamus	KAL uh muhs	kăl′ȧ mŭs	ˈkæl ə məs
calcimine	KAL si main	kăl′sĭ mīn	ˈkæl sɪ maɪn,
	KAL si min	kăl′sĭ mĭn	-mɪn, -sə-
	§ 50(34)	§ 47(3)	
calcine (v.)	kal SAIN	kăl sīn′	kæl ˈsaɪn
	KAL sain	kăl′sīn	ˈkæl saɪn
	KAL sin	kăl′sĭn § 12	ˈkæl sɪn
—— (n.)	KAL sain	kăl′sīn	ˈkæl saɪn
	KAL sin	kăl′sĭn § 47(2)	ˈkæl sɪn
calcium	KAL si uhm	kăl′sĭ ŭm	ˈkæl sɪ əm
caldron	KAWL druhn	kôl′drŭn	ˈkɔl drən
calf	kahf	käf	kɑf, kæf; *E also*
	kaf	kȧf §§ 20(5),	kɑf
		47(1)	

	SIMPLIFIED	DIACRITICAL	PHONETIC
calf's-foot	KAHVZ *fŏŏt* KAVZ *fŏŏt* *Not infreq.:* KAHFS *fŏŏt* KAFS *fŏŏt*	kävz′fŏŏt′ kȧvz′foot′ § 20(5) *Not infreq.:* käfs′fŏŏt′ kȧfs′fŏŏt′ § 51(8)	'kɑvz ˌfʊt, 'kævz-; *E also* 'kɑvz- *Not infreq.:* 'kɑfs ˌfʊt, 'kæfs-; *E also* 'kɑfs-
Caliban	KAL i ban	kăl′ĭ băn	'kæl ɪ bæn
caliph, calif	KAY lif KAL if	kā′lĭf kăl′ĭf § 47(1)	'ke lɪf 'kæl ɪf
calk, caulk	kawk	kôk	kɔk
calm	kahm	käm	kɑm; *E also* kam
caloric	kuh LOR ik kuh LAWR ik	kȧ lŏr′ĭk kȧ lôr′ĭk §§ 20(2), 24(9)	kə 'lɑr ɪk, -'lɔr-, -'lɒr-
calumnious	kuh LUHM ni uhs	kȧ lŭm′nĭ ŭs § 50(25)	kə 'lʌm nɪ əs
calumny	KAL uhm ni	kăl′ŭm nĭ	'kæl əm nɪ
calve	kahv kav	käv kȧv § 20(5)	kɑv, kæv; *E also* kav
calved (p.t. of *calve*)	kahvd kavd	kävd kȧvd §§ 20(5), 50(4)	kɑvd, kævd; *E also* kavd
calves	kahvz kavz	kävz kȧvz § 48(3)	kɑvz, kævz; *E also* kavz
calyx	KAY liks KAL iks	kā′lĭks kăl′ĭks § 47(1)	'ke lɪks 'kæl ɪks
cambric	KAYM brik	kām′brĭk	'kem brɪk
Camelot	KAM uh lot	kăm′ĕ lŏt	'kæm ə lɑt, *ES also* -lɒt
camera	KAM uhr uh	kăm′ĕr ȧ	'kæm ər ə
camouflage (n.)	KAM ŏŏ flahzh KAM uh flahzh	kăm′ŏŏ fläzh kăm′ŏŏ fläzh	'kæm ʊ flɑʒ 'kæm ə flɑʒ
—— (v.)	*kam* ŏŏ FLAHZH KAM ŏŏ flahzh KAM uh flahzh	kăm′ŏŏ fläzh′ kăm′ŏŏ fläzh § 12	ˌkæm ʊ 'flɑʒ 'kæm ʊ flɑʒ 'kæm ə flɑʒ
camp	kamp	kămp	kæmp
campaign	kam PAYN	kăm pān′	kæm 'pen
camphor	KAM fuhr	kăm′fẽr	'kæm fɚ; *ES* -fə(r)
can (v.)	kan *Unstressed:* kuhn k'n	kăn *Unstressed:* kăn k'n § 16	kæn *Unstressed:* kən kn̩
canary	kuh NEHR i kuh NAY ri	kȧ nâr′ĭ	kə 'nɛr ɪ, -'ne rɪ, *ES also* -'nɛə rɪ
cancel	KAN suhl KAN s'l	kăn′sĕl kăn′s'l §§ 24(14), 31(3)	'kæn səl 'kæn sl̩
candelabra (*plur.*)	*kan* duh LAY bruh	kăn′dĕ lā′brȧ	ˌkæn də 'le brə

	SIMPLIFIED	DIACRITICAL	PHONETIC
—— sing., with plur. "candela-bras"	kan duh LAH bruh	kăn′dĕ lä′bra͞	ˌkæn də ˈlɑ brə
	kan duh LAY bruh	kăn′dĕ lā′bra͞	ˌkæn də ˈle brə
	kan duh LAB ruh	kăn′dĕ lăb′ra͞ § 47(1)	ˌkæn də ˈlæb rə
candelabrum	kan duh LAY bruhm	kăn′dĕ lā′brŭm	ˌkæn də ˈle brəm
candidate (n.)	KAN duh dayt	kăn′dĭ dāt	ˈkæn də det
	KAN di dayt	kăn′dĭ dāt	ˈkæn dɪ det
	B., KAN duh dit	B., kăn′dĭ dĭt	B., ˈkæn də dɪt
	KAN di dit	kăn′dĭ dĭt § 51(4)	ˈkæn dɪ dɪt
—— (v.i.–colloq.)	KAN duh dayt	kăn′dĭ dāt	ˈkæn də det
	KAN di dayt	kăn′dĭ dāt	ˈkæn dɪ det
candy	KAN di	kăn′dĭ	ˈkæn dɪ
canine	KAY na͡in	kā′nīn	ˈke naɪn
	kuh NA͡IN	ka͞ nīn′	kə ˈnaɪn
	B., KAN a͡in	B., kăn′īn §§ 47(3), 51(4)	B., ˈkæn aɪn
cannot (comp. form of can not)	KAN not	kăn′nŏt	ˈkæn nɑt; ES also -nɒt
	Emph.: ka NOT	Emph.: kă nŏt′	Emph.: kæ ˈnɑt; ES also -ˈnɒt
	KAN NOT	kăn′nŏt′ § 51(11)	ˈkæn ˈnɑt; ES also -ˈnɒt
canoe	kuh NOO	ka͞ no͞o′	kə ˈnu
canon	KAN uhn	kăn′ŭn	ˈkæn ən
cañon	See canyon.		
can't (contr. of can not)	kahnt	känt	kɑnt, kænt; E also
	kant	kănt § 20(5)	kɑnt
cantata	kuhn TAH tuh	kăn tä′ta͞	kən ˈtɑ tə, kæn-,
	kan TAH tuh	kăn tä′ta͞ § 47(3)	kɑn-; E also kɒn-
canton (n., v.t.)	KAN tuhn	kăn′tŏn	ˈkæn tən
	kan TON	kăn tŏn′ § 12	kæn ˈtɑn; ES also -ˈtɒn
—— (v.–also, "to quarter," pref-erably)	kan TON	kăn tŏn′	kæn ˈtɑn; ES also -ˈtɒn
	KAN tuhn	kăn′tŏn	ˈkæn tən
cantonment	kan TON muhnt	kăn tŏn′mĕnt	kæn ˈtɑn mənt; ES also -ˈtɒn-
	KAN tuhn muhnt	kăn′tŏn mĕnt	ˈkæn tən mənt
	B., kan TOON muhnt	B., kăn to͞on′mĕnt §§ 47(2), 50(22), 51(4)	B., kæn ˈtun mənt
	In mil. circles, usu.:	In mil. circles, usu.:	In mil. circles, usu.:
	KAN tuhn muhnt	kăn′tŏn mĕnt	ˈkæn tən mənt

	SIMPLIFIED	DIACRITICAL	PHONETIC
canyon, cañon	KAN yuhn *When spelled "cañon," also:* Sp., kah NYOHN	kăn′yŭn *When spelled "cañon," also:* Sp., kä nyōn′ § 33(3)	′kæn jən *When spelled "cañon," also:* Sp., ka ′njon
caoutchouc	KOO chŏŏk kow CHOOK B., KOW chook	kōō′chŏŏk kou chŏŏk′ B., kou′chŏŏk § 47(1)	′ku tʃʊk kaʊ ′tʃuk B., ′kaʊ tʃuk
capillary	KAP uh *ler* i KAP i *ler* i B., kuh PIL uh ri	kăp′ĭ lĕr′ɪ kăp′ɪ lĕr′ɪ B., ká pĭl′á rĭ §§ 20(2), 24(9), 47(2), 51(4)	′kæp ə ˌler ɪ ′kæp ɪ ˌler ɪ B., kə ′pɪl ə rɪ
capital	KAP uh tuhl KAP uh t'l KAP i tuhl	kăp′ĭ tăl kăp′ĭ t'l kăp′ɪ tăl	′kæp ə təl ′kæp ə tḷ ′kæp ɪ təl
capitation	*kap* uh TAY shuhn *kap* i TAY shuhn	kăp′ĭ tā′shŭn kăp′ɪ tā′shŭn § 50(28)	ˌkæp ə ′te ʃən ˌkæp ɪ ′te ʃən
capitol	KAP uh tuhl KAP uh t'l KAP i tuhl	kăp′ĭ tŏl kăp′ĭ t'l kăp′ɪ tŏl	′kæp ə təl ′kæp ə tḷ ′kæp ɪ təl
capon	KAY puhn KAY pon	kā′pŏn kā′pŏn § 47(2)	′ke pən ′ke pɑn; *ES also* -pɒn
caprice	kuh PREES	ká prēs′	kə ′pris
capricious	kuh PRISH uhs	ká prĭsh′ŭs § 50(25)	kə ′prɪʃ əs, -′prɪʃ-
capsule	KAP syool KAP sool *Pop.:* KAP syuhl KAP suhl	kăp′sūl § 50(32) *Pop.:* kăp′sŭl § 51(3)	′kæp sjul, -sjʊl, -sul *Pop.:* ′kæp sjəl, -səl, -sḷ
captain	KAP tin	kăp′tĭn	′kæp tɪn, -tən
captious	KAP shuhs	kăp′shŭs § 50(25)	′kæp ʃəs
capture	KAP chuhr KAP tyuhr	kăp′tūr § 50(31)	′kæp tʃɚ, -tjɚ; *ES* -tʃə(r), -tjə(r)
Capulet	KAP yŏŏ let	kăp′ŭ lĕt	′kæp jʊ let, -jə-, -ju-
car	kahr	kär	kɑr; *ES* kɑ:(r)
caramel	KAR uh mel	kăr′á mĕl	′kær ə mel; *N.Y.C. often* kɑ: ′mel; *Midwest often* ′kɑr mḷ
carat	KAR uht	kăr′ăt	′kær ət
caravan	KAR uh van *kar* uh VAN	kăr′á văn kăr′á văn′ § 47(2)	′kær ə væn ˌkær ə ′væn

	SIMPLIFIED	DIACRITICAL	PHONETIC
caravansary	*kar* uh VAN suh ri	kär′*a* văn′s*a* rĭ	ˌkær ə 'væn sə rɪ
caravanserai	*kar* uh VAN suh raî	kăr′*a* văn′sĕ rī	ˌkær ə 'væn sə raɪ
	kar uh VAN suh ray	kăr′*a* văn′sĕ rā	ˌkær ə 'væn sə re
carbine	KAHR baîn	kär′bīn	'kɑr baɪn; *ES* 'kɑ:-
carbon	KAHR buhn	kär′bŏn	'kɑr bən; *ES* 'kɑ:-
	In chem., *often:* KAHR bon	*In chem.*, *often:* kär′bŏn § 51(6)	*In chem.*, *often:* 'kɑr bɑn; *ES* 'kɑ:-, *also* -bɒn
carburetor, carburettor	KAHR byoo *ret* uhr	kär′bû rĕt′ẽr	'kɑr bjʊ ˌret ɚ, -bjə-, -bə-,
	KAHR buh *ray* tuhr	kär′bû rā′tẽr	-ˌre tɚ; *ES* 'kɑ:-, -ə(r),
	KAHR byoo *ray* tuhr	kär′bŭ rā′tẽr	-tə(r)
caribou	KAR uh boo	kăr′*i* boō	'kær ə bu
	KAR i boo	kăr′ĭ boō § 47(2)	'kær ɪ bu
caricature	KAR i kuh chuhr	kăr′ĭ k*a* tûr	'kær ɪ kə tʃɚ, -tjɚ,
	KAR i kuh tyuhr		
	kar i kuh CHOOR	kăr′ĭ k*a* tūr′	ˌkær ɪ kə 'tʃʊr, -'tjʊr; *ES*
	kar i kuh TYOOR		-tʃə(r), -tjə(r), -'tʃʊə(r), -'tjʊə(r)
Carlyle (Thomas)	kahr LAÎL	kär līl′	kɑr 'laɪl; *ES* kɑ:
carmine	KAHR min	kär′mĭn	'kɑr mɪn, -maɪn;
	KAHR maîn	kär′mīn § 47(3)	*ES* 'kɑ:-
Carnegie (Andrew)	kahr NAY gi	kär nā′gĭ	kɑr 'ne gɪ, -'neg ɪ,
	kahr NEG i	kär nĕg′ĭ	'kɑr neg ɪ; *ES*
	KAHR neg i	kär′nĕg ĭ	kɑ:-, 'kɑ:-
carol	KAR uhl	kăr′*ŭ*l	'kær əl
carousal	kuh ROWZ uhl	k*a* rouz′*ŭ*l	kə 'raʊz əl
	kuh ROWZ 'l	k*a* rouz′ 'l § 31(3)	kə 'raʊz ḷ
carouse	kuh ROWZ	k*a* rouz′	kə 'raʊz
carriage	KAR ij	kăr′ĭj § 50(1)	'kær ɪdʒ
—— "*freight expense,*" also	KAR i ij	kăr′ĭ ĭj	'kær ɪ ɪdʒ
carry	KAR i	kăr′ĭ	'kær ɪ
cartridge	KAHR trij	kär′trĭj	'kɑr trɪdʒ; *ES* 'kɑ:-
caryatid	*kar* i AT id	kăr′ĭ ăt′ĭd	ˌkær ɪ 'æt ɪd
cascade	kas KAYD	kăs kād′	kæs 'ked
cascara	kas KEHR uh	kăs kâr′*a* § 20(2)	kæs 'ker ə, -'kær-, -'ke rə; *ES also* -'keə rə
	kas KAY ruh		
—— "*bark canoe*"	*Sp.*, KAHS kah rah	*Sp.*, käs′kä rä	*Sp.*, 'kas ka rɑ

48	SIMPLIFIED	DIACRITICAL	PHONETIC
casein	KAY si in	kā'sĕ ĭn	'ke sɪ ɪn
casement	KAYS muhnt	kās'mĕnt § 47(3)	'kes mənt, -mɛnt
	Old-fashioned:	Old-fashioned:	Old-fashioned:
	B., KAYZ muhnt	B., kāz'mĕnt	B., 'kez mənt
		§ 51(4, 8)	
cashier (n., v.t.)	kash ĬER	kăsh ē̆r'	kæʃ 'ɪər, -'ɪr, -'ir,
	ka SHĬER		kæ 'ʃɪər, -'ʃɪr,
	kash IR		-'ʃir; ES -'ɪə(r),
	ka SHIR		-'ʃɪə(r)
	kash EER	kăsh ēr' § 24(2)	
	ka SHEER		
cask	kask	kȧsk § 20(5)	kæsk; E also kask,
	kahsk		kɑsk
casket	KAS ket	kȧs'kĕt	'kæs ket, -kɪt; E
	KAS kit	kȧs'kĭt §§ 20(5),	also 'kas-, 'kɑs-
	KAHS ket	24(5)	
	KAHS kit		
Caspian (Sea)	KAS pi uhn	kăs'pĭ ăn	'kæs pɪ ən
Cassia, cassia	KASH uh	kăsh'ȧ	'kæʃ ə
	KASH i uh	kăsh'ĭ ȧ	'kæʃ ɪ ə
	KAS i uh	kăs'ĭ ȧ	'kæs ɪ ə
—— "bark,"	KASH uh	kăsh'ȧ § 47(3)	'kæʃ ə
generally			
Cassius	KASH i uhs	kăsh'ĭ ŭs	'kæʃ ɪ əs
	KAS i uhs	kăs'ĭ ŭs	'kæs ɪ əs
	KASH uhs	kăsh'ŭs	'kæʃ əs
cast	kast	kȧst § 20(5)	kæst; ES also
	kahst		kast, kɑst
caste	kast	kȧst § 20(5)	kæst; ES also
	kahst		kast, kɑst
castle	KAS 'l	kȧs' 'l §§ 20(5),	'kæs ḷ; E also
	KAHS 'l	31(3), 39(2)	'kas-, 'kɑs-
casual	KAZH yŏŏ uhl	kăzh' u̇ ăl §§ 38	'kæʒ jʊ əl,
	KAZH ŏŏ uhl	(12), 47(1)	'kæʒ ʊ-, -jʊl,
	KAZ yŏŏ uhl	kăz'u̇ ăl	'kæz jʊ əl,
		kăzh'ŏŏ ȧl	'kæz ʊl
casualty	KAZH yŏŏ uhl ti	kăzh'u̇ ăl tĭ	'kæʒ jʊ əl tɪ,
	KAZH ŏŏ uhl ti		'kæʒ ʊ-, -jʊl-,
	KAZ yŏŏ uhl ti	kăz'u̇ ăl tĭ	'kæz jʊ əl tɪ,
		kăzh'ŏŏ ăl tĭ	'kæz ʊl-
cataclysm	KAT uh kliz'm	kăt'ȧ klĭz'm	'kæt ə klɪzm̩
	KAT uh kliz uhm	§ 32(2)	'kæt ə klɪz əm
catalpa	kuh TAL puh	kȧ tăl'pȧ	kə 'tæl pə
catarrh	kuh TAHR	kȧ tär'	kə 'tɑr; ES
			-'tɑ:(r)
catastrophe	kuh TAS truh fi	kȧ tăs'trŏ fĕ	kə 'tæs trə fɪ
catastrophic	kat uh STROF ik	kăt'ȧ strŏf'ĭk	ˌkæt ə 'strɑf ɪk;
			ES also -'strɒ-
catch	kach	kăch	kætʃ

catechetical	*kat* i KET i kuhl	kăt′ĕ kĕt′ĭ kŭl	ˌkæt ɪ ˈkɛt ɪ kəl, ˌkæt ə-, -kļ
catechism	KAT i kiz'm KAT i kiz uhm	kăt′ĕ kĭz'm § 32(2)	ˈkæt ɪ kɪz m̩, ˈkæt ə-, -kɪz əm
caterpillar	KAT uhr *pil* uhr KAT uh *pil* uhr	kăt′ẽr pĭl′ẽr §§ 24(7), 48(1)	ˈkæt ɚ ˌpɪl ɚ, ˈkæt ə ˌpɪl-; *ES* ˈkæt ə ˌpɪl ə(r)
cathartic	kuh THAHR tik	kȧ thär′tĭk	kə ˈθɑr tɪk; *ES* kə ˈθɑː-, *E also* -ˈθɑː-
cathedral	kuh THEE druhl	kȧ thē′drăl	kə ˈθi drəl
catsup	KAT suhp KECH uhp	kăt′sŭp kĕch′ŭp	ˈkæt səp ˈketʃ əp
Caucasian	kaw KAY shuhn kaw KAY zhuhn kaw KASH uhn kaw KAZH uhn	kô kā′shăn kô kā′zhăn kô kăsh′ăn kô kăzh′ăn § 47(3)	kɔ ˈke ʃən kɔ ˈke ʒən kɔ ˈkæʃ ən kɔ ˈkæʒ ən
Caucasus	KAW kuh suhs	kô′kȧ săs	ˈkɔ kə səs
caucus	KAW kuhs	kô′kŭs	ˈkɔ kəs
cauliflower	KAW li *flow* uhr § 50(34)	kô′lĭ flou′ẽr	ˈkɔ lɪ ˌflaʊ ɚ; *ES* -ˌflaʊ ə(r)
cavalcade (n., v.i.)	*kav* uhl KAYD	kăv′ăl kād′ § 47(2)	ˌkæv əl ˈked, ˌkæv ļ-
—— (n.–also)	KAV uhl kayd	kăv′ăl kād §12	ˈkæv əl ked, ˈkæv ļ-
cavalry	KAV uhl ri	kăv′ăl rĭ	ˈkæv əl rɪ, ˈkæv ļ-
cavern	KAV uhrn	kăv′ẽrn	ˈkæv ɚn; *ES* -ən
caviar, caviare	*kav* i AHR KAV i *ahr* *ka* VYAR *kah* VYAHR KAH vi ahr	kăv′ĭ är′ kăv′ĭ är′ kȧ′vyär′ kä′vĭ är	ˌkæv ɪ ˈɑr, ˈkæv ɪ ˌɑr, ˌkɑ ˈvjɑr, ˈkɑ vɪ ɑr; *ES* -ˈɑː(r), -ˌɑːr, *also* ˌkɒ-, ˈkɒ-
	Occas.: ka VĬER ka VIR ka VEER kuh VĬER kuh VIR kuh VEER	*Occas.:* kă vĕr′ kă vēr′ kȧ vĕr′ §§ 24(2), 47(2) kȧ vēr′	*Occas.:* kæ ˈvɪər, -ˈvɪr, -ˈvir, kə ˈvɪər, -ˈvɪr, -ˈvir; *ES* *also* -ˈvɪə(r)
cavil	KAV il KAV 'l	kăv′ĭl kăv′ 'l	ˈkæv ɪl ˈkæv ļ
cayenne	kaȋ EN kay EN	kī ĕn′ kā ĕn′ § 47(1)	kaɪ ˈen ke ˈen
cease	sees	sēs	sis
Cecil (William)	SES il SIS il	sĕs′ĭl sĭs′ĭl	ˈsɛs ɪl, -ļ ˈsɪs ɪl, -ļ
celandine	SEL uhn daȋn	sĕl′ăn dīn	ˈsel ən daɪn

	SIMPLIFIED	DIACRITICAL	PHONETIC
celebration	*sel* i BRAY shuhn	sĕl′ĕ brā′shŭn	ˌsel ɪ 'bre ʃən, ˌsel ə-
celebrity	si LEB ruh ti si LEB ri ti	sĕ lĕb′rĭ tĭ sĕ lĕb′rĭ tĭ	sɪ 'lɛb rə tɪ, -rɪ-, sə-
celery	SEL uhr i	sĕl′ēr ĭ	'sel ər ɪ
celestial	si LES chuhl	sĕ lĕs′chăl	sɪ 'lɛs tʃəl, sə-
celibacy	SEL uh buh si SEL i buh si si LIB uh si	sĕl′ĭ bȧ sĭ sĕl′ĭ bȧ sĭ sĕ lĭb′ȧ sĭ § 47(3)	'sel ə bə sɪ 'sel ɪ bə sɪ sɪ 'lɪb ə sɪ
cellar	SEL uhr	sĕl′ēr	'sel ɚ; *ES* -ə(r)
celluloid	SEL yŏŏ loid	sĕl′û loid	'sel jʊ lɔɪd, -jə-, -ju-
Celt	selt *B.,* kelt	sĕlt *B.,* kĕlt § 51(4)	selt *B.,* kɛlt
Celtic	SEL tik *B.,* KEL tik	sĕl′tĭk *B.,* kĕl′tĭk § 51(4)	'sel tɪk *B.,* 'kɛl tɪk
cement (n., v., adj.)	si MENT	sĕ mĕnt′	sɪ 'mɛnt, sə-
—— (n. – also occasionally)	SEM uhnt	sĕm′ĕnt §§ 12, 47(3)	'sem ənt
cemetery	SEM i *ter* i	sĕm′ĕ tĕr′ĭ	'sem ɪ ˌtɛr ɪ
census	SEN suhs	sĕn′sŭs	'sen səs
centaur	SEN tawr	sĕn′tôr	'sen tɔr; *ES* -tɔə(r)
centime	SAHN teem *F.,* sahN TEEM	sän′tēm *F.,* sän′tēm′ § 20(14)	'sɑn tim *F.,* sã 'tim
centipede	SEN tuh peed SEN ti peed SEN ti ped	sĕn′tĭ pēd sĕn′tĭ pēd sĕn′tĭ pĕd	'sen tə pid 'sen tɪ pid 'sen tɪ pɛd
centrifugal	sen TRIF yŏŏ guhl	sĕn trĭf′û găl	sen 'trɪf jʊ gəl, -gl̩
century	SEN chŏŏ ri SEN chuh ri SEN tyŏŏ ri	sĕn′tû rĭ § 5̃0(33)	'sen tʃʊ rɪ 'sen tʃə rɪ 'sen tjʊ rɪ
cereal	SĬER i uhl SIR i uhl SEER i uhl	sēr′ĕ ăl § 24(2) sēr′ĕ ăl	'sɪər ɪ əl, 'sɪr-, 'sir-; *ES* 'sɪər-
cerebellum	*ser* i BEL uhm *ser* uh BEL uhm	sĕr′ĕ bĕl′ŭm	ˌsɛr ɪ 'bɛl əm ˌsɛr ə 'bɛl əm
cerebral	SER i bruhl SER uh bruhl	sĕr′ĕ brăl	'ser ɪ brəl 'ser ə brəl
cerebrum	SER i bruhm SER uh bruhm	sĕr′ĕ brŭm	'ser ɪ brəm 'ser ə brəm
cerement	SĬER muhnt SIR muhnt SEER muhnt	sēr′mĕnt §§ 24(2), 50(22) sēr′mĕnt	'sɪər mənt, 'sɪr-, 'sir-; *ES also* 'sɪə-

	SIMPLIFIED	DIACRITICAL	PHONETIC
ceremony	SER i *moh* ni SER uh *moh* ni *B.*, SER i muhn i	sĕr′ĕ mō′nĭ § 51(4) *B.*, sĕr′ĕ mŭn ĭ	′sɛr ɪ ˌmo nɪ ′sɛr ə ˌmo nɪ *B.*, ′sɛr ɪ mə nɪ
Ceres	SEE reez	sē′rēz	′si riz, ′sɪ-
certain	SUHR tin SUHR t′n	sûr′tĭn sûr′t′n § 33(2)	′sɝ tɪn, -tṇ; *ES* *also* ′sɜ-
certainly	SUHR tin li SUHR t′n li	sûr′tĭn lĭ sûr′t′n lĭ § 50(20)	′sɝ tɪn lɪ, -tṇ-; *ES* *also* ′sɜ-
certificate (n.)	suhr TIF uh kit suhr TIF i kit	sẽr tĭf′ĭ kĭt sẽr tĭf′ĭ kĭt	sɚ ′tɪf ə kɪt, -′tɪf ɪ-; *ES* sə ′tɪf-
—— (v.t.)	suhr TIF uh kayt suhr TIF i kayt	sẽr tĭf′ĭ kāt sẽr tĭf′ĭ kāt § 20(8, 9)	sɚ ′tɪf ə ket, -′tɪf ɪ-; *ES* sə ′tɪf-
cerulean	si ROO li uhn	sĕ rōō′lĕ ăn § 40(4)	sɪ ′ru lɪ ən, sə-
Cervantes (**Saavedra, de** **Miguel**)	ther VAHN tays *Angl.:* suhr VAN teez	thĕr vän′tās *Angl.:* sẽr văn′tēz § 51(1)	*Sp.*, θɛr ′βan tes *Angl.:* sɚ ′væn tiz; *ES* sə ′væn-
chafe	chayf	chāf	tʃef
chaff	chaf chahf	chăf § 20(5)	tʃæf; *E also* tʃɑf, tʃɑf
chagrin (n.)	shuh GRIN *B.*, shuh GREEN SHAG rin	shȧ grĭn′ *B.*, shȧ grēn′ shăg′rĭn	ʃə ′grɪn *B.*, ʃə ′grin ′ʃæg rɪn
—— (v.t.)	shuh GRIN shuh GREEN	shȧ grĭn′ shȧ grēn′ §§ 12, 22(7), 47(3), 51(4)	ʃə ′grɪn ʃə ′grin
chaise	shayz	shāz	ʃez
chalet	sha LAY SHAL ay *F.*, shah LE	shă lā′ shăl′ȧ *F.*, shȧ′lĕ′	ʃæ ′le, ′ʃæl e, -ɪ; *F.*, ʃɑ ′le
challis	SHAL i *Less often:* *B.*, CHAL is	shăl′ĭ § 47(3) *Less often:* *B.*, chăl′ĭs § 51(4, 8)	′ʃæl ɪ *Less often:* *B.*, ′tʃæl ɪs
chameleon	kuh MEE li uhn kuh MEEL yuhn	kȧ mē′lĕ ăn kȧ mēl′yŭn § 24(15)	kə ′mi lɪ ən kə ′mil jən
chamois (n.)	SHAM i *sha* MWAH *shah* MWAH	shăm′ĭ shȧ′mwä′ §§ 38(2), 47(3)	′ʃæm ɪ, ′ʃæm ɔɪ ˌʃæ ′mwɑ, ˌʃa-
—— (v.t.)	SHAM i	shăm′ĭ	ʃæm ɪ
champagne	sham PAYN	shăm pān′	ʃæm ′pen
champaign	sham PAYN *B.*, CHAM payn	shăm pān′ *B.*, chăm′pān §§ 47(2), 51(4)	ʃæm ′pen *B.*, ′tʃæm pen

	SIMPLIFIED	DIACRITICAL	PHONETIC
champion	CHAM pi uhn	chăm′pĭ ŭn § 28(9)	'tʃæm pɪ ən
chance	chans chahns	chăns §§ 20(5), 39(3)	tʃæns; *E also* tʃɑns, tʃɒns
chandelier	*shan* duh LĬER *shan* duh LIR *shan* duh LEER	shăn′dĕ lĕr′ § 24(2) shăn′dĕ lēr′	ˌʃæn də 'lɪər, -'lɪr, -'lir; *ES* -'lɪə(r)
chanson	SHAN suhn *F., shah*N SAWN	shăn′sŏn *F.,* shän′sôɴ′ § 20(14)	'ʃæn sən *F.,* ʃɑ̃ 'sɔ̃ [-'sõ]
chanticleer	CHAN ti klĭer CHAN ti klir CHAN ti kleer	chăn′tĭ klĕr § 24(2) chăn′tĭ klēr	'tʃæn tɪ klɪər, -klɪr, -klir; *ES* -klɪə(r)
chaos	KAY os	kā′ŏs	'ke ɑs; *ES also* -ɒs
chaotic	kay OT ik	kā ŏt′ĭk	ke 'ɑt ɪk; *ES also* -'ɒt-
chaperon (v.)	SHAP uhr ohn SHAP uh rohn	shăp′ĕr ōn	'ʃæp ər on 'ʃæp ə ron
—— (n. – "ac- companying person": fem. often spelled "chaperone")	SHAP uhr ohn SHAP uh rohn	shăp′ĕr ōn	'ʃæp ər on 'ʃæp ə ron
—— (n. – "hood.")	SHAP uhr ohn SHAP uh rohn SHAP uh rawn SHAP uh ron	shăp′ĕr ōn shăp′ĕr ŏn §§ 34(7), 47(3), 51(11)	'ʃæp ər on, -ə ron, -ər ɔn, -ə rɔn, -ər ɒn, -ə rɒn
charlatan	SHAHR luh tuhn	shär′lȧ tăn	'ʃɑr lə tən, -tn̩; *ES* 'ʃɑ:-, *E also* 'ʃa:-
Charlemagne	SHAHR li mayn SHAHR luh mayn	shär′lĕ mān shär′lĕ mān	'ʃɑr lɪ men, -lə-; *ES* 'ʃɑ:-; *F.,* ʃar lə 'maɲ
charmeuse	shahr MUHZ	shär mûz′	ʃɑr 'mɜz; *ES* ʃɑ:-, *E also often* ʃa:-; *F.,* ʃar 'mø:z
Charon	KAY rahn KEHR uhn KAY ron	kā′rŏn kâr′ŏn kā′rŏn	'ke rən, 'kɛr ən, 'kær-, 'ke rɑn; *ES also* 'kɛə rən, *E also* -rɒn
chary	CHEHR i CHAY ri	châr′ɪ §§ 20(9), 47(2)	'tʃɛr ɪ, 'tʃær ɪ, 'tʃe rɪ; *ES also* 'tʃɛə rɪ
Charybdis	kuh RIB dis	kȧ rĭb′dĭs	kə 'rɪb dɪs
chasm	KAZ 'm KAZ uhm	kăz′ 'm § 32(2)	'kæz m̩ 'kæz əm

chassis (n. sing.)	SHAS i	shăs′ĭ	′ʃæs ɪ
	SHAS is	shăs′ĭs § 47(2)	′ʃæs ɪs
—— (n. pl.)	SHAS iz	shăs′ĭz	′ʃæs ɪz
chaste	chayst	chāst	tʃest
chasten	CHAYS ′n	chās′ ′n §§ 33(2), 39(2)	′tʃes ņ, -ən
chastise	chas TAĪZ	chăs tīz′	tʃæs ′taɪz
chastisement	CHAS tiz muhnt	chăs′tĭz mĕnt	′tʃæs tɪz mənt
	chas TAĪZ muhnt	chăs tīz′mĕnt § 50(22)	tʃæs ′taɪz mənt
chastity	CHAS tuh ti	chăs′tĭ tĭ	′tʃæs tə tɪ
	CHAS ti ti	chăs′tĭ tĭ	′tʃæs tɪ tɪ
château	sha TOH	shă tō′	ʃæ ′to
	F., shah TOH	F., shä′tō′	F., ʃɑ ′to
chatelaine	SHAT uh layn	shăt′ĕ lān	′ʃæt ə len
	F., shah t' LEN	F., shä′t′ lĕn′	F., ʃɑ ′tlen
chauffeur	shoh FUHR	shō fûr′	ʃo ′fɝ; ES also -′fɜ(r)
	SHOH fuhr	shō′fēr §§ 24(22), 47(1)	′ʃo fɝ; ES -fə(r)
chef	shef	shĕf	ʃef
Chelsea	CHEL si	chĕl′sĕ	′tʃel sɪ
chemise	shi MEEZ	shĕ mēz′	ʃɪ ′miz
	shuh MEEZ	shĕ mēz′	ʃə ′miz
Cheops	KEE ops	kē′ŏps	′ki ɑps; ES also -ɒps
Chesapeake	CHES uh peek	chĕs′á pēk	′tʃes ə pik
chestnut	CHES nuht	chĕs′nŭt	′tʃes nʌt
	CHEST nuht	chĕst′nŭt	′tʃest nʌt
	CHEST nuht	chĕst′nŭt §§ 39(2), 40(6)	′tʃest nət
chevalier	shev uh LĪER	shĕv′á lēr′	ˌʃev ə ′lɪər, -′lɪr,
	shev uh LIR	§ 24(2)	-′lir; ES -′lɪə(r)
	shev uh LEER	shĕv′á lēr′	
chew	choo	choo	tʃu
	chyoo	chū §§ 48(2), 50(32)	tʃju
Chicago	shi KAW goh	shĭ kô′gō	ʃɪ ′kɔ go, -′kɑ-,
	shi KAH goh	shĭ kä′gō	-′kɒ-, ʃə-
chicken	CHIK en	chĭk′ĕn	′tʃɪk en
	CHIK in	chĭk′ĭn § 24(5)	′tʃɪk ɪn
chieftain	CHEEF tin	chēf′tĭn	′tʃif tɪn
	CHEEF tuhn	chēf′tĕn	′tʃif tən
chiffon	SHIF on	shĭf′ŏn	′ʃɪf ɑn, -ɒn
	shi FON	shĭ fŏn′	ʃɪ ′fɑn, -′fɒn
	F., shi FAWN	F., shĕ′fôn′ § 20(14)	F., ʃɪ ′fɔ̃ [-′fõ]

	SIMPLIFIED	DIACRITICAL	PHONETIC
chiffonier, chiffonnier	*shif* uh NĬER *shif* uh NIR *shif* uh NEER	shĭf′ŏ nēr′ §§ 24(2), 47(2) shĭf′ŏ nēr′	ˌʃɪf ə ˈnɪər, -ˈnɪr, -ˈnir; *ES* -ˈnɪə(r)
chilblain	CHIL *blayn*	chĭl′blān′	ˈtʃɪl ˌblen
children	CHIL druhn	chĭl′drĕn	ˈtʃɪl drən, -drɪn
Chile	CHIL i *Sp.*, CHEE lay	chĭl′ĕ *Sp.*, chē′lå	ˈtʃɪl ɪ *Sp.*, ˈtʃi le
Chilean,	CHIL i uhn	chĭl′ĕ ăn	ˈtʃɪl ɪ ən
chimera, chimaera	kaī MEE ruh ki MEE ruh	kī mē′rȧ kĭ mē′rȧ § 47(1)	kaɪ ˈmi rə kɪ ˈmi rə
chimerical	kaī MER i kuhl ki MER i kuhl	kī mĕr′Ĭ kȧl kĭ mĕr′Ĭ kȧl	kaɪ ˈmɛr ɪ kəl, kɪ ˈmɛr-, -ɪ kl̩
chimney	CHIM ni	chĭm′nĭ	ˈtʃɪm nɪ
chimpanzee	*chim* pan ZEE chim PAN zi	chĭm′păn zē′ chĭm păn′zĕ	ˌtʃɪm pæn ˈzi tʃɪm ˈpæn zɪ
chinchilla	chin CHIL uh	chĭn chĭl′ȧ	tʃɪn ˈtʃɪl ə
Chinese	*chaī* NEEZ *chaī* NEES	chĭ′nēz′ chĭ′nēs′ §§ 11, 38 (6), 47(1), 50(7)	ˌtʃaɪ ˈniz ˌtʃaɪ ˈnis
Chinook	chi NOOK chi NŎŎK	chĭ nōōk′ chĭ nŏŏk′	tʃɪ ˈnuk tʃɪ ˈnʊk
chisel	CHIZ ′l	chĭz′ ′l § 31(3)	ˈtʃɪz l̩
chivalric (See *chivalry*.)	SHIV uhl rik shi VAL rik	shĭv′ăl rĭk shĭ văl′rĭk § 47(1)	ˈʃɪv əl rɪk, ˈtʃɪv-, ʃɪ ˈvæl-, tʃɪ-
chivalry	SHIV uhl ri	shĭv′ăl rĭ §§ 22(7), 47(3)	ˈʃɪv əl rɪ
	Occas. or hist.: B., CHIV uhl ri	*Occas. or hist.:* B., chĭv′ăl rĭ § 51(4, 11)	*Occas. or hist.:* B., ˈtʃɪv əl rɪ
chloride (n.)	KLOH raīd KLAW raīd KLOH rid KLAW rid	klō′rīd klō′rĭd §§ 28(7), 34(3), 47(3), 50(34)	ˈklo raɪd ˈklɔ raɪd ˈklo rɪd ˈklɔ rɪd
—— (v.i.)	KLOH raīd KLAW raīd	klō′rīd § 50(34)	ˈklo raɪd ˈklɔ raɪd
chlorine	KLOH reen KLAW reen KLOH rin KLAW rin	klō′rēn klō′rĭn §§ 28(7), 34(3), 47(3)	ˈklo rin ˈklɔ rin ˈklo rɪn ˈklɔ rɪn
chloroform	KLOH ruh fawrm KLAW ruh fawrm	klō′rŏ fôrm § 34(3)	ˈklo rə fɔrm, ˈklɔ-; *ES* -fɔəm
chocolate	CHAWK uh lit CHOK uh lit	chŏk′ŏ lĭt §§ 34(7), 50(2)	ˈtʃɔk ə lɪt, ˈtʃɒk-, ˈtʃɔk ˌlɪt, ˈtʃɒk-
choir	kwair § 50(34)	kwīr	kwaɪr; *ES* kwaɪə(r)

	SIMPLIFIED	DIACRITICAL	PHONETIC
choler	KOL uhr	kŏl′ẽr	kɑl ɚ; ES 'kɑl ə(r), 'kɒl-
cholera	KOL uhr uh	kŏl′ẽr ȧ	'kɑl ər ə; ES also 'kɒl-
choleric	KOL uhr ik	kŏl′ẽr ĭk	'kɑl ər ɪk; ES also 'kɒl-
chore	chohr chawr	chōr § 34(3)	tʃor, tʃɔr; ES tʃoə(r), E also tʃɔə(r)
chorister	KOR is tuhr KAWR is tuhr	kŏr′ĭs tẽr kôr′ĭs tẽr § 34(5, 7)	'kɑr ɪs tɚ, 'kɔr-, 'kɒr-; ES -tə(r)
chorus	KOH ruhs KAW ruhs	kō′rŭs §§ 28(8), 34(3)	'ko rəs 'kɔ rəs
christen	KRIS 'n	krĭs′ 'n § 33(2)	'krɪs n̩
Christendom	KRIS 'n duhm	krĭs′ 'n dŭm § 33(2)	'krɪs n̩ dəm
Christian	KRIS chuhn KRIST yuhn	krĭs′chăn krĭst′yăn § 47(3)	'krɪs tʃən 'krɪst jən
Christianity	*kris* chi AN uh ti *kris* chi AN i ti *kris* ti AN uh ʝi	krĭs′chĭ ăn′ĭ tĭ krĭs′chĭ ăn′ĭ tĭ krĭs′tĭ ăn′ĭ tĭ §§ 38(12), 47(3)	ˌkrɪs tʃɪ 'æn ə tɪ, -ɪ tɪ, -tɪ 'æn-, -'tʃæn ə tɪ
Christmas	KRIS muhs KRIST muhs	krĭs′mȧs krĭst′mȧs	'krɪs məs 'krɪst məs
chrysanthemum	kris AN thuh muhm kriz AN thuh muhm	krĭs ăn′thē̆ mŭm krĭz ăn′thē̆ mŭm § 47(1)	krɪs 'æn θə məm krɪz 'æn θə məm
chrysolite	KRIS uh la͡it	krĭs′ŏ līt	'krɪs ə laɪt
church	*chuhrch*	chûrch §§ 22(5), 40(6)	tʃɝtʃ; ES also tʃɜtʃ
churl	*chuhrl*	chûrl § 40(6)	tʃɝl; ES also tʃɜl
cicada	si KAY duh si KAH duh	sĭ kā′dȧ sĭ kä′dȧ	sɪ 'ke də sɪ 'kɑ də
Cicero	SIS uh roh	sĭs′ĕ rō	'sɪs ə ro
cigar	si GAHR	sĭ gär′	sɪ 'gɑr; ES -'gɑ:(r), E also -'gɑ:(r)
cigarette	*sig* uh RET	sĭg′ȧ rĕt′	ˌsɪg ə 'rɛt
cinchona	sin KOH nuh	sĭn kō′nȧ	sɪn 'ko nə
Cincinnati	*sin* suh NAT i *Locally, often:* *sin* suh NAT uh	sĭn′sĭ năt′ĭ *Locally, often:* sĭn′sĭ năt′ȧ § 51(6)	ˌsɪn sə 'næt ɪ *Locally, often:* ˌsɪn sə 'næt ə
cincture	SINGK chuhr SINGK tyuhr	sĭngk′tū̆r §§ 33(4), 50(31)	'sɪŋk tʃɚ, -tjɚ; ES -tʃə(r), -tjə(r)
cinema	SIN i muh	sĭn′ĕ mȧ	'sɪn ɪ mə, 'sɪn ə-

	SIMPLIFIED	DIACRITICAL	PHONETIC
cinnamon	SIN uh muhn	sĭn'ȧ mŭn	'sın ə mən
Circe	SUHR si SUHR see	sûr'sĕ	'sɝ sı, -si; *ES also* 'sɜ-
circuit	SUHR kit	sûr'kĭt	'sɝ kıt; *ES also* 'sɜ-
circuitous	suhr KYOO uh tuhs suhr KYOO i tuhs	sēr kū'ĭ tŭs sēr kū'ĭ tŭs § 48(2)	sə 'kju ə təs, -ı təs; *ES* sə-
circumspect	SUHR kuhm spekt	sûr'kŭm spĕkt	'sɝ kəm spekt; *ES* *also* 'sɜ-
circumstance	SUHR kuhm stans *B.*, SUHR kuhm stuhns	sûr'kŭm stăns *B.*, sûr'kŭm stăns § 51(4)	'sɝ kəm stæns; *B.*, -stəns; *ES* *also* 'sɜ-
circumstances	SUHR kuhm stan siz *B.*, SUHR kuhm stuhn siz	sûr'kŭm stăn sĭz *B.*, sûr'kŭm stăn sĭz §§ 48(3), 51(4)	'sɝ kəm stæn sız; *B.*, -stən-; *ES* *also* 'sɜ-
cistern	SIS tuhrn	sĭs'tẽrn	'sıs tɚn; *ES* -tən
cite	saīt § 50(34)	sīt	saıt
citizen	SIT uh zuhn SIT uh z'n *Gaining ground:* SIT uh suhn	sĭt'ĭ zĕn sĭt'ĭ z'n *Gaining ground:* sĭt'ĭ sĕn § 51(5)	'sıt ə zən, -ı zən, -zṇ *Gaining ground:* 'sıt ə sən, -sṇ
citizenship	SIT uh zuhn *ship* SIT i zuhn *ship*	sĭt'ĭ zĕn shĭp' sĭt'ĭ zĕn shĭp'	'sıt ə zən ˌʃıp, -ı zən, -zṇ-, -sən-, -sṇ-
citron	SIT ruhn	sĭt'rŭn	'sıt rən
city	SIT i	sĭt'ĭ	'sıt ı
civet	SIV et SIV it	sĭv'ĕt sĭv'ĭt § 24(5)	'sıv ɛt 'sıv ıt
civilian	si VIL yuhn	sĭ vĭl'yăn § 28(9)	sı 'vıl jən
civilization	*siv* uh li ZAY shuhn *siv* i li ZAY shuhn *siv* uh laī ZAY shuhn *siv* i laī ZAY shuhn	sĭv'ĭ lĭ zā'shŭn sĭv'ĭ lĭ zā'shŭn sĭv'ĭ lī zā'shŭn sĭv'ĭ lī zā'shŭn § 28(3)	ˌsıv ə lı 'ze ʃən, ˌsıv ı-, -laı-, ˌsıv ḷ ı- ˌsıv ḷ aı-
clandestine	klan DES tin	klăn dĕs'tĭn	klæn 'dɛs tın
clangor	KLANG guhr KLANG uhr	klăng'gẽr klăng'ẽr §§ 33(4), 47(3)	'klæŋ gɚ, 'klæŋ ɚ; *ES* -gə(r), -ə(r)
clapboard	KLAP bohrd KLAP bawrd KLAB uhrd	klăp'bōrd klăb'ẽrd §§ 1, 34(3), 35 (1), 47(3)	'klæp bord, -bɔrd, 'klæb ɚd; *ES* 'klæp bɔəd, 'klæb əd, *E also* 'klæp bɔəd

	SIMPLIFIED	DIACRITICAL	PHONETIC
claret	KLAR uht	klăr′ĕt	'klær ət
clarinet	*klar* uh NET	klăr′ĭ nĕt′	ˌklær ə 'net
	klar i NET	klăr′ĭ nĕt′	ˌklær ɪ 'net
	KLAR uh net	klăr′ĭ nĕt	'klær ə net
	KLAR uh nit	klăr′ĭ nĭt § 47(1)	'klær ə nɪt
clasp	klasp	klásp	klæsp; *E also*
	klahsp	§ 20(5)	klasp, klɑsp
class	klas	klás	klæs; *E also* klas,
	klahs	§ 20(5)	klɑs
classic	KLAS ik	klăs′ĭk	'klæs ɪk
Claudius (I)	KLAW di uhs	klô′dĭ ŭs	'klɔ dɪ əs
cleanliness	KLEN li nes	klĕn′lĭ nĕs	'klɛn lɪ nes
	KLEN li nis	klĕn′lĭ nĭs	'klɛn lɪ nɪs
		§§ 24(5), 50(23)	
cleanly (adj.)	KLEN li	klĕn′lĭ § 50(20)	'klɛn lɪ
cleanly (adv.)	KLEEN li	klēn′lĭ § 50(20)	'klin lɪ
clearly	KLĬER li	klē̦r′lĭ	'klɪər lɪ, 'klɪr-,
	KLIR li	§§ 24(2), 50(20)	'klɪr-; *ES*
	KLEER li	klēr′lĭ	'klɪə(r)-
clematis	KLEM uh tis	klĕm′*a* tĭs	'klem ə tɪs
clement	KLEM uhnt	klĕm′ĕnt	'klem ənt
Cleopatra	*klee* uh PAY truh	klē′ŏ pā′tr*a*	ˌkli ə 'pe trə
	klee oh PAY truh		ˌkli o 'pe trə
	klee uh PAH truh	klē′ŏ pä′tr*a*	ˌkli ə 'pɑ trə
	klee oh PAH truh		ˌkli o 'pɑ trə
	klee uh PAT ruh	klē′ŏ păt′r*a*	ˌkli ə 'pæt rə
	klee oh PAT ruh		ˌkli o 'pæt rə
clerk	*kluhrk*	klûrk §§ 40(6),	klɜk; *ES also*
		47(2)	klɜk
client	KLAI͡ uhnt	klī′ĕnt	'klaɪ ənt
	§ 50(34)		
climate	KLAI͡ mit	klī′mĭt § 50(2)	'klaɪ mɪt
	§ 50(34)		
climatic	klai͡ MAT ik	klī măt′ik	klaɪ 'mæt ɪk
climb	klai͡m § 50(34)	klīm §§ 1, 21(1),	klaɪm
		22(2)	
clinic	KLIN ik	klĭn′ĭk	'klɪn ɪk
clinician	kli NISH uhn	klĭ nĭsh′ăn	klɪ 'nɪʃ ən
cloak	klohk	klōk	klok
cloth	klawth	klôth §§ 34(7),	klɔθ
	kloth	39(5, 6)	klɒθ
clothe	klohth̶	klōth̶ § 39(6)	kloð
clothes (n. pl.:	klohth̶z	klōth̶z §§ 39(5),	kloðz
has no sing.)		47(2)	
	Colloq.:	*Colloq.:*	*Colloq.:*
	klohz	klōz § 51(3)	kloz
clothier	KLOTH̶ yuhr	klōth̶′yĕr § 28(9)	'kloð jɚ; *ES*
			-jə(r)

	SIMPLIFIED	DIACRITICAL	PHONETIC
cloths (n. pl. of *cloth*)	klawthz klothz klawths kloths	klŏthz klŏths §§ 39(5), 51(11)	klɔðz klɒðz klɔθs klɒθs
—— "*pieces of cloth*"	klawthz klothz	klŏthz § 39(5), 51(11)	klɔðz klɒðz
—— "*kinds of cloth*," esp.	klawths kloths	klŏths §§ 39(5), 51(11)	klɔθs klɒθs
cloy	kloi	kloi	klɔɪ
clue	kloo	klōō §§ 40(4), 48(2)	klu
coadjutor	koh AJ ōŏ tuhr *koh* uh JOO tuhr	kō ăj′ōŏ tēr kō′ă jōō′tēr	ko ˈædʒ ʊ tɚ, -ə tɚ, ˌko ə ˈdʒu tɚ; *ES* -tə(r)
coagulate	koh AG yōŏ layt	kō ăg′ʉ lāt	ko ˈæg jʊ let, -jə-, -ju-
coagulation	koh *ag* yōŏ LAY shuhn	kō ăg′ʉ lā′shŭn	ko ˌæg jʊ ˈle ʃən, -jə-, -ju-
coalesce	*koh* uh LES	kō′ă lĕs′	ˌko ə ˈlɛs
coalescence	*koh* uh LES uhns *koh* uh LES ′ns	kō′ă lĕs′ĕns kō′ă lĕs′ ′ns § 33(2)	ˌko ə ˈlɛs əns ˌko ə ˈlɛs n̩s
coalition	*koh* ul LISH uhn	kō′ă lĭsh′ŭn	ˌko ə ˈlɪʃ ən
coarse	kohrs kawrs	kōrs § 34(3)	kors, kɔrs; *ES* koəs, *E also* kɔəs
cobalt	KOH bawlt KOH bolt	kō′bôlt kō′bŏlt § 47(3)	ˈko bɔlt, −bɑlt, -bɒlt
cobra	KOH bruh	kō′bră § 47(1)	ˈko brə
cocaine	koh KAYN KOH kayn KOH kuh een KOH kuh in	kō kān′ kō′kān kō′kă ēn kō′kă ĭn § 47(1)	ko ˈken ˈko ken ˈko kə in ˈko kə ɪn
cochineal	*koch* uh NEEL *koch* i NEEL KOCH uh neel	kŏch′ĭ nēl′ koch′ĭ nēl′ kŏch′ĭ nēl § 47(3)	ˌkɑtʃ ə ˈnil, -ɪ ˈnil, ˈkɑtʃ ə nil, -ɪ nil; *ES also* ˌkɒtʃ-, ˈkɒtʃ-
cochlea	KOK li uh	kŏk′lĕ ă	ˈkɑk lɪ ə; *ES also* ˈkɒk-
cockatoo	*kok* uh TOO KOK uh *too*	kŏk′ă tōō′ kŏk′ă tōō′ § 11	ˌkɑk ə ˈtu, ˈkɑk ə ˌtu; *ES also* ˌkɒk-, ˈkɒk-
cockatrice	KOK uh tris *B.*, KOK uh trais	kŏk′ă trĭs §§ 47(2), 51(4) *B.*, kŏk′ă trīs	ˈkɑk ə trɪs; *ES also* ˈkɒk- *B.*, ˈkɒk ə traɪs
cocoa	KOH koh	kō′kō	ˈko ko
cocoon	kuh KOON	kŏ kōōn′	kə ˈkun

	SIMPLIFIED	DIACRITICAL	PHONETIC
coerce	koh UHRS	kŏ ûrs′	ko ˈɜˈs; *ES also* -ˈɜs
coffee	KAWF i KOF i	kŏf′ĭ § 34(7)	ˈkɔf ɪ ˈkɒf ɪ
cogent	KOH juhnt	kŏ′jĕnt	ˈko dʒənt
cognac	KOH nyak KON yak	kŏ′nyăk kŏn′yăk § 47(1)	ˈko njæk ˈkɑn jæk; *ES also* ˈkɒn-
		F., kŏ′nyàk′	*F.,* kö ˈɲak
cognizance	KOG ni zuhns § 47(3)	kŏg′nĭ zăns	ˈkɑg nɪ zəns; *ES also* ˈkɒg-
	Also, esp. in law: KON i zuhns	*Also, esp. in law:* kŏn′ĭ zăns § 51(11)	*Also, esp. in law:* ˈkɑn ɪ zəns; *ES also* ˈkɒn-
cognizant	KOG ni zuhnt	kŏg′nĭ zănt	ˈkɑg nɪ zənt; *ES also* ˈkɒg-
	Also, esp. in law: KON i zuhnt	*Also, esp. in law:* kŏn′ĭ zănt	*Also, esp. in law:* ˈkɑn ɪ zənt; *ES also* ˈkɒn-
coherence	koh HIER uhns koh HIR uhns koh HEER uhns	kŏ hēr′ĕns § 24(2) kŏ hēr′ĕns	ko ˈhɪər əns, -ˈhɪr-, -ˈhir; *ES* -ˈhɪər-
cohesion	koh HEE zhuhn	kŏ hē′zhŭn § 50(28)	ko ˈhi ʒən
coincidence	koh IN suh duhns koh IN si duhns	kŏ ĭn′sĭ dĕns kŏ ĭn′sĭ dĕns	ko ˈɪn sə dəns ko ˈɪn sɪ dəns
coincident	koh IN suh duhnt koh IN si duhnt	kŏ ĭn′sĭ dĕnt kŏ ĭn′sĭ dĕnt	ko ˈɪn sə dənt ko ˈɪn sɪ dənt
colander	KUHL uhn duhr KOL uhn duhr	kŭl′ăn dẽr kŏl′ăn dẽr § 47(1)	ˈkʌl ən dɚ ˈkɑl-; *ES* -də(r), *also* ˈkɒl-
cold	kohld	kōld § 22(2)	kold
Coleridge (S.T.)	KOHL rij	kōl′rĭj	ˈkol rɪdʒ
collapse	kuh LAPS	kŏ lăps′	kə ˈlæps
collate	kuh LAYT ko LAYT	kŏ lāt′ kŏ lāt′	kə ˈlet kɑ ˈlet; *ES also* kɒ-
	KO layt	kŏ′lāt	ˈkɑ let; *ES also* ˈkɒ-
colleague (n.)	KOL eeg	kŏl′ēg	ˈkɑl ig; *ES also* ˈkɒl-
—— (v.i.)	kuh LEEG	kŏ lēg′ §§ 12, 34(13)	kə ˈlig, kɑ-; *ES also* kɒ-
collect (v.)	kuh LEKT	kŏ lĕkt′	kə ˈlɛkt
—— (n.)	KOL ekt	kŏl′ĕkt § 12	ˈkɑl ɛkt; *ES also* ˈkɒl-
college	KOL ej KOL ij	kŏl′ĕj kŏl′ĭj § 24(5)	ˈkɑl ɛdʒ, -ɪdʒ; *ES also* ˈkɒl-
collegiate (n., adj.)	kuh LEE ji it	kŏ lē′jĭ ĭt § 28(9)	kə ˈli dʒɪ ɪt, -dʒɪt

collier	KOL yuhr	kŏl′yēr § 28(9)	ˈkɑl jɚ; *ES* -jə(r), *also* ˈkɒl-
colliery	KOL yuhr i	kŏl′yēr ĭ	ˈkɑl jər ɪ; *ES also* ˈkɒl-
collision	kuh LIZH uhn	kŏ lĭzh′ŭn	kə ˈlɪʒ ən
collocation	*kol* oh KAY shuhn	kŏl′ō kā′shŭn	ˌkɑl o ˈke ʃən; *ES also* ˌkɒl-
colloquial	kuh LOH kwi uhl	kŏ lō′kwĭ ăl § 28(9)	kə ˈlo kwɪ əl
collusion	kuh LOO zhuhn kuh LYOO zhuhn	kŏ lū′zhŭn §§ 48(2), 50(32)	kə ˈlu ʒən kə ˈlju ʒən
cologne	kuh LOHN	kŏ lōn′	kə ˈlon
colonel	KUHR nuhl KUHR n′l	kûr′něl kûr′ n′l § 31(3)	ˈkɝ nəl, -n̩; *ES also* ˈkɜ-
colonnade	*kol* uh NAYD	kŏl′ŏ nād′	ˌkɑl ə ˈned; *ES also* ˌkɒl-
Colorado	*kol* uh RAH doh *kol* uh RAD oh	kŏl′ŏ rä′dō kŏl′ŏ răd′ō	ˌkɑl ə ˈra do, -ˈræd o; *ES also* ˌkɒl-
colossal	kuh LOS uhl kuh LOS ′l	kŏ lŏs′ăl kŏ lŏs′ ′l	kə ˈlɑs əl, -ˈlas l̩; *ES also* -ˈlɒs-
Colosseum	*kol* uh SEE uhm	kŏl′ŏ sē′ŭm	ˌkɑl ə ˈsi əm; *ES also* ˌkɒl-
Colossus, colossus	kuh LOS uhs	kŏ lŏs′ŭs	kə ˈlɑs əs; *ES also* -ˈlɒs-
colt	kohlt	kōlt	kolt
Columbia	kuh LUHM bi uh kuh LUHM bi yuh	kŏ lŭm′bĭ *a* kŏ lŭm′bĭ y*a* § 28(9)	kə ˈlʌm bɪ ə kə ˈlʌm bɪ jə, -bjə
columbine (n.)	KOL uhm bain	kŏl′ŭm bīn	ˈkɑl əm baɪn; *ES also* ˈkɒl-
—— (adj.)	KOL uhm bain KOL uhm bin § 50(34)	kŏl′ŭm bīn kŏl′ŭm bĭn	ˈkɑl əm baɪn, -bɪn; *ES also* -ˈkɒl-
column	KOL uhm	kŏl′ŭm	ˈkɑl əm; *ES also* ˈkɒl-
—— (*newspaper: often spelled "colyum"*)	*Generally dial. or humorous:* KOL yuhm	*Generally dial. or humorous:* kŏl′yŭm § 51(2, 11)	*Generally dial. or humorous:* ˈkɑl jəm; *ES also* ˈkɒl-
columnist (See the dial. or humor. pronunciation of *column*.)	KOL uhm nist KOL uhm ist	kŏl′ŭm nĭst kŏl′ŭm ĭst	ˈkɑl əm nɪst; *ES also* ˈkɒl- ˈkɑl əm ɪst; *ES also* ˈkɒl-
	Dial. or humor.: KOL yuhm ist	*Dial. or humor.:* kŏl′yŭm ĭst § 51(2, 11)	*Dial. or humor.:* ˈkɑl jəm ɪst; *ES also* ˈkɒl-
coma	KOH muh	kō′m*a*	ˈko mə
comb	kohm	kōm § 21(1)	kom

	SIMPLIFIED	DIACRITICAL	PHONETIC
combat (n., adj.)	KOM bat KUHM bat	kŏm′băt kŭm′băt § 1, 12	'kɑm bæt, 'kʌm-; *ES also* 'kɒm-
—— (v.)	KOM bat KUHM bat kuhm BAT	kŏm′băt kŭm′băt kŏm băt′ §§ 34(10), 47(3)	'kɑm bæt, 'kʌm-, kəm 'bæt; *ES* *also* 'kɒm-
combatant	KOM buh tuhnt KUHM buh tuhnt	kŏm′bå tănt kŭm′bå tănt	'kɑm bə tənt, 'kʌm-; *ES also* 'kɒm-
combatants	KOM buh tuhnts KUHM buh tuhnts	kŏm′bå tănts kŭm′bå tănts § 48(3)	'kɑm bə tənts, 'kʌm-; *ES also* 'kɒm-
combative	KOM buh tiv KUHM buh tiv kuhm BAT iv	kŏm′bå tĭv kŭm′bå tĭv kŏm băt′ĭv § 50(3)	'kɑm bə tɪv, 'kʌm-, kəm 'bæt ɪv; *ES also* 'kɒm-
combine (v.)	kuhm BA͞IN	kŏm bīn′	kəm 'baɪn
—— (n.)	KOM ba͞in kuhm BA͞IN	kŏm′bīn kŏm bīn′ § 12	'kɑm baɪn, kəm 'baɪn; *ES* *also* 'kɒm-
come	*kuhm* *Occas. unstressed:* kuhm k'm	kŭm § 40(6) *Occas. unstressed:* kŭm §§ 1, 16, 51(8)	kʌm *Occas. unstressed:* kəm km̩
comely	KUHM li	kŭm′lĭ	'kʌm lɪ
comfit	KUHM fit KOM fit	kŭm′fĭt kŏm′fit	'kʌm fɪt, 'kɑm-; *ES also* 'kɒm-
comfort	KUHM fuhrt	kŭm′fẽrt §§ 1, 35(2)	'kʌm fɚt; *ES* -fət
comfortable	KUHM fuhrt uh b'l	kŭm′fẽrt å b'l	'kʌm fɚt ə bl̩; *ES* -fət-
coming	KUHM ing	kŭm′ĭng	'kʌm ɪŋ
comity	KOM uh ti KOM i ti	kŏm′ĭ tĭ kŏm′ĭ tĭ	'kɑm ə tɪ, -ɪ tɪ; *ES* *also* 'kɒm-
comma	KOM uh	kŏm′å	'kɑm ə; *ES also* 'kɒm-
command	kuh MAND kuh MAHND	kŏ månd′ § 20(5)	kə 'mænd; *ES* *also* -'mand, -'mɑnd
commandant	*kom* uhn DAHNT *kom* uhn DANT	kŏm′ăn dänt′ kŏm′ăn dänt′	ˌkɑm ən 'dɑnt, -'dænt; *ES also* ˌkɒm-
commensurate (adj.)	kuh MEN sho͝o rit	kŏ mĕn′sho͝o rit	kə 'mɛn ʃʊ rɪt
—— (v.)	kuh MEN sho͝o rayt	kŏ mĕn′sho͝o rāt § 34(13)	kə 'mɛn ʃʊ ret
comment (n.)	KOM ent	kŏm′ĕnt § 47(2)	'kɑm ɛnt; *ES also* 'kɒm-

—— (v.)	KOM ent	kŏm′ĕnt §§ 12, 51(8)	ˈkɑm ɛnt; *ES also* ˈkɒm-
	Occas.: kuh MENT	*Occas.:* kŏ mĕnt′	*Occas.:* kə ˈmɛnt
commissariat	*kom* uh SEHR i at *kom* uh SAY ri at *kom* i SEHR i at	kŏm′ĭ sâr′ĭ ăt §§ 20(2), 47(2) kŏm′ĭ sâr′ĭ ăt	ˌkɑm ə ˈsɛr ɪ æt, -ˈsær-, -ˈse rɪ-, ˌkɑm ɪ-; *ES also* ˌkɒm-, -ˈsɛə rɪ-
commissary	KOM uh *ser* i	kŏm′ĭ sĕr′ ĭ §§ 20(2), 24(9)	ˈkɑm ə ˌsɛr ɪ; *ES also* ˈkɒm-
	B., KOM uh suhr i	*B.*, kŏm′ĭ sĕr ĭ	*B.*, ˈkɒm ə sə rɪ
commissioner	kuh MISH uhn uhr	kŏ mĭsh′ŭn ẽr	kə ˈmɪʃ ən ɚ; *ES* -ən ə(r)
commode	kuh MOHD	kŏ mōd′ § 34(13)	kə ˈmod, kɑ-
commodious	kuh MOH di uhs	kŏ mō′dĭ ŭs §§ 28(9), 50(25)	kə ˈmo dɪ əs
commonalty	KOM uhn uhl ti	kŏm′ŭn ăl tĭ	ˈkɑm ən əl tɪ; *ES also* ˈkɒm-
commonweal	KOM uhn *weel*	kŏm′ŭn wēl′	ˈkɑm ən ˌwil; *ES also* ˈkɒm-
communal	KOM yōō nuhl kuh MYOO nuhl kuh MYOO n'l	kŏm′ū năl kŏ mū′năl kŏ mū′n'l §§ 31(3), 47(3), 48(2)	ˈkɑm jʊ nəl, -ju-, kə ˈmju nəl, kɑ-, -n̩]; *ES also* ˈkɒm-, kɒ-
commune (v.i.)	kuh MYOON *In poetry, often:* KOM yoon	kŏ mūn′ *In poetry, often:* kŏm′ūn	kə ˈmjun *In poetry, often:* ˈkɑm jun; *ES also* ˈkɒm-
—— (n.)	KOM yoon	kŏm′ūn §§ 12, 48(2)	ˈkɑm jun; *ES also* ˈkɒm-
communicable	kuh MYOO nuh kuh b'l kuh MYOO ni kuh b'l	kŏ mū′nĭ kȧ b'l kŏ mū′nĭ kȧ b'l § 48(2)	kə ˈmju nə kə b̩ kə ˈmju nɪ kə b̩
communism	KOM yōō nĭz'm KOM yōō nĭz uhm	kŏm′ū nĭz'm	ˈkɑm jʊ nɪz m̩, -nɪz əm, -ju-; *ES also* ˈkɒm-
compact (adj., v.t.)	kuhm PAKT	kŏm păkt′	kəm ˈpækt
—— (n.)	KOM pakt	kŏm′păkt § 11	ˈkɑm pækt; *ES also* ˈkɒm-
company	KUHM puh ni	kŭm′pȧ nĭ § 1	ˈkʌm pə nɪ
comparable	KOM puh ruh b'l	kŏm′pȧ rȧ b'l	ˈkɑm pə rə b̩, -prə-; *ES also* ˈkɒm-
comparative	kuhm PAR uh tiv	kŏm păr′ȧ tĭv	kəm ˈpær ə tɪv

	SIMPLIFIED	DIACRITICAL	PHONETIC
compare	kuhm PEHR	kŏm pâr′	kəm 'pɛr, -'pær; *ES* -'pææə(r), *E also* -'pɛə(r)
comparison	kuhm PAR uh suhn	kŏm păr′ĭ sŭn	kəm 'pær ə sən, -ɪ sən, -sn̩
	kuhm PAR uh s'n	kŏm păr′ĭ s'n	
compass	KUHM puhs	kŭm′pȧs § 1	'kʌm pəs
compatriot	kuhm PAY tri uht	kŏm pā′trĭ ŭt	kəm 'pe trɪ ət
	kuhm PAT ri uht	kŏm păt′rĭ ŭt § 47(3)	kəm 'pæt rɪ ət
compeer	kom PĬER	kŏm pḙr′	kam 'pɪər, -'pɪr,
	kom PIR	§ 24(2)	-'pir, 'kam pir,
	kom PEER	kŏm pēr′	-pɪr; *ES also*
	KOM peer	kŏm′pēr	kɒm-, 'kɒm-, -pɪə(r)
compensate	KOM pen sayt	kŏm′pĕn sāt	'kam pɛn set,
	KOM puhn sayt	kŏm′pĕn sāt § 47(3)	-pən-; *ES also* 'kɒm-
	Not infreq.:	*Not infreq.:*	*Not infreq.:*
	kuhm PEN sayt	kŏm pĕn′sāt	kəm 'pɛn set,
	kom PEN sayt	kŏm pĕn′sāt § 51(8)	kam-; *ES also* kɒm-
competence	KOM pi tuhns	kŏm′pḙ tĕns	'kam pɪ təns, -pə-;
	KOM puh tuhns		*ES also* 'kɒm-
competent	KOM pi tuhnt	kŏm′pḙ tĕnt	'kam pɪ tənt, -pə-; *ES also* 'kɒm-
complacence	kuhm PLAY suhns	kŏm plā′sĕns	kəm 'ple səns
	kuhm PLAY s'ns	kŏm plā′s'ns § 33(2)	kəm 'ple sn̩s
complaisance	kuhm PLAY zuhns	kŏm plā′zăns	kəm 'ple zəns
	kuhm PLAY suhns	kŏm plā′săns	kəm 'ple səns
	KOM play *zans*	kŏm′plā zăns′	'kam ple ˌzæns
	kom play ZANS	kŏm′plā zăns′	ˌkam ple 'zæns; *ES also* 'kɒm-, ˌkɒm-
complaisant	kuhm PLAY zuhnt	kŏm plā′zănt	kəm 'ple zənt
	kuhm PLAY suhnt	kŏm plā′sănt	kəm 'ple sənt
	KOM play *zant*	kŏm′plā zănt′	'kam ple ˌzænt
	kom play ZANT	kŏm′plā zănt′	ˌkam ple 'zænt; *ES also* 'kɒm-, ˌkɒm-
complement (n.)	KOM pli muhnt	kŏm′plḙ mĕnt § 47(2)	'kam plɪ mənt; *ES also* 'kɒm-
—— (v.t.)	KOM pli ment	kŏm′plḙ mĕnt § 50(22)	'kam plɪ mɛnt; *ES also* 'kɒm-

	SIMPLIFIED	DIACRITICAL	PHONETIC
complex (adj.)	kom PLEKS KOM pleks	kŏm plĕks′ kŏm′plĕks §§ 11, 12	kam 'plɛks 'kam plɛks; *ES* *also* kɒm-, 'kɒm-
—— (n.)	KOM pleks	kŏm′plĕks	'kam plɛks; *ES* *also* 'kɒm-
—— (v.t.)	kuhm PLEKS	kŏm plĕks′	kəm 'plɛks
compliment (n.)	KOM pluh muhnt KOM pli muhnt	kŏm′plĭ mĕnt kŏm′plĭ mĕnt § 50(22)	'kam plə mənt, -plɪ-; *ES also* 'kɒm-
—— (v.)	KOM pluh ment KOM pli ment	kŏm′plĭ mĕnt kŏm′plĭ mĕnt § 47(3)	'kam plə mɛnt, -plɪ-; *ES also* 'kɒm-
component	kuhm POH nuhnt	kŏm pō′nĕnt	kəm 'po nənt
comport	kuhm POHRT kuhm PAWRT	kŏm pōrt′ § 34(3)	kəm 'port, -'pɔrt; *ES* -'poət, *E* *also* -'pɔət
composite	kuhm POZ it *B.*, KOM puh zit	kŏm pŏz′ĭt §§ 47(3), 51(4) *B.*, kŏm′pŏ zĭt	kəm 'paz ɪt; *ES* *also* kɒm- *B.*, 'kɒm pə zɪt
compost	KOM pohst	kŏm′pōst § 47(1)	'kam post; *ES* *also* 'kɒm-
composure	kuhm POH zhuhr	kŏm pō′zhēr	kəm 'po ʒɚ; *ES* -ʒə(r)
compound (v.)	kom POWND	kŏm pound′	kam 'paʊnd, kəm-; *ES also* kɒm-
—— (adj.)	KOM pownd kom POWND	kŏm′pound kŏm pound′ § 11	'kam paʊnd, kam 'paʊnd; *ES also* 'kɒm-, kɒm-
—— (n.)	KOM pownd	kŏm′pound § 12	'kam paʊnd; *ES* *also* 'kɒm-
compress (v.t.)	kuhm PRES	kŏm prĕs′	kəm 'prɛs
—— (n.)	KOM pres	kŏm′prĕs § 12	'kam prɛs; *ES* *also* 'kɒm-
compromise	KOM pruh maiz § 50(34)	kŏm′prŏ mīz	'kam prə maɪz; *ES also* 'kɒm-
comptroller	kuhn TROHL uhr	kŏn trōl′ēr	kən 'trol ɚ; *ES* -ə(r)
compulsory	kuhm PUHL suh ri	kŏm pŭl′sŏ rĭ	kəm 'pʌl sə rɪ
comrade	KOM rad KOM rid KOM rayd KUHM rid	kŏm′răd kŏm′rĭd kŏm′rād kŭm′rĭd § 47(3)	'kam ræd, -rɪd, -red, 'kʌm rɪd; *ES also* 'kɒm-
concave (adj.)	KON kayv kon KAYV KONG kayv	kŏn′kāv kŏn kāv′ kŏng′kāv §§ 11, 33(4), 47(2)	'kan kev, 'kɒŋ-, kan 'kev; *ES* *also* 'kɒn-, 'kɒŋ-

	SIMPLIFIED	DIACRITICAL	PHONETIC
—— (n., v.)	KON kayv	kŏn′kāv	ˈkɑn kev; *ES also* ˈkɒn-
conceit	kuhn SEET	kŏn sēt′	kən ˈsit
concentrate (v.)	KON suhn trayt KON sen trayt	kŏn′sĕn trāt kŏn′sĕn trāt	ˈkɑn sən tret, -sɛn-; *ES also* ˈkɒn-
	kon SEN trayt kuhn SEN trayt	kŏn sĕn′trāt kŏn sĕn′trāt § 47(3)	kɑn ˈsɛn tret, kən-; *ES also* kɒn-
—— (n., adj.)	KON suhn trayt	kŏn′sĕn trāt	ˈkɑn sən tret, -sn̩-; *ES also* ˈkɒn-
concert (v.)	kuhn SUHRT	kŏn sûrt′	kən ˈsɝt; *ES also* -ˈsɜt
—— (n., adj.)	KON suhrt	kŏn′sûrt § 12	ˈkɑn sɝt; *ES also* ˈkɒn sɜt
concerto	kohn CHER toh kon CHER toh kuhn CHER toh kuhn SUHR toh	kŏn chĕr′tō kŏn chĕr′tō kŏn chĕr′tō kŏn sûr′tō § 47(1)	kon ˈtʃɛr to, kən-, kɑn-, kən ˈsɝ to, kɑn-; *ES* -ˈtʃɛə to, *also* kɒn-, -ˈsɜ-
conch	kongk *Occas.:* konch	kŏngk *Occas.:* kŏnch	kɑŋk, kɒŋk *Occas.:* kɑntʃ, kɒntʃ
conclude	kuhn KLOOD	kŏn klōōd′ §§ 40(4), 47(2), 48(2)	kən ˈklud
concomitant	kon KOM uh tuhnt kon KOM i tuhnt	kŏn kŏm′ĭ tănt kŏn kŏm′ĭ tănt	kɑn ˈkɑm ə tənt, -ˈkɑm ɪ-; *ES* *also* -ˈkɒm-
concord	KON kawrd KONG kawrd	kŏn′kôrd kŏng′kôrd § 33(4)	ˈkɑn kɔrd, ˈkɑŋ-; *ES* -kɔəd, *also* ˈkɒn-, ˈkɒŋ-
Concord (**Mass.**)	KONG kuhrd	kŏng′kĕrd	ˈkɑŋ kɚd; *ES* -kəd, *also* ˈkɒŋ-; *towns outside* *New England,* ˈkɑn kɔrd; *ES* -kɔəd, *also* ˈkɒn-
concordance	kon KAWR duhns kuhn KAWR duhns	kŏn kôr′dăns kŏn kôr′dăns	kɑn ˈkɔr dəns, kən-, -dn̩s; *ES* -ˈkɔə-, *also* kɒn-
concourse	KON kohrs KON kawrs KONG kohrs KONG kawrs	kŏn′kōrs kŏng′kōrs §§ 33(4), 34(3)	ˈkɑn kors, -kɔrs, ˈkɑŋ-; *ES* -koəs, *also* ˈkɒn-, *E* *also* -kɔəs
concrete (adj., n.)	KON kreet kon KREET	kŏn′krēt kŏn krēt′ §§ 11, 34(4)	ˈkɑn krit, kɑn ˈkrit; *ES* *also* ˈkɒn-, kɒn-

	SIMPLIFIED	DIACRITICAL	PHONETIC
—— (n. – also, "concrete form or object; artificial stone"; esp.)	kon KREET	kŏn krēt′	kɑn ′krit; ES also kɒn-
—— (v.)	kon KREET	kŏn krēt′ § 47(2)	kɑn ′krit; ES also kɒn-
—— (v. – also, form of, or cover with, concrete"; preferably)	KON kreet	kŏn′krēt § 51(11)	′kɑn krit; ES also ′kɒn-
concubine	KONG kyo͞o bain	kŏng′kŭ bīn § 33(4)	′kaŋ kjʊ baɪn, -kju-, ′kɑn-; ES also ′kɒŋ-, ′kɒn-
condemn	kuhn DEM	kŏn dĕm′ § 33(1)	kən ′dem
condolence	kuhn DOH luhns	kŏn dō′lĕns	kən ′do ləns; not infreq., ′kɑn də ləns; ES also ′kɒn-
condone	kuhn DOHN	kŏn dōn′	kən ′don
conduct (n.)	KON duhkt	kŏn′dŭkt § 40(6)	′kɑn dʌkt; ES also ′kɒn-
—— (v.)	kuhn DUHKT	kŏn dŭkt′ § 12	kən ′dʌkt
conduit	KON dit	kŏn′dĭt § 47(3)	′kɑn dɪt, -dwɪt; ES also ′kɒn-
	In engin., esp.: KON do͞o it	In engin., esp.: kŏn′do͞o ĭt § 51(6)	In engin., esp.: ′kɑn dʊ ɪt; ES also ′kɒn-
	Occas.: KUHN dit	Occas.: kŭn′dĭt § 51(8)	Occas.: ′kʌn dɪt
confessor	kuhn FES uhr	kŏn fĕs′ĕr	kən ′fes ɚ; ES -ə(r)
	Occas., esp. in church matters: KON fes uhr	Occas., esp. in church matters: kŏn′fĕs ēr § 47(2)	Occas., esp. in church matters: ′kɑn fes ɚ; ES -ə(r), also ′kɒn-
confidant (n. masc.), confidante (n. fem.)	kon fuh DANT kon fi DANT KON fuh dant KON fi dant	kŏn′fĭ dănt′ kŏn′fĭ dănt′ kŏn′fĭ dănt′ kŏn′fĭ dănt′ § 47(2)	ˌkɑn fə ′dænt, -fɪ-, ′kɑn fə ˌdænt, -fɪ-; ES also ˌkɒn-, ′kɒn-
confident	KON fuh duhnt KON fi duhnt	kŏn′fĭ dĕnt kŏn′fĭ dĕnt	′kɑn fə dənt, -fɪ-; ES also ′kɒn-
confine (v.)	kuhn FAIN	kŏn fīn′	kən ′faɪn
—— (n.)	KON fain § 50(34)	kŏn′fīn § 12	′kɑn faɪn; ES also ′kɒn-
	In poetry, often: kuhn FAIN	In poetry, often: kŏn fīn′ § 51(11)	In poetry, often: kən ′faɪn

confines (n. pl.)	KON faïnz	kŏn′fīnz	′kɑn faɪnz
	kuhn FAĪNZ	kŏn fīnz′	kən ′faɪnz; *ES also* ′kɒn faɪnz
confiscate	KON fis kayt	kŏn′fĭs kāt	′kɑn fɪs ket
	kuhn FIS kayt	kŏn fĭs′kāt § 47(3)	kən ′fɪs ket, kɑn-; *ES also* ′kɒn-, kɒn-
conflict (n.)	KON flikt	kŏn′flĭkt	′kɑn flɪkt; *ES also* ′kɒn-
—— (v.i.)	kuhn FLIKT	kŏn flĭkt′ § 12	kən ′flɪkt
confusion	kuhn FYOO zhuhn	kŏn fū′zhŭn § 48(2)	kən ′fju ʒən
congeal	kuhn JEEL	kŏn jēl′	kən ′dʒil
congenial	kuhn JEEN yuhl	kŏn jēn′yăl	kən ′dʒin jəl
	kuhn JEE ni uhl	kŏn jē′nĭ ăl §§ 28(9), 47(2)	kən ′dʒi nɪ əl
congenital	kuhn JEN i tuhl	kŏn jĕn′Ĭ tăl	kən ′dʒen ɪ təl
	kuhn JEN i t'l	kŏn jĕn′Ĭ t'l § 31(3)	kən ′dʒen ɪ tl̩
conger	KONG guhr	kŏng′gēr § 33(4)	′kɑŋ gɚ; *ES* -gə(r), *also* ′kɒŋ-
congestion	kuhn JES chuhn	kŏn jĕs′chŭn	kən ′dʒes tʃən
congratulate	kuhn GRACH ŏŏ layt	kŏn grăt′ủ lāt	kən ′grætʃ ʊ let, -′grætʃ ə-,
	kuhn GRAT yŏŏ layt	§§ 33(4), 50(33)	-′græt jʊ-, -jə-, -ju-
Congress, congress (n.)	KONG gres	kŏng′grĕs	′kɑŋ gres, -grɪs;
	KONG gris	kŏng′grĭs §§ 24(5), 33(4)	*ES also* ′kɒŋ-
—— (v.i. – "*assemble*")	kuhn GRES	kŏn grĕs′ §§ 12, 34(13)	kən ′gres, kɑn-
—— "*attend a congress*"	KONG gres	kŏng′grĕs	′kɑŋ gres, -grɪs;
	KONG gris	kŏng′grĭs	*ES also* ′kɒŋ-
congressional	kuhn GRESH uhn uhl	kŏn grĕsh′ŭn ăl	kən ′greʃ ən əl,
	kuhn GRESH uhn 'l	kŏn grĕsh′ŭn 'l § 31(3)	-ən l̩, -′greʃ nəl
congruent	KONG grŏŏ uhnt	kŏng′grŏŏ ĕnt § 33(4)	′kɑŋ grʊ ənt, *ES also* ′kɒŋ-
conical	KON i kuhl	kŏn′Ĭ kăl § 31(3)	′kɑn ɪ kəl, -kl̩; *ES also* ′kɒn-
conifer	KOH ni fuhr	kō′nĭ fēr	′ko nɪ fɚ, ′kɑn ɪ-;
	KON i fuhr	kŏn′Ĭ fēr	*ES* -fə(r), *also* ′kɒn-
conjecture	kuhn JEK chuhr	kŏn jĕk′tūr	kən ′dʒek tʃɚ,
	kuhn JEK tyuhr	§ 50(32)	-tjɚ; *ES* -tʃə(r), -tjə(r)

	SIMPLIFIED	DIACRITICAL	PHONETIC
conjugal	KON jŏŏ guhl	kŏn′jŏŏ găl	ˈkɑn dʒʊ gəl, -gl̩; *ES also* ˈkɒn-
conjure (n.)	KUHN juhr	kŭn′jĕr § 12	ˈkʌn dʒɚ; *ES* -dʒə(r)
—— (v. – *"request earnestly"*)	kuhn JŎŎR	kŏn jŏŏr′	kən ˈdʒʊr; *ES* -ˈdʒʊə(r)
—— *"affect by conjuration"*	KUHN juhr	kŭn′jĕr	ˈkʌn dʒɚ; *ES* -dʒə(r)
—— *"summon or constrain; charm; juggle"*	KUHN juhr KON juhr	kŭn′jĕr kŏn′jĕr	ˈkʌn dʒɚ, ˈkɑn-; *ES* -dʒə(r), *also* ˈkɒn-
connoisseur	*kon* i SUHR *kon* i SŎŎR *kon* i SOOR	kŏn′ĭ sûr′ kŏn′ĭ sūr′ § 47(3)	ˌkɑn ɪ ˈsɝ, -ˈsʊr; *ES also* -ˈsɜ(r), ˌkɒn-, *ES* -ˈsʊə(r)
connubial	kuh NYOO bi uhl kuh NOO bi uhl	kŏ nū′bĭ ăl §§ 48(2), 50(32)	kə ˈnju bɪ əl kə ˈnu bɪ əl
conquer	KONG kuhr	kŏng′kĕr	ˈkɑŋ kɚ, ˈkɒŋ-, ˈkɔŋ-; *ES* -kə(r)
conquest	KONG kwest KON kwest	kŏng′kwĕst kŏn′kwĕst § 33(4)	ˈkɑŋ kwɛst, ˈkɑn-; *ES also* ˈkɒŋ-, ˈkɒn-
consanguinity	*kon* sang GWIN uh ti *kon* sang GWIN i ti	kŏn′săng gwĭn′ĭ tĭ kŏn′săng gwĭn′ĭ tĭ § 50(16)	ˌkɑn sæŋ ˈgwɪn ə tɪ, -ɪ tɪ; *ES also* ˌkɒn-
conscience	KON shuhns	kŏn′shĕns § 38(9, 12)	ˈkɑn ʃəns; *ES also* ˈkɒn-
conscientious	*kon* shi EN shuhs	kŏn′shĭ ĕn′shŭs § 50(25)	ˌkɑn ʃɪ ˈɛn ʃəs; *ES* *also* ˌkɒn-
conscious	KON shuhs	kŏn′shŭs § 50(25)	ˈkɑn ʃəs; *ES also* ˈkɒn-
consciousness	KON shuhs nes KON shuhs nis	kŏn′shŭs nĕs kŏn′shŭs nĭs § 24(5)	ˈkɑn ʃəs nɛs, -nɪs; *ES also* ˈkɒn-
conscript (v.t.)	kuhn SKRIPT	kŏn skrĭpt′	kən ˈskrɪpt
—— (adj., n.)	KON skript	kŏn′skrĭpt § 12	ˈkɑn skrɪpt; *ES* *also* ˈkɒn-
conscription	kuhn SKRIP shuhn	kŏn skrĭp′shŭn § 50(30)	kən ˈskrɪp ʃən
conserve (v.t.)	kuhn SUHRV	kŏn sûrv′	kən ˈsɝv; *ES also* -ˈsɜv
—— (n.)	kuhn SUHRV KON *suhrv*	kŏn sûrv′ kŏn′sûrv §§ 12, 40(6)	kən ˈsɝv, ˈkɑn sɜv; *ES* *also* -ˈsɜv, -sɜv, -ˈkɒn-
considerable	kuhn SID uhr uh b'l	kŏn sĭd′ēr ȧ b'l § 9	kən ˈsɪd ər ə bl̩

consistory	kuhn SIS tuh ri KON sis tuhr i	kŏn sĭs′tŏ rĭ kŏn′sĭs tēr ĭ § 47(3)	kən ′sɪs tə rɪ ′kɑn sɪs tər ɪ; *ES* *also* ′kɒn-
console (v.)	kuhn SOHL	kŏn sōl′ § 34(13)	kən ′sol
console (n.)	KON sohl	kŏn′sōl	′kɑn sol; *ES also* ′kɒn-
consommé	*kon* suh MAY *F., kawN saw* MAY	kŏn′sŏ mā′ § 20(14) *F.,* kôn′sô′mā′	ˌkɑn sə ′me; *ES* *also* ˌkɒn- *F.,* kɔ̃ sə ′me [kō-]
consonant	KON suh nuhnt	kŏn′sŏ nănt	′kɑn sə nənt; *ES* *also* ′kɒn-
consort (n.)	KON sawrt	kŏn′sôrt § 12	′kɑn sɔrt; *ES* -sɔət, *also* ′kɒn-
—— (v.)	kuhn SAWRT	kŏn sôrt′	kən ′sɔrt; *ES* -′sɔət
conspiracy	kuhn SPIR uh si	kŏn spĭr′*à* sĭ	kən ′spɪr ə sɪ
constable	KON stuh b′l KUHN stuh b′l	kŏn′st*à* b′l kŭn′st*à* b′l §§ 1, 34(10)	′kɑn stə bl̩, ′kʌn-; *ES also* ′kɒn-
constituency	kuhn STICH ŏŏ uhn si kuhn STIT yŏŏ uhn si	kŏn stĭt′û ĕn sĭ § 50(33)	kən ′stɪtʃ ʊ ən sɪ, -′stɪt jʊ-, -ju-
constitution	*kon* stuh TYOO shuhn *kon* stuh TOO shuhn *kon* sti TYOO shuhn *kon* sti TOO shuhn	kŏn′stĭ tū′shŭn kŏn′stĭ tū′shŭn §§ 40(4), 48(2), 50(30)	ˌkɑn stə ′tju ʃən, -stə ′tu-, -stɪ ′tju-, -′tu-; *ES also* ˌkɒn-
construe	kuhn STROO KON stroo	kŏn strōō′ kŏn′strōō § 47(3)	kən ′stru, kɑn-, ′kɑn stru; *ES* *also* kɒn-, ′kɒn-
consul	KON suhl	kŏn′sŭl § 31(3)	′kɑn səl, -sl̩; *ES* *also* ′kɒn-
consular	KON syuh luhr KON suh luhr KON syŏŏ luhr KON sŏŏ luhr	kŏn′sû lēr § 40(11)	′kɑn sjə lɚ, -sə-, -sjʊ-, -sʊ-, -sjə-, ′kɑn sl̩-; *ES* -lə(r)
consume	kuhn SYOOM kuhn SOOM	kŏn sūm′ §§ 34(13), 50(32)	kən ′sjum kən ′sum
consummate (adj.)	kuhn SUHM it	kŏn sŭm′ĭt § 47(2)	kən ′sʌm ɪt
—— (v.)	KON suh mayt	kŏn′sŭ māt §§ 20 (8, 9), 50(2)	′kɑn sə met; *ES* *also* ′kɒn-
contagious	kuhn TAY juhs	kŏn tā′jŭs § 50(25)	kən ′te dʒəs

	SIMPLIFIED	DIACRITICAL	PHONETIC
contain	kuhn TAYN	kŏn tān′ § 34(13)	kən 'ten
contemn	kuhn TEM	kŏn tĕm′	kən 'tɛm
contemplate	KON tuhm playt	kŏn′tĕm plāt §§ 47(2), 50(2)	'kɑn təm plet; ES also 'kɒn-
	Occas.:	Occas.:	Occas.:
	kuhn TEM playt	kŏn tĕm′plāt § 51(8)	kən ˌtɛm plet
contemplative	kuhn TEM pluh tiv	kŏn tĕm′plɑ tĭv	kən 'tɛm plə tɪv
	KON tuhm *play* tiv	kŏn′tĕm plā′tĭv §§ 47(1), 50(17)	'kɑn təm ˌple tɪv; *ES also* 'kɒn-
contemptuous	kuhn TEMP chŏŏ uhs	kŏn tĕmp′tŭ ŭs	kən 'tɛmp tʃʊ əs
	kuhn TEMP tyŏŏ uhs	§§ 35(2), 50(25, 33)	kən 'tɛmp tjʊ əs
content (n. – "*what is con-tained*")	KON tent	kŏn′tĕnt	'kɑn tɛnt; *ES also* 'kɒn-
	Occas.:	Occas.:	Occas.:
	kuhn TENT	kŏn tĕnt′	kən 'tɛnt
content (adj. – "*satisfied*"; v.t. – "*please*"; n. – "*satisfaction*")	kuhn TENT	kŏn tĕnt′	kən 'tɛnt
contentious	kuhn TEN shuhs	kŏn tĕn′shŭs § 50(25)	kən 'tɛn ʃəs
contest (n.)	KON test	kŏn′tĕst § 12	'kɑn tɛst; *ES also* 'kɒn-
—— (v.)	kuhn TEST	kŏn tĕst′	kən 'tɛst
contiguous	kuhn TIG yŏŏ uhs	kŏn tĭg′ŭ ŭs § 50(25)	kən 'tɪg jʊ əs, -ju-
continence	KON tuh nuhns	kŏn′tĭ nĕns	'kɑn tə nəns, -tɪ-;
	KON ti nuhns	kŏn′tĭ nĕns	*ES also* 'kɒn-
contour	KON tŏŏr	kŏn′tŏŏr	'kɑn tʊr,
	kon TŎŎR	kŏn tŏŏr′ § 47(2)	kɑn 'tʊr; *ES* -tʊə(r), -'tʊə(r), *also* 'kɒn-, kɒn-
contract (n.)	KON trakt	kŏn′trăkt	'kɑn trækt; *ES also* 'kɒn-
—— (adj.)	kuhn TRAKT	kŏn trăkt′ § 11	kən 'trækt
—— (v.)	kuhn TRAKT	kŏn trăkt′ § 12	kən 'trækt
—— "*agree by contract,*" *also*	KON trakt	kŏn′trăkt § 51(11)	'kɑn trækt; *ES also* 'kɒn-
contractile	kuhn TRAK til	kŏn trăk′tĭl § 28(5), 50(13)	kən 'træk tɪl, -tļ
contractor	KON trak tuhr	kŏn′trăk tĕr	'kɑn træk tɚ,
	kuhn TRAK tuhr	kŏn trăk′tĕr	kən 'træk tɚ; *ES* -tə(r), *also* 'kɒn-

	SIMPLIFIED	DIACRITICAL	PHONETIC
—— *"contracting muscle,"* commonly	kuhn TRAK tuhr	kŏn trăk′tēr § 51(11)	kən ′træk tɚ; *ES* -tə(r)
contrariety	*kon* truh RĀI uh ti § 50(34)	kŏn′trȧ rī′ĕ tĭ	ˌkɑn trə ′raɪ ə tɪ; *ES also* ˌkɒn-
contrariwise	KON trer i *wāiz*	kŏn′trĕr ĭ wīz′	′kɑn trer ɪ ˌwaɪz,
	KON truh ri *wāiz* § 50(34)	kŏn′trȧ rĭ wīz′ §§ 20(2), 24(9)	-trə rɪ-; *ES also* ′kɒn-
	Dial. or *colloq.,* often:	*Dial.* or *colloq.,* often:	*Dial.* or *colloq.,* often:
	kon TRER ri *wāiz*	kŏn trĕr′ĭ wīz′ § 51(2, 3)	kɑn ′trer ɪ ˌwaɪz; *ES also* kɒn-
contrary	KON trer i	kŏn′trĕr ĭ §§ 20 (2), 24(9), 51(4)	′kɑn trer ɪ; *ES also* ′kɒn-
	B., KON truh ri *Dial.* or *colloq.* (*esp. when meaning "perverse"*):	*B.,* kŏn′trȧ rĭ *Dial.* or *colloq.* (*esp. when meaning "perverse"*):	*B.,* ′kɒn trə rɪ *Dial.* or *colloq.* (*esp. when meaning "perverse"*):
	kon TRER i	kŏn trĕr′ĭ § 51(2, 3)	kɑn ′trer ɪ; *ES also* kɒn-
contrast (v.)	kuhn TRAST	kŏn trăst′	kən ′træst
—— (n.)	KON trast	kŏn′trăst § 12	′kɑn træst; *ES also* ′kɒn-
contrite (n., adj.)	KON trait § 50(34)	kŏn′trīt	′kɑn traɪt; *ES also* ′kɒn-
	In poetry (adj. only), also:	*In poetry (adj. only), also:*	*In poetry (adj. only), also:*
	kuhn TRAIT	kŏn trīt′ § 51(11)	kən ′traɪt
contrition	kuhn TRISH uhn	kŏn trĭsh′ŭn § 50(13)	kən ′trɪʃ ən
controversial	*kon* truh VUHR shuhl	kŏn′trŏ vûr′shăl	ˌkɑn trə ′vɝ ʃəl; *ES also* -′vɝ-
controversy	KON truh *vuhr* si	kŏn′trŏ vûr′sĭ	′kɑn trə ˌvɝ sɪ; *ES also* ′kɒn-, -ˌvɝ-
controvert	KON truh *vuhrt*	kŏn′trŏ vûrt	′kɑn trə vɝt,
	kon truh VUHRT	kŏn′trŏ vûrt′ §§ 11, 40(6), 47(1)	ˌkɑn trə ′vɝt; *ES also* ′kɒn-, ˌkɒn-, -vɝt, -′vɝt
contumacious	*kon* tyo͝o MAY shuhs	kŏn′tṳ mā′shŭs	ˌkɑn tjʊ ′me ʃəs, -tʊ-, -tju-, -tu-; *ES also* ˌkɒn-
	kon to͝o MAY shuhs	§ 50(25, 32)	
contumacy	KON tyo͝o muh si	kŏn′tṳ mȧ sĭ	′kɑn tjʊ mə sɪ,
	KON to͝o muh si	§ 50(32)	-tʊ-, -tju-, -tu-; *ES also* ′kɒn-

contumely	KON tyŏŏ *mee* li KON tŏŏ *mee* li KON tyŏŏ mi li KON tŏŏ mi li	kŏn′tû mē′lĭ kŏn′tû mē lĭ § 47(1)	'kɑn tjʊ ˌmi lɪ, -tʊ-, -tju-, -tu-, -mɪ lɪ; *ES also* 'kɒn-
convenient	kuhn VEEN yuhnt	kŏn vēn′yĕnt §§ 24(15), 28(9) 47(3)	kən 'vin jənt, -'vi nɪ ənt
conventicle (n.)	kuhn VEN ti k'l	kŏn vĕn′tĭ k'l	kən 'vɛn tɪ kḷ
conversant	KON vuhr suhnt KON vuhr s'nt *Occas.:* kuhn VUHR suhnt	kŏn′vēr sănt kŏn′vēr s'nt § 33(2) *Occas.:* kŏn vûr′sănt § 51(8)	'kɑn və sənt, -sṇt; *ES* -və-, *also* 'kɒn- *Occas.:* kən 'vɝ sənt, -sṇt: *ES also* -'vɝ-
converse (v. – "*talk*")	kuhn VUHRS	kŏn vûrs′ § 12	kən 'vɝs; *ES also* -'vɝs
—— (n.)	KON *vuhrs*	kŏn′vûrs § 40(6)	'kɑn vɝs; *ES also* 'kɒn vɝs
converse (adj., n. – "*opposite*")	KON vuhrs	kŏn′vûrs § 11	'kɑn vɝs; *ES also* 'kɒn vɝs
conversion	kuhn VUHR shuhn kuhn VUHR zhuhn	kŏn vûr′shăn kŏn vûr′zhăn § 50(28)	kən 'vɝ ʃən, -ʒən; *ES also* -'vɝ-
convert (v.)	kuhn VUHRT	kŏn vûrt′	kən 'vɝt; *ES also* -'vɝt
—— (n., adj.)	KON vuhrt	kŏn′vûrt § 12	'kɑn vɝt; *ES also* 'kɒn vɝt
convex (adj.)	KON veks kon VEKS	kŏn′vĕks kŏn vĕks′ § 11	'kɑn vɛks, kɑn 'vɛks; *ES also* 'kɒn-, kɒn-
—— (n.)	KON veks	kŏn′vĕks	'kɑn vɛks; *ES also* 'kɒn-
—— (v.)	KON veks kuhn VEKS	kŏn′vĕks kŏn vĕks′	'kɑn vɛks kən 'vɛks; *ES also* 'kɒn-
convict (v.t.)	kuhn VIKT	kŏn vĭkt′	kən 'vɪkt
—— (n.)	KON vikt	kŏn′vĭkt § 12	'kɑn vɪkt; *ES also* 'kɒn-
convivial	kuhn VIV i uhl kuhn VIV i yuhl	kŏn vĭv′ĭ ăl kŏn vĭv′ĭ yăl § 47(2)	kən 'vɪv ɪ əl kən 'vɪv ɪ jəl
convoy (n.)	KON voi	kŏn′voi	'kɑn vɔɪ; *ES also* 'kɒn-
—— (v.t.)	kon VOI kuhn VOI	kŏn voi′ kŏn voi′ § 12	kɑn 'vɔɪ, kən-; *ES also* kɒn-
cony	KOH ni *Occas.:* KUHN i	kō′nĭ § 47(2) *Occas.:* kŭn′ĭ § 1	'ko nɪ *Occas.:* 'kʌn ɪ
cook	kŏŏk	kŏŏk § 34(22)	kʊk

co-operate (v.i.)	koh OP uhr ayt koh OP uh rayt	kŏ ŏp′ĕr āt § 20(8, 9)	ko ′ɑp ər et, -ə ret; *ES also* -′ɒp-
—— (adj.)	koh OP uhr it	kŏ ŏp′ĕr ăt	ko ′ɑp ər ɪt; *ES also* -′ɒp-
coping	KOHP ing	kōp′ĭng § 50(14)	′kop ɪŋ
coppice	KOP is	kŏp′ĭs	′kɑp ɪs; *ES also* ′kɒp-
copse	kops	kŏps	kɑps; *ES also* kɒps
coquetry	KOH kuh tri KOH ki tri koh KET ri	kō′kĕ trĭ kō′kĭ trĭ kŏ kĕt′rĭ	′ko kə trɪ ′ko kɪ trɪ ko ′ket rɪ
coquette	koh KET	kŏ kĕt′	ko ′ket
coracle	KOR uh k′l KAWR uh k′l	kŏr′å k′l kôr′å k′l § 34(4, 5)	′kɑr ə kļ, ′kɔr-, ′kɒr-
coral	KOR uhl KAWR uhl	kŏr′ăl kôr′ăl § 34(5, 7)	′kɑr əl, ′kɔr-, ′kɒr-, ′kor-
cordial	KAWR juhl KAWRD yuhl *B.*, KAWR di uhl	kôr′jăl kôrd′yăl *B.*, kôr′dĭ ăl §§ 47(2), 51(4)	′kɔr dʒəl ′kɔrd jəl *B.*,′kɔr dɪ əl; *ES* ′kɔə-
cordiality	kawr JAL uh ti kawr JAL i ti *kawr* di AL uh ti *kawr* di AL i ti	kôr jăl′ĭ tĭ kôr jăl′ĭ tĭ kôr′dĭ ăl′ĭ tĭ kôr′dĭ ăl′ĭ tĭ § 50(16)	kɔr ′dʒæl ə tɪ -ɪ tɪ, ˌkɔr dɪ ′æl ə tɪ, -ɪ tɪ; *ES* kɔə-, ˌkɔə-
cordillera	*kawr* dil YEHR uh kawr DIL uhr uh	kôr′dĭl yâr′å kôr dĭl′ĕr å § 47(2)	ˌkɔr dɪl ′jer ə kɔr ′dɪl ər ə; *ES also* ˌkɔə-, kɔə-, -′jɛə rə
Cordovan	KAWR duh vuhn KAWR doh vuhn kawr DOH vuhn	kôr′dŏ văn kôr dō′văn	′kɔr də vən, -do-, kɔr ′do vən; *ES* ′kɔə-, kɔə-
corduroy	KAWR duh roi KAWR jŏŏ roi KAWR dyŏŏ roi *kawr* duh ROI *kawr* jŏŏ ROI *kawr* dyŏŏ ROI	kôr′dŭ roi kôr′dū roi kôr′dŭ roi′ kôr′dū roi′ §§ 47(3), 50(33)	′kɔr də rɔɪ, -dʒʊ-, -djʊ-, ˌkɔr də ′rɔɪ, -dʒʊ-, -djʊ-; *ES* ′kɔə-, ˌkɔə-
cormorant	KAWR muh ruhnt	kôr′mŏ rănt	′kɔr mə rənt; *ES* ′kɔə-
cornet	KAWR net KAWR nit *Often, esp. in U.S. when referring to wind instru- ment:* kawr NET	kôr′nĕt kôr′nĭt § 50(10) *Often, esp. in U.S. when referring to wind instru- ment:* kôr nĕt′ §§ 47(1), 51(10)	′kɔr net, -nɪt; *ES* ′kɔə- *Often, esp. in U.S. when referring to wind instru- ment:* kɔr ′net; *ES* kɔə-

	SIMPLIFIED	DIACRITICAL	PHONETIC
corollary	KOR uh *ler* i KAWR uh *ler* i *B.*, kuh ROL uh ri	kŏr′ŏ lĕr′ĭ kôr′ŏ lĕr′ĭ *B.*, kŏ rŏl′*á* rĭ §§ 34(5, 7), 47(3)	ˈkɑr ə ˌlɛr ɪ, ˈkɔr-, ˈkɒr- *B.*,kə ˈrɒl ə rɪ
coronal (n.)	KOR uh nuhl KOR uh n'l KAWR uh nuhl KAWR uh n'l	kŏr′ŏ năl kŏr′ŏ n'l kôr′ŏ năl kôr′ŏ n'l	ˈkɑr ə nəl, ˈkɔr-, ˈkɒr-, -nļ
—— (adj.)	kuh ROH nuhl KOR uh nuhl KOR uh n'l KAWR uh nuhl KAWR uh n'l	kŏ rō′năl kŏr′ŏ năl kŏr′ŏ n'l kôr′ŏ năl kôr′ŏ n'l §§ 34 (5, 7), 47(3)	kə ˈro nəl, -nļ, ˈkɑr ə nəl, ˈkɔr-, ˈkɒr-, -nļ
coronet	KOR uh net KAWR uh net KOR uh nit KAWR uh nit	kŏr′ŏ nĕt kôr′ŏ nĕt kŏr′ŏ nĭt kôr′ŏ nĭt § 24(5)	ˈkɑr ə nɛt, ˈkɔr-, ˈkɒr-, -nɪt
corporal	KAWR puh ruhl	kôr′pŏ răl § 9	ˈkɔr pə rəl, -prəl; *ES* ˈkɔə-
corporeal	kawr POH ri uhl kawr PAW ri uhl	kôr pō′rĕ ăl § 34(3)	kɔr ˈpo rɪ əl, -ˈpɔ-; *ES* kə ˈpo-, *E* *also* -ˈpɔ-
corps (n. sing. and pl.)	*Sing.:* kohr kawr *Pl.:* kohrz kawrz	*Sing.:* kōr *Pl.:* kōrz §§ 34(3), 38(2), 48(3)	*Sing.:* kor, kɔr; *ES* koə(r), *E also* kɔə(r) *Pl.:* korz, kɔrz; *ES* koəz, *E also* kɔəz
corpse	kawrps *Rarely:* kawrs	kôrps *Rarely:* kôrs § 51(8)	kɔrps; *ES* kɔəps *Rarely:* kɔrs; *ES* kɔəs
corpuscle	KAWR *puhs* 'l	kôr′pŭs 'l §§ 22(3), 40(6)	ˈkɔr pʌs ļ, -pəs-; *ES* ˈkɔə-
corral (n.)	kuh RAL kuh RAHL	kŏ răl′ kŏ räl′	kə ˈræl kə ˈrɑl
—— (v.t.)	kuh RAL	kŏ răl′	kə ˈræl
correlate (v.)	KOR uh layt KAWR uh layt *kor* uh LAYT *kawr* uh LAYT	kŏr′ĕ lāt kôr′ĕ lāt kŏr′ĕ lāt′ kôr′ĕ lāt′	ˈkɑr ə let, ˈkɔr-, ˈkɒr-, ˌkɑr ə ˈlet, ˌkɔr-, ˌkɒr-
—— (n.)	KOR uh layt KAWR uh layt	kŏr′ĕ lāt kôr′ĕ lāt	ˈkɑr ə let, ˈkɔr-, ˈkɒr-
—— (adj.)	KOR uh lit KAWR uh lit	kŏr′ĕ lăt kôr′ĕ lăt §§ 20(8, 9), 34(5, 7), 47(3)	ˈkɑr ə lɪt, ˈkɔr-, ˈkɒr-

	SIMPLIFIED	DIACRITICAL	PHONETIC
corridor	KOR i dawr KOR i duhr KAWR i duhr	kŏr′ĭ dôr kŏr′ĭ dēr kôr′ĭ dēr §§ 34 (5, 7), 47(2)	′kar ɪ dɔr, ′kɒr-, -dɚ, ′kɔr ɪ dɚ; *ES* -dəə(r), -də(r)
	In political geog- *raphy, usu.:* KOR i dawr	*In political geog-* *raphy, usu.:* kŏr′ĭ dôr	*In political geog-* *raphy, usu.:* ′kar ɪ dɔr, ′kɒr-; *ES* -dəə(r)
corroborate (v.t.)	kuh ROB uh rayt	kǒ rŏb′ǒ rāt § 50(2)	kə ′rab ə ret; *ES* *also* -′rɒb-
corrugate (v.)	KOR yo͝o gayt KAWR yo͝o gayt KOR o͞o gayt KAWR o͞o gayt	kŏr′u̇ gāt kôr′u̇ gāt kŏr′o͞o gāt kôr′o͞o gāt §§ 34(5, 7), 47(1)	′kar jʊ get, ′kɔr-, ′kɒr-, -jə-, ′kar ʊ-, ′kɔr ʊ-, ′kɒr-, ′kar ə-, ′kɔr-, ′kɒr-
—— (adj.)	KOR yo͝o git KAWR yo͝o git KOR o͞o git KAWR o͞o git	kŏr′u̇ gĭt kôr′u̇ gĭt kŏr′o͞o gĭt kôr′o͞o gĭt § 20(8, 9)	′kar jʊ gɪt, ′kɔr-, ′kɒr-, -jə-, ′kar ʊ-, ′kɔr-, ′kɒr-, ′kar ə-, ′kɔr-, ′kɒr-
corsage	kawr SAHZH KAWR sij	kôr säzh′ kôr′sĭj § 47(2)	kɔr ′saʒ; *ES* kɔə- ′kɔr sɪdʒ; *ES* ′kɔə-
corsair	KAWR sehr	kôr′sâr	′kɔr sɛr, -sær; *ES* ′kɔə sæə(r), *E* *also* -sɛə(r)
corse (usu. poetic)	kawrs	kôrs § 47(2)	kɔrs; *ES* kɔəs
cosmetic	koz MET ik	kŏz mĕt′ĭk	kaz ′mɛt ɪk; *ES* *also* kɒz-
cosmetics	koz MET iks	kŏz mĕt′ĭks § 48(3)	kaz ′mɛt ɪks; *ES* *also* kɒz-
cosmopolitan	*koz* muh POL uh tuhn	kŏz′mǒ pŏl′ĭ tăn	ˌkaz mə ′pal ə tən, -tn̩; *ES also* ˌkɒz mə ′pɒl-
cosmopolite	koz MOP uh la͞it § 50(34)	kŏz mŏp′ǒ līt	kaz ′map ə laɪt; *ES also* kɒz ′mɒp-
Cossack	KOS uhk KOS ak	kŏs′ǎk kŏs′ăk	′kas ək, ′kɒs-, -æk
Costa Rica	KOS tuh REE kuh KAWS tuh REE kuh	kŏs′tȧ rē′kȧ kôs′tȧ rē′kȧ	′kas tə ′ri kə, ′kɔs-, ′kɒs-, ′kos-
costume (n.)	KOS tyoom KOS toom	kŏs′tūm §§ 47(3), 48(2), 51(4)	kas ′tjum, kɒs-, -′tum
	B., kos TYOOM	*B.,* kŏs tūm′	*B.,* kɒs ′tjum
—— (v.t.)	kos TYOOM kos TOOM	kŏs tūm′ §§ 12, 50(32)	kas ′tjum, kɒs-, -′tum

	SIMPLIFIED	DIACRITICAL	PHONETIC
—— (adj.)	KOS tyoom KOS toom	kŏs′tūm § 50(32)	'kɑs tjum, 'kɒs-, -tum
costuming	kos TYOOM ing kos TOOM ing	kŏs tūm′ĭng §§ 48(2), 50(32)	kɑs 'tjum ɪŋ, kɒs-, -'tum-
coterie	KOH tuh ri KOH tuh ree	kō′tĕ rĭ kō′tĕ rē § 47(2)	'ko tə rɪ 'ko tə ri
cotyledon	*kot* uh LEE duhn *kot* i LEE duhn	kŏt′ĭ lē′dŭn kŏt′ĭ lē′dŭn	ˌkɑt ə 'li dən, ˌkɑt ɪ-; *ES also* ˌkɒt-
couchant	KOWCH uhnt	kouch′ănt	'kautʃ ənt
cough	kawf kof	kŏf §§ 26(2), 34(7)	kɔf kɒf
couldn't (contr. of "could not")	KOŎD n't	koŏd′n't §§ 1, 16, 31(2)	'kʊd n̩t; *unstressed,* 'kəd n̩t
council	KOWN suhl KOWN s'l	koun′sĭl koun′s'l § 31(3)	'kaʊn səl 'kaʊn sl̩
counsel	KOWN suhl	koun′sĕl § 31(3)	'kaʊn səl, -sl̩
counterfeit	KOWN tuhr fit	koun′tĕr fĭt	'kaʊn tɚ fɪt; *ES* -tə-
countersign (n.)	KOWN tuhr sa͡in	koun′tĕr sīn′	'kaʊn tɚ ˌsaɪn; *ES* -tə-
—— (v.t.)	KOWN tuhr sa͡in *kown* tuhr SA͡IN	koun′tĕr sīn′ koun′tĕr sīn′ §§ 47(1)	'kaʊn tɚ ˌsaɪn ˌkaʊn tɚ 'saɪn; *ES* -tə-
coup	koo	kōō	ku
coupé	*koo* PAY	kōō′pā′	ˌku 'pe
—— *(automobile)* also colloq.	koop	kōōp § 51(11)	kup
coupon	KOO pon KYOO pon *B.,* KOO pawng KOO pawn	kōō′pŏn kū′pŏn *B.,* kōō′pông kōō′pôn §§ 48(2), 51(4)	'ku pɑn, 'kju-, -pɒn *B.,* 'ku pɒŋ 'ku pɒn
courage	KUHR ij	kûr′ĭj §§ 26(3), 50(1)	'kɝ ɪdʒ; *ES also* 'kɜr-, 'kʌr-
courier	KOŎR i uhr KUHR i uhr	koŏr′ĭ ẽr kûr′ĭ ẽr § 47(2)	'kʊr ɪ ɚ, 'kɝ-; *ES* 'kʊr ɪ ə(r), *also* 'kɜr-, 'kʌr-
courteous	KUHR ti uhs	kûr′tĕ ŭs § 47(3)	'kɝ tɪ əs; *ES also* 'kɜ-
courtesan, courtezan	KOHR ti zuhn KAWR ti zuhn	kōr′tĕ zăn §§ 34(3), 47(3)	'kor tɪ zən, 'kɔr-; *ES* 'koə-, *E also* 'kɔə-
	Often: KUHR ti zuhn	*Often:* kûr′tĕ zăn	*Often:* 'kɝ tɪ zən; *ES also* 'kɜ-

courtesy (n., adj.)	KUHR tuh si	kûr′tĕ sĭ	ˈkɝ tə sɪ, -tɪ-,
	KUHR ti si	kûr′tĭ sĭ	ˈkor tə-, ˈkɔr-;
	KOHR tuh si	kōr′tĕ sĭ	ES ˈkoə-, also
	KAWR tuh si	§§ 34(3), 47(3)	ˈkɜ-, E also
			ˈkɔə-
courtier	KOHR ti uhr	kōr′tĭ ēr	ˈkor tɪ ɚ, ˈkɔr-,
	KAWR ti uhr		ˈkort jɚ, ˈkɔrt-;
	KOHRT yuhr	kōrt′yēr	ES ˈkoə tɪ ə(r),
	KAWRT yuhr	§ 34(3)	ˈkoət jə(r), E
			also ˈkɔə-, ˈkɔət-
cousin	KUHZ ′n	kŭz′ ′n	ˈkʌz n̩
covenant	KUHV uh nuhnt	kŭv′ĕ nănt	ˈkʌv ə nənt
Covent (Garden)	KOV uhnt	kŏv′ĕnt	ˈkɑv ənt, ˈkʌv-;
	KUHV uhnt	kŭv′ĕnt	ES also ˈkɒv-
•Coventry	KOV uhn tri	kŏv′ĕn trĭ	ˈkɑv ən trɪ, ˈkʌv-;
(England)	KUHV uhn tri	kŭv′ĕn trĭ	ES also ˈkɒv-
covert	KUHV uhrt	kŭv′ērt	ˈkʌv ɚt; ES -ət
covet	KUHV et	kŭv′ĕt	ˈkʌv ɛt
	KUHV it	kŭv′ĭt § 24(5)	ˈkʌv ɪt
covetous	KUHV uh tuhs	kŭv′ĕ tŭs	ˈkʌv ə təs
	KUHV i tuhs	kŭv′ĭ tŭs § 50(25)	ˈkʌv ɪ təs
covey	KUHV i	kŭv′ĭ	ˈkʌv ɪ
cowardice	KOW uhr dis	kou′ēr dĭs	ˈkaʊ ɚ dɪs; ES
			-ə dɪs
Cowper (William)	KOO puhr	kŏŏ′pēr	ˈku pɚ, ˈkaʊ-; ES
—poet	KOW puhr	kou′pēr § 1	-pə(r)
coxswain,	KOK s′n	kŏk′s′n	ˈkɑk sn̩, -swen; ES
cockswain	KOK swayn	kŏk′swān	also ˈkɒk-
		§§ 1, 42(3)	
coyote	KA͡I oht	kī′ōt	ˈkaɪ ot
	ka͡i OH ti	kī ō′tĕ	kaɪ ˈo tɪ
cozen	KUHZ ′n	kŭz′ ′n	ˈkʌz n̩
crabbed	KRAB ed	krăb′ĕd	ˈkræb ɛd
	KRAB id	krăb′ĭd §§ 24(5),	ˈkræb ɪd
		50(5)	
cranberry	KRAN ber i	krăn′bĕr′ĭ	ˈkræn ˌber ɪ
	KRAN buhr i	krăn′bĕr ĭ	ˈkræn bər ɪ
cranny	KRAN i	krăn′ĭ	ˈkræn ɪ
cravat	kruh VAT	krȧ văt′	krə ˈvæt
crayon	KRAY uhn	krā′ŏn	ˈkre ən
	KRAY on	krā′ŏn § 34(13)	ˈkre ɑn, -ɒn
creature	KREE chuhr	krē′tûr	ˈkri tʃɚ, -tjɚ; ES
	KREE tyuhr	§ 50(31)	-tʃə(r), -tjə(r)
credence	KREE duhns	krē′dĕns	ˈkri dəns
	KREE d′ns	krē′d′ns § 33(2)	ˈkri dn̩s
credulity	kri DYOO luh ti	krĕ dū′lĭ tĭ	krɪ ˈdju lə tɪ
	kri DOO luh ti		krɪ ˈdu lə tɪ
	kri DYOO li ti	krĕ dū′lĭ tĭ	krɪ ˈdju lɪ tɪ
	kri DOO li ti	§§ 48(2), 50(32)	krɪ ˈdu lɪ tɪ

credulous	KREJ ŏŏ luhs	krĕd′û lŭs	ˈkredʒ ʊ ləs, -ə ləs,
	KRED yŏŏ luhs	§ 50(25, 33)	ˈkred jʊ-
creek	kreek	krēk	krik
	Colloq.:	*Colloq.:*	*Colloq.:*
	krik	krĭk § 51(3)	krɪk
Creole	KREE ohl	krē′ōl	ˈkri ol
cretonne	kri TON	krē tŏn′	krɪ ˈtan, -ˈtɒn,
	KREE ton	krē′tŏn § 47(1)	ˈkri tan, -tɒn
crevice	KREV is	krĕv′ĭs	ˈkrɛv ɪs
crew	kroo	krōō §§ 40(4),	kru
		48(2)	
cribbage	KRIB ij	krĭb′ĭj § 50(1)	ˈkrɪb ɪdʒ
Crimea	krai͡ MEE uh	krī mē′a	kraɪ ˈmi ə
	kri MEE uh	krĭ mē′a	krɪ ˈmi ə
	§ 50(34)		
crinoline	KRIN uh lin	krĭn′ŏ lĭn	ˈkrɪn ə lɪn
	KRIN uh leen	krĭn′ŏ lēn § 47(3)	ˈkrɪn ə lin
crises (n. pl.)	KRAI͡ seez	krī′sēz § 48(3)	ˈkraɪ siz
crisis (n. sing.	KRAI͡ sis	krī′sĭs	ˈkraɪ sɪs
—See *crises.*)	§ 50(34)		
critic	KRIT ik	krĭt′ĭk	ˈkrɪt ɪk
critique	kri TEEK	krĭ tēk′	krɪ ˈtik
crochet (*"knit-*	kroh SHAY	krō shā′	kro ˈʃe
ting; to knit")	*Pop.:*	*Pop.:*	*Pop.:*
	KROH shay	krō′shā § 51(3)	ˈkro ʃe
crocodile	KROK uh dai͡l	krŏk′ŏ dīl § 47(2)	ˈkrɑk ə daɪl; *ES*
	§ 50(34)		*also* ˈkrɒk-
Croesus	KREE suhs	krē′sŭs	ˈkri səs
crone	krohn	krōn	kron
crooked	KRŎŎK ed	krŏŏk′ĕd	ˈkrʊk ɛd
	KRŎŎK id	krŏŏk′ĭd § 24(5)	ˈkrʊk ɪd
—— *"having a*	krŏŏkt	krŏŏkt	krʊkt
curved part (or			
crook)"			
croquet	krok KAY	krŏ kā′	kro ˈke
	Pop.:	*Pop.:*	*Pop.:*
	KROH kay	krō′kā § 51(3)	ˈkro ke
cross	kraws	krôs	krɔs
	kros	§§ 34(7), 47(3)	krɒs
croup	kroop	krōōp § 48(2)	krup
crucial	KROO shuhl	krōō′shŭl § 48(2)	ˈkru ʃəl
cruel	KROO uhl	krōō′ĕl	ˈkru əl
	KROO il	krōō′ĭl § 48(2)	ˈkru ɪl
cruise	krooz	krōōz § 48(2)	kruz
cruse	kroos	krōōs	krus
	krooz	krōōz §§ 47(3),	kruz
		48(2)	
crux	*kruhks*	krŭks § 40(6)	krʌks

	SIMPLIFIED	DIACRITICAL	PHONETIC
crystalline	KRIS tuhl in KRIS tuhl ain *In poetry, also:* kris TAL in kris TAL ain	krĭs′tăl ĭn krĭs′tăl īn *In poetry, also:* krĭs tăl′ĭn krĭs tăl′īn §§ 28(6), 31(3), 47(3), 51(11)	ˈkrɪs təl ɪn, -aɪn, -tḷ- *In poetry, also:* krɪs ˈtæl ɪn krɪs ˈtæl aɪn
cuckoo	KOŌK oo	koŏk′oō	ˈkʊk u
cucumber	KYOO *kuhm* buhr	kū′kŭm bēr §§ 40(6), 48(2)	ˈkju kʌm bɚ; *ES* -bə(r)
cudgel	KUHJ uhl	kŭj′ĕl	ˈkʌdʒ əl
cuirass	kwi RAS	kwĕ răs′ § 47(2)	kwɪ ˈræs
cuirassier	*kwee* ruh SĬER *kwee* ruh SIR *kwee* ruh SEER	kwē′ră sēr′ § 24(2) kwē′ră sēr′	ˌkwi rə ˈsɪər, -ˈsɪr, -ˈsir, ˌkwɪ-; *ES* -ˈsɪə(r)
culinary	KYOO li *ner* i *B.,* KYOO li nuhr i	kū′lĭ nĕr′ĭ *B.,* kū′lĭ nēr ĭ §§ 20(2), 24(9), 48(2), 51(4)	ˈkju lɪ ˌnɛr ɪ *B.,* ˈkju lɪ nə rɪ
culture	KUHL chuhr KUHL tyuhr	kŭl′tûr § 50(31)	ˈkʌl tʃɚ, -tjɚ; *ES* -tʃə(r), -tjə(r)
culvert	KUHL vuhrt	kŭl′vērt	ˈkʌl vɚt; *ES* -vət
cumulative	KYOO myoŏ *lay* tiv KYOO myoŏ luh tiv	kū′mû lā′tĭv kū′mû lȧ tĭv §§ 48(2), 50(32)	ˈkju mjʊ ˌle tɪv, -mjə-, -mju-, -mjʊ lə-, -mjə lə-
cuneiform	kyoŏ NEE uh fawrm kyoŏ NEE i fawrm KYOO ni uh *fawrm* KYOO ni i *fawrm*	kû nē′ĭ fôrm kû nē′ĭ fôrm kū′nĕ ĭ fôrm′ kū′nĕ ĭ fôrm′ §§ 47(2), 48(2), 50(32)	kjʊ ˈni ə fɔrm, -ˈni ɪ-, kju-; *ES* -fɔəm ˈkju nɪ ə ˌfɔrm, -nɪ ɪ-; *ES* -ˌfɔəm
cuniform	KYOO nuh fawrm KYOO ni fawrm	kū′nĭ fôrm kū′nĭ fôrm § 48(2)	ˈkju nə fɔrm, -nɪ-; *ES* -fɔəm
cupboard	KUHB uhrd	kŭb′ērd § 35(1)	ˈkʌb ɚd; *ES* -əd
cupidity	kyoŏ PID uh ti kyoŏ PID i ti	kû pĭd′ĭ tĭ kû pĭd′ĭ tĭ §§ 48(2), 49(16)	kjʊ ˈpɪd ə tɪ, -ɪ tɪ, kju-
cupola	KYOO puh luh	kū′pȯ lȧ § 48(2)	ˈkju pə lə
curator	kyoŏ RAY tuhr *In law, also:* KYOO ruh tuhr	kû rā′tēr § 48(2) *In law, also:* kū′rȧ tēr § 51(6)	kjʊ ˈre tɚ, kju-; *ES* -tə(r) *In law, also:* ˈkju rə tɚ; *ES* -tə(r)
curd	*kuhrd*	kûrd § 40(6)	kɝd; *ES also* kɜd

	SIMPLIFIED	DIACRITICAL	PHONETIC
cure	kyŏŏr kyoor	kūr §§ 34(21), 40(4), 48(2), 50(32)	kjʊr; *ES* kjʊə(r)
curio	KYŎŎ ri oh KYOO ri oh	kū′rĭ ō §§ 40(4), 48(2), 50(32)	'kjʊ rɪ o; *ES* 'kjʊə rɪ o
curious	KYŎŎ ri uhs KYOO ri uhs	kū′rĭ ŭs §§ 40(4), 48(2), 49(25), 50(32)	'kjʊ͞rɪ əs; *ES* 'kjʊə rɪ əs
currant	KUHR uhnt	kûr′ănt	'kɝ ənt; *ES also* 'kɜr-, 'kʌr-
current	KUHR uhnt	kûr′ĕnt	'kɝ ənt; *ES also* 'kɜr-, 'kʌr-
curriculum	kuh RIK yŏŏ luhm	kŭ rĭk′û lŭm	kə 'rɪk jʊ ləm, -jə-, -ju-
curtail (v.t.)	*kuhr* TAYL kuhr TAYL	kûr tāl′ § 40(7)	kɝ 'tel, kə-; *ES* *also* kɜ-, kə-
curtain	KUHR tin KUHR t'n	kûr′tĭn kûr′t'n	'kɝ tɪn, -tṇ, -tən; *ES also* 'kɜ-
curtsy	KUHRT si	kûrt′sĭ	'kɝt sɪ; *ES also* 'kɜt-
curvet (n.)	KUHR vet	kûr′vĕt	'kɝ vɛt, -vɪt; *ES* *also* 'kɜ-
—— (v.i.)	*kuhr* VET kuhr VET KUHR vet	kûr vĕt′ §§ 12, 40(6, 7), 47(2) kûr′vĕt	kɝ 'vɛt, kə-, 'kɝ vɛt, -vɪt; *ES also* kɜ-, 'kɜ-, *ES* kə-
cushion	KŎŎSH uhn KŎŎSH in	kŏŏsh′ŭn kŏŏsh′ĭn § 47(1)	'kʊʃ ən 'kʊʃ ɪn
cuspidor	KUHS pi dawr	kŭs′pĭ dôr § 47(2)	'kʌs pɪ dɔr; *ES* -dɔə(r)
cyanogen	saī AN uh jen § 50(34)	sī ăn′ŏ jĕn	saɪ 'æn ə dʒɛn, -dʒɪn, -dʒən
cycle	SAĪ k'l § 50(34)	sī′k'l	'saɪ kḷ
cyclic	SAĪ klik SIK lik § 50(34)	sī′klĭk sĭk′lĭk § 47(3)	'saɪ klɪk 'sɪk lɪk
cyclone	SAĪ klohn	sī′klōn	'saɪ klon
cymbal	SIM buhl	sĭm′băl § 31(3)	'sɪm bəl, -bḷ
cynic	SIN ik	sĭn′ĭk	'sɪn ɪk
cynosure, Cynosure	SAĪ nuh shŏŏr SIN uh shŏŏr SIN uh zhŏŏr	sī′nŏ shŏŏr sĭn′ŏ shŏŏr sĭn′ŏ zhŏŏr § 47(3)	'saɪ nə ʃʊr, 'sɪn ə-, 'sɪn ə ʒʊr; *ES* -ʃʊə(r), -ʒʊə(r)
cyst	sist	sist	sɪst
czar	zahr	zär	zɑr; *ES* zɑ:(r), *E* *also* za:(r)
	Occas.: tsahr	*Occas.:* tsär §§ 22(3), 47(3)	*Occas.:* tsɑr; *ES* tsɑ:(r), *E also* tsa:(r)

Czech	chek	chĕk chĕк § 22(10)	tʃek
Czechoslovakia, Czecho-Slovakia	*chek* uh sluh VAH ki uh	chĕk′ŏ slŏ vä′kĭ *à*	ˌtʃek ə slə ′vɑ kɪ ə
	chek oh sloh VAH ki uh	chĕk′ō slō vä′kĭ *à*	ˌtʃek o slo ′vɑ kɪ ə
	chek uh sloh VAK i uh	chĕk′ŏ slō văk′ĭ *à*	ˌtʃek ə slo ′væk ɪ ə
	chek oh sloh VAK i uh	chĕk′ō slō văk′ĭ *à*	ˌtʃek o slo ′væk ɪ ə

D

dace	days § 50(34)	dās	des
Daedalus	DED uh luhs *B.*, DEE duh luhs	dĕd′*à* lŭs *B.*, dē′d*à* lŭs § 51(4)	′dɛd ə ləs *B.*, ′di də ləs
dahlia	DAHL yuh DAL yuh DAYL yuh	däl′y*à* dăl′y*à* dāl′y*à* § 47(3)	′dɑl jə ′dæl jə ′del jə
dairy	DEHR i DAY ri	dâr′ĭ § 20(2)	′dɛr ɪ, de rɪ; *ES* *also* ′dɛə rɪ
dais	DAY is days § 50(34)	dā′ĭs dās §§ 1, 47(3)	′de ɪs des
dalliance	DAL i uhns	dăl′ĭ *ă*ns § 28(8)	′dæl ɪ əns, ′dæl jəns
damage	DAM ij	dăm′ĭj § 50(1)	′dæm ɪdʒ
damask	DAM uhsk	dăm′*à*sk	′dæm əsk
damn	dam	dăm	dæm
damned	damd	dămd §§ 33(1), 50(4)	dæmd
	Poet. or rhet.: DAM ned DAM nid	*Poet. or rhet.:* dăm′nĕd dăm′nĭd §§ 24(5), 51(11)	*Poet. or rhet.:* ′dæm nɛd ′dæm nɪd
damning	DAM ing DAM ning	dăm′ĭng dăm′nĭng §§ 33(1), 50(14)	′dæm ɪŋ ′dæm nɪŋ
dance	dans dahns	dáns § 20(5)	dæns; *E also* dans, dɑns

	SIMPLIFIED	DIACRITICAL	PHONETIC
dandelion	DAN di $\widehat{lai}$ uhn § 50(34)	dăn′dĕ lī′ŭn § 47(2)	′dæn dɪ ˌlaɪ ən, ′dæn dl̩ ˌaɪ-
Danish	DAYN ish	dān′ĭsh	′den ɪʃ
Dante	DAN ti It., DAHN tay	dăn′tĕ It., dän′tå	′dæn tɪ It., ′dɑn te
Danube	DAN yoob F., dah NOOB	dăn′ūb F., dä nüb′	′dæn jub F., dɑ ′nyb
Dartmouth	DAHRT muhth	därt′mŭth	′dɑrt məθ; ES ′dɑːt-, E also ′dɑːt-
data	DAY tuh DAH tuh DAT uh	dā′tå dä′tå dăt′å § 47(1)	de tə dɑ tə ′dæt ə
daub	dawb	dôb	dɔb
daughter	DAW tuhr	dô′tēr	′dɔ tɚ; ES -tə(r)
daunt	dawnt dahnt	dônt dänt §§ 34(4), 47(3)	dɔnt dɑnt
dauphin	DAW fin	dô′fĭn	′dɔ fɪn
dawdle	DAW d'l	dô′d′l	′dɔ dl̩
days	dayz	dāz § 48(3)	dez
dazzling	DAZ ling	dăz′lĭng § 50(14)	′dæz lɪŋ, -l̩ŋ
deaf	def *Dial. and arch.:* deef	dĕf §§ 24(17), 47(2) *Dial. and arch.:* dēf § 51(2)	dɛf *Dial. and arch.:* dif
debar	di BAHR	dĕ bär′ § 49(2)	dɪ ′bɑr; ES -′bɑː(r)
debate	di BAYT	dĕ bāt′	dɪ ′bet
debauch	di BAWCH	dĕ bôch′	dɪ ′bɔtʃ
debonair, debonaire	*deb* uh NEHR	dĕb′ŏ nâr′ § 20(2)	ˌdɛb ə ′nɛr, -′nær; ES -′næə(r), E also -′nɛə(r)
debris (See *débris*.)	de BREE DEB ree	dĕ brē′ dĕb′rē § 38(2)	dɛ ′bri ′dɛb ri
débris (See *debris*.)	day BREE duh BREE B., DAY bree DEB ree	då brē′ dŭh brē′ B., dā′brē dĕb′rē § 51(4)	de ′bri də ′bri B., ′de bri ′dɛb ri
debt	det	dĕt § 21(1)	dɛt
debut (n., v.i.)	day BOO DAY boo de BYOO DAY byoo F., day BOO	då bü′ dā′bü dĕ bū′ dā′bū F., då bü′	de ′by ′de by dɛ ′bju ′de bju F., de ′by
—— (n. – also)	B., DAY boo DEB oo	B., dā′bōō dĕb′ōō § 51(4)	B., ′de bu ′dɛb u

debutant (n. masc.)	*deb* yŏŏ TAHNT DEB yuh tuhnt *day* byŏŏ TAHNT *deb* oo TAHNT *F.*, *day* boo ᴛᴀʜN	dĕb′û tänt′ dĕb′û tănt dā′bû tänt′ dĕb′ōō tänt′ *F.*, dȃ′bü tä͡n′ § 20(14)	ˌdɛb jʊ 'tɑnt, ˌde bjʊ-; -bʊ-, 'dɛb jə ˌtənt, -ˌtænt, ˌdɛb ʊ 'tɑnt *F.*, de by 'tȃ
debutante (n. fem.)	*deb* yŏŏ TAHNT DEB yuh tant	dĕb′û tänt′ dĕb′û tănt	ˌdɛb jʊ 'tɑnt 'dɛb jə tænt
decade	DEK ayd *B.*, DEK uhd de KAYD	dĕk′ād § 11 *B.*, dĕk′ăd dĕ kād′ §§ 11, 51(4)	'dɛk ed *B.*, 'dɛk əd dɛ 'ked
decadence	di KAY duhns DEK uh duhns	dĕ kā′dĕns dĕk′a dĕns § 33(2)	dɪ 'ke dəns, -dn̩s 'dɛk ə dəns, -dn̩s
decadent	di KAY duhnt DEK uh duhnt	dĕ kā′dĕnt dĕk′a dĕnt	dɪ 'ke dənt, -dn̩t 'dɛk ə dənt, -dn̩t
decay	di KAY	dĕ kā′	dɪ 'ke
decease	di SEES	dĕ sēs′	dɪ 'sis
deceases	di SEES iz	dĕ sēs′ĭz §§ 48(3), 50(6)	dɪ 'sis ɪz
decedent	di SEE duhnt	dĕ sē′dĕnt § 33(2)	dɪ 'si dənt, -dn̩t
decent	DEE suhnt DEE s'nt	dē′sĕnt dē′s'nt	'di sənt 'di sn̩t
deciduous	di SIJ ŏŏ uhs di SID yŏŏ uhs	dĕ sĭd′û ŭs § 50(25, 33)	dɪ 'sɪdʒ ʊ əs dɪ 'sɪd jʊ əs
decimate	DES uh mayt DES i mayt	dĕs′ĭ māt dĕs′ĭ māt	'dɛs ə met 'dɛs ɪ met
decision	di SIZH uhn	dĕ sĭzh′ŭn	dɪ 'sɪʒ ən
declare	di KLEHR	dĕ klâr′	dɪ 'klɛr, -'klær; *ES* -'klæə(r) *E also* -'klɛə(r)
décolleté	day KOL tay *day* kol TAY *F.*, *day* kawl TAY	dā kŏl′tā dā′kŏl tā′ *F.*, dȃ′kôl′tā′	de 'kɑl te, -'kɒl- ˌde kɑl 'te, -kɒl- *F.*, de kôl 'te
decorative	DEK uh *ray* tiv DEK uh ruh tiv	dĕk′ŏ rā′tĭv dĕk′ŏ ra tĭv § 50(17)	'dɛk ə ˌre tɪv 'dɛk ə rə tɪv
decorous	DEK uh ruhs di KOH ruhs di KAW ruhs	dĕk′ŏ rŭs dĕ kō′rŭs §§ 34(3), 47(3)	'dɛk ə rəs dɪ 'ko rəs dɪ 'kɔ rəs
decorum	di KOH ruhm di KAW ruhm	dĕ kō′rŭm § 34(3)	dɪ 'ko rəm dɪ 'kɔ rəm
decoy (v., adj.)	di KOI	dĕ koi′	dɪ 'kɔɪ
—— (n.)	di KOI DEE koi	dĕ koi′ dē′koi § 12	dɪ 'kɔɪ 'di kɔɪ
decrease (v.)	dee KREES di KREES	dĕ krēs′ dĕ krēs′	di 'kris dɪ 'kris

	SIMPLIFIED	DIACRITICAL	PHONETIC
—— (n.)	DEE krees	dē′krēs	'di kris
	dee KREES	dē krēs′	di 'kris
	di KREES	dĭ krēs′ §§ 11, 12	dɪ 'kris
decrepit	di KREP it	dĭ krĕp′ĭt	dɪ 'krɛp ɪt
decry	di KRAῙ § 50(34)	dĭ krī′ § 49(2)	dɪ 'kraɪ
deduce	di DYOOS	dĭ dūs′ §§ 48(2),	dɪ 'djus
	di DOOS	49(2), 50(32)	dɪ 'dus
defect	di FEKT	dĭ fĕkt′	dɪ 'fɛkt
	DEE fekt	dē′fĕkt § 47(1)	'di fɛkt
defects	di FEKTS	dĭ fĕkts′	dɪ 'fɛkts
	DEE fekts	dē′fĕkts §§ 48(3),	'di fɛkts
		50(6)	
deficiency	di FISH uhn si	dĭ fĭsh′ĕn sĭ	dɪ 'fɪʃ ən sɪ
deficit	DEF uh sit	dĕf′ĭ sĭt	'def ə sɪt
	DEF i sit	dĕf′ῐ sĭt § 47(1)	'def ɪ sɪt
defile (v.t. –	di FAῙL § 50(34)	dĭ fīl′	dɪ 'faɪl
"make filthy")			
defile (n. –	di FAῙL	dĭ fīl′	dɪ 'faɪl
"passage")	DEE fail § 50(34)	dē′fīl § 47(3)	'di faɪl
—— (v. –	di FAῙL § 50(34)	dĭ fīl′ § 12	dɪ 'faɪl
"march off")			
definite	DEF uh nit	dĕf′ĭ nĭt	'def ə nɪt
	DEF i nit	dĕf′ῐ nĭt	'def ɪ nɪt
definitive	di FIN uh tiv	dĭ fĭn′ĭ tĭv	dɪ 'fɪn ə tɪv
	di FIN i tiv	dĭ fĭn′ῐ tĭv	dɪ 'fɪn ɪ tɪv
degradation	deg ruh DAY shuhn	dĕg′rȧ dā′shŭn	ˌdɛg rə 'de ʃən
deify	DEE uh faῙ	dē′ĭ fī	'di ə faɪ
	DEE i faῙ § 50(34)	dē′ῐ fī	'di ɪ faɪ
deign	dayn	dān	den
deity	DEE uh ti	dē′ĭ tĭ	'di ə tɪ
	DEE i ti	dē′ῐ tĭ	'di ɪ tɪ
deleterious	del i TῙER i uhs	dĕl′ĕ tēr′ῐ ŭs	ˌdɛl ɪ 'tɪər ɪ əs,
	del i TIR i uhs	§§ 24(2), 50(25)	-'tɪr-, -'tir-; ES
	del i TEER i uhs	dĕl′ĕ tēr′ῐ ŭs	-'tɪər-
delicate	DEL uh kit	dĕl′ĭ kĭt	'dɛl ə kɪt
	DEL i kit	dĕl′ῐ kĭt	'dɛl ɪ kɪt
delicious	di LISH uhs	dĭ lĭsh′ŭs	dɪ 'lɪʃ əs
delight	di LAῙT § 50(34)	dĭ līt′ § 26(2)	dɪ 'laɪt
delinquent	di LING kwuhnt	dĭ lĭng′kwĕnt § 33(4)	dɪ 'lɪŋ kwənt
delirious	di LIR i uhs	dĭ lĭr′ῐ ŭs § 50(25)	dɪ 'lɪr ɪ əs
delivery	di LIV uhr i	dĭ lĭv′ēr ῐ § 9	dɪ 'lɪv ər ɪ, -'lɪv rɪ
delude	di LOOD	dĭ lūd′ §§ 48(2),	dɪ 'lud
	di LYOOD	50(32)	dɪ 'ljud
deluge	DEL yooj	dĕl′ûj	'dɛl judʒ

delusive	di LOO siv di LYOO siv	dĕ lū′sĭv §§ 48(2), 50(32)	dɪ ˈlu sɪv dɪ ˈlju sɪv
demand	di MAND di MAHND	dĕ mȧnd′ § 20(5)	dɪ ˈmænd; *E also* -ˈmand, -ˈmɑnd
demeanor	di MEEN uhr	dĕ mēn′ĕr	dɪ ˈmin ɚ; *ES* -ə(r)
demesne	di MAYN di MEEN	dĕ mān′ dĕ mēn′ §§ 38(2), 47(1)	dɪ ˈmen dɪ ˈmin
democracy	di MOK ruh si	dĕ mŏk′rȧ sĭ	dɪ ˈmɑk rə sɪ; *ES* *also* -ˈmɒk-
demolition	*dem* uh LISH uhn *dee* muh LISH uhn	dĕm′ŏ lĭsh′ŭn dē′mŏ lĭsh′ŭn § 47(2)	ˌdɛm ə ˈlɪʃ ən ˌdi mə ˈlɪʃ ən
demon	DEE muhn	dē′mŭn	ˈdi mən
demoniac	di MOH ni ak	dĕ mō′nĭ ăk	dɪ ˈmo nɪ æk
demoniacal	*dee* muh NAI uh kuhl	dē′mŏ nī′ȧ kăl §§ 31(3), 47(2)	ˌdi mə ˈnaɪ ə kəl, -kl̩
demonic	di MON ik dee MON ik	dĕ mŏn′ĭk dē mŏn′ĭk	dɪ ˈmɑn ɪk, di-; *ES* *also* -ˈmɒn-
demonology	*dee* muhn OL uh ji	dē′mŭn ŏl′ŏ jĭ § 47(2)	ˌdi mən ˈɑl ə dʒɪ; *ES also* -ˈɒl-
demonstrable	di MON struh b'l	dĕ mŏn′strȧ b'l	dɪ ˈmɑn strə bl̩; *ES also* -ˈmɒn-
	DEM uhn struh b'l	dĕm′ŭn strȧ b'l § 47(1)	ˈdɛm ən strə bl̩
demonstrate	DEM uhn strayt di MON strayt	dĕm′ŭn strāt dĕ mŏn′strāt § 47(3)	ˈdɛm ən stret dɪ ˈmɑn stret; *ES* *also* -ˈmɒn-
demur	di MUHR	dĕ mûr′	dɪ ˈmɝ; *ES also* -ˈmɜ(r)
demure	di MYOOR di MYOOR	dĕ mūr′ § 40(4)	dɪ ˈmjʊr; *ES* -ˈmjʊə(r)
demurrer	di MUHR uhr	dĕ mûr′ĕr	dɪ ˈmɝ ɚ; *ES also* -ˈmɜr-, -ˈmʌr-, *ES* -ə(r)
denounce	di NOWNS	dĕ nouns′ § 49(2)	dɪ ˈnaʊns
denunciation	di *nuhn* si AY shuhn	dĕ nŭn′sĭ ā′shŭn	dɪ ˌnʌn sɪ ˈe ʃən
	di *nuhn* shi AY shuhn	dĕ nŭn′shĭ ā′shŭn § 47(3)	dɪ ˌnʌn ʃɪ ˈe ʃən
deny	di NAI § 50(34)	dĕ nī′	dɪ ˈnaɪ
deplore	di PLOHR di PLAWR	dĕ plōr′ § 34(3)	dɪ ˈplor, -ˈplɔr; *ES* -ˈploə(r), *E also* -ˈplɔə(r)
deposition	*dep* uh ZISH uhn *dee* puh ZISH uhn	dĕp′ŏ zĭsh′ŭn dē′pŏ zĭsh′ŭn § 47(3)	ˌdɛp ə ˈzɪʃ ən ˌdi pə ˈzɪʃ ən

depot (n., v.t.)	DEE poh	dē′pō	'di po
	B., DEP oh	*B.*, dĕp′ō § 51(4)	*B.*, 'dɛp o
	Mil. usage (n.):	*Mil. usage (n.):*	*Mil. usage (n.):*
	DEP oh	dĕp′ō §§ 47(3), 51(6)	'dɛp o
depravity	di PRAV uh ti	dĕ prăv′ĭ tĭ	dɪ 'præv ə tɪ
	di PRAV i ti	dĕ prăv′ĭ tĭ	dɪ 'præv ɪ tɪ
deprecate	DEP ri kayt	dĕp′rĕ kāt	'dɛp rɪ ket
deprecation	*dep* ri KAY shuhn	dĕp′rĕ kā′shŭn	ˌdɛp rɪ 'ke ʃən
deprecatory	DEP ri kuh *toh* ri	dĕp′rĕ kȧ tō′rĭ	'dɛp rɪ kə ˌto rɪ
	DEP ri kuh *taw* ri	§§ 34(3), 51(4)	'dɛp rɪ kə ˌtɔ rɪ
	B., DEP ri *kay* tuhr i	*B.*, dĕp′rĕ kā′tēr ĭ	*B.*, 'dɛp rɪ ˌke tə rɪ
depreciate	di PREE shi ayt	dĕ prē′shĭ āt § 38(12)	dɪ 'pri ʃɪ et
depredate	DEP ri dayt	dĕp′rĕ dāt	'dɛp rɪ det
depredation	*dep* ri DAY shuhn	dĕp′rĕ dā′shŭn	ˌdɛp rɪ 'de ʃən
deprivation	*dep* ruh VAY shuhn	dĕp′rĭ vā′shŭn	ˌdɛp rə 've ʃən
	dep ri VAY shuhn	dĕp′rĭ vā′shŭn	ˌdɛp rɪ 've ʃən
depth	depth	dĕpth	dɛpθ
depths	depths	dĕpths §§ 48(3), 50(6)	dɛpθs
deputy	DEP yŏŏ tĭ	dĕp′ů tĭ	'dɛp ju tɪ, -jə-, -ju-
derelict	DER uh likt	dĕr′ĕ lĭkt	'dɛr ə lɪkt
	DER i likt	dĕr′ĕ lĭkt	'dɛr ɪ lɪkt
dereliction	*der* uh LIK shuhn	dĕr′ĕ lĭk′shŭn	ˌdɛr ə 'lɪk ʃən
	der i LIK shuhn	dĕr′ĕ lĭk′shŭn	ˌdɛr ɪ 'lɪk ʃən
derision	di RIZH uhn	dĕ rĭzh′ŭn	dɪ 'rɪʒ ən
derisive	di RĀI siv § 50(34)	dĕ rī′sĭv § 50(17)	dɪ 'raɪ sɪv
derivation	*der* uh VAY shuhn	dĕr′ĭ vā′shŭn	ˌdɛr ə 've ʃən
	der i VAY shuhn	dĕr′ĭ vā′shŭn	ˌdɛr ɪ 've ʃən
derogation	*der* uh GAY shuhn	dĕr′ŏ gā′shŭn	ˌdɛr ə 'ge ʃən
derogatory	di ROG uh *toh* ri	dĕ rŏg′ȧ tō′rĭ	dɪ 'rɑg ə ˌto rɪ,
	di ROG uh *taw* ri	§§ 34(3), 51(4)	-'rɒg-, -ə ˌtɔ rɪ
	B., di ROG uh tuhr i	*B.*, dĕ rŏg′ȧ tēr ĭ	*B.*, dɪ 'rɒg ə tə rɪ
dervish	DUHR vish	dûr′vĭsh	'dɝ vɪʃ; *ES also* 'dɜ-
descant (n.)	DES kant	dĕs′kănt	'dɛs kænt
—— (v.)	des KANT	dĕs kănt′	dɛs 'kænt, dɪs-
descend	di SEND	dĕ sĕnd′	dɪ 'sɛnd
descent	di SENT	dĕ sĕnt′	dɪ 'sɛnt
describe	di SKRĀIB § 50(34)	dĕ skrīb′	dɪ 'skraɪb

	SIMPLIFIED	DIACRITICAL	PHONETIC
desert (n. – "reward or punishment")	di ZUHRT	dĕ zûrt′	dɪ 'zɝt; *ES also* -'zɜt
desert (n. – "barren region"; adj. – "dry")	DEZ uhrt	dĕz′ērt	'dɛz ɚt; *ES* -ət
—— (adj. – also, "forsaken; deserted": arch.)	di ZUHRT	dĕ zûrt′	dɪ 'zɝt; *ES also* -'zɜt
desert (v. – "abandon")	di ZUHRT	dĕ zûrt′	dɪ 'zɝt; *ES also* -zɜt
deserve	di ZUHRV	dĕ zûrv′	dɪ 'zɝv; *ES also* -'zɜv
desiccate (v.)	DES uh kayt DES i kayt	dĕs′ĭ kāt dĕs′ĭ kāt §§ 20 (8, 9), 47(3)	'dɛs ə ket 'dɛs ɪ ket
—— (adj.)	DES uh kit DES i kit	dĕs′ĭ kĭt dĕs′ĭ kĭt	'dɛs ə kɪt 'dɛs ɪ kɪt
desideratum	di *sid* uhr AY tuhm di *sid* uh RAY tuhm	dĕ sid′ēr ā′tŭm	dɪ ˌsɪd ər 'e təm dɪ ˌsɪd ə 're təm
design	di ZAIN § 50(34)	dĕ zīn′ § 47(2)	dɪ 'zaɪn
designate (v.t.)	DEZ ig nayt DES ig nayt	dĕz′ĭg nāt dĕs′ĭg nāt	'dɛz ɪg net 'dɛs ɪg net
—— (adj.)	DEZ ig nit DES ig nit	dĕz′ĭg nĭt dĕs′ĭg nĭt §§ 20 (8, 9), 47(3)	'dɛz ɪg nɪt 'dɛs ɪg nɪt
desire	di ZAIR § 50(34)	dĕ zīr′	dɪ 'zaɪr; *ES* -'zaɪə(r)
desist	di ZIST	dĕ zĭst′ §§ 47(3), 49(2)	dɪ 'zɪst, -'sɪst
desolate (adj.)	DES uh lit	dĕs′ŏ lĭt § 20(8, 9)	'dɛs ə lɪt
—— (v.t.)	DES uh layt	dĕs′ŏ lāt	'dɛs ə let
despair	di SPEHR	dĕ spâr′	dɪ 'spɛr, -'spær; *ES* -'spæə(r), *E also* -'spɛə(r)
despaired	di SPEHRD	dĕ spârd′	dɪ 'spɛrd, -'spærd; *ES* -'spæəd, *E also* -'spɛəd
despatch	dis PACH	dĭs păch′	dɪs 'pætʃ
desperado	*des* puhr AY doh *des* puh RAY doh *des* puhr AH doh *des* puh RAH doh	dĕs′pēr ā′dō dĕs′pēr ä′dō § 47(2)	ˌdɛs pər 'e do ˌdɛs pə 're do ˌdɛs pər 'ɑ do ˌdɛs pə 'rɑ do
despicable	DES pi kuh b'l *Not infreq.:* des PIK uh b'l	dĕs′pĭ ká b'l *Not infreq.:* dĕs pĭk′á b'l § 51(8)	'dɛs pɪ kə bļ *Not infreq.:* dɛs 'pɪk ə bļ, dɪs-

	SIMPLIFIED	DIACRITICAL	PHONETIC
despise	di SPĀIZ § 50(34)	dĕ spīz′	dɪ 'spaɪz
despot	DES puht	dĕs′pŏt	'dɛs pət, -pɑt; *ES*
	DES pot	dĕs′pŏt	*also* -pɒt
dessert	di ZUHRT	di zûrt′ § 47(2)	dɪ 'zɝt; *ES also*
			-zɜt
	Dial.:	*Dial.:*	*Dial.:*
	DEZ uhrt	dĕz′ērt § 51(2)	'dɛz ɚt; *ES* -ɜt
desuetude	DES wi tyood	dĕs′wĕ tūd	'dɛs wɪ tjud
	DES wi tood	§§ 48(2),	'dɛs wɪ tud
		50(32), 51(4)	
	B., DEE swi	*B.*, dē′swĕ tūd	*B.*, 'di swɪ tjud
	tyood		
desultory	DES uhl *toh* ri	dĕs′ŭl tō′rĭ §§ 31	'dɛs əl ˌto rɪ,
	DES uhl *taw* ri	(3), 34(3), 51(4)	-ˌtɔ-, 'dɛs]-
	B., DES uhl tuhr i	*B.*, dĕs′ŭl tēr ĭ	*B.*, 'dɛs əl tə rɪ,
			-]-
detachment	di TACH muhnt	dĕ tach′mĕnt	di 'tætʃ mənt
detail (n.)	di TAYL	dĕ tāl′	dɪ 'tel
	DEE tayl	dē′tāl § 12	'di tel
—— (v.)	di TAYL	dĕ tāl′ § 47(1)	dɪ 'tel
detective	di TEK tiv	dĕ tĕk′tĭv § 50(17)	dɪ 'tɛk tɪv
detestation	*dee* tes TAY	dē′tĕs tā′shŭn	ˌdi tɛs 'te ʃən
	shuhn		
	det es TAY shuhn	dĕt′ĕs tā′shŭn	ˌdet ɛs 'te ʃən
		§ 47(2)	
detour	di TŌOR	dĕ tōor′	dɪ 'tur; *ES*
	di TOOR	dĕ tōor′	-'tʊə(r)
	DEE tōor	dē′tōor § 40(4)	'di tur; *ES*
			-tʊə(r)
Detroit	di TROIT	dĕ troit′	dɪ 'trɔɪt
deuce	dyoos	dūs §§ 48(2),	djus
	doos	50(32)	dus
Deutschland	DOICH *lahnt*	doich′länt′	'dɔɪtʃ ˌlɑnt; *G.*,
			'dɔytʃ-
devastate	DEV uhs tayt	dĕv′ăs tāt § 47(2)	'dɛv əs tet
devastation	*dev* uhs TAY	dĕv′ăs tā′shŭn	ˌdɛv əs 'te ʃən
	shuhn		
device	di VĀIS § 50(34)	dĕ vīs′	dɪ 'vaɪs
devil	DEV ’l	dĕv′ ’l	'dɛv ḷ
devise	di VĀIZ § 50(34)	dĕ vīz′	dɪ 'vaɪz
devoir	duh VWAHR	dĕ vwär′	də 'vwɑr; *ES*
			-'vwɑ:(r)
	DEV wahr	dĕv′wär	'dɛv wɑr; *ES*
			-wɑ:(r)
devotee	*dev* uh TEE	dĕv′ ô tē′	ˌdɛv ə 'ti, ˌdɛv o-
dew	dyoo	dū §§ 40(4),	dju
	doo	48(2), 50(32)	du

	SIMPLIFIED	DIACRITICAL	PHONETIC
dexterous	DEK stuhr uhs	děk′stẽr ŭs § 9	'dɛk stər əs, -strəs
diabetes	da͡i uh BEE teez § 50(34) *Colloq.:*	dī′a̍ bē′tēz § 47(1) *Colloq.:*	ˌdaɪ ə 'bi tiz *Colloq.:*
	da͡i uh BEE tis	dī′a̍ bē′tĭs § 51(3)	ˌdaɪ ə 'bi tɪs
diabetic	da͡i uh BET ik	dī′a̍ bĕt′ĭk	ˌdaɪ ə 'bɛt ɪk
	da͡i uh BEE tik § 50(34)	dī′a̍ bē′tĭk § 47(3)	ˌdaɪ ə 'bi tɪk
diagnose	da͡i uhg NOHS	dī′ăg nōs′	ˌdaɪ əg 'nos
	da͡i uhg NOHZ § 50(34)	dī′ăg nōz′ § 47(3)	ˌdaɪ əg 'noz
diagnosis	da͡i uhg NOH sis	dī′ăg nō′sĭs	ˌdaɪ əg 'no sɪs
diagnostician	da͡i uhg nos TISH uhn § 50(34)	dī′ăg nŏs tĭsh′ăn	ˌdaɪ əg nɑs 'tɪʃ ən; *ES also* -nɒs-
dial	DA͡I uhl § 50(34)	dī′ăl	'daɪ əl
diameter	dai AM i tuhr § 50(34)	dī ăm′ĕ tẽr § 28(3)	daɪ 'æm ə tɚ; *ES* -tə(r)
diamond	DA͡I uh muhnd *Pop.:*	dī′a̍ mănd *Pop.:*	'daɪ ə mənd *Pop.:*
	DA͡I muhnd § 50(34)	dī′mănd § 51(3)	'daɪ mənd
Diana	dai AN uh § 50(34)	dī ăn′a̍ § 47(2)	daɪ 'æn ə
diapason	da͡i uh PAY zuhn	dī′a̍ pā′zăn	ˌdaɪ ə 'pe zən
	da͡i uh PAY z'n	dī′a̍ pā′z'n	ˌdaɪ ə 'pe zn̩
	da͡i uh PAY suhn	dī′a̍ pā′săn	ˌdaɪ ə 'pe sən
	da͡i uh PAY s'n § 50(34)	dī′a̍ pā′s'n § 33(2)	ˌdaɪ ə 'pe sn̩
diaphragm	DA͡I uh fram § 50(34)	dī′a̍ frăm § 25(5)	'daɪ ə fræm
diarrhea, diarrhoea	da͡i uh REE uh § 50(34)	dī′a̍ rē′a̍	ˌdaɪ ə 'ri ə
dice	dais § 50(34)	dīs	daɪs
dicker	DIK uhr	dĭk′ẽr	'dɪk ɚ; *ES* -ə(r)
dictate (v.)	DIK tayt dik TAYT	dĭk′tāt dĭk tāt′	'dɪk tet dɪk 'tet
—— (n.)	DIK tayt	dĭk′tāt § 12	'dɪk tet
dictator	dik TAY tuhr DIK tayt uhr	dĭk tā′tẽr dĭk′tāt ẽr § 47(1)	dɪk 'te tɚ, 'dɪk tet ɚ; *ES* -tə(r), -ə(r)
dictatorial	dik tuh TOH ri uhl dik tuh TAW ri uhl	dĭk′ta̍ tō′rĭ ăl § 34(3)	ˌdɪk tə 'to rɪ əl ˌdɪk tə 'tɔ rɪ əl

	SIMPLIFIED	DIACRITICAL	PHONETIC

dictionary	DIK shuhn *er* i
	B., DIK shuhn
	  uhr i
	DIK shuhn ri
		dĭk′shŭn ĕr′ĭ
		B., dĭk′shŭn ēr ĭ
		
		dĭk′shŭn rĭ
		§§ 20(2), 24(9),
		51(4)
			′dɪk ʃən ˌɛr ɪ
			B., ′dɪk ʃən ə rɪ,
			  -ʃən rɪ, -ʃn̩ ə rɪ

didactic	daī DAK tik di DAK tik § 50(34)	dī dăk′tĭk dĭ dăk′tĭk § 47(3)	daɪ ′dæk tɪk dɪ ′dæk tɪk
didn't	DID 'nt	dĭd′ 'nt	′dɪd n̩t
Dido	DAĪ doh § 50(34)	dī′dō	′daɪ do
dietary	DAĪ uh *ter* i *B.*, DAĪ uh tuhr i § 50(34)	dī′ĕ tĕr′ĭ *B.*, dī′ĕ tĕr ĭ §§ 20 (2), 24(9), 51(4)	′daɪ ə ˌtɛr ɪ *B.*, ′daɪ ə tə rɪ
dietetic	*daī* uh TET ik § 50(34)	dī′ĕ tĕt′ĭk	ˌdaɪ ə ′tɛt ɪk
different	DIF uhr uhnt	dĭf′ĕr ĕnt §§ 9, 49(3)	′dɪf ər ənt, ′dɪf rənt
differentiate (v.)	*dif* uhr EN shi ayt *dif* uh REN shi ayt	dĭf′ĕr ĕn′shĭ āt § 20(8, 9)	ˌdɪf ər ′en ʃɪ et ˌdɪf ə ′ren ʃɪ et
diffidence	DIF uh duhns DIF i duhns	dĭf′ĭ dĕns dĭf′ĭ dĕns	′dɪf ə dəns ′dɪf ɪ dəns
diffident	DIF uh duhnt DIF i duhnt	dĭf′ĭ dĕnt dĭf′ĭ dĕnt	′dɪf ə dənt ′dɪf ɪ dənt
diffuse (adj.)	di FYOOS	dĭ fūs′ § 48(2)	dɪ ′fjus
—— (v.)	di FYOOZ	dĭ fūz′ §§ 48(2), 50(32)	dɪ ′fjuz
diffusion	di FYOO zhuhn	dĭ fū′zhŭn § 48(2)	dɪ ′fju ʒən
diffusive	di FYOO siv	dĭ fū′sĭv § 48(2)	dɪ ′fju sɪv
digest (n.)	DAĪ jest	dī′jĕst § 12	′daɪ dʒest
—— (v.)	di JEST daī JEST § 50(34)	dĭ jĕst′ dī jĕst′ § 47(1)	dɪ ′dʒest, də- daɪ ′dʒest
digestion	di JES chuhn daī JES chuhn	dĭ jĕs′chŭn dī jĕs′chŭn	dɪ ′dʒes tʃən, də-, daɪ-
digestive	di JES tiv daī JES tiv § 50(34)	dĭ jĕs′tĭv dī jĕs′tĭv § 50(17)	dɪ ′dʒes tɪv, də-, daɪ-
digit	DIJ it	dĭj′ĭt	′dɪdʒ ɪt
digress	di GRES daī GRES § 50(34)	dĭ grĕs′ dī grĕs′ § 47(1)	dɪ ′gres daɪ ′gres
digression	di GRESH uhn daī GRESH uhn	dĭ grĕsh′ŭn dī grĕsh′ŭn	dɪ ′greʃ ən daɪ ′greʃ ən
digressive	di GRES iv daī GRES iv § 50(34)	dĭ grĕs′ĭv dī grĕs′ĭv § 50(17)	dɪ ′gres ɪv daɪ ′gres ɪv

	SIMPLIFIED	DIACRITICAL	PHONETIC
dilate	dai͡ LAYT di LAYT § 50(34)	dī lāt′ dǐ lāt′, § 47(3)	daɪ ˈlet dɪ ˈlet
dilatory	DIL uh *toh* ri DIL uh *taw* ri B., DIL uh tuhr i	dǐl′*à* tō′rǐ §§ 34(3), 51(4) B., dǐl′*à* tẽr ǐ	ˈdɪl ə ˌto rɪ ˈdɪl ə ˌtɔ rɪ B., ˈdɪl ə tə rɪ
dilemma	di LEM uh dai͡ LEM uh § 50(34)	dǐ lĕm′*à* dī lĕm′*à* § 47(2)	dɪ ˈlɛm ə daɪ ˈlɛm ə
dilettante	*dil* uh TAN ti *It.,* *dee* let TAHN tay	dǐl′*ĕ* tän′tǐ *It.,* dē′lĕt tän′tā	ˌdɪl ə ˈtæn tɪ *It.,* ˌdi lɛt ˈtɑn te
dilettanti	*dil* uh TAN ti	dǐl′*ĕ* tän′tē	ˌdɪl ə ˈtæn tɪ
dilute	di LOOT di LYOOT dai͡ LOOT dai͡ LYOOT	dǐ lūt′ dī lūt′ §§ 47(3), 48(2), 50(32)	dɪ ˈlut dɪ ˈljut daɪ ˈlut daɪ ˈljut
diminution	*dim* i NYOO shuhn *dim* i NOO shuhn	dǐm′ǐ nū′shǔn § 50(30, 32)	ˌdɪm ɪ ˈnju ʃən ˌdɪm ɪ ˈnu ʃən
diminutive	di MIN yŏŏ tǐv	dǐ mǐn′û tǐv	dɪ ˈmɪn ju tɪv, -jə-, -ju-
dinghy, dingy, dingey (n. – "*small boat*")	DING gi *Often:* DING i *Occas.:* DEENGK i deenk	dǐng′gǐ § 33(4) *Often:* dǐng′ǐ § 50(8, 9) *Occas.:* dēngk′ǐ dēnk	ˈdɪŋ gɪ *Often:* ˈdɪŋ ɪ *Occas.:* ˈdiŋk ɪ dink
dingy (adj. – "*faded*")	DIN ji	dǐn′jǐ	ˈdɪn dʒɪ
dinosaur	DAI͡ nuh sawr § 50(34)	dī′nŏ sôr	ˈdaɪ nə sɔr; *ES* -sɔə(r)
diocesan	dai͡ OS i suhn dai͡ OS i zuhn DAI͡ uh *see* suhn § 50(34)	dī ŏs′ĕ sǎn dī ŏs′ĕ zǎn dī′ŏ sē′sàn § 47(3)	daɪ ˈɑs ɪ sən, -zən, -sn̩, -zn̩, ˈdaɪ ə ˌsi sən, -sn̩; *ES also* daɪ ˈɒs ɪ-
diocese	DAI͡ uh sees B., DAI͡ uh sis	dī′ŏ sēs B., dī′ŏ sǐs §§ 47 (3), 50(34), 51(4)	ˈdaɪ ə sis B., ˈdaɪ ə sɪs
Diogenes	dai͡ OJ i neez § 50(34)	dī ŏj′ĕ nēz	daɪ ˈɑdʒ ɪ niz; *ES* *also* -ˈɒdʒ-
Dionysius	*dai͡* uh NISH i uhs *dai͡* uh NAI si uhs	dī′ŏ nǐsh′ǐ ǔs dī′ŏ nī′sǐ ǔs	ˌdaɪ ə ˈnɪʃ ɪ əs ˌdaɪ ə ˈnaɪ sɪ əs
diphtheria	dif THĪER i uh dif THIR i uh dif THEER i uh	dǐf thẽr′ǐ *à* §§ 24(2), 35(4), 47(3) dǐf thēr′ǐ *à*	dɪf ˈθɪər ɪ ə, -ˈθɪr-, -ˈθir-, dɪp-; *ES* -ˈθɪər-, *S also* -ˈθɛr-

	SIMPLIFIED	DIACRITICAL	PHONETIC
diphthong	DIF thawng DIF thong	dĭf′thŏng §§ 34 (7), 35(4), 47(3)	'dɪf θɔŋ, 'dɪp- 'dɪf θɒŋ, 'dɪp-
diploma	di PLOH mŭh	dĭ plō′má	dɪ 'plo mə
diplomacy	di PLOH muh si	dĭ plō′má sĭ	dɪ 'plo mə sɪ
diplomatist	di PLOH muh tist	dĭ plō′má tĭst	dɪ 'plo mə tɪst
direct	duh REKT di REKT daī REKT	dĕ rĕkt′ dĭ rĕkt′ dī rĕkt′ § 11	də 'rɛkt dɪ 'rɛkt daɪ 'rɛkt
direction	duh REK shuhn di REK shuhn daī REK shuhn	dĕ rĕk′shŭn dĭ rĕk′shŭn dī rĕk′shŭn	də 'rɛk ʃən dɪ 'rɛk ʃən daɪ 'rɛk ʃən
directly	duh REKT li di REKT li daī REKT li § 50(34)	dĕ rĕkt′lĭ dĭ rĕkt′lĭ dī rĕkt′lĭ § 50(20)	də 'rɛkt lɪ dɪ 'rɛkt lɪ daɪ 'rɛkt lɪ
dirigible	DIR i juh b'l DIR i ji b'l	dĭr′ĭ jǔ b'l dĭr′ĭ jĭ b'l	'dɪr ɪ dʒə bḷ, -ə dʒɜ-, -dʒɪ-
dirk	*duhrk*	dûrk § 40(6)	dɝk; *ES also* dɜk
disable	dis AY b'l	dĭs ā′b'l §§ 47(2), 49(3)	dɪs 'e bḷ
disarm	dis AHRM	dĭs ärm′ §§ 47(2), 49(3)	dɪs 'arm; *ES* -'ɑ:m, *E also* -'a:m
disaster	di ZAS tuhr di ZAHS tuhr	dĭ zȧs′tēr §§ 20(5), 49(3)	dɪ 'zæs tɚ; *ES* -tə(r), *E also* -'zas-, -'zɑs-
disastrous	di ZAS truhs di ZAHS truhs	dĭ zȧs′trŭs §§ 20(5), 49(3), 50(25)	dɪ 'zæs trəs; *E also* -'zas-, -'zɑs-
disband	dis BAND	dĭs bănd′ §§ 47(2), 49(3)	dɪs 'bænd
disburse	dis BUHRS	dĭs bûrs′ §§ 47(2), 49(3)	dɪs 'bɝs; *ES also* -'bɜs
discard (v.)	dis KAHRD	dĭs kärd′ §§ 12, 49(3)	dɪs 'kard; *ES* -'kɑ:d, *E also* -'ka:d
—— (n.)	DIS kahrd	dĭs′kärd	'dɪs kard; *ES* -kɑ:d, *E also* -ka:d
discern	di ZUHRN di SUHRN	dĭ zûrn′ dĭ sûrn′ §§ 38 (6, 9), 49(3)	dɪ 'zɝn, -'sɝn; *ES* *also* -'zɜn, -'sɜn
discernible	di ZUHR nuh b'l di ZUHR ni b'l di SUHR nuh b'l] di SUHR ni b'l	dĭ zûr′nǔ b'l dĭ zûr′nĭ b'l dĭ sûr′nǔ b'l dĭ sûr′nĭ b'l	dɪ 'zɝ nə bḷ, -nɪ-, -'sɝ-; *ES also* -'zɜ-, -'sɜ-

	SIMPLIFIED	DIACRITICAL	PHONETIC
discernment	di ZUHRN muhnt di SUHRN muhnt	dĭ zûrn′mĕnt dĭ sûrn′mĕnt § 38(6)	dɪ ′zɜn mənt, -′sɜn-; *ES also* -′zɜn-, -′sɜn-
discharge	dis CHAHRJ	dĭs chärj′ § 38(6)	dɪs ′tʃɑrdʒ; *ES* -′tʃɑːdʒ, *E also* -′tʃɑːdʒ
discipline	DIS uh plin DIS i plin	dĭs′ĭ plĭn dĭs′ĭ plĭn	′dɪs ə plɪn ′dɪs ɪ plɪn
discomfit	dis KUHM fit	dĭs kŭm′fĭt § 38(6)	dɪs ′kʌm fɪt
discomfiture	dis KUHM fi chuhr dis KUHM fi tyuhr	dĭs kŭm′fĭ tûr §§ 49(3), 50(31)	dɪs ′kʌm fɪ tʃɚ, -ˌtʃʊr, -tjɚ, -ˌtjʊr; *ES* -tʃə(r), -ˌtʃʊə(r), -tjə(r), -ˌtjʊə(r)
disconcerting	*dis* kuhn SUHR ting	dĭs′kŏn sûr′tĭng	ˌdɪs kən ′sɜ tɪŋ; *ES also* -′sɜ-
disconnected	*dis* kuh NEK ted *dis* kuh NEK tid	dĭs′kŏ nĕk′tĕd dĭs′kŏ nĕk′tĭd §§ 24(5), 38(6)	ˌdɪs kə ′nɛk təd ˌdɪs kə ′nɛk tɪd
disconsolate	dis KON suh lit	dĭs kŏn′sŏ lĭt §§ 9, 38(6)	dɪs ′kɑn sə lɪt, -sl̩ɪt; *ES also* -′kɒn-
discord (n.)	DIS kawrd	dĭs′kôrd	′dɪs kɔrd; *ES* -kɔəd
—— (v.i.)	dis KAWRD	dĭs kôrd′ § 12	dɪs ′kɔrd; *ES* -′kɔəd
discount (v.)	DIS kownt dis KOWNT	dĭs′kount dĭs kount′ §§ 12, 38(6)	′dɪs kaʊnt dɪs ′kaʊnt
—— (n.)	DIS kownt	dĭs′kount § 47(3)	′dɪs kaʊnt
discourse (n.)	dis KOHRS dis KAWRS DIS kohrs DIS kawrs	dĭs kōrs′ dĭs′kōrs §§ 34(3), 47(1), 49(3)	dɪs ′kors, -′kɔrs, ′dɪs kors, -kɔrs; *ES* -′koəs, -koəs, *E also* -′kɔəs, -kɔəs
—— (v.)	dis KOHRS dis KAWRS	dĭs kōrs′ §§ 12, 34(3)	dɪs ′kors, -′kɔrs; *ES* -′koəs, *E also* -′kɔəs
discourteous	dis KUHR ti uhs	dĭs kûr′tĕ ŭs § 38(6)	dɪs ′kɜ tɪ əs; *ES also* -′kɜ-
discourtesy	dis KUHR ti si	dĭs kûr′tĕ sĭ § 38(6)	dɪs ′kɜ tɪ sɪ; *ES also* -′kɜ-

discrepancy	dis KREP uhn si	dĭs krĕp′ăn sĭ	dɪs ′krɛp ən sɪ
	di SKREP uhn si	§§ 47(2), 49(3), 51(8)	dɪ ′skrɛp ən sɪ
	Occas.:	*Occas.:*	*Occas.:*
	DIS krep uhn si	dĭs′krĕp ăn sĭ	′dɪs krɛp ən sɪ
discretion	dis KRESH uhn	dĭs krĕsh′ŭn	dɪs ′krɛʃ ən
discursive	dis KUHR siv	dĭs kûr′sĭv § 38(6)	dɪs ′kɝ sɪv; *ES also* -′kɜ-
disdain	dis DAYN	dĭs dān′ §§ 38(6), 47(2), 49(3)	dɪs ′den, dɪz-
disease	di ZEEZ	dĭ zēz′ §§ 38(6), 49(3)	dɪ ′ziz
disgrace	dis GRAYS	dĭs grās′ § 47(2)	dɪs ′gres
disgust	dis GUHST	dĭs gŭst′	dɪs ′gʌst, dɪz-
disheveled, dishevelled	di SHEV uhld	dĭ shĕv′ĕld	dɪ ʃɛv əld
	di SHEV ′ld	dĭ shĕv′ ld	dɪ ʃɛv l̩d
dishonest	dis ON est	dĭs ŏn′ĕst	dɪs ′ɑn ɛst, -ɪst;
	dis ON ist	dĭs ŏn′ĭst §§ 24 (5), 47(2), 49(3)	*ES also* -′ɒn-
disinter	*dis* in TUHR	dĭs′ĭn tûr′ § 38(6)	ˌdɪs ɪn ′tɝ; *ES also* -′tɜ(r)
disinterested	dis IN tuhr es ted	dĭs ĭn′tẽr ĕs tĕd	dɪs ′ɪn tər ɛs tɛd
	dis IN tuhr is tid	dĭs ĭn′tẽr ĭs tĭd	dɪs ′ɪn tər ɪs tɪd
	dis IN tris tid	dis ĭn′trĭs tĭd §§ 24(5), 38(6̣), 47(2), 50(5)	dɪs ′ɪn trɪs tɪd, -trɛs-
disparagement	dis PAR ij muhnt	dĭs păr′ĭj mĕnt	dɪs ′pær ɪdʒ mənt,
	di SPAR ij muhnt	§ 50(22)	dɪ ′spær-
disparate	DIS puh rayt	dĭs′pȧ răt	′dɪs pə ret
	DIS puh rit	dĭs′pȧ rĭt	′dɪs pə rɪt
dispatch	dis PACH	dĭs păch′	dɪs ′pætʃ
dispensary	dis PEN suh ri	dĭs pĕn′sȧ rĭ	dɪs ′pen sə rɪ
dispersion	dis PUHR shuhn	dĭs pûr′shŭn	dɪs ′pɝ ʃən, -ʒən,
	dis PUHR zhuhn	dĭs pûr′zhŭn §§ 47(1), 50(28)	dɪ ′spɝ-; *ES also* -′pɝ-, -′spɝ-
dispossess	*dis* puh ZES	dĭs′pŏ zĕs′ § 38(6)	ˌdɪs pə ′zɛs
disputable	DIS pyo͞o tuh b'l	dĭs′pū tȧ b'l	′dɪs pjʊ tə bl̩
	dis PYOOT uh b'l	dĭs pūt′ȧ b'l §§ 47(3), 48(2)	dɪs ′pjut ə bl̩
disputant	DIS pyo͞o tuhnt	dĭs′pū tănt	′dɪs pjʊ tənt, -pju-, -tn̩t
	dis PYOO tuhnt	dĭs pū′tănt §§ 47(2), 48(2)	dɪs ′pju tənt, -tn̩t
disputatious	*dis* pyo͞o TAY shuhs	dĭs′pū tā′shŭs § 48(2)	ˌdɪs pjʊ ′te ʃəs, -pju-
dispute	dis PYOOT	dĭs pūt′ §§ 48(2), 50(32)	dɪs ′pjut
	di SPYOOT		dɪ ′spjut
disreputable	dis REP yo͞o tuh b'l	dĭs rĕp′ů tȧ b'l § 38(6)	dɪs ′rɛp jʊ tə bl̩, -jə-, -ju-

	SIMPLIFIED	DIACRITICAL	PHONETIC
dissect	di SEKT	dĭ sĕkt′	dɪ 'sɛkt
dissemble	di SEM b'l	dĭ sĕm′b'l § 38(6)	dɪ 'sɛm bl̩
dissent	di SENT	dĭ sĕnt′	dɪ 'sɛnt
dissolute	DIS uh loot	dĭs′ŏ lūt	'dɪs ə lut
	DIS uh lyoot	§§ 48(2), 50(32)	'dɪs ə ljut
dissolution	*dis* uh LOO shuhn	dĭs′ŏ lū′shŭn	ˌdɪs ə 'lu ʃən
	dis uh LYOO shuhn	§§ 48(2), 50(30, 32)	ˌdɪs ə 'lju ʃən
dissolvable	di ZOL vuh b'l	dĭ zŏl′v*a* b'l § 38(6)	dɪ 'zɑl və bl̩, -'zɒl-
dissolve	di ZOLV	dĭ zŏlv′ § 38(6)	dɪ 'zɑlv, -'zɒlv
dissonance	DIS uh nuhns	dĭs′ŏ năns § 38(6)	'dɪs ə nəns
distich	DIS tik	dĭs′tĭk	'dɪs tɪk
distinct	dis TINGKT	dĭs tĭngkt′ § 33(4)	dɪs 'tɪŋkt
distinctly	dis TINGKT li	dĭs tĭngkt′lĭ § 50(20)	dɪs 'tɪŋkt lɪ
district	DIS trikt	dĭs′trĭkt	'dɪs trɪkt
diurnal	dai UHR nuhl	dī ûr′năl	daɪ 'ɝ nəl, -nl̩; *ES*
	dai UHR n'l § 50(34)	dī ûr′n'l	*also* -'ɝ-
divan	DAI van	dī′văn	'daɪ væn
	di VAN	dĭ văn′	dɪ 'væn
—— "*Turkish court; reception room; mattress; book*," preferably	di VAN	dĭ văn′ §§ 47(3), 51(11)	dɪ 'væn
divergent	dai VUHR juhnt	dī vûr′jĕnt	daɪ 'vɝ dʒənt,
	di VUHR juhnt	dĭ vûr′jĕnt	dɪ-; *ES also* -'vɝ-
divers (adj. – *arch.*)	DAI vuhrz § 50(34)	dī′vērz	'daɪ vɚz; *ES* -vəz
diverse (adj., adv.)	dai VUHRS	dī vûrs′	daɪ 'vɝs, də-, dɪ-,
	DAI *vuhrs*	dī′vûrs	'daɪ vɝs; *ES*
	duh VUHRS	dŭ vûrs′	*also* -'vɝs, -vɜs
	di VUHRS § 50(34)	dĭ vûrs′ §§ 40(6), 47(3)	
diversion	duh VUHR shuhn	dŭ vûr′shŭn	də 'vɝ ʃən, dɪ-,
	di VUHR shuhn	dĭ vûr′shŭn	daɪ-, də 'vɝ ʒən,
	duh VUHR zhuhn	dŭ vûr′zhŭn	dɪ-, daɪ-; *ES*
	di VUHR zhuhn	dĭ vûr′zhŭn	*also* -'vɝ-
	dai VUHR shuhn	dī vûr′shŭn	
	dai VUHR zhuhn § 50(34)	dī vûr′zhŭn § 50(28)	
divert	dai VUHRT	dī vûrt′	daɪ 'vɝt, də-, dɪ-;
	duh VUHRT	dŭ vûrt′	*ES also* -'vɝt
	di VUHRT § 50(34)	dĭ vûrt′	

	SIMPLIFIED	DIACRITICAL	PHONETIC
divest	daī VEST duh VEST di VEST § 50(34)	dī vĕst′ dĭ vĕst′ dĭ vĕst′	daɪ 'vɛst də 'vɛst dɪ 'vɛst
divide	duh VĀID di VĀID § 50(34)	dĭ vīd′ dĭ vīd′	də 'vaɪd dɪ 'vaɪd
divine	duh VĀIN di VĀIN § 50(34)	dĭ vīn′ dĭ vīn′	də 'vaɪn dɪ 'vaɪn
division	duh VIZH uhn di VIZH uhn	dĭ vĭzh′ŭn dĭ vĭzh′ŭn	də 'vɪʒ ən dɪ 'vɪʒ ən
divulge	duh VUHLJ di VUHLJ	dĭ vŭlj′ dĭ vŭlj′ § 47(1)	də 'vʌldʒ, dɪ-, daɪ-
do	doo *Unstressed (before vowels):* dŏŏ *Unstressed (before consonants):* duh	dōō *Unstressed (before vowels):* dŏŏ *Unstressed (before consonants):* dŭ § 16	du *Unstressed (before vowels):* dʊ *Unstressed (before consonants):* də
docile	DOS il	dŏs′ĭl §§ 28(5), 47(3)	'dɑs ɪl; *ES also* 'dɒs-
docility	doh SIL uh ti doh SIL i ti	dṓ sĭl′ĭ tĭ dṓ sĭl′ĭ tĭ	do 'sɪl ə tɪ, -ɪ tɪ, dɑ-; *ES also* dɒ-
doctor	DOK tuhr	dŏk′tẽr	'dɑk tɚ; *ES* -tə(r), *also* 'dɒk-
doctorate (n.)	DOK tuhr it	dŏk′tẽr ĭt §§ 9, 20(8, 9)	'dɑk tər ɪt, -trɪt; *ES also* 'dɒk-
—— (v.t.)	DOK tuhr ayt	dŏk′tẽr āt	'dɑk tər et; *ES also* 'dɒk-
doctrinal	DOK tri nuhl DOK tri n'l *B.,* dok TRĀI nuhl § 50(34)	dŏk′trĭ năl dŏk′trĭ n'l *B.,* dŏk trī′năl § 51(4)	'dɑk trɪ nəl, -n̩l; *ES also* 'dɒk- *B.,* dɒk 'traɪ nəl, -n̩l̩
dog	dawg dog	dŏg § 34(7)	dɔg dɒg
dogged	DAWG ed DOG ed DAWG id DOG id	dŏg′ĕd dŏg′ĭd §§ 24(5), 34(7), 50(5)	'dɔg ɛd 'dɒg ɛd 'dɔg ɪd 'dɒg ɪd
doggerel	DAWG uhr uhl DOG uhr uhl	dŏg′ẽr ĕl §§ 9, 34(7)	'dɔg ər əl, 'dɒg-, 'dɔg rəl, 'dɒg-
dogma	DAWG muh DOG muh	dŏg′må § 34(7)	'dɔg mə 'dɒg mə
dogmatic	dawg MAT ik dog MAT ik	dŏg măt′ĭk § 34(7)	dɔg 'mæt ɪk dɒg 'mæt ɪk
dogmatism	DAWG muh tiz'm DOG muh tiz'm	dŏg′må tĭz'm § 34(7)	'dɔg mə tɪzm̩, 'dɒg-, -tɪz əm

dogmatize	DAWG muh taīz	dŏg′má tīz	'dɔg mə taɪz
	DOG muh taīz	§§ 34(7), 50(34)	'dɒg mə taɪz
doings	DOO ingz	dōō′ĭngz §§ 48(3)	'du ɪŋz
	Joc.:	*Joc.:*	*Joc.:*
	DOO inz	dōō′ĭnz § 51(11)	'du ɪnz
doit	doit	doit	dɔɪt
dolor	DOH luhr	dō′lẽr	'do lɚ; *ES* -lə(r)
dolorous	DOL uhr uhs	dŏl′ẽr ŭs	'dɑl ər əs, 'do lər-;
	DOH luhr uhs	dō′lẽr ŭs § 47(2)	*ES also* 'dɒl ər-
domain	doh MAYN	dŏ mān′	do 'men
dome	dohm	dōm	dom
domicile	DOM uh sil	dŏm′ĭ sĭl	'dɑm ə sɪl, -sl̩-,
	DOM i sil	dŏm′ĭ sĭl	'dɑm ɪ-; *ES also*
		§§ 28(5), 47(1)	'dɒm-
	B., DOM i saīl	*B.,* dŏm′ĭ sīl	*B.,* 'dɒm ɪ saɪl
		§§ 50(34), 51(4)	
dominant	DOM uh nuhnt	dŏm′ĭ nănt	'dɑm ə nənt,
	DOM i nuhnt	dŏm′ĭ nănt	'dɑm ɪ-; *ES*
			also 'dɒm-
dominion	duh MIN yuhn	dŏ mĭn′yŭn	də 'mɪn jən
don	don	dŏn	dɑn; *ES also* dɒn
donate	DOH nayt	dō′nāt	'do net
	B., doh NAYT	*B.,* dŏ nāt′	*B.,* do 'net
		§§ 47(1), 51(4)	
donee	*doh* NEE	dō′nē′	ˌdo 'ni
donkey	DONG ki	dŏng′kĭ § 47(2)	'dɑŋ kɪ, 'dɒŋ-,
			'dɒŋ-
	Formerly:	*Formerly:*	*Formerly:*
	DUHNK ki	dŭnk′kĭ § 51(2)	'dʌnk kɪ
donor	DOH nuhr	dō′nẽr	'do nɚ; *ES* -nə(r)
	In law, esp.:	*In law, esp.:*	*In law, esp.:*
	DOH nawr	dō′nôr	'do nor, ˌdo 'nɔr;
	doh NAWR	dō′nôr′ § 51(6)	*ES* -nɔə(r),
			-'nɔə(r)
door	dohr	dōr §§ 34(3, 20)	dor, dɔr; *ES*
	dawr		doə(r), *E also*
			dɔə(r)
Dorian	DOH ri uhn	dō′rĭ ăn § 34(3)	'do rɪ ən
	DAW ri uhn		'dɔ rɪ ən
Doric	DOR ik	dŏr′ĭk	'dɑr ɪk, 'dɔr-,
	DAWR ik	dôr′ĭk § 34(5, 7)	'dɒr-
dormouse	DAWR *mows*	dôr′mous′	'dɔr ˌmaʊs; *ES*
	§ 50(34)		'dɔə-
dotage	DOHT ij	dōt′ĭj	'dot ɪdʒ
dotard	DOH tuhrd	dō′tẽrd	'do tɚd; *ES* -təd
doth	*duhth*	dŭth	dʌθ
	Unstressed:	*Unstressed:*	*Unstressed:*
	duhth	dŭth §§ 16, 40(6)	dəθ

doubled	DUHB 'ld	dŭb′ 'ld § 50(4)	'dʌb ļd
doubloon	*duhb* LOON	dŭb lōōn′ § 40(6)	dʌb 'lun
doubt	dowt § 50(34)	dout § 21(1)	daʊt
dough	doh	dō	do
doughty	DOW ti	dou′tĭ	'daʊ tɪ
dozen	DUHZ 'n	dŭz′ 'n	'dʌz n̩
drachm	dram	drăm § 22(9)	dræm
draft	draft drahft	dȧft § 20(5)	dræft; *E also* draft, drɑft
drama	DRAH muh DRAM uh	drä′mȧ drăm′ȧ § 47(3)	'drɑ mə 'dræm ə
dramatic	druh MAT ik	drȧ măt′ĭk	drə 'mæt ɪk
dramatist	DRAM uh tist	drăm′ȧ tĭst	'dræm ə tɪst
dramatize	DRAM uh taiz § 50(34)	drăm′ȧ tīz	'dræm ə taɪz
draught (var. of "*draft*")	draft drahft	drȧft §§ 20(5), 26(2)	dræft; *E also* draft, drɑft
drawing	DRAW ing	drô′ĭng	'drɔ ɪŋ
dreary	DRĬER i DRIR i DREER i	drẹr′ĭ § 24(2) drēr′ĭ	'drɪər ɪ, 'drɪr ɪ, 'drir ɪ; *ES* 'drɪər ɪ
dredge	drej	drĕj	drɛdʒ
drift	drift	drĭft	drɪft
drivel	DRIV 'l	driv′ 'l	'drɪv ļ
droll	drohl	drōl	drol
drollery	DROHL uhr i	drōl′ẽr ĭ	'drol ər ɪ
dromedary	DROM uh *der* i DRUHM uh *der* i	drŏm′ĕ dĕr′ĭ drŭm′ĕ dĕr′ĭ	'drɑm ə ˌder ɪ, 'drʌm-; *ES also* 'drɒm-
	B., DRUHM uh duhr i DROM uh duhr i	*B.,* drŭm′ĕ dēr ĭ drŏm′ĕ dēr i §§ 20(2), 24(9), 47(1), 51(4)	*B.,* 'drʌm ə də rɪ, 'drɒm-, -drɪ
dross	draws dros	drôs §§ 34(7), 50(34)	drɔs drɒs
drought	drowt	drout	draʊt
drouth	drowth	drouth	draʊθ
drowned	drownd	dround § 50(5)	draʊnd
drudge	*druhj*	drŭj § 40(6)	drʌdʒ
Druid, druid	DROO id	drōō′ĭd	'dru ɪd
dryad, Dryad	DRAĪ ad DRAĪ uhd § 50(34)	drī′ăd drī′ăd	'draɪ æd 'draɪ əd
dual	DYOO uhl DOO uhl	dū′ăl §§ 48(2), 50(32)	'dju əl 'du əl

	SIMPLIFIED	DIACRITICAL	PHONETIC
dubious	DYOO bi uhs DOO bi uhs	dū′bĭ ŭs §§ 48(2), 50(25, 32)	'dju bɪ əs 'du bɪ əs
ducal	DYOO kuhl DOO kuhl	dū′kăl §§ 48(2), 50(32)	'dju kəl, 'du-, -kl̩
ducat	DUHK uht	dŭk′ăt	'dʌk ət
duchess	DUHCH es DUHCH is	dŭch′ĕs dŭch′ĭs § 24(5)	'dʌtʃ ɛs 'dʌtʃ ɪs
duchy	DUHCH i	dŭch′ĭ	'dʌtʃ ɪ
ductile	DUHK til	dŭk′tĭl § 28(5)	'dʌk tɪl, -tl̩
due	dyoo doo	dū §§ 40(4), 48(2), 50(32)	dju du
duel	DYOO uhl DOO uhl	dū′ĕl §§ 48(2), 50(32)	'dju əl 'du əl
dues (n. pl.)	dyooz dooz	dūz §§ 48(2, 3), 50(6, 32)	djuz duz
duet	dyoo ET doo ET	dû ĕt′ §§ 48(2), 50(32)	dju 'ɛt du 'ɛt
duke	dyook dook	dūk §§ 40(4), 48(2), 50(32)	djuk duk
dulcet	DUHL set DUHL sit	dŭl′sĕt dŭl′sĭt § 24(5)	'dʌl sɛt 'dʌl sɪt
dulcimer	DUHL suh muhr DUHL si muhr	dŭl′sĭ mēr dŭl′sĭ mēr	'dʌl sə mɚ, -sɪ-; *ES* -mə(r)
duly	DYOO li DOO li	dū′lĭ §§ 48(2), 50(32)	'dju lɪ 'du lɪ
dungeon	DUHN juhn	dŭn′jŭn	'dʌn dʒən
dupe	dyoop doop	dūp §§ 48(2), 50(32)	djup dup
duplex	DYOO pleks DOO pleks	dū′plĕks §§ 48(2), 50(32)	'dju plɛks 'du plɛks
duplicate (adj., n.)	DYOO pluh kit DOO pluh kit DYOO pli kit DOO pli kit	dū′plĭ kăt dū′plĭ kăt	'dju plə kɪt 'du plə kɪt 'dju plɪ kɪt 'du plɪ kɪt
—— (v.t.)	DYOO pluh kayt DOO pluh kayt DYOO pli kayt DOO pli kayt	dū′plĭ kāt dū′plĭ kāt §§ 20(8, 9), 48 (2), 50(2, 32)	'dju plə ket 'du plə ket 'dju plɪ ket 'du plɪ ket
duplicity	dyoo PLIS uh ti doo PLIS uh ti dyoo PLIS i ti doo PLIS i ti	dû plĭs′ĭ tĭ dû plĭs′ĭ tĭ §§ 48(2), 50(32)	dju 'plɪs ə tɪ du 'plɪs ə tɪ dju 'plɪs ɪ tɪ du 'plɪs ɪ tɪ
durable	DYOO͝O ruh b'l DO͝O ruh b'l DYOO ruh b'l DOO ruh b'l	dū′rȧ b'l §§ 40(4), 48(2), 50(32)	'djʊ rə bl̩ 'dʊ rə bl̩

	SIMPLIFIED	DIACRITICAL	PHONETIC
duress (n.)	DYOO̅ res DO̅O̅ res DYOO res DOO res dyo̅o̅ RES do̅o̅ RES	dū′rĕs dŭ rĕs′ §§ 12, 40(4), 47(2)	ˈdjʊ rɛs, -rɪs ˈdʊ rɛs, -rɪs djʊ ˈrɛs dʊ ˈrɛs
—— (v.t.)	dyo̅o̅ RES do̅o̅ RES	dŭ rĕs′ §§ 48(2), 50(32)	djʊ ˈrɛs dʊ ˈrɛs
Durham	DUHR uhm	dûr′ăm	ˈdɝ əm; ES also ˈdɝr-, ˈdʌr-
during	DYOO̅R ing DO̅O̅R ing DYOOR ing DOOR ing	dūr′ĭng §§ 40(4), 48(2), 50(14, 32)	ˈdjʊr ɪŋ ˈdʊr ɪŋ
Dutchman	DUHCH muhn	dŭch′măn § 50(21)	ˈdʌtʃ mən
duteous	DYOO ti uhs DOO ti uhs	dū′tĕ ŭs §§ 48(2), 50(25, 32)	ˈdju tɪ əs ˈdu tɪ əs
duty	DYOO ti DOO ti	dū′tĭ §§ 40(4), 48(2), 50(32)	ˈdju tɪ ˈdu tɪ
dynamic	dai NAM ik di NAM ik § 50(34)	dī năm′ĭk dĭ năm′ĭk	daɪ ˈnæm ɪk dɪ ˈnæm ɪk
dynamite	DA͡I nuh ma͡it § 50(34) *Occas. or rarely:* DIN uh ma͡it	dī′nȧ mīt § 47(2) *Occas. or rarely:* dĭn′ȧ mīt § 51(8)	ˈdaɪ nə maɪt *Occas. or rarely:* ˈdɪn ə maɪt
dynamo	DA͡I nuh moh § 50(34)	dī′nȧ mō	ˈdaɪ nə mo
dynamometer	da͡i nuh MOM i tuhr din uh MOM i tuhr § 50(34)	dī′nȧ mŏm′ĕ tēr dĭn′ȧ mŏm′ĕ tēr	ˌdaɪ nə ˈmɑm ɪ tɚ, ˌdɪn ə-; ES -tə(r), also -ˈmɒm-
dynastic	dai NAS tik di NAS tik § 50(34)	dī năs′tĭk dĭ năs′tĭk	daɪ ˈnæs tɪk dɪ ˈnæs tɪk
dynasty	DA͡I nuhs ti *B.,* DIN uhs ti § 50(34)	dī′năs tĭ *B.,* dĭn′ăs tĭ §§ 47(3), 51(4)	ˈdaɪ nəs tɪ, -næs- *B.,* ˈdɪn əs tɪ
dysentery	DIS uhn *ter* i *B.,* DIS uhn tri	dĭs′ĕn tĕr′ĭ *B.,* dĭs′ĕn trĭ § 51(4)	ˈdɪs ən ˌtɛr ɪ, -ŋ- *B.,* ˈdɪs ən trɪ, ˈdɪs ŋ-
dyspepsia	dis PEP shuh dis PEP si uh	dĭs pĕp′shȧ dĭs pĕp′sĭ ȧ § 47(2)	dɪs ˈpɛp ʃə dɪs ˈpɛp sɪ ə

E

earn	*uhrn*	ûrn § 40(6)	ɝn; *ES also* ɜn
earthenware	UHR thuhn *wehr*	ûr′thĕn wâr′	'ɝ θən ˌwɛr, -ˌwær; *ES also* 'ɜ-, *ES* -ˌwæə(r), *E also* -ˌwɛə(r)
eastward	EEST wuhrd	ēst′wērd § 47(2)	'ist wɝd; *ES* -wəd
ebullition	*eb* uh LISH uhn	ĕb′ŭ lĭsh′ŭn	ˌɛb ə 'lɪʃ ən
eccentric	ek SEN trik	ĕk sĕn′trĭk § 49(4)	ɛk 'sɛn trɪk, ɪk-
Ecclesiastes	e *klee* zi AS teez	ĕ klē′zĭ ăs′tēz § 49(4)	ɛ ˌkli zɪ 'æs tiz, ɪ ˌkli-
ecclesiastic	e *klee* zi AS tik	ĕ klē′zĭ ăs′tĭk § 49(4)	ɛ ˌkli zɪ 'æs tɪk, ɪ ˌkli-
echo	EK oh	ĕk′ō § 22(8)	'ɛk o
éclat	ay KLAH	â klä′ § 47(2)	e 'klɑ; *F.*, e 'kla
eclipse	i KLIPS	ĕ klĭps′	ɪ 'klɪps
eclogue	EK lawg EK log	ĕk′lŏg § 34(7)	'ɛk lɔg 'ɛk lɒg
economic	*ee* kuh NOM ik *ek* uh NOM ik	ē′kŏ nŏm′ĭk ĕk′ŏ nŏm′ĭk § 47(1)	ˌi kə 'nɑm ɪk, ˌɛk ə-; *ES also* -'nɒm-
economical	*ee* kuh NOM i kuhl *ek* uh NOM i kuhl	ē′kŏ nŏm′ĭ kăl ĕk′ŏ nŏm′ĭ kăl § 47(2)	ˌi kə 'nɑm ɪ kəl, ˌɛk ə-, -kl̩; *ES also* -'nɒm-
economics	*ee* kuh NOM iks *ĕk* uh NOM iks	ē′kŏ nŏm′ĭks ĕk′ŏ nŏm′ĭks	ˌi kə 'nɑm ɪks, ˌɛk ə-; *ES also* -'nɒm-
economist	i KON uh mist	ĕ kŏn′ŏ mĭst	ɪ 'kɑn ə mɪst, i-; *ES also* -'kɒn-
economize	i KON uh ma͡iz § 50(34)	ĕ kŏn′ŏ mīz	ɪ 'kɑn ə maɪz, i-; *ES also* -'kɒn-
economy	i KON uh mi	ĕ kŏn′ŏ mĭ	ɪ 'kɑn ə mɪ, i-; *ES also* -'kɒn-
ecstasy	EK stuh si	ĕk′stá sĭ	'ɛk stə sɪ
edge	ej	ĕj	ɛdʒ
edible	ED uh b'l ED i b'l	ĕd′ĭ b'l ĕd′ĭ b'l	'ɛd ə bl̩ 'ɛd ɪ bl̩

	SIMPLIFIED	DIACRITICAL	PHONETIC
edict	EE dikt	ē′dĭkt	′i dɪkt
edifice	ED uh fis	ĕd′ĭ fĭs	′ɛd ə fɪs
	ED i fis	ĕd′ĭ fĭs	′ɛd ɪ fɪs
Edinburgh (Scotland)	ED in buh ruh	ĕd′ĭn bŭ rŭ	′ɛd ɪn bə rə,
	ED in *buhr* oh	ĕd′ĭn bûr′ō § 1	-ˌbɝ o; *ES also* -ˌbɝ ro, -ˌbʌ-
edition	i DISH uhn	ĕ dĭsh′ŭn § 50(30)	ɪ ′dɪʃ ən, i-
educate	EJ o͝o kayt	ĕd′û kāt § 50(33)	′ɛdʒ ʊ ket, ′ɛd jʊ-,
	ED yo͞o kayt		′ɛdʒ ə-
education	*ej* o͝o KAY shuhn	ĕd′û kā′shŭn	ˌɛdʒ ʊ ′ke ʃən,
	ed yo͞o KAY shuhn	§ 50(30, 33)	ˌɛd jʊ-, ˌɛdʒ ə-
educe	i DYOOS	ĕ dūs′	ɪ ′djus
	i DOOS	§§ 48(2), 50(32)	ɪ ′dus
e′er	ehr	âr	ɛɝ; *ES* ɛə(r)
	ayr	ār §§ 20(2), 47(2)	eɝ
eerie, eery	EE ri	ē′rĭ	′i rɪ, ′ɪər ɪ, ′ɪr ɪ,
	ĬER i	ēr′ĭ	′ir ɪ; *ES* ′ɪər ɪ
	IR i	§ 24(2)	
	EER i	ēr′ĭ	
effect	e FEKT	ĕ fĕkt′	ɛ ′fɛkt
	uh FEKT	ĭ fĕkt′	ə ′fɛkt
	i FEKT	ĭ fĕkt′ § 49(4)	ɪ ′fɛkt
effectual	e FEK cho͝o uhl	ĕ fĕk′tû ăl	ɛ ′fɛk tʃʊ əl, ə′-
	e FEK tyo͝o uhl	§ 50(33)	ɛ ′fɛk tjʊ əl, ə′-
effeminate (n., adj.)	e FEM uh nit	ĕ fĕm′ĭ nĭt	ɛ ′fɛm ə nɪt,
	uh FEM uh nit	ĭ fĕm′ĭ nĭt	ə ′fɛm-, ɪ ′fɛm ɪ-
	i FEM i nit	ĕ fĕm′ĭ nĭt § 20(8, 9)	
—— (v.)	e FEM uh nayt	ĕ fĕm′ĭ nāt	ɛ ′fɛm ə net
efferent	EF uhr uhnt	ĕf′ēr ĕnt	′ɛf ər ənt
effete	e FEET	ĕ fēt′	ɛ ′fit
	uh FEET	ĭ fēt′	ə ′fit
	i FEET	ĭ fēt′ § 49(4)	ɪ ′fit
efficacious	*ef* uh KAY shuhs	ĕf′ĭ kā′shŭs	ˌɛf ə ′ke ʃəs
	ef i KAY shuhs	ĕf′ĭ kā′shŭs § 50(25)	ˌɛf ɪ ′ke ʃəs
efficacy	EF uh kuh si	ĕf′ĭ kȧ sĭ	′ɛf ə kə sɪ
	EF i kuh si	ĕf′ĭ kȧ sĭ	′ɛf ɪ kə sɪ
effigy	EF uh ji	ĕf′ĭ jĭ	′ɛf ə dʒɪ
	EF i ji	ĕf′ĭ jĭ	′ɛf ɪ dʒɪ
effluence	EF lo͝o uhns	ĕf′lû ĕns § 48(2)	′ɛf lʊ əns
effrontery	e FRUHN tuhr i	ĕ frŭn′tēr ĭ	ɛ ′frʌn tər ɪ,
	i FRUHN tuhr i	ĕ frŭn′tēr ĭ § 49(4)	ɪ ′frʌn-, ə ′frʌn-
effulgence	e FUHL juhns	ĕ fŭl′jĕns	ɛ ′fʌl dʒəns
	i FUHL juhns	ĕ fŭl′jĕns	ɪ ′fʌl dʒəns
egg	eg	ĕg	ɛg

	SIMPLIFIED	DIACRITICAL	PHONETIC
eglantine	EG luhn tain § 50(34)	ĕg′lăn tīn § 47(3)	ˈɛg lən taɪn, -tɪn
egotism	EE goh tiz'm EG oh tĭz'm	ē′gŏ tĭz'm ĕg′ŏ tĭz'm § 47(3)	ˈi go tɪzm̩, -gə-, ˈɛg o-, ˈɛg ə-, -tɪz əm
egregious	i GREE juhs i GREE ji uhs	ē grē′ jŭs ē grē′jĭ ŭs §§ 47(2), 50(25)	ɪ ˈgri dʒəs ɪ ˈgri dʒɪ əs
egress (n.)	EE gres	ē′grĕs	ˈi grɛs
—— (v.i.)	i GRESS	ē grĕss′	ɪ ˈgrɛs, i-
eider down (n.)	AI duhr down	ī′dĕr doun	ˈaɪ dɚ daʊn; ES -də-
eider-down (adj.)	AI duhr *down* § 50(34)	ī′dĕr doun′	ˈaɪ dɚ ˌdaʊn; ES -də-
eight	ayt	āt	et
eighth	aytth	ātth	etθ
eighths	aytths	ātths §§ 48(3), 50(6)	etθs
eights	ayts	āts §§ 48(3), 50(6)	ets
either	EE thuhr AI thuhr § 50(34)	ē′thēr ī′thēr §§ 24(20), 47(3)	ˈi ðɚ, ˈaɪ ðɚ; ES -ðə(r)
ejaculate	i JAK yŏŏ layt	ē jăk′ū̇ lāt	ɪ ˈdʒæk jʊ let, -jə-, -ju-, i-
elaborate (adj.)	i LAB uh rit	ē lăb′ŏ rĭt §§ 20 (8, 9), 50(2)	ɪ ˈlæb ə rɪt, -ˈlæb rɪt, ə ˈlæb-
—— (v.)	i LAB uh rayt	ē lăb′ŏ rāt	ɪ ˈlæb ə ret, ə ˈlæb-
elastic	i LAS tik	ē lăs′tĭk	ɪ ˈlæs tɪk, ə ˈlæs-
El Dorado	el duh RAH doh	ĕl dŏ rä′dō	ɛl də ˈra do
elect	i LEKT	ē lĕkt′ § 49(4)	ɪ ˈlɛkt, ə ˈlɛkt
election	i LEK shuhn	ē lĕk′shŭn	ɪ ˈlɛk ʃən, ə'-
elective	i LEK tiv	ē lĕk′tĭv § 49(4)	ɪ ˈlɛk tɪv, ə'-
electoral	i LEK tuhr uhl	ē lĕk′tēr ăl § 49(4)	ɪ ˈlɛk tər əl, ə'-
electric	i LEK trik	ē lĕk′trĭk § 49(4)	ɪ ˈlɛk trɪk, ə'-
electrician	i *lek* TRISH uhn *el* ek TRISH uhn	ē lĕk′trĭsh′ăn ĕl′ĕk trĭsh′ăn § 11	ɪ ˌlɛk ˈtrɪʃ ən, ə ˌlɛk-, ˌɛl ɛk-
electricity	i *lek* TRIS uh ti i *lek* TRIS i ti *el* ek TRIS uh ti *el* ek TRIS i ti	ē lĕk′trĭs′ĭ̇ tĭ ē lĕk′trĭs′ī̇ tĭ ĕl′ĕk trĭs′ĭ̇ tĭ ĕl′ĕk trĭs′ī̇ tĭ §§ 11, 47(3)	ɪ ˌlɛk ˈtrɪs ə tɪ, -ɪ tɪ, i ˌlɛk-, ə ˌlɛk-, ˌɛl ɛk-, i ˌlɛk-
electron	i LEK tron	ē lĕk′trŏn § 49(4)	ɪ ˈlɛk tran, ə ˈlɛk-; *ES also* -trɒn
elevate	EL i vayt	ĕl′ē̇ vāt	ˈɛl ɪ vet, ˈɛl ə-
eleven	i LEV uhn	ē lĕv′ĕn § 24(14)	ɪ ˈlɛv ən, -n̩, ə'-

elf	elf	ĕlf	ɛlf
Eli	EE lai͡ § 50(34)	ē′lī	'i laɪ
elicit	i LIS it	ĕ lĭs′ĭt	ɪ 'lɪs ɪt
eligible	EL i juh b'l	ĕl′ĭ jĭ b'l	'ɛl ɪ dʒə bḷ
	EL i ji b'l	ĕl′ĭ jĭ b'l	'ɛl ɪ dʒɪ bḷ
Elisha	i LAI shuh § 50(34)	ĕ lī′shȧ	ɪ 'laɪ ʃə, ə 'laɪ ʃə
elixir	i LIK suhr	ĕ lĭk′sēr	ɪ 'lɪk sɚ; *ES* -sə(r)
Elizabethan	i *liz* uh BEE thuhn	ĕ lĭz′ȧ bē′thăn	ɪ ˌlɪz ə 'bi θən, -'bɛθ ən, ə ˌlɪz-
	i *liz* uh BETH uhn	ĕ lĭz′ȧ bĕth′ăn	
ellipse	e LIPS	ĕ lĭps′	ɛ 'lɪps
	i LIPS	ĭ lĭps′	ɪ 'lɪps, ə 'lɪps
ellipsis	e LIP sis	ĕ lĭp′sĭs	ɛ 'lɪp sɪs, ɪ 'lɪp-, ə 'lɪp-
	i LIP sis	ĭ lĭp′sĭs	
elliptic	e LIP tik	ĕ lĭp′tĭk	ɛ 'lɪp tɪk, ɪ 'lɪp-, ə 'lɪp-
	i LIP tik	ĭ lĭp′tĭk	
elm	elm	ĕlm § 9	ɛlm
elongate (v.)	i LAWNG gayt	ĕ lŏng′gāt	ɪ 'lɔŋ get
	i LONG gayt		ɪ 'lɒŋ get
	B., EE lawng gayt	*B.*, ē′lŏng gāt §§ 20(8, 9), 33(4), 34(7)	*B.*, 'i lɔŋ get
	EE long gayt		'i lɒŋ get
elongation	i *lawng* GAY shuhn	ĕ lŏng′gā′shăn	ɪ ˌlɔŋ 'ge ʃən
	i *long* GAY shuhn		ɪ ˌlɒŋ 'ge ʃən
	ee lawng GAY shuhn	ē′lŏng gā′shăn	ˌi lɔŋ 'ge ʃən
	ee long GAY shuhn	§§ 33(4), 34(7), 50(30)	ˌi lɒŋ 'ge ʃən
elucidate	i LOO suh dayt	ĕ lū′sĭ dāt	ɪ 'lu sə det
	i LYOO suh dayt		ɪ 'lju sə det
	i LOO si dayt	ĕ lū′sĭ dāt	ɪ 'lu sɪ det
	i LYOO si dayt	§§ 48(2), 49(5), 50(2, 32)	ɪ 'lju sɪ det
elude	i LOOD	ĕ lūd′ §§ 47(2), 48(2), 50(32)	ɪ 'lud
	i LYOOD		ɪ 'ljud
elusion	i LOO zhuhn	ĕ lū′zhŭn §§ 9, 48 (2), 50(28, 32)	ɪ 'lu ʒən,
	i LYOO zhuhn		ɪ 'lju-, -ʒṇ
elusive	i LOO siv	ĕ lū′sĭv §§ 48(2). 50(32)	ɪ 'lu sɪv
	i LYOO siv		ɪ 'lju sɪv
elusory	i LOO suh ri	ĕ lū′sŏ rĭ §§ 48(2), 50(32)	ɪ 'lu sə rɪ
	i LYOO suh ri		ɪ 'lju sə rɪ
elves	elvz	ĕlvz §§ 48(3), 50(6)	ɛlvz
Elysian	i LIZH uhn	ĕ lĭzh′ăn	ɪ 'lɪʒ ən
	i LIZ i uhn	ĕ lĭz′ĭ ăn	ɪ 'lɪz ɪ ən
	i LIZ yuhn	ĕ lĭz′yăn §§ 28(9), 47(3)	ɪ 'lɪz jən

	SIMPLIFIED	DIACRITICAL	PHONETIC
Elysium	i LIZH i uhm	ĕ lĭzh′ĭ ŭm	ɪ 'lɪʒ ɪ əm
	i LIZ i uhm	ĕ lĭz′ĭ ŭm	ɪ 'lɪz ɪ əm
	i LIZ i yuhm	ĕ lĭz′ĭ yŭm	ɪ 'lɪz ɪ jəm
		§§ 28(9), 47(1)	ɪ 'lɪz əm
emaciate (v.t.)	i MAY shi ayt	ĕ mā′shĭ āt	ɪ 'me ʃɪ et
		§ 49(4)	
emanate	EM uh nayt	ĕm′a̤ nāt	'ɛm ə net
emanation	*em* uh NAY shuhn	ĕm′a̤ nā′shŭn	ˌɛm ə 'ne ʃən
emasculate (v.t.)	i MAS kyŏŏ layt	ĕ măs′kṳ lāt	ɪ 'mæs kju let,
			-kjə-, -kju-
—— (adj.)	i MAS kyŏŏ lit	ĕ măs′kṳ lăt §§ 20	ɪ 'mæs kju lɪt,
		(8, 9), 50(2)	-kjə-, -kju-
embitter	em BIT uhr	ĕm bĭt′ĕr § 49(5)	ɛm 'bɪt ɚ, ɪm-;
			ES -ə(r)
embrasure (n.,	em BRAY zhuhr	ĕm brā′zhĕr	ɛm 'bre ʒɚ; *ES*
v.t.)		§§ 40(11), 47(2)	-ʒə(r)
—— (n. also –	*em* bruh ZHŎŎR	ĕm′bra̤ zhŏŏr′	ˌɛm brə 'ʒʊr; *ES*
"fortification")		§ 51(11)	-'ʒʊə(r)
embroider	em BROI duhr	ĕm broi′dĕr	ɛm 'brɔɪ dɚ, ɪm-;
			ES -də(r)
embryo	EM bri oh	ĕm′brĭ ō	'ɛm brɪ o
emendation	*ee* men DAY	ē′mĕn dā′shŭn	ˌi mɛn 'de ʃən,
	shuhn		ˌɛm ɛn-,
	em en DAY shuhn	ĕm′ĕn dā′shŭn	ˌi mən-,
		§ 47(3)	ˌɛm ən-
emetic	i MET ik	ĕ mĕt′ĭk	ɪ 'mɛt ɪk
emigrant	EM uh grant	ĕm′ĭ grănt	'ɛm ə grænt
	EM uh gruhnt	ĕm′ĭ grănt	'ɛm ə grənt
	EM i gruhnt	ĕm′ĭ grănt	'ɛm ɪ grənt
emir, emeer	uh MĬER	ĕ mēr′	ə 'mɪər, ə 'mɪr,
	uh MIR	§§ 24(2), 47(2)	ə 'mir; *ES*
	uh MEER	ĕ mēr′	ə 'mɪə(r)
emolument	i MOL yŏŏ muhnt	ĕ mŏl′ṳ mĕnt	ɪ 'mɑl ju mənt,
		§ 50(22)	-jə-, -ju-; *ES*
			also -'mɒl-
emperor	EM puhr uhr	ĕm′pēr ēr	'ɛm pər ɚ; *ES*
			-pər ə(r)
empire	EM pair § 50(34)	ĕm′pīr	'ɛm paɪr; *ES*
			-paɪə(r)
empiric	em PIR ik	ĕm pĭr′ĭk § 47(2)	ɛm 'pɪr ɪk
empiricism	em PIR uh siz'm	ĕm pĭr′ĭ sĭz'm	ɛm 'pɪr ə sɪzm̩,
	em PIR i siz'm	ĕm pĭr′ĭ sĭz'm § 9	-'pɪr ɪ-, -sɪz əm
employ	em PLOI	ĕm ploi′ § 49(5)	ɛm 'plɔɪ, ɪm-
employee	*em* ploi EE	ĕm′ploi ē′	ˌɛm plɔɪ 'i, ˌɪm-,
	em PLOI ee	ĕm ploi′ē § 11	ɛm 'plɔɪ i, ɪm-
emporium	em POH ri uhm	ĕm pō′rĭ ŭm	ɛm 'po rɪ əm
	em PAW ri uhm	ĕm pô′rĭ ŭm	ɛm 'pɔ rɪ əm
		§ 34(3)	

	SIMPLIFIED	DIACRITICAL	PHONETIC
empyreal	em PIR i uhl	ĕm pĭr′ĕ ăl	ɛm ′pɪr ɪ əl
	em puh REE uhl	ĕm′pĭ rē′ăl	ˌɛm pə ′ri əl
	em pi REE uhl	ĕm′pĭ rē′ăl	ˌɛm pɪ ′ri əl
	em paî REE uhl	ĕm′pī rē′ăl	ˌɛm paɪ ′ri əl
	§ 50(34)	§ 47(3)	
empyrean	*em* puh REE uhn	ĕm′pĭ rē′ăn	ˌɛm pə ′ri ən,
	em pi REE uhn	ĕm′pĭ rē′ăn	-pɪ-, -paɪ-,
	em paî REE uhn	ĕm′pī rē′ăn	ɛm ′pɪr ɪ ən
		§ 47(3)	
enabling	en AY bling	ĕn ā′blĭng § 49(5)	ɛn ′e blɪŋ, -b!ɪŋ
enamor, enamour	en AM uhr	ĕn ăm′ēr § 49(5)	ɛn ′æm ɚ, ɪn-; *ES*
			-ə(r)
enchant	en CHANT	ĕn chănt′	ɛn ′tʃænt, ɪn-; *E*
	en CHAHNT	§§ 20(5), 49(5)	*also* -′tʃant,
			-′tʃɑnt
encomium	en KOH mi uhm	ĕn kō′mĭ ŭm	ɛn ′ko mɪ əm
		§ 28(9)	
encore (interj.)	ahng KOHR	äng kōr′	ɑŋ ′kor, -′kɔr; *ES*
	ahng KAWR	äng kôr′	-′koə(r), *E also*
			-′kɔə(r)
—— (n.)	AHNG kohr	äng′kōr	′ɑŋ kor, -kɔr,
	AHNG kawr		ɑ̃ ′kor, -′kɔr;
	ahɴ KOHR	äɴ′kōr′	*ES* -koə(r),
	ahɴ KAWR	§§ 34(3), 47(1)	-′koə(r), *E also*
			-′kɔə(r),
			-kɔə(r)
—— (v.t.)	ahng KOHR	äng kōr′	ɑŋ ′kor, -′kɔr,
	ahng KAWR		′ɑŋ kor, -kɔr;
	AHNG kohr	äng′kōr	*ES* -′koə(r),
	AHNG kawr	§§ 34(3), 47(1)	-koə(r), *E also*
			-′kɔə(r),
			-kɔə(r)
endeavor,	en DEV uhr	ĕn dĕv′ēr § 24(5)	ɛn ′dɛv ɚ, ɪn-; *ES*
endeavour			-ə(r)
endue (v.t.)	en DYOO	ĕn dū′	ɛn ′dju, -′du-, ɪn-
	en DOO	§§ 48(2), 50(32)	
endurance	en DYOOR uhns	ĕn dūr′ăns	ɛn ′djʊr əns,
	en DOOR uhns		-′dʊr-, ɪn-
	en DYOOR uhns	§§ 40(4), 48(2),	
	en DOOR uhns	50(32)	
endure	en DYOOR	ĕn dūr′	ɛn ′djʊr, -′dʊr,
	en DOOR		ɪn-; *ES*
	en DYOOR	§§ 34(21), 40(4,	-′djʊə(r),
	en DOOR	11), 48(2), 49(5)	-′dʊə(r)
Endymion	en DIM i uhn	ĕn dĭm′ĭ ŏn	ɛn ′dɪm ɪ ən
enervate (v.t.)	EN uhr vayt	ĕn′ēr vāt	′ɛn ɚ vet; *ES*
			-ə vet
	Occas.:	*Occas.:*	*Occas.:*
	i NUHR vayt	ĕ nûr′vāt § 51(8)	ɪ ′nɝ vet; *ES also*
			ɪ ′nɜ-

	SIMPLIFIED	DIACRITICAL	PHONETIC
—— (adj.)	i NUHR vayt i NUHR vit	ĕ nûr′văt §§ 20 (8, 9), 47(3)	ɪ 'nɝ vet, -vɪt; *ES* *also* ɪ 'nɝ-
enfranchise	en FRAN chaiz § 50(34)	ĕn frăn′chĭz	ɛn 'fræn tʃaɪz
enfranchisement	en FRAN chiz muhnt	ĕn frăn′chĭz mĕnt	ɛn 'fræn tʃɪz mən
engine	EN juhn *Dial. or humor.:* EN jain § 50(34)	ĕn′jĭn *Dial. or humor:.* ĕn′jīn § 51(2, 11)	'ɛn dʒən *Dial. or humor.:* 'ɛn dʒaɪn
engineer	*en* juh NĬER *en* juh NIR *en* juh NEER	ĕn′jĭ nẽr′ § 24(2) ĕn′jĭ nēr′	ˌɛn dʒə 'nɪər, -'nɪr, -'nir; *ES* -'nɪə(r)
England	ING gluhnd	ĭng′glănd	'ɪŋ glənd
English	ING glish	ĭng′glĭsh	'ɪŋ glɪʃ
engraft	en GRAFT en GRAHFT	ĕn gráft′ §§ 20(5), 49(5)	ɛn 'græft; *E also* -'graft, -'grɑft
engross	en GROHS	ĕn grōs′	ɛn 'gros, ɪn-
enhance	en HANS en HAHNS	ĕn háns′ § 20(5)	ɛn 'hæns, ɪn-; *E* *also* -'hans, -'hɑns
enigma	i NIG muh	ĕ nĭg′má § 49(4)	ɪ 'nɪg mə
enigmatic	*ee* nig MAT ik *en* ig MAT ik	ē′nĭg măt′′ĭk ĕn′ĭg măt′′ĭk § 47(3)	ˌi nɪg 'mæt ɪk ˌɛn ɪg 'mæt ɪk
ennui (n.)	AHN wee *F., ahɴ* NWEE	än′wē *F., ä*ɴ*′nwē′*	'an wi *F., ã* 'nɥi
—— (v.t.)	ahn NWEE	än nwē′ § 12	an 'nwi
enormity	i NAWR muh ti i NAWR mi ti	ĕ nôr′mĭ tĭ ĕ nôr′mĭ tĭ	ɪ 'nɔr mə tɪ, -mɪ-; *ES* ɪ 'nɔə-
ensanguine	en SANG gwin	ĕn sǎng′gwĭn § 33(4)	ɛn 'sæŋ gwɪn
ensconce	en SKONS	ĕn skŏns′ § 39(3)	ɛn 'skɑns; *ES also* -'skɒns
ensign (n.)	EN sain EN suhn § 50(34) *In mil. circles,* *gen.:* EN suhn	ĕn′sīn ĕn′sĭn *In mil. circles,* *gen.:* ĕn′sĭn § 51(6)	ɛn 'saɪn, -'sən, -'sn̩ *In mil. circles,* *gen.:* 'ɛn sən, -sn̩
—— (v.t. – *Her.*)	en SAIN § 50(34)	ĕn sīn′ § 12	ɛn 'saɪn
ensilage	EN suh lij EN si lij	ĕn′sĭ lĭj ĕn′sĭ lĭj	'ɛn sə lɪdʒ, -sɪ-, -sl̩ ɪdʒ
enslave	en SLAYV	ĕn slāv′ § 49(5)	ɛn 'slev, ɪn-
entente	*F., ahɴ* ᴛᴀʜɴᴛ *Angl.:* ahn ᴛᴀʜɴᴛ	än′tänt′ *Angl.:* än tänt′ § 51(1)	*F., ã* 'tã:t *Angl.:* an 'tant
enterprise	EN tuhr praiz EN tuh praiz	ĕn′tēr prīz ĕn′tĕ prīz § 48(1)	'ɛn tɚ praɪz, -tə praɪz; *ES* -tə-

	SIMPLIFIED	DIACRITICAL	PHONETIC
enthusiasm	en THYOO zi az'm en THOO zi az'm	ĕn thū′zĭ ăz'm §§ 40(4), 48(2), 50(32)	ɛn ˈθju zɪ æzm̩, -ˈθu-, -æz əm, ɪn-
enthusiast	en THYOO zi ast en THOO zi ast	ĕn thū′zĭ ăst §§ 48(2), 50(32)	ɛn ˈθju zɪ æst ɛn ˈθu zɪ æst, ɪn-
entire	en TAIR § 50(34) *Emph., sometimes:* EN tair § 50(34)	ĕn tīr′ § 24(4) *Emph., sometimes:* ĕn′tīr § 51(11)	ɛn ˈtaɪr, ɪn-; *ES* -ˈtaɪə(r) *Emph., sometimes:* ˈɛn taɪr, ˈɪn-; *ES* -taɪə(r)
entomology	*en* tuh MOL uh ji	ĕn′tŏ mŏl′ŏ jĭ	ˌɛn tə ˈmɑl ə dʒɪ; *ES also* -ˈmɒl-
entrails	EN traylz *Colloq. or dial.:* EN truhlz	ĕn′trālz *Colloq. or dial.:* ĕn′trĕlz § 51(2, 3)	ˈɛn trelz *Colloq. or dial.:* ˈɛn trəlz
entrance (n.)	EN truhns	ĕn′trăns	ˈɛn trəns
entrance (v.t. – "*delight*")	en TRANS en TRAHNS	ĕn trăns′ § 20(5)	ɛn ˈtræns, ɪn-; *E* *also* -ˈtrans, -ˈtrɑns
entreaty	en TREET i	ĕn trēt′ĭ § 49(5)	ɛn ˈtrit ɪ, ɪn-
enumerate	i NYOO muhr ayt i NYOO muh rayt i NOO muhr ayt i NOO muh rayt	ĕ nū′mĕr āt §§ 48(2), 50(2, 32)	ɪ ˈnju mər et ɪ ˈnju mə ret ɪ ˈnu mər et ɪ ˈnu mə ret
enunciate	i NUHN shi ayt i NUHN si ayt	ĕ nŭn′shĭ āt ĕ nŭn′sĭ āt § 47(2)	ɪ ˈnʌn ʃɪ et ɪ ˈnʌn sɪ et
envelop (v.t.)	en VEL uhp	ĕn vĕl′ŭp §§ 24(4), 49(5)	ɛn ˈvɛl əp, ɪn-
envelope	EN vuh lohp ON vuh lohp AHN vuh lohp	ĕn′vĕ lōp ŏn′vĕ lōp än′vĕ lōp § 47(1)	ˈɛn və lop, ˈɑn-, ˈɒn-, -vɪ-, ɛn ˈvɛl əp, ɪn-; *F.,* ã ˈvlöp
envenom	en VEN uhm	ĕn vĕn′ŭm	ɛn ˈvɛn əm
environ	en VAI ruhn § 50(34)	ĕn vī′răn § 49(5)	ɛn ˈvaɪ rən, ɪn-
environment	en VAI ruhn muhnt § 50(34)	ĕn vī′răn mĕnt § 50(22)	ɛn ˈvaɪ rən mənt
environs	en VAI ruhnz EN vuh ruhnz EN vɪ ruhnz	ĕn vī′rănz ĕn′vĕ rănz ĕn′vĭ rănz § 47(3), 48(3)	ɛn ˈvaɪ rənz, ɪn- ˈɛn və rənz ˈɛn vɪ rənz
envoy (v., n.)	EN voi	ĕn′voi	ˈɛn vɔɪ
enzyme	EN zaim EN zim § 50(34)	ĕn′zīm ĕn′zĭm	ˈɛn zaɪm ˈɛn zɪm
epaulet	EP uh let	ĕp′ŏ lĕt	ˈɛp ə lɛt
ephemeral	uh FEM uhr uhl i FEM uhr uhl	ĕ fĕm′ĕr ăl ĕ fĕm′ĕr ăl	ə ˈfɛm ər əl ɪ ˈfɛm ər əl
Ephesian	i FEE zhuhn i FEE zi uhn	ĕ fē′zhăn ĕ fē′zĭ ăn § 39(9)	ɪ ˈfi ʒən ɪ ˈfi zɪ ən

	SIMPLIFIED	DIACRITICAL	PHONETIC
ephod	EF od EE fod	ĕf′ŏd ē′fŏd	'ɛf ɑd, -əd, 'i fɑd, -fəd; *ES also* -ɒd, -fɒd
epicurean	*ep* i kyōō REE uhn	ĕp′ĭ kû rē′ăn §§ 47(2), 48(2)	ˌɛp ɪ kjʊ 'ri ən
epileptic	*ep* uh LEP tik *ep* i LEP tik	ĕp′ĭ lĕp′tĭk ĕp′ĭ lĕp′tĭk	ˌɛp ə 'lɛp tɪk ˌɛp ɪ 'lɛp tɪk
episcopal	i PIS kuh puhl	ĕ pĭs′kŏ păl	ɪ 'pɪs kə pəl, -p!̣
Episcopalian	i *pis* kuh PAY li uhn i *pis* kuh PAYL yuhn	ĕ pĭs′kŏ pā′lĭ ăn ĕ pĭs′kŏ pāl′yăn § 28(9)	ɪ ˌpɪs kə 'pe lɪ ən ɪ ˌpɪs kə 'pel jən
episcopate	i PIS kuh payt i PIS kuh pit	ĕ pĭs′kŏ pât §§ 20(8, 9), 49(4)	ɪ 'pɪs kə pet ɪ 'pɪs kə pɪt
epistle	i PIS ′l	ĕ pĭs′ ′l § 49(4)	ɪ 'pɪs !̣
epistolary	i PIS tuh *ler* i *B.*, i PIS tuh luhr i	ĕ pĭs′tŏ lĕr′ĭ *B.*, ĕ pĭs′tŏ lĕr ĭ §§ 13, 20(2), 24(9), 51(4)	ɪ 'pɪs tə ˌler ɪ *B.*, ɪ 'pɪs tə lə rɪ
epitaph	EP uh taf EP uh tahf EP i taf EP i tahf	ĕp′ĭ tăf ĕp′ĭ tàf § 20(5)	'ɛp ə tæf, 'ɛp ɪ-; *ES also* -taf, -tɑf
epithet	EP uh thet EP i thet	ĕp′ĭ thĕt ĕp′ĭ thĕt	'ɛp ə θɛt 'ɛp ɪ θɛt
epitome	i PIT uh mi	ĕ pĭt′ŏ mē	ɪ 'pɪt ə mɪ
epitomize	i PIT uh maⁱz § 50(34)	ĕ pĭt′ŏ mīz	ɪ 'pɪt ə maɪz
epoch	EP uhk *B.*, EE pok	ĕp′ŏk §§ 22(8), 47(3) *B.*, ē′pŏk § 51(4)	'ɛp ək, -ɑk; *ES* *also* -ɒk *B.*, 'i pɒk
equable	EK wuh b'l EE kwuh b'l	ĕk′wà b'l ē′kwà b'l § 47(3)	'ɛk wə b!̣ 'i kwə b!̣
equality	i KWOL uh ti ee KWOL i ti	ĕ kwŏl′ĭ tĭ ē kwŏl′ĭ tĭ § 50(16)	ɪ 'kwɑl ə tɪ, -'kwɒl-, -ɪ tɪ, i 'kwɑl-, -'kwɒl-
equanimity	*ee* kwuh NIM uh ti *ee* kwuh NIM i ti *ek* wuh NIM uh ti *ek* wuh NIM i ti	ē′kwà nĭm′ĭ tĭ ē′kwà nĭm′ĭ tĭ ĕk′wà nĭm′ĭ tĭ ĕk′wà nĭm′ĭ tĭ	ˌi kwə 'nɪm ə tɪ ˌi kwə 'nɪm ɪ tɪ ˌɛk wə 'nɪm ə tɪ ˌɛk wə 'nɪm ɪ tɪ
equation	i KWAY zhuhn ee KWAY zhuhn i KWAY shuhn ee KWAY shuhn	ĕ kwā′zhŭn ē kwā′zhŭn ĕ kwā′shŭn ē kwā′shŭn §§ 47(1), 50(30)	ɪ 'kwe ʒən i 'kwe ʒən ɪ 'kwe ʃən i 'kwe ʃən
equator	i KWAY tuhr ee KWAY tuhr	ĕ kwā′tẽr ē kwā′tẽr	ɪ 'kwe tɚ, i 'kwe-; *ES* -tə(r)

	SIMPLIFIED	DIACRITICAL	PHONETIC
equidistant	*ee* kwi DIS tuhnt	ē′kwĭ dĭs′tănt	ˌi kwɪ ˈdɪs tənt
equilibrate	*ee* kwi LAI͡ brayt	ē′kwĭ lī′brāt	ˌi kwɪ ˈlaɪ bret
	i KWIL uh brayt	ĕ kwĭl′ĭ brāt	ɪ ˈkwɪl ə bret
	ee KWIL i brayt	ē kwĭl′ĭ brāt	i ˈkwɪl ɪ bret
equilibrium	*ee* kwuh LIB ri uhm	ē′kwĭ lĭb′rĭ ŭm	ˌi kwə ˈlɪb rɪ əm
	ee kwi LIB ri uhm	ē′kwĭ lĭb′rĭ ŭm	ˌi kwɪ ˈlɪb rɪ əm
equinoctial	*ee* kwuh NOK shuhl	ē′kwĭ nŏk′shăl	ˌi kwə ˈnɑk ʃəl, -kwɪ-, ˌɛk wə-.
	ee kwi NOK shuhl	ē′kwĭ nŏk′shăl	-wɪ-; *ES also*
	ek wuh NOK shuhl	ek′wĭ nŏk′shăl	-ˈnɒk-
equinox	EE kwuh noks	ē′kwĭ nŏks	ˈi kwə nɑks, -kwɪ-,
	EE kwi noks	ē′kwĭ nŏks	ˈɛk wə-, -wɪ-;
	EK wuh noks	ĕk′wĭ nŏks	*ES also* -nɒks
equip	i KWIP	ĕ kwĭp′	ɪ ˈkwɪp
equipage	EK wuh pij	ĕk′wĭ pĭj	ˈɛk wə pɪdʒ
	EK wi pij	ĕk′wĭ pĭj § 50(1)	ˈɛk wɪ pɪdʒ
equipoise	EE kwuh poiz	ē′kwĭ poiz	ˈi kwə pɔɪz
	EE kwi poiz	ē′kwĭ poiz	ˈi kwɪ pɔɪz
	EK wuh poiz	ĕk′wĭ poiz	ˈɛk wə pɔɪz
	EK wi poiz	ĕk′wĭ poiz	ˈɛk wɪ pɔɪz
equitable	EK wi tuh b'l	ĕk′wĭ tȧ b'l	ˈɛk wɪ tə bl̩
equity	EK wuh ti	ĕk′wĭ tĭ	ˈɛk wə tɪ
	EK wi ti	ĕk′wĭ tĭ	ˈɛk wɪ tɪ
equivalent (n.)	i KWIV uh luhnt	ĕ kwĭv′ȧ lĕnt	ɪ ˈkwɪv ə lənt
era	EE ruh	ē′rȧ	ˈi rə, ˈɪər ə, ˈɪr ə,
	ĬER uh	ēr′ȧ	ˈir ə; *ES* ˈɪər ə
	IR uh	§ 24(2)	
	EER uh	ēr′ȧ	
eradicate	i RAD uh kayt	ĕ răd′ĭ kāt	ɪ ˈræd ə ket
	i RAD i kayt	ĕ răd′ĭ kāt	ɪ ˈræd ɪ ket
ere	ehr	âr §§ 20(2), 47(2)	ɛr, ær; *ES* ɛə(r), æə(r)
erect	i REKT	ĕ rĕkt′ § 49(4)	ɪ ˈrɛkt
eremite	ER i mait͡ § 50(34)	ĕr′ĕ mīt	ˈɛr ɪ maɪt, ˈɛr ə-
ergo	UHR goh	ûr′gō	ˈɝ go; *ES also* ˈɜ-
	In Elizabethan times:	*In Elizabethan times:*	*In Elizabethan times:*
	AR gaw	âr′gô § 51(2)	ˈær gɔ; *ES* ˈæə gɔ
ergot	UHR guht	ûr′gŏt	ˈɝ gət, -gɑt; *ES*
	UHR got	ûr′gŏt	*also* ˈɜ-, -gɒt
Eros	ĬER os	ēr′ŏs	ˈɪər ɑs, -ɒs, ˈɪr-,
	IR os	§ 24(2)	ˈir-, ˈɛr-; *ES*
	EER os	ēr′ŏs	ˈɪər ɒs
	ER os	ĕr′ŏs	
erosion	i ROH zhuhn	ĕ rō′zhŭn § 50(28)	ɪ ˈro ʒən

	SIMPLIFIED	DIACRITICAL	PHONETIC
err	*uhr*	ûr § 40(6)	ɝ; *ES also* ɜ(r)
errata	e RAY tuh	ĕ rā′tȧ	ɛ ′re tə
	i RAY tuh	ĭ rā′tȧ	ɪ ′re tə
	i RAH tuh	ĭ rä′tȧ	ɪ ′rɑ tə
erratic	e RAT ik	ĕ răt′ĭk	ɛ ′ræt ɪk, ɪ ′ræt-, ə ′ræt-
erratum	e RAY tuhm	ĕ rā′tŭm	ɛ ′re təm
	i RAY tuhm	ĭ rā′tŭm	ɪ ′re təm
	i RAH tuhm	ĭ rä′tŭm	ɪ ′rɑ təm
erred	*uhrd*	ûrd § 40(6)	ɝd; *ES also* ɜd
erudite	ER ŏŏ daìt	ĕr′ŏŏ dīt	′ɛr ʊ daɪt,
	ER yŏŏ daìt § 50(34)	ĕr′û dīt § 40(11)	′ɛr jʊ-, -ju-
erudition	*er* ŏŏ DISH uhn	ĕr′ŏŏ dĭsh′ŭn	ˌɛr ʊ ′dɪʃ ən,
	er yŏŏ DISH uhn	ĕr′û dĭsh′ŭn	ˌɛr jʊ-, -ju-
erysipelas	*er* i SIP uh luhs	ĕr′ĭ sĭp′ĕ lȧs	ˌɛr ɪ ′sɪp ə ləs,
	er i SIP i luhs	ĕr′ĭ sĭp′ĭ lȧs	ˌɪr ɪ-, ˌɪr ɪ-,
	ir i SIP uh luhs	ĭr′ĭ sĭp′ĕ lȧs	ˌɪər ɪ-, -ɪ ləs,
	eer i SIP uh luhs	ēr′ĭ sĭp′ĕ lȧs	-′sɪp l̩-
Esau	EE saw	ē′sô	′i sɔ
escapade	*es* kuh PAYD	ĕs′kȧ pād′	ˌɛs kə ′ped
	ES kuh payd	ĕs′kȧ pād	′ɛs kə ped
escape	es KAYP	ĕs kāp′	ɛs ′kep, ɪs-,
	e SKAYP		ɛ ′skep, ɪ ′skep,
	is KAYP	ĭs kāp′	ə ′skep
	i SKAYP	§ 38(9)	
eschew	es CHOO	ĕs chŏŏ′	ɛs ′tʃu
	es CHYOO	ĕs chū′ §§ 40(4), 48(2)	ɛs ′tʃju
escorted	es KAWRT ed	ĕs kôrt′ĕd	ɛs ′kɔrt ɛd, -ɪd,
	e SKAWRT ed § 24(5)		ɛ ′skɔrt-, ɪ′-; *ES*
	es KAWRT id	ĕs kôrt′ĭd	-′kɔət-, -′skɔət-
escutcheon	es KUCH uhn	ĕs kŭch′ŭn	ɛs ′kʌtʃ ən, ɛ ′skʌtʃ-, ɪ ′skʌtʃ-
esophagus, oesophagus	i SOF uh guhs	ĕ sŏf′ȧ gŭs	ɪ ′sɑf ə gəs, i ′sɑf-;
	ee SOF uh guhs	ē sŏf′ȧ gŭs	*ES also* -′sɒf-
esoteric	*es* oh TER ik	ĕs′ŏ tĕr′ĭk	ˌɛs o ′tɛr ɪk, ˌɛs ə-
espionage	ES pi uh nij	ĕs′pĭ ŏ nĭj	′ɛs pɪ ə nɪdʒ,
	es pi uh NAHZH	ĕs′pĭ ŏ näzh′	ˌɛs pɪ ə ′nɑʒ,
	es PAI uh nij	ĕs pī′ŏ nĭj	ɛs ′paɪ ə nɪdʒ,
	e SPAI uh nij		ɛ ′spaɪ-,
–espionnage (*F.*)	*F.*, *es pyo* NAHZH	*F.*, ĕs′pyŏ′nàzh′ §§ 47(3), 50(1)	ə ′spaɪ-; *F.*, ɛs pjɔ̃ ′na:ʒ
espousal	es POWZ uhl	ĕs pouz′ăl	ɛs ′paʊz əl, ɪs-, -l̩,
	es POWZ ʼl	ĕs pouz′ ʼl	ɛ ′spaʊz, ɪ′-
espouse	es POWZ	es pouz′	ɛs ′paʊz, ɪs-, ɛ ′spaʊz, ɪ′-

	SIMPLIFIED	DIACRITICAL	PHONETIC
esprit	*es* PREE ES pree	ĕs′prē′ ĕs′prē	ˌɛs ˈpri, ɛ ˈspri, ˈɛs pri
essay (v.)	e SAY	ĕ sā′	ɛ ˈse, ə ˈse
—— (n.)	ES ay	ĕs′ā	ˈɛs e, ˈɛs ɪ
—— *"exertion; an attempt,"* often	e SAY	ĕ sā′ §§ 12, 51(11)	ɛ ˈse, ˈɛ se
essayist	ES ay ist	ĕs′ā ĭst § 47(2)	ˈɛs e ɪst
essential	e SEN shuhl i SEN shuhl	ĕ sĕn′shăl ĭ sĕn′shăl	ɛ ˈsɛn ʃəl, ɪ ˈsɛn-, ə ˈsɛn-
estate	es TAYT is TAYT	ĕs tāt′ ĭs tāt′	ɛs ˈtet, ɪs-, ə ˈstet
Esther	ES tuhr	ĕs′tēr § 39(7)	ˈɛs tɚ; *ES* -tə(r)
estranged	es TRAYNJD is TRAYNJD	ĕs trānjd′ ĭs trānjd′ § 50(4)	ɛs ˈtrendʒd, ɪs-, ə ˈstrendʒd
estuary	ES chŏŏ *er* i ES tyŏŏ *er* i *B.,* ES tyŏŏ uhr i	ĕs′tū ĕr′ĭ §§ 20(2), 24(9), 50(33), 51(4) *B.,* ĕs′tū ĕr ĭ	ˈɛs tʃʊ ˌɛr ɪ ˈɛs tjʊ ˌɛr ɪ *B.,* ˈɛs tjʊ ə rɪ
eternal	i TUHR nuhl i TUHR n'l	ĕ tûr′năl ĕ tûr′n'l	ɪ ˈtɝ nəl, -nl̩; *ES also* -ˈtɝ-
ethereal	i THĬER i uhl i THIR i uhl i THEER i uhl	ĕ thēr′ĕ ăl § 24(2) ĕ thēr′ĕ ăl	ɪ ˈθɪər ɪ əl, -ˈθɪr-, -ˈθir-; *ES* -ˈθɪər-
ethical	ETH i kuhl	ĕth′ĭ kăl	ˈɛθ ɪ kəl, -kl̩
etiquette	ET i ket *B., et* i KET	ĕt′ĭ kĕt *B.,* ĕt′ĭ kĕt′ § 51(4)	ˈɛt ɪ kɛt *B.,* ˌɛt ɪ ˈkɛt
Etna (**Mount**)	Et nuh	ĕt′ná	ˈɛt nə
étude	*ay* TOOD ay TYOOD ay TOOD	ā′ tüd′ ā tūd′ 	*F.,* e ˈtyd e ˈtjud e ˈtud
Eucharist	YOO kuh rist	ū′ká rĭst	ˈju kə rɪst
eulogy	YOO luh ji	ū′lŏ jĭ	ˈju lə dʒɪ
euphonious	yoo FOH ni uhs	ũ fō′nĭ ŭs § 50(25)	ju ˈfo nɪ əs
euphony	YOO fuh ni	ū′fŏ nĭ	ˈju fə nɪ
Euphrates	yoo FRAY teez *In Elizabethan times, often:* YOO fruh *teez*	ũ frā′tēz *In Elizabethan times, often:* ū′frá tēz′ § 51(2)	ju ˈfre tiz *In Elizabethan times, often:* ˈju frə ˌtiz
Euripides	yŏŏ RIP i deez	ũ rĭp′ĭ dēz	jʊ ˈrɪp ɪ diz
European	*yŏŏ* ruh PEE uhn *yoo* ruh PEE uhn	ū′rŏ pē′ăn §§ 34(21), 40(4)	ˌjʊ rə ˈpi ən
Eustachian (tube)	yoo STAY ki uhn yŏŏ STAY ki uhn	ũ stā′kĭ ăn	ju ˈste kɪ ən, jʊ-, -ˈste ʃən
evaluation	i *val* yŏŏ AY shuhn	ĕ′văl ũ ā′shăn § 50(30)	ɪ ˌvæl jʊ ˈe ʃən, -ju-

	SIMPLIFIED	DIACRITICAL	PHONETIC
evanescent	*ev* uh NES uhnt *ev* uh NES 'nt	ĕv′*á* nĕs′ĕnt ĕv′*á* nĕs′ 'nt § 24(14)	ˌɛv ə 'nɛs ənt ˌɛv ə 'nɛs n̩t
evangelical	*ee* van JEL i kuhl *ev* uhn JEL i kuhl	ē′văn jĕl′ĭ kăl ĕv′*ăn* jĕl′ĭ kăl § 47(3)	ˌi væn 'dʒɛl ɪ kəl, ˌɛv ən-, -kl̩
evasion	i VAY zhuhn	ĕ vā′zhŭn § 50(28)	ɪ 've ʒən
evasive	i VAY siv	ĕ vā′sĭv § 50(17)	ɪ 've sɪv
even	EE vuhn	ē′vĕn	'i vən
evening	EEV ning	ĕv′nĭng	'iv nɪŋ
event	i VENT	ĕ vĕnt′	ɪ 'vɛnt
eventually	i VEN chŏŏ uhl i i VEN tyŏŏ uhl i	ĕ vĕn′tŭ ăl ĭ §§ 49̃(4), 50(20, 33)	ɪ 'vɛn tʃʊ əl ɪ, -tjʊ-, -tʃʊ lɪ, -tjʊ-
every	EV uhr i EV ri	ĕv′ĕr ĭ ĕv′rĭ §§ 9, 47(3)	'ɛv ər ɪ 'ɛv rɪ
evidently	EV uh duhnt li EV i duhnt li *Emph., occas.:* *ev* uh DENT li *ev* i DENT li	ĕv′ĭ dĕnt lĭ ĕv′ĭ dĕnt lĭ *Emph., occas.:* ĕv′ĭ dĕnt′lĭ ĕv′ĭ dĕnt′lĭ § 51(11)	'ɛv ə dənt lɪ, 'ɛv ɪ-, -dɛnt- *Emph., occas.:* ˌɛv ə 'dɛnt lɪ ˌɛv ɪ 'dɛnt lɪ
evil	EE v'l EE vil	ē′v′l ē′vĭl	'i vl̩ 'i vɪl
evolution	*ev* uh LOO shuhn *ev* uh LYOO shuhn	ĕv′ŏ lū′shŭn §§ 40(3), 48(2), 50(30, 32)	ˌɛv ə 'lu ʃən ˌɛv ə 'lju ʃən ˌɛv l̩ 'ju ʃən
ewe	yoo *Often (hist. var.),* *commonly dial.:* yoh	ū § 24(22) *Often (hist. var.),* *commonly dial.:* yō § 51(2, 11)	ju *Often (hist. var.),* *commonly dial.:* jo
ewer	YOO uhr	ū′ĕr § 40(4)	'ju ɚ, 'jʊ-; *ES* -ə(r)
exact	eg ZAKT ig ZAKT	ĕg zăkt′ ĭg zăkt′ § 49(6)	ɛg 'zækt ɪg 'zækt
exaggerate	eg ZAJ uhr ayt eg ZAJ uh rayt ig ZAJ uhr ayt ig ZAJ uh rayt	ĕg zăj′ĕr āt ĭg zăj′ĕr āt § 49(6)	ɛg 'zædʒ ər et ɛg 'zædʒ ə ret ɪg 'zædʒ ər et ɪg 'zædʒ ə ret
exalt	eg ZAWLT ig ZAWLT	ĕg zôlt′ ĭg zôlt′ § 49(6)	ɛg 'zɔlt ɪg 'zɔlt
exaltation	*eg* zawl TAY shuhn	ĕg′zôl tā′shŭn	ˌɛg zɔl 'te ʃən
exasperate (v.t.)	eg ZAS puhr ayt eg ZAS puh rayt ig ZAS puhr ayt ig ZAS puh rayt	ĕg zăs′pĕr āt ĭg zăs′pĕr āt §§ 49(6), 50(2)	ɛg 'zæs pər et ɛg 'zæs pə ret ɪg 'zæs pər et ɪg 'zæs pə ret
excavate	EKS kuh vayt	ĕks′*ká* vāt § 49(6)	'ɛks kə vet

	SIMPLIFIED	DIACRITICAL	PHONETIC
exceed	ek SEED	ĕk sēd′	ɛk 'sid
	ik SEED	ĭk sēd′ § 49(6)	ɪk 'sid
excellent	EK suh luhnt	ĕk′sĕ lĕnt	'ɛk sə lənt, -sļ ənt
excelsior (n.)	ek SEL si uhr	ĕk sĕl′sĭ ēr	ɛk 'sɛl sɪ ɚ, ɪk-; *ES* -ə(r)
—— (adj.)	ek SEL si awr	ĕk sĕl′sĭ ôr	ɛk 'sɛl sɪ ɔr, -sɪ ɚ,
	ek SEL si uhr	ĕk sĕl′sĭ ēr	ɪk-; *ES* -əə(r), -ə(r)
exceptionable	ek SEP shuhn uh b'l	ĕk sĕp′shŭn á b'l	ɛk 'sɛp ʃən ə bļ, ɪk-, -ʃnə bļ
	ik SEP shuhn uh b'l	ĭk sĕp′shŭn á b'l	
exceptionally	ek SEP shuhn uhl i	ĕk sĕp′shŭn ăl ĭ	ɛk 'sɛp ʃən əl ɪ,
	ek SEP shuhn 'l i	ĕk sĕp′shŭn 'l ĭ	ɪk-, -ʃən ļ ɪ,
	ik SEP shuhn uhl i	ĭk sĕp′shŭn ăl ĭ	-ʃnə lɪ
	ik SEP shuhn 'l i	ĭk sĕp′shŭṇ 'l ĭ § 49(6)	
excess (n.)	ek SES	ĕk sĕs′	ɛk 'sɛs
	ik SES	ĭk sĕs′ § 49(6)	ɪk 'sɛs
—— (adj.)	ek SES	ĕk sĕs′	ɛk 'sɛs
	ik SES	ĭk sĕs′	ɪk 'sɛs
	EK ses	ĕk′sĕs § 11	'ɛk sɛs
exchequer (n.)	eks CHEK uhr	ĕks chĕk′ēr	ɛks 'tʃɛk ɚ, ɪks-,
	EKS chek uhr	ĕks′chĕk ēr § 12	'ɛks tʃɛk-, 'ɪks-; *ES* -ə(r)
—— (v.t.)	eks CHEK uhr	ĕks chĕk′ēr	ɛks 'tʃɛk ɚ, ɪks-; *ES* -ə(r)
excise (n. –	ek SAIZ	ĕk sīz′	ɛk 'saɪz
"duty; import")	ik SAIZ	ĭk sīz′	ɪk 'saɪz
	EK saiz § 50(34)	ĕk′sīz §§ 12, 49(6)	'ɛk saɪz
excise (v.t. –	ek SAIZ	ĕk sīz′	ɛk 'saɪz
"impose tax")	ik SAIZ § 50(34)	ĭk sīz′ § 49(6)	ɪk 'saɪz
excise (adj.–	EK saiz	ĕk′sīz	'ɛk saɪz
"having to do	ek SAIZ	ĕk sīz′	ɛk 'saɪz
with excises")	ik SAIZ § 50(34)	ĭk sīz′ §§ 11, 49(6)	ɪk 'saɪz
excise (v.t. –	ek SAIZ	ĕk sīz′	ɛk 'saɪz
"cut out")	ik SAIZ § 50(34)	ĭk sīz′ § 49(6)	ɪk 'saɪz
excision	ek SIZH uhn	ĕk sĭzh′ŭn	ɛk 'sɪʒ ən
	ik SIZH uhn	ĭk sĭzh′ŭn	ɪk 'sɪʒ ən
exclaim	eks KLAYM	ĕks klām′	ɛks 'klem
	ek SKLAYM		ɛk 'sklem
	iks KLAYM	ĭks klām′	ɪks 'klem
	ik SKLAYM	§ 49(6)	ɪk 'sklem
exclude	eks KLOOD	ĕks klo͞od′	ɛks 'klud
	ek SKLOOD		ɛk 'sklud
	iks KLOOD	ĭks klo͞od′	ɪks 'klud
	ik SKLOOD	§§ 40(4), 48(2), 49(6)	ɪk 'sklud
excrement	EKS kri muhnt	ĕks′krĕ mĕnt	'ɛks krɪ mənt

	SIMPLIFIED	DIACRITICAL	PHONETIC
excrescence	eks KRES uhns	ĕks krĕs′ĕns	ɛks ′krɛs əns,
	ek SKRES uhns		ɪks ′krɛs-,
	eks KRES 'ns	ĕks krĕs′ 'ns	ɛk ′skrɛs-,
	iks KRES uhns	ĭks krĕs′ĕns	ɪk ′skrɛs-,
	ik SKRES uhns	§§ 33(2), 49(6)	-ns
	iks KRES 'ns	ĭks krĕs′ 'ns	
excretory	EKS kri *toh* ri	ĕks′krĕ tō′rĭ	′ɛks krɪ ˌto rɪ
	EKS kri *taw* ri		′ɛks krɪ ˌtɔ rɪ
	eks KREE tuh ri	ĕks krē′tŏ rĭ	ɛks ′kri tə rɪ
	ek SKREE tuh ri	§§ 34(3), 47(3)	ɛk ′skri tə ri
excursion	eks KUHR zhuhn	ĕks kûr′zhŭn	ɛks ′kɝ ʒən,
	ek SKUHR zhuhn		ɛk ′skɝ-,
	eks KUHR shuhn	ĕks kûr′shŭn	ɪks ′kɝ-,
	ek SKUHR shuhn		ɪk ′skɝ-,
	iks KUHR zhuhn	ĭks kûr′zhŭn	ɛks ′kɝ ʃən,
	ik SKUHR zhuhn		ɛk ′skɝ-,
	iks KUHR shuhn	ĭks kûr′shŭn	ɪks ′kɝ-,
	ik SKUHR shuhn	§§ 47(1), 49(6),	ɪk ′skɝ-; *ES*
		50(28)	*also* -′kɝ-,
			-′skɝ-
excuse (v.)	eks KYOOZ	ĕks kūz′	ɛks ′kjuz
	ek SKYOOZ		ɛk ′skjuz
	iks KYOOZ	ĭks kūz′	ɪks ′kjuz
	ik SKYOOZ		ɪk ′skjuz
—— (n.)	eks KYOOS	ĕks kūs′	ɛks ′kjus
	ek SKYOOS		ɛk ′skjus
	iks KYOOS	ĭks kūs′	ɪks ′kjus
	ik SKYOOS	§§ 38(4), 49(6)	ɪk ′skjus
execrable	EK si kruh b'l	ĕk′sĕ krȧ b'l	′ɛk sɪ krə bl̩
execrate	EK si krayt	ĕk′sĕ krāt	′ɛk sɪ kret
execute	EK si kyoot	ĕk′sĕ kūt § 48(2)	′ɛk sɪ kjut
executive	eg ZEK yŏŏ tiv	ĕg zĕk′û tĭv	ɛg ′zɛk jʊ tɪv,
	ig ZEK yŏŏ tiv	ĭg zĕk′û tĭv	-ju-, ɪg-,
	ek SEK yŏŏ tiv	ĕk sĕk′û tĭv	ɛk ′sɛk-,
	ik SEK yŏŏ tiv	ĭk sĕk′û tĭv	ɪk ′sɛk-
		§§ 47(1), 49(6)	
executor (*Law*)	eg ZEK yŏŏ tuhr	ĕg zĕk′û tēr	ɛg ′zɛk jʊ tɚ,
	ig ZEK yŏŏ tuhr	ĭg zĕk′û tēr	-jə-, -ju-, ɪg-,
	ek SEK yŏŏ tuhr	ĕk sĕk′û tēr	ɛk ′sɛk-,
	ik SEK yŏŏ tuhr	ĭk sĕk′û tēr	ɪk ′sɛk-; *ES*
		§47(1)	-tə(r)
—— "*a doer or agent*"	EK si *kyoo* tuhr	ĕk′sĕ kū′tēr	′ɛk sɪ ˌkju tɚ; *ES*
		§ 51(11)	-tə(r)
exemplary	eg ZEM pluh ri	ĕg zĕm′plȧ rĭ	ɛg ′zɛm plə rɪ, ɪg-,
	ig ZEM pluh ri	ĭg zĕm′plȧ rĭ	′ɛg zəm ˌplɛr ɪ,
	EG zuhm *pler* i	ĕg′zĕm plĕr′ĭ	-plər ɪ,
	EG zuhm pluhr i	ĕg′zĕm plĕr ĭ	′ɛk sɛm-
		§§ 20(2), 47(3),	
		49(6)	
exempt	eg ZEMPT	ĕg zĕmpt′	ɛg ′zɛmpt
	ig ZEMPT	ĭg zĕmpt′ § 49(6)	ɪg ′zɛmpt

exercise	EK suhr saiz § 50(34)	ĕk′sẽr sīz	'ɛk sɚ saɪz; *ES* -sə-
exert	eg ZUHRT ig ZUHRT	ĕg zûrt′ ĭg zûrt′ § 49(6)	ɛg 'zɝt, ɪg-; *ES* *also* -'zɝt
exhalation	*eks* huh LAY shuhn *ek* suh LAY shuhn *eg* zuh LAY shuhn	ĕks′há lā′shŭn ĕk′sá lā′shŭn ĕg′zá lā′shŭn § 47(3)	ˌɛks hə 'le ʃən ˌɛk sə 'le ʃən ˌɛg zə 'le ʃən
exhale	eks HAYL eg ZAYL	ĕks hāl′ ĕg zāl′ §§ 47(3), 49(6)	ɛks 'hel ɛg 'zel, ɪg-
exhaust	eg ZAWST ig ZAWST	ĕg zôst′ ĭg zôst′ §§ 27(1), 47(3), 49(6)	ɛg 'zɔst ɪg 'zɔst
exhaustion	eg ZAWS chuhn ig ZAWS chuhn	ĕg zôs′chŭn ĭg zôs′chŭn §§ 47(2), 49(6)	ɛg 'zɔs tʃən ɪg 'zɔs tʃən
exhibit	eg ZIB it ig ZIB it	ĕg zĭb′ĭt ĭg zĭb′ĭt §§ 47(2), 49(6)	ɛg 'zɪb ɪt ɪg 'zɪb ɪt
exhilarate	eg ZIL uh rayt ig ZIL uh rayt	ĕg zĭl′á rāt ĭg zĭl′á rāt §§ 27(1), 47(2), 49(6)	ɛg 'zɪl ə ret ɪg 'zɪl ə ret
exhort	eg ZAWRT ig ZAWRT	ĕg zôrt′ ĭg zôrt′ §§ 27(1), 47(2), 49(6)	ɛg 'zɔrt, ɪg-, ɛgz 'hɔrt; *ES* -'zɔət, -'hɔət
exigency	EK suh juhn si EK si juhn si	ĕk′sŭ jĕn sĭ ĕk′sĭ jĕn sĭ	'ɛk sə dʒən sɪ 'ɛk sɪ dʒən sɪ
exile	EK sail EG zail § 50(34)	ĕk′sīl ĕg′zīl §§ 47(3), 49(6)	'ɛk saɪl 'ɛg zaɪl; *v. also* ɪg 'zaɪl
exist	eg ZIST ig ZIST	ĕg zĭst′ ĭg zĭst′ § 49(6)	ɛg 'zɪst ɪg 'zɪst
exists	eg ZISTS ig ZISTS	ĕg zĭsts′ ĭg zĭsts′ § 50(6)	ɛg 'zɪsts ɪg 'zɪsts
exit	EK sit EG zit	ĕk′sĭt ĕg′zĭt § 49(6)	'ɛk sɪt 'ɛg zɪt
exodus	EK suh duhs	ĕk′sŏ dŭs	'ɛk sə dəs
exorbitant	eg ZAWR bi tuhnt ig ZAWR bi tuhnt	ĕg zôr′bĭ tănt ĭg zôr′bĭ tănt § 49(6)	ɛg 'zɔr bɪ tənt, ɪg-; *ES* -'zɔə-
exotic	eks OT ik eg ZOT ik	ĕks ŏt′ĭk ĕg zŏt′ĭk § 47(1)	ɛks 'ɑt ɪk, ɛg 'zɑt-, ɪg-; *ES* *also* -'ɒt-, -'zɒt-
expatiate (v.)	eks PAY shi ayt ek SPAY shi ayt	ĕks pā′shĭ āt § 20(8, 9)	ɛks 'pe ʃɪ et, ɛk 'spe-, ɪk 'spe-

	SIMPLIFIED	DIACRITICAL	PHONETIC
expect	eks PEKT iks PEKT	ĕks pĕkt′ ĭks pĕkt′ § 49(6)	ɛks 'pɛkt, ɪks-, ɪk 'spɛkt
expediency	eks PEE di uhn si ek SPEE di uhn si	ĕks pē′dĭ ĕn sĭ	ɛks 'pi dɪ ən sɪ, ɛk 'spi-, ɪk 'spi-
expedient	eks PEE di uhnt ek SPEE di uhnt	ĕks pē′dĭ ĕnt	ɛks 'pi dɪ ənt, ɛk 'spi-, ɪk-
expedite	EKS pi da͡it § 50(34)	ĕks′pĕ dīt	'ɛks pɪ daɪt
expeditious	*eks* pi DISH uhs	ĕks′pĕ dĭsh′ŭs § 50(25)	ˌɛks pɪ 'dɪʃ əs
expenditure	eks PEN di chuhr ek SPEN di chuhr eks PEN di tyuhr ek SPEN di tyuhr iks PEN di chuhr ik SPEN di chuhr iks PEN di tyuhr ik SPEN di tyuhr	ĕks pĕn′dĭ tu̯r ĭks pĕn′dĭ tu̯r §§ 49(6), 50(31)	ɛks 'pɛn dɪ tʃɚ, -ˌtʃʊr, -tjɚ, -ˌtjʊr, ɪks-, ɛk 'spɛn-, ɪk-; *ES* -tʃə(r), -ˌtʃʊə(r), -tjə(r), -ˌtjʊə(r)
experience	eks PĬER i uhns ek SPĬER i uhns eks PIR i uhns ek SPIR i uhns eks PEER i uhns ek SPEER i uhns ik SPĬER i uhns ik SPIR i uhns ik SPEER i uhns	ĕks pḗr′ĭ ĕns §§ 24(2, 4), 49(6) ĕks pēr′ĭ ĕns ĭks pḗr′ĭ ĕns ĭks pēr′ĭ ĕns	ɛks 'pɪər ɪ əns, -'pɪr-, -'pir-, ɛk 'spɪər-, -'spɪr-, -'spir-, ɪks 'pɪər-, -'pɪr-, -'pir-, ɪk 'spɪər-, -'spɪr-, -'spir-; *ES* -'pɪər-, -'spɪər-
experiment (n.)	eks PER uh muhnt ek SPER uh muhnt eks PER i muhnt ek SPER i muhnt iks PER uh muhnt ik SPER uh muhnt	ĕks pĕr′ĭ mĕnt ĕks pĕr′ĭ mĕnt ĭks pĕr′ĭ mĕnt	ɛks 'pɛr ə mənt ɛk 'spɛr ə mənt ɛks 'pɛr ɪ mənt ɛk 'spɛr ɪ mənt ɪks 'pɛr ə mənt ɪk 'spɛr ə mənt
—— (v.)	eks PER uh ment ek SPER uh ment eks PER i ment ek SPER i ment iks PER uh ment ik SPER uh ment	ĕks pĕr′ĭ mĕnt ĕks pĕr′ĭ mĕnt ĭks pĕr′ĭ mĕnt §§ 49(6), 50(22)	ɛks 'pɛr ə mɛnt ɛk 'spɛr ə mɛnt ɛks 'pɛr ɪ mɛnt ɛk 'spɛr ɪ mɛnt ɪks 'pɛr ə mɛnt ɪk 'spɛr ə mɛnt
expert (n.)	EKS *puhrt* EK *spuhrt*	ĕks′pûrt § 47(2)	'ɛks pɝt, 'ɛk spɝt; *ES also* -pɝt, -spɝt
—— (adj.)	eks PUHRT ek SPUHRT EKS *puhrt*	ĕks pûrt′ § 11 ĕks′pûrt	ɛks 'pɝt, ɛk 'spɝt, 'ɛks pɝt; *ES* *also* -'pɝt, -'spɝt, -pɝt

	SIMPLIFIED	DIACRITICAL	PHONETIC
expiate	EKS pi ayt	ĕks′pĭ āt	'ɛks pɪ et
expire	ek SPAIR	ĕk spīr′	ɛk 'spaɪr, ɪk-; *ES*
	ik SPAIR	ĭk spīr′ § 49(6)	-'spaɪə(r)
	§ 50(34)		
explain	eks PLAYN	ĕks plān′	ɛks 'plen
	ek SPLAYN		ɛk 'splen
	iks PLAYN	ĭks plān′	ɪks 'plen
	ik SPLAYN	§ 49(6)	ɪk 'splen
expletive	EKS pli tĭv	ĕks′plĕ tĭv	'ɛks plɪ tɪv
explicit (adj. –	eks PLIS it	ĕks plĭs′ĭt	ɛks 'plɪs ɪt
"clear"; v.t. –	ek SPLIS it		ɛk 'splɪs ɪt
"make defi-	iks PLIS it	ĭks plĭs′ĭt § 49(6)	ɪks 'plɪs ɪt
nite")	ik SPLIS it		ɪk 'splɪs ɪt
exploit (n.)	EKS ploit	ĕks′ploit	'ɛks plɔɪt,
	eks PLOIT	§ 47(1)	ɛks 'plɔɪt, ɪks-,
	ek SPLOIT	ĕks ploit′	ɛk 'splɔɪt, ɪk-
—— (v.)	eks PLOIT	ĕks ploit′	ɛks 'plɔɪt, ɪks-,
	ek SPLOIT		ɛk 'splɔɪt, ɪk-
	iks PLOIT	ĭks ploit′	
	ik SPLOIT	§ 47(1)	
exponent	eks POH nuhnt	ĕks pō′nĕnt	ɛks 'po nənt, ɪks-,
	ek SPOH nuhnt		ɛk 'spo-, ɪk-
export (n., adj.)	EKS pohrt	ĕks′pōrt	'ɛks port, -pərt;
	EKS pawrt	§ 34(3)	*ES* -poət, *E*
			also -pɔət
—— (v.t.)	eks POHRT	ĕks pōrt′	ɛks 'port, ɪks-,
	ek SPOHRT		ɛk 'sport, ɪk-,
	eks PAWRT		-'pərt, -'spərt;
	ek SPAWRT	§ 34(3)	*ES* -'poət,
			-'spoət, *E also*
			-'pɔət, -'spɔət
	Often, esp. in	*Often, esp. in*	*Often, esp. in*
	contrast with	*contrast with*	*contrast with*
	"import":	*"import"*:	*"import"*:
	EKS pohrt	ĕks′pōrt	'ɛks port, -pərt;
	EKS pawrt	§§ 34(3), 51(11)	*ES* -poət, *E*
			also -pɔət
expose	eks POHZ	ĕks pōz′	ɛks 'poz
	ek SPOHZ		ɛk 'spoz
	iks POHZ	ĭks pōz′	ɪks 'poz
	ik SPOHZ	§ 49(6)	ɪk 'spoz
exposé	*eks* poh ZAY	ĕks′pŏ zā′	ˌɛks po 'ze
	B., eks POH zay	*B.*, ĕks pō′zā	*B.*, ɛks 'po ze
		§ 51(4)	
exquisite	EKS kwi zit	ĕks′kwĭ zĭt	'ɛks kwɪ zɪt
	Occas., *often for*	*Occas.*, *often for*	*Occas.*, *often for*
	emphasis:	*emphasis*:	*emphasis*:
	eks KWIZ it	ĕks kwĭz′ĭt	ɛks 'kwɪz ɪt
	ek SKWIZ it		ɛk 'skwɪz ɪt
	iks KWIZ it	ĭks kwĭz′ĭt	ɪks 'kwɪz ɪt
	ik SKWIZ it	§ 51(11)	ɪk 'skwɪz ɪt

	SIMPLIFIED	DIACRITICAL	PHONETIC
extant	EKS tuhnt ek STANT ik STANT	ĕks′tănt ĕk stănt′ ĭk stănt′ § 47(2)	'ɛks tənt ɛk 'stænt ɪk 'stænt
extempore	eks TEM puh ri ek STEM puh ri	ĕks tĕm′pŏ rĕ	ɛks 'tɛm pə rɪ, ɪks-, ɛk 'stɛm-, ɪk-, -ri
extend	eks TEND ek STEND iks TEND ik STEND	ĕks tĕnd′ ĭks tĕnd′ § 49(6)	ɛks 'tɛnd ɛk 'stɛnd ɪks 'tɛnd ɪk 'stɛnd
extinct	eks TINGKT ek STINGKT iks TINGKT ik STINGKT	ĕks tĭngkt′ ĭks tĭngkt′ §§ 33(4), 49(6)	ɛks 'tɪŋkt ɛk 'stɪŋkt ɪks 'tɪŋkt ɪk 'stɪŋkt
extinguish	eks TING gwish ek STING gwish iks TING gwish ik STING gwish	ĕks tĭng′gwĭsh ĭks tĭng′gwĭsh §§ 33(4), 49(6)	ɛks 'tɪŋ gwɪʃ ɛk 'stɪŋ gwɪʃ ɪks 'tɪŋ gwɪʃ ɪk 'stɪŋ gwɪʃ
extirpate (v.t.)	EK stuhr payt eks TUHR payt ek STUHR payt	ĕk′stẽr pāt ĕks tûr′pāt § 47(2)	'ɛk stɚ pet, ɛks 'tɝ-, ɪks-, ɛk 'stɝ-, ɪk-; ES -stə-, also -'tɝ-, -'stɝ-
extol, extoll (v.t.)	eks TOL ek STOL eks TOHL ek STOHL iks TOHL ik STOHL	ĕks tŏl′ ĕks tōl′ ĭks tōl′ § 47(3)	ɛks 'tɑl, -'tɒl, -'tol, ɛk 'stɑl, -'stɒl, -'stol, ɪks 'tol, ɪk 'stol, ɪk 'stɑl, -'stɒl
extract (v.)	eks TRAKT ek STRAKT iks TRAKT ik STRAKT	ĕks trăkt′ ĭks trăkt′ §§ 12, 49(6)	ɛks 'trækt ɛk 'strækt ɪks 'trækt ɪk 'strækt
—— (n.)	EKS trakt	ĕks′trăkt	'ɛks trækt
extraditable	EKS truh *dait* uh b'l	ĕks′tr*ȧ* dīt′*ȧ* b'l	'ɛks trə ˌdaɪb ə bļ
extradite	EKS truh *dait* § 50(34)	ĕks′tr*ȧ* dīt	'ɛks trə daɪt
extraneous	eks TRAY ni uhs ek STRAY ni uhs	ĕks trā′nĕ ŭs § 24(15)	ɛks 'tre nɪ əs, ɪks-, ɛk 'stre-, ɪk-
extraordinary (adj.) *Special Note:* **For every pro- nunciation given in the simplified col- umn as eks, ek, or *eks*, or in the diacritical col-**	eks TRAWR duh *ner* i ek STRAWR duh *ner* i eks TRAWR di *ner* i ek STRAWR di *ner* i *eks* truh AWR duh ner ĭ	ĕks trôr′dĭ nĕr′ĭ ĕks trôr′dĭ nĕr′ĭ ĕks′tr*ȧ* ôr′dĭ nĕr ĭ	ɛks 'trɔr də ˌnɛr ɪ, ɪks-, ɛk 'strɔr-, ɪk-, -dɪ ˌnɛr ɪ, ˌɛks trə 'ɔr də nɛr ɪ, -tri-, ˌɪks-, -dɪ-, -dn̩-; ES -'trɔə-, -'strɔə-

umn as ĕks or ĕks′, you may substitute respectively iks, ik, or *iks* in the simplified column, or ĭks or ĭks′ in the diacritical column.	*eks* truh AWR di ner ĭ *B.,* iks TRAWR duh nuhr i ik STRAWR duh nuhr i iks TRAWR d′n ri ik STRAWR d′n ri	ĕks′trȧ ôr′dĭ nĕr ĭ *B.,* ĭks trôr′dĭ nĕr ĭ ĭks trôr′d′n rĭ §§ 20(2), 24(4), 51(4)	*B.,* ɪks ′trɔr də nə rɪ, -dn̩ rɪ, ɪk ′strɔr-; *ES* -′trɔə-, -′strɔə-
—— *"sent upon a special service,"* esp.	*eks* truh AWR duh ner i *eks* truh AWR di ner i	ĕks′trȧ ôr′dĭ nĕr ĭ ĕks′trȧ ôr′dĭ nĕr ĭ	ˌɛks trə ′ɔr də ner ɪ, -trɪ-, -dɪ-, -dn̩-; *ES* -′ɔə-
extreme	eks TREEM ek STREEM iks TREEM ik STREEM	ĕks trēm′ ĭks trēm′ §§ 11, 49(6)	ɛks ′trim ɛk ′strim ɪks ′trim ɪk ′strim
extricable	EKS tri kuh b′l	ĕks′trĭ kȧ b′l	′ɛks trɪ kə bl̩
extricate (v.t.)	EKS truh kayt EKS tri kayt	ĕks′trĕ kāt ĕks′trĭ kāt § 50(2)	′ɛks trə ket ′ɛks trɪ ket
exuberance	eg ZYOO buhr uhns eg ZOO buhr uhns ig ZYOO buhr uhns ig ZOO buhr uhns	ĕg zū′bēr ăns ĭg zū′bēr ăns §§ 48(2), 49(6), 50(32)	ɛg ′zju bər əns ɛg ′zu bər əns ɪg ′zju bər əns ɪg ′zu bər əns
exuberant	eg ZYOO buhr uhnt eg ZOO buhr uhnt ig ZYOO buhr uhnt ig ZOO buhr uhnt	ĕg zū′bēr ănt ĭg zū′bēr ănt §§ 48(2), 50(32)	ɛg ′zju bər ənt ɛg ′zu bər ənt ɪg ′zju bər ənt ɪg ′zu bər ənt
exude	eks YOOD ek SYOOD eg ZYOOD eg ZOOD ig ZYOOD ig ZOOD	ĕks ūd′ ĕg zūd′ ĭg zūd′ §§ 47(1), 48(2), 49(6), 50(32)	ɛks ′jud, ɛk ′sjud, ɪk-, ɛg ′zjud, -′zud, ɪg ′zjud, -′zud, ɛk ′ʃjud, -′ʃud
exult	eg ZUHLT ig ZUHLT	ĕg zŭlt′ ĭg zŭlt′ § 49(6)	ɛg ′zʌlt ɪg ′zʌlt
exultation	*ek suhl* TAY shuhn *eg zuhl* TAY shuhn	ĕk′sŭl tā′shăn ĕg′zŭl tā′shăn §§ 40(6), 47(1)	ˌɛk sʌl ′te ʃən ˌɛg zʌl ′te ʃən
eyrie, eyry	EHR i ĬER i IR i EER i Â͡I ri § 50(34)	âr′ĭ ē̠r′ĭ § 24(2) ēr′ĭ ī′rĭ	′er ɪ, ′ær ɪ, ′ɪər ɪ, ′ɪr ɪ, ′ir ɪ, ′aɪ rɪ, *ES also* ′ɛər ɪ, ′æər ɪ, ′ɪər ɪ, ′aɪ ə rɪ

F

Fabian	FAY bi uhn	fā′bĭ ăn § 28(9)	′fe bɪ ən
façade	fuh SAHD	fȧ säd′	fə ′sɑd
	fa SAHD	fă säd′ § 47(2)	fæ ′sɑd
facet	FAS et	făs′ĕt	′fæs ɛt
	FAS it	făs′ĭt § 24(5)	′fæs ɪt
facetious	fuh SEE shuhs	fȧ sē′shŭs	fə ′si ʃəs
facial	FAY shuhl	fā′shăl § 47(2)	′fe ʃəl
facile	FAS il	făs′ĭl §§ 28(5), 31(3)	′fæs ɪl, ′fæs ļ
fact	fakt	făkt	fækt
factious	FAK shuhs	făk′shŭs	′fæk ʃəs
factitious	fak TISH uhs	făk tĭsh′ŭs	fæk ′tɪʃ əs
factor	FAK tuhr	făk′tĕr	′fæk tɚ; ES -tə(r)
factory	FAK tuh ri	făk′tŏ rĭ § 9	′fæk tə rɪ, -trɪ
factotum	fak TOH tuhm	făk tō′tŭm	fæk ′to təm
Fahrenheit	FAR uhn haı̑t	fär′ĕn hīt	′fær ən haɪt
	FAHR uhn haı̑t § 50(34)	fär′ĕn hīt § 47(3)	′fɑr ən haɪt
fail	fayl	fāl	fel
failing	FAYL ing	fāl′ĭng § 50(14)	′fel ɪŋ
failure	FAYL yuhr	fāl′ûr	′fel jɚ; ES -jə(r)
fairy	FEHR i	fâr′ĭ	′fer ɪ, ′fær ɪ; ES ′fæær ɪ, E also ′feər ɪ
falchion	FAWL chuhn	fôl′chŭn	′fɔl tʃən
	FAWL shuhn	fôl′shŭn § 47(2)	′fɔl ʃən
falcon	FAWL kuhn	fôl′kŭn	′fɔl kən
	FAW kuhn	fô′kŭn	′fɔ kən
	Among hawk-hunters, esp.:	*Among hawk-hunters, esp.:*	*Among hawk-hunters, esp.:*
	FAW kuhn	fô′kŭn §§ 47(3) 51(6)	′fɔ kən
falconer	FAWL kuhn uhr	fôl′kŭn ĕr	′fɔl kən ɚ,
	FAW kuhn uhr	fô′kŭn ĕr § 47(1)	′fɔ kən ɚ; ES -ə(r)
falconry	FAWL kuhn ri	fôl′kŭn rĭ	′fɔl kən rɪ
	FAW kuhn ri	fô′kŭn rĭ § 47(1)	′fɔ kən rɪ
fallacious	fuh LAY shuhs	fă lā′shŭs	fə ′le ʃəs

fallacy	FAL uh si	făl′à sĭ	'fæl ə sɪ
fallen	FAWL uhn	fôl′ĕn § 9	'fɔl ən, fɔln
familiar	fuh MIL yuhr	fà mĭl′yẽr § 28(9)	fə 'mɪl jɚ; ES -jə(r)
familiarity	fuh *mil* i AR uh ti	fà mĭl′ĭ ăr′ĭ tĭ	fə ˌmɪl ɪ 'ær ə tɪ,
	fuh *mil* i AR i ti	fà mĭl′ĭ ăr′ĭ tĭ	-ɪ tɪ,
	fuh *mil* YAR uh ti	fà mĭl′yăr′ĭ tĭ §§ 47(2), 50(16)	-ˌmɪl 'jær ə-, -ˌmɪl jɪ 'ær-
familiarize	fuh MIL yuhr a͡iz § 50(34)	fà mĭl′yẽr īz	fə 'mɪl jər aɪz
family	FAM uh li	făm′ĭ lĭ	'fæm ə lɪ, -ɪ lɪ,
	FAM i li	făm′ĭ lĭ § 9	'fæm lɪ
fanatic	fuh NAT ik	fà năt′ĭk § 33(2)	fə 'næt ɪk
fancy	FAN si	făn′sĭ	'fæn sɪ
fantasy	FAN tuh si	făn′tà sĭ	'fæn tə sɪ
	FAN tuh zi	făn′tà zĭ	'fæn tə zɪ
farce	fahrs	färs	fɑrs; ES fɑːs; E also fɑːs
farcical	FAHR si kuhl	fär′sĭ kăl	'fɑr sɪ kəl, -kḷ; ES 'fɑː-
farewell (n., v.)	*fehr* WEL	fâr′wĕl′	ˌfɛr 'wɛl, ˌfær-; ES ˌfæə(r)-; E also ˌfeə(r)-
—— (adj.)	*fehr* WEL	fâr′wĕl′	ˌfɛr 'wɛl, 'fɛr ˌwɛl,
	FEHR *wel*	fâr′wĕl′ § 11	ˌfær-, 'fær-; ES ˌfæə(r)-, 'fæə(r)-; E also ˌfeə(r)-, 'feə(r)-
—— (interj.)	FEHR WEL	fâr′wĕl′ § 11	'fɛr ˌwɛl, 'fær-; ES 'fæə(r)-, E also 'feə(r)-
—— interj. also	*fehr* WEL	fâr′wĕl′	ˌfɛr 'wɛl, ˌfær-,
	FEHR *wel*	fâr′wĕl′ § 11	'fɛr ˌwɛl, 'fær-; ES ˌfæə(r)-, 'fæə(r)-, E also ˌfeə(r)-, 'feə(r)-
farrier	FAR i uhr	fär′ĭ ẽr	'fær ɪ ɚ; ES -ɪ ə(r)
farthest	FAHR t̶h̶est	fär′t̶h̶ĕst	'fɑr ðɛst, -ðɪst; ES 'fɑː-; E also 'fɑː-
	FAHR t̶h̶ist	fär′t̶h̶ĭst §§ 24(5), 50(9)	
fashion	FASH uhn	făsh′ŭn § 9	'fæʃ ən
fast (v.t., n.)	fast	fàst	fæst; E also fɑst,
	fahst	§§ 20(5), 47(2)	fɑst
fast (adj., adv.)	fast	fàst § 20(5)	fæst; E also fɑst,
	fahst		fɑst
fasten	FAS 'n	fàs′ 'n	'fæs n̩; E also
	FAHS 'n	§§ 1, 20(5)	'fɑs-, 'fɑs-

fastidious	fas TID i uhs	făs tĭd′ĭ ŭs § 28(9)	fæs ′tɪd ɪ əs
fathomless	FATH uhm les	făth′ŭm lĕs	′fæð əm lɛs
	FATH uhm lis	făth′ŭm lĭs §§ 24(5), 50(18)	′fæð əm lɪs
fatigue	fuh TEEG	fȧ tēg′	fə ′tig
fatuity	fuh TYOO uh ti	fȧ tū′ĭ tĭ	fə ′tju ə ɪ
	fuh TOO uh ti		fə ′tu ə ɪ
	fuh TYOO i ti	fȧ tŭ′ĭ tĭ	fə ′tju ɪ ɪ
	fuh TOO i ti	§§ 48(2), 50(32)	fə ′tu ɪ ɪ
fatuous	FACH ŏŏ uhs	făt′û ŭs	′fætʃ ʊ əs,
	FAT yŏŏ uhs	§ 50(25, 32)	′fæt jʊ-, -ju-
faucet	FAW set	fô′sĕt	′fɔ sɛt
	FAW sit	fô′sĭt §§ 24(5), 50(10)	′fɔ sɪt
fault	fawlt	fôlt § 1	fɔlt
favor, favour	FAY vuhr	fā′vẽr	′fe vɚ; ES -və(r)
fealty	FEE uhl ti	fē′ăl tĭ	′fi əl tɪ, ′fil tɪ
feature	FEE chuhr	fē′tûr	′fi tʃɚ, -tjɚ; ES
	FEE tyuhr	§ 50(31)	-tʃə(r), -tjə(r)
February	FEB rŏŏ er i	fĕb′rŏŏ ĕr′ĭ §§ 20(2), 24(9)	′fɛb rʊ ˌɛr ɪ,
	B., FEB roo uhr i	B., fĕb′rŏŏ ĕr ĭ §§ 13, 51(4)	B., ′fɛb ru ə rɪ
	Pop.:	Pop.:	Pop.:
	FEB yŏŏ er i	fĕb′yŏŏ ĕr′ĭ	′fɛb jʊ ˌɛr ɪ
	B., FEB yŏŏ uhr i	B., fĕb′yŏŏ ĕr i §§ 48(1)	B., ′fɛb ju ə rɪ
federal	FED uhr uhl	fĕd′ĕr ăl § 9	′fɛd ər əl, ′fɛd rəl
feign	fayn	fān	fen
feint	faynt	fānt	fent
felicitate	fi LIS uh tayt	fė lĭs′ĭ tāt	fɪ ′lɪs ə tet, -ɪ tet,
	fi LIS i tayt	fė lĭs′ĭ tāt § 50(2)	fə-
felicitous	fi LIS uh tuhs	fė lĭs′ĭ tŭs	fɪ ′lɪs ə təs, -ɪ təs,
	fi LIS i tuhs	fė lĭs′ĭ tŭs	fə-
felicity	fi LIS uh ti	fė lĭs′ĭ tĭ	fɪ ′lɪs ə tɪ, -ɪ tɪ, fə-
	fi LIS i ti	fė lĭs′ĭ tĭ § 50(16)	
fellow	FEL oh	fĕl′ō § 34(25)	′fɛl o, -ə
felon	FEL uhn	fĕl′ŭn	′fɛl ən
felony	FEL uh ni	fĕl′ŏ nĭ	′fɛl ə nɪ
femur	FEE muhr	fē′mẽr	′fi mɚ; ES -mə(r)
ferment (n.)	FUHR ment	fûr′mĕnt	′fɝ mɛnt; ES also ′fɜ-
—— (v.)	fuhr MENT	fẽr mĕnt′ §§ 12, 50(22)	fɚ ′mɛnt; ES fə-
ferret	FER et	fĕr′ĕt	′fɛr ɛt
	FER it	fĕr′ĭt § 24(5)	′fɛr ɪt

	SIMPLIFIED	DIACRITICAL	PHONETIC
ferrule ("*metal ring or cap*")	FER uhl FER ool FER ool	fĕr′ĭl fĕr′ool fĕr′ool § 47(1)	ˈfɛr əl ˈfɛr ul ˈfɛr ʊl
fertile	FUHR tuhl FUHR t'l FUHR til	fûr′tĭl fûr′t'l fûr′tĭl § 47(2)	ˈfɝ təl, -tl̩, -tɪl; *ES also* ˈfɝ-
	B., FUHR tail § 50(34)	*B.,* fûr′tīl §§ 28(5), 51(4)	*B.,* ˈfɝ taɪl; *ES also* ˈfɝ-
ferule ("*rod*")	FER ool FER il	fer′ool fĕr′ĭl § 47(3)	ˈfɛr ul, -ɪl, -əl, ˈfɛr uːl, ˈfɛr jul
festoon	fes TOON	fĕs toon′	fɛs ˈtun
fetid	FET id FEE tid	fĕt′ĭd fē′tĭd § 47(2)	ˈfɛt ɪd ˈfi tɪd
fetish, fetich	FEE tish FET ish	fē′tĭsh fĕt′ĭsh § 47(3)	ˈfi tɪʃ ˈfɛt ɪʃ
feud ("*strife*")	fyood	fūd § 48(2)	fjud
feudatory	FYOO duh *toh* ri FYOO duh *taw* ri	fū′dá tō′rĭ §§ 34(3), 48(2), 50(32)	ˈfju də ˌto rɪ ˈfju də ˌtɔ rɪ
	B., FYOO duh tuhr i	*B.,* fū′dá tēr ĭ § 51(4)	*B.,* ˈfju də tə rɪ
few	fyoo	fū § 48(2)	fju
fiancé (n. masc.), **fiancée** (n. fem.)	*fee* ahn SAY fi AHN say *F., fee ahɴ* SAY	fē′än sā′ fê än′sā *F.,* fē′äɴ′sā′	ˌfi ɑn ˈse, -ən- fɪ ˈɑn se, fi- *F.,* fjã ˈse
fiat	FAI at FAI uht § 50(34)	fī′ăt fī′ăt	ˈfaɪ æt ˈfaɪ ət
fidelity	fai DEL uh ti fai DEL i ti fi DEL uh ti fi DEL i ti	fī dĕl′ĭ tĭ fī dĕl′ĭ tĭ fĭ dĕl′ĭ tĭ fĭ dĕl′ĭ tĭ	faɪ ˈdɛl ə tɪ faɪ ˈdɛl ɪ tɪ fɪ ˈdɛl ə tɪ fɪ ˈdɛl ɪ tɪ
fidget	FIJ et FIJ it	fĭj′ĕt fĭj′ĭt § 24(5)	ˈfɪdʒ ɛt ˈfɪdʒ ɪt
fief	feef	fēf	fif
fiendish	FEEND ish	fēnd′ĭsh	ˈfind ɪʃ, ˈfin dɪʃ
fiery	FAI ri FAI uhr i § 50(34)	fī′rĭ fī′ēr ĭ § 47(2)	ˈfaɪ rɪ ˈfaɪ ər ɪ
fifth	fifth	fĭfth	fɪfθ
fifths	fifths	fĭfths §§ 39(5), 48(3), 50(6)	fɪfθs
figure	FIG yuhr	fĭg′ûr	ˈfɪg jɚ, ˈfɪg ɚ; *ES* -jə(r), -ə(r)
filament (n.)	FIL uh muhnt	fĭl′á mĕnt	ˈfɪl ə mənt
filbert	FIL buhrt	fĭl′bêrt	ˈfɪl bɚt; *ES* -bət
filial	FIL i uhl FIL yuhl	fĭl′ĭ ăl fĭl′yăl §§ 28(9), 47(2)	ˈfɪl ɪ əl ˈfɪl jəl

	SIMPLIFIED	DIACRITICAL	PHONETIC
fillet	FIL et FIL it *In cookery, often:* FIL ay FIL i	fĭl′ĕt fĭl′ĭt § 24(5) *In cookery, often:* fĭl′ā fĭl′ĭ	'fɪl ɛt 'fɪl ɪt *In cookery, often:* 'fɪl e 'fɪl ɪ
fillip	FIL uhp FIL ip	fĭl′ŭp fĭl′ĭp	'fɪl əp 'fɪl ɪp
film	film	fĭlm	fɪlm
finale	fi NAH lay fi NAH li	fĕ nä′lā fĕ nä′lĕ	fɪ 'nɑ le, -lɪ; *It.,* fi 'nɑː le
finality	fai NAL uh ti fai NAL i ti § 50(34)	fī năl′ĭ tĭ fī năl′ĭ tĭ § 50(16)	faɪ 'næl ə tɪ faɪ 'næl ɪ tɪ
finally	FAI nuhl i	fī′năl ĭ § 31(3)	'faɪ nəl ɪ, -nḷ ɪ
finance (n.)	fi NANS fai NANS FAI nans § 50(34)	fĭ năns′ fī năns′ fī′năns §§ 11, 12, 47(1)	fɪ 'næns, faɪ-, fə-. 'faɪ næns
—— (v.t.)	fi NANS fai NANS	fĭ năns′ fī năns′	fɪ 'næns, faɪ-, fə-
financial	fi NAN shuhl fai NAN shuhl	fĭ năn′shăl fī năn′shăl	fɪ 'næn ʃəl, faɪ-, fə-
financially	fi NAN shuhl i fai NAN shuhl i	fĭ năn′shăl lĭ fī năn′shăl lĭ § 50(20)	fɪ 'næn ʃəl ɪ, faɪ-, fə-
financier (n., v.)	*fin* uhn SIER *fin* uhn SIR *fin* uhn SEER *fai* nan SIER *fai* nan SIR *fai* nan SEER	fĭn′ăn sēr′ § 24(2) fī′năn sēr′ fī′năn sēr′	ˌfɪn ən 'sɪər, -'sɪr, -'sir, ˌfaɪ næn 'sɪər, -'sɪr, -'sir; *ES* -'sɪə(r)
—— (n. – *also*)	fi NAN si uhr	fĭ năn′sĭ ĕr § 47(3)	fɪ 'næn sɪ ɚ; *ES* -sɪ ə(r)
finger	FING guhr	fĭng′gĕr	'fɪŋ gɚ; *ES* -gə(r)
finite	FAI nait § 50(34)	fī′nīt	'faɪ naɪt
fiord, fjord	fyawrd fyohrd	fyôrd fyōrd	fjɔrd, fjord; *ES* fjɔəd, *E also* fjɔəd
first	*fuhrst*	fûrst § 40(6)	fɜst; *ES also* fɝst
first-class	FUHRST KLAS FUHRST KLAHS	fûrst′klås′ §§ 11, 20(5)	'fɜst 'klæs; *ES* *also* 'fɝst-, -'klas, -'klɑs
first-rate (adj., adv.)	FUHRST RAYT	fûrst′rāt′ § 11	'fɜst 'ret; *ES also* 'fɝst-
—— (n.)	FUHRST *rayt*	fûrst′rāt′	'fɜst ˌret; *ES also* 'fɝst-
fish	fish	fĭsh	fɪʃ

	SIMPLIFIED	DIACRITICAL	PHONETIC
fissure	FISH uhr	fĭsh′ẽr	'fɪʃ ɚ; ES -ə(r)
fist	fist	fĭst	fɪst
fists	fists	fĭsts §§ 48(3), 50(6)	fɪsts
fistula	FIS chŏŏ luh FIS tyŏŏ luh	fĭs′tṳ là § 50(33)	'fɪs tʃʊ lə, -tjʊ-, tju-
five	faiv § 50(34)	fīv	faɪv
fixture	FIKS chuhr FIKS tyuhr	fĭks′tûr § 50(31)	'fɪks tʃɚ, -tjɚ; ES -tʃə(r), -tjə(r)
fjord	See *fiord*.		
flaccid	FLAK sid	flăk′sĭd	'flæk sɪd
flaccidity	flak SID uh ti flak SID i ti	flăk sĭd′ĭ tĭ flăk sĭd′ĭ tĭ	flæk 'sɪd ə tɪ flæk 'sɪd ɪ tɪ
flag	flag	flăg	flæg
flagitious	fluh JISH uhs	flà jĭsh′ŭs	flə 'dʒɪʃ əs
flagrant	FLAY gruhnt	flā′grănt	'fle grənt
flamboyant	flam BOI uhnt	flăm boi′ănt	flæm 'bɔɪ ənt
flamen	FLAY men	flā′mĕn	'fle mɛn
flamingo	fluh MING goh	flà mĭng′gō	flə 'mɪŋ go
flange	flanj	flănj § 25(4)	flændʒ
flannel	FLAN uhl FLAN 'l	flăn′ĕl flăn′ 'l § 31(3)	'flæn əl, 'flæn l̩
flask	flask flahsk	flàsk § 20(5)	flæsk; E also flask, flɑsk
flaunt	flawnt flahnt	flônt flänt § 47(3)	flɔnt flɑnt
fledge	flej	flĕj	flɛdʒ
flew	floo	flōō § 40(4), 48(2)	flu
flimsy	FLIM zi	flĭm′zĭ	'flɪm zɪ
flood	*fluhd*	flŭd § 40(6)	flʌd
floor	flohr flawr	flōr § 34(3, 20)	flor, flɔr; ES floə(r), E also flɔə(r)
floral	FLO ruhl FLAW ruhl	flō′răl § 34(3)	'flo rəl 'flɔ rəl
Florentine	FLOR uhn teen FLAWR uhn teen FLOR uhn tain FLAWR uhn tain FLOR uhn tin FLAWR uhn tin	flŏr′ĕn tēn flŏr′ĕn tēn flŏr′ĕn tīn flŏr′ĕn tīn flŏr′ĕn tĭn flŏr′ĕn tĭn §§ 34 (5, 7), 47(3)	'flɑr ən tin, 'flɔr-, 'flɒr- 'flɑr ən taɪn, 'flɔr-, 'flɒr- 'flɑr ən tɪn, 'flɔr-, 'flɒr-
florid	FLOR id FLAWR id	flŏr′ĭd flŏr′ĭd § 34(5, 7)	'flɑr ɪd, 'flɔr-, 'flɒr-
florist	FLOH rist FLAW rist FLOR ist	flō′rĭst §§ 34(3), 47(2) flŏr′ĭst	'flo rɪst 'flɔ rɪst 'flɑr ɪst, 'flɒr-

flotilla	floh TIL uh	flŏ tĭl′*a*	flo ˈtɪl ə
flour	flowr	flour § 28(11)	flaʊr; *ES* flaʊə(r)
flourish	FLUHR ish	flûr′ĭsh § 40(7)	ˈflɝ ɪʃ; *ES also* ˈflɜ, ˈflʌ-
floweret	FLOW uhr et FLOW uhr it § 50(34)	flou′ẽr ĕt flou′ẽr ĭt § 24(5)	ˈflaʊ ər ɛt ˈflaʊ ər ɪt, ˈflaʊ rɪt
fluctuate	FLUHK chŏŏ ayt FLUHK tyŏŏ ayt	flŭk′tŭ āt § 50(2, 33)	ˈflʌk tʃʊ et ˈflʌk tjʊ et
flue	floo	flōō §§ 40(4), 48(2)	flu
fluency	FLOO uhn si	flōō′ĕn sĭ §§ 40(4), 48(2)	ˈflu ən sɪ
fluent	FLOO uhnt	flōō′ĕnt §§ 40(4), 48(2)	ˈflu ənt
fluid	FLOO id	flōō′ĭd §§ 40(4), 48(2)	ˈflu ɪd
flute	floot	flōōt §§ 40(4), 48(2)	flut
flutist	FLOOT ist	flōō′ĭst §§ 40(4), 48(2)	ˈflut ɪst
fluvial	FLOO vi uhl	flōō′vĭ ŭl §§ 28(9), 40(4), 48(2)	ˈflu vɪ əl
foetus, fetus	FEE tuhs	fē′tŭs	ˈfi təs
fogy	FOH gi	fō′gĭ	ˈfo gɪ
foible	FOI b'l	foi′b'l	ˈfɔɪ bl̩
foliage	FOH li ij	fō′lĭ ĭj § 50(1)	ˈfo lɪ ɪdʒ
foliate (v.)	FOH li ayt	fō′lĭ āt	ˈfo lɪ et
—— (adj.)	FOH li it FOH li ayt	fō′lĭ ăt § 20(8, 9)	ˈfo lɪ ɪt ˈfo lɪ et
folio	FOH li oh FOHL yoh	fō′lĭ ō fōl′yō §§ 28(9), 47(2)	ˈfo lɪ o ˈfol jo
folk	fohk	fōk § 31(2)	fok
follicle	FOL i k'l	fŏl′ĭ k'l	ˈfɑl ɪ kl̩; *ES also* ˈfɒl-
foment (v.t.)	foh MENT	fŏ mĕnt′	fo ˈmɛnt
—— (n.)	FOH ment	fō′mĕnt §§ 12, 50(22)	ˈfo mɛnt
food	food	fōōd	fud
foot	fŏŏt	fŏŏt § 34(22)	fʊt
forage	FOR ij FAWR ij	fŏr′ĭj fôr′ĭj §§ 34(5, 7), 50(1)	ˈfɑr ɪdʒ, ˈfɔr-, ˈfɒr-
foray	FOR ay FAWR ay	fŏr′ā fôr′ā §§ 34(5, 7), 47(2)	ˈfɑr e, ˈfɔr -, ˈfɒr-

	SIMPLIFIED	DIACRITICAL	PHONETIC
forbade, forbad (p.t. of *forbid*)	fuhr BAD fawr BAD	fŏr băd′ fôr băd′ § 34(13)	fɚ 'bæd, fɔr-; *ES* fə-, fɔə-
forbear ("*hold back*")	fawr BEHR	fôr bâr′ § 11	fɔr 'bɛr, -'bær; *ES* fɔə 'bæə(r), *E* *also* -'bɛə(r)
forbear (var. of "*forebear*," meaning "*ancestor*")	FAWR behr fawr BEHR	fôr′bâr fôr bâr′	'fɔr bɛr, -bær; *ES* 'fɔə bæə(r), *E* *also* -bɛə(r) fɔr 'bɛr, -'bær; *ES* fɔə 'bæə(r) *E* *also* -'bɛə(r)
forceps	FAWR suhps FAWR seps *Among doctors,* *often:* FAWR suhps	fôr′sĕps fôr′sĕps *Among doctors,* *often:* fôr′sĕps § 51(6)	'fɔr səps, -sɛps; *ES* 'fɔə- *Among doctors,* *often:* 'fɔr səps; *ES* 'fɔə-
forcible	FOHR suh b'l FAWR suh b'l FOHR si b'l FAWR si b'l	fōr′sĭ b'l fôr′sĭ b'l § 34(3)	'fɔr sə b], 'fɔr-, -sɪ-; *ES* 'fɔə-, *E* *also* 'fɔə-
forebear ("*ancestor*")	FOHR behr FAWR behr	fōr′bâr § 34(3)	'fɔr bɛr, 'fɔr-, -bær; *ES* 'fɔə bæə(r), *E* *also* 'fɔə bɛə(r), 'fɔə-
forecast (v.)	fohr KAST fawr KAHST FOHR *kast* FAWR *kahst*	fōr kàst′ fôr′kàst′ §§ 12, 20(5), 34(3)	fɔr 'kæst, fɔr-, 'fɔr ˌkæst, 'fɔr-; *ES* fɔə-, 'fɔə-; *E also* fɔə-, 'fɔə-, -'kast, -'kast, -ˌkast, -ˌkast
—— (n.)	FOHR *kast* FAWR *kahst*	fôr′kàst′ §§ 11, 20(5), 34(3)	'fɔr ˌkæst, 'fɔr-; *ES* 'fɔə-, *E also* 'fɔə-, -ˌkast, -ˌkast
forecastle	FOHK s'l *Also, esp. as a* *literary word:* FOHR *kas* 'l FAWR *kas* 'l FOHR *kahs* 'l FAWR *kahs* 'l	fōk′s'l *Also, esp. as a* *literary word:* fôr′kàs′ 'l §§ 1, 34(5), 51(11)	'fok s] *Also, esp. as a* *literary word:* 'fɔr ˌkæs], 'fɔr-; *ES* 'fɔə-, *E also* 'fɔə-, -ˌkas-, -ˌkas-
foreclose	fohr KLOHZ fawr KLOHZ	fōr klōz′ § 34(5)	fɔr 'kloz, fɔr-; *ES* fɔə-, *E also* fɔə-
forefather	FOHR *fah* thuhr FAWR *fah* thuhr	fōr′fä′thēr §§ 34(5), 47(2)	'fɔr ˌfɑ ðɚ, 'fɔr-; *ES* 'fɔə ˌfɑ ðə(r), *E also* 'fɔə-, -ˌfɑ-

	SIMPLIFIED	DIACRITICAL	PHONETIC
forehead	FOR ed FOR id FAWR id	fŏr′ĕd fŏr′ĭd fôr′ĭd §§ 27(1), 34(7), 47(3)	'fɑr ɛd, 'fɒr-, -ɪd, 'fɔr ɪd, -əd, 'for hɛd, 'fɔr-
foreign	FOR in FAWR in	fŏr′ĭn fôr′ĭn § 34(7)	'fɑr ɪn, 'fɔr-, 'fɒr-, -ən
forensic	fuh REN sik	fŏ rĕn′sĭk	fə 'rɛn sɪk, fo-
forest	FOR est FOR ist FAWR ist	fŏr′ĕst fŏr′ĭst fôr′ĭst §§ 24(5), 34(7)	'fɑr ɛst, 'fɔr-, 'fɒr-, -ɪst, -əst

forfeiture	FAWR fuh chuhr
	FAWR fuh tyuhr
	FAWR fi chuhr
	FAWR fi tyuhr
		fôr′fĭ̆ tūr
		
		fôr′fĭ tūr
		§ 50(31)
			'fɔr fə tʃɚ, -tjɚ,
			  -fɪ-; ES -tʃə(r),
			  -tjə(r)

formaldehyde	fawr MAL di haïd	fôr măl′dĕ̇ hīd	fɔr 'mæl dɪ haɪd; ES fəə 'mæl-

formalin,
  Formalin
	FAWR muh lin	fôr′mȧ lĭn	'fɔr mə lɪn; ES
			  'fɔə-

former	FAWR muhr	fôr′mēr	'fɔr mɚ; ES 'fɔə-

formidable	FAWR muh duh
	  b'l
	FAWR mi duh b'l
		fôr′mĭ̆ dȧ b'l
		
		fôr′mĭ dȧ b'l
			'fɔr mə də bḷ, -mɪ-;
			  ES 'fɔə-

formulary	FAWR myōō ler i
	
	B., FAWR myōō
	  luhr i
		fôr′mū lĕr′ĭ
		  §§ 13, 20(2),
		  24(9), 51(4)
		B., fôr′mū lĕr ĭ
			'fɔr mjʊ ˌlɛr ɪ,
			  -mjə-, -mju-;
			  ES 'fɔə-
			B., fɔr mjʊ lə rɪ;
			  ES fɔə-

forsooth	fuhr SOOTH fawr SOOTH	fŏr sōōth′ fôr sōōth′ § 34(13)	fɚ 'suθ; ES fə- fɔr 'suθ; ES fɔə-
fort	fohrt fawrt	fōrt §§ 34(3), 47(1)	fort fɔrt; ES foət, E also foət

forte
  ("strong point")
	fohrt
	fawrt
		fōrt
		§ 34(3)
			fort, fɔrt; ES foət,
			  E also foət

forte (Music)	FAWR tay	fôr′tā	'fɔr te, -tɪ; ES 'fɔə-

forth	fohrth
	fawrth
		fōrth
		§34(3)
			forθ, fɔrθ; ES
			  foəθ, E also
			  foəθ

forthwith	fohrth WITH fawrth WITH fohrth WITH fawrth WITH	fōrth′wĭth′ fōrth′wĭth′ §§ 39(5), 47(3)	ˌforθ 'wɪð, ˌfɔrθ-, -'wɪθ; ES ˌfoəθ-, E also ˌfɔəθ-
fortnight	FAWRT naït FAWRT nit	fôrt′nīt fôr′nĭt § 47(3)	'fɔrt naɪt, -nɪt; also 'fort-; ES 'fɔət-; also 'foət-

fortnightly	FAWRT naı͡t li § 50(34)	fôrt′nīt lĭ § 50(20)	'fɔrt naıt lı; *also* 'fort-; *ES* 'fɔət-; *also* 'foət-
fortuitous	fawr TYOO uh tuhs fawr TOO uh tuhs fawr TYOO i tuhs fawr TOO i tuhs	fôr tū′ĭ tŭs fôr tū′ĭ tŭs § 50(25, 32)	fɔr 'tju ə təs, -'tu-, -ı təs; *ES* fɔə-
fortune	FAWR chuhn FAWR tyuhn	fôr′tŭn § 50(33)	'fɔr tʃən, -tjən; *ES* 'fɔə-
forty-four	FAWR ti FOHR FAWR ti FAWR	fôr′tĭ–fōr′ § 34(3)	'fɔr tı–'for, –'fɔr; *ES* 'fɔə tı– 'foə(r), *E also* –'fɔə(r)
forum	FOH ruhm FAW ruhm	fō′rŭm § 34(3)	'fo rəm 'fɔ rəm
forward	FAWR wuhrd	fôr′wĕrd § 42(3)	'fɔr wɚd; *ES* 'fɔə wəd
	Much less freq.: FAWR uhrd	*Much less freq.:* fôr′ērd § 51(11)	*Much less freq.:* 'fɔr ɚd; *ES* 'fɔr əd
fossil	FOS il FOS 'l	fŏs′ĭl fŏs′ 'l	'fɑs ıl, 'fɒs-, -ļ
foster	FAWS tuhr FOS tuhr	fŏs′tĕr § 34(7)	'fɔs tɚ, 'fɒs-, 'fas-; *ES* -tə(r)
fought	fawt	fôt	fɔt
foulard	foo LAHRD	foō lärd′	fu 'lɑrd; *ES* -'lɑːd, *E also* -'lɑːd
found	fownd	found	faʊnd
foundry	FOWN dri	foun′drĭ	'faʊn drı
fountain	FOWN tin FOWN tuhn	foun′tĭn foun′tĕn	'faʊn tın 'faʊn tən, -tņ
four	fohr fawr	fōr § 34(5)	for fɔr; *ES* foə(r), *E* *also* fɔə(r)
fowl	fowl	foul	faʊl
foyer (n. – "*lobby;* *anteroom;* *hearth; gather-* *ing place; fur-* *nace crucible*")	FOI uhr FOI ay fwah YAY	foi′ĕr foi′ā fwä yā′ *F.,* fwå′yā′	'fɔı ɚ, 'fɔı e, fwa 'je; *ES* 'fɔı ə(r); *F.,* fwa 'je
fracas	FRAY kuhs	frā′kȧs § 47(2)	'fre kəs
fracture	FRAK chuhr FRAK tyuhr	frăk′tûr § 50(31)	'fræk tʃɚ, -tjɚ; *ES* -tʃə(r), -tjə(r)
fragile	FRAJ uhl FRAJ il	frăj′ĭl frăj′ĭl § 50(13)	'frædʒ əl 'frædʒ ıl

fragment (n.)	FRAG muhnt	frăg′mĕnt § 50(22)	′fræg mənt
fragmental	frag MEN tuhl frag MEN t'l	frăg mĕn′tăl frăg mĕn′t'l § 47(3)	fræg ′mɛn təl, tl̩, ′fræg mən-
ragmentary	FRAG muhn ter i B., FRAG muhn tuhr i	frăg′mĕn tĕr′ĭ B., frăg′mĕn tēr ĭ §§ 13, 20(2), 24(9), 51(4)	′fræg mən ˌtɛr ɪ B., ′fræg mən tər ɪ
fragrance	FRAY gruhns	frā′grăns	′fre grəns
France	frans frahns	fráns § 20(5)	fræns; E also frans, frɑns
franchise	FRAN chaiz FRAN chiz § 50(34)	frăn′chīz frăn′chĭz § 47(3)	′fræn tʃaɪz ′fræn tʃɪz
frankincense	FRANGK in sens	frăngk′ĭn sĕns	′fræŋk ɪn sɛns
fraternize	FRAT uhr naiz	frăt′ĕr nīz § 47(3)	′fræt ɚ naɪz, ′frɛt-; ES ˌfræt ə-
Frau	frow	frou	frau
fraudulent	FRAWJ o͞o luhnt FRAWJ uh luhnt FRAWD yo͞o luhnt	frôd û lĕnt §§ 40(11), 50(33)	′frɔdʒ ʊ lənt, ′frɔdʒ ə-, ′frɔd jʊ-, -jə-
frequent (adj.) —— (v.)	FREE kwuhnt fri KWENT	frē′kwĕnt § 12 frĕ kwĕnt′	′fri kwənt frɪ ′kwɛnt
frequented	fri KWENT ed fri KWENT id	frĕ kwĕnt′ĕd frĕ kwĕnt′ĭd § 24(5)	frɪ ′kwɛnt ɛd frɪ ′kwɛnt ɪd
fresco	FRES koh	frĕs′kō	′frɛs ko
friable	FRAI uh b'l § 50(34)	frī′à b'l	′fraɪ ə bl̩
fricassee	*frik* uh SEE	frĭk′à sē′ § 11	ˌfrɪk ə ′si
frieze	freez	frēz § 51(7)	friz
frigid	FRIJ id	frĭj′ĭd	′frɪdʒ ɪd
frivolity	fri VOL uh ti fri VOL i ti	frĭ vŏl′ŭ tĭ frĭ vŏl′ĭ tĭ § 50(16)	frɪ ′val ə tɪ, -ɪ tɪ; ES also -′vɒl-
frog	frog frawg	frŏg frôg § 34(7)	frag, frɒg, frɔg
from	from *Unstressed:* fruhm	frŏm *Unstressed:* frŭm § 16	fram, frɒm, frʌm *Unstressed:* frəm
frond	frond	frŏnd	frand, frɒnd
front	*fruhnt*	frŭnt §§ 1, 40(6)	frʌnt
frontal	FRUHN tuhl FRUHN t'l FRON tuhl FRON t'l	frŭn′tăl frŭn′t'l frŏn′tăl frŏn′t'l	′frʌn təl, -tl̩ ′fran təl, ′frɒn-, -tl̩

frontier	fruhn TĬER	frŭn tẹ̄r′	frʌn ˈtɪər, -ˈtɪr,
	fruhn TIR	§ 24(2)	-ˈtir; *ES*
	fruhn TEER	frŭn tēr′	-ˈtɪə(r)
	FRON tĭer	frŏn′tẹ̄r	ˈfrɑn tɪər, -tɪr,
	FRON tir		-tir, ˈfrɒn-; *ES*
	FRON teer	frŏn′tēr	-tɪə(r)
	fron TĬER	frŏn tẹ̄r′	frɑn ˈtɪər, -ˈtɪr,
	fron TIR		-ˈtir, frʌn-; *ES*
	fron TEER	frŏn tēr′ § 47(3)	-ˈtɪə(r)
frost	frawst	frȯst	frɔst
	frost	§§ 34(7), 47(2)	frɒst
froth	frawth	frȯth	frɔθ
	froth	§§ 34(7), 47(2)	frɒθ
frothy	FRAWTH i	frȯth′ĭ	ˈfrɔθ ɪ
	FROTH i	§ 34(7)	ˈfrɒθ ɪ
froward	FROH wuhrd	frō′wẽrd	ˈfro wɚd, ˈfro ɚd;
	FROH uhrd	frō′ẽrd	*ES* -wəd, -əd
fruition	froo ISH uhn	frōō ĭsh′ŭn	fru ˈɪʃ ən
frustrate (v.t.)	FRUHS trayt	frŭs′trāt	ˈfrʌs tret
fuchsia, Fuchsia	FYOO shuh	fū′shȧ	ˈfju ʃə
	FYOO shi uh	fū′shĭ ȧ §§ 22(9), 47(2)	ˈfju ʃɪ ə
	As a generic name (cap.):	*As a generic name (cap.):*	*As a generic name (cap.):*
	FŎŎK si uh	fŏŏk′sĭ ȧ § 51(11)	ˈfʊk sɪ ə
fuel	FYOO uhl	fū′ĕl	ˈfju əl
	FYOO il	fū′ĭl	ˈfju ɪl
fugitive	FYOO juh tiv	fū′jĕ tĭv	ˈfju dʒə tɪv
	FYOO ji tiv	fū′jĭ tĭv § 50(17)	ˈfju dʒɪ tɪv
fugue	fyoog	fūg	fjug
fulcrum	FUHL kruhm	fŭl′krŭm	ˈfʌl krəm
full	fŏŏl	fŏŏl	fʊl
fulminate	FUHL muh nayt	fŭl′mĕ nāt	ˈfʌl mə net
	FUHL mi nayt	fŭl′mĭ nāt	ˈfʌl mɪ net
fulsome	FŎŎL suhm	fŏŏl′sŭm	ˈfʊl səm
	FUHL suhm	fŭl′sŭm § 47(1)	ˈfʌl səm
fumigate	FYOO muh gayt	fū′mĕ gāt	ˈfju mə get
	FYOO mi gayt	fū′mĭ gāt § 48(2)	ˈfju mɪ get
fundamental	*fuhn* duh MEN tuhl	fŭn′dȧ mĕn′tăl	ˌfʌn də ˈmɛn təl
	fuhn duh MEN t'l	fŭn′dȧ mĕn′t'l	ˌfʌn də ˈmɛn tl̩
funeral	FYOO nuhr uhl	fū′nẽr ăl §§ 48(2), 50(32)	ˈfju nər əl
funereal	fyoo NĬER i uhl	fū nẹ̄r′ĕ ăl	fju ˈnɪər ɪ əl,
	fyoo NIR i uhl	§§ 24(2), 48(2)	-ˈnɪr-, -ˈnir-; *ES*
	fyoo NEER i uhl	fū nēr′ĕ ăl	-ˈnɪər-
fungi (n. pl.)	FUHN jai § 50(34)	fŭn′jī	ˈfʌn dʒaɪ

	SIMPLIFIED	DIACRITICAL	PHONETIC
fungicide	FUHN ji said § 50(34)	fŭn′jĭ sīd	'fʌn dʒɪ saɪd, -dʒə-
fungus (n. sing.)	FUHNG guhs	fŭng′gŭs	'fʌŋ gəs
furbelow	FUHR bi loh FUHR buh loh	fûr′bĕ lō fûr′bĕ lō	'fɝ bɪ lo, -bə-, -bḷo; ES also 'fɝ-
furbish	FUHR bish	fûr′bĭsh	'fɝ bɪʃ; ES also 'fɝ-
furious	FYOO ri uhs FYOO ri uhs	fū′rĭ ŭs §§ 40(4), 48(2), 50(25)	'fjʊ rɪ əs, 'fju-
fury	FYOO ri FYOO ri	fū′rĭ §§ 34(21), 40(4), 48(2)	'fjʊ rɪ, 'fju-
furze	*fuhrz*	fûrz § 40(6)	fɝz; ES also fɜz
fusillade	*fyoo* zuh LAYD *fyoo* zi LAYD	fū′zŭ lād′ fū′zĭ lād′ § 48(2)	ˌfju zə 'led, -zɪ-, -zḷ 'ed
fustian	FUHS chuhn FUHST yuhn	fŭs′chăn fŭst′yăn	'fʌs tʃən 'fʌst jən
futile	FYOO til FYOO t'l	fū′tĭl fū′t'l §§ 31(3), 47(2), 48(2)	'fju tɪl 'fju tḷ
future	FYOO chuhr FYOO tyuhr	fū′tûr §§ 48(2), 50(31, 32)	'fju tʃɚ, -tjɚ; ES -tʃə(r), -tjə(r)
futurism	FYOO chuhr iz'm FYOO chuhr iz uhm FYOO tyuhr iz'm	fū′tûr ĭz'm §§ 48(2), 50(31, 32)	'fju tʃɚ ɪzm̩, -tjɚ-, -ɪz əm
futurist	FYOO chuhr ist FYOO tyuhr ist	fū′tûr ĭst §§ 48(2), 50(33)	'fju tʃɚ ɪst, -tjə-; ES -tʃə rɪst, -tjə-
futurity	fyoo TYOO ruh ti fyoo TYOO ruh ti fyoo TYOO ri ti fyoo TYOO ri ti	fŭ tū′rŭ tĭ fŭ tū′rĭ tĭ §§ 34(21), 48(2), 50(16)	fju 'tjʊ rə tɪ, fju 'tʊ rə tɪ fju 'tjʊ rɪ tɪ, fju 'tʊ rɪ tɪ

G

gabardine, gaberdine	gab uhr DEEN GAB uhr deen	găb′ēr dēn′ găb′ēr dēn § 47(1)	ˌgæb ɚ 'din, 'gæb ɚ din; ES -ə 'din, -ə din

	SIMPLIFIED	DIACRITICAL	PHONETIC
gala	GAY luh GAH luh GAL uh	gā′lá gä′lá găl′á § 47(1)	ˈge lə ˈgɑ lə ˈgæl ə
Galahad	GAL uh had	găl′á hăd	ˈgæl ə hæd
galaxy	GAL uhk si	găl′ăk sĭ	ˈgæl ək sɪ
Galileo	gal i LEE oh It., gah lee LAY oh	găl′ĭ lē′ŏ It., gä′lē lā′ŏ	ˌgæl ɪ ˈli o, -ə ˈli o; It., ˌgɑ li ˈlɛːo
gallant (adj.)	GAL uhnt	găl′ănt § 47(2)	ˈgæl ənt
—— "attentive or courteous to women; amorous"	guh LANT GAL uhnt	gă lănt′ găl′ănt	gə ˈlænt ˈgæl ənt
—— (n.)	GAL uhnt guh LANT	găl′ănt gă lănt′	ˈgæl ənt gə ˈlænt
—— (v.)	guh LANT	gă lănt′ § 12	gə ˈlænt
gallery	GAL uhr i	găl′ĕr ĭ	ˈgæl ər ɪ
galley	GAL i	găl′ĭ	ˈgæl ɪ
Gallic	GAL ik	găl′ĭk § 47(2)	ˈgæl ɪk
gallon	GAL uhn	găl′ăn	ˈgæl ən
gallows	GAL ohz Occas.: GAL uhs	găl′ōz Occas.: găl′ŭs §§ 34(25), 47(3)	ˈgæl oz Occas.: ˈgæl əs
gamut	GAM uht	găm′ŭt	ˈgæm ət
Ganges	GAN jeez	găn′jēz	ˈgæn dʒiz
gaol	jayl	jāl	dʒel
gape	gayp gap gahp	gāp găp gäp § 47(3)	gep gæp gɑp
garage	guh RAHZH Loosely: guh RAHJ B., GAR ahzh GAR ij	gá räzh′ Loosely: gá räj′ § 51(2) B., găr′äzh găr′ĭj §§ 47(1), 51(4)	gə ˈrɑʒ, gɑ- Loosely: gə ˈrɑdʒ B., ˈgær ɑʒ ˈgær ɪdʒ
garbage	GAHR bij	gär′bĭj	ˈgɑr bɪdʒ; ES ˈgɑ:-, E also ˈgɑ:-
garden	GAHR d'n	gär′d'n §§ 24(14), 47(2)	ˈgɑr dn̩; ES ˈgɑ:-, E also ˈgɑ:-
garish	GEHR ish	gâr′ĭsh	ˈger ɪʃ, ˈgær-; ES also ˈgeər-
garniture	GAHR ni chuhr GAHR ni tyuhr	gär′nĭ tŭr § 50(31)	ˈgɑr nɪ tʃɚ; -tjɚ; ES ˈgɑ:-, -tʃə(r), -tjə(r), E also ˈgɑ:-

	SIMPLIFIED	DIACRITICAL	PHONETIC
garrison	GAR uh suhn GAR i suhn GAR uh s'n	găr′ĭ sŭn găr′ĭ sŭn găr′ĭ s'n § 47(2)	'gær ə sən 'gær ɪ sən 'gær ə sn̩
garrulity	guh ROO luh ti guh ROO li ti	gă rōō′lĭ tĭ gă rōō′lĭ tĭ § 40(4)	gə 'ru lə tɪ gə 'ru lɪ tɪ
garrulous	GAR yŏŏ luhs GAR ŏŏ luhs	găr′ŭ lŭs găr′ŏŏ lŭs § 40(11)	'gær jʊ ləs, -jə-, -ju-, 'gær ʊ ləs, 'gær ə-
gaseous	GAS i uhs	găs′ĕ ŭs §§ 24(15), 47(2)	'gæs ɪ əs, 'gæs jəs

gasoline,
   gasolene
	GAS uh leen
	gas uh LEEN
		găs′ŏ lēn
		găs′ŏ lēn′
		§§ 11, 47(3)
			'gæs ə lin, -lɪn,
			   'gæs ḷ-,
			ˌgæs ə 'lin, ˌgæs ḷ-

gasp	gasp gahsp	gȧsp § 20(5)	gæsp; *E also* gasp, gɑsp
gasping	GASP ing GAHSP ing	gȧsp′ing §§ 20(5), 50(14)	'gæsp ɪŋ; *E also* 'gasp-, 'gɑsp-
gather	GATH uhr	gath′ẽr	'gæð ɚ; *ES* -ə(r)
gauge	gayj	gāj	gedʒ
gaunt (adj.– "*lean; barren*")	gawnt gahnt	gônt gänt §§ 34(4), 47(3)	gɔnt gɑnt
gauntlet	GAWNT let GAWNT lit GAHNT let GAHNT lit	gônt′lĕt gônt′lĭt gänt′lĕt gänt′lĭt §§ 24(5), 47(3)	'gɔnt let 'gɔnt lɪt 'gɑnt let 'gɑnt lɪt
Gawain	GAH wayn GAH win	gä′wăn gä′wĭn	'gɑ wen, 'gɔ- 'gɑ wɪn
gazette	guh ZET	gȧ zĕt′	gə 'zɛt
gazetteer	*gaz* uh TĬER *gaz* uh TIR *gaz* uh TEER	găz′ĕ tẽr′ § 24(2) găz′ĕ tēr′	ˌgæz ə 'tɪər, -'tɪr, -'tir; *ES* -'tiə(r)
gelatin	JEL uh tin	jĕl′á tĭn § 47(2)	'dʒel ə tɪn, -tn̩
gendarme	zhahn DAHRM ZHAHN dahrm	zhän därm′ zhän′därm *F.*, zhän′därm′ § 47(1)	ʒɑn 'dɑrm, 'ʒɑn dɑrm; *ES* -'dɑːm, -dɑːm; *E also* -'dɑːm, -dɑːm; *F.*, ʒɑ̃ 'dɑrm
genealogist	*jen* i AL uh jist *jee* ni AL uh jist	jĕn′ĕ ăl′ŏ jĭst jē′nĕ ăl′ŏ jĭst	ˌdʒen ɪ 'æl ə dʒɪst ˌdʒi nɪ 'æl-, -nɪ 'al-, -'ɒl-
genealogy	*jen* i AL uh ji *jee* ni AL uh ji	jĕn′ĕ ăl′ŏ jĭ jē′nĕ ăl′ŏ jĭ § 47(3)	ˌdʒen ɪ 'æl ə dʒɪ, ˌdʒi nɪ 'æl-, -'al-, -'ɒl-
general	JEN uhr uhl	jĕn′ẽr ăl	'dʒen ər əl
generally	JEN uhr uhl i	jĕn′ẽr ăl ĭ § 50(20)	'dʒen ər əl ɪ

	SIMPLIFIED	DIACRITICAL	PHONETIC
generic	ji NER ik	jĕ nĕr′ĭk	dʒɪ ′nɛr ɪk, dʒə-
generous	JEN uhr uhs	jĕn′ēr ŭs	′dʒɛn ər əs
genial	JEEN yuhl	jēn′yăl	′dʒin jəl
("*conducive to growth; pertaining to genius*")	JEE ni uhl	jē′nĭ ăl § 47(2)	′dʒi nɪ əl
—— ("*nuptial; generative*")	JEE ni uhl	jē′nĭ ăl § 28(9)	′dʒi nɪ əl
genial (*Zool.* and *Anat.*)	ji NAI uhl § 50(34)	jĕ nī′ăl § 47(2)	dʒɪ ′naɪ əl
genie	JEE ni	jē′nĭ	′dʒi nɪ
genii (*one plural of "genius," n.*)	JEE ni ai § 50(34)	jē′nĭ ī	′dʒi nɪ aɪ
genius	JEEN yuhs	jēn′yŭs	′dʒin jəs
	JEE ni uhs	jē′nĭ ŭs § 47(2)	′dʒi nɪ əs
—— "*tutelar deity; familiar spirit*," esp.	JEE ni uhs	jē′nĭ ŭs § 28(9)	′dʒi nɪ əs
Genoa (Italy)	JEN oh uh	jĕn′ō ȧ	′dʒɛn o ə, ′dʒɛn ə wə
gentian	JEN shuhn	jĕn′shăn	′dʒɛn ʃən
gentile (n.)	JEN tail	jĕn′tīl	′dʒɛn taɪl
—— (*Gram.*)	JEN til	jĕn′tĭl	′dʒɛn tɪl
	JEN tail § 50(34)	jĕn′tīl § 47(2)	′dʒɛn taɪl
gentle	JEN t'l	jĕn′t'l	′dʒɛn tl̩
gentleman	JEN t'l muhn	jĕn′t'l măn § 50(21)	′dʒɛn tl̩ mən
genuine	JEN yōͦ in	jĕn′ û ĭn	′dʒɛn jʊ ɪn, -ju-
genus	JEE nuhs	jē′nŭs	′dʒi nəs
geography	ji OG ruh fi	jĕ ŏg′rȧ fĭ	dʒɪ ′ɑg rə fɪ, -′ɒg-
geometry	ji OM i tri	jĕ ŏm′ĕ tri	dʒɪ ′ɑm ɪ trɪ; *ES also* -′ɒm-
German	JUHR muhn	jûr′măn	′dʒɝ mən; *ES also* ′dʒɝ-
gerund	JER uhnd	jĕr′ŭnd	′dʒɛr ənd, -ʌnd
gesture	JES chuhr	jĕs′tûr	′dʒɛs tʃɚ, -tjɚ; *ES* -tʃə(r), -tjə(r)
	JES tyuhr	§ 50(31)	
get	get	gĕt	gɛt
geyser	GAI zuhr	gī′zēr	′gaɪ zɚ, -sɚ; *ES* -zə(r), -sə(r)
	GAI suhr	gī′sēr §§ 24(20), 47(3)	
ghastly	GAST li	gȧst′lĭ §§ 20(5), 26(2)	′gæst lɪ; *E also* ′gast-, ′gɑst-
	GAHST li		
Ghent (Belgium)	gent	gĕnt	gɛnt
ghost	gohst	gōst § 26(2)	gost
ghoul	gool	gōōl § 47(1)	gul

	SIMPLIFIED	DIACRITICAL	PHONETIC
giant	JAI͡ uhnt § 50(34)	jĭ′ănt	′dʒaɪ ənt
gibber ("*chatter* *senselessly*")	JIB uhr GIB uhr	jĭb′ēr gĭb′ēr § 47(1)	′dʒɪb ɚ, ′gɪb ɚ; *ES* -ə(r)
gibberish	JIB uhr ish GIB uhr ish	jĭb′ēr ĭsh gĭb′ēr ĭsh § 47(1)	′dʒɪb ər ɪʃ ′gɪb ər ɪʃ
gibbet	JIB et JIB it	jĭb′ĕt jĭb′ĭt § 24(5)	′dʒɪb ɛt ′dʒɪb ɪt
gibe, jibe	jaĩb § 50(34)	jīb	dʒaɪb
gibes, jibes	jaĩbz § 50(34)	jībz §§ 48(3) 50(6)	dʒaɪbz
giblet	JIB let JIB lit	jĭb′lĕt jĭb′lĭt § 24(5)	′dʒɪb let ′dʒɪb lɪt
gifts	gifts	gĭfts §§ 48(3) 50(6)	gɪfts
gigantean **gigantic**	*jai͡* gan TEE uhn *jai͡* GAN tik § 50(34)	jī′găn tē′ăn jī′găn′tĭk	ˌdʒaɪ gæn ′ti ən ˌdʒaɪ ′gæn tɪk
gill ("*respiratory* *organ*")	gil	gĭl	gɪl
gimlet	GIM let GIM lit	gĭm′lĕt gĭm′lĭt § 24(5)	′gɪm let ′gɪm lɪt
gin ("*drink*")	jin	jĭn	dʒɪn
gin ("*machine*")	jin	jĭn	dʒɪn
gingham	GING uhm	gĭng′ăm § 33(4), 50(14)	′gɪŋ əm
giraffe	juh RAF juh RAHF ji RAF ji RAHF	jĭ răf′ jĭ räf′ §§ 20(5), 47(2)	dʒə ′ræf, djɪ-; *E* *also* -′raf, -′rɑf
girl	*guhrl*	gûrl § 40(6, 7)	gɝl; *ES also* gəl
glacial	GLAY shuhl	glā′shăl § 47(3)	′gle ʃəl, -ʃɪ əl
glacier	GLAY shuhr *B.*, GLAS i uhr	glā′shēr § 47(3) *B.*, glăs′ĭ ēr § 51(4)	′gle ʃɚ, -ʃɪ ɚ; *ES* -ʃə(r), -ʃɪ ə(r) *B.*, ′glæs ɪ ɚ; *ES* - ɪ ə(r)
gladiolus, **Gladiolus**	*glad* i OH luhs gluh DAI͡ uh luhs	glăd′ĭ ō′lŭs glá dī′ð lŭs § 47(1)	ˌglæd ɪ ′o ləs glə ′daɪ ə ləs
—— *genus name* (*cap.*) properly	gluh DAI͡ uh luhs	glá dī′ð lŭs	glə ′daɪ ə ləs
—— *flower or* *plant of this* *genus (small* *letter*), usu.	*glad* i OH luhs	glăd′ĭ ō′lŭs	ˌglæd ɪ ′o ləs
glamour	GLAM uhr	glăm′ēr § 47(2)	′glæm ɚ; *ES* -ə(r)
glance	glans glahns	glàns §§ 20(5), 22(1)	glæns; *E also* glans, glɑns

glass	glas glahs	glás § 20(5)	glæs; *E also* glas, glas
glisten	GLIS 'n	glĭs′ 'n	'glɪs n̩
globular	GLOB yŏŏ luhr	glŏb′ û lĕr	'glɑb jʊ lɚ, -jə-, -ju-; *ES* -lə(r), *also* 'glɒb-
globule	GLOB yool	glŏb′ūl	'glɑb jul, -jʊl; *ES* *also* 'glɒb-
glorious	GLOH ri uhs GLAW ri uhs	glō′rĭ ŭs §§ 34(3), 50(25)	'glo rɪ əs, 'glɔ rɪ əs
glory	GLOH ri GLAW ri	glō′rĭ § 34(3)	'glo rɪ 'glɔ rɪ
glossary	GLOS uh ri	glŏs′ä rĭ	'glɑs ə rɪ, 'glɒs-
Gloucester (**England**)	GLOS tuhr GLAWS tuhr	glŏs′tēr glôs′tēr	'glɑs tɚ, 'glɒs, 'glɔs-; *ES* -tə(r)
glower ("*stare*")	GLOW uhr	glou′ēr	'glaʊ ɚ; *ES* -ə(r)
glucose	GLOO kohs	glo͞o′kōs §§ 40(4), 48(2)	'glu kos
glue	gloo	glo͞o §§ 40(4), 47(3), 48(2)	glu
gluten	GLOO tuhn GLOO t'n	glo͞o′tĕn glo͞o′t'n §§ 40(4), 48(2)	'glu tən 'glu tn̩
glycerin	GLIS uhr in	glĭs′ēr ĭn	'glɪs ər ɪn
gnash	nash	năsh	næʃ
gnat	nat	năt § 25(5)	næt
gnaw	naw	nô § 25(5)	nɔ
gneiss	nais § 50(34)	nīs	naɪs
gnome	nohm	nōm § 25(5)	nom
gnomic	NOH mik NOM ik	nō′mĭk nŏm′ĭk § 47(3)	'no mɪk 'nɑm ɪk; *ES also* 'nɒm-
goal	gohl	gōl	gol
God	god gawd	gŏd gŏd § 34(7)	gɑd, gɒd gɔd
—— *when speak-* *ing reverentially* *of the Supreme* *Being* (*cap.*), *often*	gawd	gôd	gɔd
goddess	GOD es GOD is	gŏd′ĕs gŏd′ĭs § 24(5)	'gɑd ɛs, 'gɒd-, -ɪs
Goethe	GUH tuh GAY ti	gû′tĕ	'gɜ tə, 'ge tɪ; *G.*, 'gø: tə
going	GOH ing	gō′ĭng	'go ɪŋ
golf	golf	gŏlf § 47(3)	gɑlf, gɒlf, gɔlf, gɒf, gɑf, gɒf

Golgotha	GOL guh thuh	gŏl′gŏ tha	'gɑl gə θə, 'gɒl-
gondola	GON duh luh	gŏn′dŏ la	'gɑn də lə, 'gɒn-
gondolier	*gon* duh LĬER	gŏn′dŏ lĕr′	ˌgɑn də 'lɪər,
	gon duh LIR	§ 24(2)	ˌgɒn-, -'lɪr,
	gon duh LEER	gŏn′dŏ lēr′	-'lir; *ES* -'lɪə(r)
gone	gawn	gŏn §§ 34(7),	gɔn
	gon	47(2)	gɒn
good	gŏŏd	gŏŏd § 34(22)	gʊd
gooseberry	GOOZ *ber* i	gōōz′bĕr′ĭ	'guz ˌbɛr ɪ
	GOOS *ber* i	gōōs′bĕr′ĭ	'gus ˌbɛr ɪ
	GOOS buhr i	gōōs′bēr ĭ	'gus bər ɪ
	GOOZ buhr i	gōōz′bēr ĭ	'guz bər ɪ
		§§ 34(22) 47(3)	
gorgeous	GAWR juhs	gôr′jŭs § 47(2)	'gɔr dʒəs, *ES*
			'gɔə-
gospel	GOS puhl	gŏs′pĕl § 34(7)	'gɑs pəl, 'gɒs-
gossamer	GOS uh muhr	gŏs′a mēr	'gɑs ə mɚ; *ES*
			-mə(r), *also*
			'gɒs-
Gothic	GOTH ik	gŏth′ĭk § 34(7)	'gɑθ ɪk, 'gɒθ-
gouge	gowj	gouj § 47(3)	gaʊdʒ, gudʒ
gourd	gohrd	gōrd	gord, gɔrd; *ES*
	gawrd		gɔəd, *E also*
			gɔəd
	B., gŏŏrd	*B.,* gŏŏrd § 51(4)	*B.,* gʊrd; *E* gʊəd
gout	gowt	gout	gaʊt
government	GUHV uhrn	gŭv′ērn mĕnt	'gʌv ɚn mənt, *ES*
	muhnt		-ən-
	Freq.:	*Freq.:*	*Freq.:*
	GUHV uhr	gŭv′ēr mĕnt	'gʌv ɚ mənt; *ES*
	muhnt	§ 48(1)	-ə mənt
governor	GUHV uhr nuhr	gŭv′ēr nēr	'gʌv ɚ nɚ; *ES*
			'gʌv ə nə(r)
	GUHV uh nuhr	gŭv′ē nēr	'gʌv ə nɚ; *ES*
		§§ 24(7), 37(2),	-nə(r)
		48(1)	
gradual	GRAJ yŏŏ uhl	grăd′ŭ ăl	'grædʒ ju əl,
	GRAJ ŏŏ uhl		'grædʒ ʊ-,
	GRAD yŏŏ uhl	§ 50(33)	'græd ju-
graduate	GRAJ yŏŏ it	grăd′ŭ ăt	'grædʒ ju ɪt,
(adj., n.)	GRAJ ŏŏ it		'grædʒ ʊ-, -et,
	GRAD yŏŏ it		'græd ju-
—— (v.)	GRAJ yŏŏ ayt	grăd′ŭ āt	'grædʒ ju et,
	GRAJ ŏŏ ayt		'grædʒ ʊ-,
	GRAD yŏŏ ayt	§§ 20(8, 9),	'græd ju-
		50(2)	
graft	graft	grȧft § 20(5)	græft; *E also*
	grahft		graft, grɑft
gramercy	gruh MUHR si	grȧ mûr′sĭ	grə 'mɝ sɪ; *ES*
			also -'mɜ-

	SIMPLIFIED	DIACRITICAL	PHONETIC
granary (n.)	GRAN uh ri	grăn′*á* rĭ	'græn ə rɪ
	Pop.:	*Pop.:*	*Pop.:*
	GRAYN uh ri	grān′*á* rĭ § 51(3)	'gren ə rɪ
grand	grand	grănd	grænd
		§ 23(1)	
	Before some con-	*Before some con-*	*Before some con-*
	sonants in col-	*sonants in col-*	*sonants in col-*
	loq. speech:	*loq. speech:*	*loq. speech:*
	gran	grăn § 51(3)	græn
grandam	GRAN dam	grăn′dăm	'græn dæm
	GRAN duhm	grăn′dŭm	'græn dəm
—— *when spelled*	GRAND *dam*	grănd′dăm′	'grænd ˌdæm
"granddam"			
(used of			
animals)			
grandame	GRAN daym	grăn′dām	'græn dem
	GRAN duhm	grăn′dŭm	'græn dəm
grandeur	GRAN juhr	grăn′dûr	'græn dʒɚ, -dʒʊr,
	GRAN dyŏŏr		'græn djʊr; *ES*
	GRAN dyoor	§§ 40(11),	-dʒə(r),
		50(33)	-dʒʊə(r),
			-djʊə(r)
grandiose	GRAN di ohs	grăn′dĭ ōs	'græn dɪ os
grange	graynj	grānj § 25(4)	grendʒ
grapnel	GRAP nuhl	grăp′nĕl	'græp nəl
	GRAP n'l	grăp′n'l	'græp n̩
grasp	grasp	grȧsp § 20(5)	græsp; *E also*
	grahsp		grasp, grɑsp
grass	gras	grȧs § 20(5)	græs; *E also* gras,
	grahs		grɑs
gratis	GRAY tis	grā′tĭs	'gre tɪs
	GRAT is	grăt′ĭs	'græt ɪs
gratitude	GRAT uh tyood	grăt′ĭ tūd	'græt ə tjud,
	GRAT i tyood	grăt′ĭ tūd	-ɪ tjud, -ə tud,
	GRAT uh tood	§§ 48(2), 50(32)	-ɪ tud
	GRAT i tood		
gratuitous	gruh TYOO uh	grȧ tū′ĭ tŭs	grə 'tju ə təs
	tuhs		
	gruh TYOO i	grȧ tū′ĭ tŭs	grə 'tju ɪ təs
	tuhs	§§ 48(2),	
	gruh TOO uh tuhs	50(25, 32)	grə 'tu ə təs
	gruh TOO i tuhs		grə 'tu ɪ təs
grease (n.)	grees	grēs	gris
—— (v.t.)	grees	grēs	gris
	Esp. British and	*Esp. British and*	*Esp. British and*
	Southern U.S.:	*Southern U.S.:*	*Southern U.S.:*
	greez	grēz §§ 38(4),	griz
		47(3), 51(4, 10)	

	SIMPLIFIED	DIACRITICAL	PHONETIC
greaser (See *"grease"* and *"greasy."*)	GREES uhr GREEZ uhr	grēs′ẽr grēz′ẽr § 47(1)	'gris ɚ, 'griz-; *ES* -ə(r)
greasing (See *"grease"* and *"greasy."*)	GREES ing GREEZ ing	grēs′ĭng grēz′ĭng	'gris ɪŋ 'griz ɪŋ
greasy	GREES i GREEZ i	grēs′ĭ grēz′ĭ § 47(1)	'gris ɪ 'griz ɪ
—— *"covered, smeared, or defiled with grease,"* esp.	GREES i	grēs′ĭ	'gris ɪ
—— *"slimy,"* often	GREEZ i	grēz′ĭ	'griz ɪ
—— *esp. British and Southern U.S.*	GREEZ i	grēz′ĭ	'griz ɪ
Greenwich (**England**)	GRIN ij	grĭn′ĭj §§ 1, 22(5)	'grɪn ɪdʒ, 'grɛn-, -ɪtʃ
Greenwich (**Village, N.Y.**)	GREN ich GREEN wich GRIN wich	grĕn′ĭch grēn′wĭch grĭn′wĭch §§ 1, 22(5)	'grɛn ɪtʃ 'grin wɪtʃ 'grɪn wɪtʃ
gregarious	gri GEHR i uhs gri GAY ri uhs	grĕ gâr′ĭ ŭs §§ 20(2) 50(25)	grɪ 'gɛr ɪ əs, -'gær-, '-ge rɪ-; *E also* -'gɛər-
grenadier	*gren* uh DĬER *gren* uh DIR *gren* uh DEER	grĕn′á dẽr′ § 24(2) grĕn′á dēr′	ˌgren ə 'dɪər, -'dɪr, -'dir; *ES* -'dɪə(r)
grief	greef	grēf	grif
grieving	GREEV ing	grēv′ĭng § 50(14)	'griv ɪŋ
grievous	GREEV uhs	grēv′ŭs	'griv əs
grievously	GREEV uhs li	grēv′ŭs lĭ § 50(20)	'griv əs lɪ
grimace	gri MAYS *Pop.:* GRIM is	grĭ mās′ *Pop.:* grĭm′ĭs § 51(3)	grɪ 'mes *Pop.:* 'grɪm ɪs
grimy	GRAIM i § 50(34)	grīm′ĭ	'graɪm ɪ
grindstone	GRAIND *stohn* GRAIN *stohn* § 50(34)	grīnd′stōn′ grīn′stōn′ § 23(1)	'graɪnd ˌston 'graɪn ˌston
gripe	graip § 50(34)	grīp	graɪp
gristle	GRIS 'l	grĭs′ 'l	'grɪs ļ
grocery	GROH suhr i	grō′sẽr ĭ	'gro sər ɪ
gross	grohs	grōs	gros
grotesque	groh TESK	grŏ tĕsk′	gro 'tɛsk
grouse (*"bird"*)	grows § 50(34)	grous	graʊs

grovel	GROV 'l GRUHV 'l	grŏv′ 'l grŭv′ 'l § 1	'grɑv ḷ, 'grʌv-; ES also 'grɒv-
guarantee	gar uhn TEE	găr′ăn tē′	ˌgær ən 'ti
guaranty	GAR uhn ti	găr′ăn tĭ	'gær ən tɪ
guard	gahrd	gärd §§ 25(2), 26(5), 40(13)	gɑrd; ES gɑ:d, E also gɑ:d
guardian	GAHR di uhn	gär′dĭ ăn §§ 25(2), 47(2)	'gɑr dɪ ən; ES 'gɑ:-, E also 'gɑ:-
guerdon	GUHR duhn	gûr′dŭn § 47(2)	'gɝ dən, -dṇ; ES also 'gɜ-
Guernsey	GUHRN zi	gûrn′zĭ	'gɝn zɪ; ES also 'gɜn-
guess	ges	gĕs §§ 26(5), 40(13)	gɛs
guest	gest	gĕst §§ 26(5), 40(13)	gɛst
guests	gests	gĕsts §§ 48(3), 50(6)	gɛsts
guide	gaɪd § 50(34)	gīd § 25(2)	gaɪd
guild, gild	gild	gĭld	gɪld
guillotine (n.)	GIL uh teen B., gil uh TEEN	gĭl′ô tēn B., gĭl′ô tēn′ § 51(4)	'gɪl ə tin B., ˌgɪl ə 'tin
—— (v.t.)	gil uh TEEN	gĭl′ô tēn′ §§ 12, 47(3)	ˌgɪl ə 'tin
guilt	gilt	gĭlt	gɪlt
guinea	GIN i	gĭn′ĭ	'gɪn ɪ
Guinea	GIN i	gĭn′ĭ	'gɪn ɪ
Guinevere	GWIN uh vĭer GWIN uh vir GWIN uh veer	gwĭn′ĕ vēr § 24(2) gwĭn′ĕ vēr	'gwɪn ə vɪər, -vir, -vir; ES -viə(r)
guise	gaɪz § 50(34)	gīz	gaɪz
guitar	gi TAHR	gĭ tär′	gɪ 'tɑr; ES -'tɑ:(r), E also -'tɑ:(r)
gum	guhm	gŭm § 40(6)	gʌm
gums	guhmz	gŭmz §§ 48(3), 50(6)	gʌmz
gunwale, gunnel	GUHN uhl GUHN 'l	gŭn′ĕl gŭn′ 'l §§ 1, 47(2)	'gʌn əl 'gʌn ḷ
Gustavus	guhs TAY vuhs guhs TAH vuhs	gŭs tā′vŭs gŭs tä′vŭs § 40(6)	gʌs 'te vəs gʌs 'tɑ vəs
gut	guht	gŭt § 40(6)	gʌt
gymnasium	jim NAY zi uhm	jĭm nā′zĭ ăm §§ 28(9), 47(2)	dʒɪm 'ne zɪ əm, -'zjəm

	SIMPLIFIED	DIACRITICAL	PHONETIC
gymnastic	jim NAS tik	jĭm năs′tĭk	dʒɪm ˈnæs tɪk
gyp ("swindler")	jip	jĭp	dʒɪp
gyve	jaīv § 50(34)	jīv	dʒaɪv

H

habiliment	huh BIL uh muhnt	hȧ bĭl′i̇ mĕnt	hə ˈbɪl ə mənt
	huh BIL i muhnt	hȧ bĭl′ĭ mĕnt § 50(22)	hə ˈbɪl ɪ mənt
habitable	HAB uh tuh b'l	hăb′i̇ tȧ b'l	ˈhæb ə tə bl̩
	HAB i tuh b'l	hăb′ĭ tȧ b'l	ˈhæb ɪ tə bl̩
habitual	huh BICH ŏŏ uhl	hȧ bĭt′ū ăl	hə ˈbɪtʃ ʊ əl
	huh BIT yŏŏ uhl	§ 50(33)	hə ˈbɪt jʊ əl, -ju-, -ˈbɪtʃ ʊl, -ˈbɪt jʊl
haft	haft	hȧft	hæft; E also haft, hɑft
	hahft	§ 20(5)	
Hague (The)	hayg	hāg	heg
Haiti	HAY ti	hā′tĭ	ˈhe tɪ
halcyon	HAL si uhn	hăl′sĭ ŭn § 47(2)	ˈhæl sɪ ən
half	hahf	häf	hɑf, hæf; E also haf
	haf	häf §§ 1, 20(5), 39(5)	
halibut	HAL uh buht	hăl′i̇ bŭt	ˈhæl ə bət,
	HAL i buht	hăl′ ĭ bŭt	-ɪ bət, ˈhɑl-; ES
	HOL uh buht	hŏl′i̇ bŭt	also ˈhɒl-
	HOL i buht	hŏl′ĭ bŭt § 47(3)	
Halloween, Hallowe'en	hal oh EEN Dial.: hol oh EEN	hăl′ō ēn′ Dial.: hŏl′ō ēn′ § 51(2)	ˌhæl o ˈin Dial.: ˌhɑl o ˈin; ES also ˌhɒl-
hallucination	huh loo si NAY shuhn	hȧ lū′sĭ nā′shŭn §§ 27(1), 47(2), 50(30)	hə ˌlu sɪ ˈne ʃən, -ˌlju-, -sn̩ ˈe-
	huh lyoo si NAY shuhn		
halo	HAY loh	hā′lō	ˈhe lo
halve	hahv	häv	hɑv, hæv; E also hav
	hav	häv § 20(5)	

	SIMPLIFIED	DIACRITICAL	PHONETIC
halved	hahvd havd	hävd håvd §§ 20(5), 50(4)	hɑvd, hævd; *E* *also* hɑvd
Haman	HAY muhn	hā′măn	′he mən
Handel (G. F.) *G.*, **Händel**	HAN d'l *G.*, HEN d'l	hăn′d'l *G.*, hĕn′d'l	′hæn dļ *G.*, ′hɛn dļ
handkerchief	HANG kuhr chif	hăng′kēr chĭf §§ 23(1), 47(2)	′hæŋ kɚ tʃɪʃ; *ES* -kə-
handle	HAN d'l	hăn′d'l	′hæn dļ
handsome	HAN suhm	hăn′sŭm § 23(1)	′hæn səm
hangar	HANG uhr HANG gahr	hăng′ēr hăng′gär §§ 33(4), 47(1)	′hæŋ ɚ, ′hæŋ gɑr, ′hɑŋ-; *ES* -ə(r), -gɑ:(r)
hanger	HANG uhr	hăng′ēr § 33(4)	′hæŋ ɚ; *ES* -ə(r)
hanging	HANG ing	hăng′ĭng § 50(24)	′hæŋ ɪŋ
haply	HAP li	hăp′lĭ	′hæp lɪ
harangue	huh RANG	há răng′	hə ′ræŋ
harass	HAR uhs huh RAS	hăr′ás há răs′ § 47(1)	′hær əs hə ′ræs
harbinger	HAHR bin juhr	här′bĭn jẽr	′hɑr bɪn dʒɚ; *ES* ′hɑ: bɪn dʒə(r), *E also* ′hɑ:-
harbor, harbour	HAHR buhr	här′bẽr	′hɑr bɚ; *ES* ′hɑ: bə(r), *E* *also* ′hɑ:-
harem	HAY rem HEHR em	hā′rĕm hâr′ĕm § 47(3)	′he rɛm, ′hɛr ɛm, ′hær-; *ES also* ′hæər-, *E also* ′hɛər-
harlequin, Harlequin	HAHR li kwin HAHR luh kwin HAHR li kin HAHR luh kin	här′lĕ kwĭn här′lĕ kwĭn här′lĕ kĭn här′lĕ kĭn § 47(3)	′hɑr lɪ kwɪn, -lə-, -kɪn; *ES* ′hɑ:lɪ-, -lə-, *E also* ′hɑ:-
harpsichord	HAHRP si kawrd	härp′sĭ kôrd	′hɑrp sɪ kɔrd; *ES* ′hɑ:p sɪ kɔəd
Harvard	HAHR vuhrd	här′vẽrd	′hɑr vɚd; *ES* ′hɑ: vəd, *E also* ′hɑ:-
has	*Stressed (usu.* *when meaning* *"to own" or* *"possess"):* haz *Unstressed (usu.* *as an auxiliary,* *or as a "help-* *ing" or linking* *verb):* huhz uhz	*Stressed (usu.* *when meaning* *"to own" or* *"possess"):* hăz *Unstressed (usu.* *as an auxiliary,* *or as a "help-* *ing" or linking* *verb):* hăz ăz § 16	*Stressed (usu.* *when meaning* *"to own" or* *"possess"):* hæz *Unstressed (usu.* *as an auxiliary,* *or as a "help-* *ing" or linking* *verb):* həz əz

	SIMPLIFIED	DIACRITICAL	PHONETIC
hasten	HAYS 'n	hās′ 'n § 1	′hes ṇ
haughty	HAW ti	hô′tĭ	′hɔ ɪt
haunch	hawnch hahnch	hônch hänch §§ 22(6), 47(2)	hɔntʃ, hɑntʃ, hɒntʃ
haunt	hawnt hahnt	hônt hänt § 47(3)	hɔnt hɑnt
have	*Stressed (usu. when meaning "to own" or "possess"):* hav *Unstressed (usu. as an auxiliary, except when emphatic: see "has"):* huhv uhv	*Stressed (usu. when meaning "to own" or "possess"):* hăv *Unstressed (usu. as an auxiliary, except when emphatic: see "has"):* hăv ăv § 16	*Stressed (usu. when meaning "to own" or "possess"):* hæv *Unstressed (usu. as an auxiliary, except when emphatic: see "has"):* həv əv
haversack	HAV uhr sak	hăv′ēr săk	′hæv ɚ sæk; *ES* -ə sæk
Hawaii	hah WAÎ ee huh WAÎ ee § 50(34)	hä wī′ē há wī′ē	hɑ ′waɪ i hə ′waɪ i, -′waɪ jə
Hawaiian	hah WAÎ yuhn huh WAÎ yuhn § 50(34)	hä wī′yăn há wī′yăn	hɑ ′waɪ jən hə ′waɪ jən
hawser	HAW zuhr HAW suhr	hô′zēr hô′sēr § 47(3)	′hɔ zɚ, -sɚ; *ES* -zə(r), -sə(r)
heard	*huhrd*	hûrd § 40(6)	hɝd; *ES also* hɜd
hearth	hahrth	härth § 47(2)	hɑrθ; *ES* hɑ:θ; *E also* hɑ:θ
	Poet. or dial.: *huhrth*	*Poet. or dial.:* hûrth §§ 40(6), 51(2, 11)	*Poet. or dial.:* hɝθ; *ES also* hɜθ
heathen	HEE thuhn	hē′thĕn §§ 9, 47(2)	′hi ðən
heather	HETH uhr	heth′ēr § 47(2)	′hɛð ɚ; *ES* -ə(r)
heaven	HEV uhn	hĕv′ĕn	′hɛv ən
Hebrides	HEB ri deez	hĕb′rĭ dēz	′hɛb rɪ diz
Hecate, Hekate	HEK uh ti HEK uh tee	hĕk′á tĕ hĕk′á tē	′hɛk ə tɪ ′hɛk ə ti
	In poetry, often: HEK it	*In poetry, often:* hĕk′ăt § 51(11)	*In poetry, often:* ′hɛk ɪt
hecatomb	HEK uh tom HEK uh toom	hĕk′á tŏm hĕk′á tōōm § 47(3)	′hɛk ə tɑm, -tum, -tom; *ES also* -tɒm
hectic	HEK tik	hĕk′tĭk	′hɛk tɪk
hedgerow	HEJ *roh*	hĕj′rō′	′hɛdʒ ˌro

	SIMPLIFIED	DIACRITICAL	PHONETIC
heifer	HEF uhr	hĕf′ẽr	′hɛf ɚ; *ES* -ə(r)
height	haīt § 50(34)	hīt	haɪt
	Occas. (and always when spelled "highth"), but gen. dial.:	*Occas. (and always when spelled "highth"), but gen. dial.:*	*Occas. (and always when spelled "highth"), but gen. dial.:*
	haītth	hītth	haɪtθ
	B., haīth § 50(34)	*B.,* hīth § 51(2, 4, 8)	*B.,* haɪθ
heinous	HAY nuhs	hā′nŭs § 50(25)	′he nəs
heir	ehr	âr §§ 1, 27(1)	ɛr, ær; *ES* æə(r), *E also* ɛə(r)
heirloom	EHR LOOM	âr′lo͞om′ § 11	′ɛr ′lum, ′ær-; *ES* ′æə(r)-, *E also* ′ɛə(r)-
heliotrope	HEE li uh trohp	hē′lĭ ŏ trōp § 28(9)	′hi lɪ ə trop, ′hil jə-
Hellenic	he LEN ik	hĕ lĕn′ĭk	hɛ ′lɛn ɪk
	he LEE nik	hĕ lē′nĭk § 47(3)	hɛ ′li nɪk
helm	helm	hĕlm	hɛlm
helmsman	HELMZ muhn	hĕlmz′măn § 50(21)	′hɛlmz mən
help	help	hĕlp	hɛlp
hemoglobin, haemoglobin	*hee* moh GLOH bin	hē′mŏ glō′bĭn	ˌhi mo ′glo bɪn, -mə-, ˌhɛm o-, ˌhɛm ə-
	hem oh GLOH bin	hĕm′ŏ glō′bĭn	
hemorrhage	HEM uh rij	hĕm′ŏ rĭj § 50(1)	′hɛm ə rɪdʒ
Henry	HEN ri	hĕn′rĭ	′hɛn rɪ
heraldic	he RAL dik	hĕ răl′dĭk	hɛ ′ræl dɪk
herb	*uhrb*	ûrb	ɝb; *ES also* ɜb
	huhrb	hûrb §§ 1, 27(11), 40(6), 47(3)	hɝb; *ES also* hɜb
herbage (See *herb*.)	UHR bij	ûr′bĭj	′ɝ bɪdʒ; *ES also* ′ɜ-
	HUHR bij	hûr′bĭj §§ 47(2), 50(1)	′hɝ bɪdʒ; *ES also* ′hɜ-
herculean, Herculean	huhr KYOO li uhn	hûr kū′lĕ ăn	hɝ ′kju lɪ ən; *ES also* hɜ-
	huhr kyo͞o LEE uhn	hûr′kû lē′ăn	ˌhɝ kjʊ ′li ən, -kjə-, -kju-; *ES also* ˌhɜ-
Hercules	HUHR kyo͞o leez	hûr′kû lēz	′hɝ kjʊ liz, -kjə-, -kju-; *ES also* ′hɜ-
herd	*huhrd*	hûrd § 40(6)	hɝd; *ES also* hɜd
here	hĭer	hēr § 24(2)	hɪər, hɪr, hir; *ES* hɪə(r)
	hir		
	heer	hēr	

	SIMPLIFIED	DIACRITICAL	PHONETIC
hereditary	hi RED i *ter* i *B.*, hi RED i tuhr i	hḗ rĕd′ĭ tĕr′ĭ *B.*, hḗ rĕd′ĭ tĕr ĭ §§ 13, 20(2), 24(9), 27(1), 51(4)	hɪ 'red ɪ ˌter ɪ, hə- *B.*, hɪ 'red ɪ tə rɪ
heresy	HER uh si	hĕr′ĕ sĭ	'her ə sɪ
heretic	HER uh tik	hĕr′ĕ tĭk §§ 1, 27(1)	'her ə tɪk
heretical	hi RET i kuhl	hḗ rĕt′ĭ kăl	hɪ 'ret ɪ kəl, hə-, -kl̩
herewith	hĭer WITH hir WITH heer WITH hĭer WITH hir WITH heer WITH	hẹr wĭth′ § 24(2) hẹr wĭth′ hẹr wĭth′ § 39(5), 47(3) hẹr wĭth′	hɪər 'wɪð, hɪr-, hir-; *ES* hɪər- hɪər 'wɪθ, hɪr-, hir-; *ES* hɪə-
Hermes	HUHR meez	hûr′mēz	'hɝ miz; *ES also* 'hɜ-
hero	HĬER oh HIR oh HEER oh	hẹr′ō § 24(2) hẹr′ō	'hɪər o, 'hɪr-, 'hir-; *ES* 'hɪər o
heroin, Heroin	HER oh in HĬER oh in HIR oh in HEER oh in hi ROH in	hĕr′ō ĭn hẹr′ō ĭn § 24(2) hḗ rō′ĭn	'her o ɪn, 'hɪr-, 'hɪr-, 'hir-, hɪ 'ro ɪn; *ES* 'hɪər o-
heroine	HER oh in	hĕr′ō ĭn § 47(2)	'her o ɪn
heroism	HER oh iz'm HER oh iz uhm	hĕr′ō ĭz′m̩ § 50(15)	'her o ɪzm̩ 'her o ɪz əm
hesitate	HEZ uh tayt HEZ i tayt	hĕz′ĭ tāt hĕz′ĭ tāt §§ 47(2), 50(2)	'hez ə tet 'hez ɪ tet
heterodox	HET uhr uh doks	hĕt′ĕr ŏ dŏks § 9	'het ər ə dɑks, 'het rə-; *ES also* -dɒks
heterogeneous	*het* uhr uh JEE ni uhs	hĕt′ĕr ŏ jē′nĕ ŭs § 24(15)	ˌhet ər ə 'dʒi nɪ əs, ˌhet rə 'dʒin jəs
heyday	HAY *day*	hā′dā′	'he ˌde
hiatus	haꙮ AY tuhs § 50(34)	hī ā′tŭs	haɪ 'e təs
Hiawatha	*haꙮ* uh WAW thuh *haꙮ* uh WOTH uh *hee* uh WOTH uh	hī′ȧ wô′thȧ hī′ȧ wŏth′ȧ hē′ȧ wŏth′ȧ	ˌhaɪ ə 'wɔ θə, -'wɑθ ə, -'wɒθ-, ˌhi ə 'wɑθ ə, -'wɒθ-
hibernate	HAꙮ buhr nayt § 50(34)	hī′bĕr nāt § 47(2)	'haɪ bɚ net; *ES* -bə-
hidalgo	hi DAL goh	hĭ dăl′gō	hɪ 'dæl go
hideous	HID i uhs	hĭd′ĕ ŭs	'hɪd ɪ əs

	SIMPLIFIED	DIACRITICAL	PHONETIC
hierarchy	HĀI uhr *ahr* ki	hī′ēr är′kĭ	′haɪ ər ˌɑr kɪ, *ES* -ˌɑː kɪ, *E also* -ˌɑ:-
hieroglyphic	*hai͡* uhr uh GLIF ik	hī′ēr ŏ glĭf′ĭk	ˌhaɪ ər ə ′glɪf ɪk, ˌhaɪ rə-
highth	See *height.*	*Dial. var. of* "*height*," page 146.	
highwayman *n.* ("*highway robber*")	HĀI *way* muhn hai͡ WAY muhn	hī′wā′măn hī wā′măn § 50(21)	′haɪ ˌwe mən haɪ ′we mən
hilarious	hi LEHR i uhs hi LAY ri uhs hai͡ LEHR i uhs hai͡ LAY ri uhs	hĭ lâr′ĭ ŭs hī lâr′ĭ ŭs §§ 47(3), 50(25)	hɪ ′lɛr ɪ əs, -′lær-, -′le rɪ-, hə-, haɪ-; *ES also* -′læər-, -′lɛər-
hilarity	hi LAR uh ti hi LAR i ti hai͡ LAR uh ti hai͡ LAR i ti	hĭ lăr′ĭ tĭ hĭ lăr′ĭ tĭ hī lăr′ĭ tĭ hī lăr′ĭ tĭ § 47(3)	hɪ ′lær ə tɪ, haɪ-, -ɪ tɪ; *ES also* -′læər-
hindrance	HIN druhns	hĭn′drăns	′hɪn drəns
Hindu, **Hindoo**	HIN doo HIN DOO *B.,* hin DOO	hĭn′dōō hĭn′dōō′ *B.,* hĭn dōō′ §§ 47(3), 51(4)	′hɪn du ′hɪn ′du *B.,* hɪn ′du
hippopotamus	*hip* uh POT uh muhs	hĭp′ŏ pŏt′*a* mŭs § 47(2)	ˌhɪp ə ′pɑt ə məs; *ES also* -′pɒt-
his	hiz *Unstressed:* iz	hĭz *Unstressed:* ĭz § 16	hɪz *Unstressed:* ɪz
historian	his TOH ri uhn his TAW ri uhn	hĭs tō′rĭ ăn § 34(3)	hɪs ′to rɪ ən hɪs ′tɔ rɪ ən
historiographer	his *toh* ri OG ruh fuhr his *taw* ri OG ruh fuhr	hĭs tō′rĭ ŏg′rȧ fēr § 34(3)	hɪs ˌto rɪ ′ɑg rə fɚ, -ˌtɔ-, -′ɒg-; *ES* -fə(r)
history	HIS tuh ri	hĭs′tô rĭ § 9	′hɪs tə rɪ, -trɪ
hoarse	hohrs hawrs	hōrs § 34(3)	hors, hɔrs; *ES* hoəs, *E also* hɔəs
hobgoblin	HOB *gob* lin	hŏb′gŏb′lĭn	′hɑb ˌgab lɪn; *ES also* ′hɒb ˌgɒb-
hocus–pocus	HOH kuhs–POH kuhs	hō′kŭs–pō′kŭs	′ho kəs–′po kəs
hog	hog hawg	hŏg hôg §§ 34(7), 47(3)	hɑg, hɒg, hɔg

	SIMPLIFIED	DIACRITICAL	PHONETIC
hoist	hoist *Dial.:* haist § 50(34)	hoist *Dial.:* hīst § 51(4)	hɔist *Dial.:* haɪst
holocaust	HOL uh kawst	hŏl′ŏ kôst	'hal ə kɔst; *ES* *also* 'hɒl-
homage	HOM ij OM ij	hŏm′ĭj ŏm′ĭj §§ 1, 47(2), 50(1)	'ham ɪdʒ, 'am-; *ES* 'hɒm-, 'ɒm-
homicidal	*hom* uh SAID uhl *hom* i SAID uhl *hom* uh SAID 'l *hom* i SAID 'l	hŏm′ĭ sīd′ăl hŏm′ĭ sīd′ăl hŏm′ĭ sīd′ 'l hŏm′ĭ sīd′ 'l	ˌham ə 'saɪd əl, ˌham ɪ-, -'saɪd l̩; *ES also* ˌhɒm-
homicide	HOM uh said HOM i said § 50(34)	hŏm′ĭ sīd hŏm′ĭ sīd	'ham ə saɪd, 'ham ɪ-; *ES also* 'hɒm-
homiletic	*hom* uh LET ik *hom* i LET ik	hŏm′ĭ lĕt′ĭk hŏm′ĭ lĕt′ĭk	ˌham ə 'let ɪk, ˌham ɪ-; *ES also* ˌhɒm-
homily	HOM uh li HOM i li	hŏm′ĭ lĭ hŏm′ĭ lĭ	'ham ə lɪ, -ɪ lɪ; *ES* *also* 'hɒm-
homogeneous	*hoh* muh JEE ni uhs *hoh* moh JEE ni uhs *hom* oh JEE ni uhs *hom* uh JEE ni uhs	hō′mŏ jē′nĕ ŭs hŏm′ŏ jē′nĕ ŭs §§ 28(9), 47(3), 50(25)	ˌho mə 'dʒi nɪ əs, -mo-, ˌham o-, ˌham ə-; *ES* *also* ˌhɒm-
honest	ON est ON ist	ŏn′ĕst ŏn′ĭst §§ 1, 24(5), 27(1)	'an ɛst, -ɪst; *ES* *also* 'ɒn-
honey	HUHN i	hŭn′ĭ § 1	'hʌn ɪ
Honolulu	*hoh* noh LOO loo *More commonly:* *hon* uh LOO loo *hon* uh LOO luh *Among natives:* HOH NOH LOO LOO	hō′nŏ lōō′lōō *More commonly:* hŏn′ŏ lōō′lōō hŏn′ŏ lōō′lŭ *Among natives:* hō′nŏ′lōō′lōō′ § 51(3, 6)	ˌho no 'lu lu *More commonly:* ˌhan ə 'lu lu -'lu lə; *ES also* ˌhɒn- *Among natives:* 'ho 'no 'lu 'lu ho no 'lu lu
honor, honour	ON uhr	ŏn′ẽr §§ 1, 27(1)	'an ɚ; *ES* -ə(r), *also* 'ɒn-
honorable, honourable	ON uhr uh b'l	ŏn′ẽr *á* b'l	'an ər ə bl̩; *ES also* 'ɒn-
honorary	ON uhr *er* i *B.*, ON uhr uhr i	ŏn′ẽr ĕr′ĭ §§ 20(2), 24(9) *B.*, ŏn′ẽr ẽr ĭ §§ 13, 51(4)	'an ər ˌɛr ɪ; *ES* *also* 'ɒn- *B.*, 'ɒn ər ə rɪ
hood	hŏŏd	hŏŏd § 34(22)	hʊd
hoof	hoof hŏŏf	hōōf § 34(22) 	huf hʊf

hook	hŏŏk	hŏŏk	hʊk
hoop	hoop hŏŏp	hōōp § 34(22)	hup hʊp
hoot (*"shout"*)	hoot	hōōt § 34(22)	hut
horizon	huh RĀI z'n § 50(34)	hŏ rī′z'n § 47(2)	hə ˈraɪ zn̩
horoscope	HOR uh skohp HAWR uh skohp	hŏr′ŏ skōp hôr′ŏ skōp § 34(5, 7)	ˈhɑr ə skop, ˈhɔr-, ˈhɒr-
horrid	HOR id HAWR id	hŏr′ĭd hôr′ĭd § 34(5, 7)	ˈhɑr ɪd ˈhɔr, ˈhɒr-
horrors	HOR uhrz HAWR uhrz	hŏr′ērz hôr′ērz §§34(5,7), 50(6)	ˈhɑr ɚz, ˈhɔr-, -hɒr-; *ES* -əz
horse	hawrs	hôrs § 34(3, 5)	hɔrs; *ES* hɒəs
hosanna	hoh ZAN uh	hŏ zăn′à	ho ˈzæn ə
hosiery	HOH zhuhr i	hō′zhēr ĭ § 9	ˈho ʒɚ ɪ, -ʒrɪ
hospice	HOS pis	hŏs′pĭs	ˈhas pɪs, -hɒs-
hospitable	HOS pi tuh b'l *Gaining ground:* hos PIT uh b'l	hŏs′pĭ tà b'l *Gaining ground:* hŏs pĭt′à b'l § 51(5)	ˈhas pɪ tə bl̩, ˈhɒs- *Gaining ground:* has ˈpɪt ə bl̩, hɒs-
hospital	HOS pit uhl HOS pit 'l	hŏs′pĭt ál hŏs′pĭt 'l §§ 1, 27(1), 34(7)	ˈhas pɪt əl, ˈhɒs-, -pɪt l̩
hospitalization	*hos* pit 'l i ZAY shuhn *hos* pit 'l ai ZAY shuhn	hŏs′pĭt 'l ĭ zā′shŭn hŏs′pĭt 'l ī zā′shŭn	ˌhas pɪt l̩ ɪ ˈze ʃən, ˌhɒs-, -l̩ aɪ ˈze ʃən, -ə ˈze-
hostage	HOS tij	hŏs′tĭj §§ 34(7), 47(2), 50(1)	ˈhas tɪdʒ, *ES also* ˈhɒs-
hostel	HOS tuhl HOS t'l	hŏs′tĕl hŏs′t'l § 47(2)	ˈhas təl, -tl̩; *ES* *also* ˈhɒs-
hostelry	HOS tuhl ri	hŏs′tĕl rĭ § 47(2)	ˈhas təl rɪ, -tl̩-; *ES* *also* ˈhɒs-
hostile	HOS til	hŏs′tĭl	ˈhas tɪl; *ES also* ˈhɒs-
	B., HOS tail § 50(34)	*B.,* hŏs′tīl §§ 28(5), 34(7), 47(2), 51(4)	*B.,* ˈhɒs taɪl
hotel	hoh TEL	hō tĕl′	ho ˈtɛl
hour	owr	our §§1, 27(1)	aʊr; *ES* aʊə(r)
houri	HOO ri HOW ri	hōō′rĭ hou′rĭ §§ 34(21), 47(3)	ˈhu rɪ, ˈhʊ- ˈhaʊ rɪ
house (n.)	hows	hous § 39(5)	haʊs
—— (v.)	howz	houz § 38(4)	haʊz

housewife (n.)	HOWS *waif*	hous′wīf′	′haʊs ˌwaɪf
	Occas.:	*Occas.:*	*Occas.:*
	HUHZ if	hŭz′ĭf	′hʌz ɪf
—— *"little bag for needles, patching cloth, etc.,"* usually	B., HUHZ if § 50(34)	B., hŭz′ĭf § 47(2)	B., ′hʌz ɪf
housewifery	HOWS *waif* uhr i	hous′wīf′ēr ĭ	′haʊs ˌwaɪf ər ɪ
	HOWS *waif* uh ri	hous′wīf′ē rĭ	′haʊs ˌwaɪf ə rɪ
	HOWS *waif* ri	hous′wīf′rĭ	′haʊs ˌwaɪf rɪ
	HUHZ if ri	hŭz′ĭf rĭ § 47(2)	′hʌz ɪf rɪ
housing	HOWZ ing	houz′ĭng	′haʊz ɪŋ
Houston (Texas)	HYOOS tuhn	hūs′tŭn	′hjus tən
hovel	HOV uhl	hŏv′ĕl	′hʌv əl, ′hʌv-, -l̩;
	HUHV uhl	hŭv′ĕl	*ES also* ′hɒv-
	HUHV ′l	hŭv′ ′l	
hover	HUHV uhr	hŭv′ēr	′hʌv ɚ, ′hɑv-; *ES*
	HOV uhr	hŏv′ēr §§ 1, 47(3)	-ə(r), *also* ′hɒv-
how	how	hou	haʊ
howbeit	how BEE it	hou bē′ĭt	haʊ ′bi ɪt
howl	howl	houl	haʊl
hue	hyoo	hū § 51(7)	hju
huge	hyooj	hūj	hjudʒ
Hugo (Victor Marie)	HYOO goh	hū′gō	′hju go
hulk	*huhlk*	hŭlk § 40(6)	hʌlk
human	HYOO muhn	hū′mǎn § 1	′hju mən, ′ju-
humane	hyoo MAYN	hū mān′	hju ′men
humble	HUHM b′l	hŭm′b′l	′hʌm bl̩
	Occas. (esp. in the South):	*Occas. (esp. in the South):*	*Occas. (esp. in the South):*
	UHM b′l	ŭm′b′l §§ 1, 27(1), 47(2), 51(8, 10)	′ʌm bl̩
humid	HYOO mid	hū′mĭd	′hju mɪd
humidity	hyoo MID uh ti	hū mĭd′ĭ tĭ	hju ′mɪd ə tɪ
	hyoo MID i ti	hū mĭd′ĭ tĭ § 50(16)	hju ′mɪd ɪ tɪ
humiliate	hyoo MIL i ayt	hū mĭl′ĭ āt	hju ′mɪl ɪ et
humility	hyoo MIL uh ti	hū mĭl′ĭ tĭ	hju ′mɪl ə tɪ
	hyoo MIL i ti	hū mĭl′ĭ tĭ	hju ′mɪl ɪ tɪ
humor, humour	HYOO muhr	hū′mēr	′hju mɚ, ′ju-; *ES*
	YOO muhr	ū′mēr §§ 1, 27(1), 47(3)	-mə(r)

	SIMPLIFIED	DIACRITICAL	PHONETIC
—— in the normal senses of *"state of mind or disposition of feeling; mood,"* and in all the verb senses, often	YOO muhr	ū′mēr	'ju mɚ; *ES* -mə(r)
humorist, humourist	HYOO muhr ist YOO muhr ist	hū′mēr ĭst ū′mēr ĭst § 47(2)	'hju mər ɪst 'ju mər ɪst
humorous, humourous	HYOO muhr uhs YOO muhr uhs	hū′mēr ŭs ū′mēr ŭs	'hju mər əs 'ju mər əs
humus	HYOO muhs	hū′mŭs	'hju məs
hundred	HUHN druhd	hŭn′drĕd	'hʌm drəd, -drɪd
hung	*huhng*	hŭng §§ 40(6), 50(24)	hʌŋ
Hungary	HUHNG guh ri	hŭng′gá rĭ	'hʌŋ gə rɪ
hungry	HUHNG gri	hŭng′grĭ	'hʌŋ grɪ
hurly–burly	HUHR li–*buhr* li	hûr′lĭ–bûr′lĭ	'hɝ lɪ–ˌbɝ lɪ; *ES also* 'hɜ lɪ–ˌbɜ lɪ
hurrah (interj., n., v.)	hŏŏ RAW huh RAW huh RAH hŏŏ RAH	hŏŏ rô′ hŭ rô′ hŭ rä′ hŏŏ rä′	hʊ 'rɔ hə 'rɔ hə 'rɑ hʊ 'rɑ
—— (n.–also)	HOO rah	hōō′rä § 47(2)	'hu rɑ
hurricane	HUHR i kayn HUHR i kin HUHR i kuhn	hûr′ĭ kān hûr′ĭ kĭn hûr′ĭ kĕn § 40(7)	'hɝ ɪ ken, -kɪn, -kən; *ES also* 'hɜ rɪ-, 'hʌ-
husbandry	HUHZ buhnd ri	hŭz′bănd rĭ	'hʌz bənd rɪ
hussar	hŏŏ ZAHR *huh* ZAHR	hŏŏ zär′ hŭ zär′	hʊ 'zɑr, hʌ-; *ES* 'zɑ:(r), *E also* 'za:(r)
hussy	HUHZ i HUHS i	hŭz′ĭ hŭs′ĭ	'hʌz ɪ 'hʌs ɪ
hustle	HUHS ′l	hŭs′ ′l	'hʌs ļ
hybrid	HAI brid § 50(34)	hī′brĭd § 47(2)	'haɪ brɪd
hydrangea, Hydrangea	hai DRAN ji uh hai DRAYN ji uh hai DRAYN juh	hī drăn′jĕ á hī drān′jĕ á hī drān′já § 47(1)	haɪ 'dræn dʒɪ ə haɪ 'dren dʒɪ ə haɪ 'dren dʒə
hydraulic	hai DRAW lik § 50(34)	hī drô′lĭk	haɪ 'drɔ lɪk
hydrochloric	*hai* druh KLOH rik *hai* druh KLAW rik *hai* druh KLOR ik	hī′drŏ klō′rĭk § 34(3) hī′drŏ klŏr′ĭk	ˌhaɪ drə 'klo rɪk, -'klɔ-, -'klɑr-; *ES also* -'klɒr-

	SIMPLIFIED	DIACRITICAL	PHONETIC
hydrometer	haī DROM i tuhr § 50(34)	hī drŏm′ĕ tēr	haɪ ʹdrɑm ɪ tɚ; *ES* -tə(r), *also* -ʹdrɒm-
hydrophobia	*haī* druh FOH bi uh § 50(34)	hī′drŏ fō′bĭ *a* § 28(9)	ˌhaɪ drə ʹfo bɪ ə
hyena, hyaena	haī EE nuh § 50(34)	hī ē′n*a*	haɪ ʹi nə
hygiene	HAī jeen HAī ji een § 50(34)	hī′jēn hī′jĭ ēn § 47(3)	ʹhaɪ dʒin ʹhaɪ dʒɪ in
hygienic	*haī* ji EN ik *haī* JEE nik	hī′jĭ ĕn′ĭk hī jē′nĭk § 47(1)	ˌhaɪ dʒɪ ʹɛn ɪk haɪ ʹdʒi nɪk
hygienist	HAī ji uhn ist	hī′jĭ ĕn ĭst	ʹhaɪ dʒɪ ən ɪst
hymeneal	*haī* muh NEE uhl	hī′mĕ nē′ăl	ˌhaɪ mə ʹni əl
hymn	him	hĭm § 33(1)	hɪm
hyperbole	haī PUHR buh lee haī PUHR buh li	hī pûr′bŏ lē hī pûr′bŏ lē	haɪ ʹpɝ bə li, -lɪ; *ES also* -ʹpɝ bə-
hyperbolic	*haī* puhr BOL ik	hī′pēr bŏl′ĭk	ˌhaɪ pɚ ʹbɑl ɪk; *ES* -pə-, *also* -ʹbɒl-
hyperbolical	*haī* puhr BOL i kuhl	hī′pēr bŏl′ĭ kăl	ˌhaɪ pɝ ʹbɑl ɪ kəl; *ES also* -pɝ ʹbɒl-
hypochondriac	*haī* puh KON dri ak *hip* uh KON dri ak	hī′pŏ kŏn′drĭ ăk hĭp′ŏ kŏn′drĭ ăk	ˌhaɪ pə ʹkɑn drɪ æk, ˌhɪp ə-; *ES also* -ʹkɒn-
hypochondriacal	*haī* puh kon DRAī uh kuhl *hip* uh kon DRAī uh kuhl	hī′pŏ kŏn drī′*a* kăl hĭp′ŏ kŏn drī′*a* kăl	ˌhaɪ pə kɑn ʹdraɪ ə kəl, ˌhɪp ə-; *ES also* -kɒn-
hypocrisy	hi POK ruh si hi POK ri si	hĭ pŏk′rĭ sĭ hĭ pŏk′rĭ sĭ	hɪ ʹpɑk rə sɪ, -rɪ-; *ES also* -ʹpɒk-
hypocrite	HIP uh krit	hĭp′ŏ krĭt	ʹhɪp ə krɪt
hypotenuse	haī POT i nyoos haī POT i noos hi POT i nyoos hi POT i noos	hī pŏt′ĕ nūs hĭ pŏt′ĕ nūs §§ 47(1), 50(32, 34)	haɪ ʹpɑt ɪ njus, -nus, hɪ-, -ʹpɑt n̩-; *ES also* -ʹpɒt-
hyssop	HIS uhp § 50(34)	hĭs′ŭp § 47(2)	ʹhɪs əp
hysteria	his TĪER i uh his TIR i uh his TEER i uh	hĭs tēr′ĭ *a* § 24(2) hĭs tēr′ĭ *a*	hɪs ʹtɪər ɪ ə, -ʹtɪr-, -ʹtir-; *ES* -ʹtɪər-
hysterics	his TER iks	hĭs tĕr′ĭks	hɪs ʹtɛr ɪks

I

ibis	$\widehat{\text{AI}}$ bis § 50(34)	ī′bĭs	ˈaɪ bɪs
ichneumon	ik NYOO muhn ik NOO muhn	ĭk nū′mŏn § 50(32)	ɪk ˈnju mən ɪk ˈnu mən
icicle	$\widehat{\text{AI}}$ sik 'l § 50(34)	ī′sĭk 'l	ˈaɪ sɪk ļ
iconoclast	$\widehat{\text{ai}}$ KON uh klast § 50(34)	ī kŏn′ŏ klăst	aɪ ˈkɑn ə klæst; *ES also* -ˈkɒn-
iconoclastic	$\widehat{\text{ai}}$ kon uh KLAS tik	ī kŏn′ŏ klăs′tĭk	aɪ ˌkɑn ə ˈklæs tɪk; *ES also* -ˌkɒn-
idea (n.)	$\widehat{\text{ai}}$ DEE uh $\widehat{\text{ai}}$ DI uh § 50(34)	ī dē′à ī dē′à §§ 24(2), 28(3)	aɪ ˈdi ə aɪ ˈdɪ ə
	Sometimes because of sentence rhythm (partic- ularly when a stress immedi- ately follows): $\widehat{\text{AI}}$ di uh *A provincialism when pro- nounced consistently:* $\widehat{\text{AI}}$ di uh	*Sometimes because of sentence rhythm (partic- ularly when a stress immedi- ately follows):* ī′dĕ à *A provincialism when pro- nounced consistently:* ī′dĕ à § 51(2)	*Sometimes because of sentence rhythm (partic- ularly when a stress immedi- ately follows):* ˈaɪ dɪ ə *A provincialism when pro- nounced consistently:* ˈaɪ dɪ ə
ideal	$\widehat{\text{ai}}$ DEE uhl $\widehat{\text{ai}}$ DI uhl § 50(34)	ī dē′ăl ī dē′ăl §§ 24(2), 31(2)	aɪ ˈdi əl, -ˈdil, -ˈdɪ əl
idealism	$\widehat{\text{ai}}$ DEE uhl iz'm $\widehat{\text{ai}}$ DEE uhl iz uhm	ī dē′ăl ĭz'm § 50(15)	aɪ ˈdi əl ɪzm̩, -ˈdil-, -ˈdɪ əl-, -ɪz əm
idealist	$\widehat{\text{ai}}$ DEE uhl ist	ī dē′ăl ĭst	aɪ ˈdi əl ɪst, -ˈdil-, -ˈdɪ əl-
ideality	$\widehat{ai}$ di AL uh ti $\widehat{ai}$ di AL i ti	ī′dĕ ăl′ĭ tĭ ī′dĕ ăl′ĭ tĭ § 50(16)	ˌaɪ dɪ ˈæl ə tɪ ˌaɪ dɪ ˈæl ɪ tɪ
idealization	$\widehat{ai}$ *dee* uhl i ZAY shuhn $\widehat{ai}$ *dee* uhl $\widehat{ai}$ ZAY shuhn	ī dē′ăl ĭ zā′shŭn ī dē′ăl ī zā′shŭn § 47(1)	aɪ ˌdi əl ɪ ˈze ʃən, -ˌdɪ- aɪ ˌdi əl aɪ ˈze ʃən

	SIMPLIFIED	DIACRITICAL	PHONETIC
idealize	aî DEE uhl aîz § 50(34)	ī dē′ăl ĭz	aɪ 'di əl aɪz, -'dɪ-
identify	aî DEN tuh faî aî DEN ti faî § 50(34)	ī děn′tĭ fī ī děn′tĭ fī	aɪ 'dɛn tə faɪ aɪ 'dɛn tɪ faɪ
idiosyncrasy	*id* i uh SING kruh si *id* i oh SING kruh si	ĭd′ĭ ŏ sĭng′krả sĭ § 33(4)	ˌɪd ɪ ə 'sɪŋ krə sɪ, ˌɪd ɪ o-, -'sɪn krə-
idle	AÎ d'l § 50(34)	ī′d'l	'aɪ dl̩
idol	AÎ duhl AÎ d'l § 50(34)	ī′dŭl ī′d'l	'aɪ dəl 'aɪ dl̩
idolatry	aî DOL uh tri § 50(34)	ī dŏl′ả trĭ	aɪ 'dɑl ə trɪ; *ES also* -'dɒl-
idyl, idyll	AÎ duhl AÎ dil § 50(34)	ī′dĭl ī′dĭl § 47(1)	'aɪ dəl, -dl̩- 'aɪ dɪl
idylist	AÎ duhl ist § 50(34)	ī′dĭl ĭst	'aɪ dəl ɪst, -dl̩-
idyllic	aî DIL ik i DIL ik § 50(34)	ī dĭl′ĭk ĭ dĭl′ĭk	aɪ 'dɪl ɪk ɪ 'dɪl ɪk
if	if	ĭf	ɪf, f
ignoble	ig NOH b'l	ĭg nō′b'l	ɪg 'no bl̩
ignominious	*ig* nuh MIN i uhs	ĭg′nŏ mĭn′ĭ ŭs § 50(25)	ˌɪg nə 'mɪn ɪ əs
ignominy	IG nuh min i	ĭg′nŏ mĭn ĭ	'ɪg nə mɪn ɪ
ignore	ig NOHR ig NAWR	ĭg nōr′ § 34(3)	ɪg 'nor, -'nɔr; *ES* -'noə(r), *E also* -'nɔə(r)
Iliad	IL i uhd	ĭl′ĭ ăd	'ɪl ɪ əd
illegitimate (n., adj.)	*il* li JIT uh mit *il* li JIT i mit	ĭl′lĕ jĭt′ĭ mĭt ĭl′lĕ jĭt′ĭ mĭt	ˌɪl ɪ 'dʒɪt ə mɪt, -ɪ mɪt, ˌɪl lɪ-
—— (v.t.)	*il* li JIT uh mayt *il* li JIT i mayt	ĭl′lĕ jĭt′ĭ māt ĭl′lĕ jĭt′ĭ māt § 49(7)	ˌɪl ɪ 'dʒɪt ə met, -ɪ met, ˌɪl lɪ-
illicit	il LIS it i LIS it	ĭl lĭs′ĭt ĭ lĭs′ĭt § 49(7)	ɪl 'lɪs ɪt ɪ 'lɪs ɪt
illimitable	il LIM it uh b'l	ĭl lĭm′ĭt ả b'l § 49(7)	·ɪl 'lɪm ɪt ə bl̩, ɪ 'lɪm-
Illinois	*il* uh NOI *il* i NOI *il* uh NOIZ *il* i NOIZ	ĭl′ĭ noi′ ĭl′ĭ noi′ ĭl′ĭ noiz′ ĭl′ĭ noiz′ § 38(2)	ˌɪl ə 'nɔɪ, ˌɪl ɪ 'nɔɪ ˌɪl ə 'nɔɪz ˌɪl ɪ 'nɔɪz
illuminate (v.)	i LOO muh nayt i LYOO muh nayt i LOO mi nayt i LYOO mi nayt	ĭ lū′mĭ nāt §§ 20(8,9), 49 (7), 50(1, 32) ĭ lū′mĭ nāt	ɪ 'lu mə net ɪ 'lju mə net ɪ 'lu mɪ net ɪ 'lju mɪ net

	SIMPLIFIED	DIACRITICAL	PHONETIC
—— (n., adj.)	i LOO muh nit i LYOO muh nit	ĭ lū′mĭ năt §§ 20(8, 9), 49(7)	ɪ ′lu mə nɪt ɪ ′lju mə nɪt
	i LOO mi nit i LYOO mi nit	ĭ lū′mĭ năt	ɪ ′lu mɪ nɪt ɪ ′lju mɪ nɪt
illumination	i *loo* muh NAY shuhn	ĭ lū′mĭ nā ′shŭn	ɪ ˌlu mə ′ne ʃən
	i *lyoo* muh NAY shuhn		ɪ ˌlju mə ′ne ʃən
	i *loo* mi NAY shuhn	ĭ lū′mĭ nā′shŭn	ɪ ˌlu mɪ ′ne ʃən
	i *lyoo* mi NAY shuhn	§§ 48(2), 50(30)	ɪ ˌlju mɪ ′ne ʃən
illusion	i LOO zhuhn i LYOO zhuhn	ĭ lū′zhŭn §§ 48(2), 49(7), 50(32)	ɪ ′lu ʒən ɪ ′lju ʒən
illusive	i LOO siv i LYOO siv	ĭ lū′sĭv §§ 48(2), 49(7), 50(17, 32)	ɪ ′lu sɪv ɪ ′lju sɪv
illusory	i LOO suh ri i LYOO suh ri	ĭ lū′sŏ rĭ §§ 48(2), 49(7), 50(32)	ɪ ′lu sə rɪ ɪ ′lju sə rɪ
illustrate	IL uhs trayt i LUHS trayt	ĭl′ŭs trāt ĭ lŭs′trāt § 47(3)	′ɪl əs tret ɪ ′lʌs tret
illustration	*il* uhs TRAY shuhn	ĭl′ŭs trā′shŭn	ˌɪl əs ′tre ʃən, ɪ ˌlʌs-
illustrative	i LUHS truh tiv IL uhs *tray* tiv	ĭ lŭs′trᴀ̇ tĭv ĭl′ŭs trā′tĭv	ɪ ′lʌs trə tɪv ′ɪl əs ˌtre tɪv
illustrator	IL uhs *tray* tuhr	ĭl′ŭs trā′tēr	′ɪl əs ˌtre tɚ; *ES* -tə(r)
	i LUHS tray tuhr	ĭ lŭs′trā tēr	ɪ ′lʌs tre tɚ; *ES* -tə(r)
illustrious	i LUHS tri uhs	ĭ lŭs′trĭ ŭs	ɪ ′lʌs trɪ əs
image	IM ij	ĭm′ĭj	′ɪm ɪdʒ
imagery	IM ij ri IM ij uhr i	ĭm′ĭj rĭ ĭm′ĭj ēr ĭ § 47(2)	′ɪm ɪdʒ rɪ ′ɪm ɪdʒ ər ɪ
imaginative	i MAJ uh *nay* tiv i MAJ i *nay* tiv i MAJ uh nuh tiv i MAJ i nuh tiv	ĭ măj′ĭ nā′tĭv ĭ măj′ĭ nā′tĭv ĭ măj′ĭ nᴀ̇ tĭv ĭ măj′ĭ nᴀ̇ tĭv	ɪ ′mædʒ ə ˌne tɪv ɪ ′mædʒ ɪ ˌne tɪv ɪ ′mædʒ ə nə tɪv ɪ ′mædʒ ɪ nə tɪv
imbecile	IM bi sil IM bi s'l	ĭm′bĕ sĭl ĭm′bĕ s'l	′ɪm bɪ sɪl ′ɪm bɪ sl̩
	B., IM bi seel IM bi sail	*B.*, ĭm′bĕ sēl ĭm′bĕ sīl §§ 28(5), 47(2), 51(4)	*B.*, ′ɪm bɪ sil ′ɪm bɪ saɪl
imbecility	*im* bi SIL uh ti *im* bi SIL i ti	ĭm′bĕ sĭl′ĭ tĭ ĭm′bĕ sĭl′ĭ tĭ § 50(16)	ˌɪm bɪ ′sɪl ə tɪ ˌɪm bɪ ′sɪl ɪ tɪ
imbroglio	im BROHL yoh	ĭm brōl′yō § 47(2)	ɪm ′brol jo

	SIMPLIFIED	DIACRITICAL	PHONETIC
imbrue	im BROO	ĭm brōō′ § 40(4)	ɪm 'bru
imbue	im BYOO	ĭm bū′ § 49(9)	ɪm 'bju
imitative	IM uh *tay* tiv	ĭm′ĭ tā′tĭv	'ɪm ə ˌte tɪv
	IM i *tay* tiv	ĭm′ĭ tā′tĭv	'ɪm ɪ ˌte tɪv
	IM uh tuh tiv	ĭm′ĭ tȧ tĭv	'ɪm ə tə tɪv
immaculate (adj.)	i MAK yŏŏ lit	ĭ măk′ů lĭt	ɪ 'mæk jʊ lɪt, -jə-, -ju-
—— (v.t.)	i MAK yŏŏ layt	ĭ măk′ů lāt § 49(9)	ɪ 'mæk jʊ let, -ju-, -jə-
immature	*im* uh TYOOR	ĭm′ȧ tūr′	ˌɪm ə 'tjʊr, -'tʃʊr;
	im uh TYOOR	§§ 34(21), 40(4)	ES -'tjʊə(r), -'tʃʊə(r)
	im uh TOOR		ˌɪm ə 'tʊr; ES
	im uh TOOR		-'tʊə(r)
immediate	i MEE di uht	ĭ mē′dĭ ĭt	ɪ 'mi dɪ ət
	i MEE di it	ĭ mē′dĭ ĭt § 28(9)	ɪ 'mi dɪ ɪt
immediately	i MEE di uht li	ĭ mē′dĭ ĭt lĭ	ɪ 'mi dɪ ət lɪ
	i MEE di it li	ĭ mē′dĭ ĭt lĭ	ɪ 'mi dɪ ɪt lɪ
immense	i MENS	ĭ měns′	ɪ 'mɛns
immersion	i MUHR shuhn	ĭ mûr′shŭn	ɪ 'mɝ ʃən; ES also -'mɜ-
	Gaining ground:	*Gaining ground:*	*Gaining ground:*
	i MUHR zhuhn	ĭ mûr′zhŭn §§ 50(28), 51(5)	ɪ 'mɝ ʒən; ES also -'mɜ-
immigrant	IM uh gruhnt	ĭm′ĭ grȧnt	'ɪm ə grənt
	IM uh grant	ĭm′ĭ grănt	'ɪm ə grænt
	IM i grant	ĭm′ĭ grănt	'ɪm ɪ grænt
imminent	IM uh nuhnt	ĭm′ĭ něnt	'ɪm ə nənt
	IM i nuhnt	ĭm′ĭ něnt	'ɪm ɪ nənt
immobile	im MOH bil	ĭm mō′bĭl	ɪm 'mo bɪl
	i MOH bil	ĭ mō′bĭl	ɪ 'mo bɪl
	im MOH beel	ĭm mō′bēl	ɪm 'mo bil
	i MOH beel	ĭ mō′bēl §§ 28(5), 49(8)	ɪ 'mo bil
immortal	i MAWR tuhl	ĭ môr′tăl	ɪ 'mɔr təl, -tl̩; ES
	i MAWR t'l	ĭ môr′t'l § 49(8)	-'mɔə-
immune	i MYOON	ĭ mūn′ § 48(2)	ɪ 'mjun
immunize	IM yŏŏ naiz	ĭm′ů nīz	'ɪm jʊ naɪz, -jə-,
	ɪ MYOON aiz § 50(34)	ĭ mūn′īz § 49(8)	-ju-, ɪ 'mju naɪz
immure	i MYOOR	ĭ mūr′ §§ 34(21), 48(2)	ɪ 'mjʊr; ES
	i MYOOR		ɪ 'mjʊə(r)
impartiality	*im* pahr shi AL uh ti	ĭm′pär shĭ ăl′ĭ tĭ	ˌɪm pɑr ʃɪ 'æl ə tɪ,
	im pahr shi AL i ti	ĭm′pär shĭ ăl′ɪ tĭ	-ɪ tɪ, -pɑr 'ʃæl ə-;
	im pahr SHAL uh ti	ĭm′pär shăl′ĭ tĭ §§ 28(9), 47(2), 50(16)	ES -'pɑ-, E also -'pɑ-
imperial	im PĬER i uhl	ĭm pēr′ĭ ăl	ɪm 'pɪər ɪ əl,
	im PIR i uhl	§ 24(2)	-'pɪr-, -'pir-; ES
	im PEER i uhl	ĭm pēr′ĭ ăl	-'pɪər-

	SIMPLIFIED	DIACRITICAL	PHONETIC
imperturbable	*im* puhr TUHR buh b'l	ĭm′pẽr tûr′bà b'l	ˌɪm pɚ ′tɝ bə bļ, *ES also* -pə ′tɝ-
imperturbably	*im* puhr TUHR buh bli	ĭm′pẽr tûr′bà blĭ § 50(20)	ˌɪm pɚ ′tɝ bə blɪ; *ES also* -pə ′tɝ-
impervious	im PUHR vi uhs	ĭm pûr′vĭ ŭs § 28(9)	ɪm ′pɝ vɪ əs; *ES also* -′pɝ-
impetuosity	im *pech* ŏŏ OS uh ti	ĭm pĕt′ů ŏs′ĭ tĭ	ɪm ˌpɛtʃ ʊ ′ɑs ə tɪ, -ɪ tɪ,
	im *pech* ŏŏ OS i ti		-ˌpɛt jʊ ′ɑs-; *ES*
	im *pet* yŏŏ OS uh ti	ĭm pĕt′ů ŏs′ĭ tĭ	*also* -′ɒs-
	im *pet* yŏŏ OS i ti	§ 50(33)	
impetuous	im PECH ŏŏ uhs	ĭm pĕt′ů ŭs	ɪm ′pɛtʃ ʊ əs
	im PET yŏŏ uhs	§ 50(25,33)	ɪm ′pɛt jʊ əs, -ju-
impetus	IM pi tuhs	ĭm′pĕ tŭs	′ɪm pɪ təs, -pə-
impiety	im PAI uh ti § 50(34)	ĭm pī′ĕ tĭ	ɪm ′paɪ ə tɪ
impinge	im PINJ	ĭm pĭnj′	ɪm ′pɪndʒ
impious	IM pi uhs	ĭm′pĭ ŭs § 28(9)	′ɪm pɪ əs
implacable	im PLAY kuh b'l	ĭm plā′kà b'l	ɪm ′ple kə bļ
	im PLAK uh b'l	ĭm plăk′à b'l § 47(1)	ɪm ′plæk ə bļ
impolitik	im POL uh tik	ĭm pŏl′ĭ tĭk	ɪm ′pɑl ə tɪk,
	im POL i tik	ĭm pŏl′ĭ tĭk	-ɪ tɪk; *ES also* -′pɒl-
import (v.)	im POHRT	ĭm pōrt′ § 34(3)	ɪm ′port, -′pɔrt;
	im PAWRT		*ES* -′poət, *E also* -′poət
	Freq., esp in contrast with "export":	*Freq., esp. in contrast with "export":*	*Freq., esp. in contrast with "export":*
	IM pohrt	ĭm′pōrt § 34(3)	′ɪm port, -pɔrt;
	IM pawrt		*ES* -poət, *E also* -poət
—— (n.)	IM port	ĭm′pōrt § 34(3)	′ɪm port, -pɔrt;
	IM pawrt		*ES* -poət, *E also* -poət
importunate (v.t.)	im PAWR chŏŏ nayt	ĭm pôr′tů nāt	ɪm ′pɔr tʃʊ net, -tʃə-, -tjʊ-, -tjə-; *ES* -′pɔə-
	im PAWR chuh nayt		
	im PAWR tyŏŏ nayt		
—— (adj.)	im PAWR chŏŏ nit	ĭm pôr′tů nĭt §§ 20(8, 9), 50(2, 33)	ɪm ′pɔr tʃʊ nɪt, -tʃə-, -tjʊ-, -tjə-; *ES* -′pɔə-
	im PAWR chuh nit		
	im PAWR tyŏŏ nit		

	SIMPLIFIED	DIACRITICAL	PHONETIC
importune (v.)	*im* pawr TYOON	ĭm′pôr tūn′	‚ɪm pər ′tjun,
	im pawr TOON	§§ 34(13),	-′tun, -pə-; *ES*
		48(2),　50(33),	-pɔə-, -pə-
		51(8)	
	Occas.:	*Occas.:*	*Occas.:*
	im PAWR chuhn	ĭm pôr′tŭn	ɪm ′pɔr tʃən; *ES*
			-′pɔə-
impostor	im POS tuhr	ĭm pŏs′tẽr	ɪm ′pɑs tɚ; *ES*
			-tə(r), *also*
			-′pɒs-
imposture	im POS chuhr	ĭm pŏs′tŭr	ɪm ′pɑs tʃɚ; *ES*
		§ 50(33)	-tʃə(r),　*also*
			-′pɒs-
impotence	IM puh tuhns	ĭm′pŏ tĕns	′ɪm pə təns
impotency	IM puh tuhn si	ĭm′pŏ tĕn sĭ	′ɪm pə tən sɪ
impotent	IM puh tuhnt	ĭm′pŏ tĕnt	′ɪm pə tənt
impracticable	im PRAK ti kuh b'l	ĭm prăk′tĭ ká b'l	ɪm ′præk tɪ kə bļ
imprecate	IM pri kayt	ĭm′prĕ kāt	′ɪm prɪ ket
imprecation	*im* pri KAY shuhn	ĭm′prĕ kā′shŭn	‚ɪm prɪ ′ke ʃən
imprecatory	IM pri kuh *toh* ri	ĭm′prĕ ká tō′rĭ	′ɪm prɪ kə ‚to rɪ
	IM pri kuh *taw* ri	§§ 34(3), 47(2),	′ɪm prɪ kə ‚tɔ rɪ
		51(4)	
	B., IM pri *kay* tuhr i	*B.,* ĭm′prĕ kā′tẽr ĭ	*B.,* ′ɪm prɪ ‚ke tə rɪ
impregnable	im PREG nuh b'l	ĭm prĕg′ná b'l	ɪm ′preg nə bļ
impregnate (v.)	im PREG nayt	ĭm prĕg′nāt	ɪm ′preg net
—— (adj.)	im PREG nit	ĭm prĕg′năt § 20(8, 9)	ɪm ′preg nɪt
impresario	*im* pre SAH ri oh	ĭm′prä sä′rĭ ō	‚ɪm pre ′sɑ rɪ o,
	im pri SAH ri oh	§§ 20(8),　47(1)	-prɪ-, -pre-, -′se-
impress (v.)	im PRES	ĭm′prĕs′ § 12	ɪm ′pres
—— (n.)	IM pres	ĭm′prĕs	′ɪm pres
imprint (v.t.)	im PRINT	ĭm prĭnt′ § 12	ɪm ′prɪnt
—— (n.)	IM print	ĭm′prĭnt	′ɪm prɪnt
impromptu	im PROMP tyoo	ĭm prŏmp′tū	ɪm ′prɑmp tju,
	im PROMP too	§ 48(2)	-tu-; *ES also* -′prɒmp-
improvisation	*im* pruh vai ZAY shuhn	ĭm′prŏ vī zā′shŭn	‚ɪm prə vaɪ ′ze ʃən,
	im prov i ZAY shuhn	ĭm′prŏv ĭ zā′ shŭn § 47(3)	‚ɪm prɑv ɪ ′ze ʃən, -′se-; *ES also* -′prɒv-
improvise	IM pruh vaiz	ĭm′prŏ vīz	′ɪm prə vaɪz
	im pruh VAIZ § 50(34)	ĭm′prŏ vīz′ § 47(3)	‚ɪm prə ′vaɪz
impugn	im PYOON	ĭm pūn′ §§ 48(2), 50(32)	ɪm ′pjun

impulse (n.)	IM *puhls*	ĭm′pŭls′ § 40(6)	'ɪm ˌpʌls
—— (v.t.)	im PUHLS	ĭm pŭls′ § 12	ɪm 'pʌls
imputation	*im* pyŏŏ TAY shuhn	ĭm′pŭ tā′shŭn	ˌɪm pjʊ 'te ʃən, -pju-
inadvertent	*in* uhd VUHR tuhnt	ĭn′ăd vûr′tĕnt	ˌɪn əd 'vɝ tənt, -tn̩t; *ES also* -'vɝ-
inalienability	ĭn *ayl* yuhn uh BIL uh ti	ĭn āl′yĕn *ȧ* bĭl′′ĭ tĭ	ɪn ˌel jən ə 'bɪl ə tɪ
	in *ayl* yuhn uh BIL i ti	ĭn āl′yĕn *ȧ* bĭl′ĭ tĭ	ɪn ˌel jən ə 'bɪl ɪ tɪ
	in *ay* li uhn uh BIL uh ti	ĭn ā′lĭ ĕn *ȧ* bĭl′′ĭ tĭ § 49(9)	ɪn ˌe lɪ ən ə 'bɪl ə tɪ
inalienable	in AYL yuhn uh b'l	ĭn āl′yĕn *ȧ* b'l	ɪn 'el jən ə bl̩
	in AY li uhn uh b'l	ĭn ā′lĭ ĕn *ȧ* b'l § 49(9)	ɪn 'e lɪ ən ə bl̩
inanition	*in* uh NISH uhn	ĭn′*ȧ* nĭsh′ŭn	ˌɪn ə 'nɪʃ ən
	in a NISH uhn	ĭn′ă nĭsh′ŭn	ˌɪn æ 'nɪʃ ən
inapplicable	in AP li kuh b'l	ĭn ăp′lĭ k*ȧ* b'l § 49(9)	ɪn 'æp lɪ kə bl̩
inarticulate	*in* ahr TIK yŏŏ lit	ĭn′är tĭk′û lăt § 49(9)	ˌɪn ar 'tɪk jʊ lɪt, -jə-, -ju-; *ES* -ɑ: 'tɪk-, *E also* -ɑ: 'tɪk-
inaugurate (v.t.)	in AW gyŏŏ rayt	ĭn ô′gû rāt	ɪn 'ɔ gjʊ ret, -gjə-, -gju-
incalculable	in KAL kyŏŏ luh b'l	ĭn kăl′kû l*ȧ* b'l § 49(9)	ɪn 'kæl kjʊ lə bl̩, -kjə-, -kju-
incandescent	*in* kuhn DES uhnt	ĭn′kăn dĕs′ĕnt	ˌɪn kən 'des ənt
	in kuhn DES 'nt	ĭn′kăn dĕs′ 'nt	ˌɪn kən 'des nt̩
incarnate (v.)	in KAHR nayt	ĭn kär′nāt	ɪn 'kar net; *ES* -'kɑ:-, *E also* -'ka:-
—— (adj.)	in KAHR nit	ĭn kär′năt	ɪn 'kar nɪt, -net;
	in KAHR nayt	§§ 20(8, 9), 49(9)	*ES* -'kɑ:-, *E also* -'ka:-
incendiarism	in SEN di uh riz'm	ĭn sĕn′dĭ *ȧ* rĭz'm §§ 28(9), 50(15)	ɪn 'sen dɪ ə rɪzm̩, -rɪz əm
	in SEN di uh riz uhm		
incendiary	in SEN di *er* i	ĭn sĕn′dĭ ĕr′ĭ	ɪn 'sen dɪ ˌer ɪ
	B., in SEN di uhr i	*B.*, ĭn sĕn′dĭ ēr ĭ § 51(4)	*B.*, ɪn 'sen dɪ ə rɪ
incense ("*perfume*")	IN sens	ĭn′sĕns § 47(2)	'ɪn sens
incense ("*anger*")	in SENS	ĭn sĕns′	ɪn 'sens
incisive	in SAI siv § 50(34)	ĭn sī′sĭv § 50(17)	ɪn 'saɪ sɪv, -zɪv

	SIMPLIFIED	DIACRITICAL	PHONETIC
incisor	in SAI zuhr § 50(34)	ĭn sī′zẽr	ɪn ˈsaɪ zɚ; *ES* -zə(r)
inclement	in KLEM uhnt	ĭn klĕm′ĕnt	ɪn ˈklɛm ənt
incline (v.)	in KLAIN	ĭn klīn′	ɪn ˈklaɪn
—— (n.)	IN klain	ĭn′klīn	ˈɪn klaɪn
	in KLAIN § 50(34)	ĭn klīn′ § 12	ɪn ˈklaɪn
include	in KLOOD	ĭn klo͞od′ § 40(4)	ɪn ˈklud
inclusive	in KLOO siv	ĭn klo͞o′sĭv §§ 40(4), 47(2)	ɪn ˈklu sɪv, -zɪv
incognito	in KOG ni toh	ĭn kŏg′nĭ tō	ɪn ˈkɑg nɪ to, -ˈkɒg-
incombustible	*in* kuhm BUHS tuh b'l	ĭn′kŏm bŭs′tĭ b'l	ˌɪn kəm ˈbʌs tə bļ
	in kuhm BUHS ti b'l	ĭn′kŏm bŭs′tĭ b'l § 49(9)	ˌɪn kəm ˈbʌs tɪ bļ
incomparable (*adj.*)	in KOM puh ruh b'l	ĭn kŏm′pá rá b'l § 49(9)	ɪn ˈkɑm pə rə bļ; *ES also* -ˈkɒm-
incompatible	*in* kuhm PAT uh b'l	ĭn′kŏm păt′ĭ b'l	ˌɪn kəm ˈpæt ə bļ
	in kuhm PAT i b'l	ĭn′kŏm păt′ĭ b'l § 49(9)	ˌɪn kəm ˈpæt ɪ bļ
incompetent	in KOM pi tuhnt	ĭn kŏm′pē tĕnt § 49(9)	ɪn ˈkɑm pɪ tənt; *ES also* -ˈkɒm-
incomplete	*in* kuhm PLEET	ĭn′kŏm plēt′ § 49(9)	ˌɪn kəm ˈplit
incongruent	in KONG gro͞o uhnt	in kŏng′gro͞o ĕnt § 49(9)	ɪn ˈkɑŋ grʊ ənt; *ES also* -ˈkɒŋ-
incongruity	*in* kong GROO uh ti	ĭn′kŏng gro͞o′ĭ tĭ	ˌɪn kɑŋ ˈgru ə tɪ, -ɪ tɪ, -kən ˈgru-, -kən-; *ES also* -kɒŋ-, -kɒn-
	in kong GROO i ti	ĭn′kŏng gro͞o′ĭ tĭ §§ 33(4), 47(2), 48(2)	
incongruous	in KONG gro͞o uhs	ĭn kŏng′gro͞o ŭs	ɪn ˈkɑŋ grʊ əs; *ES* *also* -ˈkɒŋ-
incorporate (v.)	in KAWR puh rayt	ĭn kôr′pŏ rāt § 20(8, 9)	ɪn ˈkɔr pə ret; *ES* -ˈkɔə-
—— (adj.)	in KAWR puh rit	ĭn kôr′pŏ rât	ɪn ˈkɔr pə rɪt, -prɪt; *ES* -ˈkɔə-
incorporation	in *kawr* puh RAY shuhn	ĭn kôr′pŏ rā′shŭn	ɪn ˌkɔr pə ˈre ʃən; *ES* -ˌkɔə-
incorrigible	in KOR i juh b'l in KOR i ji b'l in KAWR i juh b'l in KAWR i ji b'l	ĭn kŏr′ĭ jĭ b'l ĭn kŏr′ĭ jĭ b'l ĭn kôr′ĭ jĭ b'l ĭn kôr′ĭ jĭ b'l § 34(5, 7)	ɪn ˈkɑr ɪ dʒə bļ, -ɪ dʒɪ-, -ˈkɔr-, -ˈkɒr-; *ES often* -ˈkɒr-
increase (v.)	in KREES	ĭn krēs′	ɪn ˈkris
—— (n.)	IN krees	ĭn′krēs §§ 12, 33(4)	ˈɪn kris

incredulity	*in* kri DYOO luh ti	ĭn′krĕ dū′lĭ tĭ	ˌɪn krɪ ˈdju lə tɪ
	in kri DOO luh ti		ˌɪn krɪ ˈdu lə tɪ
	in kri DYOO li ti	ĭn′krĕ dū′lĭ tĭ	ˌɪn krɪ ˈdju lɪ tɪ
	in kri DOO li ti	§§ 48(2), 49(9), 50(16, 32)	ˌɪn krɪ ˈdu lɪ tɪ
increment	IN kri muhnt	ĭn′krĕ mĕnt	ˈɪn krɪ mənt
	ING kri muhnt	ĭng′krĕ mĕnt § 47(2)	ˈɪŋ krɪ mənt
incubate	IN kyōŏ bayt	ĭn′kû bāt	ˈɪn kjʊ bet
	ING kyōŏ bayt	ĭng′kû bāt §§ 47(2), 50(1, 24)	ˈɪŋ kjʊ-, -kjə-, -kyu-
incubus	IN kyōŏ buhs	ĭn′kû bŭs	ˈɪn kjʊ bəs,
	ING kyōŏ buhs	ĭng′kû bŭs § 47(2)	ˈɪŋ kjʊ-, -kjə-, -kju-
inculcate	in KUHL kayt	ĭn kŭl′kāt	ɪn ˈkʌl ket
	IN *kuhl* kayt	ĭn′kŭl kāt §§ 40(6), 47(3)	ˈɪn kʌl ket
indecision	*in* di SIZH uhn	ĭn′dĕ sĭzh′ŭn § 49(9)	ˌɪn dɪ ˈsɪʒ ən
indecisive	*in* di SAI siv § 50(34)	ĭn′dĕ sĭ′sĭv § 49(9)	ˌɪn dɪ ˈsaɪ sɪv
indecorous	in DEK uh ruhs	ĭn dĕk′ŏ rŭs	ɪn ˈdɛk ə rəs
	in di KOH ruhs	ĭn′dĕ kō′rŭs § 47(3)	ˌɪn dɪ ˈko rəs; *EN also* -ˈkɔ-
indecorum	*in* di KOH ruhm	ĭn′dĕ kō′rŭm	ˌɪn dɪ ˈko rəm
	in di KAW ruhm	§§ 34(3), 49(9)	ˌɪn dɪ ˈkɔ rəm
indefatigability	*in* di *fat* uh guh BIL uh ti	ĭn′dĕ făt′ĭ *gá* bĭl′ĭ tĭ	ˌɪn dɪ ˌfæt ə gə ˈbɪl ə tɪ
	in di *fat* i guh BIL i ti	ĭn′dĕ făt′ĭ *gá* bĭl′ĭ tĭ	ˌɪn dɪ ˌfæt ɪ gə ˈbɪl ɪ tɪ
indefatigable	*in* di FAT uh guh b'l	ĭn′dĕ făt′ĭ *gá* b′l	ˌɪn dɪ ˈfæt ə gə bl̩
	in di FAT i guh b'l	ĭn′dĕ făt′ĭ *gá* b′l	ˌɪn dɪ ˈfæt ɪ gə bl̩
indefeasible	*in* di FEE zuh b'l	ĭn′dĕ fē′zĭ b′l	ˌɪn dɪ ˈfi zə bl̩
	in di FEE zi b'l	ĭn′dĕ fē′zĭ b′l	ˌɪn dɪ ˈfi zɪ bl̩
indenture	in DEN chuhr	ĭn dĕn′tûr	ɪn ˈdɛn tʃɚ, -tjɚ;
	in DEN tyuhr	§ 50(33)	*ES* -tʃə(r), -tjə(r)
indeterminate	*in* di TUHR muh nit	ĭn′dĕ tûr′mĭ nät	ˌɪn dɪ ˈtɝ mə nit; *ES* -ˈtɜ-
	in di TUHR mi nit	ĭn′dĕ tûr′mĭ nät § 50(2)	ˌɪn dɪ ˈtɝ mɪ nɪt; *ES also* -ˈtɜ-
Indian	IN di uhn	ĭn′dĭ ăn §§ 28(9), 38(12), 47(2)	ˈɪn dɪ ən, -djən
indicative (adj.)	in DIK uh tiv	ĭn dĭk′*á* tĭv	ɪn ˈdɪk ə tɪv
—— *"pointing out; suggestive,"* often	B., IN duh *kay* tiv	B., ĭn′dĭ kā′tĭv	B., ˈɪn də ˌke tɪv

	SIMPLIFIED	DIACRITICAL	PHONETIC
indict	in DĀIT § 50(34)	ĭn dīt′	ɪn 'daɪt
indictment	in DĀIT muhnt § 50(34)	ĭn dīt′mĕnt § 50(22)	ɪn 'daɪt mənt
indigenous	in DIJ i nuhs	ĭn dĭj′ĕ nŭs § 50(25)	ɪn 'dɪdʒ ɪ nəs
indigent	IN duh juhnt IN di juhnt	ĭn′dĭ jĕnt ĭn′dĭ jĕnt	'ɪn də dʒənt 'ɪn dɪ dʒənt
indigestion	*in* duh JES chuhn *in* di JES chuhn	ĭn′dĭ jĕs′chŭn ĭn′dĭ jĕs′chŭn	ˌɪn də 'dʒɛs tʃən ˌɪn dɪ 'dʒɛs tʃən
indisputability	in *dis* pyŏŏ tuh BIL uh ti in *dis* pyŏŏ tuh BIL i ti *in* dis PYOOT uh bil uh ti *in* di SPYOOT uh bil uh ti *in* dis PYOOT uh bil i ti *in* di SPYOOT uh bil i ti	ĭn dĭs′pŭ tă bĭl′ĭ tĭ ĭn dĭs′pŭ tă bĭl′ĭ tĭ ĭn′dĭs pūt′ă bĭl ĭ tĭ ĭn′dĭs pūt′ă bĭl ĭ tĭ	ɪn ˌdɪs pju tə 'bɪl ə tɪ, -pju-, -ɪ tɪ ˌɪn dɪs 'pjut ə bɪl ə tɪ ˌɪn dɪ 'spjut ə bɪl ə tɪ ˌɪn dɪs 'pjut ə bɪl ɪ tɪ ˌɪn dɪ 'spjut ə bɪl ɪ tɪ
indisputable	in DIS pyŏŏ tuh b'l *in* dis PYOOT uh b'l *in* di SPYOOT uh b'l	ĭn dĭs′pŭ tă b'l ĭn′dĭs pūt′ă b'l §§ 47(1), 50(32)	ɪn 'dɪs pju tə bļ ˌɪn dɪs 'pjut ə bļ ˌɪn dɪ 'spjut ə bļ
indissolubility	*in* di *sol* yŏŏ BIL uh ti *in* di *sol* yŏŏ BIL i ti	ĭn′dĭ sŏl′ŭ bĭl′ĭ tĭ ĭn′dĭ sŏl′ŭ bĭl′ĭ tĭ	ˌɪn dɪ ˌsɑl ju 'bɪl ə tɪ, -ju-, -jə-, -ɪ tɪ; *ES also* -ˌsɒl-
—— *also, esp. in the non-literal senses,*	in *dis* uh lŏŏ BIL uh ti in *dis* uh lyŏŏ BIL uh ti in *dis* uh lŏŏ BIL i ti in *dis* uh lyŏŏ BIL i ti	ĭn dĭs′ŏ lŭ bĭl′ĭ tĭ ĭn dĭs′ŏ lŭ bĭl′ĭ tĭ	ɪn ˌdɪs ə lu 'bɪl ə tɪ, -ə ljʊ-, -ə lu-, -ə lju-, -ɪ tɪ, ɪn ˌdɪs ļ jʊ-
indissoluble	*in* di SOL yŏŏ b'l	ĭn′dĭ sŏl′ŭ b'l	ˌɪn dɪ 'sɑl jʊ bļ, -jə-, -ju-; *ES also* -'sɒl-
—— *also, esp. in the non-literal senses,*	in DIS uh lŏŏ b'l in DIS uh lyŏŏ b'l	ĭn dĭs′ŏ lŭ b'l	ɪn 'dɪs ə lu bļ, -ljʊ-, -lu-, -lju-, -'dɪs ļ-
indite	in DĀIT § 50(34)	ĭn dīt′	ɪn 'daɪt
individual	*in* duh VIJ ŏŏ uhl *in* duh VID yŏŏ uhl *in* di VIJ ŏŏ uhl *in* di VID yŏŏ uhl	ĭn′dĭ vĭd′ŭ ăl ĭn′dĭ vĭd′ŭ ăl § 50(33)	ˌɪn də 'vɪdʒ ʊ əl ˌɪn də 'vɪd ju əl ˌɪn dɪ 'vɪdʒ ʊ əl ˌɪn dɪ 'vɪd ju əl

	SIMPLIFIED	DIACRITICAL	PHONETIC
indubitable	in DYOO buh tuh b'l	ĭn dū′bĭ tá b'l	ɪn ˈdju bə tə bḷ
	in DOO buh tuh b'l		ɪn ˈdu bə tə bḷ
	in DYOO bi tuh b'l	ĭn dū′bĭ tá b'l	ɪn ˈdju bɪ tə bḷ
	in DOO bi tuh b'l	§§ 48(2), 49(9), 50(32)	ɪn ˈdu bɪ tə bḷ
induce	in DYOOS	ĭn dūs′	ɪn ˈdjus
	in DOOS	§§ 48(2), 50(32)	ɪn ˈdus
industry	IN duhs tri	ĭn′dŭs trĭ	ˈɪn dəs trɪ, -dʌs-
inebriate (v.t.)	in EE bri ayt	ĭn ē′brĭ āt	ɪn ˈi brɪ et
—— (n., adj.)	in EE bri it	ĭn ē′brĭ ăt	ɪn ˈi brɪ ɪt
	in EE bri ayt	§§ 20(8, 9), 50(2)	ɪn ˈi brɪ et
inebriety	*in* i BRAI i ti § 50(34)	ĭn′ĕ brī′ĕ tĭ	ˌɪn ɪ ˈbraɪ ə tɪ
ineffable	in EF uh b'l	ĭn ĕf′á b'l	ɪn ˈɛf ə bḷ
inertia	in UHR shuh	ĭn ûr′shá	ɪn ˈɝ ʃə, -ʃɪ ə; *ES also* ɪn ˈɝ-
	in UHR shi uh	ĭn ûr′shĭ á §§ 47(1), 50(29)	
inestimable	in ES tuh muh b'l	ĭn ĕs′tĭ má b'l	ɪn ˈɛs tə mə bḷ
	in ES ti muh b'l	ĭn ĕs′tĭ má b'l	ɪn ˈɛs tɪ mə bḷ
inexhaustible	*in* eg ZAWS tuh b'l	ĭn′ĕg zôs′tĭ b'l	ˌɪn ɛg ˈzɔs tə bḷ,
	in eg ZAWS ti b'l	ĭn′ĕg zôs′tĭ b'l	ˌɪn ɪg-, -tɪ-
	in ig ZAWS tuh b'l	ĭn′ĭg zôs′tĭ b'l § 47(2)	
inexorable	in EK suh ruh b'l	ĭn ĕk′sŏ rá b'l	ɪn ˈɛk sə rə bḷ
inexpiable	in EKS pi uh b'l	ĭn ĕks′pĭ á b'l	ɪn ˈɛks pɪ ə bḷ
inexplicability	in *eks* pli kuh BIL uh ti	ĭn ĕks′plĭ ká bĭl′ĭ tĭ	ɪn ˌɛks plɪ kə ˈbɪl ə tɪ, ˌɪn ɛks-
	in *eks* pli kuh BIL i ti	ĭn ĕks′plĭ ká bĭl′ĭ tĭ	ɪn ˌɛks plɪ kə ˈbɪl ɪ tɪ, ˌɪn ɛks-
inexplicable	in EKS pli kuh b'l	ĭn ĕks′plĭ ká b'l §§ 47(1), 49(9)	ɪn ˈɛks plɪ kə bḷ ˌɪn ɪk ˈsplɪk ə bḷ
inextricable	in EKS tri kuh b'l	ĭn ĕks′trĭ ká b'l	ɪn ˈɛks trɪ kə bḷ
infamous	IN fuh muhs	ĭn′fá mŭs § 49(9)	ˈɪn fə məs
infantile	IN fuhn tail	ĭn′făn tīl	ˈɪn fən taɪl
	IN fuhn til	ĭn′făn tĭl §§ 47(3), 50(13)	ˈɪn fən tɪl
	Occas.:	*Occas.:*	*Occas.:*
	in FAN tail § 50(34)	ĭn făn′tīl § 51(8)	ɪn ˈfæn taɪl
infantine	IN fuhn tain	ĭn′făn tīn	ˈɪn fən taɪn
	IN fuhn tin § 50(34)	ĭn′făn tĭn § 47(3)	ˈɪn fən tɪn
infatuate (v.t.)	in FACH oo ayt	ĭn făt′û āt	ɪn ˈfætʃ ʊ et,
	in FAT yoo ayt		ɪn ˈfæt jʊ et, -ju-

	SIMPLIFIED	DIACRITICAL	PHONETIC
—— (n.)	in FACH ŏŏ it	ĭn făt′û ăt	ɪn 'fætʃ ʊ ɪt,
	in FAT yŏŏ it	§§ 20(8, 9), 50(2)	ɪn 'fæt jʊ ɪt, -ju-
infatuation	in *fach* ŏŏ AY shuhn	ĭn făt′û ā′shŭn	ɪn 'fætʃ ʊ 'e ʃən, ɪn ˌfæt jʊ 'e ʃən,
	in *fat* yŏŏ AY shuhn	§ 50(30)	-ju-
infectious	in FEK shuhs	ĭn fĕk′shŭs § 50(25)	ɪn 'fɛk ʃəs
infer	in FUHR	ĭn fûr′	ɪn 'fɝ; ES also -'fɜ(r)
inferable	in FUHR uh b'l	ĭn fûr′ă b'l § 47(2)	ɪn 'fɝ ə bl̩; ES also -'fɜr-
inference	IN fuhr uhns	ĭn′fĕr ĕns § 9	'ɪn fər əns
inferential	*in* fuhr EN shuhl	ĭn′fĕr ĕn′shăl	ˌɪn fər 'ɛn ʃəl
	in fuh REN shuhl		ˌɪn fə 'rɛn ʃəl
inferior	in FÏER i uhr	ĭn fēr′Ï ēr § 24(2)	ɪn 'fɪər ɪ ɚ, -'fɪr-, -'fir-; ES
	in FIR i uhr		-fɪər ɪ ə(r),
	in FEER i uhr	ĭn fēr′Ï ēr	
infidel	IN fuh duhl	ĭn′fĭ dĕl	'ɪn fə dəl
	IN fi duhl	ĭn′fĭ dĕl	'ɪn fɪ dəl
infinite	IN fuh nit	ĭn′fĭ nĭt	'ɪn fə nɪt
(adj., n., v.t.)	IN fi nit	ĭn′fĭ nĭt	'ɪn fɪ nɪt
	In church singing, n. often:	*In church singing, n. often:*	*In church singing, n. often:*
	IN fi naͶit	ĭn′fĭ nīt	'ɪn fɪ naɪt
infinitesimal	*in* fin uh TES uh muhl	ĭn′fĭn ĭ tĕs′ĭ măl	ˌɪn fɪn ə 'tɛs ə məl, -ɪ məl, -ml̩
	in fin i TES i muhl	ĭn′fĭn ĭ tĕs′Ï măl	
inflammable	in FLAM uh b'l	ĭn flăm′ă b'l	ɪn 'flæm ə bl̩
influence	IN flŏŏ uhns	ĭn′flŏŏ ĕns §§ 34(23), 40(11), 48(2)	'ɪn flʊ əns
influential	*in* flŏŏ EN shuhl	ĭn′flŏŏ ĕn′shăl §§ 34(23), 48(2)	ˌɪn flʊ 'ɛn ʃəl
influenza	*in* flŏŏ EN zuh	ĭn′flŏŏ ĕn′ză § 48(2)	ˌɪn flʊ 'ɛn zə
information	*in* fuhr MAY shuhn	ĭn′fŏr mā′shŭn § 34(13)	ˌɪn fɚ 'me ʃən; ES -fə-
ingenious	in JEEN yuhs	ĭn jēn′yŭs §§ 28(9), 47(2)	ɪn 'dʒin jəs
ingenuity	*in* ji NYOO uh ti	ĭn′jĕ nū′ĭ tĭ	ˌɪn dʒɪ 'nju ə tɪ
	in ji NOO uh ti		ˌɪn dʒɪ 'nu ə tɪ
	in ji NYOO i ti	ĭn′jĕ nū′Ï tĭ	ˌɪn dʒɪ 'nju ɪ tɪ
	in ji NOO i ti	§§ 48(2), 50(16, 32)	ˌɪn dʒɪ 'nu ɪ tɪ
ingenuous	in JEN yŏŏ uhs	ĭn jĕn′û ŭs	ɪn 'dʒɛn jʊ əs, -ju-
ingrate (adj.)	IN grayt	ĭn′grāt	'ɪn gret
	in GRAYT	ĭn grāt′ § 11	ɪn 'gret

—— (n.)	IN grayt B., in GRAYT	ĭn′grāt B., ĭn grāt′ §§ 47(2), 51(4)	′ın gret B., ın ′gret
ingratiate	in GRAY shi ayt	ĭn grā′shĭ āt	ın ′gre ʃı et
ingredient	in GREE di uhnt	ĭn grē′dĭ ĕnt	ın ′gri dı ənt
inherent	in HĬER uhnt in HIR uhnt in HEER uhnt	ĭn hĕr′ĕnt § 24(2) ĭn hēr′ĕnt	ın ′hıər ənt -′hır-, -′hir-; ES -′hıər-
inhospitable	in HOS pi tuh b'l	ĭn hŏs′pĭ tå b'l	ın ′hɑs pı tə bļ; ES also -′hɒs-
	Gaining ground: *in* hos PIT uh b'l	*Gaining ground:* ĭn′hŏs pĭt′å b'l § 51(5)	*Gaining ground:* ˌın hɑs ′pıt ə bļ; ES also -hɒs-
inhuman	in HYOO muhn	ĭn hū′măn § 48(2)	ın ′hju mən, ın ′ju-
iniquitous	i NIK wuh tuhs i NIK wi tuhs	ĭ nĭk′wĭ tŭs ĭ nĭk′wĭ tŭs	ı ′nık wə təs ı ′nık wı təs
initial	i NISH uhl	ĭ nĭsh′ăl	ı ′nıʃ əl
initiate (v.)	i NISH i ayt	ĭ nĭsh′ĭ āt	ı ′nıʃ ı et
—— (n., adj.)	i NISH i it i NISH i ayt	ĭ nĭsh′ĭ ăt §§ 20(8, 9), 50(2)	ı ′nıʃ ı ıt ı ′nıʃ ı et
initiatory	i NISH i uh *toh* ri i NISH i uh *taw* ri B., i NISH i uh tuhr i	ĭ nĭsh′ĭ å tō′rĭ §§ 34(3), 51(4) B., ĭ nĭsh′ĭ å tēr ĭ	ı ′nıʃ ı ə ˌto rı ı ′nıʃ ı ə ˌtɔ rı B., ı ′nıʃ ı ə tə rı
injure	IN juhr	ĭn′jĕr	′ın dʒɚ; ES -dʒə(r)
injurious	in JOOR i uhs	ĭn jōōr′ĭ ŭs §§ 34(21), 48(2)	ın ′dʒʊr ı əs
inlaid (p.t. of *in- lay*)	in LAYD IN *layd*	ĭn lād′ ĭn′lād′	ın ′led ′ın ˌled
—— as part. adj., usually	IN *layd*	ĭn′lād′ § 47(1)	′ın ˌled
inlay (v.t.)	in LAY	ĭn lā′	ın ′le
—— (n.)	IN *lay*	ĭn′lā′ § 47(2)	′ın ˌle
innate	IN nayt i NAYT in NAYT	ĭn′nāt ĭ nāt′ ĭn nāt′ §§ 11, 47(3)	′ın net ı ′net ın ′net
innocent	IN uh suhnt IN uh s'nt	ĭn′ŏ sĕnt ĭn′ŏ s'nt	′ın ə sənt ′ın ə sņt
innuendo	*in* yŏŏ EN doh	ĭn′ŭ ĕn′dō § 48(2)	ˌın jʊ ′ɛn do, -ju-
inoculate	in OK yŏŏ layt	ĭn ŏk′ŭ lāt	ın ′ɑk jʊ let, -jə-, -ju-; ES also -′ɒk-

	SIMPLIFIED	DIACRITICAL	PHONETIC
inopportune	in *op* uhr TYOON in *op* uhr TOON	ĭn ŏp′ŏr tūn′ §§ 48(2), 49(9), 50(32)	ɪn ˌɑp ɚ ˈtjun, -ˈtun; *ES* -ˌɑp ə-, *also* -ˌɒp-
inquire	in KWAIR § 50(34)	ĭn kwīr′	ɪn ˈkwaɪr; *ES* -ˈkwaɪə(r)
inquiry	in KWAIR i IN kwuh ri IN kwi ri	ĭn kwīr′ĭ ĭn′kwĭ rĭ ĭn′kwĭ rĭ § 47(1)	ɪn ˈkwaɪr ɪ ˈɪn kwə rɪ ˈɪn kwɪ rɪ
insane	in SAYN	ĭn sān′ § 11	ɪn ˈsen
insatiable	in SAY shi uh b'l in SAY shuh b'l	ĭn sā′shĭ *a* b'l ĭn sā′shá b'l § 47(2)	ɪn ˈse ʃɪ ə bl̩ ɪn ˈse ʃə bl̩
insatiate	in SAY shi it	ĭn sā′shĭ ăt §§ 47(2), 50(2)	ɪn ˈse ʃɪ ɪt
inscrutable	in SKROO tuh b'l	ĭn skrōō′tá b'l	ɪn ˈskru tə bl̩
insert (v.t.)	in SUHRT	ĭn sûrt′ § 12	ɪn ˈsɝt; *ES also* -ˈsɜt
—— (n.)	IN suhrt	ĭn′sûrt	ˈɪn sɝt; *ES also* -sɜt
insidious	in SID i uhs	ĭn sĭd′ĭ ŭs § 28(9)	ɪn ˈsɪd ɪ əs
insight	IN *sait* § 50(34)	ĭn′sīt′	ˈɪn ˌsaɪt
insignia	in SIG ni uh	ĭn sĭg′nĭ *a* § 28(9)	ɪn ˈsɪg nɪ ə
insinuate	in SIN yŏŏ ayt	ĭn sĭn′û āt	ɪn ˈsɪn jʊ et, -ju-
insinuation	in *sin* yŏŏ AY shuhn	ĭn sĭn′û ā′shŭn	ɪn ˌsɪn jʊ ˈe ʃən, -ju-
insoluble	in SOL yŏŏ b'l	ĭn sŏl′û b'l	ɪn ˈsɑl jʊ bl̩, -ju-; *ES also* -ˈsɒl-
insomnia	in SOM ni uh	ĭn sŏm′nĭ *a*	ɪn ˈsɑm nɪ ə; *ES* *also* -ˈsɒm-
instead	in STED	ĭn stĕd′	ɪn ˈstɛd
instinct (n.)	IN stingkt	ĭn′stĭngkt	ˈɪn stɪŋkt
—— (adj.)	in STINGKT	ĭn stĭngkt′ § 33(4)	ɪn ˈstɪŋkt
institute	IN stuh tyoot IN stuh toot IN sti tyoot IN sti toot	ĭn′stĭ tūt ĭn′stĭ tūt §§ 48(2), 50(32)	ˈɪn stə tjut ˈɪn stə tut ˈɪn stɪ tjut ˈɪn stɪ tut
institution	*in* stuh TYOO shuhn *in* stuh TOO shuhn *in* sti TYOO shuhn *in* sti TOO shuhn	ĭn′stĭ tū′shŭn ĭn′stĭ tū′shŭn §§ 48(2), 50(32)	ˌɪn stə ˈtju ʃən ˌɪn stə ˈtu ʃən ˌɪn stɪ ˈtju ʃən ˌɪn stɪ ˈtu ʃən
insular	IN syŏŏ luhr IN sŏŏ luhr IN suh luhr	ĭn′sû lẽr § 50(32) ĭn′sŭ lẽr	ˈɪn sjʊ lɚ, -sju-, -sʊ-, -sə-; *ES* -lə(r)

	SIMPLIFIED	DIACRITICAL	PHONETIC
insularity	*in* syŏŏ LAR uh ti	ĭn′sû lăr′ĭ tĭ	ˌɪn sjʊ ˈlær ə tɪ
	in sŏŏ LAR uh ti	§ 50(16, 32)	ˌɪn sʊ ˈlær ə tɪ
	in suh LAR uh ti	ĭn′sŭ lăr′ĭ tĭ	ˌɪn sə ˈlær ə tɪ
	in syŏŏ LAR i ti	ĭn′sû lăr′ĭ tĭ	ˌɪn sjʊ ˈlær ɪ tɪ
	in sŏŏ LAR i ti		ˌɪn sʊ ˈlær ɪ tɪ
	in suh LAR i ti	ĭn′sŭ lăr′ĭ tĭ	ˌɪn sə ˈlær ɪ tɪ
insulate (v.t.)	IN syŏŏ layt	ĭn′sû lāt	ˈɪn sjʊ let, -sju-
	IN sŏŏ layt	§ 50(2, 32)	ˈɪn sʊ let
	IN suh layt	ĭn′sŭ lāt	ˈɪn sə let
insulation	*in* syŏŏ LAY shuhn	ĭn′sû lā′shŭn	ˌɪn sjʊ ˈle ʃən, -sju-
	in sŏŏ LAY shuhn	§ 50(30, 32)	ˌɪn sʊ ˈle ʃən
	in suh LAY shuhn	ĭn′sŭ lā′shŭn	ˌɪn sə ˈle ʃən
insulator	IN syŏŏ *lay* tuhr	ĭn′sû lā′tẽr	ˈɪn sjʊ ˌle tɚ, -sʊ-, -sə-; *ES*
	IN sŏŏ *lay* tuhr		
	IN suh *lay* tuhr	ĭn′sŭ lā′tẽr	-tə(r)
insult (v.)	in SUHLT	ĭn sŭlt′ § 12	ɪn ˈsʌlt
—— (n.)	IN *suhlt*	ĭn′sŭlt § 40(6)	ˈɪn sʌlt
insurance	in SHŎŎR uhns	ĭn shŏŏr′ăns § 34(21)	ɪn ˈʃʊr əns
integer	IN ti juhr	ĭn′tĕ jẽr	ˈɪn tɪ dʒɚ, -tə-; *ES* -dʒə(r)
integral	IN ti gruhl	ĭn′tĕ grăl	ˈɪn tɪ grəl
integrity	in TEG ruh ti	ĭn tĕg′rĭ tĭ	ɪn ˈteg rə tɪ
	in TEG ri ti	ĭn tĕg′rĭ tĭ	ɪn ˈteg rɪ tɪ
integument	in TEG yŏŏ muhnt	ĭn tĕg′û mĕnt § 50(22)	ɪn ˈteg jʊ mənt, -jə-, -ju-
intent	in TENT	ĭn tĕnt′	ɪn ˈtent
interdict (n.)	IN tuhr dikt	ĭn′tẽr dĭkt § 12	ˈɪn tɚ dɪkt; *ES* -tə-
—— (v.t.)	*in* tuhr DIKT	ĭn′tẽr dĭkt′	ˌɪn tɚ ˈdɪkt; *ES* -tə-
interest	IN tuhr est	ĭn′tẽr ĕst	ˈɪn tər est
	IN tuhr ist	ĭn′tẽr ĭst	ˈɪn tər ɪst
	B., IN trist	*B.*, ĭn′trĭst § 51(4)	*B.*, ˈɪn trɪst
interesting	IN tuhr es ting	ĭn′tẽr ĕs tĭng	ˈɪn tər es tɪŋ
	IN tuhr is ting	ĭn′tẽr ĭs tĭng	ˈɪn tər ɪs tɪŋ
	B., IN tris ting	*B.*, ĭn′trĭs tĭng §§ 47(1), 51(4)	*B.*, ˈɪn trɪs tɪŋ
interloper	IN tuhr *lohp* uhr	ĭn′tẽr lōp′ẽr § 47(3)	ˈɪn tɚ ˌlop ɚ; *ES* ˈɪn tə ˌlop ə(r)
interment	in TUHR muhnt	ĭn tûr′mĕnt § 50(22)	ɪn ˈtɝ mənt; *ES also* -ˈtɜ-
interpolate	in TUHR puh layt	ĭn tûr′pŏ lāt	ɪn ˈtɝ pə let, -pɪ-; *ES also* -ˈtɜ-
interpose	*in* tuhr POHZ	ĭn′tẽr pōz′	ˌɪn tɚ ˈpoz; *ES also* -tə-

	SIMPLIFIED	DIACRITICAL	PHONETIC
interposition	*in* tuhr puh ZISH uhn	ĭn′tēr pŏ zĭsh′ŭn § 47(2)	ˌɪn tɚ pə ′zɪʃ ən; *ES also* -tə-
interpretation	in *tuhr* pri TAY shuhn	ĭn tûr′prĕ tā′ shŭn	ɪn ˌtɚ prɪ ′te ʃən; *ES also* -ˌtɚ-
interpretative	in TUHR pri *tay* tiv	ĭn tûr′prĕ tā′tĭv	ɪn ′tɚ prɪ ˌte tɪv. *ES also* -′tɚ-
	in TUHR pri tuh tiv	ĭn tûr′prĕ tă tĭv	ɪn ′tɚ prɪ tə tɪv; *ES also* -′tɚ-
interpreter	in TUHR pruh tuhr	ĭn tûr′prĕ tēr	ɪn ′tɚ prə tɚ, -prɛ-, -prɪ-; *ES*
	in TUHR pre tuhr	ĭn tûr′prĕ tēr	*also* -′tɚ-, *ES* -tə(r)
	in TUHR pri tuhr	ĭn tûr′prĭ tēr	
interrogative	*in* tuh ROG uh tiv	ĭn′tĕ rŏg′ă tĭv	ˌɪn tə ′rɑg ə tɪv, -′rɒg-
interrogatory	*in* tuh ROG uh *toh* ri	ĭn′tĕ rŏg′ă tō′rĭ §§ 34(3), 51(4)	ˌɪn tə ′rɑg əˉ ˌto rɪ, -′rɒg-, -ˌtə rɪ
	in tuh ROG uh *taw* ri		
	B., *in* tuh ROG uh tuhr i	B., ĭn′tĕ rŏg′ă tēr ĭ	B., ˌɪn tə ′rɒg ə tə rɪ
interstice	in TUHR stis	ĭn tûr′stĭs	ɪn ′tɚ stɪs,
	IN tuhr stis	ĭn′tēr stĭs § 47(3)	′ɪn tɚ-; *ES also* -′tɚ-, *ES* -tə-
intertwine (v.)	*in* tuhr TWAIN	ĭn′tēr twīn′	ˌɪn tɚ ′twaɪn; *ES* -tə-
—— (n.)	IN tuhr *twain* § 50(34)	ĭn′tēr twīn′ § 12	′ɪn tɚ ˌtwaɪn; *ES* -tə-
intestacy	in TES tuh si	ĭn tĕs′tă sĭ	ɪn ′tɛs tə sɪ
intestate	in TES tayt	ĭn tĕs′tāt § 50(2)	ɪn ′tɛs tet
	in TES tit		ɪn ′tɛs tɪt
intestinal	in TES tuh nuhl	ĭn tĕs′tĭ năl	ɪn ′tɛs tə nəl,
	in TES ti nuhl	ĭn tĕs′tĭ năl	-tɪ-, -nḷ
	B., *in* tes TAI nuhl	B., ĭn′tĕs tī′năl	B., ˌɪn tɛs ′taɪ nəl
	in tes TAI n'l § 50(34)	ĭn′tĕs tī′n'l § 51(4)	ˌɪn tɛs ′taɪ nḷ
intimate (v.t.)	IN tuh mayt	ĭn′tĭ māt	′ɪn tə met
	IN ti mayt	ĭn′tĭ māt	′ɪn tɪ met
—— (n., adj.)	IN tuh mit	ĭn′tĭ mĭt	′ɪn tə mɪt
	IN ti mit	ĭn′tĭ mĭt § 20(8, 9)	′ɪn tɪ mɪt
intractable	in TRAK tuh b'l	ĭn trăk′tă b'l § 49(9)	ɪn ′træk tə bḷ
intrepid	in TREP id	ĭn trĕp′ĭd	ɪn ′trɛp ɪd
intrepidity	*in* tri PID uh ti	ĭn′trĕ pĭd′ĭ tĭ	ˌɪn trɪ ′pɪd ə tɪ
	in tri PID i ti	ĭn′trĕ pĭd′ĭ tĭ	ˌɪn trɪ ′pɪd ɪ tɪ
intricacy	IN truh kuh si	ĭn′trĭ kă sĭ	′ɪn trə kə sɪ
	IN tri kuh si	ĭn′trĭ kă sĭ	′ɪn trɪ kə sɪ

	SIMPLIFIED	DIACRITICAL	PHONETIC
intricate (adj.)	IN truh kit IN tri kit	ĭn′trĭ kĭt ĭn′trĭ kĭt	'ın trə kıt 'ın trı kıt
intrigue (n.)	in TREEG IN treeg	ĭn trēg′ ĭn′trēg	ın 'trig 'ın trig
—— (v.)	in TREEG	ĭn trēg′ §§ 12, 47(1)	ın 'trig
introduce	*in* truh DYOOS *in* truh DOOS	ĭn′trŏ dūs′ § 50(32)	ˌın trə 'djus ˌın trə 'dus
introvert (n., adj.)	IN truh *vuhrt*	ĭn′trŏ vûrt′	'ın trə ˌvɜt; *ES* *also* -ˌvɜt
—— (v.)	*in* truh VUHRT	ĭn′trŏ vûrt′	ˌın trə 'vɜt; *ES* *also* -'vɜt
intrusion	in TROO zhuhn	ĭn trōō′zhŭn § 40(4)	ın 'tru ʒən
intuitional	*in* tyŏŏ ISH uhn uhl *in* tŏŏ ISH uhn uhl *in* tyŏŏ ISH uhn 'l *in* tŏŏ ISH uhn 'l	ĭn′tŭ ĭsh′ŭn ăl ĭn′tŭ ĭsh′ŭn 'l § 50(32)	ˌın tjʊ 'ıʃ ən əl ˌın tʊ 'ıʃ ən əl ˌın tjʊ 'ıʃ ən l̩ ˌın tʊ 'ıʃ ən l̩
intuitive	in TYOO uh tiv in TOO uh tiv in TYOO i tiv in TOO i tiv	ĭn tū′ĭ tĭv ĭn tū′ĭ tĭv § 50(17, 32)	ın 'tju ə tıv ın 'tu ə tıv ın 'tju ı tıv ın 'tu ı tıv
inundate	IN *uhn* dayt in UHN dayt	ĭn′ŭn dāt ĭn ŭn′dāt §§ 40(6), 47(1)	'ın ʌn det, -ən- ın 'ʌn det
inundation	*in uhn* DAY shuhn	ĭn′ŭn dā′shŭn § 40(6)	ˌın ʌn 'de ʃən, -ən 'de-
inure	in YŎŎR in YOOR *B.*, in YAWR	ĭn ūr′ §§ 34(21), 40(4), 51(4) *B.*, ĭn yôr′	ın 'jʊr; *ES* -'jʊə(r) *B.*, ın 'jɔr; *ES* -'jɔə(r)
invalid (n., v.– *"person in ill health"; "make infirm"*)	IN vuh lid *B.*, IN vuh leed *in* vuh LEED	ĭn′vȧ lĭd *B.*, ĭn′vȧ lēd ĭn′vȧ lēd′ §§ 47(2), 51(4)	'ın və lıd *B.*, 'ın və lıd ˌın və 'lid
—— (adj.–*"not well"*)	IN vuh lid *B.*, IN vuh leed	ĭn′vȧ lĭd *B.*, ĭn′vȧ lēd § 51(4)	'ın və lıd *B.*, 'ın və lid
invalid (*"void"*)	in VAL id	ĭn văl′ĭd	ın 'væl ıd
invariable	in VEHR i uh b'l in VAY ri uh b'l	ĭn vâr′ĭ ȧ b'l § 20(2)	ın 'vɛr ı ə b l̩, -'vær-, -'ve rı-; *E also* -'veər-
invasion	in VAY zhuhn	ĭn vā′zhŭn	ın 've ʒən
invective	in VEK tiv	ĭn věk′tĭv	ın 'vɛk tıv
inveigh	in VAY	ĭn vā′	ın 've
inveigle	in VEE g'l in VAY g'l	ĭn vē′g'l ĭn vā′g'l § 47(1)	ın 'vi g l̩ ın 've g l̩

	SIMPLIFIED	DIACRITICAL	PHONETIC
inventory	IN vuhn *toh* ri IN vuhn *taw* ri *B.,* IN vuhn tuhr i IN vuhn tri	ĭn′vĕn tō′rĭ §§ 34(3), 51(4) *B.,* ĭn′vĕn tẽr ĭ ĭn′vĕn trĭ	'ɪn vən ˌto rɪ 'ɪn vən ˌtɔ rɪ *B.,* 'ɪn vən tə rɪ 'ɪn vən trɪ
inverse (n., adj.)	in VUHRS IN vuhrs	ĭn vûrs′ ĭn′vûrs §§ 11, 47(2)	ɪn 'vɝs, 'ɪn vɝs; *ES also* -'vɝs, -vɝs
—— (v.t.)	in VUHRS	ĭn vûrs′	ɪn 'vɝs; *ES also* -'vɝs
inversion	in VUHR shuhn in VUHR zhuhn	ĭn vûr′shŭn ĭn vûr′zhŭn § 50(28)	ɪn 'vɝ ʃən ɪn 'vɝ ʒən *ES also* -'vɝ-
inviolable	in VAI uh luh b'l	ĭn vī′ŏ lȧ b'l	ɪn 'vaɪ ə lə bļ
inviolate	in VAI uh lit in VAI uh layt	ĭn vī′ŏ lât ĭn vī′ŏ lât § 50(2, 34)	ɪn 'vaɪ ə lɪt ɪn 'vaɪ ə let
iodide	AI uh daɪd AI uh did § 50(34)	ī′ŏ dīd ī′ŏ dĭd §§ 28(7), 47(2)	'aɪ ə daɪd 'aɪ ə dɪd
iodine	AI uh daɪn AI uh din AI uh deen *Chemists prefer:* AI uh deen AI uh din	ī′ŏ dīn ī′ŏ dĭn ī′ŏ dēn *Chemists prefer:* ī′ŏ dēn ī′ŏ dĭn §§ 28(7), 47(3), 51(6)	'aɪ ə daɪn 'aɪ ə dɪn 'aɪ ə din *Chemists prefer:* 'aɪ ə din 'aɪ ə dɪn
Ionic	aɪ ON ik § 50(34)	ī ŏn′ĭk	aɪ 'ɑn ɪk, -'ɒn-
iota	aɪ OH tuh § 50(34)	ī ō′tȧ	aɪ 'o tə
Iowa	AI uh wuh AI oh uh *Among Iowans:* AI uh way § 50(34)	ī′ŏ wȧ ī′ŏ ă *Among Iowans:* ī′ŏ wā	'aɪ ə wə 'aɪ o ə *Among Iowans:* 'aɪ ə we
irascible	ai RAS uh b'l ai RAS i b'l i RAS uh b'l i RAS i b'l § 50(34)	ĭ răs′ĭ b'l ĭ răs′ĭ b'l ĭ răs′ĭ b'l ĭ răs′ĭ b'l § 47(1)	aɪ 'ræs ə bļ aɪ 'ræs ɪ bļ ɪ 'ræs ə bļ ɪ 'ræs ɪ bļ
irate	AI rayt ai RAYT § 50(34)	ī′rāt ī rāt′ § 47(3)	'aɪ ret aɪ 'ret
iridescent	*ir* uh DES uhnt *ir* i DES ent *ir* uh DES 'nt	ĭr′ĭ dĕs′ĕnt ĭr′ĭ dĕs′ĕnt ĭr′ĭ dĕs′ 'nt § 47(2)	ˌɪr ə 'dɛs ənt ˌɪr ɪ 'dɛs ɛnt ˌɪr ə 'dɛs ņt
iris, Iris	AI ris § 50(34)	ī′rĭs	'aɪ rɪs

	SIMPLIFIED	DIACRITICAL	PHONETIC
iron	$\widehat{AI}$ uhrn *Occas.:* $\widehat{AI}$ ruhn	ī′ẽrn *Occas.:* ī′rŭn § 51(8)	ˈaɪ ɚn; *ES* -ən *Occas.:* ˈaɪ rən
ironical	aî RON i kuhl § 50(34)	ī rŏn′ĭ kăl	aɪ ˈrɑn ɪ kəl, -kl̩; *ES also* -ˈrɒn-
ironworks	$\widehat{AI}$ uhrn *wuhrks*	ī′ẽrn wûrks′	ˈaɪ ɚn ˌwɝks; *ES* -ən-, *also* -ˌwɜks
irony (*"sort of* *humor"*)	$\widehat{AI}$ ruh ni § 50(34)	ī′rŏ nĭ §§ 47(2), 51(7)	ˈaɪ rə nɪ
irradiate (v.)	i RAY di ayt	ĭ rā′dĭ āt § 49(10)	ɪ ˈre dɪ et
irrational	ir RASH uhn uhl ir RASH uhn 'l	ĭr răsh′ŭn ăl ĭr răsh′ŭn 'l § 49(10)	ɪr ˈræʃ ən əl ɪr ˈræʃ ən l̩; *ES* *also* ɪə ˈræʃ-
irreconcilable	ir *rek* uhn $\widehat{SAIL}$ uh b'l ir REK uhn *sail* uh b'l	ĭr rĕk′ŏn sīl′*a* b'l ĭr rĕk′ŏn sīl′*a* b'l §§ 47(3), 49(10)	ɪr ˌrek ən ˈsaɪl ə bl̩; *ES also* ɪə ˌrek- ɪr ˈrɛk ən ˌsaɪl ə bl̩; *ES also* ɪə ˈrek-
irrecoverable	*ir* ri KUHV uhr uh b'l	ĭr′rĕ kŭv′ẽr *a* b'l § 49(10)	ˌɪr rɪ ˈkʌv ɚ ə bl̩; *ES also* ˌɪə rɪ-
irrelevant	ir REL i vuhnt	ĭr rĕl′ĕ vănt § 49(10)	ɪr ˈrel ɪ vənt; *ES* *also* ɪə ˈrel-
irreligious	*ir* ri LIJ uhs	ĭr′rĕ lĭj′ŭs § 49(10)	ˌɪr rɪ ˈlɪdʒ əs, *ES* *also* ˌɪə rɪ-
irremediable	*ir* ri MEE di uh b'l	ĭr′rĕ mē′dĭ *a* b'l § 49(10)	ˌɪr rɪ ˈmi dɪ ə bl̩; *ES also* ˌɪə rɪ-
irreparable	i REP uh ruh b'l	ĭ rĕp′*a* r*a* b'l § 49(10)	ɪ ˈrep ə rə bl̩; *ES* *also* ɪə ˈrep-
irrepressible	*ir* ri PRES uh b'l *ir* ri PRES i b'l	ĭr′rĕ prĕs′ĭ b'l ĭr′rĕ prĕs′ĭ b'l § 49(10)	ˌɪr rɪ ˈpres ə bl̩, -ɪ bl̩; *ES also* ˌɪə rɪ-
irreproachable	*ir* ri PROHCH uh b'l	ĭr′rĕ prōch′*a* b'l	ˌɪr rɪ ˈprotʃ ə bl̩; *ES also* ˌɪə rɪ-
irresistible	*ir* ri ZIS tuh b'l *ir* ri ZIS ti b'l	ĭr′rĕ zĭs′tĭ b'l ĭr′rĕ zĭs′tĭ b'l § 49(10)	ˌɪr rɪ ˈzɪs tə bl̩, -tɪ-; *ES also* ˌɪə rɪ-
irresolute	i REZ uh loot i REZ uh lyoot	ĭ rĕz′ŏ lūt §§ 48(2), 49(10), 50(32)	ɪ ˈrez ə lut, -ljut, -ˈrez l̩-; *ES also* ɪə ˈrez-
irrespective	*ir* ri SPEK tiv	ĭr′rĕ spĕk′tĭv § 49(10)	ˌɪr rɪ ˈspek tɪv; *ES* *also* ˌɪə rɪ-
irresponsible	*ir* ri SPON suh b'l *ir* ri SPON si b'l	ĭr′rĕ spŏn′sĭ b'l ĭr′rĕ spŏn′sĭ b'l § 49(10)	ˌɪr rɪ ˈspɑn sə bl̩, -sɪ bl̩; *ES also* ˌɪə rɪ-, -ˈspɒn-
irretrievable	*ir* ri TREEV uh b'l	ĭr′rĕ trēv′*a* b'l § 49(10)	ˌɪr rɪ ˈtriv ə bl̩; *ES* *also* ˌɪə rɪ-
irreverence	i REV uhr uhns	ĭ rĕv′ẽr ĕns § 49(10)	ɪ ˈrev ɚ əns; *ES* *also* ɪə ˈrɛv-

	SIMPLIFIED	DIACRITICAL	PHONETIC
irreverent	i REV uhr uhnt	ĭ rĕv′ēr ĕnt § 49(10)	ɪ ˈrɛv ər ənt; *ES also* ɪə ˈrɛv-
irrevocability	i *rev* uh kuh BIL uh ti i *rev* uh kuh BIL i ti	ĭ rĕv′ŏ ká bĭl′ĭ tĭ ĭ rĕv′ŏ ká bĭl′ĭ tĭ § 49(10)	ɪ ˌrɛv ə kə ˈbɪl ə tɪ, -ɪ tɪ; *ES also* ɪə ˌrɛv-
irrevocable	i REV uh kuh b′l	ĭ rĕv′ŏ ká b′l § 49(10)	ɪ ˈrɛv ə kə bl̩; *ES also* ɪə ˈrɛv-
isinglass	AI zing *glas* AI zing *glahs*	ī′zĭng glàs′ § 20(5)	ˈaɪ zɪŋ ˌglæs; *E also* -ˌglas, -ˌglas
Isis	AI sis § 50(34)	ī′sĭs	ˈaɪ sɪs
Islam	IS luhm IZ luhm is LAHM	ĭs′lám ĭz′lám ĭs läm′ § 47(3)	ˈɪs ləm ˈɪz ləm ɪs ˈlam
island	AI luhnd § 50(34)	ī′lănd § 38(2)	ˈaɪ lənd
isle	ail § 50(34)	īl § 38(2)	aɪl
isolate (v.t.)	AI suh layt IS uh layt	ī′sŏ lāt ĭs′ŏ lāt § 47(3)	ˈaɪ sə let, -sl̩-, ˈɪs ə-, ˈɪs l̩-
isolation	*ai* suh LAY shuhn *is* uh LAY shuhn	ī′sŏ lā′shŭn ĭs′ŏ lā′shŭn	ˌaɪ sə ˈle ʃən, -sl̩ ˈe ʃən, ˌɪs ə ˈle-, ˌɪs l̩ ˈe ʃn̩
isosceles	ai SOS uh leez	ī sŏs′ĕ lēz	aɪ ˈsɑs ə lɪz, -ˈsɑs l̩-; *ES also* -ˈsɒs-
isotherm	AI soh thuhrm	ī′sŏ thûrm	ˈaɪ so θɝm, -sə-; *ES also* -θɜm
isothermal	*ai* soh THUHR muhl	ī′sŏ thûr′măl	ˌaɪ so ˈθɝ məl, -sə-, -ml̩; *ES also* -ˈθɜ-
issue	ISH yoo ISH oo	ĭsh′ū ĭsh′o͞o §§ 38(12), 40(4), 47(2)	ˈɪʃ ju, -jʊ ˈɪʃ u, -ʊ
isthmus	IS muhs ISTH muhs IS *muhs* IST *muhs*	ĭs′mŭs isth′mŭs ĭs′mŭs ĭst′mŭs §§ 40(6), 47(3)	ˈɪs məs ˈɪsθ məs ˈɪs mʌs ˈɪst mʌs
Italian	i TAL yuhn	ĭ tăl′yăn	ɪ ˈtæl jən
italic (*"type"*)	i TAL ik	ĭ tăl′ĭk	ɪ ˈtæl ɪk
Italic (*"of Italy"*)	i TAL ik	ĭ tăl′ĭk	ɪ ˈtæl ɪk
italicize	i TAL uh saiz i TAL i saiz	ĭ tăl′ĭ sīz ĭ tăl′ĭ sīz	ɪ ˈtæl ə saɪz ɪ ˈtæl ɪ saɪz
iterate	IT uhr ayt IT uh rayt	ĭt′ēr āt ĭt′ē rāt	ˈɪt ər et ˈɪt ə ret

	SIMPLIFIED	DIACRITICAL	PHONETIC
iterative	IT uhr *ay* tiv	ĭt′ĕr ā′tĭv	ˈɪt ər ˌe tɪv
	IT uh *ray* tiv	§ 50(17)	ˈɪt ə ˌre tɪv
	IT uhr uh tiv	ĭt′ĕr *å* tĭv	ˈɪt ər ə tɪv
itinerant	a͡i TIN uhr uhnt	ī tĭn′ĕr ănt	aɪ ˈtɪn ər ənt
	i TIN uhr uhnt	ĭ tĭn′ĕr ănt	ɪ ˈtin ər ənt
itinerary	a͡i TIN uhr *er* i	ī tĭn′ĕr ĕr′ĭ	aɪ ˈtɪn ər ˌer ɪ
	a͡i TIN uh *rer* i		aɪ ˈtɪn ə ˌre rɪ
	i TIN uhr *er* i	ĭ tĭn′ĕr ĕr′ĭ	ɪ ˈtɪn ər ˌer ɪ
	i TIN uh *rer* i	§§ 13, 50(34), 51(4)	ɪ ˈtɪn ə ˈre rɪ
	B., a͡i TIN uhr uhr i	*B.,* ī tĭn′ĕr ĕr ĭ	*B.,* aɪ ˈtɪn ə rə rɪ
ivory	A͡I vuh ri § 50(34)	ī′vŏ rĭ § 9	ˈaɪ və rɪ, -vrɪ

J

Jacobin	JAK uh bin	jăk′ŏ bĭn	ˈdʒæk ə bɪn
Jacobite	JAK uh ba͡it § 50(34)	jăk′ŏ bīt	ˈdʒæk ə baɪt
Jacques (See also *Jaques.*)	zhahk	zhȧk	ʒak, ʒɑk
	jayks	jāks	dʒeks
jamb, jambe	jam	jăm	dʒæm
January	JAN yo͞o *er* i	jăn′ū̇ ĕr′ĭ §§ 20(2), 24(9)	ˈdʒæn jʊ ˌer ɪ, -ju-
	B., JAN yo͞o uhr i	*B.,* jăn′ū̇ ĕr ĭ §§ 13, 51(4)	*B.,* ˈdʒæn jʊ ə rɪ
Japanese	*jap* uh NEEZ	jăp′*å* nēz′	ˌdʒæp ə ˈniz
	jap uh NEES	jăp′*å* nēs′ §§ 11, 38(6), 47(1), 50(7)	ˌdʒæp ə ˈnis
Jaques—*son of Sir Roland de Boys in Shakespeare's "As You Like It"*	zhahk	zhäk	ʒak
	JAY kweez	jā′kwēz	ˈdʒe kwiz
	JAY kwiz	jā′kwĭz	ˈdʒe kwɪz
	jak	jăk	dʒæk
	jayks	jāks	dʒeks
—*a lord in Shakespeare's "As You Like It"; a character mentioned in "All's Well That Ends Well"* (See *Jaques.*)	JAY kweez	jā′kwēz	ˈdʒe kwiz
	JAY kwiz	jā′kwĭz	ˈdʒe kwɪz

jasmine,	JAS min	jăs′mĭn	ˈdʒæs mɪn
jasmin	JAZ min	jăz′mĭn § 47(2)	ˈdʒæz mɪn
jaundice	JAWN dis	jôn′dĭs	ˈdʒɔn dɪs
	JAHN dis	jän′dĭs § 47(3)	ˈdʒɑn dɪs, ˈdʒɒn-
jaunt	jawnt	jônt	dʒɔnt
	jahnt	jänt § 47(3)	dʒɑnt, dʒɒnt
jaunty	JAWN ti	jôn′tĭ	ˈdʒɔn tɪ
	JAHN ti	jän′tĭ § 47(1)	ˈdʒɑn tɪ, ˈdʒɒn-
Java	JAH vuh	jä′và	ˈdʒɑ və
	JAV uh	jăv′à	ˈdʒæv ə
Javanese	jav uh NEEZ	jăv′à nēz′	ˌdʒæv ə ˈniz
	jav uh NEES	jăv′à nēs′	ˌdʒæv ə ˈnis
		§§ 11, 38(6),	
		47(2), 50(6)	
javelin	JAV lin	jăv′lĭn	ˈdʒæv lɪn
	JAV uh lin	jăv′ĕ lĭn	ˈdʒæv ə lɪn
jealous	JEL uhs	jĕl′ŭs § 50(25)	ˈdʒɛl əs
jeans	jeenz	jēnz	dʒinz
	jaynz	jānz § 47(1)	dʒenz
jejune	ji JOON	jĕ jōōn′	dʒɪ ˈdʒun
		§§ 11, 47(2)	
Jena	YAY nah	yā′nä	ˈje nɑ
jeopardize	JEP uhr daiz	jĕp′ẽr dīz	ˈdʒɛp ɚ daɪz; ES
	§ 50(34)		-ə daɪz
jeopardy	JEP uhr di	jĕp′ẽr dĭ	ˈdʒɛp ɚ dɪ; ES
			-ə dɪ
Jeremiah	jer i MAI uh	jĕr′ĕ mī′à	ˌdʒɛr ɪ ˈmaɪ ə
	§ 50(34)		
Jerusalem	ji ROO suh luhm	jĕ rōō′sà lĕm	dʒɪ ˈru sə ləm,
		§ 48(2)	dʒə-, -lɛm
jessamine	JES uh min	jĕs′à mĭn	ˈdʒɛs ə mɪn
jewel	JOO uhl	jōō′ĕl	ˈdʒu əl
	JYOO uhl	jū′ĕl	ˈdʒju əl
	JYOO il	jū′ĭl	ˈdʒju ɪl
	JOO il	§§ 40(4), 47(3),	ˈdʒu ɪl
		48(2)	
jeweler,	JOO uhl uhr	jōō′ĕl ẽr	ˈdʒu əl ɚ, ˈdʒju-,
jeweller	JYOO uhl uhr	jū′ĕl ẽr	-ɪl ɚ; ES
	JYOO il uhr	jū′ĭl ẽr	-əl ə(r), -ɪl ə(r)
	JOO il uhr	§§ 48(2), 50(32)	
jewelry	JOO uhl ri	jōō′ĕl rĭ	ˈdʒu əl rɪ
	JYOO uhl ri	jū′ĕl rĭ	ˈdʒju əl rɪ
	JYOO il ri	jū′ĭl rĭ	ˈdʒju ɪl rɪ
	JOO il ri	§§ 48(2), 50(32)	ˈdʒu ɪl rɪ
job	job	jŏb	dʒɑb; ES also
			dʒɒb
Job	johb	jōb	dʒob
jocose	joh KOHS	jŏ kōs′	dʒo ˈkos

jocular	JOK yŏŏ luhr	jŏk′ŭ lēr	ˈdʒɑk jʊ lɚ, -jə-, -ju-; *ES* -lə(r), *also* ˈdʒɒk-
jocund	JOK uhnd	jŏk′ŭnd	ˈdʒɑk ənd; *ES also* ˈdʒɒk-
	JOH kuhnd	jō′kŭnd	ˈdʒo kənd
	JOK *uhnd*	jŏk′ŭnd	ˈdʒɑk ʌnd; *ES*
	§ 40(6), 47(1)		*also* ˈdʒɒk-
John	jon	jŏn	dʒɑn, dʒɒn
join	join	join	dʒɔɪn
jolt	johlt	jōlt	dʒolt
jonquil	JONG kwil	jŏng′kwĭl	ˈdʒɑŋ kwɪl,
	JON kwil	jŏn′kwĭl § 33(4)	ˈdʒɑn-; *ES also* ˈdʒɒŋ-, ˈdʒɒn-
	Occas.:	*Occas.:*	*Occas.:*
	JUHNG kwil	jŭng′kwĭl § 51(8)	ˈdʒʌŋ kwɪl
Joseph	JOH zuhf	jō′zĕf	ˈdʒo zəf
	JOH zif	jō′zĭf	ˈdʒo zɪf
jostle	JOS ′l	jŏs′ ′l	ˈdʒɑs l̩; *ES also* ˈdʒɒs-
joust	*juhst*	jŭst	dʒʌst
	joost	jōōst	dʒust
	B., jowst	*B.,* joust § 47(3), 51(4)	*B.,* dʒaʊst
jovial	JOH vi uhl	jō′vĭ ăl § 28(9)	ˈdʒo vɪ əl, -vjəl
jowl	jowl	joul	dʒaʊl
	johl	jōl § 47(3)	dʒol
jubilee	JOO buh lee	jōō′bĭ lē	ˈdʒu bə li, -bl̩ ɪ
	JOO bi lee	jōō′bĭ lē §§ 40(4), 48(2)	ˈdʒu bɪ li
Judaism	JOO day iz′m	jōō′dā ĭz′m	ˈdʒu de ɪzm̩,
	JOO di iz′m	§§ 47(2), 48(2), 50(15)	-dɪ-, -ɪz əm
Judean, Judaean	joo DEE uhn	jōō dē′ăn § 48(2)	dʒu ˈdi ən
judge	*juhj*	jŭj § 40(6)	dʒʌdʒ
judgment	JUHJ muhnt	jŭj′mĕnt § 50(22)	ˈdʒʌdʒ mənt
judicatory	JOO di kuh *toh* ri	jōō′dĭ kȧ tō′rĭ	ˈdʒu dɪ kə ˌto rɪ
	JOO di kuh *taw* ri	§§ 34(3), 40(4), 47(2), 48(2), 51(4)	ˈdʒu dɪ kə ˌtɔ rɪ
	B., JOO di kuh tuhr i	*B.,* jōō′dĭ kȧ tēr ĭ	*B.,* ˈdʒu dɪ kə tə rɪ
judicature	JOO di kuh chuhr	jōō′dĭ kȧ tûr	ˈdʒu dɪ kə tʃɚ,
	JOO di kuh tyuhr	§§ 48(2), 50(31)	-ˌtʃʊr, -tjɚ; *ES* -tʃə(r),-ˌtʃʊə(r), -tjə(r)

	SIMPLIFIED	DIACRITICAL	PHONETIC
judiciary	joo DISH i *er* i	jōō dĭsh′ĭ ẽr′ĭ §§ 13, 20(2), 24(9), 47(2), 48(2), 51(4)	dʒu ˈdɪʃ ɪ ˌɜː ɪ
	B., joo DISH i uhr i	*B.*, jōō dĭsh′ĭ ẽr ĭ	*B.*, dʒu ˈdɪʃ ɪ ə rɪ
Jugoslav	YOO goh SLAHV	yōō′gŏ släv′	ˈju go ˈslɑv
Jugo-Slav	YOO goh SLAV	yōō′gŏ slăv′ § 11	ˈju go ˈslæv
juice	joos	jōōs §§ 40(4), 47(3), 48(2)	dʒus
Juliet	JOO li et	jōō′lĭ ĕt	ˈdʒu lɪ ɛt
	JOO li uht	jōō′lĭ ĕt	ˈdʒu lɪ ət
	joo li ET	jōō′lĭ ĕt′	ˌdʒu lɪ ˈɛt
	B., JOOL yuht	*B.*, jōōl′yĕt §§ 28(9), 40(4), 48(2), 51(4)	*B.*, ˈdʒul jət
June	joon	jōōn §§ 40(4), 47(2), 48(2)	dʒun
junior	JOON yuhr	jōōn′yẽr §§ 40(4), 47(3), 48(2)	ˈdʒun jɚ; *ES* -jə(r)
jurisprudence	*joo̅r* is PROO duhns	jōōr′ĭs prōō′dĕns §§ 40(4), 48(2)	ˌdʒʊr ɪs ˈpru dəns, -dn̩s; *ES also* ˌdʒʊə rɪs-
	B., *jawr* is PROO duhns	*B.*, jôr′ĭs prōō′dĕns § 51(4)	*B.*, dʒɔr ɪs ˈpru dəns; *ES* ˌdʒɔə rɪs-
juror	JOOR uhr	jōōr′ẽr	ˈdʒʊr ɚ; *ES* -ə(r)
	B., JAWR uhr	*B.*, jôr′ẽr §§ 40(4), 48(2), 51(4)	*B.*, ˈdʒɔr ɚ; *ES* ˈdʒɔə ə(r)
jury	JOOR i	jōōr′ĭ	ˈdʒʊr ɪ
	B., JAWR i	*B.*, jôr′ĭ §§ 34(21), 40(4, 11), 48(2), 51(4)	*B.*, ˈdʒɔr ɪ; *ES* ˈdʒɔə rɪ
just (adj.)	*juhst*	jŭst § 40(6)	dʒʌst
—— (adv.)	*juhst*	jŭst	dʒʌst
	Colloq. or dial., esp. when the stress is light: jest	*Colloq. or dial., esp. when the stress is light:* jĕst § 51(2, 3)	*Colloq. or dial., esp. when the stress is light:* dʒɛst, dʒəst
justifiable	JUHS tuh *fai* uh b'l	jŭs′tĭ fī′*á* b'l	ˈdʒʌs tə ˌfaɪ ə bl̩
	JUHS ti *fai* uh b'l	jŭs′tĭ fī′*á* b'l	ˈdʒʌs tɪ ˌ faɪ ə bl̩
justification	*juhs* tuh fi KAY shuhn	jŭs′tĭ fĭ kā′shŭn	ˌdʒʌs tə fɪ ˈke ʃən
	juhs ti fi KAY shuhn	jŭs′tĭ fĭ kā′shŭn	ˌdʒʌs tɪ fɪ ˈke ʃən
jute	joot	jōōt §§ 40(4), 47(2), 48(2)	dʒut

	SIMPLIFIED	DIACRITICAL	PHONETIC
juvenile	JOO vi nil	jo͞o′vĕ nĭl	ˈdʒu vɪ nɪl
	JOO vi naïl	jo͞o′vĕ nīl	ˈdʒu vɪ naɪl
	JOO vuh nil	jo͞o′vĕ nĭl	ˈdʒu və nɪl
	§ 50(34)	§§ 28(5), 47(3)	ˈdʒu və nəl
juxtaposition	*juhks* tuh puh ZISH uhn	jŭks′ta͝ pŏ zĭsh′ŭn	ˌdʒʌks tə pə ˈzɪʃ ən

K

kaleidoscope	kuh LĀI duh skohp	ka͝ lī′dŏ skōp	kə ˈlaɪ də skop
kaleidoscopic	kuh *laï* duh SKOP ik	ka͝ lī′dŏ skŏp′ĭk	kə ˌlaɪ də ˈskɑp ɪk; *ES* also -ˈskɒp-
kangaroo	*kang* guh ROO	kăng′ga͝ ro͞o′	ˌkæŋ gə ˈru
Kansas	KAN zuhs	kăn′zȧs	ˈkæn zəs
kept	kept	kĕpt	kept
kerosene, kerosine	KER uh *seen* / *ker* uh SEEN	kĕr′ŏ sēn′ / kĕr′ŏ sēn′ § 11	ˈker ə ˌsin / ˌker ə ˈsin
kettle	KET ′l	kĕt′ ′l	ˈket ļ
	Only when spelled "kittle" (dial. var.):	*Only when spelled "kittle" (dial. var.):*	*Only when spelled "kittle" (dial. var.):*
	KIT ′l	kĭt′ ′l § 51(2)	ˈkɪt ļ
khaki	KAH ki	kä′kĭ	ˈkɑ kɪ
	KAK i	kăk′ĭ	ˈkæk ɪ
	Among the military:	*Among the military:*	*Among the military:*
	KAK ı	kăk′ɪ § 51(6)	ˈkæk ɪ
khan	kahn	kän	kɑn
	kan	kăn § 47(2)	kæn
kickshaw	KIK *shaw*	kĭk′shô′	ˈkɪk ˌʃɔ
kiln	kil	kĭl	kɪl
	kiln	kĭln §§ 1, 33(1), 47(3)	kɪln
kilometer, kilometre	KIL uh *mee* tuhr	kĭl′ŏ mē′tēr	ˈkɪl ə ˌmi tɚ; *ES* -tə(r)
	Not infreq.:	*Not infreq.:*	*Not infreq.:*
	ki LOM i tuhr	kĭ lŏm′ĕ tēr § 51(8)	kɪ ˈlam ɪ tɚ; *ES* -tə(r), *also* -ˈlɒm-

	SIMPLIFIED	DIACRITICAL	PHONETIC
kimono	ki MOH noh *Pop.:* kuh MOH nuh ki MOH nuh *Jap.*, KIM oh noh	kĭ mō′nō *Pop.:* kĭ mō′nȧ kĭ mō′nȧ *Jap.*, kĭm′ō nō § 51(3)	kɪ 'mo no *Pop.:* kə 'mo nə kɪ 'mo nə *Jap.*, 'kɪm o no
kindergarten	KIN duhr *gahr* t'n	kĭn′dĕr gär′t'n § 24(14)	'kɪn dɚ ˌgɑr tŋ; *ES* -də ˌgɑ:-, E *also* -ˌga:-
kinetic	ki NET ik ka͡i NET ik § 50(34)	kĭ nĕt′ĭk kī nĕt′ĭk § 47(1)	kɪ 'nɛt ɪk kaɪ 'nɛt ɪk
kitchen	KICH en KICH in KICH uhn	kĭch′ĕn kĭch′ĭn kĭch′ĭn § 47(1)	'kɪtʃ ɛn 'kɪtʃ ɪn 'kɪtʃ ən
knack	nak	năk § 30(1)	næk
knapsack	NAP *sak*	năp′săk′ § 30(1)	'næp ˌsæk
knave	nayv	nāv § 30(1)	nev
knead	need	nēd § 30(1)	nid
knee	nee	nē § 30(1)	ni
knew (p.t. of *know*)	nyoo noo	nū §§ 30(1), 48(2), 50(32)	nju nu
knock	nok	nŏk § 30(1)	nɑk; *ES also* nɒk
knoll	nohl	nōl § 30(1)	nol
knot	not	nŏt § 30(1)	nat; *ES also* nɒt
know	noh	nō § 30(1)	no

knowledge	NOL ej
	NOL ij
	Occas.:
	B., NOH lej
	    NOH lij
		nŏl′ĕj
		nŏl′ĭj
		Occas.:
		B., nō′lĕj
		    nō′lĭj
		§§ 22(5),
		24(5), 30(1),
		51(4)
			'nɑl ɛdʒ, -ɪdʒ; *ES*
			also 'nɒl-
			Occas.:
			B., 'no lɛdʒ
			    'no lɪdʒ

knuckle	NUHK 'l	nŭk′ 'l § 30(1)	'nʌk ḷ
Koran	koh RAHN kaw RAHN KOH ran KOH ruhn KAW ruhn	kō rän′ kô rän′ kō′răn kō′rŭn §§ 34(3), 47(3)	ko 'rɑn, -'ræn kɔ 'rɑn 'ko ræn 'ko rən 'kɔ rən
Korea (Japan)	koh REE uh	kō rē′ȧ	ko 'ri ə, kɔ-

L

labor, labour	LAY buhr	lā′bēr	′le bɚ; *ES* -bə(r)
laboratory	LAB uh ruh *toh* ri LAB uh ruh *taw* ri	lăb′ŏ rȧ tō′rĭ §§ 9, 34(3), 51(4)	′læb ə rə ˌto rɪ, -ˌtɔ rɪ, ′læb rə-
	B., LAB uh ruh tuhr i luh BOR uh tuhr i	*B.*, lăb′ŏ rȧ tēr ĭ lȧ bŏr′ȧ tēr ĭ	*B.*, ′læb ə rə tə rɪ lə ′bɒr ə tə rɪ
laborious	luh BOH ri uhs luh BAW ri uhs	lȧ bō′rĭ ŭs §§ 34(3), 50(25)	lə ′bo rɪ əs lə ′bɔ rɪ əs
Labrador	LAB ruh dawr *lab* ruh DAWR	lăb′rȧ dôr lăb′rȧ dôr′ § 47(1)	′læb rə dɔr, ˌlæb rə ′dɔr; *ES* -dɔə(r), -′dɔə(r)
labyrinth **Labyrinth**	LAB uh rinth LAB i rinth	lăb′ĭ rĭnth lăb′ĭ rĭnth	′læb ə rɪnθ ′læb ɪ rɪnθ
Lacedaemonian, **Lacedemonian**	*las* i di MOH ni uhn *las* uh di MOH ni uhn	lăs′ĕ dĕ mō′nĭ ăn lăs′ĕ dĕ mō′nĭ ăn § 28(9)	ˌlæs ɪ dɪ ′mo nɪ ən, ˌlæs ə-, -njən
lachrymal	LAK ri muhl	lăk′rĭ măl	′læk rɪ məl, -ml̩
lacquer	LAK uhr	lăk′ēr	′læk ɚ; *ES* -ə(r)
Lafayette *or* **La Fayette** (French general)	*lah* fay YET *lah* fay ET	lä′fȧ yĕt′ lä′fȧ ĕt′	ˌla fe ′jɛt, -fe ′ɛt, -fɪ-; *F.*, la fa ′jɛt
laird	lehrd	lârd	lɛrd, lærd; *ES* læəd, *E also* leəd
	Sc., layrd	*Sc.*, lärd	*Sc.*, lerd
lamb	lam	lăm § 21(1)	læm
lament	luh MENT	lȧ mĕnt′	lə ′mɛnt
lamentable	LAM uhn tuh b'l	lăm′ĕn tȧ b'l § 47(1)	′læm ən tə bl̩, -ɛn-
lamentably	LAM uhn tuh bli	lăm′ĕn tȧ blĭ § 50(20)	′læm ən tə blɪ, -ɛn-
Lancaster (England)	LANG kuhs tuhr	lăng′kăs tēr	′læŋ kəs tɚ; *ES* -tə(r)
lance	lans lahns	láns § 20(5)	læns; *E also* lans, lɑns

	SIMPLIFIED	DIACRITICAL	PHONETIC
Lancelot	LAN suh lot	lăn′sĕ lŏt	′læn sə lɑt, -′lət,
	LAHN suh lot		-sɪ-; *E also*
	LAN suh luht	lăn′sĕ lŭt	′lɑn-, ′lɒn-, *ES*
	LAHN suh luht	§ 20(5)	*also* -lɒt
landlord	LAND *lawrd*	lănd′lôrd′	′lænd ˌlɔrd; *ES*
			-ˌlɔəd
	Familiar speech, often:	*Familiar speech, often:*	*Familiar speech, often:*
	LAN *lawrd*	lăn′lôrd′	′læn ˌlɔrd; *ES*
		§§ 23(1), 51(3)	-ˌlɔəd
landscape	LAND skayp	lănd′skāp	′lænd skep
	LAN skayp	lăn′skāp § 23(1)	′læn skep
language	LANG gwij	lăng′gwĭj § 26(5)	′læŋ gwɪdʒ
languid	LANG gwid	lăng′gwĭd	′læŋ gwɪd
languor	LANG guhr	lăng′gĕr	′læŋ gɚ; *ES*
			-gə(r)
	LANG gwuhr	lăng′gwĕr § 47(3)	′læŋ gwɚ; *ES*
			-gwə(r)
lantern	LAN tuhrn	lăn′tĕrn	′læn tɚn; *ES* -tən
Laodicean	lay *od* i SEE uhn	lā ŏd′ĭ sē′ăn	le ˌɑd ɪ ′si ən; *ES*
			also -ˌɒd-
lapel	la PEL	lă pĕl′	læ ′pɛl
	luh PEL	lŭ pĕl′	lə ′pɛl
larboard	LAHR bord	lär′bōrd	′lɑr bord, -bɔrd,
	LAHR bawrd	§ 34(3)	-bɚd; *ES*
	LAHR buhrd	lär′bĕrd	′lɑ: boəd, -bəd,
			E also
			′lɑ:-, -bɔəd
larceny	LAHR suh ni	lär′sĕ nĭ	′lɑr sə nɪ, -sn̩ɪ;
			ES ′lɑ:-, *E also*
			′lɑ:-
largess,	LAHR jes	lär′jĕs	′lɑr dʒɛs, -dʒɪs;
largesse	LAHR jis	lär′jĭs § 24(5)	*ES* ′lɑ:-, *E also*
			′lɑ:-
larynx	LAR ingks	lăr′ĭngks § 47(2)	′lær ɪŋks
lass	las	lăs	læs; *E also* lɑs, lɒs
	lahs	läs § 20(5)	
last	last	läst § 20(5)	læst; *E also* lɑst,
	lahst		lɒst
latent	LAY tuhnt	lā′tĕnt § 24(14)	′le tənt, -tn̩t
latest	LAYT est	lāt′ĕst	′let ɛst
	LAYT ist	lāt′ĭst §§ 24(5),	′let ɪst
		50(9)	
lath	lath	lăth §§ 20(5),	læθ; *E also* lɑθ,
	lahth	39(5), 47(2),	lɒθ
		51(7)	
lathe	laythe	lāthe § 39(5, 6)	leð
Latin (adj., n.)	LAT in	lăt′ĭn	′læt ɪn
	LAT ′n	lăt′ ′n	′læt n̩

latitude	LAT uh tyood	lăt′ĭ tūd	′læt ə tjud
	LAT uh tood		′læt ə tud
	LAT i tyood	lăt′ĭ tūd	′læt ɪ tjud
	LAT i tood	§§ 48(2), 50(32)	′læt ɪ tud
Latium	LAY shi uhm	lā′shĭ ŭm	′le ʃɪ əm
lattice	LAT is	lăt′ĭs	′læt ɪs
laudanum	LAW duh nuhm	lô′dá năm	′lɔ də nəm, -dņəm,
	LAWD nuhm	lôd′năm § 47(3)	′lɔd nəm
laugh	lahf	läf	lɑf, læf; *E also* laf
	laf	läf §§ 20(5), 26(2)	
laughter	LAHF tuhr	läf′tĕr	′lɑf tɚ, ′læf-; *E also*
	LAF tuhr	läf′tĕr § 20(5)	′laf-, *ES* -tə(r)
launch	lawnch	lônch	lɔntʃ
	lahnch	länch §§ 22(6), 47(3)	lɑntʃ, lɒntʃ
launder	LAWN duhr	lôn′dĕr	′lɔn dɚ, ′lɑn-,
	LAHN duhr	län′dĕr § 47(2)	′lɒn-; *ES* -də(r)
laundry	LAWN dri	lôn′drĭ	′lɔn drɪ
	LAHN dri	län′drĭ § 47(3)	′lɑn drɪ, ′lɒn-
laurel	LAW ruhl	lô′rĕl	′lɔ rəl, ′lɑr əl,
	LOR uhl	lŏr′ĕl § 47(3)	′lɒr-
Lausanne	loh ZAN	lô zăn′	lo ′zæn
	F., loh ZAHN	*F.,* lô′zàn′	*F.,* lo ′zan
lava	LAH vuh	lä′vá	′lɑ və
	LAV uh	lăv′á § 47(2)	′læv ə
law	law	lô	lɔ
lawgiver	LAW *giv* uhr	lô′gĭv′ēr	′lɔ ˌgɪv ɚ; *ES* -ə(r)
lead (v.–*"guide"*)	leed	lēd	lid
lead (n.–*"metallic element"*)	led	lĕd	lɛd
leaf	leef	lēf	lif
learn	*luhrn*	lûrn § 40(6)	lɝn; *ES also* lɜn
learned (adj.)	LUHR ned	lûr′nĕd	′lɝ nɛd, -nɪd; *ES*
	LUHR nid	lûr′nĭd §§ 24(5), 50(5)	*also* ′lɜ-
leash	leesh	lēsh	liʃ
leathern	LETH uhrn	leth′ērn	′lɛð ɚn; *ES* -ən
leave	leev	lēv § 51(7)	liv
leaven	LEV uhn	lĕv′ĕn § 47(2)	′lɛv ən
lecture	LEK chuhr	lĕk′tûr	′lɛk tʃɚ, -tjɚ; *ES*
	LEK tyuhr	§ 50(31, 32)	-tʃə(r), -tjə(r)
leeward	LEE wuhrd	lē′wērd	′li wɚd; *ES* -wəd
	Naut.:	*Naut.:*	*Naut.:*
	LOO uhrd	lū′ērd	′lu ɚd, ′lju-; *ES*
	LYOO uhrd	§§ 47(3), 48(2), 50(32), 51(6)	-əd

	SIMPLIFIED	DIACRITICAL	PHONETIC
left	left	lĕft	lɛft
leg	leg	lĕg	lɛg
legate ("*ambassador*")	LEG it	lĕg′ĭt § 50(2)	'lɛg ɪt
legatee	*leg* uh TEE	lĕg′*a* tē′	ˌlɛg ə 'ti
legend	LEJ uhnd	lĕj′ĕnd	'lɛdʒ ənd
	LEE juhnd	lē′jĕnd § 47(3)	'li dʒənd
legendary	LEJ uhn *der* i *B*.,	lĕj′ĕn dĕr′ĭ *B*.,	'lɛdʒ ən ˌdɛr ɪ *B*.,
	LEJ uhn duhr i	lĕj′ĕn dĕr ĭ §§ 13, 20(2), 24(9), 51(4)	'lɛdʒ ən də rɪ
legion	LEE juhn	lē′jŭn	'li dʒən
legionnaire	*lee* juhn EHR	lē′jŭn âr′	ˌli dʒən 'ɛr, -'ær; *ES* -'æə(r), *E also* -'ɛə(r)
legislative	LEJ is *lay* tiv	lĕj′ĭs lā′tĭv	'lɛdʒ ɪs ˌle tɪv
	LEJ is luh tiv	lĕj′ĭs *la* tĭv	'lɛdʒ ɪs lə tɪv
legislatorial	*lej* is luh TOH ri uhl	lĕj′ĭs *la* tō′rĭ ăl § 34(3)	ˌlɛdʒ ɪs lə 'to rɪ əl
	lej is luh TAW ri uhl	lĕj′ĭs *la* tô′rĭ əl	ˌlɛdʒ ɪs lə 'tɔ rɪ əl
legislature	LEJ is *lay* chuhr	lĕj′ĭs lā′tûr § 50(31, 32)	'lɛdʒ ɪs ˌle tʃɚ, -tjɚ; *ES* -tʃə(r), -tjə(r)
	LEJ is *lay* tyuhr		
legitimate (adj.)	li JIT uh mit	lĕ jĭt′ĭ mĭt	lɪ 'dʒɪt ə mɪt
	li JIT i mit	lĕ jĭt′ĭ mĭt	lɪ 'dʒɪt ɪ mɪt
—— (v.t.)	li JIT uh mayt	lĕ jĭt′ĭ māt	lɪ 'dʒɪt ə met
	li JIT i mayt	lĕ jĭt′ĭ māt § 20(8, 9)	lɪ 'dʒɪt ɪ met
legume	LEG yoom	lĕg′ūm	'lɛg jum
	li GYOOM	lĕ gūm′ §§ 47(3), 48(2)	lɪ 'gjum
Leicester	LES tuhr	lĕs′tēr	'lɛs tɚ; *ES* -tə(r)
leisure	LEE zhuhr	lē′zhēr	'li ʒɚ; *ES* -ʒə(r)
	LEZH uhr	lĕzh′ēr	'lɛʒ ɚ; *ES* -ə(r)
	LEZH ŏŏr	lĕzh′ŏŏr § 47(3)	'lɛʒ ʊr; *ES* -ʊə(r)
leisurely	LEE zhuhr li	lē′zhēr lĭ	'li ʒɚ lɪ; *ES* -ʒə-
	LEZH uhr li	lĕzh′ēr lĭ § 50(20)	'lɛʒ ɚ lɪ; *ES* -ə lɪ
lemonade	*lem* uhn AYD	lĕm′ŭn ād′	ˌlɛm ən 'ed
length	length	lĕngth §§ 33(4), 50(24)	lɛŋθ
	lengkth		lɛŋkθ
lengthen	LENG thuhn	lĕng′thĕn	'lɛŋ θən
	LENGK thuhn	§§ 33(4), 50(24)	'lɛŋk θən
leniency	LEE ni uhn si	lē′nĭ ĕn sĭ	'li nɪ ən sɪ
	LEEN yuhn si	lēn′yĕn sĭ § 28(9)	'lin jən sɪ
lenient	LEE ni uhnt	lē′nĭ ĕnt	'li nɪ ənt
	LEEN yuhnt	lēn′yĕnt §§ 28(9), 47(2)	'lin jənt

	SIMPLIFIED	DIACRITICAL	PHONETIC
lenity	LEN uh ti	lĕn′ĭ tĭ	ˈlɛn ə tɪ
	LEN i ti	lĕn′ĭ tĭ § 47(1)	ˈlɛn ɪ tɪ
leonine (adj.)	LEE uh nain	lē′ŏ nīn	ˈli ə naɪn
	LEE uh nin	lē′ŏ nĭn § 47(3)	ˈli ə nɪn
	§ 50(34)		
leopard	LEP uhrd	lĕp′ĕrd § 24(21)	ˈlɛp ɚd; ES -əd
leper	LEP uhr	lĕp′ēr	ˈlɛp ɚ; ES -ə(r)
leprosy	LEP ruh si	lĕp′rŏ sĭ	ˈlɛp rə sɪ
lest	lest	lĕst	lɛst
lethargic	li THAHR jik	lĕ thär′jĭk	lɪ ˈθɑr dʒɪk; ES -ˈθɑː-, E also -ˈθɑː-
lethargy	LETH uhr ji	lĕth′ēr jĭ	ˈlɛθ ɚ dʒɪ; ES -ə dʒɪ
Lethe	LEE thee	lē′thē	ˈli θi
	LEE thi	lē′thĕ	ˈli θɪ
letter	LET uhr	lĕt′ēr	ˈlɛt ɚ; ES -ə(r)
lettuce	LET is	lĕt′ĭs	ˈlɛt ɪs
	LET uhs	lĕt′ŭs § 47(1)	ˈlɛt əs
leucocyte	LOO kuh sait	lū′kŏ sīt	ˈlu kə saɪt
	LYOO kuh sait	§§ 48(2), 50(32, 34)	ˈlju kə saɪt
Levant (n., adj.)	li VANT	lĕ vănt′ § 47(2)	lɪ ˈvænt, lə-
—— (adj. also— in earlier senses)	*Rarely:* LEV uhnt	*Rarely:* lĕv′ănt	*Rarely:* ˈlɛv ənt
Levantine	li VAN tin	lĕ văn′tĭn	lɪ ˈvæn tɪn
	li VAN tain	lĕ văn′tīn	lɪ ˈvæn taɪn
	li VAN teen	lĕ văn′tēn	lɪ ˈvæn tin
	LEV uhn tin	lĕv′ăn tĭn	ˈlɛv ən tɪn
	LEV uhn tain	lĕv′ăn tīn	ˈlɛv ən taɪn
	LEV uhn teen	lĕv′ăn tēn §§ 28(6), 47(3)	ˈlɛv ən tin
levee ("embank- ment"; "make levees on")	LEV i	lĕv′ĭ	ˈlɛv ɪ
	le VEE	lĕ vē′	lɛ ˈvi
levee, levée ("reception")	le VEE	lĕ vē′	lɛ ˈvi
	LEV i	lĕv′ĭ	ˈlɛv ɪ
	luh VEE	lĕ vē′	lə ˈvi
lever	LEE vuhr	lē′vēr	ˈli vɚ; ES -və(r)
	LEV uhr	lev′ēr § 47(3)	ˈlɛv ɚ; ES -ə(r)
leverage	LEE vuhr ij	lē′vēr ĭj	ˈli vər ɪdʒ
	LEV uhr ij	lĕv′ēr ĭj §§ 47(3), 50(1)	ˈlɛv ər ɪdʒ; ˈlɛv rɪdʒ
leviathan	li VAI uh thuhn	lĕ vī′á thăn	lɪ ˈvaɪ ə θən
levity	LEV uh ti	lĕv′ĭ tĭ	ˈlɛv ə tɪ
	LEV i ti	lĕv′ĭ tĭ	ˈlɛv ɪ tɪ

lewd	lood lyood	lūd §§ 40(4), 47(1), 48(2), 50(32)	lud ljud
liability	*lai* uh BIL uh ti *lai* uh BIL i ti	lī′*á* bĭl′*ĭ* tĭ lī′*á* bĭl′ĭ tĭ	ˌlaɪ ə ˈbɪl ə tɪ ˌlaɪ ə ˈbɪl ɪ tɪ
liable	LAI uh b'l § 50(34)	lī′*á* b'l	ˈlaɪ ə bļ
liaison	*lee ay* zawN	lē′ā′zôN′ § 20(14)	ˌli e ˈzõ *F.*, ljɛ ˈzõ [-ˈzõ]
	Angl., lee AY zuhn lee AY z'n	*Angl.*, lĕ ā′zŭn lĕ ā′z'n § 51(1)	*Angl.*, li ˈe zən li ˈe zņ
libation	lai BAY shuhn § 50(34)	lī bā′shŭn	laɪ ˈbe ʃən
liberate	LIB uhr ayt LIB uh rayt	lĭb′ĕr āt § 50(2)	ˈlɪb ər et ˈlɪb ə ret
libertine	LIB uhr teen LIB uhr tin	lĭb′ĕr tēn lĭb′ĕr tĭn §§ 28(6), 47(3)	ˈlɪb ɚ tin, -tɪn; *ES* -ə tin, -tɪn
library	LAI *brer* i *B.*, LAI bruh ri	lī′brĕr′ĭ *B.*, lī′brá rĭ §§ 13, 48(1), 51(4)	ˈlaɪ ˌbrer ɪ, -ˌber ɪ *B.*, ˈlaɪ brə rɪ, -bə rɪ
licentiate (n.)	lai SEN shi it lai SEN shi ayt	lī sĕn′shĭ ăt §§ 20(8, 9), 50(34)	laɪ ˈsɛn ʃɪ ɪt laɪ ˈsɛn ʃɪ et
—— (v.t.)	lai SEN shi ayt	lī sĕn′shĭ āt	laɪ ˈsɛn ʃɪ et
licentious	lai SEN shuhs	lī sĕn′shŭs	laɪ ˈsɛn ʃəs
lichen	LAI kuhn LAI kin *B.*, LAI ken § 54(34)	lī′kĕn lī′kĭn *B.*, lī′kĕn §§ 47(3), 51(4)	ˈlaɪ kən ˈlaɪ kɪn *B.*, ˈlaɪ kɛn
liege	leej	lēj	lidʒ
lien	LEE uhn leen	lē′ĕn lēn § 47(3)	ˈli ən, -ɛn, lin
lieu	loo lyoo	lū §§ 47(1), 48(2), 50(32)	lu lju
lieutenant	loo TEN uhnt lyoo TEN uhnt	lū tĕn′ănt §§ 47(2), 48(2), 50(32)	lu ˈtɛn ənt lju ˈtɛn ənt
lifts	lifts	lĭfts § 50(6)	lɪfts
ligature	LIG uh *choor* LIG uh chuhr LIG uh *tyoor* LIG uh tyuhr	lĭg′*á* tūr §§ 40(11), 50(31, 32)	ˈlɪg ə ˌtʃʊr, -tʃɚ, -ˌtjʊr, -tjɚ; *ES* -ˌtʃʊə(r), -tʃə(r), -ˌtjʊə(r), -tjə(r)
light	lait § 50(34)	līt § 1	laɪt

	SIMPLIFIED	DIACRITICAL	PHONETIC
light-hearted	LĀIT HÄHR ted LĀIT HÄHR tid §50(34)	līt′här′tĕd līt′här′tĭd §§ 11, 24(5)	′laɪt ′hɑr ted, -tɪd; *ES* -′hɑː-, *E* *also* -′hɑ:-
lightning	LĀIT ning § 50(34)	līt′nĭng § 50(24)	′laɪt nɪŋ
lignite	LIG nait § 50(34)	lĭg′nīt	′lɪg naɪt
lilac	LĀI luhk § 50(34)	lī′lăk	′laɪ lək
	Arch. or obs.: LĀI lak	*Arch. or obs.:* lī′lăk § 51(2)	*Arch. or obs.:* ′laɪ læk
Lille	leel	lēl	lil
lilt	lilt	lĭlt	lɪlt
Lima (Peru)	LEE mah	lē′mä	′li mɑ
Lima (Ohio)	LĀI muh § 50(34)	lī′mȧ	′laɪ mə
limn	lim	lĭm	lɪm
limner	LIM nuhr	lĭm′nĕr § 33(1)	′lɪm nɚ; *ES* -nə(r)
limning	LIM ning LIM ing	lĭm′nĭng lĭm′ĭng § 33(1)	′lɪm nɪŋ ′lɪm ɪŋ
limousine	*lim* ŏŏ ZEEN LIM uh zeen	lĭm′ŏŏ zēn′ § 11	ˌlɪm ʊ ′zin, -ə ′zin, ′lɪm ə zin
Lincoln	LING kuhn	lĭng′kŭn	′lɪŋ kən
lineage (n.–*"descent"*)	LIN i ij	lĭn′ē ĭj § 50(1)	′lɪn ɪ ɪdʒ
lineament	LIN i uh muhnt	lĭn′ē ȧ mĕnt § 50(22)	′lɪn ɪ ə mənt
linear	LIN i uhr	lĭn′ē ēr § 24(15)	′lɪn ɪ ɚ; *ES* -ɪ ə(r)
linger	LING guhr	lĭng′gēr	′lɪŋ gɚ; *ES* -gə(r)
lingerie	*la*N zh′ REE	lăn′zh′ rē′	ˌlæn ʒ ′ri, -ʒə ′ri (*F.*, læʒ ′ri)
	Pop.: LAHN zhuh ree LAN zhuh ree	*Pop.:* län′zhē rē lăn′zhē rē §§ 20(14), 47(1), 51(3)	*Pop.:* ′lɑn ʒə ri, ′læn-, læʒ ′ri; *N.Y.C. often* ˌlæn ʒə ′re
link	lingk	lĭngk § 51(7)	lɪŋk
linnet	LIN et LIN it	lĭn′ĕt lĭn′ĭt § 24(5)	′lɪn ɛt ′lɪn ɪt
linoleum	li NOH li uhm	lĭ nō′lĕ ŭm § 28(9)	lɪ ′no lɪ əm, -ljəm
lion	LĀI uhn § 50(34)	lī′ŭn	′laɪ ən
liquor	LIK uhr	lĭk′ēr	′lɪk ɚ; *ES* -ə(r)
lisle, Lisle	laīl *F.*, leel § 50(34)	līl *F.*, lēl	laɪl *F.*, lil
listen	LIS ′n	lĭs′ ′n §§ 1, 39(2)	′lɪs n̩
liter, litre	LEE tuhr	lē′tēr § 47(2)	′li tɚ; *ES* -tə(r)

	SIMPLIFIED	DIACRITICAL	PHONETIC
literacy	LIT uhr uh si	lĭt′ĕr ȧ sĭ	ˈlɪt ər ə sɪ
literal	LIT uhr uhl	lĭt′ĕr ăl	ˈlɪt ər əl
literary	LIT uhr er i B., LIT uhr uhr i	lĭt′ĕr ĕr′ĭ B., lĭt′ ĕr ĕr ĭ §§ 13, 20(2), 24(9), 51(4)	ˈlɪt ər ˌɛr ɪ B., ˈlɪt ər ə rɪ
literature	LIT uhr uh chŏŏr LIT uhr uh chuhr LIT uhr uh tyŏŏr LIT uhr uh tyuhr	lĭt′ĕr ȧ tûr §§ 9, 47(3), 50(31, 32, 33)	ˈlɪt ər ə ˌtʃʊr, -ˌtʃɚ, -ˌtjʊr, -ˌtjɚ, ˈlɪt rə-; ES -ˌtʃʊə(r), -tʃə(r), -ˌtjʊə(r), -tjə(r)
lithe	laith § 50(34)	līth § 51(7)	laɪð
litigious	li TIJ uhs	lĭ tĭj′ŭs	lɪ ˈtɪdʒ əs
little	LIT ′l	lĭt′ ′l	ˈlɪt l̩
liturgical	li TUHR ji kuhl	lĭ tûr′jĭ kăl	lɪ ˈtɝ dʒɪ kəl, -kl̩; ES also -ˈtɜ-
liturgy	LIT uhr ji	lĭt′ĕr jĭ	ˈlɪt ɚ dʒɪ; ES -ə dʒɪ
live (adj.–"living")	laiv § 50(34)	līv	laɪv
livelong	LIV lawng LIV long	lĭv′lŏng′ § 34(7)	ˈlɪv lɔŋ ˈlɪv lɒŋ
livid	LIV id	lĭv′ĭd	ˈlɪv ɪd
llama	LAH muh	lä′mȧ § 47(2)	ˈlɑ mə
llano	LAH noh Sp., LYAH noh	lä′nō Sp., lyä′nō § 31(5)	ˈlɑ no Sp., ˈlja no
loath, loth	lohth	lōth § 39(6)	loθ
loathe	lohth	lōth § 39(6)	loð
loathsome	LOHTH suhm	lōth′sŭm	ˈloð səm
locate	LOH kayt loh KAYT	lō′kāt lŏ kāt′	ˈlo ket lo ˈket
located	LOH kayt ed loh KAYT id	lō′kāt ĕd lŏ kāt′ĭd § 24(5)	ˈlo ket ɛd lo ˈket ɪd
Lochinvar	loκ in VAHR	lŏκ′ĭn vär′ § 22(10)	ˌlax ɪn ˈvar, ˌlak-, ˌlɒk-; ES -ˈva:(r), E also -ˈva:(r)
locomotive	loh kuh MOH tiv	lō′kŏ mō′tĭv	ˌlo kə ˈmo tɪv
loft	lawft loft	lŏft §§ 34(7), 47(2)	lɔft lɒft
logarithm	LAWG uh rith'm LOG uh rith'm LAWG uh rith'm LOG uh rith'm	lŏg′ȧ rĭth'm lŏg′ȧ rĭth'm §§ 34(7), 47(2)	ˈlɔg ə rɪð m̩, ˈlag-, ˈlɒg-, -rɪð əm, ˈlɔg ə rɪθ m̩, ˈlag-, ˈlɒg-, -rɪθ əm

logic	LOJ ik	lŏj′ĭk	'ladʒ ɪk; *ES also* 'lɒdʒ-
Lombard	LOM buhrd	lŏm′bẽrd	'lam bɚd, 'lʌm-,
	LUHM buhrd	lŭm′bẽrd	'lam bard; *ES*
	LOM bahrd	lŏm′bärd § 47(2)	*also* 'lɒm-, *ES* -bəd, -bɑːd, *E also* -baːd
long	lawng	lŏng	lɔŋ
	long	§§ 34(7), 47(2), 50(24)	lɒŋ
longer	LAWNG guhr	lŏng′gẽr	'lɔŋ gɚ, 'lɒŋ-; *ES*
	LONG guhr	§§ 34(7), 50(24)	-gə(r)
longest	LAWNG gest	lŏng′gĕst	'lɔŋ gest
	LONG gest		'lɒŋ gest
	LAWNG gist	lŏng′gĭst	'lɔŋ gɪst
	LONG gist	§§ 24(5), 34(7), 50(9, 24)	'lɒŋ gɪst
longevity	lon JEV uh ti	lŏn jĕv′ĭ tĭ	lan 'dʒev ə tɪ,
	lon JEV i ti	lŏn jĕv′ĭ tĭ	-ɪ tɪ; *ES also* lɒn-
long-headed	LAWNG HED ed	lŏng′hĕd′ĕd	'lɔŋ 'hed ɛd
	LONG HED ed		'lɒŋ 'hed ɛd
	LAWNG HED id	lŏng′hĕd′ĭd	'lɔŋ 'hed ɪd
	LONG HED id	§§ 11, 24(5), 34(7)	'lɒŋ 'hed ɪd
longing	LAWNG ing	lŏng′ĭng	'lɔŋ ɪŋ
	LONG ing	§§ 34(7), 50(24)	'lɒŋ ɪŋ
longitude	LON juh tyood	lŏn′jĭ tūd	'lan dʒə tjud,
	LON juh tood		-tud, -dʒɪ-; *ES*
	LON ji tyood	lŏn′jĭ tūd	*also* 'lɒn-
	LON ji tood	§§ 48(2), 50(32)	
longitudinal	*lon* juh TYOO duh nuhl, -n'l	lŏn′jĭ tū′dĭ năl	ˌlan dʒə 'tju də nəl, -tu-,
	lon juh TOO duh nuhl, -n'l	lŏn′jĭ tū′dĭ năl	-dʒɪ 'tju dɪ-, -tu-, -n̦, -dn̦];
	lon ji TYOO di nuhl, -n'l	lŏn′jĭ tū′dĭ n'l	*ES also* ˌlɒn-
	lon ji TOO di nuhl, -n'l	lŏn′ jĭ tū′ dĭ n'l §§ 48(2), 50(32)	
long-lived	LAWNG LA͡IVD	lŏng′līvd′	'lɔŋ 'laɪvd
	LONG LA͡IVD	§§ 11, 34(7), 51(8)	'lɒŋ 'laɪvd
	Not infreq.:	*Not infreq.:*	*Not infreq.:*
	LAWNG LIVD	lŏng′lĭvd′	'lɔŋ 'lɪvd
	LONG LIVD		'lɒŋ 'lɪvd
loose	loos	lo͞os § 34(22)	lus
lopsided	LOP SA͡ID ed	lŏp′sīd′ĕd	'lap 'saɪd ɛd, -ɪd;
	LOP SA͡ID id	lŏp′sīd′ĭd	*ES also* 'lɒp-
	§ 50(34)	§§ 11, 24(5)	

	SIMPLIFIED	DIACRITICAL	PHONETIC
lorgnette	*lawr* NYET *lawrn* YET	lôr′nyĕt′	ˌlɔr ′njet ˌlɔrn ′jet; *ES* -ˌlɔə-, -ˌlɔən-; *F.*, lör ′net
Los Angeles (*Note:* **Many** **regard "les"** **rather than** **"es" as the final** **syllable.**)	lohs ANG guhl es los ANG guhl es los AN juhl uhs los AN juhl eez *Sp.*, lohs AHNG hay lays laws AHNG he les	lōs ăng′gĕl ĕs lŏs ăng′gĕl ĕs lŏs ăn′jĕl ĕs lŏs ăn′jĕl ēz *Sp.*, lōs äng′hä läs lôs äng′hĕ lĕs § 25(6)	los ′æŋ gəl ɛs, lɒs-, las-, lɒs ′æn dʒəl əs, las-, -dʒəl iz *Sp.*, los ′aŋ he les lɔs ′aŋ he lɛs
loss	laws los	lŏs §§ 34(7), 47(2), 50(34)	lɔs lɒs
lotion	LOH shuhn	lō′shŭn § 50(30)	′lo ʃən
Louisiana	loo *ee* zi AN uh *loo* i zi AN uh	lōō ē′zǐ ăn′ȧ lōō′ǐ zǐ ăn′ȧ	lu ˌi zɪ ′æn ə ˌlu ɪ zɪ ′æn ə
Louisianan	loo *ee* zi AN uhn *loo* i zi AN uhn	lōō ē′zǐ ăn′ăn lōō′ǐ zǐ ăn′ăn	lu ˌi zɪ ′æn ən ˌlu ɪ zɪ ′æn ən
Louisianian	loo *ee* zi AN i uhn *loo* i zi AN i uhn	lōō ē′zǐ ăn′ǐ ăn lōō′ǐ zǐ ăn′ǐ ăn § 28(9)	lu ˌi zɪ ′æn ɪ ən ˌlu ɪ zɪ ′æn ɪ ən
lour (*"frown"*)	lowr	lour	laʊr; *ES* laʊə(r)
Louvre	LOO vr′ LOO vruh	lōō′vr′ lōō′vrĕ	′lu vr (*F.*, lu:vr) ′lu vrə
lovable	LUHV uh b′l	lŭv′ȧ b′l	′lʌv ə bl̩
lovely	LUHV li	lŭv′lǐ	′lʌv lɪ
lower (*"less* *high"; "let* *down"*)	LOH uhr	lō′ĕr	′lo ɚ; *ES* -ə(r)
lower (*"frown"*)	LOW uhr	lou′ĕr	′laʊ ɚ; *ES* -ə(r)
lozenge	LOZ enj LOZ inj	lŏz′ĕnj lŏz′ĭnj § 24(5)	′laz ɛndʒ, -ɪndʒ; *ES also* ′lɒz-
lubricant	LOO bri kuhnt LYOO bri kuhnt	lū′brǐ kănt §§ 40(4), 48(2), 50(32)	′lu brɪ kənt ′lju brɪ kənt
lubricate (v.)	LOO bri kayt LYOO bri kayt	lū′brǐ kāt §§ 48(2), 50(2, 32)	′lu brɪ ket ′lju brɪ ket
lucent	LOO suhnt LYOO suhnt LOO s′nt LYOO s′nt	lū′sĕnt lū′s′nt §§ 40(4), 48(2), 50(32)	′lu sənt ′lju sənt ′lu sn̩t ′lju sn̩t
lucid	LOO sid LYOO sid	lū′sǐd §§ 40(4), 47(2), 48(2), 50(32)	′lu sɪd ′lju sɪd

	SIMPLIFIED	DIACRITICAL	PHONETIC
lucidity	loo SID uh ti lyoo SID uh ti loo SID i ti lyoo SID i ti	lū̆ sĭd′ĭ tĭ lū̆ sĭd′ĭ tĭ §§ 48(2) 50(16, 32)	lu ′sɪd ə tɪ, lu- lju ′sɪd ə tɪ, lju- lu ′sɪd ɪ tɪ, lu- lju ′sɪd ɪ tɪ, lju-
Lucifer	LOO si fuhr LYOO si fuhr	lū′sĭ fẽr §§ 40(4), 48(2), 50(32)	′lu sɪ fɚ, ′lju-; *ES* -fə(r)
lucrative	LOO kruh tiv LYOO kruh tiv	lū′krȧ tĭv §§ 48(2), 50(17, 32)	′lu krə tɪv ′lju krə tɪv
lucre	LYOO kuhr LOO kuhr	lū′kẽr lōō′kẽr §§ 47(2), 48(2)	′lju kɚ, ′lu-; *ES* -kə(r)
lucubration	*loo* kyōō BRAY shuhn *lyoo* kyōō BRAY shuhn	lū′kū̆ brā′shŭn §§ 48(2), 50(30, 32)	ˌlu kjʊ ′bre ʃən, -kju- ˌlju kjʊ ′bre ʃən, -kju-
ludicrous	LOO di kruhs LYOO di kruhs	lū′dĭ krŭs §§ 40(4), 47(2), 48(2), 50(25, 32)	′lu dɪ krəs ′lju dɪ krəs
luggage	LUHG ij	lŭg′ĭj § 50(1)	′lʌg ɪdʒ
lugubrious	loo GYOO bri uhs lyoo GYOO bri uhs	lū̆ gū′brĭ ŭs §§ 48(2), 50(25, 32)	lu ′gju brɪ əs lju ′gju brɪ əs
Luke	look lyook	lūk §§ 48(2), 50(32)	luk ljuk
luminary	LOO muh *ner* i LYOO muh *ner* i LOO mi *ner* i LYOO mi *ner* i	lū′mĭ nẽr′ĭ lū′mĭ nẽr′ĭ §§ 13, 20(2), 24(9), 40(4), 48(2), 50(32), 51(4)	′lu mə ˌnɛr ɪ ′lju mə ˌnɛr ɪ ′lu mɪ ˌnɛr ɪ ′lju mɪ ˌnɛr ɪ
	B., LOO muh nuhr i	*B.,* lū′mĭ nẽr ĭ	*B.,* ′lu mə nə rɪ
luminous	LOO muh nuhs LYOO muh nuhs LOO mi nuhs LYOO mi nuhs	lū′mĭ nŭs lū′mĭ nŭs §§ 48(2), 50(25, 32)	′lu mə nəs ′lju mə nəs ′lu mɪ nəs ′lju mɪ nəs
lunacy	LOO nuh si LYOO nuh si	lū′nȧ sĭ §§ 48(2), 50(32)	′lu nə sɪ ′lju nə sɪ
lunatic	LOO nuh tik LYOO nuh tik	lū′nȧ tĭk §§ 40(4), 48(2), 50(32)	′lu nə tɪk ′lju nə tɪk
luncheon	LUHN chuhn	lŭn′chŭn § 22(6)	′lʌn tʃən

	SIMPLIFIED	DIACRITICAL	PHONETIC
lure (n.–"con-trivance; decoy"; v.– entice)	lŏŏr lyŏŏr loor lyoor	lūr §§ 40(4), 48(2), 50(32)	lʊr, ljʊr; *ES also* luə(r), ljʊə(r)
lurid	LŎŎ rid LYŎŎ rid LOO rid LYOO rid	lū′rĭd §§ 34(21), 40(4, 11), 48(2), 50(32)	′lʊ rɪd, ′ljʊ rɪd; *ES also* ′lʊər ɪd, ′ljʊər ɪd
luscious	LUHSH uhs	lŭsh′ŭs § 50(25)	′lʌʃ əs
lute	loot lyoot	lūt §§ 40(4), 47(3), 48(2), 50(32)	lut ljut
Lutheran	LOO thuhr uhn LYOO thuhr uhn	lū′thĕr ăn §§ 9, 40(4), 48(2), 50(32)	′lu θər ən, ′lju-, -θrən
luxuriance	*luhg* ZHŎŎR i uhns *luhk* SHŎŎR i uhns *luhks* YŎŎ ri uhns *luhks* YOO ri uhns	lŭg zhŏŏr′ĭ ăns lŭk shŏŏr′ĭ ăns lŭks ū′rĭ ăns § 40(6)	lʌg ′ʒʊr ɪ əns, lʌk ′ʃʊr-, lʌks ′jʊ rɪ əns; *ES also* -′ʒʊər-, -′ʃʊər-, -′jʊə rɪ-
luxurious	*luhg* ZHŎŎR i uhs *luhk* SHŎŎR i uhs *luhks* YŎŎ ri uhs *luhks* YOO ri uhs	lŭg zhŏŏr′ĭ ŭs lŭk shŏŏr′ĭ ŭs lŭks ū′rĭ ŭs §§ 34(21), 40(4, 6, 11), 47(3), 50(25)	lʌg ′ʒʊr ɪ əs, lʌk ′ʃʊr-, lʌks ′jʊ rɪ əs; *ES also* -′ʒʊər-, -′ʃʊər-, -′jʊə rɪ-
luxury	LUHK shŏŏ ri LUHK shuh ri LUHKS yŏŏ ri	lŭk′shŏŏ rĭ §§ 38(12), 47(3) lŭks′ŭ rĭ	′lʌk ʃʊ rɪ, -ʃə-, ′lʌg ʒə- ′lʌks jʊ rɪ
lyceum	laͤi SEE uhm	lī sē′ŭm	laɪ ′si əm
Lyons	LAͤI uhnz § 50(34)	lī′ŭnz	′laɪ ənz
lyre	laͤir § 50(34)	līr	laɪr; *ES* laɪə(r)
lyric	LIR ik	lĭr′ĭk	′lɪr ɪk
Lysander	laͤi SAN duhr § 50(34)	lī săn′dĕr	laɪ ′sæn dɚ; *ES* -də(r)

M

ma'am (colloq. contraction)	mam mahm	măm mäm	mæm mɑm
—— colloq., esp. when unaccented	muhm 'm	mŏm 'm § 47(2)	məm -m̩, -m
macaroon	*mak* uh ROON	măk'*ȧ* rōōn' § 11	ˌmæk ə 'run
Machiavelli (**Nicollȯ di Bernardo**)	*mah* kyah VEL lee *Angl.*, *mak* i uh VEL i	mä'kyä věl'lĕ *Angl.*, măk'ĭ *ȧ* věl'ĭ	ˌma kjɑ 'vɛl li *Angl.*, ˌmæk ɪ ə 'vɛl ɪ, ˌmæk jə-
Machiavellian, Machiavelian	*mak* i uh VEL i uhn *mak* i uh VEL yuhn	măk'ĭ *ȧ* věl'ĭ ăn măk'ĭ *ȧ* věl'yăn § 28(9)	ˌmæk ɪ ə 'vɛl ɪ ən, -'vɛl jən, ˌmæk jə-
machination	*mak* uh NAY shuhn *mak* i NAY shuhn	măk'ĭ nā'shŭn măk'ĭ nā'shŭn	ˌmæk ə 'ne ʃən ˌmæk ɪ 'ne ʃən
mackerel	MAK uhr uhl	măk'ēr ĕl §§ 9, 51(7)	'mæk ər əl, 'mæk rəl
madam	MAD uhm	măd'ăm	'mæd əm
madame	MAD uhm *mah* DAHM muh DAHM	măd'ăm mä'däm' mă däm' *F.*, mȧ'dȧm' § 47(1)	'mæd əm ˌma 'dɑm mə 'dɑm *F.*, ma 'dam
made	mayd	mād	med
Madeira	muh DĬER uh muh DIR uh muh DEER uh muh DAY ruh *Pg.*, mah DAY rah	mȧ dēr'*ȧ* § 24(2) mȧ dēr'*ȧ* mȧ dā'r*ȧ* *Pg.*, mä dā'rä § 47(3)	mə 'dɪər ə, -'dɪr-, -'dir-, -de rə; *ES* -'dɪər ə *Pg.*, mɑ 'de rɑ
mademoiselle	*mad mwa* ZEL *mahd mwah* ZEL *mad* uh muh ZEL *mah* duh mwah ZEL *Colloq.:* *mam* ZEL	măd'mwȧ'zĕl' §§ 47(1), 51(3) măd' ĕ mŏ zĕl' mä'dĕ mwä zĕl' *Colloq.:* mȧm'zel'	*F.*, mad mwa 'zɛl ˌmæd ə mə 'zɛl ˌma də mwa 'zɛl *Colloq.:* *F.*, mam 'zɛl

	SIMPLIFIED	DIACRITICAL	PHONETIC
madrigal	MAD ri guhl	măd′rĭ găl § 31(3)	′mæd rɪ gəl, -gl̩
magazine	*mag* uh ZEEN	măg′á zēn′	ˌmæg ə ′zin
—— *"a periodi- cal,"* also often	MAG uh zeen	măg′á zēn	′mæg ə zin
Magdalen, magdalen	MAG duh len	măg′dá lĕn	′mæg də lɛn, -lɪn, -lən
—— *"College at Oxford Uni- versity,"* usually	MAWD lin	môd′lĭn	′mɔd lɪn
Magdalene, magdalene	MAG duh leen *mag* duh LEE nee	măg′dá lēn măg′dá lē′nĕ	′mæg də lin ˌmæg də ′li ni, -nɪ
—— *in "Mary Magdalene,"* esp.	*mag* duh LEE nee	măg′dá lē′nĕ	ˌmæg də ′li ni, -nɪ
—— *"College at Cambridge Uni- versity,"* usually	MAWD lin	môd′lĭn	′mɔd lɪn
Magi	MAY jai͡ § 50(34)	mā′jī	′me dʒaɪ
magnanimity	*mag* nuh NIM uh ti	măg′ná nĭm′ĭ tĭ	ˌmæg nə ′nɪm ə tɪ
	mag nuh NIM i ti	măg′ná nĭm′ĭ tĭ	ˌmæg nə ′nɪm ɪ tɪ
magnanimous	mag NAN uh muhs	măg năn′ĭ mŭs	mæg ′næn ə məs
	mag NAN i muhs	măg năn′ĭ mŭs	mæg ′næn ɪ məs
magnesia	mag NEE shuh mag NEE zhuh *B.*, mag NEE shi uh	măg nē′shá măg nē′zhá *B.*, măg nē′shĭ á §§ 47(3), 50(27), 51(4)	mæg ′ni ʃə, -′ni ʒə, -ʒɪ ə, -zɪ ə *B.*, mæg ′nɪ ʃɪ ə
magnesium	mag NEE shi uhm mag NEE zhi uhm	măg nē′shĭ ŭm măg nē′zhĭ ŭm § 47(2)	mæg ′ni ʃɪ əm mæg ′ni ʒɪ əm mæg ′ni zɪ əm
magneto	mag NEE toh	măg nē′tō	mæg ′ni to
magnets	MAG nets MAG nits	măg′nĕts măg′nĭts § 24(5)	′mæg nɛts ′mæg nɪts
magnolia	mag NOH li uh mag NOHL yuh	măg nō′lĭ á măg nōl′yá § 28(9)	mæg ′no lɪ ə mæg ′nol jə
Magyar	MAG yahr	măg′yär § 47(3)	′mæg jɑr, ′mɑ djɑr; *ES* -jɑ:(r), -djɑ:(r), *E also* -jɑ:(r), -djɑ:(r)
	Hung., MOD yor	*Hung.*, mŏd′yŏr	*Hung.*, ′mɒd jɒr

	SIMPLIFIED	DIACRITICAL	PHONETIC
maharaja, **maharajah**	muh HAH RAH juh	má hä′rä′já	mə ′hɑ ′rɑ dʒə
	Angl.,	*Angl.,*	*Angl.,*
	mah hah RAH juh	mä′hä rä′já	ˌma hɑ ′rɑ dʒə
	mah huh RAH juh	mä′hă rä′já	ˌma hə ′rɑ dʒə
mahogany	muh HOG uh ni	má hŏg′á nĭ	mə ′hɑg ə ni, -′hɒg-
Mahomet	muh HOM et	má hŏm′ĕt	mə ′hɑm ɛt,
	muh HOM it	má hŏm′ĭt	-′hɒm-, -ɪt
	Occas.:	*Occas.:*	*Occas.:*
	MAY uh met	mā′ŏ mĕt	′me ə mɛt
	MAY uh mit	mā′ŏ mĭt	′me ə mɪt
	As a modern surname:	*As a modern surname:*	*As a modern surname:*
	MAY aw met	mā′ô mĕt	′me ɔ mɛt
	MAY aw mit	mā′ô mĭt	′me ɔ mɪt
		§§ 24(5), 51(8)	
mainsail	MAYN *sayl*	mān′sāl′	′men ˌsel
	Naut.:	*Naut.:*	*Naut.:*
	MAYN s'l	mān′s′l § 51(6)	′men sl̩
maintain	mayn TAYN	mān tān′	men ′ten
	muhn TAYN	mĕn tān′ § 47(2)	mən ′ten
maintenance	MAYN ti nuhns	mān′tĕ năns	′men tɪ nəns, -tə-
major	MAY juhr	mā′jĕr	′me dʒɚ; *ES* -dʒə(r)
malaria	muh LEHR i uh	má lâr′ĭ á	mə ′lɛr ɪ ə, -′lær-,
	muh LAY ri uh	§ 20(2)	-′le rɪ-; *ES also* -′lɛər-
malefactor	MAL i *fak* tuhr	măl′ĕ făk′tēr § 47(3)	′mæl ɪ ˌfæk tɚ; *ES* -tə(r)
malevolence	muh LEV uh luhns	má lĕv′ŏ lĕns	mə ′lɛv ə ləns
malevolent	muh LEV uh luhnt	má lĕv′ŏ lĕnt	mə ′lɛv ə lənt
malicious	muh LISH uhs	má lĭsh′ŭs	mə ′lɪʃ əs
malign	muh L͡AIN § 50(34)	má līn′	mə ′laɪn
malignant	muh LIG nuhnt	má lĭg′nănt	mə ′lɪg nənt
mall ("*shaded walk*")	mawl	môl	mɔl
	mal	măl § 47(2)	mæl
malleable	MAL i uh b'l	măl′ĕ á b′l § 28(9)	′mæl ɪ ə bl̩
mama	MAH muh	mä′má	′mɑ mə
	muh MAH	má mä′ § 47(2)	mə ′mɑ
man	man	măn § 50(21)	mæn
manage	MAN ij	măn′ĭj § 50(1)	′mæn ɪdʒ
mandarin (n., adj.)	MAN duh rin	măn′dá rĭn § 47(2)	′mæn də rɪn
—— (v.t.– *Dyeing*)	*man* duh REEN	măn′dá rēn′ § 12	ˌmæn də ′rin

	SIMPLIFIED	DIACRITICAL	PHONETIC
mandolin	MAN duh lin	măn'dŏ lĭn	'mæn də lɪn
maneuver, manoeuvre	muh NOO vuhr muh NYOO vuhr	må nōō'vĕr må nū'vĕr	mə 'nu vɚ, -'nju-; *ES* -və(r)
manganese	MANG guh nees	măng'gå nēs	'mæŋ gə nis, 'mæn-
	MANG guh neez	măng'gå nēz §§ 38(6), 47(3), 50(7)	'mæŋ gə niz, 'mæn-
manger	MAYN juhr	mān'jĕr § 25(4)	'men dʒɚ; *ES* -dʒə(r)
mania	MAY ni uh	mā'nĭ å § 28(9)	'me nɪ ə
maniac	MAY ni ak	mā'nĭ ăk § 28(9)	'me nɪ æk
maniacal	muh NAI uh kuhl § 50(34)	må nī'å kǎl	mə 'naɪ ə kəl, -kl̩
mankind ("human race")	*man* KAIND	măn'kīnd'	ˌmæn 'kaɪnd
—— "men, as distinguished from women"	MAN *kaind* § 50(34)	măn'kīnd'	'mæn ˌkaɪnd
manor	MAN uhr	măn'ĕr	'mæn ɚ; *ES* -ə(r)
Mantua	MAN chŏŏ uh MAN tyŏŏ uh MAN tŏŏ uh	măn'tû å § 50(32, 33)	'mæn tʃʊ ə, -tjʊ ə, -tju-, -tʊ ə, -tu-
manufacture	*man* yŏŏ FAK chuhr *man* yŏŏ FAK tyuhr	măn'û făk'tûr §§ 50(31,32,33)	ˌmæn ju 'fæk tʃɚ, -tjɚ, -jə-, -ju-; *ES* -tʃə(r), -tjə(r)
many	MEN i	měn'ĭ	'men ɪ
marchioness	MAHR shuhn es MAHR shuhn is	mär'shǔn ĕs mär'shǔn ĭs §§ 24(5), 50(8)	'mɑr ʃən ɛs, -ɪs; *ES* 'mɑː ʃən-, *E* *also* 'mɑ:-
marigold	MAR uh gohld MAR i gohld	măr'ĭ gōld măr'ĭ gōld	'mær ə gold 'mær ɪ gold
marital	MAR uh tuhl MAR i tuhl	măr'ĭ tăl măr'ĭ tăl	'mær ə təl, -ɪ təl, -tl̩
	B., muh RAI tuhl muh RAI t'l § 50(34)	*B.,* må rī'tăl må rī't'l § 51(4)	*B.,* mə 'raɪ təl mə 'raɪ tl̩
maritime	MAR uh taim MAR i taim MAR uh tim MAR i tim § 50(34)	măr'ĭ tīm măr'ĭ tīm măr'ĭ tĭm măr'ĭ tĭm § 47(3)	'mær ə taɪm 'mær ɪ taɪm 'mær ə tɪm 'mær ɪ tɪm
marquis	MAHR kwis	mär'kwĭs	'mɑr kwɪs; *ES* 'mɑː-, *E also* 'mɑ:-
	F., mahr KEE	*F.,* mår'kē'	*F.,* mar 'ki

	SIMPLIFIED	DIACRITICAL	PHONETIC
marquise	mahr KEEZ	mär kēz′	mɑr ′kiz; *ES* ma:-, *E also* ma:-
	F., *mahr* KEEZ	*F.*, mår′kēz′	*F.*, mar ′kiz
marriage	MAR ij	măr′ĭj	′mær ɪdʒ
Marseilles	mahr SAYLZ	mär sālz′	mɑr ′selz; *ES* ma:-, *E also* ma:-
marshmallow	MAHRSH *mal* oh	märsh′măl′ō §§ 34(25), 50(26)	′mɑrʃ ˌmæl o, -ˌmæl ə; *ES* ′ma:ʃ-, *E also* ′ma:ʃ-
martial	MAHR shuhl	mär′shăl	′mɑr ʃəl; *ES* ′ma:-, *E also* ′ma:-
martyr	MAHR tuhr	mär′tēr	′mɑr tɚ; *ES* ′ma: tə(r), *E also* ′ma:-
Mary	MEHR i	mâr′ĭ	′mɛr ɪ, ′me rɪ,
	MAY ri	mā′rĭ §§ 20(2), 47(1)	′mær ɪ; *also* ′me:rɪ; *ES also* ′mɛər ɪ
masculine	MAS kyōō lin	măs′kŭ lĭn § 20(5)	′mæs kjʊ lɪn, -kjə-, -kju-
mask	mask	måsk § 20(5)	mæsk; *E also* mɑsk, mɑsk
	mahsk		
masque	mask	måsk § 20(5)	mæsk; *E also* mɑsk, mɑsk
	mahsk		
masquerade	*mas* kuhr AYD	mås′kĕr ād′	ˌmæs kər ′ed,
	mas kuh RAYD		-kə ′red; *E also* ˌmas-, ˌmɑs-
	mahs kuhr AYD		
	mahs kuh RAYD	§ 20(5)	
Massachusetts	*mas* uh CHOO sets	măs′á chōō′sĕts	ˌmæs ə ′tʃu sɛts,
	mas uh CHOO sits	măs′á chōō′sĭts § 24(5)	-sɪts, -səts; *E also* ˌmas-, ˌmɑs-
massacre	MAS uh kuhr	măs′á kĕr	′mæs ə kɚ; *ES* -kə(r)
massacring	MAS uh kuhr ing	măs′á kĕr ĭng	′mæs ə kər ɪŋ
	MAS uh kring	măs′á krĭng	′mæs ə krɪŋ
massage	muh SAHZH	má säzh′ § 47(2)	mə ′sɑʒ
master	MAS tuhr	mås′tēr	′mæs tɚ; *ES* -tə(r), *E also* ′mas-, ′mɑs-
	MAHS tuhr	§ 20(5)	
material	muh TĬER i uhl	má tēr′ĭ ăl	mə ′tɪər ɪ əl,
	muh TIR i uhl	§ 24(11)	-′tɪr-, -′tir-; *ES* -′tɪər-
	muh TEER i uhl	má tēr′ĭ ăl	

	SIMPLIFIED	DIACRITICAL	PHONETIC
matinee, matinée	*mat* uh NAY *mat* i NAY *B.*, MAT uh nay MAT i nay	măt′ĭ nā′ măt′ĭ nā′ *B.*, măt′ĭ nā măt′ĭ nā § 51(4)	ˌmæt ə 'ne, -ɪ 'ne, ˌmæt n̩ 'e *B.*, 'mæt ə ne 'mæt ɪ ne
Matthew	MATH yoo	măth′ū §§ 39(2), 40(11)	'mæθ ju
mature	muh TYOOR muh TYOOR muh TOOR muh TOOR	má tūr′ §§ 34(21), 40(4), 48(2), 50(32)	mə 'tjʊr, -'tʊr; *ES* -'tjʊə(r), -'tʊə(r)
mausoleum, Mausoleum	*maw* suh LEE uhm	mô′sŏ lē′ŭm	ˌmɔ sə 'li əm
mauve	mohv	mōv	mov
mavis	MAY vis	mā′vĭs	'me vɪs
mayonnaise	*may* uh NAYZ	mā′ŏ nāz′ §§ 11, 47(3)	ˌme ə 'nez
mayor	MAY uhr mehr	mā′ĕr mâr	'me ɚ; *ES* -ə(r) mɛr; *ES* mɛə(r)
mayoralty	MAY uhr uhl ti MEHR uhl ti	mā′ĕr ăl tĭ mâr′ăl tĭ	'me ɚ əl tɪ; *ES* 'mɛr əl tɪ; *ES* 'mɛər-
meaningless	MEEN ing les MEEN ing lis	mēn′ĭng lĕs mēn′ĭng lĭs §§ 24(5), 50(18)	'min ɪŋ les 'min ɪŋ lɪs
meant	ment	mĕnt	mɛnt
measles	MEE z'lz	mē′z'lz	'mi z|z
measure	MEZH uhr	mĕzh′ĕr §§ 1, 38(8, 12), 40(11)	'mɛʒ ɚ; *ES* -ə(r)
mechanic	mi KAN ik	mĕ kăn′ĭk	mɪ 'kæn ɪk, mə-
medallion	mi DAL yuhn	mĕ dăl′yŭn	mɪ 'dæl jən, mə-
medial	MEE di uhl	mē′dĭ ăl § 28(9)	'mi dɪ əl
mediate (v.)	MEE di ayt	mē′dĭ āt	'mi dɪ et
—— (adj.)	MEE di it	mē′dĭ ĭt § 20(8, 9)	'mi dɪ ɪt, -ət
medicinal	mi DIS uh nuhl mi DIS i nuhl mi DIS uh n'l *In poetry, often:* MED suh nuhl *med* uh SAI nuhl § 50(34)	mĕ dĭs′ĭ năl mĕ dĭs′ĭ năl mĕ dĭs′ĭ n'l *In poetry, often:* mĕd′sĭ năl mĕd′ĭ sī′năl § 51(11)	mɪ 'dɪs ə nəl mɪ 'dɪs ɪ nəl mɪ 'dɪs ə n̩ *In poetry, often:* 'mɛd sə nəl ˌmɛd ə 'saɪ nəl
medieval, mediaeval	*mee* di EE vuhl *B.*, *med* i EE vuhl	mē′dĭ ē′văl *B.*, mĕd′ĭ ē′văl § 51(4)	ˌmi dɪ 'i vəl, -v| *B.*, ˌmɛd ɪ 'i vəl, -v|
mediocre	MEE di *oh* kuhr *mee* di OH kuhr	mē′dĭ ō′kĕr mē′dĭ ō′kĕr § 11	'mi dɪ ˌo kɚ, ˌmi dɪ 'o-; *ES* -kə(r)

mediocrity	*mee* di OK ruh ti *mee* di OK ri ti MEE di *ok* ruh ti	mē′dĭ ŏk′rĭ tĭ mē′dĭ ŏk′rĭ tĭ mē′dĭ ŏk′rĭ tĭ	ˌmi dɪ ˈak rə tɪ, -rɪ tɪ, ˈmi dɪ ˌak-; *ES* *also* -ˈɒk-, -ˌɒk-
Mediterranean	*med* uh tuh RAY ni uhn *med* i tuh RAY ni uhn	mĕd′ĭ tĕ rā′nĕ ăn mĕd′ĭ tĕ rā′nĕ ăn	ˌmɛd ə tə ˈre nɪ ən ˌmɛd ɪ tə ˈre nɪ ən
medium	MEE di uhm	mē′dĭ ŭm § 28(9)	ˈmi dɪ əm
medulla	mi DUHL uh	mĕ dŭl′*a*	mɪ ˈdʌl ə
medullary	MED uh *ler* i mi DUHL uh ri MED uh luhr i	mĕd′ŭ lĕr′ĭ mĕ dŭl′*a* rĭ mĕd′ŭ lēr ĭ §§ 20(2), 24(9), 47(2)	ˈmɛd ə ˌler ɪ, ˈmɛd ļ ˌer ɪ, mɪ ˈdʌl ə rɪ, ˈmɛd ə lər ɪ
melancholia	*mel* uhn KOH li uh	mĕl′ăn kō′lĭ *a* § 28(9)	ˌmɛl ən ˈko lɪ ə
melancholic	*mel* uhn KOL ik	mĕl′ăn kŏl′ĭk	ˌmɛl ən ˈkal ɪk; *ES also* -ˈkɒl-
melancholy (*Note: In poetry, the ac- cent is often put on the second or on the final syllable.*)	MEL uhn *kol* i *B.,* MEL uhn kuhl i	mĕl′ăn kŏl′ĭ *B.,* mĕl′ăn kŭl ĭ § 33(4), 51(4)	ˈmɛl ən ˌkal ɪ; *ES* *also* -ˌkɒl- *B.,* ˈmɛl ən kəl ɪ
melee, mélée (*"fight"*)	may LAY MAY lay MEL ay *F., me* LAY	mā lā′ mā′lā mĕl′ā *F.,* mâ′lā′	me ˈle ˈme le ˈmɛl e *F.,* mɛ ˈle
melodic	mi LOD ik	mĕ lŏd′ĭk	mɪ ˈlad ɪk; *ES* *also* -ˈlɒd-
melodious	mi LOH di uhs	mĕ lō′dĭ ŭs § 28(9)	mɪ ˈlo dɪ əs
melodrama	MEL uh *drah* muh *mel* uh DRAH muh MEL uh *dram* uh	mĕl′ŏ drä′m*a* mĕl′ŏ drä′m*a* mĕl′ŏ drăm′*a* § 47(3)	ˈmɛl ə ˌdra mə ˌmɛl ə ˈdra mə ˈmɛl ə ˌdræm ə
memoir	MEM wahr MEM wawr MEM wor	mĕm′wär mĕm′wôr mĕm′wŏr § 47(3)	ˈmɛm wɑr, -wɔr, -wɒr, ˈmi mwɑr; *ES* -wɑː(r), -wɔə(r)
memorable	MEM uh ruh b'l	mĕm′ŏ r*a* b'l § 9	ˈmɛm ə rə bļ
memories	MEM uh riz MEM uh reez	mĕm′ŏ rĭz §§ 9, 48(3), 50(6)	ˈmɛm ə rɪz, -riz, ˈmɛm rɪz, -riz
men	men	mĕn	mɛn

	SIMPLIFIED	DIACRITICAL	PHONETIC
menace	MEN uhs MEN is	mĕn′ĭs mĕn′ĭs	′mɛn əs ′mɛn ɪs
menagerie	mi NAJ uhr i muh NAZH uhr i	mĕ năj′ẽr ĭ mĕ năzh′ẽr ĭ § 47(3)	mɪ ′nædʒ ər ɪ, mə-, mə ′næʒ-
menial	MEE ni uhl MEEN yuhl	mē′nĭ ăl mēn′yăl §§ 28(9), 47(2)	′mi nɪ əl ′min jəl
meningitis	*men* in JĀI tis § 50(34)	mĕn′ĭn jĭ′tĭs	ˌmɛn ɪn ′dʒaɪ tɪs
menu	MEN yoo MAY nyoo MAY noo *F.,* muh NOO	mĕn′ū mā′nū §§ 47(1), 50(32) *F.,* mĕ nü′	′mɛn ju, -jʊ, ′mɛn u, ′me nju, -nu *F.,* mə ′ny
mercantile	MUHR kuhn til MUHR kuhn tail § 50(34)	mûr′kăn tĭl mûr′kăn tīl §§ 47(3), 50(13)	′mɝ kən tɪl, -taɪl; *ES also* ′mɜ-
merchandise	MUHR chuhn daiz § 50(34)	mûr′chăn dīz	′mɝ tʃən daɪz; *ES also* ′mɜ-
mercury	MUHR kyŏŏ ri MUHR kŏŏ ri MUHR kyuh ri	mûr′kŭ rĭ § 50(32)	′mɝ kjʊ rɪ, -kʊ-, -kju-, -ku-, -kjə-, -kə-; *ES also* ′mɜ-
mere (*"lake"*; *"marsh"*; *"simple"*)	mĭer mir meer	mẹr § 24(2) mēr	mɪər, mɪr, mir; *ES* mɪə(r)
meretricious	*mer* i TRISH uhs	mĕr′ĕ trĭsh′ŭs	ˌmɛr ɪ ′trɪʃ əs
meridian	muh RID i uhn mi RID i uhn	mĕ rĭd′ĭ ăn mĕ rĭd′ĭ ăn	mə ′rɪd ɪ ən mɪ ′rɪd ɪ ən
Messrs., messrs.	MES uhrz	mĕs′ ′rz § 47(2) *F.,* mă′syû′	′mɛs ɝz; *ES* -əz *F.,* me ′sjø
met	met	mĕt	mɛt
metabolism	me TAB uh liz′m me TAB uh liz uhm	mĕ tăb′ŏ lĭz′m § 50(15)	mɛ ′tæb ə lɪz m̩, -mə-, -lɪz əm, -′tæb l̩ ɪz-
metamorphosis	*met* uh MAWR fuh sis *met* uh mawr FOH sis	mĕt′*a* môr′fŏ sĭs mĕt′*a* môr fō′sĭs § 47(1)	ˌmɛt ə ′mɔr fə sɪs, -ə mər ′fo-; *ES* -′mɔə-, -mɔə-
meteor	MEE ti uhr	mē′tĕ ẽr § 28(9)	′mi tɪ ɚ; *ES* -ə(r)
meter, metre	MEE tuhr	mē′tẽr	′mi tɚ; *ES* -tə(r)
metric	MET rik	mĕt′rĭk	′mɛt rɪk
Michigan	MISH i guhn	mĭsh′ĭ găn	′mɪʃ ɪ gən
microscope	MĀI kruh skohp § 50(34)	mī′krŏ skōp	′maɪ krə skop
microscopic	*maĭ* kruh SKOP ik § 50(34)	mī′krŏ skŏp′ĭk	ˌmaɪ krə ′skɑp ɪk; *ES also* -′skɒp-

	SIMPLIFIED	DIACRITICAL	PHONETIC
microscopy	maī KROS kuh pi	mī krŏs′kŏ pĭ	maɪ 'krɑs kə pɪ; *ES also* -'krɒs-;
	MAĪ kruh *skoh* pi § 50(34)	mī′krŏ skō′pĭ § 47(3)	'maɪ krə ˌsko pɪ
mien	meen	mēn	min
might	maīt § 50(34)	mīt § 51(7)	maɪt
Milan (Italy)	mi LAN	mĭ lăn′	mɪ 'læn
	MIL uhn	mĭl′ăn § 11	'mɪl ən
	In poetry, often: MIL uhn	*In poetry, often:* mĭl′ăn § 51(11)	*In poetry, often:* 'mɪl ən
milch	milch	mĭlch § 22(6)	mɪltʃ
mileage	MAĪL ij § 50(34)	mīl′ĭj § 50(1)	'maɪl ɪdʒ
military	MIL uh *ter* i	mĭl′ĭ tĕr′ĭ	'mɪl ə ˌter ɪ
	MIL i *ter* i	mĭl′ĭ tĕr′ĭ §§ 13, 20(2), 24(9), 51(4)	'mɪl ɪ ˌter ɪ
	B., MIL uh tuhr i	*B.*, mĭl′ĭ tēr ĭ	*B.*, 'mɪl ə tə rɪ
militia	muh LISH uh	mŭ lĭsh′a̍	mə 'lɪʃ ə
	mi LISH uh	mĭ lĭsh′a̍	mɪ 'lɪʃ ə
millet ("*grass; grain*")	MIL et	mĭl′ĕt	'mɪl ɛt
	MIL it	mĭl′ĭt § 24(5)	'mɪl ɪt
millinery	MIL uh *ner* i	mĭl′ĭ nĕr′ĭ	'mɪl ə ˌnɛr ɪ
	MIL i *ner* i	mĭl′ĭ nĕr′ĭ	'mɪl ɪ ˌnɛr ɪ
	MIL uh nuhr i	mĭl′ĭ nēr ĭ	'mɪl ə nər ɪ
million	MIL yuhn	mĭl′yŭn	'mɪl jən
millionaire	*mil* yuhn EHR	mĭl′yŭn âr′ § 47(2)	ˌmɪl jən 'ɛr, -'ær; *ES* -'æə(r), *E also* -'ɛə(r)
mimosa	mi MOH suh	mĭ mō′sa̍	mɪ 'mo sə
	mi MOH zuh	mĭ mō′za̍ § 47(2)	mɪ 'mo zə
minaret	*min* uh RET	mĭn′a̍ rĕt′	ˌmɪn ə 'rɛt
	B., MIN uh ret	*B.*, mĭn′a̍ rĕt § 51(4)	*B.*, 'mɪn ə rɛt
mind	maīnd § 50(34)	mīnd	maɪnd
mine	maīn § 50(34)	mīn	maɪn
mineralogy	*min* uhr AL uh ji	mĭn′ēr ăl′ŏ jĭ	ˌmɪn ər 'æl ə dʒɪ
mingle	MING g'l	mĭng′g'l § 50(24)	'mɪŋ gl̩
mingling	MING gling	mĭng′glĭng	'mɪŋ glɪŋ, -gl̩ɪŋ
miniature (n., adj., v.t.)	MIN i uh chuhr	mĭn′ĭ a̍ tūr	'mɪn ɪ ə tʃɚ, -tʃʊr, -tjɚ, -ɪ tʃɚ, -ɪ tjɚ; *ES* -tʃə(r), -tʃʊə(r), -tjə(r)
	MIN i uh tyuhr		
	MIN i chuhr	mĭn′ĭ tūr	
	MIN i tyuhr	§§ 20(9), 50(31), 47(2), 51(4)	
—— (n.–also)	*B.*, MIN yuh chuhr	*B.*, mĭn′ya̍ tūr	*B.*, 'mɪn jə tʃɚ; *ES* -tʃə(r)

	SIMPLIFIED	DIACRITICAL	PHONETIC
Minneapolis	*min* i AP uh lis	mĭn′ĕ ăp′ŏ lĭs	ˌmɪn ɪ ˈæp ə lɪs, -ˈæp ļ ɪs
minority	muh NOR uh ti	mǐ nŏr′ĭ tǐ	mə ˈnɑr ə tɪ,
	mi NOR i ti	mǐ nŏr′ǐ tǐ	mɪ-, maɪ-,
	maî NOR uh ti	mī nŏr′ĭ tǐ	-ˈnɒr-
	maî NOR i ti	mī nŏr′ǐ tǐ	
	muh NAWR uh ti	mǐ nôr′ĭ tǐ	mə ˈnɔr ə tɪ
	mi NAWR i ti	mǐ nôr′ǐ tǐ	mɪ ˈnɔr ɪ tɪ
		§ 34(5, 7)	
minuet	*min* yŏŏ ET	mĭn′û ĕt′	ˌmɪn ju ˈɛt, -ju-,
	MIN yŏŏ et	mĭn′û ĕt § 47(3)	ˈmɪn ju ɛt
minute ("*sixty seconds*"; "*to time*")	MIN it	mĭn′ĭt	ˈmɪn ɪt
minute ("*small*")	mi NYOOT	mǐ nūt′	mɪ ˈnjut, mə-
	mi NOOT		mɪ ˈnut, mə-
	maî NYOOT	mī nūt′	maɪ ˈnjut
	maî NOOT	§§ 47(1), 48(2), 50(32, 34)	maɪ ˈnut
minutely ("*in an exact manner or degree*")	mi NYOOT li	mǐ nūt′lǐ	mɪ ˈnjut lɪ, mə-
	mi NOOT li		mɪ ˈnut lɪ, mə-
	maî NYOOT li	mī nūt′lǐ	maɪ ˈnjut lɪ
	maî NOOT li	§§ 48(2), 50(20, 32, 34)	maɪ ˈnut lɪ
minutiae	mi NYOO shi ee	mǐ nū′shǐ ē	mɪ ˈnju ʃɪ i
	mi NOO shi ee		mɪ ˈnu ʃɪ i
	maî NYOO shi ee	mī nū′shǐ ē	maɪ ˈnju ʃɪ i
	maî NOO shi ee	§§ 48(2), 50(32, 34)	maɪ ˈnu ʃɪ i
mirage	mi RAHZH	mǐ räzh′	mɪ ˈrɑʒ, mə-
misanthrope	MIS uhn throhp	mĭs′ăn thrōp	ˈmɪs ən θrop
	MIZ uhn throhp	mĭz′ăn thrōp § 47(1)	ˈmɪz ən θrop
misanthropist	mis AN thruh pist	mĭs ăn′thrŏ pĭst	mɪs ˈæn θrə pɪst
	mi ZAN thruh pist	mǐ zăn′thrŏ pĭst	mɪ ˈzæn θrə pɪst
misanthropy	mis AN thruh pi	mĭs ăn′thrŏ pǐ	mɪs ˈæn θrə pɪ
	mi ZAN thruh pi	mǐ zăn′thrŏ pǐ	mɪ ˈzæn θrə pɪ
miscellaneous	*mis* uh LAY ni uhs	mĭs′ĕ lā′nĕ ŭs	ˌmɪs ə ˈle nɪ əs, ˌmɪs ļ ˈe-
miscellany	MIS uh *lay* ni	mĭs′ĕ lā′nĭ §§ 47(1), 51(4)	ˈmɪs ə ˌle nɪ, ˈmɪs ļ ˌe-
	B., MIS uh luh ni	*B.,* mĭs′ĕ lå nĭ	*B.,* ˈmɪs ə lə nɪ
mischief	MIS chif	mĭs′chĭf	ˈmɪs tʃɪʃ

	SIMPLIFIED	DIACRITICAL	PHONETIC
mischievous	MIS chuh vuhs	mĭs′chĭ vŭs	′mɪs tʃə vəs
	MIS chi vuhs	mĭs′chĭ vŭs	′mɪs tʃɪ vəs
	Dial. or humorous,	*Dial. or humorous,*	*Dial. or humorous,*
	gen.:	*gen.:*	*gen.:*
	mis CHI vuhs	mĭs chĭ′vŭs	mɪs ′tʃɪ vəs
	mis CHEE vuhs	mĭs chē′vŭs	mɪs ′tʃi vəs
		§ 51(2, 11)	
misconstrue	*mis* kuhn STROO	mĭs′kŏn strōō′	ˌmɪs kən ′stru
	mis KON stroo	mĭs kŏn′strōō	mɪs ′kɑn stru; *ES*
		§§ 47(3), 48(2)	*also* -′kɒn-
miscreant	MIS kri uhnt	mĭs′krē ănt	′mɪs krɪ ənt
miserable	MIZ uhr uh b′l	mĭz′ẽr ȧ b′l § 9	′mɪz ər ə bļ,
			′mɪz rə-
mishap	mis HAP	mĭs hăp′	mɪs ′hæp
	MIS hap	mĭs′hăp	′mɪs hæp
misnomer	mis NOH muhr	mĭs nō′mēr	mɪs ′no mɚ; *ES*
			-mə(r)
Mississippi	*mis* uh SIP i	mĭs′ĭ sĭp′ɪ	ˌmɪs ə ′sɪp ɪ
	mis i SIP i	mĭs′ɪ sĭp′ɪ	ˌmɪs ɪ ′sɪp ɪ
Missouri	muh ZOOR ı	mĭ zŏŏr′ɪ	mə ′zʊr ɪ
	mi ZOOR i	mĭ zŏŏr′ɪ	mɪ ′zʊr ɪ
	muh SOOR i	mĭ sŏŏr′ɪ	mə ′sʊr ɪ
	mi SOOR i	mĭ sŏŏr′ɪ	mɪ ′sʊr ɪ
	muh ZOOR uh	mĭ zŏŏr′ȧ	mə ′zʊr ə
	mi ZOOR uh	mĭ zŏŏr′ȧ	mɪ ′zʊr ə
mistletoe	MIS ′l toh	mĭs′ ′l tō	′mɪs ļ to
	MIZ ′l toh	mĭz′ ′l tō § 47(3)	′mɪz ļ to
mitigate	MIT uh gayt	mĭt′ĭ gāt	′mɪt ə get
	MIT i gayt	mĭt′ɪ gāt	′mɪt ɪ get
mitten	MIT′ ′n	mĭt′ ′n § 47(2)	′mɪt ņ
mixture	MIKS chuhr	mĭks′tūr	′mɪks tʃɚ, -tjɚ;
	MIKS tyuhr	§§ 40(11),	*ES* -tʃə(r),
		50(31)	-tjə(r)
mobile	MOH bil	mō′bĭl	′mo bɪl
	MOH beel	mō′bēl	′mo bil
		§§ 28(5), 47(3)	
Mobile (Ala.)	moh BEEL	mō bēl′	mo ′bil
mobilize	MOH buh laiz	mō′bĭ līz	′mo bə laɪz, -bļ-
	MOH bi laiz	mō′bĭ līz	′mo bɪ laɪz
	§ 50(34)	§ 47(3)	
mock	mok	mŏk § 34(7)	mɑk, mɒk, mɔk
model	MOD ′l	mŏd′ ′l	′mɑd ļ; *ES also*
			′mɒd-
modern	MOD uhrn	mŏd′ẽrn	′mɑd ɚn; *ES* -ən,
			also ′mɒd-
modicum	MOD i kuhm	mŏd′ɪ kŭm	′mɑd ɪ kəm; *ES*
			also ′mɒd-

modulate	MOJ ŏŏ layt MOJ uh layt MOD yŏŏ layt	mŏd′û̄ lāt § 50(2, 33)	'madʒ ʊ let, 'madʒ ə let, 'mad jʊ let, -jə-; *ES also* 'mɒd-
Mohammed	moh HAM ed moh HAM id	mŏ hăm′ĕd mŏ hăm′ĭd § 24(5)	mo 'hæm ɛd mo 'hæm ɪd
moiety	MOI uh ti	moi′ĕ tĭ	'mɔɪ ə tɪ
moisten	MOIS 'n	mois′ 'n	'mɔɪs n̩
molecular	muh LEK yŏŏ luhr	mŏ lĕk′û̄ lēr	mə 'lɛk jʊ lɚ, -jə-, -ju-; *ES* -lə(r)
molecule	MOL i kyool MOH li kyool	mŏl′ĕ kūl mō′lĕ kūl §§ 47(3), 48(2)	'mal ɪ kjul, 'mo lɪ-; *ES also* 'mɒl-
molestation	*moh* les TAY shuhn *mol* es TAY shuhn	mō′lĕs tā′shŭn mŏl′ĕs tā′shŭn § 47(2)	ˌmo lɛs 'te ʃən, ˌmal ɛs 'te ʃən; *ES also* ˌmɒl-
Molière	*moh* LYEHR *mohl* YEHR *maw* LYEHR *Gaining ground:* *moh* li EHR	mō′lyâr′ *Gaining ground:* mō′lĭ âr′	ˌmo 'ljɛr; *ES* -'ljɛə(r); *F.*, mɔ 'ljɛːr *Gaining ground:* ˌmo lɪ 'ɛr; *ES* -'ɛə(r)
	B., MOH li ehr	*B.*, mō′lĭ âr § 51(4, 5)	*B.*, 'mo lɪ ɛr; *ES* -ɛə(r)
momentary	MOH muhn *ter* i *B.*, MOH muhn tuhr i	mō′mĕn tĕr′ĭ *B.*, mō′mĕn tĕr ĭ §§ 13, 51(4)	'mo mən ˌtɛr ɪ *B.*, 'mo mən tə rɪ
momentous	moh MEN tuhs	mŏ mĕn′tŭs	mo 'mɛn təs
momentum	moh MEN tuhm	mŏ mĕn′tŭm	mo 'mɛn təm
monarch	MON uhrk	mŏn′ērk	'man ɚk; *ES* 'mɒn ək
monetary	MON i *ter* i MUHN i *ter* i	mŏn′ĕ tĕr′ĭ mŭn′ĕ tĕr′ĭ	'man ɪ ˌtɛr ɪ, 'mʌn ɪ ˌtɛr ɪ; *ES also* 'mɒn-
	B., MUHN i tuhr i	*B.*, mŭn′ĕ tĕr ĭ §§ 13, 20(2), 24(9), 47(3), 51(4)	*B.*, 'mʌn ɪ tə rɪ
monetization	*mon* i ti ZAY shuhn *muhn* i ti ZAY shuhn *muhn* i tai͡ ZAY shuhn	mŏn′ĕ tĭ zā′shŭn mŭn′ĕ tĭ zā′shŭn mŭn′ĕ tī zā′shŭn § 47(1)	ˌman ɪ tɪ 'ze ʃən; *ES also* ˌmɒn- ˌmʌn ɪ tɪ 'ze ʃən ˌmʌn ɪ taɪ 'ze ʃən
money	MUHN i	mŭn′ĭ	'mʌn ɪ

mongrel	MUHNG gruhl MUHNG grel MONG gruhl	mŭng′grĕl mŭng′grĕl mŏng′grĕl § 47(1)	ˈmʌŋ grəl, -grel, ˈmaŋ-; *ES also* ˈmɒŋ-
monkey	MUHNG ki	mŭng′kĭ	ˈmʌŋ kɪ
monotonous	muh NOT uh nuhs	mŏ nŏt′ŏ nŭs	mə ˈnɑt ə nəs; *ES* *also* -ˈnɒt-
monsieur (See *Messrs.*, abbreviation of pl. *Messieurs.*)	muh SYUH(R)	mē syû′	mə ˈsjɝ; *ES also* -ˈsjə(r); *F.,* mə ˈsjø
Montaigne	mon TAYN	mŏn tān′	man ˈten; *ES also* mɒn-
Montenegro	*mon* ti NEE groh *It., mohn* tay NAY groh	mŏn′tĕ nē′grō *It.,* mōn′tå nā′grŏ	ˌman tɪ ˈni gro; *ES also* ˌmɒn- *It.,* ˌmon te ˈne gro
monument (n.)	MON yōō muhnt	mŏn′û mĕnt	ˈman jʊ mənt, -ju-, -jə-; *ES* *also* ˈmɒn-
—— (v.t.)	MON yōō ment	mŏn′û mĕnt	ˈman jʊ mɛnt, -ju-; *ES also* ˈmɒn-
moon	moon	mōōn § 34(22)	mun
Moore (Thomas)	mōōr mohr mawr	mōōr mōr § 34(3, 21)	mʊr, mor, mɔr; *ES* mʊə(r), moə(r), *E also* mɔə(r)
Moorish	MŌŌR ish	mōōr′ĭsh § 34(21)	ˈmʊr ɪʃ
moral	MOR uhl MAWR uhl	mŏr′ăl môr′ăl § 34(5, 7)	ˈmar əl, ˈmɔr-, ˈmɒr-
morale	muh RAL muh RAHL	mŏ răl′ mŏ räl′ § 47(1)	mə ˈræl, -ˈrɑl, mo-, mɔ-; *F.,* mɔ̃ ˈral
morbid	MAWR bid	môr′bĭd	ˈmɔr bɪd; *ES* ˈmɔə-
more	mohr mawr	mōr § 34(3)	mor, mɔr; *ES* moə(r), *E also* mɔə(r)
morion	MOH ri on	mō′rĭ ŏn §§ 34(3), 47(2)	ˈmo rɪ an; *ES also* -ɒn
Morpheus	MAWR fyoos *Pop.:* MAWR fi uhs	môr′fūs *Pop.:* môr′fĕ ŭs §§ 47(1), 51(3)	ˈmɔr fjus; *ES* ˈmɔə- *Pop.:* ˈmɔr fɪ əs; *ES* ˈmɔə-
morphine	MAWR feen MAWR fin	môr′fēn môr′fĭn §§ 28(6), 47(1)	ˈmɔr fin, -fɪn; *ES* ˈmɔə-
morsel	MAWR suhl MAWR s′l	môr′sĕl môr′s′l § 47(2)	ˈmɔr səl, -sl̩; *ES* ˈmɔə-

	SIMPLIFIED	DIACRITICAL	PHONETIC
mortgage	MAWR gij	môr′gĭj § 39(2)	ˈmɔr gɪdʒ; *ES* ˈmɔə-
mortise, mortice	MAWR tis	môr′tĭs	ˈmɔr tɪs; *ES* ˈmɔə-
mosaic	moh ZAY ik	mō zā′ĭk	mo ˈze ɪk
Moscow (Russia)	MOS koh *Pop.:* MOS kow	mŏs′kō *Pop.:* mŏs′kou § 51(3)	ˈmɑs ko, ˈmɒs- *Pop.:* ˈmɑs kau, ˈmɒs-
Moslem	MOZ lem MOZ luhm MOS luhm MOS lem	mŏz′lĕm mŏz′lĕm mŏs′lĕm mŏs′lĕm § 47(3)	ˈmɑz lɛm, -ləm, ˈmɑs-; *ES also* ˈmɒz-, ˈmɒs-
mosquito	muhs KEE toh muh SKEE toh	mŭs kē′tō	məs ˈki to, -tə, mə ˈski-
moths	mawthz mothz mawths moths	môthz mŏthz môths mŏths §§ 34(7), 47(1), 48(3)	mɔðz mɒðz mɔθs mɒθs
mountain	MOWN tin MOWN tuhn § 50(34)	moun′tĭn moun′tĕn § 47(1)	ˈmaʊn tɪn, -tən, -tn̩
mountebank	MOWN ti bangk	moun′tĕ băngk	ˈmaʊn tɪ bæŋk
mouth (n., adj.)	mowth	mouth	maʊθ
—— (v.)	mowth § 50(34)	mouth § 39(4, 6)	maʊð
mouthed (p.t. of *mouth*)	mowthd § 50(34)	mouthd	maʊðd
mouthed (adj.), –mouthed (combining form)	mowthd mowtht § 50(34)	mouthd moutht § 47(3)	maʊðd maʊθt
mouths (n. pl.)	mowthz	mouthz §§ 39(5), 48(3), 50(6)	maʊðz
mow ("*cut down*")	moh	mō § 47(2)	mo
mow ("*stack*")	mow	mou	maʊ
Mrs.	MIS iz MIS is	mĭs′ĭz mĭs′ĭs § 47(1)	ˈmɪs ɪz, -əz ˈmɪs ɪs, -əs
mucilage	MYOO suh lij MYOO si lij	mū′sĭ lĭj mū′sĭ lĭj § 48(2)	ˈmju sə lɪdʒ, -sl̩- ˈmju sɪ lɪdʒ
mucilaginous	*myoo* suh LAJ uh nuhs *myoo* si LAJ i nuhs	mū′sĭ lăj′ĭ nŭs mū′sĭ lăj′ĭ nŭs §§ 48(2), 50(32)	ˌmju sə ˈlædʒ ə nəs, -sl̩ ˈædʒ- ˌmju sɪ ˈlædʒ ɪ nəs
multitude	MUHL tuh tyood MUHL tuh tood MUHL ti tyood MUHL ti tood	mŭl′tĭ tūd mŭl′tĭ tūd §§ 48(2), 50(32)	ˈmʌl tə tjud ˈmʌl tə tud ˈmʌl tɪ tjud ˈmʌl tɪ tud
mundane	MUHN dayn	mŭn′dān	ˈmʌn den
Munich	MYOO nik	mū′nĭk § 48(2)	ˈmju nɪk

	SIMPLIFIED	DIACRITICAL	PHONETIC
municipal	myoo NIS uh puhl	mū nĭs′ĭ păl	mju 'nıs ə pəl, -pļ
	myoo NIS i puhl	mū nĭs′ĭ păl	mju 'nıs ı pəl
		§ 48(2)	
muscle	MUHS 'l	mŭs′ 'l	'mʌs ļ
museum	myoo ZEE uhm	mū zē′ŭm	mju 'zi əm
mushroom	MUHSH room	mŭsh′rŏŏm	'mʌʒ rum
	MUHSH rŏŏm	§ 34(22)	'mʌʒ rʊm
musician	myoo ZISH uhn	mū zĭsh′ăn	mju 'zıʃ ən
		§ 48(2)	
muskrat	MUHSK *rat*	mŭsk′răt′	'mʌsk ˌræt
muslin	MUHZ lin	mŭz′lĭn	'mʌz lın
mustache,	muhs TASH	mŭs tàsh′	məs 'tæʃ,
moustache	muhs TAHSH	§§ 20(5), 22(7),	mə 'stæʃ; *E also*
		47(3), 51(4)	-'taʃ, -'taʃ,
			-'staʃ, -'staʃ
	MUHS tash	mŭs′tăsh	'mʌs tæʃ
	B., mŏŏs TAHSH	*B.,* mŏŏs tàsh′	*B.,* mʊs 'taʃ
mustn't	MUHS 'nt	mŭs′ 'nt	'mʌs ņt
mutable	MYOO tuh b'l	mū′tȧ b'l § 48(2)	'mju tə bļ
mute	myoot	mūt § 48(2)	mjut
mutual	MYOO chŏŏ uhl	mū′tŭ ăl	'mju tʃʊ əl
	MYOO tyŏŏ uhl	§§ 48(2), 50(32)	'mju tjʊ əl
myriad	MIR i uhd	mĭr′ĭ ăd	'mır ı əd
myself	mai͡ SELF	mī sĕlf′	maı 'sɛlf
	Unstressed:	*Unstressed:*	*Unstressed:*
	mai͡ SELF	mī sĕlf′	maı 'sɛlf
	muh SELF	mȧ sĕlf′ §§ 16,	mə 'sɛlf
		47(2)	
mysterious	mis TĬER i uhs	mĭs tẽr′ĭ ŭs	mıs 'tıər ı əs,
	mis TIR i uhs	§§ 24(2), 50(25)	-'tır-, -'tir-; *ES*
	mis TEER i uhs	mĭs tēr′ĭ ŭs	-'tıər-
mystery	MIS tuhr i	mĭs′tĕr ĭ	'mıs tər ı, 'mıs trı
("secret")			
mythology	mi THOL uh ji	mĭ thŏl′ŏ jĭ	mı 'θɑl ə dʒı; *ES*
			also -'θɒl-

N

naiad, **Naiad**	NAY ad NAY yad NĀI ad § 50(34)	nā′ăd nā′yăd nī′ăd § 47(3)	'ne æd, 'ne jæd, -jəd, 'naı æd, -əd
naïve, naive **naïveté, naïvete**	nah EEV nah *eev* TAY	nä ēv′ § 47(2) nä ēv′tā′ § 47(2)	nɑ 'iv nɑ ˌiv 'te
nape	nayp *Dial. or colloq.:* nap	năp *Dial. or colloq.:* năp § 51(2, 3)	nep *Dial. or colloq.:* næp
naphtha	NAF thuh NAP thuh	năf′thả năp′thả §§ 35(4), 47(3)	'næf θə 'næp θə
narrate	na RAYT	nă rāt′ § 47(2)	næ 'ret
nasal	NAY zuhl NAY z'l	nā′zăl nā′z'l	'ne zəl 'ne z̩l
nasturtium	nuh STUHR shuhm	nả stûr′shăm § 47(2)	nə 'stɝ ʃəm, næ-; *ES also* -'stɜ-
nasty	NAS ti NAHS ti	nảs′ti § 20(5)	'næs tɪ; *E also* 'nas-, 'nɑs-
nation	NAY shuhn	nā′shăn §§ 9, 50(30)	'ne ʃən
national	NASH uhn uhl NASH uhn 'l	năsh′ăn ăl năsh′ăn 'l	'ne ʒən əl 'ne ʒən l̩
natural	NACH uh ruhl NAT yŏŏ ruhl	năt′ủ răl §§ 49(11), 50(33)	'næʧ ə rəl 'næt jʊ rəl
naturalization	*nach* uh ruhl i ZAY shuhn *nat* yŏŏ ruhl i ZAY shuhn *nach* uh ruhl aī ZAY shuhn *nat* yŏŏ ruhl aī ZAY shuhn	năt′ủ răl ĭ zā′shăn năt′ủ răl ī zā′shăn § 50(30, 33, 34)	ˌnæʧ ə rəl ɪ 'ze ʃən ˌnæt jʊ rəl ɪ 'ze ʃən ˌnæʧ ə rəl aɪ 'ze ʃən ˌnæt jʊ rəl aɪ 'ze ʃən
nature	NAY chuhr NAY tyuhr	nā′tủr §§ 40(11), 50(31)	'ne tʃɚ, -tjɚ; *ES* -tʃə(r), -tjə(r)

naughty	NAW ti	nô′tĭ	′nɔ tɪ
nausea	NAW shi uh	nô′shĕ å	′nɔ ʃɪ ə
	NAW si uh	nô′sĕ å	′nɔ sɪ ə
	NAW shuh	nô′shå	′nɔ ʃə
		§§ 38(12), 47(3)	
nauseate	NAW shi ayt	nô′shĕ āt	′nɔ ʃɪ et
	NAW si ayt	nô′sĕ āt § 38(12)	′nɔ sɪ et
nauseous	NAW shuhs	nô′shŭs	′nɔ ʃəs
	NAW shi uhs	nô′shĕ ŭs	′nɔ ʃɪ əs
	NAW si uhs	nô′sĭ ŭs	′nɔ sɪ əs
		§§ 38(7, 12), 47(3)	
near	nĭer	nēr	nɪər, nɪr, nir; *ES*
	nir	§ 24(2)	nɪə(r)
	neer	nēr	
necessarily	NES uh *ser* uh li	nĕs′ĕ sĕr′ĭ lĭ	′nɛs ə ˌsɛr ə lɪ
	NES i *ser* i li	nĕs′ĕ sĕr′ĭ lĭ	-ɪ ′sɛr ɪ-; *ES*
		§§ 20(2), 24(9), 50(20), 51(11)	*also* -ˌsɛər-
	Emph.:	*Emph.:*	*Emph.:*
	nes uh SEHR uh li	nĕs′ĕ sâr′ĭ lĭ	ˌnɛs ə ′sɛr ə lɪ,
			-ɪ ′sɛr ɪ-; *ES*
	nes i SEHR i li	nĕs′ĕ sâr′ĭ lĭ	*also* -′sɛər-
necessary	NES uh *ser* i	nĕs′ĕ sĕr′ĭ	′nɛs ə ˌsɛr ɪ,
	NES i *ser* i	nĕs′ĕ sĕr′ĭ	-ɪ ˌsɛr-, -ɪ ˌsɛ rɪ;
		§§ 20(2), 24(9), 47(1)	*ES also* -ˌsɛər-
	B., NES uh suhr i	*B.*, nĕs′ĕ sĕr ĭ	*B.*, ′nɛs ə sə rɪ
		§§ 13, 51(4)	
neckromancer	NEK ruh *man* suhr	nĕk′rŏ măn′sĕr	′nɛk rə ˌmæn sɚ,
	NEK roh *man* suhr		-ro-; *ES* -sə(r)
necromancy	NEK ruh *man* si	nĕk′rŏ măn′sĭ	′nɛk rə ˌmæn sɪ
	NEK roh *man* si		′nɛk ro ˌmæn sɪ
nectarine	*nek* tuhr EEN	nĕk′tĕr ēn′	ˌnɛk tər ′in
	NEK tuhr in	nĕk′tĕr ĭn	′nɛk tər ɪn
	NEK tuhr een	nĕk′tĕr ēn § 47(1)	′nɛk tər in
ne′er (*chiefly poetic*)	nehr	nâr	nɛr, ner; *ES*
	nayr	nār § 47(2)	nɛə(r)
nefarious	ni FEHR i uhs	nĕ fâr′ĭ ŭs	nɪ ′fɛr ɪ əs,
	ni FAY ri uhs	§§ 20(2), 50(25)	-′fær-, -′fe rɪ;-
			ES also -′fɛər-
neither	NEE t͟huhr	nē′t͟hĕr	′ni ð˞, ′naɪ-; *ES*
	NAI t͟huhr	nī′t͟hĕr	-ðə(r)
		§§ 24(20), 47(3)	
Nemesis	NEM i sis	nĕm′ĕ sĭs	′nɛm ɪ sɪs
neophyte	NEE oh faı̆t	nē′ŏ fīt	′ni o faɪt, -ə-

	SIMPLIFIED	DIACRITICAL	PHONETIC
nephew	NEF yoo *B.*, NEV yoo	nĕf′ū *B.*, nĕv′ū §§ 1, 35(4), 47(3), 51(4)	'nɛf ju, -jʊ *B.*, 'nɛv ju, -jʊ
nether	NETH uhr	nĕth′ẽr	'nɛð ɚ; *ES* -ə(r)
neuralgia	nyŏŏ RAL juh nŏŏ RAL juh nyŏŏ RAL ji uh nŏŏ RAL ji uh	nū răl′já nū răl′jĭ á §§ 47(1), 48(2), 50(32)	njʊ 'ræl dʒə, nʊ-, nju-, nu- njʊ 'ræl dʒɪ ə, nʊ-, nju-, nu-
neuter	NYOO tuhr NOO tuhr	nū′tẽr §§ 48(2), 50(32)	'nju tɚ, 'nu-; *ES* -tə(r)
neutral	NYOO truhl NOO truhl	nū′trăl §§ 48(2), 50(32)	'nju trəl 'nu trəl
Nevada	nuh VAD uh nuh VAH duh	nĕ văd′á nĕ vä′dá	nə 'væd ə nə 'vɑ də
new	nyoo noo	nū §§ 40(4), 48(2), 50(32)	nju nu
Newfoundland (n.)	*nyoo* fuhn(d) LAND *noo* fuhn(d) LAND NYOO fuhnd *land* NOO fuhnd *land* *nyoo* fownd LAND *noo* fownd LAND	nū′fŭn(d) lănd′ nū′fănd lănd′ nū′found lănd′ §§ 47(2), 48(2), 50(32)	ˌnju fən(d) 'lænd ˌnu fən(d) 'lænd 'nju fənd ˌlænd 'nu fənd ˌlænd ˌnju faʊnd 'lænd ˌnu faʊnd 'lænd
—— "*intelligent dog*"	nyoo FOWND luhnd noo FOWND luhnd	nŭ found′lănd	nju 'faʊnd lənd nu 'faʊnd lənd 'nu fənd lənd
—— (adj.–usu- ally)	nyoo FOWND luhnd noo FOWND luhnd	nŭ found′lănd §§ 47(2), 48(2), 50(32)	nju 'faʊnd lənd nu 'faʊnd lənd
New Orleans	nyoo AWR li uhnz noo AWR li uhnz nyoo AWR lyuhnz noo AWR lyuhnz *Also, especially in the phrases:* nyoo awr LEENZ noo awr LEENZ	nū ôr′lĕ ănz nū ôr′lyănz §§ 48(2), 50(32) *Also, especially in the phrases:* nū ôr lēnz′ §§ 48(2), 50(32)	nju 'ɔr lɪ ənz, nu-; *ES* -'ɔə- nju 'ɔr ljənz, nu-; *ES* -'ɔə- *Also, especially in the phrases:* nju ɔr 'linz, nu-; *ES* -'ɔə-
news	nyooz nooz	nūz §§ 40(4), 48(2), 50(32)	njuz nuz

	SIMPLIFIED	DIACRITICAL	PHONETIC
newspaper	NYOOZ *pay* puhr NOOZ *pay* puhr NYOOS *pay* puhr NOOS *pay* puhr	nūz′pā′pēr nūs′pā′pēr §§ 40(4), 48(2), 50(32)	′njuz ˌpe pɚ, ′nuz-, ′njus ˌpe pɚ, ′nus-; *ES* -pə(r)
Niagara	naī AG uh ruh § 50(34)	nī ăg′*á* r*á* § 9	naɪ ′æg ə rə, -′æg rə
Nicaragua	*nik* uh RAH gwuh	nĭk′*á* rä′gw*á*	ˌnɪk ə ′rɑ gwə
nicety	NAI suh ti NAI si ti § 50(34)	nī′sĕ tĭ nī′sĭ tĭ	′naɪ sə ɪt ′naɪ sɪ ɪt
niche	nich	nĭch § 47(1)	nɪtʃ
nicotine	NIK uh teen NIK uh tin	nĭk′ŏ tēn nĭk′ŏ tĭn § 47(1)	′nɪk ə tin ′nɪk ə tɪn
Niger	NAI juhr § 50(34)	nī′jēr	′naɪ dʒɚ; *ES* -dʒə(r)
nightingale	NAIT in gayl NAIT ing gayl § 50(34)	nīt′ĭn gāl nīt′ĭng gāl §§ 33(4), 47(1)	′naɪt ɪn gel ′naɪt ɪŋ gel
ninety	NAIN ti § 50(34)	nīn′tĭ	′naɪn tɪ
nocturnal	nok TUHR nuhl nok TUHR n'l	nŏk tûr′năl nôk tûr′n'l	nak ′tɜ nəl, -nl̩; *ES also* -′tɜ-, *also* nɒk-
nodule	NOD yool NOJ ool	nŏd′ūl nŏj′ōōl	′nad jul, ′nadʒ ul; *ES also* ′nɒd-, ′nɒdʒ-
nomad	NOH mad *B*., NOM uhd	nō′măd § 47(3) *B*., nŏm′ăd § 51(4)	′no mæd *B*., ′nɒm əd
nomenclature	NOH muhn *klay* chuhr NOH muhn *klay* tyuhr *B*., noh MEN kluh chuhr	nō′mĕn klā′tūr §§ 47(3), 50(31), 51(4) *B*., nŏ mĕn′klá tūr	′no mən ˌkle tʃɚ, -tjɚ; *ES* -tʃə(r), tjə(r) *B*., no ′mɛn klə tʃɚ; *ES* -tʃə(r)
nominative	NOM uh nuh tiv NOM uh *nay* tiv NOM i *nay* tiv	nŏm′*ĭ* n*á* tĭv nŏm′*ĭ* nā′tĭv nŏm′ĭ nā′tĭv	′nam ə nə tɪv, -ə ˌne-, -ɪ ˌne-; *ES also* ′nɒm-
——"*nominated*," usually	NOM uh *nay* tiv NOM i *nay* tiv	nŏm′*ĭ* nā′tĭv nŏm′ĭ nā′tĭv	′nam ə ˌne trv, -ɪ ˌne-; *ES also* ′nɒm-
nonchalance	NON shuh luhns *non* shuh LAHNS	nŏn′sh*á* lăns nŏn′sh*á* läns′	′nan ʃə ləns, ˌnan ʃə ′lans; *ES also* ′nɒn-, ˌnɒn-
nonchalant	NON shuh luhnt *non* shuh LAHNT	nŏn′sh*á* lănt nŏn′sh*á* länt′	′nan ʃə lənt, ˌnan ʃə ′lant; *ES also* ′nɒn-, ˌnɒn-

	SIMPLIFIED	DIACRITICAL	PHONETIC
none (*"not any"*)	*nuhn*	nŭn §§ 34(10), 40(6)	nʌn
nonpareil	*non* puh REL	nŏn′pȧ rĕl′	ˌnɑn pə 'rɛl; *ES also* ˌnɒn-
nook	nŏŏk	nŏŏk § 34(22)	nʊk
noose (n.)	noos	nōōs	nus
—— (v.t.)	noos	nōōs	nus
	nooz	nōōz §§ 34(22), 47(2)	nuz
Norfolk	NAWR fuhk	nôr′fŭk	'nɔr fək; *ES* -'nɔə-
not	not	nŏt	nɑt; *ES also* nɒt
	Unstressed: n't, nt	*Unstressed:* n't, nt § 16	*Unstressed:* nt, n̩t, -t, n̩-
nothing	NUHTH ing	nŭth′ĭng §§ 34(10), 50(24)	'nʌθ ɪŋ
notoriety	*noh* tuh RAI uh ti	nō′tṓ rī′ĕ tĭ	ˌno tə 'raɪ ə tɪ
	noh tuh RAI i ti	nō′tṓ rī′ĕ tĭ	ˌno tə 'raɪ ɪ tɪ
notorious	noh TOH ri uhs	nō tō′rĭ ŭs	no 'to rɪ əs
	noh TAW ri uhs	§§ 34(3), 50(25)	no 'tɔ rɪ əs
novel	NOV uhl	nŏv′ĕl	'nɑv əl, -l̩; *ES also* 'nɒv-
	NOV 'l	nŏv′ 'l § 47(2)	
novice	NOV is	nŏv′ĭs	'nɑv ɪs; *ES also* 'nɒv-
novitiate, noviciate	noh VISH i it	nō vĭsh′ĭ ȧt	no 'vɪʃ ɪ ɪt
	noh VISH i ayt	§ 50(2)	no 'vɪʃ ɪ et
now	now	nou	naʊ
nowhere	NOH hwehr	nō′hwâr §§ 42(4), 49(23)	'no hwɛr, -hwær; *ES* -hwæə(r), *E also* -hwɛə(r)
noxious	NOK shuhs	nŏk′shŭs	'nɑk ʃəs; *ES also* 'nɒk-
nucleus	NYOO kli uhs	nū′klḗ ŭs	'nju klɪ əs
	NOO kli uhs	§§ 48(2), 50(32)	'nu klɪ əs
nude	nyood	nūd §§ 40(4),	njud
	nood	48(2), 50(32)	nud
nuisance	NYOO suhns	nū′sȧns	'nju səns
	NOO suhns		'nu səns
	NYOO s'ns	nū′s'ns §§ 40(4),	'nju sn̩s
	NOO s'ns	48(2), 50(32)	'nu sn̩s
numeral	NYOO muhr uhl	nū′mẽr ăl	'nju mər əl
	NOO muhr uhl	§§ 40(4), 48(2), 50(32)	'nu mər əl
			'njum rəl, 'num-
numerous	NYOO muhr uhs	nū′mẽr ŭs	'nju mər əs
	NOO muhr uhs	§§ 40(4), 48(2), 50(32)	'nu mər əs
			'njum rəs, 'num-
nunnery	NUHN uhr i	nŭn′ẽr ĭ	'nʌn ər ɪ
nuptial	NUHP shuhl	nŭp′shăl	'nʌp ʃəl

nutrient	NYOO tri uhnt	nū′trĭ ĕnt	'nju trɪ ənt
	NOO tri uhnt	§§ 48(2), 50(32)	'nu trɪ ənt
nutriment	NYOO truh muhnt	nū′trĭ mĕnt	'nju trə mənt
	NOO truh muhnt		'nu trə mənt
	NYOO tri muhnt	nū′trĭ mĕnt	'nju trɪ mənt
	NOO tri muhnt	§§ 48(2), 50(22, 32)	'nu trɪ mənt
nymph	nimf	nĭmf § 35(2)	nɪmf, nɪmpf

O

oar	ohr	ōr § 34(3)	or, ɔr; *ES* ɔə(r), *E also* ɔə(r)
	awr		
oases (n. pl. of *oasis*)	oh AY seez	ō ā′sēz	o 'e siz
	OH uh seez	ō′a̍ sēz §§ 48(3), 50(6)	'o ə siz
oasis	oh AY sis	ō ā′sĭs	o 'e sɪs
	OH uh sis	ō′a̍ sĭs § 47(3)	'o ə sɪs
oath	ohth	ōth § 39(5)	oθ
oaths (n. pl.)	ohthz	ōthz §§ 39(5), 47(3), 48(3), 50(6)	oðz
obduracy	OB dyŏŏ ruh si	ŏb′dŭ ra̍ sĭ	'ab djʊ rə sɪ, -djə-, -dju-, -dʊ-, -də-; *ES also* 'ɒb-
	OB dyuh ruh si		
	OB dŏŏ ruh si		
	ob DYOO ruh si	ŏb dū′ra̍ sĭ	ab 'djʊ rə sɪ, -'dʊ-, -'dju-, -'du-; *ES also* ɒb-
	ob DOO ruh si		
	ob DYOO ruh si	§§ 40(4), 47(2), 50(32)	
	ob DOO ruh si		
obdurate (adj.)	OB dyŏŏ rit	ŏb′dŭ ra̍t	'ab djʊ rɪt, -ret, -dʊ-, -djə-, -dju-, -də-; *ES also* 'ɒb-
	OB dŏŏ rit		
	OB dyŏŏ rayt		
	OB dŏŏ rayt		
	Often, esp. in poetry:	*Often, esp. in poetry:*	*Often, esp. in poetry:*
	ob DYOO rit	ŏb dū′ra̍t	ab 'djʊ rɪt, -'dʊ-, -'dju-, -'du-; *ES also* ɒb-
	ob DOO rit	§§ 20(8, 9), 47(3), 50(2, 32), 51(11)	

	SIMPLIFIED	DIACRITICAL	PHONETIC
obedience	uh BEE di uhns	ŏ bē′dĭ ĕns	ə 'bi dɪ əns
	oh BEE di uhns	§ 28(9)	o 'bi dɪ əns
obeisance	oh BAY suhns	ŏ bā′săns	o 'be səns
	oh BAY s'ns	ŏ bā′s'ns	o 'be sn̩s
	oh BEE suhns	ŏ bē′săns	o 'bi səns
	oh BEE s'ns	ŏ bē′s'ns § 47(1)	o 'bi sn̩s
obelisk	OB uh lisk	ŏb′ĕ lĭsk	'ab ə lɪsk, 'ab l̩ ɪsk; *ES also* 'ɒb-
Oberon	OH buhr on	ō′bĕr ŏn	'o bər ɑn, -bə rɑn,
	OH buh ron		-rən, 'ab ər ɑn,
	OB uhr on	ŏb′ĕr ŏn	-ə rɑn, -rən; *ES*
	OB uhr uhn	ŏb′ĕr ŭn § 47(2)	*also* -ɒn, -rɒn
obese	oh BEES	ŏ bēs′	o 'bis
obesity	oh BEES uh ti	ŏ bēs′ĭ tĭ	o 'bis ə tɪ
	oh BEES i ti	ŏ bēs′ĭ tĭ	o 'bis ɪ tɪ
	oh BES uh ti	ŏ bĕs′ĭ tĭ	o 'bɛs ə tɪ
	oh BES i ti	ŏ bĕs′ĭ tĭ § 47(1)	o 'bɛs ɪ tɪ
obituary	uh BICH o͝o *er* i	ŏ bĭt′û ĕr′ĭ	ɪ 'bɪtʃ ʊ ˌɛrˌɪ
	oh BICH o͝o *er* i	§§ 20(2), 24(9),	o 'bɪtʃ ʊ ˌɛrˌɪ
	uh BIT yo͝o *er* i	50(33), 51(4)	ə 'bɪt jʊ ˌɛrˌɪ
	oh BIT yo͝o *er* i		o 'bɪt jʊ ˌɛrˌɪ, -ju-
	B., uh BIT yo͝o	*B.,* ŏ bĭt′û ēr ĭ	*B.,* ə 'bɪt jʊ ə rɪ,
	uhr i		o 'bɪt-
object (n.)	OB jekt	ŏb′jĕkt	'ab dʒɛkt, -dʒɪkt;
	OB jikt	ŏb′jikt § 24(5)	*ES also* 'ɒb-
—— (v.)	uhb JEKT	ŏb jĕkt′ § 12	əb 'dʒɛkt
oblige	uh BLAIJ	ŏ blīj′ § 47(2)	ə 'blaɪdʒ
oblique	uhb LEEK	ŏb lēk′	əb 'lik, ab-, ə 'b-
	uhb LAIK	ŏb līk′ § 47(3)	əb 'laɪk, ab-, ə 'b-
	Military, usu.:	*Military, usu.:*	*Military, usu.:*
	uhb LAIK	ŏb līk′ § 51(6)	əb 'laɪk, ə 'b-; *ES also* ɒb-
obloquy	OB luh kwi	ŏb′lŏ kwĭ	'ab lə kwɪ; *ES also* 'ɒb-
obnoxious	uhb NOK shuhs	ŏb nŏk′shŭs § 34(13)	əb 'nak ʃəs, ab-; *ES also* -'nɒk-, ɒb-
obscenity	uhb SEN uh ti	ŏb sĕn′ĭ tĭ	əb 'sɛn ə tɪ,
	ob SEN i ti	ŏb sĕn′ĭ tĭ	-'si nə-,
	uhb SEE nuh ti	ŏb sē′nĭ tĭ	ab 'sɛn ə-,
	ob SEE ni ti	ŏb sē′nĭ tĭ §§ 34(13), 47(1)	-'si nɪ-; *ES also* ɒb-
obsequies	OB si kwiz	ŏb′sĕ kwĭz	'ab sɪ kwɪz; *ES also* 'ɒb-
	OB si kweez		
obsequious	uhb SEE kwi uhs	ŏb sē′kwĭ ŭs	əb 'si kwɪ əs
obsolete	OB suh leet	ŏb′sŏ lēt	'ab sə lit; *ES also* 'ɒb-
obstacle	OB stuh k'l	ŏb′stă k'l	'ab stə kl̩, -stɪ-;
	OB sti k'l	ŏb′stĭ k'l	*ES also* 'ɒb-

	SIMPLIFIED	DIACRITICAL	PHONETIC
obstinate	OB stuh nit OB sti nit	ŏb′stĭ nĭt ŏb′stĭ nĭt	ˈɑb stə nɪt, -stɪ-; *ES also* ˈɒb-
obtuse	uhb TYOOS uhb TOOS	ŏb tūs′ §§ 11, 48(2), 50(32)	əb ˈtjus əb ˈtus
occasion	uh KAY zhuhn	ŏ kā′zhŭn	ə ˈke ʒən
occult (n., adj.)	uh KUHLT o KUHLT OK *uhlt*	ŏ kŭlt′ ŏ kŭlt′ ŏk′ŭlt	ə ˈkʌlt, ɑ-, ˈɑk ʌlt; *ES also* ɒ-, ˈɒk-
—— (v.)	uh KUHLT o KUHLT	ŏ kŭlt′ ŏ kŭlt′ §§ 11, 40(6), 47(1)	ə ˈkʌlt, ɑ ˈkʌlt; *ES also* ɒ ˈkʌlt
occultism	uh KUHL tiz′m o KUHL tiz′m OK uhl tiz′m	ŏ kŭl′tĭz′m ŏ kŭl′tĭz′m ŏk′ŭl tĭz′m § 50(15)	ə ˈkʌl tɪz m̩, ɑ ˈkʌl-, ˈɑk əl-, -əm; *ES also* ɒ ˈkʌl-, ˈɒk əl-
ocean	OH shuhn	ō′shŭn § 22(1)	ˈo ʃən
oceanic	*oh* shi AN ik	ō′shē ăn′ĭk § 22(1)	ˌoˈʃɪ ˈæn ɪk
octave	OK tayv OK tiv	ŏk′tāv ŏk′tĭv	ˈɑk tev, -tɪv; *ES also* ˈɒk-
octavo	ok TAY voh ok TAH voh	ŏk tā′vō ŏk tä′vō	ɑk ˈte vo, -ˈtɑ-; *ES also* ɒk-
octopus	OK tuh puhs	ŏk′tŏ pŭs	ˈɑk tə pəs; *ES also* ˈɒk-
	Latin: ok TOH puhs	*Latin:* ŏk tō′pŭs §§ 47(3), 51(11)	*Latin:* ɑk ˈto pəs; *ES also* ɒk-
odious	OH di uhs *B.*, OHD yuhs	ō′dĭ ŭs *B.*, ōd′yŭs §§ 28(9), 47(2), 50(25), 51(4)	ˈo dɪ əs *B.*, ˈod jəs
Odysseus	oh DIS yoos oh DIS i uhs	ŏ dĭs′ūs ŏ dĭs′ĕ ŭs	o ˈdɪs jus o ˈdɪs ɪ əs
Odyssey	OD uh si OD i si	ŏd′ĭ sĭ ŏd′ĭ sĭ	ˈɑd ə sɪ, -ɪ sɪ; *ES also* ˈɒd-
off	awf of	ôf § 34(7)	ɔf ɒf
offense, offence	uh FENS	ŏ fĕns′	ə ˈfɛns
offer	AWF uhr OF uhr	ôf′ēr § 34(7)	ˈɔf ɚ, ˈɒf ɚ; ˈɑf ɚ; *ES* -ə(r)
office	AWF is OF is	ôf′ĭs § 34(7)	ˈɔf ɪs, ˈɒf ɪs, ˈɑf ɪs
official	uh FISH uhl	ŏ fĭsh′ăl	ə ˈfɪʃ əl
officious	uh FISH uhs	ŏ fĭsh′ŭs	ə ˈfɪʃ əs
offset (n., adj.)	AWF *set* OF *set*	ôf′sĕt′	ˈɔf ˌsɛt ˈɒf ˌsɛt
—— (v.)	*awf* SET *of* SET	ôf′sĕt′	ˌɔf ˈsɛt ˌɒf ˈsɛt
	AWF *set* OF *set*	ôf′sĕt′	ˈɔf ˌsɛt ˈɒf ˌsɛt

—— *Printing*	AWF *set*	ôf′sĕt′ §§ 11, 12, 34(7)	′ɔf ˌsɛt
often	AWF uhn OF uhn AWF ’n OF ’n *Esp. in singing:* AWF tuhn OF tuhn	ôf′ĕn ŏf′ĕn ôf′ ’n ŏf′ ’n *Esp. in singing:* ôf′tĕn §§ 1, 34(7), 39(2), 47(1)	′ɔf ən ′ɒf ən ′ɔf n̩ ′ɒf n̩ *Esp. in singing:* ′ɔf tən ′ɒf tən
ogle	OH g’l	ō′g’l	′o gl̩
ogre	OH guhr	ō′gĕr	′o gɚ; *ES* -gə(r)
ohm, Ohm	ohm	ōm	om
oil	oil	oil	ɔɪl
oily	OIL i	oil′ĭ	′ɔɪl ɪ
old	old	ōld	old
oleomargarine	*oh* li oh MAHR juh reen *oh* li oh MAHR guh reen *oh* li oh MAHR guh rin	ō′lē ō mär′jȧ rēn ō′ lē ō mär′ gȧ rēn ō′lē ō mär′gȧ rĭn § 47(3)	ˌo lɪ o ′mɑr dʒə rin, - lɪ ə-, -rɪn, -′mɑr gə-; *ES* -′mɑ:-, *E also* -′mɑ:-
olfactory	ol FAK tuh ri	ŏl făk′tô rĭ § 9	ɑl ′fæk tə rɪ, -′fæk trɪ; *ES* *also* ɒl-
Omar Khayyám	OH muhr kaī̂ YAM OH muhr kaī̂ YAWM OH mahr kaī̂ YAHM	ō′mȧr kī yäm′ ō′mȧr kī yôm′ ō′mär kī yäm′	′o mɚ kaɪ ′jɑm, -′jɒm, kaɪ ′ɑm, -′æm, -′jæm; *ES* -mə(r) ′o mɑr kaɪ ′jɑm; *ES* -mɑ:(r)-, -mɑ:(r)-
omega	oh MEE guh OH me guh oh MEG uh OH muh guh	ō mē′gȧ ō′mĕ gȧ ō mĕg′ȧ ō′mĕ gȧ § 47(3)	o ′mi gə ′o mɛ gə o ′mɛg ə ′o mə gə
omelet, **omelette**	OM uh let OM let OM lit	ŏm′ĕ lĕt ŏm′lĕt ŏm′lĭt §§ 24(5), 47(3)	′ɑm ə lɛt, -ɪ-, ′ɑm lɛt, -lɪt; *ES* *also* ′ɒm-
omen	OH men OH muhn	ō′mĕn ō′mĕn	′o mɛn ′o mən
ominous	OM uh nuhs OM i nuhs	ŏm′ĭ nŭs ŏm′ĭ nŭs	′ɑm ə nəs, -ɪ nəs; *ES also* ′ɒm-
omnipotent	om NIP uh tuhnt	ŏm nĭp′ŏ tĕnt	ɑm ′nɪp ə tənt; *ES also* ɒm-
omnipresent	*om* ni PREZ uhnt *om* ni PREZ ’nt	ŏm′nĭ prĕz′ĕnt ŏm′nĭ prĕz′ ’nt	ˌɑm nɪ ′prɛz ənt, -n̩t; *ES also* ˌɒm-

	SIMPLIFIED	DIACRITICAL	PHONETIC
omniscience	om NISH uhns	ŏm nĭsh′ĕns	am ′nɪʃ əns; *ES* also ɒm-
	B., om NIS i uhns	*B.,* ŏm nĭs′ĭ ĕns §§ 47(2), 51(4)	*B.,* ɒm ′nɪs ɪ əns
on	on	ŏn §§ 16, 34(6)	an, ɒn, ɔn
once	*wuhns*	wŭns §§ 39(3), 40(6), 42(3)	wʌns
onerous	ON uhr uhs	ŏn′ĕr ŭs	′an ər əs; *ES also* ′ɒn-
onion	UHN yuhn	ŭn′yŭn § 26(4)	′ʌn jən, -jɪn
only	OHN li	ōn′lĭ	′on lɪ
onyx	ON iks	ŏn′ĭks	′an ɪks; *ES also* ′ɒn-
	OH niks	ō′nĭks § 47(3)	′o nɪks
ooze	ooz	ōōz § 34(22)	uz
open	OH puhn	ō′pĕn § 47(1)	′o pən, -pn̩, -pm̩
opening	OH puhn ing	ō′pĕn ĭng	′o pən ɪŋ
	OHP ning	ōp′nĭng	′op nɪŋ
open-minded	OH puhn MA͡IND ed	ō′pĕn mīnd′ĕd	′o pən ′maɪnd ɛd
	OH puhn MA͡IND id § 50(34)	ō′pĕn mīnd′ĭd §§ 11, 24(5)	′o pən ′maɪnd ɪd
opera	OP uhr uh	ŏp′ĕr ȧ § 9	′ap ər ə, ′ap rə; *ES also* ′ɒp-
operative (adj.)	OP uhr *ay* tiv	ŏp′ĕr ā′tĭv	′ap ər ˌe tɪv,
	OP uhr uh tiv	ŏp′ĕr ȧ tĭv § 9	-ə tɪv, ′ap rə tɪv; *ES also* ′ɒp-
ophthalmia	of THAL mi uh	ŏf thăl′mĭ ȧ § 28(9)	af ′θæl mɪ ə, -mjə; *ES also* ɒf-
ophthalmic	of THAL mik	ŏf thăl′mĭk § 47(3)	af ′θæl mɪk; *ES also* ɒf-
opiate (n., adj.)	OH pi ayt	ō′pĭ āt	′o pɪ et
	OH pi it	ō′pĭ ĭt	′o pɪ ɪt
—— (v.t.)	OH pi ayt	ō′pĭ āt § 20(8, 9)	′o pɪ et
opined	oh PA͡IND § 50(34)	ŏ pīnd′ § 50(4)	o ′paɪnd
opinion	uh PIN yuhn	ŏ pĭn′yŭn §§ 28(9), 34(12)	ə ′pɪn jən
opponent	uh POH nuhnt	ŏ pō′nĕnt	ə ′po nənt
opportune	*op* uhr TYOON	ŏp′ŏr tūn′	ˌap ɚ ′tjun, -′tun,
	op uhr TOON		′ap ɚ tjun,
	OP uhr tyoon	ŏp′ŏr tūn §§ 11,	-tun; *ES*
	OP uhr toon	47(2), 48(2), 50(32)	-ə ′tjun,
			-ə ′tun, -ə tjun,
			-ə tun, *also* ˌɒp-, ɒp-

opportunity	*op* uhr TYOON uh ti	ŏp′ŏr tū′nĭ tĭ	‚ap ɚ 'tjun ə tɪ, -'tun-, -ɪ tɪ; *ES*
	op uhr TOON i ti		-ə 'tjun-,
	op uhr TYOON i ti	ŏp′ŏr tū′nĭ tĭ	-ə 'tun-, *also*
	op uhr TOON i ti	§§ 48(2), 50(32)	‚ɒp-
oppression	uh PRESH uhn	ŏ prĕsh′ăn § 50(28)	ə 'prɛʃ ən
opprobrius	uh PROH bri uhs	ŏ prō′brĭ ăs	ə 'pro brɪ əs
optimist	OP tuh mist	ŏp′tĭ mĭst	'ap tə mɪst, -tɪ-;
	OP ti mist	ŏp′tĭ mĭst	*ES also* 'ɒp-
opulent	OP yŏŏ luhnt	ŏp′ û lĕnt	'ap jʊ lənt, -jə-, -ju-; *ES also* 'ɒp-
oral	OH ruhl	ō′răl § 34(3)	'o rəl
	AW ruhl		'ɔ rəl
orange	OR enj	ŏr′ĕnj	'ar ɛndʒ, 'ɔr-,
	OR inj	ŏr′ĭnj	'ɒr-, -ɪndʒ,
	AWR inj	ôr′ĭnj § 34(5, 7)	-əndʒ
oranges	OR enj iz	ŏr′ĕnj ĭz	'ar ɛndʒ ɪz, 'ɔr-,
	OR inj iz	ŏr′ĭnj ĭz	'ɒr-, -ɪndʒ-,
	AWR inj iz	ôr ĭnj ĭz § 34(5, 7), 48(3)	-əndʒ-
orator	OR uh tuhr	ŏr′á tēr	'ar ə tɚ, 'ɔr-,
	AWR uh tuhr	ôr′á tēr § 34(5, 7)	'ɒr-; *ES* -tə(r)
orchestra	AWR kes truh	ôr′kĕs trá	'ɔr kɛs trə, -kɪs-;
	AWR kis truh	ôr′kĭs trá	*ES* 'ɔə-
orchestral	awr KES truhl	ôr kĕs′trăl	ɔr 'kɛs trəl,
	AWR kes truhl	ôr′kĕs trăl § 47(3)	'ɔr kɛs-; *ES* 'ɔə-
orchid	AWR kid	ôr′kĭd	'ɔr kɪd; *ES* 'ɔə-
ordeal	awr DEE uhl	ôr dē′ăl	ɔr 'di əl, -'dil,
	awr DEEL	ôr dēl′	'ɔr di əl, -dɪ-;
	AWR dee uhl	ôr′dē ăl	*ES* ɔə-, 'ɔə-
	AWR di uhl	ôr′dĭ ăl § 47(1)	
ordinance	AWR duh nuhns	ôr′dĭ năns	'ɔr də nəns,
	AWR di nuhns	ôr′dĭ năns	-dn əns, -dɪ-; *ES* 'ɔə-
ore	ohr	ōr § 34(3)	or, ɔr; *ES* ɔə(r),
	awr		*E also* ɔə(r)
organization	*awr* guhn i ZAY shuhn	ôr′găn ĭ zā′shŭn	‚ɔr gən ɪ 'ze ʃən, -gən ə-, -aɪ 'ze-
	awr guhn a͡i ZAY shuhn § 50(34)	ôr′găn ī zā′shŭn § 47(3)	*ES* ‚ɔə gən-
orgy	AWR ji	ôr′jĭ	'ɔr dʒɪ; *ES* 'ɔə-
Orient, orient (n., v.t.)	OH ri ent	ō′rĭ ĕnt	'o rɪ ɛnt
	AW ri ent		'ɔ rɪ ɛnt

	SIMPLIFIED	DIACRITICAL	PHONETIC
—— (adj., n. *also*)	OH ri uhnt AW ri uhnt	ō′rĭ ĕnt § 34(3)	′o rɪ ənt ′ɔ rɪ ənt
oriental	*oh* ri EN tuhl *aw* ri EN tuhl *oh* ri EN t'l *aw* ri EN t'l	ō′rĭ ĕn′tăl ō′rĭ ĕn′t'l § 34(3)	ˌo rɪ ′ɛn təl ˌɔ rɪ ′ɛn təl ˌo rɪ ′ɛn tl̩ ˌɔ rɪ ′ɛn tl̩
orientate	OH ri en *tayt* AW ri en *tayt* *oh* ri EN tayt *aw* ri EN tayt	ō′rĭ ĕn tāt′ ō′rĭ ĕn′tāt §§ 34(3), 47(3), 50(2)	′o rɪ ɛn ˌtet ′ɔ rɪ ɛn ˌtet ˌo rɪ ′ɛn tet ˌɔ rɪ ′ɛn tet
orifice	OR uh fis OR i fis AWR uh fis AWR i fis	ŏr′ĭ fĭs ŏr′ĭ fĭs ôr′ĭ fĭs ôr′ĭ fĭs § 34(5, 7)	′ar ə fɪs, ′ɔr-, ′ɒr-, -ɪ fɪs
origin	OR uh jin OR i jin AWR uh jin AWR i jin	ŏr′ĭ jĭn ŏr′ĭ jĭn ôr′ĭ jĭn ôr′ĭ jĭn § 34(5, 7)	′ar ə dʒɪn, ′ɔr-, ′ɒr-, -ɪ dʒɪn
Orion	oh RĀI uhn § 50(34)	ō rī′ŏn	o ′raɪ ən
ornament (n.)	AWR nuh muhnt	ôr′nȧ mĕnt	′ɔr nə mənt; *ES* ′ɔə-
—— (v.t.)	AWR nuh ment	ôr′nȧ mĕnt § 47(2)	′ɔr nə mɛnt; *ES* ′ɔə-
ornate	awr NAYT AWR nayt	ôr nāt′ ôr′nāt §§ 11, 47(2)	ɔr ′net; *ES* ɔə- ′ɔr net; *ES* ′ɔə-
Orphean	awr FEE uhn	ôr fē′ăn § 47(2)	ɔr ′fi ən; *ES* ɔə-
Orpheus	AWR fyoos *Freq.*: AWR fi uhs	ôr′fūs *Freq.*: ôr′fē ŭs § 51(9)	′ɔr fjus; *ES* ′ɔə- *Freq.*: ′ɔr fɪ əs; *ES* ′ɔə-
osmosis	os MOH sis oz MOH sis	ŏs mō′sĭs ŏz mō′sĭs § 47(2)	as ′mo sɪs, az-; *ES* *also* ɒs-, ɒz-
ostler	OS luhr	ŏs′lēr	′as lɚ; *ES* -lə(r), *also* ′ɒs-
ostrich	OS trich *Occas.*: OS trij	ŏs′trĭch § 34(7) *Occas.*: ŏs′trĭj § 51(8)	′ɒs trɪtʃ, ′ɔs-, ′as- *Occas.*: ′ɒs trɪdʒ, ′ɔs-, ′as-
other	UHTH uhr	ŭth′ēr § 34(10)	ʌð ɚ; *ES* -ə(r)
ought	awt	ôt	ɔt
our	owr	our	aʊr; *ES* aʊə(r)
oust	owst § 50(34)	oust	aʊst
outcast (v.t.)	owt KAST owt KAHST	out kȧst′ §§ 11, 12, 20(5)	aʊt ′kæst; *E also* ′kast, -′kast

	SIMPLIFIED	DIACRITICAL	PHONETIC
—— (adj., n.)	OWT *kast* OWT *kahst*	out′kȧst′ § 49(11)	'aʊt ˌkæst; *E also* -ˌkast, -ˌkɑst
overalls	OH vuhr *awlz*	ō′vĕr ôlz′ § 49(12)	'o vər ˌɔlz
overbalance	*oh* vuhr BAL uhns	ō′vĕr băl′ăns §§ 47(2), 49(12)	ˌo və˞ 'bæl əns; *ES* ˌo və-
overflow (v.)	*oh* vuhr FLOH	ō′vĕr flō′ §§ 11, 14	ˌo və˞ 'flo, *ES* ˌo və-
—— (n.)	OH vuhr *floh*	ō′vĕr flō′ § 49(12)	'o və˞ ˌflo; *ES* -və-
overlap (v.)	*oh* vuhr LAP	ō′vĕr lăp′ §§ 11, 14	ˌo və˞ 'læp; *ES* ˌo və-
—— (n.)	OH vuhr *lap*	ō′vĕr lăp′ § 49(12)	'o və˞ ˌlæp; *ES* -və-
overlook (v.t.)	*oh* vuhr LOOK	ō′vĕr lŏŏk′ §§ 11, 14	ˌo və˞ 'lʊk; *ES* ˌo və-
	OH vuhr *look*	ō′vĕr lŏŏk′ § 49(12)	'o və˞ ˌlʊk; *ES* -və-
overseer	OH vuhr *see* uhr	ō′vĕr sē′ĕr	'o və˞ ˌsi ə˞, 'o və si ə(r)
	oh vuhr SĪER *oh* vuhr SIR *oh* vuhr SEER OH vuhr sĭer OH vuhr sir	ō′vĕr sẽr′ §§ 24(2), 49(12) ō′vĕr sēr′ ō′vĕr sẽr §§ 24(2), 47(3), 49(12)	ˌo və˞ 'sɪər, -'sɪr, -'sir; *ES* ˌo və 'sɪə(r) 'o və˞ sɪər, -sɪr, -sir; *ES* 'o və sɪə(r)
	OH vuhr seer	ō′vĕr sēr	
overt	OH *vuhrt* oh VUHRT	ō′vûrt ō vûrt′ § 40(6)	'o vɝt, o 'vɝt; *ES* *also* -vɜt, -'vɜt
overture	OH vuhr chuhr OH vuhr tyuhr	ō′vĕr tūr § 50(31)	'o və˞ tʃə˞, -ˌtʃʊr, -tjə˞; *ES* -və tʃə(r), -ˌtʃʊə(r), -tjə(r)
oxide	OK sa͞id OK sid § 50(34)	ŏk′sīd ok′sĭd §§ 28(7), 47(2)	'ɑk saɪd, -sɪd; *ES* *also* 'ɒk-
oyster	OIS tuhr	ois′tĕr	'ɔɪs tə˞; *ES* -tə(r)

P

	SIMPLIFIED	DIACRITICAL	PHONETIC
padre	PAH dri *Sp., It.,* PAH dray	pä′drĭ *Sp., It.,* pä′dră	′pa drɪ *Sp., It.,* ′pɑ: dre; *Sp. also,* ′pɑ ðre
paean	PEE uhn	pē′ăn	′pi ən
pageant	PAJ uhnt *Occas.:* PAY juhnt	păj′ĕnt § 47(3) *Occas.:* pā′jĕnt § 51(8)	′pædʒ ənt *Occas.:* ′pe dʒənt
pajamas	puh JAH muhz puh JAM uhz	pȧ jä′mȧz pȧ jăm′ȧz	pə ′dʒɑ məz pə ′dʒæm əz
palace	PAL is PAL uhs	păl′ĭs păl′ȧs	′pæl ɪs ′pæl əs
palate	PAL it PAL uht	păl′ĭt păl′ȧt	′pæl ɪt ′pæl ət
palatial	puh LAY shuhl	pȧ lā′shăl	pə ′le ʃəl
palaver	puh LAV uhr puh LAH vuhr	pȧ lăv′ēr pȧ lä′vēr § 47(3)	pə ′læv ɚ, -′lɑ vɚ; *ES* -ə(r), -və(r)
Palestine	PAL es tain PAL is tain § 50(34)	păl′ĕs tīn păl′ĕs tīn § 28(6)	′pæl ɛs tɑɪn, -ɪs-, -əs-, -tin
palfrey	PAWL fri PAL fri	pôl′frĭ păl′frĭ § 47(3)	′pɔl frɪ ′pæl frɪ
palisade	*pal* uh SAYD *pal* i SAYD	păl′ȧ sād′ păl′ĭ sād′	ˌpæl ə ′sed ˌpæl ɪ ′sed
palladium	puh LAY di uhm	pȧ lā′dĭ ŭm	pə ′le dɪ əm
palliate (v.t.)	PAL i ayt	păl′ĭ āt	′pæl ɪ et
palliative	PAL i *ay* tiv PAL i uh tiv	păl′ĭ ā′tĭv păl′ĭ ȧ tĭv § 28(9)	′pæl ɪ ˌe tɪv ′pæl ɪ ə tɪv
palm (*"hand"*)	pahm	päm	pɑm
palmetto	pal MET oh	păl mĕt′ō	pæl ′mɛt o
palmy (*"abound- ing in palms"*)	PAHM i	päm′ĭ § 51(7)	′pɑm ɪ
palpable	PAL puh b'l	păl′pȧ b'l	′pæl pə bļ
palsied	PAWL zid	pôl′zĭd	′pɔl zɪd
palsy	PAWL zi	pôl′zĭ	′pɔl zɪ
palter	PAWL tuhr	pôl′tēr	′pɔl tɚ; *ES* -tə(r)
paltry	PAWL tri	pôl′trĭ	′pɔl trɪ

	SIMPLIFIED	DIACRITICAL	PHONETIC
pamphlet	PAM flet PAM flit	păm′flĕt păm′flĭt §§ 24(5), 50(10)	′pæm flɛt ′pæm flɪt ′pæmp flɪt
panacea	*pan* uh SEE uh	păn′á sē′á	ˌpæn ə ′si ə
pancreas	PAN kri uhs PANG kri uhs	păn′krĕ ăs păng′krĕ ăs § 47(2)	′pæn krɪ əs ′pæŋ krɪ əs
panegyric	*pan* i JIR ik	păn′ĕ jĭr′ĭk	ˌpæn ɪ ′dʒɪr ɪk
pannier	PAN yuhr PAN i uhr	păn′yēr păn′ĭ ēr §§ 28(9), 47(2)	ˌpæn jɚ, ′pæn ɪ ɚ; *ES* -jə(r), -ə(r)
panoply	PAN uh pli	păn′ŏ plĭ	′pæn ə plɪ
panorama	*pan* uh RAM uh *pan* uh RAH muh	păn′ŏ răm′á păn′ŏ rä′má § 47(3)	ˌpæn ə ′ræm ə ˌpæn ə ′rɑ mə
Pantheon, pantheon	păn THEE uhn PAN thi on PAN thi uhn	păn thē′ŏn păn′thĕ ŏn păn′thĕ ăn § 47(3)	pæn ′θi ən, ′pæn θɪ ɑn, -ən; *ES also* ′pæn θɪ ɒn
pantomime	PAN tuh maim § 50(34)	păn′tŏ mīm	′pæn tə maɪm
papa (*"father"*)	PAH puh *B.,* puh PAH	pä′pá § 47(2) *B.,* pá pä′ § 51(4)	′pɑ pə *B.,* pə ′pɑ
papal	PAY puhl	pā′păl	′pe pəl, -pl̩
papyrus	puh PAI ruhs § 50(34)	pá pī′rŭs	pə ′paɪ rəs
parable	PAR uh b'l	păr′á b'l	′pær ə bl̩
parabola	puh RAB uh luh	pá răb′ŏ lá	pə ′ræb ə lə
parabolical	*par* uh BOL i kuhl	păr′á bŏl′ĭ kăl	ˌpær ə ′bɑl ɪ kəl; *ES also* -′bɒl-
parade	puh RAYD	pá rād′	pə ′red
paradox	PAR uh doks	păr′á dŏks	′pær ə dɑks; *ES* *also* -dɒks
paraffin	PAR uh fin	păr′ă fĭn	′pær ə fɪn
paraffine	PAR uh fin PAR uh feen	păr′ă fĭn păr′ă fēn	′pær ə fɪn ′pær ə fin
paragon	PAR uh gon PAR uh guhn	păr′á gŏn păr′á gŭn	′pær ə gɑn, -gən; *ES also* -gɒn
parallelogram	*par* uh LEL uh gram	păr′ă lĕl′ŏ grăm	ˌpær ə ′lɛl ə græm
paraphernalia	*par* uh fuhr NAY li uh *par* uh fuhr NAYL yuh *par* uh fuh NAY li uh	păr′á fēr nā′lĭ á păr′á fēr nāl′yá §§ 28(9), 48(1)	ˌpær ə fɚ ′ne lɪ ə, -′nel jə, (*by dis- similation*) -fə ′ne lɪ-, -′nel jə, *ES* -fə-
parasitic	*par* uh SIT ik	păr′á sĭt′ĭk	ˌpær ə ′sɪt ɪk
parasol	PAR uh sawl PAR uh sol	păr′á sŏl §§ 34(7), 47(2)	′pær ə sɔl, -sɒl, -sɑl

	SIMPLIFIED	DIACRITICAL	PHONETIC
parent	PEHR uhnt PAY ruhnt	pâr′ĕnt §§ 20(2), 47(2)	'pɛr ənt, 'pær-, 'pe rənt; *ES* *also* 'peər-
pariah	puh RAI uh PAY ri uh § 50(34)	pȧ rī′ȧ pā′rĭ ȧ § 47(3)	pə 'raɪ ə 'pe rɪ ə
—— *"member of* *a low caste,"*	PAH ri uh PAR i uh	pä′rĭ ȧ păr′ĭ ȧ § 51(11)	'pɑ rɪ ə 'pær ɪ ə
Parisian	puh RIZH uhn puh RIZ i uhn	pȧ rĭzh′ăn pȧ rĭz′ĭ ăn § 47(3)	pə 'rɪʒ ən pə 'rɪz ɪ ən
Parisienne	*pah ree* ZYEN *pa ree* ZYEN	pȧ′rē′zyĕn′	pa ri 'zyɛn, pæ-
parity	PAR uh ti PAR i ti	păr′ĭ tĭ păr′ĭ tĭ	'pær ə tɪ 'pær ɪ tɪ
parley	PAHR li	pär′lĭ	'pɑr lɪ; *ES* 'pɑ:-, *E also* 'pa:-
parliament (n.)	PAHR luh muhnt PAHR li muhnt	pär′lŭ mĕnt pär′lĭ mĕnt § 50(22)	'pɑr lə mənt, -lɪ-; *ES* 'pɑ:-, *E also* 'pa:-
parliamentarily	*pahr luh* MEN *tuh ruh li* *pahr li* MEN *tuh* *ruh li*	pär′lŭ mĕn′tȧ rĭ lĭ pär′lĭ mĕn′tȧ rĭ lĭ	ˌpɑr lə 'mɛn tə rə lɪ, ˌpɑr lɪ-; *ES* ˌpɑ lə-, -lɪ-, *E* *also* ˌpa:-
parliamentary	*pahr luh* MEN *tuh ri* *pahr li* MEN *tuh* *ri*	pär′lŭ mĕn′tȧ rĭ pär′lĭ mĕn′tȧ rĭ	ˌpɑr lə 'mɛn tə rɪ, -lɪ-; *ES* ˌpɑ:-, *E also* ˌpa:-
parochial	puh ROH ki uhl	pȧ rō′kĭ ăl § 28(9)	pə 'ro kɪ əl, -kjəl
parole	puh ROHL	pȧ rōl′	pə 'rol
Parthenon	PAHR thi non PAHR thi nuhn	pär′thē nŏn pär′thē nŭn	'pɑr θɪ nɑn, -nən; *ES* 'pɑ: θɪ-, *also* -nɒn, *E* *also* 'pa:-
partiality	*pahr shi* AL *uh ti* *pahr shi* AL *i ti* pahr SHAL *uh ti*	pär′shĭ ăl′ĭ tĭ pär′shĭ ăl′ĭ tĭ pär shăl′ĭ tĭ §§ 20(9), 47(2)	ˌpɑr ʃɪ 'æl ə tɪ, -ɪ tɪ, pɑr 'ʃæl-; *ES* ˌpɑ: ʃɪ, pɑ: 'ʃæl-, *E also* ˌpa:-, pa:-
participial	*pahr tuh* SIP *i uhl* *pahr ti* SIP *i uhl*	pär′tĭ sĭp′ĭ ăl pär′tĭ sĭp′ĭ ăl	ˌpɑr tə 'sɪp ɪ əl, -tɪ-; *ES* ˌpɑ:-, *E also* ˌpa:-
participle	PAHR tuh si p'l PAHR ti si p'l	pär′tŭ sĭ p'l pär′tĭ sĭ p'l	'pɑr tə sɪ pl̩, -tɪ-; *ES* 'pɑ:-, *E also* 'pa:-

	SIMPLIFIED	DIACRITICAL	PHONETIC
particular	puhr TIK yŏŏ luhr pahr TIK yŏŏ luhr puh TIK yŏŏ luhr	pẽr tĭk′û lẽr pär tĭk′û lẽr § 48(1)	pɚ 'tɪk jʊ lɚ, par-, -jə-, -ju-, *(by dissimila-tion)* pə 'tɪk-; *ES* pə-, pɑ:-, -lə(r), *E also* pɑ:-
particularly	puhr TIK yŏŏ luhr li pahr TIK yŏŏ luhr li puh TIK yŏŏ luhr li	pẽr tĭk′û lẽr lĭ pär tĭk′û lẽr lĭ §§ 48(1), 50(20)	pɚ 'tɪk jʊ lɚ lɪ, par-, -jə-, -ju-, *(by dissimila-tion)* pə 'tɪk-; *ES* pə-, pɑ:-, -lə-, *E also* pɑ:-
partner	PAHRT nuhr	pärt′nẽr	'pɑrt nɚ; *ES* 'pɑːt nə(r), *E also* 'pɑːt-
partridge	PAHR trij	pär′trĭj	'pɑr trɪdʒ; *ES* 'pɑ:-, *E also* 'pɑ:-
party	PAHR ti	pär′tĭ	'pɑr tɪ; *ES* 'pɑ:-, *E also* 'pɑ:-
parvenu	PAHR vi nyoo PAHR vi noo PAHR vuh nyoo PAHR vuh noo	pär′vē nū pär′vĕ nū §§ 48(2), 50(32)	'pɑr vɪ nju, -nu, -və-; *ES* 'pɑ:-, *E also* 'pɑ:-; *F.,* par və 'ny
pasha, pacha	puh SHAH PAH shuh PASH uh	pȧ shä′ pä′shȧ păsh′ȧ § 47(2)	pə 'ʃɑ 'pɑ ʃə 'pæʃ ə
pass	pas pahs	pás § 20(5)	pæs; *E also* pas, pɑs
passable	PAS uh b'l PAHS uh b'l	pás′ȧ b'l § 20(5)	'pæs ə bl̩; *E also* 'pas-, 'pɑs-
passage	PAS ij	păs′ĭj § 50(1)	'pæs ɪdʒ
passive	PAS iv	păs′ĭv § 47(2)	'pæs ɪv
past	past pahst	pást § 20(5)	pæst; *E also* past, pɑst
Pasteur (Louis)	*pahs* TUHR pas TUHR	päs′tûr′ păs tûr′	ˌpɑs 'tɝ, 'pæs-; *ES also* -'tɜ(r); *F.,* pas 'tœːr
pasteurize	PAS tuhr a͡iz PAS tuh ra͡iz *Pop.:* PAS chuhr a͡iz PAS tyuhr a͡iz § 50(34)	păs′tẽr īz *Pop.:* păs′tûr īz §§ 20(5), 47(1), 51(3)	'pæs tər aɪz 'pæs tə raɪz *Pop.:* 'pæs tʃər aɪz, -tʃʊr-, -tjər-, -tər-, 'pɒs-
pastor	PAS tuhr PAHS tuhr	pás′tẽr § 20(5)	'pæs tɚ; *ES* -tə(r), *E also* 'pas-, 'pɑs-

	SIMPLIFIED	DIACRITICAL	PHONETIC
pastoral	PAS tuh ruhl	pås′tŏ răl	′pæs tə rəl; *E also*
	PAHS tuh ruhl	§ 9	′pas-, ′pɒs-
pasture	PAS chuhr	pås′tûr	′pæs tʃɚ, -tjɚ; *ES*
	PAHS chuhr		-tʃə(r), -tjə(r),
	PAS tyuhr	§§ 20(5), 50(31)	*E also* ′pas-,
	PAHS tyuhr		′pɒs-
patent	PAT uhnt	păt′ĕnt	′pæt ənt, -n̩t
	PAY tuhnt	pā′tĕnt	′pe tənt, -n̩t
		§§ 24(14), 47(2)	
—— *"open; not closed; obvious,"* usually	PAY tuhnt	pā′tĕnt	′pe tənt, -n̩t
—— in all other senses, usually	PAT uhnt	păt′ĕnt § 51(11)	′pæt ənt, -n̩t
pathos	PAY thos	pā′thŏs	′pe θas; *ES also* -θɒs
patience	PAY shuhns	pā′shĕns § 39(3)	′pe ʃəns
patriarch	PAY tri ahrk	pā′trĭ ärk	′pe trɪ ark; *ES* -ɑːk, *E also* -ɑːk
patrimony	PAT ruh *moh* ni	păt′rĭ mō′nĭ	′pæt rə ˌmo nɪ
	PAT ri *moh* ni	păt′rĭ mō′nĭ	′pæt rɪ ˌmo nɪ
	B., PAT ruh muhn i	*B.,* păt′rĭ mŭn ĭ § 51(4)	*B.,* ′pæt rə mən ɪ
patriot	PAY tri uht	pā′trĭ ŭt	′pe trɪ ət
	PAT ri uht	păt′rĭ ŭt § 47(3)	′pæt rɪ ət
patriotic	*pay* tri OT ik	pā′trĭ ŏt′ĭk	ˌpe trɪ ′at ɪk; *ES also* -′ɒt-
	B., pat ri OT ik	*B.,* păt′rĭ ŏt′ĭk §§ 47(1), 51(4)	*B.,* ˌpæt rɪ ′ɒt ɪk
patron	PAY truhn	pā′trŭn	′pe trən
	PAT ruhn	păt′rŭn § 47(3)	′pæt rən
patronage	PAY truhn ij	pā′trŭn ĭj	′pe trən ɪdʒ
	PAT ruhn ij	păt′rŭn ĭj § 47(3)	′pæt rən ɪdʒ
patroness	PAY truhn es	pā′trŭn ĕs	′pe trən ɛs
	PAY truhn is	pā′trŭn ĭs	′pe trən ɪs
	PAT ruhn es	păt′rŭn ĕs	′pæt rən ɛs
	PAT ruhn is	păt′rŭn ĭs §§ 24(5), 50(8)	′pæt rən ɪs
patronize	PAY truhn a͡iz	pā′trŭn īz	′pe trən aɪz
	PAT ruhn a͡iz § 50(34)	păt′rŭn īz § 47(3)	′pæt rən aɪz
pattern	PAT uhrn	păt′ĕrn	′pæt ɚn; *ES* -ən
paunch	pawnch	pônch	pɔntʃ
	pahnch	pänch §§ 22(6), 47(3)	pantʃ
pavilion	puh VIL yuhn	på vĭl′yŭn	pə ′vɪl jən

	SIMPLIFIED	DIACRITICAL	PHONETIC
pecan	pi KAN pi KAHN	pĕ kăn′ pĕ kän′ § 47(3)	pɪ 'kæn, -'kɑn, 'pi kæn
peculate	PEK yŏŏ layt	pĕk′ û lāt	'pɛk ju let, -jə-, -ju-
peculation	*pek* yŏŏ LAY shuhn	pĕk′ û lā′shŭn	ˌpɛk ju 'le ʃən, -jə-, -ju-
peculiar	pi KYOOL yuhr	pĕ kūl′yĕr §§ 48(2), 50(32)	pɪ 'kjul jɚ; ES -jə(r)
peculiarity	pi *kyoo* li AR uh ti pi *kyoo* li AR i ti pi *kyool* YAR uh ti	pĕ kū′lĭ ăr′ĭ tĭ pĕ kū′lĭ ăr′ĭ tĭ pĕ kūl′yăr′ĭ tĭ §§ 28(9), 47(1), 48(2), 50(32)	pɪ ˌkju lɪ 'ær ə tɪ pɪ ˌkju lɪ 'ær ɪ tɪ pɪ ˌkjul 'jær ə tɪ pɪ ˌkjul ɪ jær ə tɪ
peculiarly	pi KYOOL yuhr li	pĕ kūl′yĕr lĭ §§ 48(2), 50(2, 32)	pɪ 'kjul jɚ lɪ; ES -jə-
pecuniary	pi KYOO ni *er* i	pĕ kū′nĭ ĕr′ĭ §§ 20(2), 24(9), 47(2), 48(2)	pɪ 'kju nɪ ˌɛr ɪ
	B., pi KYOO nyuhr i	*B.,* pĕ kū′nyĕr ĭ	*B.,* pɪ 'kju njə rɪ
	pi KYOO ni uhr i	pĕ kū′nĭ ĕr ĭ §§ 13, 51(4)	pɪ 'kju nɪ ə rɪ
pedant	PED uhnt	ped′ănt	'pɛd ənt, -ṇt
pedantic	pi DAN tik	pĕ dăn′tĭk	pɪ 'dæn tɪk
pedantry	PED uhnt ri	pĕd′ănt rĭ	'pɛd ənt rɪ, -ṇt-
pedestal	PED es tuhl PED is tuhl PED is t'l	pĕd′ĕs tăl pĕd′ĭs tăl pĕd′ĭs t'l	'pɛd ɛs təl 'pɛd ɪs təl 'pɛd ɪs tḷ
pediment	PED uh muhnt PED i muhnt	pĕd′ĭ mĕnt pĕd′ĭ mĕnt § 50(22)	'pɛd ə mənt 'pɛd ɪ mənt
Pegasus	PEG uh suhs	pĕg′*a* sŭs	'pɛg ə səs
pellucid	puh LOO sid puh LYOO sid	pĕ lū′sĭd §§ 48(2), 50(32)	pə 'lu sɪd pə 'lju sɪd
penal	PEE nuhl PEE n'l	pē′năl pē′n'l	'pi nəl 'pi nḷ
penalize	PEE nuhl a͡iz PEE n'l a͡iz PEN uhl a͡iz § 50(34)	pē′năl ĭz pē′n'l ĭz pĕn′ăl ĭz § 47(1)	'pi nəl aɪz 'pi nḷ aɪz 'pɛn əl aɪz 'pɛn ḷ aɪz
penalty	PEN uhl ti PEN 'l ti	pĕn′ăl tĭ pĕn′ 'l tĭ § 31(3)	'pɛn əl tɪ 'pɛn ḷ tɪ
penance	PEN uhns	pĕn′ăns	'pɛn əns
pendulum	PEN jŏŏ luhm PEN dyŏŏ luhm	pĕn′dŭ lŭm § 50(33)	'pɛn dʒu ləm, -dʒə-, -dʒu-, -djʊ-, -djə-, -dju-
Penelope	pi NEL uh pi	pĕ nĕl′ŏ pĕ	pɪ 'nɛl ə pɪ

peninsula	puhn IN syŏŏ luh	pĕn ĭn′sŭ l*a*	pən ′ɪn sjʊ lə,
	puhn IN sŏŏ luh		pə ′nɪn-, -sʊ-,
	puhn IN suh luh	pĕn ĭn′sŭ l*a*	-sjə-, -sə-, -sju-,
	puh NIN suh luh	§ 50(32)	-su-, -ʃʊ-
peninsular	puhn IN syŏŏ luhr	pĕn ĭn′sŭ lēr	pən ′ɪn sjʊ lɚ,
			pə ′nɪn-, -sʊ-,
	puhn IN sŏŏ luhr		-sjə-, -sə-, -sju-,
	puhn IN suh luhr	pĕn ĭn′sŭ lēr	-su-, -ʃʊ-; *ES*
	puh NIN suh luhr		-lə(r)
penitentiary	*pen* uh TEN shuh ri	pĕn′*i* tĕn′sh*a* rĭ	ˌpen ə ′ten ʃə rɪ
	pen i TEN shuh ri	pĕn′*i̇* tĕn′sh*a* rĭ	ˌpen ɪ ′ten ʃə rɪ
penury	PEN yŏŏ ri	pĕn′*u̇* rĭ	′pen jʊ rɪ, -jə-,
			-ju-
peony	PEE uh ni	pē′ŏ nĭ	′pi ə nɪ
people	PEE p'l	pē′p'l § 24(21)	′pi pḷ
Pepys	peeps	pēps	pips
(Samuel)	peps	pĕps	pɛps
	PEP is	pĕp′ĭs	′pep ɪs
perambulate	puhr AM byŏŏ layt	pĕr ăm′bŭ lāt	pər ′æm bjʊ let,
		§ 50(2, 32)	pə ′ræm-,
	puh RAM byŏŏ layt		-bjə-, -bju-
percale	puhr KAYL	pĕr kāl′	pɚ ′kel, -′kæl; *ES*
	puhr KAL	pĕr kăl′	pə-
percolate (v.)	PUHR kuh layt	pûr′kŏ lāt	′pɝ kə let; *ES also*
			′pɜ-
——(n.)	PUHR kuh lit	pûr′kŏ lăt	′pɝ kə lɪt, -let;
	PUHR kuh layt	§§ 20(8, 9),	*ES also* ′pɜ-
		50(2)	
percolator	PUHR kuh *lay* tuhr	pûr′kŏ lā′tēr	′pɝ kə ˌle tɚ; *ES also* ′pɜ-, *ES* -tə(r)
peregrinate (v.)	PER i gri nayt	pĕr′ĕ grĭ nāt	′per ɪ grɪ net
peregrination	*per* i gri NAY shuhn	pĕr′ĕ grĭ nā′shŭn	ˌper ɪ grɪ ′ne ʃən
peremptorily	puhr EMP tuh ri li	pĕr ĕmp′tŏ rĭ lĭ	pər ′emp tə rɪ lɪ
	puh REMP tuh ri li		pə ′remp tə rɪ lɪ
	PER uhmp *toh* ri li	pĕr′ĕmp tō′rĭ lĭ	′per əmp ˌto rɪ lɪ
	PER uhmp *taw* ri li		′per əmp ˌtɔ rɪ lɪ
	PER uhmp tuhr i li	pĕr′ĕmp tēr ĭ lĭ §§ 34(3), 47(1), 50(20)	′per əmp tər ɪ lɪ

	SIMPLIFIED	DIACRITICAL	PHONETIC
peremptory	puhr EMP tuh ri	pĕr ĕmp′tŏ rĭ	pər ˈɛmp tə rɪ
	puh REMP tuh ri		pə ˈrɛmp tə rɪ
	PER uhmp *toh* ri	pĕr′ĕmp tō′rĭ	ˈpɛr əmp ˌto rɪ
	PER uhmp *taw* ri		ˈpɛr əmp ˌtɔ rɪ
	PER uhmp tuhr i	pĕr′ĕmp tĕr ĭ	ˈpɛr əmp tər ɪ
		§§ 34(3), 47(1)	
perennial	puhr EN i uhl	pĕr ĕn′ĭ ăl	pər ˈɛn ɪ əl
	puh REN i uhl	§ 28(9)	pə ˈrɛn ɪ əl
perfect (n., adj.)	PUHR fekt	pûr′fĕkt	ˈpɝ fɛkt, -fɪkt; *ES*
	PUHR fikt	pûr′fĭkt	*also* ˈpɝ-
—— (v.)	puhr FEKT	pĕr fĕkt′	pə ˈfɛkt, ˈpɝ fɛkt,
	PUHR fekt	pûr′fĕkt	ˈpɝ fɪkt; *ES*
	PUHR fikt	pûr′fĭkt	pə-, *also* ˈpɝ-
		§§ 24(5), 47(3)	
perfidious	puhr FID i uhs	pĕr fĭd′ĭ ŭs	pə ˈfɪd ɪ əs; *ES*
		§ 47(2)	pə-
perfume (v.)	puhr FYOOM	pĕr fūm′	pə ˈfjum; *ES* pə-
		§§ 12, 48(2)	
—— (n.)	PUHR fyoom	pûr′fūm § 47(2)	ˈpɝ fjum; *ES* ˈpɝ-
	Occas.:	*Occas.:*	*Occas.:*
	puhr FYOOM	pĕr fūm′	pə ˈfjum; *ES* pə-
		§§ 50(32), 51(8)	
perhaps	puhr HAPS	pĕr hăps′	pə ˈhæps; *ES* pə-
	Often:	*Often:*	*Often:*
	puhr APS	pĕr ăps′ § 51(9)	pə ˈæps; *ES* pə-
perilous	PER uh luhs	pĕr′ĭ lŭs	ˈpɛr ə ləs
	PER i luhs	pĕr′ĭ lŭs § 50(25)	ˈpɛr ɪ ləs
period	PĬER i uhd	pēr′ĭ ŭd	ˈpɪər ɪ əd, ˈpɪr-,
	PIR i uhd	§ 24(2)	ˈpir-; *ES* ˈpɪər-
	PEER i uhd	pēr′ĭ ŭd	
periodic ("*occur-ring regularly; intermittent*")	pĭer i OD ik	pēr′ĭ ŏd′ĭk	ˌpɪər ɪ ˈɑd ɪk,
	pir i OD ik	§ 24(2)	ˌpɪr-, ˌpir-; *ES*
	peer i OD ik	pēr′ĭ ŏd′ĭk	ˌpɪər-, *also* -ˈɒd-
permit (v.)	puhr MIT	pĕr mĭt′ § 12	pə ˈmɪt; *ES* pə-
—— (n.–"*leave; consent; license*")	PUHR mit	pûr′mĭt	ˈpɝ mɪt, pə ˈmɪt;
	puhr MIT	pĕr mĭt′ § 47(2)	*ES also* ˈpɝ-,
			ES pə-
pernicious	puhr NISH uhs	pĕr nĭsh′ŭs	pə ˈnɪʃ əs; *ES* pə-
peroration	*per* uh RAY shuhn	pĕr′ŏ rā′shŭn	ˌpɛr ə ˈre ʃən
		§ 50(30)	
	per oh RAY shuhn		ˌpɛr o ˈre ʃən
perpetuity	*puhr* pi TYOO uh ti	pûr′pĕ tū′ĭ tĭ	ˌpɝ pɪ ˈtju ə tɪ,
	puhr pi TOO uh ti		-ˈtu-, -ɪ tɪ; *ES*
	puhr pi TYOO i ti	pûr′pĕ tū′ĭ tĭ	*also* ˌpɝ-
	puhr pi TOO i ti	§§ 48(2), 50(32)	
persecute	PUHR si kyoot	pûr′sĕ kūt § 48(2)	ˈpɝ sɪ kjut; *ES*
			also ˈpɝ-

	SIMPLIFIED	DIACRITICAL	PHONETIC
persecutory	PUHR si *kyoo* tuh ri	pûr′sĕ kū′tŏ rĭ	ˈpɝ sɪ ˌkju tə rɪ, ˌpɝ sɪ ˈkju-; *ES*
	puhr si KYOO tuh ri	pûr′sĕ kū′tŏ rĭ § 48(2)	*also* ˈpɝ-, ˌpɝ-
perseverance	*puhr* si VĬER uhns	pûr′sĕ vĕr′ăns § 24(2)	ˌpɝ sɪ ˈvɪər əns, -ˈvɪr-, -ˈvir-;
	puhr si VIR uhns		*ES also* ˌpɝ-,
	puhr si VEER uhns	pûr′sĕ vēr′ăns	*ES* -vɪər-
Persia	PUHR zhuh	pûr′zhᴀ́	ˈpɝ ʒə, -ʃə; *ES*
	PUHR shuh	pûr′shᴀ́ § 50(27)	*also* ˈpɝ-
persiflage	PUHR si flahzh	pûr′sĭ fläzh	ˈpɝ sɪ flɑʒ,
	per si FLAHZH	pĕr′sĭ fläzh′	ˌper sɪ ˈflɑʒ; *ES*
	F., *per see* FLAHZH	F., pĕr′sĕ′fläzh′ § 47(3)	*also* ˈpɝ-, ˌpeə-; F., per si ˈflɑːʒ
persist	puhr SIST	pĕr sĭst′	pɚ ˈsɪst, -ˈzɪst; *ES*
	puhr ZIST	pĕr zĭst′ § 47(1)	pə-
persistence	puhr SIS tuhns	pĕr sĭs′tĕns	pɚ ˈsɪs təns, -ˈzɪs-;
	puhr ZIS tuhns	pĕr zĭs′tĕns	*ES* pə-
persistent	puhr SIS tuhnt	pĕr sĭs′tĕnt	pɚ ˈsɪs tənt, -ˈzɪs-;
	puhr ZIS tuhnt	pĕr zĭs′tĕnt	*ES* pə-
person	PUHR s′n	pûr′s′n	ˈpɝ sn̩; *ES also* ˈpɝ-
personal	PUHR suhn uhl	pûr′sŭn ăl § 33(2)	ˈpɝ sən əl, -sn̩ l̩; *ES also* ˈpɝ-
personality	*puhr* suh NAL uh ti	pûr′sŭ năl′ĭ tĭ	ˌpɝ sə ˈnæl ə tɪ, -sn̩ ˈæl-, -ɪ tɪ;
	puhr suh NAL i ti	pûr′sŭ năl′Ĭ tĭ	*ES also* ˌpɝ-
personnel	*puhr* suh NEL	pûr′sŏ nĕl′ § 47(2)	ˌpɝ sə ˈnɛl; *ES also* ˌpɝ-
perspiration	*puhr* spuh RAY shuhn	pûr′spĭ rā′shăn	ˌpɝ spə ˈre ʃən, -spɪ-; *ES also* ˌpɝ-
	puhr spi RAY shuhn	pûr′spĭ rā′shăn	
perspire	puhr SPAIR § 50(34)	pĕr spīr′	pɚ ˈspaɪr; *ES* pə ˈspaɪə(r)
persuasive	puhr SWAY siv	pĕr swā′sĭv § 47(2)	pɚ ˈswe sɪv; *ES* pə-
peruse	pi ROOZ	pĕ rōōz′	pɪ ˈruz
	puh ROOZ	pĕ rōōz′ § 48(2)	pə ˈruz
perverse	puhr VUHRS	pĕr vûrs′	pɚ ˈvɝs; *ES* pə-, *also* -ˈvɝs
perversion	puhr VUHR zhuhn	pĕr vûr′zhăn	pɚ ˈvɝ ʒən, -ʃən; *ES* pə-, *also* -ˈvɝ-
	puhr VUHR shuhn	pĕr vûr′shăn §§ 47(1), 50(28)	
pestle	PES ′l	pĕs′ ′l	ˈpɛs l̩
	PES t′l	pĕs′t′l § 47(2)	ˈpɛs tl̩
petal	PET ′l	pĕt′ ′l § 47(2)	ˈpɛt l̩
petition	pi TISH uhn	pĕ tĭsh′ăn	nɛ ʒɪt̚ ən

	SIMPLIFIED	DIACRITICAL	PHONETIC
phalanx	FAY langks	fā′lăngks	′fe læŋks
	FAL angks	făl′ăngks § 47(3)	′fæl æŋks
Pharaoh	FEHR oh	fâr′ō	′fɛr o, ′fe ro,
	FAY roh	fā′rō	′fɛr e o, -ɪ o; *ES*
	FEHR ay oh	fâr′ā ō § 47(3)	*also* ′fɛər o
pharyngeal	fuh RIN ji uhl	fă rĭn′jĕ ăl	fə ′rɪn dʒɪ əl
	far in JEE uhl	făr′ĭn jē′ăl	ˌfær ɪn ′dʒi əl
		§ 47(3)	
pharynx	FAR ingks	făr′ĭngks	′fær ɪŋks
phenomenon	fi NOM i non	fē nŏm′ē nŏn	fɪ ′nam ɪ nan; *ES*
			also -′nɒm ɪ nɒn
	B., fi NOM i	*B.*, fē nŏm′ē năn	*B.*, fɪ ′nɒm ɪ nən
	nuhn	§ 51(4)	
philanthropic	*fil* uhn THROP ik	fĭl′ăn thrŏp′ĭk	ˌfɪl ən ′θrap ɪk;
			ES also -′θrɒp-
philanthropist	fi LAN thruh pist	fĭ lăn′thrŏ pĭst	fɪ ′læn θrə pɪst
philanthropy	fi LAN thruh pi	fĭ lăn′thrŏ pĭ	fɪ ′læn θrə pi
Philistine (n.)	fuh LIS tin	fĭ lĭs′tĭn	fə ′lɪs tɪn
	FIL uhs tin	fĭl′ĭs tĭn	′fɪl əs tɪn
	FIL uhs teen	fĭl′ĭs tēn	′fɪl əs tin
	FIL is tain	fĭl′ĭs tīn	′fɪl ɪs taɪn
	fil IS teen	fĭl ĭs′tēn § 47(2)	fɪl ′ɪs tin
—— (adj.)	fuh LIS tin	fĭ lĭs′tĭn	fə ′lɪs tɪn
	FIL is tin	fĭl′ĭs tĭn § 28(6)	′fɪl ɪs tɪn
philosophic	*fil* uh SOF ik	fĭl′ŏ sŏf′ĭk	ˌfɪl ə ′saf ɪk; *ES*
		§ 47(2)	*also* -′sɒf-
phlegm	flem	flĕm	flɛm
phlegmatic	fleg MAT ik	flĕg măt′ĭk	flɛg ′mæt ɪk
		§ 47(2)	
Phoebe	FEE bi	fē′bē	′fi bɪ
phonograph	FOH nuh graf	fō′nŏ gráf	′fo nə græf; *E also*
	FOH nuh grahf	§ 20(5)	-graf, -graf
photographer	fuh TOG ruh fuhr	fŏ tŏg′rà fēr	fə ′tag rə fɚ, fo-,
			-′tɒg-; *ES*
			-′tɒg-, -fə(r)
physic	FIZ ik	fĭz′ĭk	′fɪz ɪk
physician	fuh ZISH uhn	fă zĭsh′ăn	fə ′zɪʃ ən
	fi ZISH uhn	fĭ zĭsh′ăn	fɪ ′zɪʃ ən
physicist	FIZ uh sist	fĭz′ĭ sĭst	′fɪz ə sɪst
	FIZ i sist	fĭz′ĭ sĭst	′fɪz ɪ sɪst
physiognomy	*fiz* i OG nuh mi	fĭz′ĭ ŏg′nŏ mĭ	ˌfɪz ɪ ′ag nə mɪ,
	fiz i ON uh mi	fĭz′ĭ ŏn′ŏ mĭ	-ɪ ′an ə-; *ES*
		§ 47(2)	*also* -′ɒg-, -′ɒn-
physique	fi ZEEK	fĭ zēk′	fɪ ′zik
pianist	pi AN ist	pĭ ăn′ĭst	pɪ ′æn ɪst
	PEE uh nist	pē′à nĭst § 47(3)	′pi ə nɪst

	SIMPLIFIED	DIACRITICAL	PHONETIC
piano (n.– *"stringed instrument of percussion"*)	pi AN oh pi AH noh	pĭ ăn′ō pĭ ä′nō § 47(2)	pɪ ˈæn o pɪ ˈɑ no
—— (adj., adv.)	pi AH noh	pĭ ä′nō	pɪ ˈɑ no
pianoforte	pi *an* uh FOHR ti pi *an* oh FOHR ti pi *an* uh FAWR ti pi *an* oh FAWR ti pi AN uh fohrt pi AN oh fohrt pi AN uh fawrt pi AN oh fawrt	pĭ ăn′ō fōr′tê § 34(3) pĭ ăn′ō fōrt §§ 34(3), 47(3)	pɪ ˌæn ə ˈfor tɪ, -ˈfɔr-, -ˌæn o-, -te; *ES* -ˈfoə-, *E also* -ˈfɔə- pɪ ˈæn ə fort, -fɔrt, -ˈæn o-; *ES* -foət, *E also* -fɔət
piazza	pi AZ uh	pĭ ăz′à	pɪ ˈæz ə
picot	PEE koh	pē′kō § 47(2)	ˈpi ko
picture	PIK chuhr PIK tyuhr	pĭk′tûr § 50(31)	ˈpɪk tʃɚ, -tjɚ; *ES* -tʃə(r), -tjə(r)
picturesque	*pik* chuhr ESK *pik* chuh RESK *pik* tyuhr ESK *pik* tyuh RESK	pĭk′tûr ĕsk′ § 50(33)	ˌpɪk tʃər ˈɛsk ˌpɪk tʃə ˈrɛsk ˌpɪk tjər ˈɛsk ˌpɪk tjə ˈrɛsk
pierce	pi͡ers pirs peers	pērs §§ 24(2), 47(2) pērs	pɪərs, pɪrs, pirs; *ES* pɪəs
Pierre (South Dakota)	pi͡er pir peer	pēr § 24(2) pēr	pɪər, pɪr, pir; *ES* pɪə(r)
piety	PAI͡ uh ti § 50(34)	pī′ĕ tĭ §§ 28(2), 34(24)	ˈpaɪ ə tɪ
pincers	PIN suhrz	pĭn′sĕrz	ˈpɪn sɚz; *ES* -səz
pioneer	*pai͡* uh NIER *pai͡* uh NIR *pai͡* uh NEER § 50(34)	pī′ō nēr′ §§ 24(2), 50(34) pī′ō nēr′	ˌpaɪ ə ˈnɪər, -ˈnɪr, -ˈnir; *ES* -ˈnɪə(r)
pious	PAI͡ uhs § 50(34)	pī′ŭs	ˈpaɪ əs
piquancy	PEE kuhn si	pē′kăn sĭ	ˈpi kən sɪ
piquant	PEE kuhnt	pē′kănt § 47(2)	ˈpi kənt
pique (*"anger"*)	peek	pēk § 51(7)	pik
Pisa	PEE zuh *It.*, PEE sah	pē′zà *It.*, pē′sä	ˈpi zə *It.*, ˈpi: sɑ
pismire	PIS *mai͡r* § 50(34)	pĭs′mīr′ § 47(2)	ˈpɪs ˌmaɪr; *ES* -ˌmaɪə(r)
piteous	PIT i uhs	pĭt′ê ŭs § 24(15)	ˈpɪt ɪ əs
pituitary	pi TYOO i ter i pi TOO i *ter* i *B.*, pi TYOO i tuhr i	pĭ tū′ĭ tĕr′ĭ §§ 20(2), 24(9), 40(4), 47(2), 48(2), 51(4) *B.*, pĭ tū′ĭ tēr ĭ	pɪ ˈtju ɪ ˌtɛr ɪ pɪ ˈtu ɪ ˌtɛr ɪ *B.*, pɪ ˈtju ɪ tə rɪ

	SIMPLIFIED	DIACRITICAL	PHONETIC
placard (n.)	PLAK ahrd PLAK uhrd	plăk′ärd plăk′ǎrd	'plæk ɑrd, -ɚd; *ES* -ɑːd, -əd; *E* *also* -aːd
—— (v.)	pluh KAHRD PLAK ahrd	plȧ kärd′ plăk′ärd §§ 12, 47(3)	plə 'kɑrd, plæ-, 'plæk ɑrd; *ES* -'kɑːd, -ɑːd, *E* *also* -'kaːd, -aːd
placid	PLAS id	plăs′ĭd	'plæs ɪd
plagiarism	PLAY ji uh riz'm PLAY ji uh riz uhm PLAY juh riz'm	plā′jĭ ȧ rĭz'm §§ 47(2), 50(15) plā′jȧ rĭz'm	'ple dʒɪ ə rɪzm̩, -dʒə rɪzm̩, -ə rɪz əm, -dʒə rɪz əm
plague	playg	plāg §§ 26(6), 40(13)	pleg
	Dial. or colloq.: pleg	*Dial. or colloq.:* plĕg § 51(2, 3)	*Dial. or colloq.:* plɛg
plaid	plad *Sc.,* playd	plăd *Sc.,* plād	plæd *Sc.,* pled
plait (n., v.t.)	playt pleet	plāt plēt § 47(2)	plet plit
—— "a braid; plaited fiber," often	plat playt	plăt plāt	plæt plet
—— "interweave; braid; felt," often	plat pleet	plăt plēt	plæt plit
plant	plant plahnt	plȧnt §§ 20(5), 47(2)	plænt; *E also* plant, plɑnt
plantain	PLAN tin	plăn′tĭn § 47(2)	'plæn tɪn
plasma	PLAZ muh	plăz′mȧ § 47(2)	'plæz mə
plateau	pla TOH	plȧ tō′	plæ 'to
play	play	plā	ple
plead (pres. t.)	pleed	plēd	plid
plebeian	pli BEE yuhn pli BEE uhn	plĕ bē′yăn plĕ bē′ăn § 47(2)	plɪ 'bi jən plɪ 'bi ən
plebeianism	pli BEE yuhn iz'm pli BEE uhn iz'm	plĕ bē′yăn ĭz'm plĕ bē′ăn ĭz'm § 50(15)	plɪ 'bi jən ɪzm̩, -'bi ən-, -ɪz əm
plebiscite	PLEB i sait PLEB i sit PLEE bi sait § 50(34)	plĕb′ĭ sīt plĕb′ĭ sĭt plē′bĭ sīt § 47(3)	'plɛb ɪ saɪt 'plɛb ɪ sɪt 'pli bɪ saɪt
Pleiades	PLEE yuh deez PLEE uh deez PLAI uh deez § 50(34)	plē′yȧ dēz plē′ȧ dēz plī′ȧ dēz §§ 47(3), 50(6)	'pli jə diz 'pli ə diz plaɪ ə diz
plenary	PLEE nuh ri PLEN uh ri	plē′nȧ rĭ plĕn′ȧ rĭ § 47(2)	'pli nə rɪ 'plɛn ə rɪ

	SIMPLIFIED	DIACRITICAL	PHONETIC
plenipotentiary	*plen* i puh TEN shi *er* i	plĕn′ĭ pŏ tĕn′shĭ ĕr′ĭ	ˌplɛn ɪ pə 'tɛn ʃɪ ˌɛr ɪ
	plen i puh TEN shi *ay* ri	plĕn′ĭ pŏ tĕn′shĭ ã′rĭ	ˌplɛn ɪ pə 'tɛn ʃɪ ˌe rɪ
	plen i puh TEN shi uhr i	plĕn′ĭ pŏ tĕn′shĭ ẽr ĭ	ˌplɛn ɪ pə 'tɛn ʃɪ ər ɪ
	plen i puh TEN shuh ri	plĕn′ĭ pŏ tĕn′shȧ rĭ §§ 20(2), 24(9), 47(3)	ˌplɛn ɪ pə 'tɛn ʃə rɪ
plenty	PLEN ti	plĕn′tĭ	'plɛn tɪ
pleurisy	PLŌOR uh si	plŏŏr′ĭ̆ sĭ	'plʊr ə sɪ
	PLŌOR i si	plŏŏr′ĭ sĭ	'plʊr ɪ sɪ
	PLŌOR i si	plŏŏr′ĭ sĭ §§ 40(4), 47(3), 48(2)	'plʊr ɪ sɪ
plexus	PLEK suhs	plĕk′sŭs	'plɛk səs
plod	plod	plŏd	plɑd; *ES also* plɒd
plover	PLUHV uhr	plŭv′ẽr	'plʌv ɚ, 'plo vɚ; *ES* -ə(r), -və(r)
	PLOH vuhr	plō′vẽr	
plumber	PLUHM uhr	plŭm′ẽr	'plʌm ɚ; *ES* -ə(r)
plume	ploom	plŏŏm §§ 40(4), 47(2), 48(2)	plum
plural	PLŌOR uhl	plŏŏr′ăl §§ 40(4), 47(2), 48(2)	'plʊr əl
pneumatic	nyoo MAT ik	nû mắt′ĭk	nju 'mæt ɪk
	noo MAT ik	§§ 35(1), 48(2), 50(32)	nu 'mæt ɪk
pneumonia	nyoo MOH ni uh	nû mō′nĭ ȧ	nju 'mo nɪ ə, nu-,
	noo MOH ni uh	§§ 28(9), 35(1),	-'mon jə
	nyoo MOHN yuh	48(2), 50(32)	
	noo MOHN yuh		
poem	POH em	pō′ĕm	'po ɛm, -ɪm, -əm
	POH im	pō′ĭm § 24(5)	
poet	POH et	pō′ĕt	'po ɛt, -ɪt, -ət
	POH it	pō′ĭt § 24(5)	
poetaster	POH et *as* tuhr	pō′ĕt ăs′tẽr	'po ɛt ˌæs tɚ,
	POH it *as* tuhr	pō′ĭt ăs′tẽr	ˌpo ɛt ˈæs-,
	poh et AS tuhr	pō′ĕt ăs′tẽr	-ɪt-, -ət-; *ES*
	poh it AS tuhr	pō′ĭt ăs′tẽr § 47(1)	-tə(r)
poignancy	POIN yuhn si	poin′yăn sĭ	'pɔɪn jən sɪ
	POIN uhn si	poin′ăn sĭ	'pɔɪn ən sɪ
poignant	POIN yuhnt	poin′yănt	'pɔɪn jənt
	POIN uhnt	poin′ănt	'pɔɪn ənt
point	point	point	pɔɪnt
poison	POI z'n	poi′z'n § 9	'pɔɪ zn̩

police	puh LEES *Dial. or* *humorous:* POH lees POH lis	pŏ lēs′ *Dial. or* *humorous:* pō′lēs pō′lĭs § 51(2, 11)	pə ′lis *Dial. or* *humorous:* ′po lis ′po lɪs
policeman	puh LEES muhn	pŏ lēs′măn § 50(21)	pə ′lis mən
politic	POL uh tik POL i tik	pŏl′ĭ tĭk pŏl′ĭ tĭk	′pɑl ə tɪk, -ɪ tɪk; *ES also* ′pɒl-
pollen	POL uhn	pŏl′ĕn	′pɑl ən; *ES also* ′pɒl-
poltroon	pol TROON	pŏl trōōn′	pɑl ′trun; *ES* pɒl-
polygamy	puh LIG uh mi	pŏ lĭg′á mĭ	pə ′lɪg ə mɪ
polyglot	POL i glot	pŏl′ĭ glŏt	′pɑl ɪ glɑt; *ES* *also* ′pɒl ɪ glɒt
pomegranate	POM *gran* it PUHM *gran* it puhm GRAN it *puhm* GRAN it pom GRAN it	pŏm′grăn′ĭt pŭm′grăn′ĭt pŏm grăn′ĭt pŭm grăn′ĭt pŏm grăn′ĭt §§ 40(6), 47(3), 50(2)	′pɑm ˌgræn ɪt, ′pʌm-, pəm ′græn-, pʌm-, pɑm-; *ES also* ′pɒm ˌgræn-, pɒm ′græn-
pommel (n., v.t.)	PUHM uhl PUHM ′l	pŭm′ĕl pŭm′ ′l	′pʌm əl, -]-, ′pɑm; *ES also* ′pɒm-
—— (n.–also)	POM ′l	pŏm′ ′l § 1	′pɑm], -əl; *ES* *also* ′pɒm-
pond	pond	pŏnd	pɑnd, pɔnd, pɒnd
poor	pŏŏr	pŏŏr §§ 24(5), 34(21), 40(4)	pʊr; *ES* pʊə(r), poə(r), *E also* pɔə(r)
popular	POP yŏŏ luhr	pŏp′û lēr	′pɑp jʊ lɚ, -jə-, -ju-; *ES* -lə(r), *also* ′pɒp-
porcelain	POHR suh lin PAWR suh lin POHRS lin PAWRS lin	pōr′sĕ lĭn pōrs′lĭn §§ 34(3), 47(3)	′por sə lɪn, ′pɔr-, ′pors lɪn, ′pɔrs-; *ES* ′poə-, ′poəs-, *E also* ′pɔə-, ′pɔəs-
pore	pohr pawr	pōr § 34(3)	por, pɔr; *ES* poə(r), *E also* pɔə(r)
pork	pohrk pawrk	pōrk § 34(3)	pork, pɔrk; *ES* poək, *E also* pɔək
porpoise	PAWR puhs	pôr′pŭs § 47(2)	′pɔr pəs; *ES* ′pɔə-
port	pohrt pawrt	pōrt § 34(3)	port, pɔrt; *ES* poət, *E also* pɔət

	SIMPLIFIED	DIACRITICAL	PHONETIC
portend	pohr TEND pawr TEND	pōr tĕnd′ pôr tend′ § 34(3)	por ′tend, pər-; *ES* poə-, *E also* pɔə-
portent	POHR tent PAWR tent	pōr′tĕnt §§ 34(3), 47(2), 51(4)	′por tent, ′pər-; *ES* ′poə-, *E also* ′pɔə-
	B., POHR tuhnt PAWR tuhnt	*B.,* pōr′tĕnt pôr′tĕnt	*B.,* ′por tənt, ′pər-; *ES* ′poə-, *E also* -′pɔə-
portentous	pohr TEN tuhs pawr TEN tuhs	pōr tĕn′tŭs §§ 34(3), 50(25)	por ′tɛn təs, pər-; *ES* poə-, *E also* pɔə-
Portia	POHR shi uh PAWR shi uh POHR shuh PAWR shuh	pōr′shĭ *a* pōr′sh*a* §§ 34(3), 50(29)	′por ʃɪ ə, ′pər-; ′por ʃə, ′pər-; *ES* ′poə-, *E also* ′pɔə-
portiere, portière	pohr TYEHR pawr TYEHR pohr ti EHR pawr ti EHR	pōr tyâr′ pōr tĭ âr′ *F.,* pôr′tyâr′	por ′tjer, pər-, -tɪ ′ɛr; *ES* poə-, pɔə-, *E* *also* -′tjeə(r), -′ɛə(r); *F.,* pör ′tjeːr
portion	POHR shuhn PAWR shuhn	pōr′shŭn §§ 34(3), 50(30)	′por ʃən, ′pər-; *ES* ′poə-, *E also* ′pɔə-
portmanteau	pohrt MAN toh pawrt MAN toh	pōrt măn′tō § 34(3)	port ′mæn to, pərt-; *ES* poət-, *E also* pɔət-
portrait	POHR trayt PAWR trayt POHR trit PAWR trit	pōr′trāt pōr′trĭt § 34(3)	′por tret, ′pər-, -trɪt; *ES* ′poə-, *E also* ′pɔə-
portray	pohr TRAY pawr TRAY	pōr trā′ § 34(3)	por ′tre, pər-; *ES* poə-, *E also* ′pɔə-
Portuguese	POHR choo geez PAWR choo geez POHR choo gees PAWR choo gees	pōr′tŭ gēz pōr′tŭ gēs §§ 38(6), 50(7)	′por tʃu giz, ′pər-, -gis, -tʃə-; *ES* ′poə-, *E also* ′pɔə-
positive	POZ uh tiv POZ i tiv	pŏz′ĭ tĭv pŏz′ĭ tĭv § 50(17)	′paz ə tɪv, -ɪ tɪv; *ES also* ′pɒz-
positively	POZ uh tiv li POZ i tiv li	pŏz′ĭ tĭv lĭ pŏz′ĭ tĭv lĭ § 50(20)	′paz ə tɪv lɪ, -ɪ tɪv-; *ES also* ′pɒz-
	Emph., occ.: poz i TIV li	*Emph., occ.:* pŏz′ĭ tĭv′lĭ § 51(11)	*Emph., occ.:* ˌpaz ɪ ′tɪv lɪ; *ES* *also* ˌpɒz-
possess	puh ZES	pŏ zĕs′ § 47(2)	pə ′zɛs
post	pohst	pōst	post

	SIMPLIFIED	DIACRITICAL	PHONETIC
posterior	pos TĬER i uhr pos TIR i uhr pos TEER i uhr	pŏs tẽr′ĭ ẽr § 24(2) pŏs tēr′ĭ ẽr	pɑs ′tɪər ɪ ɚ, -′tɪr-, -′tir-; *ES* -′tɪər ɪ ə(r), *also* pɒs-
posthumous	POS chŏŏ muhs POS tyŏŏ muhs	pŏs′tŭ mŭs §§ 47(2), 50(25, 33)	′pɑs tʃʊ məs, -tjʊ-, -tju-; *ES* *also* ′pɒs-
postscript	POHST skript POHS skript	pōst′skrĭpt pōs′skrĭpt § 47(1)	′post skrɪpt ′pos skrɪpt
posture	POS chuhr POS tyuhr	pŏs′tûr § 50(31)	′pɑs tʃɚ, -tjɚ; *ES* -tʃə(r), -tjə(r), *also* ′pɒs-
potato	puh TAY toh	pŏ tā′tō § 34(12)	pə ′te to, -tə
potent	POH tuhnt	pō′tĕnt § 24(14)	′po tənt, -tṇt
Poughkeepsie	puh KIP si	pŏ kĭp′sĭ	pə ′kɪp sɪ
poultice	POHL tis	pōl′tĭs	′pol tɪs
poultry	POHL tri	pōl′trĭ	′pol trɪ
Prague	prahg prayg	präg prāg	prɑg preg
prairie	PREHR i PRAY ri	prâr′ĭ §§ 20(2), 47(2)	′prɛr ɪ, ′prɛ rɪ; *ES* *also* ′prɛər ɪ
prayer (*"act of praying"*)	prehr	prâr § 47(2)	prɛr, prær; *ES* præə(r), *E also* prɛə(r)
prayer (*"one who prays"*)	PRAY uhr	prā′ẽr	′pre ɚ; *ES* -ə(r)
preamble	PREE *am* b'l pri AM b'l	prē′ăm′b'l prē ăm′b'l § 49(13)	′pri ˌæm bḷ prɪ ′æm bḷ
precarious	pri KEHR i uhs pri KAY ri uhs	prē kâr′ĭ ŭs § 49(13)	prɪ ′kɛr ɪ əs, -′kær-, -′ke rɪ-; *ES also* -′kɛər-
precede	pree SEED	prē sēd′ §§ 11, 49(13)	prɪ ′sid
precedence	pri SEED uhns pree SEED uhns PRES i duhns	prē sēd′ĕns prē sēd′ĕns prĕs′ĭ dĕns	prɪ ′sid əns prɪ ′sid əns ′prɛs ɪ dəns
precedent (adj.)	pri SEED uhnt pree SEED uhnt PRES i duhnt	prē sēd′ĕnt prē sēd′ĕnt prĕs′ĭ dĕnt	prɪ ′sid ənt prɪ ′sid ənt ′prɛs ɪ dənt
—— (n.)	PRES i duhnt	prĕs′ĕ dĕnt § 47(2)	′prɛs ɪ dənt
—— (v.t.)	PRES i dent	prĕs′ĕ dĕnt	′prɛs ɪ dent
preceptor	pri SEP tuhr	prē sĕp′tẽr	prɪ ′sɛp tɚ; *ES* -tə(r)
precinct (n.)	PREE singkt	prē′sĭngkt	′pri sɪŋkt
precise	pri SAIS § 50(34)	prē sīs′ § 49(13)	prɪ ′saɪs

	SIMPLIFIED	DIACRITICAL	PHONETIC
precision	pri SIZH uhn	prĕ sĭzh′ŭn	prɪ 'sɪʒ ən
preclude	pri KLOOD	prĕ klōōd′ §§ 40(4), 47(2), 48(2)	prɪ 'klud
precocious	pri KOH shuhs	prĕ kō′shŭs	prɪ 'ko ʃəs
precocity	pri KOS uh ti pri KOS i ti	prĕ kŏs′ĭ tĭ prĕ kŏs′ĭ tĭ	prɪ 'kɑs ə tɪ, -ɪ tɪ; ES also -'kɒs-
precursor	pri KUHR suhr pree KUHR suhr	prĕ kûr′sĕr prĕ kûr′sēr	prɪ 'kɝ sɚ, prɪ-; ES also -'kɝ-, Eɔ -sə(r)
predatory	PRED uh *toh* ri PRED uh *taw* ri B., PRED uh tuhr i	prĕd′á tō′rĭ §§ 34(3), 51(4) B., prĕd′á tēr ĭ	'prɛd ə ˌto rɪ 'prɛd ə ˌtɔ rɪ B., 'prɛd ə tə rɪ
predecessor	*prĕd* i SES uhr PRED i *ses* uhr B., PREE di *ses* uhr *pree* di SES uhr	prĕd′ĕ sĕs′ĕr prĕd′ĕ sĕs′ĕr § 47(3) B., prē′dĕ sĕs′ĕr prē′dĕ sĕs′ĕr § 51(4)	ˌprɛd ɪ 'sɛs ɚ, 'prɛd ɪ ˌsɛs-; ES -ə(r) B., 'pri dɪ ˌsɛs ɚ, ˌpri dɪ 'sɛs-; ES -ə(r)
predilection	*pree* di LEK shuhn *pred* uh LEK shuhn *pred* i LEK shuhn	prē′dĭ lĕk′shŭn prĕd′ĭ lĕk′shŭn prĕd′ĭ lĕk′shŭn	ˌpri dɪ 'lɛk ʃən ˌprɛd ə 'lɛk ʃən ˌprɛd ḷ 'ɛk ʃən ˌprɛd ɪ 'lɛk ʃən
preface	PREF is	prĕf′ĭs	'prɛf ɪs, -əs
prefer	pri FUHR	prĕ fûr′ § 49(13)	prɪ 'fɝ; ES also -'fɝ(r)
preferable	PREF uhr uh b'l	prĕf′ēr á b'l § 9	'prɛf ər ə bḷ, 'prɛf rə bḷ
preferment	pri FUHR muhnt	prĕ fûr′mĕnt § 50(22)	prɪ 'fɝ mənt; ES also -'fɝ-
prefix (n.)	PREE fiks	prē′fĭks	'pri fɪks
—— (v.t.)	pree FIKS	prē fĭks′	pri 'fɪks
——"*put before another thing; add, as a prefix,*"	pri FIKS	prĕ fĭks′ § 49(13)	prɪ 'fɪks
prejudice	PREJ ŏŏ dis	prĕj′ŏŏ dĭs §§ 40(11), 47(2)	'prɛdʒ ʊ dɪs, 'prɛdʒ ə-
prelate	PREL it	prĕl′ĭt § 50(2)	'prɛl ɪt
prelude (n., v.)	PREL yood PREE lood PREE lyood	prĕl′ūd prē′lūd F., prĕ lüd′	'prɛl jud 'pri lud 'pri ljud
—— (occasionally, verb also)	pri LOOD pri LYOOD	prĕ lūd′ §§ 12, 48(2)	prɪ 'lud prɪ 'ljud

	SIMPLIFIED	DIACRITICAL	PHONETIC
premature	*pree* muh TYOOR *pree* muh TYOOR *pree* muh TOOR *pree* muh TOOR	prē′mȧ tūr′ §§ 11, 40(4), 47(3), 49(13), 50(32)	ˌpri mə ˈtjʊr, -ˈtʊr; *ES* -ˈtjuə(r), -ˈtʊə(r)
	PREE muh *choŏr* PREE muh *tyoŏr* PREE muh *toŏr*	prē′mȧ tūr′ §§ 47(1), 50(33)	ˈpri mə ˌtʃʊr, -ˌtjʊr, -ˌtʊr; *ES* -ˌtʃuə(r), -ˌtjuə(r), -ˌtʊə(r)
	B., *prem* uh TYOOR PREM uh *tyoŏr*	*B.*, prĕm′ȧ tūr′ prĕm′ȧ tūr § 51(4)	*B.*, ˌprɛm ə ˈtjʊr, ˈprɛm ə tjʊr; *ES* -ˈtjuə(r), -tjuə(r)
premier (adj.)	PREE mi uhr PREM yuhr	prē′mĭ ẽr prĕm′yẽr	ˈpri mi ɚ, ˈprɛm jɚ; *ES* -ə(r), -jə(r)
—— (n., v.i.)	PREE mi uhr pri MIER pri MIR pri MEER PREM yuhr	prē′mĭ ẽr prĕ mẽr′ prĕ mẽr′ prĕm′yẽr §§ 24(2), 47(3)	ˈpri mi ɚ, prɪ ˈmɪər, -ˈmɪr, -ˈmir, ˈprɛm jɚ, ˈprɛm ɪ ɚ; *ES* -ə(r), -ˈmɪə(r), -jə(r)
premise (n.)	PREM is	prĕm′ĭs	ˈprɛm ɪs
—— (v.)	pri MAIZ § 50(34)	prĕ mīz′	prɪ ˈmaɪz, ˈprɛm ɪs
preparatory	pri PAR uh *toh* ri pri PAR uh *taw* ri *B.*, pri PAR uh tuhr i pri PAR uh tri	prĕ păr′ȧ tō′rĭ §§ 34(3), 51(4) *B.*, prĕ păr′ȧ tẽr ĭ prĕ păr′ȧ trĭ	prɪ ˈpær ə ˌto rɪ prɪ ˈpær ə ˌtɔ rɪ *B.*, prɪ ˈpær ə tə rɪ prɪ ˈpær ə trɪ
preponderant	pri PON duhr uhnt	prĕ pŏn′dẽr ănt §§ 9, 49(13)	prɪ ˈpɑn dər ənt; *ES also* -ˈpɒn-
prerogative	pri ROG uh tiv	prĕ rŏg′ȧ tĭv § 50(3)	prɪ ˈrɑg ə tɪv, -ˈrɒg-
presage (n.)	PRES ij	prĕs′ĭj	ˈprɛs ɪdʒ
—— (v.)	pri SAYJ	prĕ sāj′	prɪ ˈsedʒ
Presbyterian	*prez* buh TIER i uhn *prez* buh TIR i uhn	prĕz′bĭ tẽr′ĭ ăn § 24(2)	ˌprez bə ˈtɪər ɪ ən, -bɪ-, -ˈtɪr-, -ˈtir-; *ES* -ˈtɪər-
	prez buh TEER i uhn	prĕz′bĭ tẽr′ĭ ăn	
	pres buh TIER i uhn *pres* buh TIR i uhn	prĕs′bĭ tẽr′ĭ ăn §§ 24(2), 47(1)	ˌpres bə ˈtɪər ɪ ən, -bɪ-, -ˈtɪr-, -ˈtir-; *ES* -ˈtɪər-
	pres buh TEER i uhn	prĕs′bĭ tẽr′ĭ ăn	

	SIMPLIFIED	DIACRITICAL	PHONETIC
prescience	PREE shi uhns	prē′shĭ ĕns	ˈpri ʃɪ əns
	PRESH i uhns	prĕsh′ĭ ĕns	ˈpreʃ ɪ əns
		§ 47(2)	
prescribe	pri SKRAIB	prē skrīb′	prɪ ˈskraɪb
	§ 50(34)		
prescription	pri SKRIP shuhn	prē skrĭp′shŭn	prɪ ˈskrɪp ʃən
present (v.)	pri ZENT	prē zĕnt′	prɪ ˈzɛnt
—— (adj., n.)	PREZ uhnt	prĕz′ĕnt	ˈprez ənt
	PREZ ′nt	prĕz′ ′nt	ˈprez n̩t
		§ 24(14)	
——(n.–*Military*)	pri ZENT	prē zĕnt′	prɪ ˈzɛnt
presentation	*prez* uhn TAY shuhn	prĕz′ĕn tā′shŭn	ˌprez ən ˈte ʃən
			ˌprez n̩ ˈte ʃən
	pree zen TAY shuhn	prē′zĕn tā′shŭn	ˌpri zɛn ˈte ʃən
presentiment	pri ZEN tuh muhnt	prē zĕn′tĭ mĕnt	prɪ ˈzɛn tə mənt
	pri ZEN ti muhnt	prē zĕn′tĭ mĕnt	prɪ ˈzɛn tɪ mənt
	pri SEN tuh muhnt	prē sĕn′tĭ mĕnt	prɪ ˈsɛn tə mənt
	pri SEN ti muhnt	prē sĕn′tĭ mĕnt	prɪ ˈsɛn tɪ mənt
		§ 47(1)	
preserve	pri ZUHRV	prē zûrv′	prɪ ˈzɝv; *ES also* -ˈzɜv
prestige	pres TEEZH	prĕs tēzh′	pres ˈtiʒ
	PRES tij	prĕs′tĭj § 47(3)	ˈpres tɪdʒ
presumable	pri ZYOOM uh b'l	prē zūm′ȧ b'l	prɪ ˈzjʊm ə bl̩
	pri ZOOM uh b'l	§§ 48(2), 50(32)	prɪ ˈzum ə bl̩
presumption	pri ZUHMP shuhn	prē zŭmp′shŭn	prɪ ˈzʌmp ʃən
		§ 35(2)	
presumptive	pri ZUHMP tiv	prē zŭmp′tĭv	prɪ ˈzʌmp tɪv
presumptuous	pri ZUHMP choo uhs	prē zŭmp′tû ŭs	prɪ ˈzʌmp tʃʊ əs
		§ 50(25, 33)	
	pri ZUHMP tyoo uhs		prɪ ˈzʌmp tjʊ əs
pretend	pri TEND	prē tĕnd′	prɪ ˈtɛnd
pretense, pretence	pri TENS	prē tĕns′	prɪ ˈtɛns
	PREE tens	prē′tĕns, § 11	ˈpri tɛns
pretext (n.)	PREE tekst	prē′tĕkst § 47(2)	ˈpri tɛkst
	Occas.:	*Occas.:*	*Occas.:*
	pri TEKST	prē tĕkst′	prɪ ˈtɛkst
		§ 51(8)	
—— (v.t.)	pri TEKST	prē tĕkst′ § 12	prɪ ˈtɛkst
prettily (adv.–See *pretty*.)	PRIT uh li	prĭt′ĭ lĭ	ˈprɪt ə lɪ
	PRIT i li	prĭt′ĭ lĭ § 50(20)	ˈprɪt ɪ lɪ
pretty	PRIT i	prĭt′ĭ	ˈprɪt ɪ
	Unstressed, occ.:	*Unstressed, occ.:*	*Unstressed, occ.:*
	P'RT i	p'rt′ĭ § 16	ˈpr̩t ɪ

	SIMPLIFIED	DIACRITICAL	PHONETIC
prevalence	PREV uh luhns	prĕv′á lĕns	ˈprɛv ə ləns
prevalent	PREV uh luhnt	prĕv′á lĕnt	ˈprɛv ə lənt
prevaricate	pri VAR uh kayt	prĕ văr′ĭ kāt	prɪ ˈvær ə ket
	pri VAR i kayt	prĕ văr′ĭ kāt	prɪ ˈvær ɪ ket
preventive	pri VEN tiv	prĕ vĕn′tĭv § 49(13)	prɪ ˈvɛn tɪv
Priam	PRA͞I uhm	prī′ăm	ˈpraɪ əm
	PRA͞I am § 50(34)	prī′ăm	ˈpraɪ æm
primarily	PRA͞I mer uh li	prī′mĕr ĭ lĭ	ˈpraɪ mɛr ə lɪ
	PRA͞I mer i li	prī′mĕr ĭ lĭ	ˈpraɪ mɛr ɪ lɪ
	PRA͞I muh ruh li	prī′má rĭ lĭ	ˈpraɪ mə rə lɪ
	PRA͞I muh ri li	prī′má rĭ lĭ	ˈpraɪ mə rɪ lɪ
	Emph., also:	*Emph., also:*	*Emph., also:*
	prai MEHR uh li	prī mâr′ĭ lĭ	praɪ ˈmɛr ə lɪ,
	prai MEHR i li § 50(34)	prī mâr′ĭ lĭ §§ 11, 20(2), 24(9), 50(20), 51(11)	-ˈmær-, -ˈme rɪ-, -ɪ lɪ; *ES also* -ˈmæær-, *E also* -ˈmɛər-
primer (*"book"*)	PRIM uhr	prĭm′ĕr § 51(7)	ˈprɪm ɚ; *ES* -ə(r)
primer (*"preparer"*)	PRA͞IM uhr § 50(34)	prīm′ĕr § 51(7)	ˈpraɪm ɚ; *ES* -ə(r)
primogeniture	*prai* moh JEN uh chuhr	prī′mŏ jĕn′ĭ tûr	ˌpraɪ mo ˈdʒɛn ə tʃɚ, -ˌtʃʊr,
	prai moh JEN uh tyuhr		-tjɚ, -mə-, -ˈdʒɛn ɪ-; *ES*
	prai moh JEN i chuhr	prī′mŏ jĕn′ĭ tûr § 50(31)	-tʃə(r), -ˌtʃʊə(r),
	prai moh JEN i tyuhr		-tjə(r)
primordial	prai MAWR di uhl § 50(34)	prī môr′dĭ ăl	praɪ ˈmɔr dɪ əl; *ES* -ˈmɔə dɪ-
princess	PRIN ses	prĭn′sĕs	ˈprɪn sɛs
	PRIN sis	prĭn′sĭs §§ 24(5), 50(8)	ˈprɪn sɪs
prism	PRIZ′M	prĭz′m	ˈprɪzm̩
	PRIZ ′m		ˈprɪz m̩
	PRIZ uhm	§§ 9, 32(2), 50(15)	ˈprɪz əm
prison	PRIZ ′n	prĭz′ ′n	ˈprɪz n̩
pristine	PRIS teen	prĭs′tēn	ˈprɪs tin
	PRIS tin	prĭs′tĭn § 47(3)	ˈprɪs tɪn
	B., PRIS ta͞in § 50(34)	*B.,* prĭs′tīn §§ 28(6), 51(4)	*B.,* ˈprɪs taɪn
privacy	PRA͞I vuh si § 50(34)	prī′vá sĭ § 47(3)	ˈpraɪ və sɪ
privilege	PRIV uh lij	prĭv′ĭ lĭj	ˈprɪv ə lɪdʒ
	PRIV i lij	prĭv′ĭ lĭj	ˈprɪv ɪ lɪdʒ

	SIMPLIFIED	DIACRITICAL	PHONETIC
probably	PROB uh bli	prŏb'*a* blĭ § 50(20)	'prab ə blɪ; *ES* *also* 'prɒb-
probity	PROB uh ti PROB i ti PROH buh ti PROH bi ti	prŏb'*i* tĭ prŏb'ĭ tĭ prō'bĭ tĭ prō'bĭ tĭ §§ 47(1), 50(16)	'prab ə tɪ, -ɪ tɪ; *ES also* 'prɒb- 'pro bə tɪ 'pro bɪ tɪ
procedure	pruh SEE juhr pruh SEE dyuhr	prō sē'dûr § 40(11), 49(14), 50(33)	prə 'si dʒɚ, -djɚ, pro-; *ES* -dʒə(r), -djə(r)
proceed (v.) proceeds (n. pl.)	pruh SEED PROH seedz	prō sēd' § 49(14) prō'sēdz §§ 47(2), 48(3)	prə 'sid, pro- 'pro sidz
process (n., v.t.)	PROS es *B.*, PROH ses	prŏs'ĕs *B.*, prō'sĕs § 51(4)	'pras ɛs; *ES also* 'prɒs- *B.*, 'pro sɛs
processes (n. pl.)	PROS es ez PROS es iz *B.*, PROH ses iz *Among anatom- ists, occ.:* PROS es eez *B.*, PROH ses eez	prŏs'ĕs ĕz prŏs'ĕs ĭz *B.*, prō'sĕs ĭz *Among anatom- ists, occ.:* prŏs'ĕs ēz *B.*, prō'sĕs ēz §§ 48(3), 51(4)	'pras ɛs ɛz, -ɛs ɪz; *ES also* 'prɒs- *B.*, 'pro sɛs ɪz *Among anatom- ists, occ.:* 'pras ɛs iz; *ES* *also* 'prɒs- *B.*, 'pro sɛs iz
procession	pruh SESH uhn	prō sĕsh'ŭn § 49(14)	prə 'sɛʃ ən, pro-
procurator	PROK yŏŏ *ray* tuhr	prŏk'û rā'tēr	'prak jʊ ˌre tɚ, -ju-; *ES also* 'prɒk-, *ES* -tə(r)
prodigal	PROD uh guhl PROD i guhl PROD uh g'l	prŏd'*i* gŭl prŏd'ĭ gŭl prŏd'*i* g'l	'prad ə gəl, -ɪ gəl, -gl̩; *ES also* 'prɒd-
prodigy	PROD uh ji PROD i ji	prŏd'*i* jĭ prŏd'ĭ jĭ	'prad ə dʒɪ, -ɪ dʒɪ; *ES also* 'prɒd-
produce (v.)	pruh DYOOS pruh DOOS	prō dūs' §§ 40(4), 47(2), 48(2), 50(32)	prə 'djus, -'dus, pro-
—— (n., adj.)	PROD yoos	prŏd'ūs	'prad jus; *ES also* 'prɒd-
production	pruh DUHK shuhn	prō dŭk'shŭn § 49(14)	prə 'dʌk ʃən, pro-
profanation	*prof* uh NAY shuhn	prŏf'*a* nā'shŭn	ˌpraf ə 'ne ʃən; *ES* *also* ˌprɒf-
professor	pruh FES uhr	prō fĕs'ēr	prə 'fɛs ɚ, pro-; *ES* -ə(r)

SIMPLIFIED	DIACRITICAL	PHONETIC
proffer PROF uhr	prŏf'ẽr	'prɑf ɚ; *ES also* 'prɒf-, *ES* -ə(r)
profile (n.) PROH fa͡il *B.,* PROH feel	prō'fīl *B.,* prō'fēl §§ 47(3), 51(4)	'pro faɪl *B.,* 'pro fil
profligacy PROF luh guh si PROF li guh si	prŏf'lĭ gȧ sĭ prŏf'lĭ gȧ sĭ	'prɑf lə gə sɪ, -lɪ-; *ES also* 'prɒf-
progenitor proh JEN uh tuhr proh JEN i tuhr	prŏ jĕn'ĭ tẽr prŏ jĕn'ĭ tẽr	pro 'dʒɛn ə tɚ, -ɪ tɚ; *ES* -ə tə(r), -ɪ tə(r)
program (n.) PROH gram *Gaining ground:* PROH gruhm	prō'grăm § 47(1) *Gaining ground:* prō'grăm § 51(5)	'pro græm *Gaining ground:* 'pro grəm
progress (n.) PROG res *B.,* PROH gres	prŏg'rĕs §§ 12, 47(3) *B.,* prō'grĕs § 51(4)	'prɑg rɛs; *ES also* 'prɒg- *B.,* 'pro grɛs
—— (v.) pruh GRES	prŏ grĕss' § 49(14)	prə 'grɛs, pro-
project (v.) pruh JEKT	prŏ jĕkt' §§ 11, 49(14)	prə 'dʒɛkt, pro-
—— (n.) PROJ ekt PROJ ikt	prŏj'ĕkt prŏj'ĭkt § 47(3)	'prɑdʒ ɛkt, -ɪkt; *ES also* 'prɒdʒ-
projectile pruh JEK til proh JEK til	prŏ jĕk'tĭl §§ 28(5), 49(14), 50(13)	prə 'dʒɛk tɪl pro 'dʒɛk tɪl
proletarian *proh* li TEHR i uhn *proh* li TAY ri uhn	prō'lĕ târ'ĭ ăn prō'lĕ tā'rĭ ăn § 47(1)	ˌpro lɪ 'tɛr ɪ ən, -'tær-, -'te rɪ-, ˌprɑl ɪ-; *ES also* ˌprɒl-, -'tɛər-, *E* -'tɛɚ-
proletariat *proh* li TEHR i uht *proh* li TAY ri uht	prō'lĕ târ'ĭ ăt	ˌpro lɪ 'tɛr ɪ ət, -'tær-, -'te rɪ-, ˌprɑl ɪ-; *ES also* ˌprɒl-, -'tɛər-, *E* -'tɛɚ-
prolific pruh LIF ik	prŏ lĭf'ĭk	prə 'lɪf ɪk, pro-
prolix proh LIKS PROH liks	prŏ lĭks' prō'lĭks § 11	pro 'lɪks 'pro lɪks
prolixity proh LIK suh ti proh LIK si ti	prŏ lĭk'sĭ tĭ prŏ lĭk'sĭ tĭ	pro 'lɪk sə tɪ pro 'lɪk sɪ tɪ
prologue, prolog PROH lawg PROH log	prō'lôg §§ 34(7), 47(3), 49(14)	'pro lɔg, -lɒg, -lag
promenade *prom* i NAHD *prom* i NAYD	prŏm'ĕ näd' prŏm'ĕ nād' § 47(3)	ˌprɑm ɪ 'nɑd, ˌprɑm ɪ 'ned; *ES also* ˌprɒm-

	SIMPLIFIED	DIACRITICAL	PHONETIC
Prometheus	pruh MEE thyoos pruh MEE thi uhs	prŏ mē′thūs prŏ mē′thĕ ŭs	prə ′mi θjus, -θɪ əs, pro-
prominent	PROM uh nuhnt PROM i nuhnt	prŏm′ĭ nĕnt prŏm′ĭ nĕnt	′pram ə nənt, -ɪ nənt; *ES also* ′prɒm-

promulgate	pruh MUHL gayt
	B., PROM uhl
	   gayt
	   PROH *muhl*
	   gayt
		prŏ mŭl′gāt
		B., prŏm′ŭl gāt
		
		prō′mŭl gāt
		  §§ 40(6),
		  47(3), 51(4)
			prə ′mʌl get
			B., ′prɒm əl get
			
			′pro mʌl get

promulgation	*proh muhl* GAY
	  shuhn
	B., prom uhl GAY
	  shuhn
		prŏ′mŭl gā′shŭn
		
		B., prŏm′ŭl gā′
		  shŭn
		  §§ 40(6), 47(1)
			ˌpro mʌl ′ge ʃən
			
			B., ˌprɒm əl ′ge
			  ʃən

pronunciation	pruh *nuhn* si AY
	  shuhn
	pruh *nuhn* shi AY
	  shuhn
		prŏ nŭn′sĭ ā′shŭn
		
		prŏ nŭn′shĭ ā′
		  shŭn § 47(3)
			prə ˌnʌn sɪ ′e ʃən
			
			prə ˌnʌn ʃɪ ′e ʃən

propaganda	*prop* uh GAN duh	prŏp′*a* găn′d*a*	ˌprap ə ′gæn də; *ES also* ˌprɒp-

property	PROP uhr ti	prŏp′ēr tĭ	′prap ɚ tɪ; *ES*
			  also ′prɒp-, *ES*
			  -ə tɪ

prophecy	PROF i si	prŏf′ĕ sĭ	′praf ɪ sɪ; *ES also* ′prɒf-

prophesy	PROF i sai
	  § 50(34)
		prŏf′ĕ sī	′praf ɪ saɪ; *ES*
			  also ′prɒf-

propitiate (v.)	pruh PISH i ayt	prŏ pĭsh′ĭ āt	prə ′pɪʃ ɪ et, pro-

propitiatory	pruh PISH i uh
	  toh ri
	pruh PISH i uh
	  taw ri
	B., pruh PISH i
	  uh tuhr i
		prŏ pĭsh′ĭ *a* tō′rĭ
		
		B., prŏ pĭsh′ĭ *a*
		  tēr ĭ §§ 13,
		  34(3), 51(4)
			prə ′pɪʃ ɪ ə ˌto rɪ,
			  -ˌtɔ rɪ, pro-
			
			B., prə ′pɪʃ ɪ ə tə rɪ

propitious	pruh PISH uhs	prŏ pĭsh′ŭs	prə ′pɪʃ əs, pro-
propose	pruh POHZ	prŏ pōz′ § 49(14)	prə ′poz
prosaic	proh ZAY ik	prŏ zā′ĭk	pro ′ze ɪk

proscribe	proh SKRAIB
	  § 50(34)
		prŏ skrĭb′
		  § 49(14)
			pro ′skraɪb

prosecute	PROS i kyoot	prŏs′ĕ kūt
		  §§ 48(2), 50(32)
			′pras ɪ kjut; *ES*
			  also ′prɒs-

proselyte	PROS uh lait
	  § 50(34)
		prŏs′ĕ līt § 31(3)	′pras ə laɪt; *ES*
			  also ′prɒs-

protect	pruh TEKT	prŏ tĕkt′ § 49(14)	prə ′tɛkt

	SIMPLIFIED	DIACRITICAL	PHONETIC
protégé (masc.), **protégée** (fem.)	PROH tuh zhay *proh tay* ZHAY	prō′tĕ zhā *F.,* prŏ′tă′zhā′	ˈpro tə ʒe *F.,* prɔ te ˈʒe
protein	PROH ti in PROH tee in PROH teen	prō′tĕ ĭn prō′tē ĭn prō′tēn	ˈpro tɪ ɪn ˈpro ti ɪn ˈpro tin
protest (v.)	pruh TEST	prō tĕst′ § 12	prə ˈtɛst, pro-
—— (n.)	PROH test	prō′tĕst § 47(2)	ˈpro tɛst
protestant (n., adj.)	PROT uhs tuhnt PROT is tuhnt	prŏt′ĕs tănt prŏt′ĭs tănt	ˈprat əs tənt, -ɪs-; *ES also* ˈprɒt-
—— (n. also– *"maker of a protest; a declared lover"*)	pruh TES tuhnt proh TES tuhnt	prō tĕs′tănt § 51(11)	prə ˈtɛs tənt pro ˈtɛs tənt
Protestantism	PROT uhs tuhnt iz′m PROT is tuhnt iz′m PROT is tuhnt iz uhm	prŏt′ĕs tănt ĭz′m prŏt′ĭs tănt ĭz′m § 50(15)	ˈprat əs tənt ɪzm̩, -ɪs-, -ɪz əm; *ES also* ˈprɒt-
Proteus	PROH tyoos PROH ti uhs	prō′tūs prō′tĕ ŭs	ˈpro tjus ˈpro tɪ əs
prototype	PROH tuh taip § 50(34)	prō′tŏ tīp	ˈpro tə taɪp
Provençal	*proh* vahn SAHL *F., praw vahN* SAHL	prō′vän säl′ *F.,* prŏ′vän′säl′	ˌpro van ˈsal *F.,* pr‥ vã ˈsal
provincial	pruh VIN shuhl	prō vĭn′shăl	prə ˈvɪn ʃəl
proviso	pruh VAI zoh § 50(34)	prō vī′zō	prə ˈvaɪ zo
provocative	pruh VOK uh tiv	prō vŏk′à tĭv § 47(3)	prə ˈvak ə tɪv, -ˈvok-; *ES also* -ˈvɒk-
provost (n., v.i.)	PROV uhst *Mil.:* proh VOH PROH VOH	prŏv′ŭst *Mil.:* prō vō′ prō′vō′ § 51(6)	ˈprav əst; *ES also* ˈprɒv- *Mil.:* pro ˈvo ˈpro ˈvo
—— *attributively*	PROH voh	prō′vō § 11	ˈpro vo
prowess	PROW es PROW is	prou′ĕs prou′ĭs § 24(5)	ˈpraʊ ɛs ˈpraʊ ɪs
proxy	PROK si	prŏk′sĭ	ˈprak sɪ; *ES also* ˈprɒk-
prude	prood	prōōd § 48(2)	prud
psalm	sahm	säm § 35(1)	sam
psalmist	SAHM ist	säm′ĭst § 47(3)	ˈsam ɪst ˈsæl mɪst
psalmody	SAL muh di SAHM uh di	săl′mŏ dĭ säm′ŏ dĭ § 47(3)	ˈsæl mə dɪ ˈsam ə dɪ

	SIMPLIFIED	DIACRITICAL	PHONETIC
pseudonym	SYOO duh nim SOO duh nim PSYOO duh nim PSOO duh nim	sū′dŏ nĭm psū′dŏ nĭm §§ 35(1), 40(4), 48(2)	ˈsju də nɪm ˈsu də nɪm ˈpsju də nɪm ˈpsu də nɪm
pshaw	shaw *Hum., often:* pshaw	shô § 35(1) *Hum., often:* pshô § 51(11)	ʃɔ *Hum., often:* pʃə
Psyche	SAI ki PSAI ki § 50(34)	sī′kĕ psī′kĕ § 35(1)	ˈsaɪ kɪ ˈpsaɪ kɪ
psychiatric	*sai* ki AT rik *psai* ki AT rik § 50(34)	sī′kĭ ăt′rĭk psī′kĭ ăt′rĭk § 35(1)	ˌsaɪ kɪ ˈæt rɪk ˌpsaɪ kɪ ˈæt rɪk
psychiatrist	sai KAI uh trist psai KAI uh trist SAI ki *at* rist PSAI ki *at* rist § 50(34)	sī kĭ′*ȧ* trĭst psī kĭ′*ȧ* trĭst sī′kĭ ăt′rĭst psī′kĭ ăt′rĭst § 35(1)	saɪ ˈkaɪ ə trɪst psaɪ ˈkaɪ ə trɪst ˈsaɪ kɪ ˌæt rɪst ˈpsaɪ kɪ ˌæt rɪst
psychiatry	sai KAI uh tri psai KAI uh tri SAI ki *at* ri PSAI ki *at* ri § 50(34)	sī kĭ′*ȧ* trĭ psī kĭ′*ȧ* trĭ sī′kĭ ăt′rĭ psī′kĭ ăt′rĭ § 35(1)	saɪ ˈkaɪ ə trɪ psaɪ ˈkaɪ ə trɪ ˈsaɪ kɪ ˌæt rɪ ˈpsaɪ kɪ ˌæt rɪ
psychic	SAI kik PSAI kik § 50(34)	sī′kĭk psī′kĭk § 35(1)	ˈsaɪ kɪk ˈpsaɪ kɪk
psychology	sai KOL uh ji psai KOL uh ji § 50(34)	sī kŏl′ŏ jĭ psī kŏl′ŏ jĭ § 35(1)	saɪ ˈkɑl ə dʒɪ, psaɪ-; *ES also* -ˈkɒl-
ptomaine, ptomain	TOH mayn toh MAYN *Rarely or tech.:* TOH may een TOH muh in	tō′mān tō mān′ *Rarely or tech.:* tō′mȧ ēn tō′mȧ ĭn §§ 11, 47(1), 51(8)	ˈto men to ˈmen *Rarely or tech.:* ˈto me in ˈto mə ɪn
puberty	PYOO buhr ti	pū′bẽr tĭ § 48(2)	ˈpju bɚ tɪ; *ES* -bə tɪ
public	PUHB lik	pŭb′lĭk	ˈpʌb lɪk
pueblo	PWEB loh	pwĕb′lō § 47(2)	ˈpwɛb lo
puerile	PYOO uhr il *B.,* PYOO uhr ail	pū′ẽr ĭl *B.,* pū′ẽr īl §§ 28(5), 34(21), 47(2), 48(2), 50(34), 51(4)	ˈpju ər ɪl *B.,* ˈpju ər aɪl

	SIMPLIFIED	DIACRITICAL	PHONETIC
puissance	PYOO i suhns	pū′ĭ săns	′pju ɪ sǝns
	pyoo IS uhns	pủ ĭs′ăns	pju ′ɪs ǝns
	pyoo IS ′ns	pủ ĭs′ ′ns	pju ′ɪs ṇs
	PWIS uhns	pwĭs′ăns	′pwɪs ǝns
	PWIS ′ns	pwĭs′ ′ns	′pwɪs ṇs
		§§ 47(3), 48(2)	
puissant	PYOO i suhnt	pū′ĭ sănt	′pju ɪ sǝnt
	PYOO i s'nt	pū′ĭ s'nt	′pju ɪ sṇt
	pyoo IS uhnt	pủ ĭs′ănt	pju ′ɪs ǝnt
	pyoo IS ′nt	pủ ĭs′ ′nt	pju ′ɪs ṇt
	PWIS uhnt	pwĭs′ănt	′pwɪs ǝnt
	PWIS ′nt	pwĭs′ ′nt § 48(2)	′pwɪs ṇt
pulley	POOL i	pŏŏl′ĭ	′pʊl ɪ
pulmonary	PUHL muh ner i	pŭl′mŏ nĕr′ĭ	′pʌl mǝ ˌnɛr ɪ ɪ
	B., PUHL muh nuhr i	B., pŭl′mŏ nĕr ĭ §§ 13, 20(2), 24(9), 51(4)	B., ′pʌl mǝ nǝ rɪ
pulpit	POOL pit	pŏŏl′pĭt	′pʊl pɪt
pumice	PUHM is	pŭm′ĭs § 47(2)	′pʌm ɪs
pumpkin	PUHMP kin *Colloq.:* PUHNG kin	pŭmp′kĭn *Colloq.:* pŭng′kĭn § 51(3)	′pʌmp kɪn *Colloq.:* ′pʌŋ kɪn
punctilious	*puhngk* TIL i uhs *puhngk* TIL yuhs	pŭngk tĭl′ĭ ŭs pŭngk tĭl′yŭs §§ 28(9), 33(4), 40(6), 47(2)	pʌŋk ′tɪl ɪ ǝs pʌŋk ′tɪl jǝs
punctual	PUHNGK chŏŏ uhl PUHNGK tyŏŏ uhl	pŭngk′tŭ ăl §§ 33(4), 50(33)	′pʌŋk tʃʊ ǝl ′pʌŋk tjʊ ǝl
puncture	PUHNGK chuhr PUHNGK tyuhr	pŭngk′tûr § 50(31)	′pʌŋk tʃɚ, -tjɚ; *ES* -tʃǝ(r), -tjǝ(r)
pungent	PUHN juhnt	pŭn′jĕnt	′pʌn dʒǝnt
purblind	PUHR *blaind* § 50(34)	pûr′blīnd′	′pɝ ˌblaɪnd; *ES also* ′pɝ-
purée (n.)	pyŏŏ RAY PYOO ray PYOO ray pŏŏ RAY	pủ rā′ pū′rā *F.,* pü′rā′ § 48(2)	pjʊ ′re ′pjʊ re pʊ ′re *F.,* py ′re
purport (v.t.)	*puhr* POHRT *puhr* PAWRT puhr POHRT puhr PAWRT	pûr pōrt′ §§ 34(3), 40(6, 7)	pɝ ′port, pǝ-, -′pɔrt; *ES also* pɝ-, *ES* pǝ-, -′poǝt, *E also* -′pɔǝt
	PUHR pohrt PUHR pawrt	pûr′pōrt	′pɝ port, -pɔrt; *ES also* ′pɝ-, -poǝt, *E also* -pɔǝt

	SIMPLIFIED	DIACRITICAL	PHONETIC
—— (n.)	PUHR pohrt PUHR pawrt	pûr′pōrt §§ 12, 34(3)	'pɝ port, -pərt; *ES also* 'pɜ-, -poət, *E also* -pəət
purpose	PUHR puhs	pûr′pŭs	'pɝ pəs; *ES also* 'pɜ-
pursuivant	PUHR swi vuhnt	pûr′swĭ vănt	'pɝ swɪ vənt; *ES* *also* 'pɜ-
pusillanimous	*pyoo* suh LAN uh muhs *pyoo* si LAN i muhs	pū′sĭ lăn′ĭ mŭs pū′sĭ lăn′Ĭ mŭs § 48(2)	ˌpju sə 'læn ə məs ˌpju sḷ 'æn ə məs ˌpju sɪ 'læn ɪ məs
put	pŏŏt	pŏŏt	pʊt
putrefaction	*pyoo* tri FAK shuhn	pū′trĕ făk′shŭn § 48(2)	ˌpju trɪ 'fæk ʃən
putrefy	PYOO tri faī § 50(34)	pū′trĕ fī § 48(2)	'pju trɪ faɪ
putter (*"keep busy* *uselessly"*)	PUHT uhr	pŭt′ĕr	'pʌt ɚ; *ES* -ə(r)
Pygmalion	pig MAY li uhn pig MAYL yuhn	pĭg mā′lĭ ŏn pĭg māl′yŏn § 28(9)	pɪg 'me lɪ ən pɪg 'mel jən
pyorrhea, **pyorrhoea**	*paī* uh REE uh § 50(34)	pī′ŏ rē′á	ˌpaɪ ə 'ri ə
pyramid	PIR uh mid	pĭr′á mĭd	'pɪr ə mɪd
pyramidal	pi RAM i duhl pi RAM i d'l	pĭ răm′Ĭ dăl pĭ răm′Ĭ d'l	pɪ 'ræm ɪ dəl pɪ 'ræm ɪ dḷ
Pyrenees	PIR i neez	pĭr′ĕ nēz	'pɪr ɪ niz
pyrites (*"any of a* *number of* *metallic-looking* *sulphides"*)	paī RAĪ teez puh RAĪ teez pi RAĪ teez PAĪ raīts § 50(34)	pī rī′tēz pǔ rī′tēz pĭ rī′tēz pī′rīts	paɪ 'raɪ tiz pə 'raɪ tiz pɪ 'raɪ tiz 'paɪ raɪts
Pythagoras	pi THAG uh ruhs	pĭ thăg′ŏ răs	pɪ 'θæg ə rəs
Pythias	PITH i uhs	pĭth′Ĭ ăs	'pɪθ ɪ əs

Q

quadrille ("*game of cards*"; "*a square dance*")	kwuh DRIL	kwŏ drĭl′ §§ 47(3), 51(4)	kwə 'drɪl, kwɑd 'rɪl, kwɒd-
	B., kuh DRIL	*B.*, ká drĭl′	*B.*, kə 'drɪl
quadruple (adj.)	KWOD rōō p'l kwod ROO p'l	kwŏd′rōō p'l kwŏd rōō′p'l	'kwɑd rʊ pļ, kwɑd 'ru-, 'kwɒd-, kwɒd-
—— (n.)	KWOD rōō p'l	kwŏd′rōō p'l	'kwɑd rʊ pļ, 'kwɒd-
—— (v.)	kwod ROO p'l KWOD rōō p'l	kwŏd rōō′p'l kwŏd′rōō p'l §§ 11, 12, 47(1)	kwɑd 'ru pļ, 'kwɑd rʊ-, kwɒd-, 'kwɒd-
quaff	kwaf kwahf	kwȧf §§ 20(5), 47(2)	kwæf, kwɒf, kwɑf, kwɔf; *E also* kwaf
quagmire	KWAG ma͡ir KWOG ma͡ir § 50(34)	kwăg′mīr′ kwŏg′mīr′	'kwæg ˌmaɪr, 'kwɑg-, 'kwɒg-; *ES* -ˌmaɪə(r)
qualm	kwahm kwawm	kwäm kwôm § 47(3)	kwɑm kwɔm
quandary	KWON duh ri	kwŏn′dá rĭ	'kwan də rɪ, 'kwɒn-, -drɪ
	B., kwon DEHR i	*B.*, kwŏn dâr′ɪ §§ 9, 47(3), 51(4)	*B.*, kwɒn 'der ɪ; *ES also* -'deər ɪ
quantitative	KWON tuh *tay* tiv KWON ti *tay* tiv	kwŏn′tĭ tā′tĭv kwŏn′tĭ tā′tĭv	'kwan tə ˌte tɪv, 'kwɒn-, -tɪ ˌte-
quantity	KWON tuh ti KWON ti ti	kwŏn′tĭ tĭ kwŏn′tĭ tĭ	'kwan tə tɪ, 'kwɒn-, -tɪ tɪ
quarantine (n.)	KWOR uhn teen KWAWR uhn teen	kwŏr′ăn tēn kwôr′ăn tēn	'kwar ən tin, 'kwɔr-, 'kwɒr-
—— (v.)	KWOR uhn teen KWAWR uhn teen *kwor* uhn TEEN *kwawr* uhn TEEN	kwŏr′ăn tēn kwôr′ăn tēn kwŏr′ăn tēn′ kwôr′ăn tēn′ §§ 12, 34(5, 7), 47(1)	'kwar ən tin, 'kwɔr-, 'kwɒr-, ˌkwar ən 'tin, ˌkwɔr-, ˌkwɒr-

	SIMPLIFIED	DIACRITICAL	PHONETIC
quarrel	KWOR uhl KWAWR uhl	kwŏr′ĕl kwôr′ĕl § 34(5, 7)	′kwar əl, ′kwɔr-, ′kwɒr-
quartz	kwawrts	kwôrts § 39(9)	kwɔrts; ES kwɔəts
quash	kwosh	kwŏsh § 34(7)	kwɑʃ, kwɒʃ
quasi, quasi-	KWAY saī KWAH si § 50(34)	kwā′sī kwä′sĭ	′kwe saɪ ′kwɑ sɪ ′kwe zaɪ
quay (also **key**)	kee F., ke	kē F., kĕ	ki F., kɛ
queer	kwĭer kwir kweer	kwēr § 24(2) kwēr	kwɪər, kwɪr, kwir; ES kwɪə(r)
querulous	KWER yŏŏ luhs KWER ŏŏ luhs	kwĕr′ū lŭs kwĕr′ŏŏ lŭs § 47(3)	′kwɛr jʊ ləs, -jə-, -ju-, -ʊ ləs, -ə ləs
query	KWĬER i KWIR i KWEER i	kwēr′ĭ § 24(2) kwēr′ĭ	′kwɪər ɪ, ′kwɪr-, ′kwir-; ES kwɪər-
question	KWES chuhn	kwĕs′chŭn §§ 38(12), 39(1), 40(11)	′kwɛs tʃən
quick	kwik	kwĭk	kwɪk
quiddity	KWID uh ti KWID i ti	kwĭd′ĭ tĭ kwĭd′ĭ tĭ § 50(16)	′kwɪd ə tɪ ′kwɪd ɪ tɪ
quiescent	kwaī ES uhnt kwaī ES ′nt § 50(34)	kwī ĕs′ĕnt kwī ĕs′ ′nt	kwaɪ ′ɛs ənt kwaɪ ′ɛs n̩t
quiet	KWAī uht § 50(34)	kwī′ĕt	′kwaɪ ət
quietus	kwaī EE tuhs § 50(34)	kwī ē′tŭs	kwaɪ ′i təs
Quincy (**Florida**)	KWIN si	kwĭn′sĭ	′kwɪn sɪ
Quincy (**Mass.**)	KWIN zi	kwĭn′zĭ	′kwɪn zɪ
quinine	KWAī naīn § 50(34) B., kwi NEEN KWIN een	kwī′nīn B., kwĭ nēn′ kwĭn′ēn §§ 47(3), 51(4)	′kwaɪ naɪn B., kwɪ ′nin ′kwɪn in
quoit	kwoit B., koit	kwoit B., koit §§ 47(3), 51(4)	kwɔɪt B., kɔɪt
quondam	KWON dam	kwŏn′dăm	′kwan dæm, ′kwɒn-
quorum	KWOH ruhm KWAW ruhm	kwō′rŭm § 34(3)	′kwo rəm ′kwɔ rəm

	SIMPLIFIED	DIACRITICAL	PHONETIC
quoth	kwohth *Formerly, also:* kwuhth	kwōth *Formerly, also:* kwŭth §§ 16, 47(3), 51(2)	kwoθ *Formerly, also:* kwəθ
quotient	KWOH shuhnt	kwō′shĕnt	'kwo ʃənt

R

rabbi	RAB ai RAB i § 50(34)	răb′ī răb′ĭ § 47(2)	'ræb aɪ 'ræb ɪ
rabies	RAY bi eez RAY beez	rā′bĭ ēz rā′bēz § 47(1)	're bɪ iz, 'ræ-, 're biz, 'ræ-
raceme	ruh SEEM ray SEEM ra SEEM	rȧ sēm′ rā sēm′ ră sēm′ § 47(2)	rə 'sim re 'sim ræ 'sim
racial	RAY shuhl	rā′shŭl §§ 38(12), 47(2)	're ʃəl, -ʃɪ əl
radiate	RAY di ayt	rā′dĭ āt	're dɪ et
radiation	*ray* di AY shuhn	rā′dĭ ā′shŭn	ˌre dɪ 'e ʃən
radiator	RAY di *ay* tuhr	rā′dĭ ā′tēr	're dɪ ˌe tɚ; *ES* -tə(r)
radio	RAY di oh	rā′dĭ ō	're dɪ o
radish	RAD ish	răd′ĭsh	'ræd ɪʃ
raft	raft rahft	råft § 20(5)	ræft; *E also* raft, raft
ragout	ra GOO	ră go͞o′	ræ 'gu, rə-
raillery	RAYL uhr i RAL uhr i	rāl′ēr ĭ răl′ēr ĭ § 47(3)	'rel ər ɪ 'ræl ər ɪ
raisin	RAY z'n	rā′z'n	're zn̩
rajah, raja	RAH juh	rä′jȧ § 47(2)	'ra dʒə
rampart	RAM pahrt RAM puhrt	răm′pärt răm′pērt	'ram part, -pɚt; *ES* -paːt, -pət, *E also* -paːt
Ramses (II)	RAM seez	răm′sēz	'ræm siz
rancid	RAN sid	răn′sĭd	'ræn sɪd
rancor, rancour	RANG kuhr	răng′kēr	'ræŋ kɚ; *ES* kə(r)
ransack	RAN sak	răn′săk	'ræn sæk

Raphael ("*archangel*")	RAF ay el RAY fay el RAF i uhl RAH fay el RAY fi uhl	răf′â ĕl rā′fâ ĕl răf′ĭ ĕl rä′fâ ĕl rā′fĭ ĕl	'ræf e ɛl, -ɪ ɛl 're fe ɛl 'ræf ɪ əl 'ra fe ɛl 're fɪ əl
Raphael ("*painter*")	RAF ay el RAF i uhl RAH fay el	răf′â ĕl răf′ĭ ĕl rä′fâ ĕl § 51(7)	'ræf e ɛl 'ræf ɪ əl 'ra fe ɛl
rapier	RAY pi uhr	rā′pĭ ēr § 28(9)	're pɪ ɚ, -pjɚ; *ES* -ə(r), -pjə(r)
rapine	RAP in	răp′ĭn § 28(6)	'ræp ɪn
rapture	RAP chuhr RAP tyuhr	răp′tûr § 50(31)	'ræp tʃɚ, -tjɚ; *ES* -tʃə(r), -tjə(r)
rarity	RAR uh ti REHR uh ti REHR i ti	răr′ĭ tĭ râr′ĭ tĭ râr′ĭ tĭ § 47(2)	'rær ə tɪ 'rer ə tɪ 'rer ɪ tɪ
rasp	rasp rahsp	råsp §§ 20(5), 47(2)	ræsp; *E also* rasp, rɑsp
raspberry	RAZ *ber* i *B.*, RAHZ buhr i	răz′bĕr′ĭ *B.*, răz′bĕr ĭ §§ 35(1), 47(3), 51(4)	'ræz ˌber ɪ *B.*, 'raz bə rɪ; *E also* 'raz-
rasping	RASP ing RAHSP ing	råsp′ĭng §§ 20(5), 50(24)	'ræsp ɪŋ; *E also* 'rasp-, 'rɑsp-
rather	RATH uhr RAHTH uhr	råth′ēr §§ 20(5), 47(3)	'ræð ɚ; *ES also* 'rað-, 'rɑð-, *ES* -ə(r)
ratio	RAY shoh RAY shi oh *Latin:* RAY shi oh	rā′shō rā′shĭ ō *Latin:* rā′shĭ ō §§ 47(1), 51(11)	're ʃo 're ʃɪ o *Latin:* 're ʃɪ o
ration	RASH uhn RAY shuhn *Military men prefer:* RASH uhn	răsh′ŭn rā′shŭn *Military men prefer:* răsh′ŭn §§ 47(3), 51(6)	'ræʃ ən 're ʃən *Military men prefer:* 'ræʃ ən
rationing	RASH uhn ing RAY shuhn ing	răsh′ŭn ĭng rā′shŭn ĭng	'ræʃ ən ɪŋ 're ʃən ɪŋ
rattan	ra TAN	ră tăn′	ræ 'tæn
ravine ("*gorge*")	ruh VEEN	rá vēn′ § 51(7)	rə 'vin
reading	REED ing	rēd′ĭng	'rid ɪŋ
Reading	RED ing	rĕd′ĭng	'rɛd ɪŋ
real ("*genuine; actual*")	REE uhl RI uhl	rē′ăl rĕ̜′ăl §§ 24(2), 31(2)	'ri əl 'rɪ əl ril

	SIMPLIFIED	DIACRITICAL	PHONETIC
realization	*ree* uhl i ZAY shuhn	rē′ăl ĭ zā′shŭn	ˌri əl ɪ ˈze ʃən
	ree uhl a͜i ZAY shuhn	rē′ăl ī zā′shŭn	ˌri əl aɪ ˈze ʃən
	ri uhl a͜i ZAY shuhn § 50(34)	rḙ′ăl ī zā′shŭn § 24(2)	ˌrɪ əl aɪ ˈze ʃən
realize	REE uhl a͜iz	rē′ăl īz	ˈri əl aɪz
	RI uhl a͜iz § 50(34)	rḙ′ăl īz § 24(2)	ˈrɪ əl aɪz
really	REE uhl i	rē′ăl ĭ	ˈri əl ɪ
	RI uhl i	rḙ′ăl ĭ §§ 24(2), 50(20)	ˈrɪ əl ɪ / ˈril ɪ
rear	rĭer / rir / reer	rēr § 24(2) / rẽr	rɪər, rɪr, rir; *ES* rɪə(r)
rebate (n., v.– *"discount"*)	REE bayt / ri BAYT	rē′bāt / rĕ bāt′	ˈri bet / rɪ ˈbet
—— (v. especially)	ri BAYT	rĕ bāt′ §§ 12, 47(1)	rɪ ˈbet
rebel (n., adj.)	REB uhl / REB ′l	rĕb′ĕl / rĕb′ ′l	ˈreb əl / ˈreb l̩
—— (v.i.)	ri BEL	rĕ bĕl′ § 12	rɪ ˈbel
rebound (v.)	ri BOWND	rĕ bound′ § 49(15)	rɪ ˈbaʊnd
—— (n.)	ri BOWND / REE *bownd*	rĕ bound′ / rē′bound′ § 12	rɪ ˈbaʊnd / ˈri ˌbaʊnd
—— (adj.)	ree BOWND	rē bound′	ri ˈbaʊnd
recalcitrant	ri KAL si truhnt	rĕ kăl′sĭ trănt	rɪ ˈkæl sɪ trənt
recall (v.t.)	ri KAWL	rĕ kôl′ § 49(15)	rɪ ˈkɔl
—— (n.)	ri KAWL / REE *kawl*	rĕ kôl′ / rē′kôl′ § 12	rɪ ˈkɔl / ˈri ˌkɔl
receipt	ri SEET	rĕ sēt′ § 35(1)	rɪ ˈsit
recess (v.)	ri SES	rĕ sĕs′ § 12	rɪ ˈses
—— (n.)	ri SES / REE ses	rĕ sĕs′ / rē′sĕs § 47(1)	rɪ ˈses / ˈri ses
—— *"period of intermission or suspension of business,"* usually	REE ses	rē′sĕs § 51(11)	ˈri ses
—— all other meanings, especially	ri SES	rĕ sĕs′	rɪ ˈses
recipe	RES uh pee / RES i pee / RES i pi	rĕs′ĭ pē / rĕs′ĭ pē / rĕs′ĭ pĭ	ˈres ə pi / ˈres ɪ pi / ˈres ɪ pɪ

	SIMPLIFIED	DIACRITICAL	PHONETIC
reciprocity	*res* uh PROS uh ti *res* i PROS i ti	rĕs′ĭ prŏs′ĭ tĭ rĕs′ĭ prŏs′ĭ tĭ	ˌres ə ′prɑs ə tɪ; -ɪ tɪ; *ES also* -′prɒs-
recitative (n.–*Music*)	*res* i tuh TEEV	rĕs′ĭ tá̇ tēv′ § 51(7)	ˌrɛs ɪ tə ′tiv
recitative (adj.) —— "*that repeats or recites; narra- tive*"	RES uh *tay* tiv RES i *tay* tiv ri SAIT uh tiv § 50(34)	rĕs′ĭ tā′tĭv rĕs′ĭ tā′tĭv rĕ sīt′á̇ tĭv	′rɛs ə ˌte tɪv ′rɛs ɪ ˌte tɪv rɪ ′saɪt ə tɪv
—— "*pertaining to, or having the style or manner of, recitative*"	*res* i tuh TEEV	rĕs′ĭ tá̇ tēv′ § 51(7, 11)	ˌrɛs ɪ tə ′tiv
recline	ri KLAIN⁀ § 50(34)	rĕ klīn′ § 49(15)	rɪ ′klaɪn
recluse (n.)	ri KLOOS REK loos REK lyoos	rĕ klōōs′ rĕk′lūs §§ 12, 40(4), 48(2)	rɪ ′klus ′rɛk lus ′rɛk ljus
—— (adj.)	ri KLOOS	rĕ klōōs′	rɪ ′klus
recognizable	REK uhg *na⁀iz* uh b'l	rĕk′ŏg nīz′á̇ b'l § 47(2)	′rɛk əg ′naɪz ə bl̩
recognizance	ri KOG ni zuhns *In law, esp.:* ri KON i zuhns	rĕ kŏg′nĭ zăns § 47(3) *In law, esp.:* rĕ kŏn′ĭ zăns § 51(6)	rɪ ′kɑg nɪ zəns, -′kɒg- *In law, esp.:* rɪ ′kɑn ɪ zəns, -′kɒn-
recognize	REK uhg naiz⁀ § 50(34)	rĕk′ŏg nīz	′rɛk əg naɪz
recoil	ri KOIL	rĕ koil′	rɪ ′kɔɪl
reconcilable (adj., n.)	REK uhn *sai⁀l* uh b'l	rĕk′ŏn sīl′á̇ b'l	′rɛk ən ˌsaɪl ə bl̩
reconcile (v.)	REK uhn sail⁀ § 50(34)	rĕk′ŏn sīl	′rɛk ən saɪl
reconciliable (adj.)	*rek* uhn SIL i uh b'l	rĕk′ŏn sĭl′ĭ á̇ b'l § 28(9)	ˌrɛk ən ′sɪl ɪ ə bl̩
reconciliation	*rek* uhn *sil* i AY shuhn	rĕk′ŏn sĭl′ĭ ā′shŭn	ˌrɛk ən ˌsɪl ɪ ′e ʃən
recondite	REK uhn da⁀it ri KON da⁀it § 50(34)	rĕk′ŭn dīt rĕ kŏn′dīt § 47(3)	′rɛk ən daɪt, rɪ ′kɑn-; *ES also* -′kɒn-
reconnoiter, reconnoitre	*rek* uh NOI tuhr *ree* kuh NOI tuhr	rĕk′ŏ noi′tēr rē′kŏ noi′tēr	ˌrɛk ə ′nɔɪ tɚ, ˌri kə-; *ES -tə(r)
record (n., adj.)	REK uhrd B., REK awrd	rĕk′ērd B., rĕk′ôrd § 51(4)	′rɛk ɚd; *ES* -əd B., ′rɛk ɔrd; *ES -əd

	SIMPLIFIED	DIACRITICAL	PHONETIC
—— (v.)	ri KAWRD	rĕ kôrd′ § 12	rɪ ˈkɔrd; *ES* -ˈkɔəd
recount (v.t.–"*tell*")	ri KOWNT	rĕ kount′ § 49(15)	rɪ ˈkaʊnt
recourse (n.)	ri KOHRS ri KAWRS REE kohrs REE kawrs	rĕ kōrs′ rē′kōrs §§ 34(3), 49(15)	rɪ ˈkors, -ˈkɔrs, ˈri kors, -kɔrs; *ES* -ˈkoəs, -koəs; *E also* -ˈkɔəs, -kɔəs
recreant	REK ri uhnt	rĕk′rĕ ănt	ˈrek rɪ ənt
recreate (v.–"*refresh*")	REK ri ayt	rĕk′rĕ āt § 51(11)	ˈrek rɪ et
re-create (v.t.– "*create anew*")	*ree* kri AYT *ree* kree AYT	rē′krē ‐āt′ rē′krē āt′	ˌri krɪ ˈet ˌri kri ˈet
recreation	*rek* ri AY shuhn	rĕk′rĕ ā′shŭn	ˌrek rɪ ˈe ʃən
recriminate	ri KRIM uh nayt ri KRIM i nayt	rĕ krĭm′ĭ nāt rĕ krĭm′ĭ nāt	rɪ ˈkrɪm ə net rɪ ˈkrɪm ɪ net
recrimination	ri *krim* uh NAY shuhn ri *krim* i NAY shuhn	rĕ krĭm′ĭ nā′shŭn rĕ krĭm′ĭ nā′shŭn	rɪ ˌkrɪm ə ˈne ʃən rɪ ˌkrɪm ɪ ˈne ʃən
recriminatory	ri KRIM uh nuh *toh* ri ri KRIM uh nuh *taw* ri ri KRIM i nuh *toh* ri ri KRIM i nuh *taw* ri	rĕ krĭm′ĭ nȧ tō′rĭ rĕ krĭm′ĭ nȧ tō′rĭ § 34(3)	rɪ ˈkrɪm ə nə ˌto rɪ rɪ ˈkrɪm ə nə ˌtə rɪ rɪ ˈkrɪm ɪ nə ˌto rɪ rɪ ˈkrɪm ɪ nə ˌtə rɪ
recruit	ri KROOT	rĕ krōŏt′ §§ 40(4), 48(2)	rɪ ˈkrut
recuperate	ri KYOO puhr ayt ri KOO puhr ayt	rĕ kū′pĕr āt §§ 48(2), 50(32)	rɪ ˈkju pər et, -ˈku-, -pə ret
recuperative	ri KYOO puhr *ay* tiv ri KOO puhr *ay* tiv ri KYOO puhr uh tiv ri KOO puhr uh tiv	rĕ kū′pĕr ā′tĭv rĕ kū′pĕr ȧ tĭv §§ 48(2), 50(17, 32)	rɪ ˈkju pər ˌe tɪv, -ˈku-, -pər ə tɪv, -pə ˌre-, -rə-
red	red	rĕd	red
redolent	RED uh luhnt	rĕd′ŏ lĕnt	ˈred ə lənt
redoubtable	ri DOWT uh b'l	rĕ dout′ȧ b'l	rɪ ˈdaʊt ə bl̩
redress (v.)	ri DRES	rĕ drĕs′	rɪ ˈdres
—— (n.)	ri DRES REE dres	rĕ drĕs′ rē′drĕs § 12	rɪ ˈdres ˈri drɛs
reduce	ri DYOOS ri DOOS	rĕ dūs′ §§ 48(2), 50(32)	rɪ ˈdjus rɪ ˈdus

refectory	ri FEK tuh ri	rĕ fĕk′tŏ rĭ	rɪ ˈfɛk tə rɪ
refer	ri FUHR	rĕ fûr′ § 49(15)	rɪ ˈfɜ; *ES also* -ˈfɜ(r)
referable	REF uhr uh b'l	rĕf′ĕr *a* b'l § 47(1)	ˈref ər ə bļ, ˈref rə bļ
	B., ri FUHR uh b'l	*B.*, rĕ fûr′*a* b'l § 51(4)	*B.*, rɪ ˈfɜ ə bļ; *ES* -ˈfɜr ə-
referee	*ref* uhr EE *ref* uh REE	rĕf′ĕr ē′	ˌref ər ˈi ˌref ə ˈri
refine	ri FAIN § 50(34)	rĕ fīn′	rɪ ˈfaɪn
reflex (adj., n.)	REE fleks	rē′flĕks § 11	ˈri flɛks
—— (v.t.)	ri FLEKS	rĕ flĕks′ § 12	rɪ ˈflɛks
reflexive	ri FLEK siv	rĕ flĕk′sĭv § 50(17)	rɪ ˈflɛk sɪv
refuge	REF yooj	rĕf′ūj	ˈref judʒ
refulgent	ri FUHL juhnt	rĕ fŭl′jĕnt	rɪ ˈfʌl dʒənt
refund (v.–*"pay back"*)	ri FUHND	rĕ fŭnd′ § 12	rɪ ˈfʌnd
—— (n.)	ri FUHND REE fuhnd	rĕ fŭnd′ rē′fŭnd	rɪ ˈfʌnd ˈri fʌnd
refund (v.t.– *"change into a new form"*)	ree FUHND	rē fŭnd′ § 51(7)	ri ˈfʌnd
refuse (*"say no"*)	ri FYOOZ	rĕ fūz′ § 48(2)	rɪ ˈfjuz
refuse (*"waste"*)	REF yoos	rĕf′ūs § 51(7)	ˈref jus, -juz
refutable	REF yŏŏ tuh b'l ri FYOOT uh b'l	rĕf′û ta b'l rĕ fūt′*a* b'l §§ 47(2), 48(2)	ˈref jʊ tə bļ rɪ ˈfjut ə bļ
refute	ri FYOOT	rĕ fūt′ § 48(2)	rɪ ˈfjut
regardless	ri GAHRD les ri GAHRD lis	rĕ gärd′lĕs rĕ gärd′lĭs §§ 24(5), 50(18)	rɪ ˈgɑrd lɛs, -lɪs; *ES* -ˈgɑːd-, *E also* -ˈgɑːd-
regime, régime	ray ZHEEM ri ZHEEM	rā zhēm′	re ˈʒim rɪ ˈʒim
regimen	REJ uh men REJ i men	rĕj′*i* mĕn rĕj′ĭ mĕn	ˈredʒ ə mɛn ˈredʒ ɪ men
regular	REG yŏŏ luhr	rĕg′û lēr	ˈreg jʊ lɚ, -jə-, -ju-; *ES* -lə(r)
regulate	REG yŏŏ layt	rĕg′û lāt	ˈreg jʊ let, -jə-, -ju-
reinforce	*ree* in FOHRS *ree* in FAWRS	rē′ĭn fōrs′ §§ 34(3), 49(15)	ˌri ɪn ˈfors, -ˈfɔrs; *ES* -ˈfoəs, *E also* -ˈfɔəs
rejuvenate	ri JOO vi nayt	rĕ jōō′vĕ nāt § 48(2)	rɪ ˈdʒu vɪ net

	SIMPLIFIED	DIACRITICAL	PHONETIC
relaxation	*ree* lak SAY shuhn *ree* laks AY shuhn *rel* ak SAY shuhn *rel* aks AY shuhn	rē′lăk sā′shŭn rĕl′ăk sā′shŭn §§ 47(2), 49(15), 50(30)	ˌri læk ′se ʃən ˌri læks ′e ʃən ˌrel æk ′se ʃən ˌrel æks ′e ʃən
release	ri LEES	rē lēs′	rɪ ′lis
relevant	REL i vuhnt	rĕl′ĕ vănt	′rel ɪ vənt
reluctance	ri LUHK tuhns	rē lŭk′tăns	rɪ ′lʌk təns
remedial	ri MEE di uhl	rē mē′dĭ ăl	rɪ ′mi dɪ əl
remembrance	ri MEM bruhns	rē mĕm′brăns	rɪ ′mɛm brəns
reminiscent	*rem* uh NIS uhnt *rem* i NIS uhnt *rem* uh NIS ′nt	rĕm′ĭ nĭs′ĕnt rĕm′ĭ nĭs′ĕnt rĕm′ĭ nĭs′ ′nt	ˌrem ə ′nɪs ənt ˌrem ɪ ′nɪs ənt ˌrem ə ′nɪs n̩t
remonstrance	ri MON struhns	rē mŏn′străns	rɪ ′man strəns; *ES* *also* -′mɒn-
remonstrate	ri MON strayt	rē mŏn′strāt	rɪ ′man stret; *ES* *also* -′mɒn-
rendezvous	RAHN duh voo REN duh voo *F.*, *rahn* day VOO	rän′dĕ vōō rĕn′dĕ vōō *F.*, rän′då vōō′ §§ 38(2), 47(3)	′ran də vu ′ren də vu *F.*, rã de ′vu
renunciation	ri *nuhn* si AY shuhn ri *nuhn* shi AY shuhn	rē nŭn′sĭ ā′shŭn rē nŭn′shĭ ā′shŭn § 47(3)	rɪ ˌnʌn sɪ ′e ʃən rɪ ˌnʌn ʃɪ ′e ʃən
reorganize	ree AWR guhn aiz ree AWR guh naiz § 50(34)	rē ôr′găn īz § 49(15)	ri ′or gən aɪz, -gə naɪz; *ES* -′ɔə gən-, -gə naɪz
reparable	REP uh ruh b′l	rĕp′å rå b′l	′rep ə rə bl̩
reparation	*rep* uh RAY shuhn	rĕp′å rā′shŭn	ˌrep ə ′re ʃən
repartee	*rep* uhr TEE *rep* ahr TEE	rĕp′ēr tē′ rĕp′är tē′	ˌrep ɚ ′ti, -ɑr ′ti; *ES* -ə ′ti, -ɑː-
repast	ri PAST ri PAHST	rē pàst′ § 20(5)	rɪ ′pæst; *E also* -′past, -′pɑst
repertoire	REP uhr twahr REP uhr twawr *F.*, *ray* puhr TWAHR	rĕp′ēr twär rĕp′ēr twôr *F.*, rå′pĕr twär′ § 47(1)	′rep ɚ twɑr, -twɔr; *ES* -ə twɑː(r), -twɔə(r) *F.*, re per ′twaːr
repertory	REP uhr *toh* ri REP uhr *taw* ri *B.*, REP uhr tuhr i	rĕp′ēr tō′rĭ §§ 34(3), 51(4) *B.*, rĕp′ēr tĕr ĭ	′rep ɚ ˌto rɪ, -ˌtɔ-; *ES* ′rep ə- *B.*, ′rep ɚ tə rɪ; *ES* -ə tə-
replica	REP li kuh	rĕp′lĭ kå	′rep lɪ kə
repose ("*rest; sleep*")	ri POHZ	rē pōz′ § 49(15)	rɪ ′poz
repose ("*put*")	ri POHZ	rē pōz′ § 51(11)	rɪ ′poz

	SIMPLIFIED	DIACRITICAL	PHONETIC
reprieve	ri PREEV	rē prēv′	rɪ ˈpriv
reprimand (n.)	REP ri mand REP ri mahnd	rĕp′rĭ mȧnd	ˈrep rɪ mænd; E also -mand, -mɑnd
—— (v.t.)	REP ri mand REP ri mahnd *rep* ri MAND *rep* ri MAHND	rĕp′rĭ mȧnd rĕp′rĭ mȧnd′ §§ 12, 20(5), 47(2), 49(15)	ˈrep rɪ mænd, ˌrep rɪ ˈmænd; E also -mand, -mɑnd, -ˈmand, -ˈmɑnd
reprint (v.t.)	ree PRINT	rē prĭnt′	ri ˈprɪnt
—— (n.)	REE *print* ree PRINT	rē′prĭnt′ rē prĭnt′ §§ 12, 49(15)	ˈri ˌprɪnt ri ˈprɪnt
reprisal	ri PRAIZ uhl ri PRAIZ ′l § 50(34)	rē prīz′ăl rē prīz′ ′l § 31(3)	rɪ ˈpraɪz əl rɪ ˈpraɪz l̩
reptile	REP til	rĕp′tĭl §§ 28(5), 47(2)	ˈrep tɪl
reputable	REP yŏŏ tuh b'l	rĕp′ û tȧ b'l	ˈrep jʊ tə bl̩, -jə-; -ju-
request	ri KWEST	rē kwĕst′	rɪ ˈkwest
requiem, Requiem	REE kwi uhm REK wi uhm	rē′kwĭ ĕm rĕk′wĭ ĕm § 47(3)	ˈri kwɪ əm ˈrek wɪ əm
requisite	REK wuh zit REK wi zit	rĕk′wĭ zĭt rĕk′wĭ zĭt	ˈrek wə zɪt ˈrek wɪ zɪt
requital	ri KWAIT uhl ri KWAIT ′l § 50(34)	rē kwīt′ăl rē kwīt′ ′l § 31(3)	rɪ ˈkwaɪt əl rɪ ˈkwaɪt l̩
requite	ri KWAIT § 50(34)	rē kwīt′	rɪ ˈkwaɪt
rescind	ri SIND	rē sĭnd′	rɪ ˈsɪnd
research	ri SUHRCH REE suhrch	rē sûrch′ rē′sûrch §§ 11, 47(1), 49(15)	rɪ ˈsɝtʃ, ˈri sɝtʃ; ES also -ˈsɜtʃ, -sɜtʃ
reservoir	REZ uhr vwawr REZ uh vwawr REZ uhr vwahr REZ uh vwahr REZ uhr vawr	rĕz′ẽr vwôr rĕz′ẽr vwär §§ 47(3), 48(1) rĕz′ẽr vôr	ˈrez ɚ vwɔr, -vɔr, -ə vwɔr, -ɚ vwɑr; ES -ə vwɔə(r), -vɔə(r), -vwɑ:(r)
residual	ri ZIJ ŏŏ uhl ri ZID yŏŏ uhl	rē zĭd′û ăl § 50(33)	rɪ ˈzɪdʒ ʊ əl rɪ ˈzɪd jʊ əl, -ju-
residuary	ri ZIJ ŏŏ er i ri ZID yŏŏ *er* i B., ri ZID yŏŏ uhr i	rē zĭd′û ẽr′ĭ §§ 13, 20(2), 24(9), 51(4) B., rē zĭd′û ẽr ĭ	rɪ ˈzɪdʒ ʊ ˌɛr ɪ rɪ ˈzɪd jʊ ˌɛr ɪ, -ju- B., rɪ ˈzɪd jʊ ə rɪ

	SIMPLIFIED	DIACRITICAL	PHONETIC
residue	REZ uh dyoo	rĕz′ĭ dū	′rez ə dju
	REZ uh doo		′rez ə du
	REZ i dyoo	rĕz′ĭ dū	′rez ı dju
	REZ i doo	§ 48(2)	′rez ı du
residuum	ri ZIJ ŏŏ uhm	rĕ zĭd′ū ŭm	rı ′zıdʒ ʊ əm
	ri ZID yŏŏ uhm	§ 49(15, 33)	rı ′zıd jʊ əm, -ju-
resin	REZ in	rĕz′ĭn	′rez ın
	REZ ′n	rĕz′ ′n § 33(2)	′rez n̩
resist	ri ZIST	rĕ zĭst′	rı ′zıst
resonance	REZ uh nuhns	rĕz′ŏ năns	′rez ə nəns
resource	ri SOHRS	rĕ sōrs′	rı ′sors, -′sɔrs,
	ri SAWRS		′ri sors, -sɔrs;
	REE sohrs	rē′sōrs	ES -′soəs, -soəs;
	REE sawrs	§§ 34(3), 47(1)	E also -′sɔəs, -sɔəs
respects (n. pl.)	ri SPEKTS	rĕ spĕkts′ § 48(3)	rı ′spekts
respiratory	ri SPAIR uh toh ri	rĕ spīr′a̍ tō′rĭ	rı ′spaır ə ˌto rı
	ri SPAIR uh taw ri		rı ′spaır ə ˌtɔ rı
	RES puh ruh toh ri	rĕs′pĭ ra̍ tō′rĭ	′res pə rə ˌto rı
	RES puh ruh taw ri		′res pə rə ˌtɔ rı
	RES pi ruh toh ri	rĕs′pĭ ra̍ tō′rĭ	′res pı rə ˌto rı
	RES pi ruh taw ri § 50(34)	§§ 34(3), 47(3)	′res pı rə ˌtɔ rı
respire	ri SPAIR § 50(34)	rĕ spīr′	rı ′spaır; ES -′spaıə(r)
respite	RES pit	rĕs′pĭt	′res pıt
restaurant	RES tuh ruhnt	rĕs′tŏ rănt	′res tə rənt
	RES tuh rahnt	rĕs′tŏ ränt § 47(3)	′res tə rɑnt
restitution	res tuh TYOO shuhn	rĕs′tĭ tū′shŭn	ˌres tə ′tju ʃən
	res tuh TOO shuhn		ˌres tə ′tu ʃən
	res ti TYOO shuhn	rĕs′tĭ tū′shŭn	ˌres tı ′tju ʃən
	res ti TOO shuhn	§§ 48(2), 50(30, 32)	ˌres tı ′tu ʃən
restorative	ri STOHR uh tiv	rĕ stōr′a̍ tĭv	rı ′stor ə tıv
	ri STAWR uh tiv	§§ 34(3), 50(17)	rı ′stɔr ə tıv
resume	ri ZYOOM	rĕ zūm′	rı ′zjum
	ri ZOOM	§§ 40(4), 48(2), 49(15), 50(32)	rı ′zum

	SIMPLIFIED	DIACRITICAL	PHONETIC
résumé	*ray* zyōō MAY	rā′zŭ mā′	ˌre zjʊ ˈme
	ray zōō MAY		ˌre zʊ ˈme
	REZ ōō may	rĕz′ŭ mā	ˈrez ʊ me
	REZ yōō may		ˈrez jʊ me
	Pop.:	*Pop.:*	*Pop.:*
	rez ōō MAY	rĕz′ŭ mā′	ˌrez ʊ ˈme
	rez yōō MAY	§ 51(3)	ˌrez jʊ ˈme
resuscitate	ri SUHS *i* tayt	rĕ sŭs′ĭ tāt	rɪ ˈsʌs ə tet
	ri SUHS i tayt	rĕ sŭs′ĭ tāt	rɪ ˈsʌs ɪ tet
resuscitation	ri *suhs* uh TAY shuhn	rĕ sŭs′ĭ tā′shŭn	rɪ ˌsʌs ə ˈte ʃən
	ri *suhs* i TAY shuhn	rĕ sŭs′ĭ tā′shŭn	rɪ ˌsʌs ɪ ˈte ʃən
resuscitative	ri SUHS uh *tay* tiv	rĕ sŭs′ĭ tā′tĭv	rɪ ˈsʌs ə ˌte tɪv
	ri SUHS i *tay* tiv	rĕ sŭs′ĭ tā′tĭv	rɪ ˈsʌs ɪ ˌte tɪv
retail (n., adj.)	REE tayl	rē′tāl § 11	ˈri tel
—— (v.)	REE tayl	rē′tāl	ˈri tel
	ri TAYL	rĕ tāl′ §§ 12, 47(1)	rɪ ˈtel
—— *"relate in detail; repeat,"* esp.	ri TAYL	rĕ tāl′	rɪ ˈtel
retailer	REE tayl uhr	rē′tāl ēr	ˈri tel ɚ, rɪ ˈtel-;
	ri TAYL uhr	rĕ tāl′ēr § 47(3)	*ES* -ə(r)
retinue	RET i nyoo	rĕt′ĭ nū	ˈret ɪ nju, -nu,
	RET i noo	§§ 48(2), 50(32)	ˈret n̩ ju
retort	ri TAWRT	rĕ tôrt′	rɪ ˈtɔrt; *ES* -ˈtɔət
retrograde	RET roh grayd	rĕt′rŏ grād	ˈret ro gred,
	REE troh grayd	rē′ trŏ grād § 47(3)	ˈri tro-, -rə-, -trə-
retrospect	RET roh spekt	rĕt′rŏ spĕkt	ˈret ro spekt,
	REE troh spekt	rē′trŏ spĕkt § 47(3)	ˈri tro-, -rə-, -trə-
revenue	REV uh nyoo	rĕv′ĕ nū	ˈrev ə nju
	REV uh noo	§§ 48(2), 50(32)	ˈrev ə nu
reverie	REV uhr i	rĕv′ēr ĭ § 47(2)	ˈrev ər ɪ
reversion	ri VUHR shuhn	rĕ vûr′shŭn	rɪ ˈvɝ ʃən, -ʒən;
	ri VUHR zhuhn	rĕ vûr′zhŭn §§ 47(1), 50(28)	*ES also* -ˈvɜ-
revolt	ri VOHLT	rĕ vōlt′	rɪ ˈvolt, -ˈvɑlt; *ES*
	ri VOLT	rĕ vŏlt′ § 47(2)	*also* -ˈvɒlt
revolution	*rev* uh LOO shuhn	rĕv′ŏ lū′shŭn	ˌrev ə ˈlu ʃən
	rev uh LYOO shuhn	§§ 40(4), 48(2), 49(15), 50(30, 32)	ˌrev ə ˈlju ʃən
			ˌrev l̩ ˈju ʃən

	SIMPLIFIED	DIACRITICAL	PHONETIC
revolutionary	*rev* uh LOO shuhn *er* i	rĕv′ŏ lū′shŭn ēr′ĭ § 48(2)	ˌrɛv ə ′lu ʃən ˌɛr ɪ
	rev uh LYOO shuhn *er* i		ˌrɛv ə ′lju ʃən ˌɛr ɪ
	B., *rev* uh LOO shuhn uhr i	*B.*, rĕv′ŏ lū′shŭn ēr ĭ §§ 13, 51(4)	*B.*, ˌrɛv ə ′lu ʃən ə rɪ
Reynard	REN uhrd RAY nahrd RAY nuhrd	rĕn′ērd rā′närd rā′nērd § 47(3)	′rɛn ɚd, ′re nɑrd, -nɚd; *ES* -əd, -nɑːd, -nəd; *E also* -nɑːd
rhapsodical	rap SOD i kuhl	răp sŏd′ĭ kăl	ræp ′sɑd ɪ kəl; *ES also* -′sɒd-
rhapsody	RAP suh di	răp′sŏ dĭ	′ræp sə dɪ
rheum	room	rōōm §§ 37(5), 40(4)	rum
rhododendron	*roh* duh DEN druhn	rō′dŏ dĕn′drŏn	ˌro də ′dɛn drən
rhubarb	ROO bahrb	rōō′bärb § 40(4)	′ru bɑrb; *ES* -bɑːb, *E also* -bɑːb
rhythm	rĭth′m rĭth′m	rĭth′m rĭth′m §§ 9, 47(2)	rɪðm̩, ′rɪð əm, rɪθm̩, ′rɪθ əm
ribald	RIB uhld RIB ′ld	rĭb′ăld rĭb′ ′ld § 31(3)	′rɪb əld ′rɪb l̩
Richelieu	*ree* shuh LYUH *Angl.:* REESH uh loo RISH uh loo *rish* uh LOO	rē′shĕ lyû′ *Angl.:* rēsh′ē lōō rĭsh′ē lōō rĭsh′ē lōō′ §§ 48(2), 51(1)	*F.*, ri ʃə ′ljø *Angl.:* ′riʃ ə lu, ′rɪʃ-, ˌrɪʃ ə ′lu, -′lju
ridiculous	ri DIK yŏŏ luhs	rĭ dĭk′û lŭs	rɪ ′dɪk jʊ ləs, -jə-, -ju-
righteous	RAI chuhs § 50(34)	rī′chŭs §§ 40(11), 47(3)	′raɪ tʃəs
rigmarole	RIG muh rohl	rĭg′ma rōl	′rɪg mə rol
rind	raind § 50(34)	rīnd	raɪnd
rinse	rins	rĭns § 39(3)	rɪns
Rio de Janeiro	REE oh day zhuh NAY roh	rē′ō dā zha nā′rō	′ri o de ʒə ′ne ro
	REE oh day zhuh NEH roh	rē′ō dā zha nâ′rō	′ri o de ʒə ′nɛ ro
	REE oh di juh NEE roh	rē′ō dĭ ja nē′rō	′ri o dɪ dʒə ′ni ro
	Pg., REE ŏŏ ŧħuh zhuh NAY rŏŏ REE ŏŏ di zhuh NAY rŏŏ	*Pg.*, rē′ŏŏ ŧħĕ zha nā′rŏŏ rē′ŏŏ dĕ zha nā′rŏŏ	*Pg.*, ′ri ʊ ðə ʒə ′ne rʊ, -ʒa ′ne i rʊ, -dɪ ʒə ′ne rʊ
rise (v., n.)	raiz § 50(34)	rīz	raɪz

	SIMPLIFIED	DIACRITICAL	PHONETIC
—— (n. also—rarely)	rais § 50(34)	rīs §§ 38(4), 48(3)	raɪs
risible	RIZ uh b'l RIZ i b'l	rĭz′ĭ b'l rĭz′ĭ b'l	ˈrɪz ə bl̩ ˈrɪz ɪ bl̩
risks	risks	rĭsks §§ 48(3), 50(6)	rɪsks
roar	rohr rawr	rōr § 34(3)	ror, rɔr; *ES* roə(r), *E also* rɔə(r)
roaring	ROHR ing RAWR ing	rōr′ĭng §§ 34(3), 50(24)	ˈror ɪŋ, ˈrɔr-; *ES* ˈroər-, *E also* ˈrɔər-
robust	roh BUHST	rŏ bŭst′ § 11	ro ˈbʌst
role, rôle	rohl	rōl	rol
romance (n.— "*tale*")	roh MANS ROH mans	rŏ măns′ rō′măns	ro ˈmæns, rə- ˈro mæns
—— (v.)	roh MANS	rŏ măns′ §§ 12, 47(1)	ro ˈmæns, rə-
Romeo	ROH mi oh	rō′mĕ ō	ˈro mɪ o
roof	roof roŏf	rōōf § 34(22)	ruf rʊf
room	room roŏm	rōōm §§ 34(22), 40(4), 47(1)	rum rʊm
Roosevelt	ROH zuh velt *Also, esp. in some* *stress patterns:* ROHZ velt ROOS velt	rō′zĕ vĕlt *Also, esp. in some* *stress patterns:* rōz′vĕlt rōōs′vĕlt § 51(11)	ˈro zə vɛlt *Also, esp. in some* *stress patterns:* ˈroz vɛlt ˈrus vɛlt
root	root roŏt	rōōt § 34(22)	rut rʊt
Rosalind	ROZ uh lind ROZ uh laind § 50(34)	rŏz′á lĭnd rŏz′á līnd	ˈraz ə lɪnd, -laɪnd, ˈraz l̩ ɪnd; *ES* *also* ˈrɒz-
roseate (adj.)	ROH zi ayt ROH zi it	rō′zĕ ăt rō′zĕ ĭt	ˈro zɪ et ˈro zɪ ɪt
—— (v.t.—rare)	ROH zi ayt	rō′zĕ āt § 20(8, 9)	ˈro zɪ et
rosin	ROZ in ROZ 'n	rŏz′ĭn rŏz′ 'n	ˈraz ɪn, -n̩; *ES* *also* ˈrɒz-
rotary	ROH tuh ri	rō′tá rĭ	ˈro tə rɪ
rotate (v.)	ROH tayt *B.*, roh TAYT	rō′tāt *B.*, rŏ tāt′ § 51(4)	ˈro tet *B.*, ro ˈtet
—— (adj.)	ROH tayt	rō′tāt	ˈro tet
rouge	roozh	rōōzh	ruʒ
roundabout	ROWND uh *bowt* § 50(34)	round′á bout′	ˈraʊnd ə ˌbaʊt

	SIMPLIFIED	DIACRITICAL	PHONETIC
roundelay	ROWN duh lay § 50(34)	roun′dĕ lā	'raʊn də le 'raʊn dļ e
Rousseau	*roo* SOH	rōō′sō′	ˌru 'so
rout	rowt § 50(34)	rout § 51(7)	raʊt
route	root	rōōt § 47(1)	rut
—— *"delivery route,"* often	rowt	rout § 51(11)	raʊt
—— in special fields (*e.g.,* among military men and rail-road men), often	rowt § 50(34)	rout § 51(6)	raʊt
—— colloquially	rowt § 50(34)	rout § 51(3)	raʊt
routine	roo TEEN	rōō tēn′ § 11	ru 'tin
rowel	ROW uhl § 50(34)	rou′ĕl	'raʊ əl
rubric	ROO brik	rōō′brĭk § 48(2)	'ru brɪk
rudiments	ROO duh muhnts ROO di muhnts	rōō′dĭ mĕnts rōō′dĭ mĕnts § 48(3)	'ru də mənts 'ru dɪ mənts
ruffian	RUHF i uhn RUHF yuhn	rŭf′ĭ ăn rŭf′yăn §§ 28(9), 47(1)	'rʌf ɪ ən 'rʌf jən
ruin	ROO in	rōō′ĭn §§ 40(4), 48(2)	'ru ɪn
rule	rool	rōōl §§ 40(4), 48(2)	rul
rumor, rumour	ROO muhr	rōō′mēr §§ 40(4), 48(2)	'ru mɚ; *ES* -mə(r)
rung	*ruhng*	rŭng § 40(6)	rʌŋ
rupture	RUHP chuhr RUHP tyuhr	rŭp′tûr § 50(31)	'rʌp tʃɚ, -tjɚ; *ES* -tʃə(r), -tjə(r)
rural	RŌŌR uhl	rŏŏr′ăl §§ 34(21), 40(4), 48(2)	'rʊr əl
ruse	rooz	rōōz §§ 40(4), 48(2)	ruz
Russia	RUHSH uh	rŭsh′á	'rʌʃ ə
rustle	RUHS ′l	rŭs′ ′l	'rʌs ļ
ruthless	ROOTH les ROOTH lis	rōōth′lĕs rōōth′lĭs §§ 24(5), 50(18)	'ruθ lɛs 'ruθ lɪs

S

sacerdotal	*sas* uhr DOH tuhl	săs′ēr dō′tăl	ˌsæs ɚ ˈdo təl, -tḷ;
	sas uhr DOH t'l	săs′ēr dō′t'l	*ES* -ə ˈdo-
		§ 31(3)	
sachem	SAY chuhm	sā′chĕm	ˈse tʃəm
sachet	sa SHAY	să shā′	sæ ˈʃe
	B., SASH ay	B., săsh′ā	B., ˈsæʃ e
		§ 51(4)	
sacrifice (n.)	SAK ruh fais	săk′rĭ fīs	ˈsæk rə faɪs
(*Note: For the*	SAK ri fais	săk′rĭ fīs	ˈsæk rɪ faɪs
verb as well as	SAK ruh faiz	săk′rĭ fīz	ˈsæk rə faɪz
the noun, the	SAK ri faiz	săk′rĭ fīz	ˈsæk rɪ faɪz
pronunciation	§ 50(34)	§§ 22(1), 47(3)	
with "s" is now			
more frequent.)			
—— (v.)	SAK ruh faiz	săk′rĭ fīz	ˈsæk rə faɪz
	SAK ri faiz	săk′rĭ fīz	ˈsæk rɪ faɪz
	SAK ruh fais	săk′rĭ fīs	ˈsæk rə faɪs
	SAK ri fais	săk′rĭ fīs	ˈsæk rɪ faɪs
	§ 50(34)	§ 47(3)	
sacrilege	SAK ruh lej	săk′rĭ lĕj	ˈsæk rə ledʒ
	SAK ri lej	săk′rĭ lĕj	ˈsæk rɪ ledʒ
	SAK ruh lij	săk′rĭ lĭj	ˈsæk rə lɪdʒ
	SAK ri lij	săk′rĭ lĭj	ˈsæk rɪ lɪdʒ
sacrilegious	*sak* ruh LEE juhs	săk′rĭ lē′jŭs	ˌsæk rə ˈli dʒəs
	sak ri LEE juhs	săk′rĭ lē′jŭs	ˌsæk rɪ ˈli dʒəs
	sak ruh LIJ uhs	săk′rĭ lĭj′ŭs	ˌsæk rə ˈlɪdʒ əs
	sak ri LIJ uhs	săk′rĭ lĭj′ŭs	ˌsæk rɪ ˈlɪdʒ əs
		§ 50(25)	
sad	sad	săd	sæd
safety	SAYF ti	sāf′tĭ	ˈsef tɪ
saffron	SAF ruhn	săf′rŭn § 47(2)	ˈsæf rən
	Occas.:	*Occas.:*	*Occas.:*
	SAF uhrn	săf′ĕrn § 51(8)	ˈsæf ɚn; *ES* -ən
saga	SAH guh	sä′gȧ	ˈsɑ gə
	SAY guh	sā′gȧ § 47(1)	ˈse gə
sagacious	suh GAY shuhs	sȧ gā′shŭs	sə ˈge ʃəs
		§ 50(25)	

	SIMPLIFIED	DIACRITICAL	PHONETIC
Sahara	suh HAH ruh suh HEHR uh	sȧ hä′rȧ sȧ hâr′ȧ § 47(1)	sə ′hɑ rə, -′her-, -′he rə; *ES also* -′hɛər ə
said	sed *Unstressed:* suhd	sĕd *Unstressed:* sĕd § 16	sed *Unstressed:* səd
sail	sayl	sāl	sel
saint	saynt *Unstressed or un- accented, as in "Saint Louis," esp. British:* B., sint suhnt s'n	sānt *Unstressed or un- accented, as in "Saint Louis," esp. British:* B., sȧnt sĕnt s'n §§ 16, 51(4)	sent *Unstressed or un- accented, as in "Saint Louis," esp. British:* B., sınt, sənt, sn̩t, sın, sən, sn̩
Saint Louis, **St. Louis** (See *saint.*)	saynt LOO is saynt LOO i	sȧnt lōō′ĭs sȧnt lōō′ĭ §§ 38(2), 48(2)	sent ′lu ıs sent ′lu ı
saith (arch.)	seth	sĕth	sɛθ
salary	SAL uh ri	săl′ȧ rĭ	′sæl ə rı
salient	SAY li uhnt	sā′lĭ ĕnt § 28(9)	′se lı ənt, ′sel jənt
saline (adj.)	SAY lain͡ § 50(34)	sā′līn § 47(2)	′se laın
—— (n.)	SAY lain͡ B., suh LAIN͡	sā′līn B., sȧ līn′ § 51(4)	′se laın B., sə ′laın
Salisbury	SAWLZ *ber* i SAWLZ buhr i	sôlz′bĕr′ĭ sôlz′bĕr ĭ § 13	′sɔlz ˌbɜɹ ı ′sɔlz bə rı
salivary	SAL uh *ver* i SAL i *ver* i B., SAL uh vuhr i	săl′ĭ vĕr′ĭ săl′ĭ vĕr′ĭ B., săl′ĭ vĕr ĭ §§ 13, 20(2), 24(9), 50(4)	′sæl ə ˌver ı ′sæl ı ˌver ı B., ′sæl ə və rı
salmon	SAM uhn	săm′ŭn	′sæm ən
salon	*sah* LAWN sa LON	sȧ′lôɴ′ sȧ lŏn′ § 20(14)	F., sa ′lɔ̃ [-′lõ] sæ ′lɑn, -′lɒn
salt	sawlt	sôlt §§ 20(6), 31(2)	sɔlt
salubrious	suh LOO bri uhs suh LYOO bri uhs	sȧ lū′brĭ ŭs §§ 40(4), 48(2), 50(25)	sə ′lu brı əs sə ′lju brı əs
salutary	SAL yŏŏ *ter* i B., SAL yŏŏ tuhr i	săl′ū tĕr′ĭ B., săl′ū tĕr ĭ §§ 13, 20(2), 24(9), 51(4)	′sæl jʊ ˌter ı, -jə-, -ju- B., ′sæl jʊ tə rı
salute	suh LOOT suh LYOOT	sȧ lūt′ §§ 40(4, 11), 48(2)	sə ′lut sə ′ljut

	SIMPLIFIED	DIACRITICAL	PHONETIC
salvage	SAL vij	săl′vĭj § 50(1)	′sæl vɪdʒ
salve (n.– "*ointment*")	sahv sav	säv săv § 51(7)	sɑv sæv
salve (v.–"*save*")	salv	sălv § 51(7)	sælv
salve (interj.)	SAL vi	săl′vĕ § 51(7)	′sæl vɪ
salver (n.– "*tray*")	SAL vuhr	săl′vẽr	′sæl vɚ; *ES* -və(r)
sample	SAM p'l SAHM p'l	săm′p'l § 20(5)	′sæm pḷ; *E also* ′sam-, ′sɑm-
sanction	SANGK shuhn	săngk′shŭn § 33(4)	′sæŋk ʃən
sanctuary	SANGK chŏŏ er i SANGK tyŏŏ er i *B.*, SANGK tyŏŏ uhr i	săngk′tŭ ĕr′ĭ §§ 20(2), 24(9), 33(4) *B.*, săngk′tŭ ẽr ĭ §§ 13, 51(4)	′sæŋk tʃʊ ˌɛr ɪ ′sæŋk tjʊ ˌɛr ɪ *B.*, ′sæŋk tjʊ ə rɪ
San Diego	san di AY goh	săn dĕ ā′gō	sæn dɪ ′e go, -di-
sandwich	SAND wich *Familiar speech, often:* SAN wich	sănd′wĭch *Familiar speech, often:* săn′wĭch §§ 23(1), 51(3)	′sænd wɪtʃ *Familiar speech, often:* ′sæn wɪtʃ
sanguine	SANG gwin	săng′gwĭn § 50(24)	′sæŋ gwɪn
sanitarium	*san* uh TEHR i uhm *san* i TEHR i uhm *san* uh TAY ri uhm	săn′ĭ târ′ĭ ŭm §§ 20(2), 24(9)	ˌsæn ə ′tɛr ɪ əm, -ɪ ′tɛr-, -′te rɪ-; *ES also* -′tɛər-
San Jose (Costa Rica)	sahn hoh SAY sahn hoh ZAY	sän hŏ sā′ sän hŏ zā′	sɑn ho ′se sɑn ho ′ze
San Jose (Calif.)	san hoh SAY san hoh ZAY	săn hŏ sā′ săn hŏ zā′	sæn ho ′se sæn ho ′ze
San Juan	san HWAHN *Sp.*, sahn HWAHN	săn hwän′ *Sp.*, sän hwän′	sæn ′hwɑn *Sp.*, sɑn ′hwɑn
sank	sangk	săngk	sæŋk
Santa Fé (Argentina)	SAHN tah FAY SAN tuh FAY	sän′tä fā′ săn′tá fā′	′sɑn tɑ ′fe ′sæn tə ′fe *Sp.*, ˌsɑn tɑ ′fe
Santa Fe (New Mexico)	SAN tuh FAY	săn′tá fā′	′sæn tə ′fe, -ˌfe
Santiago	*sahn* ti AH goh	sän′tĕ ä′gō	ˌsɑn tɪ ′ɑ go, ˌsæn-, -′e-, *Sp.*, sɑn ti ′a go
sapience	SAY pi uhns	sā′pĭ ĕns § 28(9)	′se pɪ əns, -pjəns
sapient	SAY pi uhnt	sā′pĭ ĕnt § 28(9)	′se pɪ ənt, -pjənt
Saracen	SAR uh suhn	săr′á sĕn	′sær ə sən, -sn̩

	SIMPLIFIED	DIACRITICAL	PHONETIC
sarcophagus	sahr KOF uh guhs	sär kŏf′á gŭs	sɑr ′kɑf ə gəs; *ES* sɑ:-, *also* -′kɒf-, *E also* sɑ:-
sardine ("*fish*")	sahr DEEN SAHR deen	sär dēn′ sär′dēn §§ 47(3), 51(7)	sɑr ′din, ′sɑr din; *ES* sɑ:-, ′sɑ:-, *E also* sɑ:-, ′sɑ:-
sarsaparilla	*sahr* suh puh RIL uh	sär′sá pá rĭl′á § 9	ˌsɑr sə pə ′rɪl ə, -spə-, ˌsæ-; *ES* ˌsɑ:-, *E also* ˌsɑ:-
satiate (v.)	SAY shi ayt	sā′shĭ āt	′se ʃɪ et
—— (adj.)	SAY shi it	sā′shĭ ăt § 20(8, 9)	′se ʃɪ ɪt
satiety	suh TAI uh ti § 50(34)	sá tī′ĕ tĭ	sə ′taɪ ə tɪ, sæ ′taɪ-
satin (n.)	SAT in SAT ′n	săt′ĭn săt′ ′n § 33(2)	′sæt ɪn ′sæt n̩
satire	SAT air § 50(34)	săt′īr § 47(2)	′sæt aɪr; *ES* -aɪə(r)
satirical	suh TIR i kuhl	sá tĭr′ĭ kăl	sə ′tɪr ɪ kəl, sæ-
satisfactory	*sat* is FAK tuh ri	săt′ĭs făk′tŏ rĭ § 9	ˌsæt ɪs ′fæk tə rɪ, -trɪ
satisfactorily	*sat* is FAK tuh ruh li	săt′ĭs făk′tŏ rĭ lĭ §§ 9, 50(20)	ˌsæt ɪs ′fæk tə rə lɪ, -trə lɪ
satrap	SAY trap SAT rap *B.*, SAT ruhp	sā′trăp săt′răp *B.*, săt′răp §§ 47(1), 51(4)	′se træp ′sæt ræp *B.*, ′sæt rəp
saturate (v.t.)	SACH o͝o rayt SAT yo͞o rayt	săt′u͡ rāt	′sæt ʃ ʊ ret, -ə ret, ′sæt ju-, -jə-
—— (adj.)	SACH uh rit SAT yuh rit	săt′u͡ răt §§ 20(8, 9), 50(2)	′sæt ʃ ə rɪt ′sæt jə rɪt
Saturday	SAT uhr di SAT uhr day	săt′ẽr dĭ săt′ẽr dă § 20(9)	′sæt ɚ di, -de; *ES* -ə dɪ, -ə de
saturnine	SAT uhr nain § 50(34)	săt′ẽr nīn § 47(2)	′sæt ɚ naɪn; *ES* -ə naɪn
satyr	SAT uhr SAY tuhr	săt′ẽr sā′tẽr § 47(3)	′sæt ɚ, ′se tɚ; *ES* -ə(r), -tə(r)
saucy	SAW si	sô′sĭ	′sɔ sɪ
sauerkraut	SOWR *krowt*	sour′kraut′	′saʊr ˌkraʊt; *ES* ′saʊə ˌkraʊt
saunter	SAWN tuhr SAHN tuhr	sôn′tẽr sän′tẽr § 47(3)	′sɔn tɚ, ′sɑn-; *ES* -tə(r)
sausage	SAW sij	sô′sĭj §§ 22(5), 50(1)	′sɔ sɪdʒ, ′sɒ-, ′sɑ-
sauté	soh TAY	sō tā′	so ′te
savage	SAV ij	săv′ĭj § 50(1)	′sæv ɪdʒ

	SIMPLIFIED	DIACRITICAL	PHONETIC
savant	suh vahN *sah* vahN SAV uhnt suh VAHNT	sȧ vän′ sä′vän′ săv′ănt §§ 20(14), 47(1)	*Fr.*, sa ′vã; ′sæv ənt, sə ′vænt, -′vɑnt
savory	SAY vuhr i	sā′vĕr ĭ § 9	′se vər ɪ, -vrɪ
saw (*"tool"; p.t.* of *"see"*)	saw	sô	sɔ
say	say	sā	se
says	sez *Unstressed:* suhz	sĕz *Unstressed:* sĕz §§ 16, 50(6)	sɛz *Unstressed:* səz
scallop	SKOL uhp SKAL uhp	skŏl′ŭp skăl′ŭp § 47(3)	′skɑl əp, ′skæl-; *ES also* ′skɒl-
scalp	skalp	skălp	skælp
scared (*"alarmed;* *driven by fear"*)	skehrd	skârd	skɛrd, skæərd; *ES* skææd, *E also* skɛəd
	Colloq. and dial.: skehrt	*Colloq. and dial.:* skârt § 51(2, 3)	*Colloq. and dial.:* skɛrt, skæært; *ES* skæət, *E also* skɛət
scarred (*"marred"*)	skahrd	skärd	skɑrd; *ES* skɑːd, *E also* skaːd
scathe	skayth	skāth § 47(2)	skeð
scenario	si NAH ri oh si NEHR i oh shay NAH ri oh *It.*, shay NAH ree oh	sĕ nä′rĭ ō sĕ nâr′ĭ ō shā nä′rĭ ō *It.*, shā nä′rē ō § 47(1)	sɪ ′nɑ rɪ o sɪ ′ner ɪ o, -′nær-; *ES also* -′nɛər- ʃe ′nɑ rɪ o *It.*, ʃe ′nɑː ri o, -rjo
scenic	SEE nik SEN ik	sē′nĭk sĕn′ĭk § 47(3)	′si nɪk ′sɛn ɪk
scepter	SEP tuhr	sĕp′tēr	′sɛp tɚ; *ES* -tə(r)
schedule	SKEJ ool SKED yool	skĕd′ūl §§ 47(2), 50(33)	′skɛdʒ ul, -ʊl ′skɛd jul
schism	SIZ ′m	sĭz′ ′m §§ 22(9), 32(2)	′sɪz m̩, ′sɪz əm
schismatic	siz MAT ik	sĭz măt′ĭk	sɪz ′mæt ɪk
Schleswig- Holstein	SHLAYS vik HOHL shtain SHLES wig HOHL stain	shlās′vĭk hōl′shtīn § 30(2) shlĕs′wĭg hōl′stīn	*G.*, ′ʃleːs vɪx ′hol ʃtaɪn, ′ʃlɛs-; ′ʃlɛs wɪg ′hol staɪn
school	skool	skō͞ol § 34(22)	skul
schoolman (*"a* *Scholastic"*)	SKOOL muhn	skō͞ol′măn § 50(21)	′skul mən

—— *"one who teaches in or manages a school"*	SKOOL *man*	skōōl′măn′ § 51(11)	'skul ˌmæn
science	SAI͡ uhns § 50(34)	sī′ĕns	'saɪ əns
scientific	*sai͡* uhn TIF ik § 50(34)	sī′ĕn tĭf′ĭk	ˌsaɪ ən 'tɪf ɪk
scion	SAI͡ uhn § 50(34)	sī′ŭn	'saɪ ən
scissors	SIZ uhrz	sĭz′ĕrz § 38(9)	'sɪz ɚz; *ES* -əz
scourge	*skuhrj*	skûrj § 40(6)	skɝdʒ; *ES also* skɜdʒ
scratch	skrach	skrăch	skrætʃ
Scripture, scripture	SKRIP chuhr SKRIP tyuhr	skrĭp′tūr § 50(31)	'skrɪp tʃɚ, -tjɚ; *ES* -tʃə(r), -tjə(r)
sculpture	SKUHLP chuhr SKUHLP tyuhr	skŭlp′tūr § 50(31)	'skʌlp tʃɚ, -tjɚ; *ES* -tʃə(r), -tjə(r)
scurrility	skuh RIL uh ti skuh RIL i ti *skuh* RIL uh ti	skŭ rĭl′ĭ tĭ skŭ rĭl′ĭ tĭ § 40(7)	skə 'rɪl ə tɪ, skɝ 'ɪl-, -ɪtɪ; *ES also* skɜ 'rɪl-, skʌ-
scurrilous	SKUHR uh luhs SKUHR i luhs	skûr′ĭ lŭs skûr′ĭ lŭs § 40(7)	'skɝ ə ləs, -ɪ ləs; *ES also* 'skɜr-, 'skʌr-
Scylla	SIL uh	sĭl′ă	'sɪl ə
scythe	saith͡	sīth § 38(9)	saɪð
seamstress	SEEM stres SEEM stris SEM stris	sēm′strĕs sēm′strĭs sĕm′strĭs §§ 24(5), 47(2), 50(8)	'sim strɛs 'sim strɪs 'sɛm strɪs
season	SEE z'n	sē′z'n	'si zn̩
sebaceous	si BAY shuhs	sĕ bā′shŭs § 49(16)	sɪ 'be ʃəs
secondary	SEK uhn *der* i *B.,* SEK uhn duhr i	sĕk′ŭn dĕr′ĭ *B.,* sĕk′ŭn dĕr ĭ §§ 13, 20(2), 24(9), 51(4)	'sɛk ən ˌder ɪ *B.,* 'sɛk ən də rɪ
second-hand (adj., adv.)	SEK uhnd HAND	sĕk′ŭnd hănd′	'sɛk ənd 'hænd
secondhand (n.)	SEK uhnd *hand*	sĕk′ŭnd hănd′ § 11	'sɛk ənd ˌhænd
secretary˙	SEK ri *ter* i *B.,* SEK ri tuhr i	sĕk′rĕ tĕr′ĭ §§ 20(2), 24(9), 48(1) *B.,* sĕk′rĕ tĕr ĭ §§ 13, 51(4)	'sɛk rɪ ˌter ɪ, *by dissimilation* 'sɛk ə ˌter ɪ *B.,* 'sɛk rɪ tə rɪ

secrete	si KREET	sĕ krēt′ § 49(16)	sɪ 'krit
secretive	si KREE tiv	sĕ krē′tĭv § 49(16)	sɪ 'kri tɪv
sects	sekts	sĕkts § 48(3)	sɛkts
secular	SEK yŏŏ luhr	sĕk′ū lēr	'sɛk jʊ lɚ, -jə-, -ju-; *ES* -lə(r)
secure	si KYOOR si KYOOR	sĕ kūr′ §§ 34(21), 48(2), 49(16), 50(32)	sɪ 'kjʊr; *ES* -'kjʊə(r)
sedan	si DAN	sĕ dăn′ § 49(16)	sɪ 'dæn
sedative	SED uh tiv	sĕd′a̤ tĭv § 50(3)	'sɛd ə tɪv
sedentary	SED uhn *ter* i	sĕd′ĕn tēr′ĭ §§ 20(2), 24(9)	'sɛd ən ˌter ɪ, 'sɛd n̩ ˌter ɪ
	B., SED uhn tuhr i	*B.*, sĕd′ĕn tēr ĭ §§ 13, 51(4)	*B.*, 'sɛd ən tə rɪ
seduce	si DYOOS	sĕ dūs′ §§ 48(2), 49(16), 50(32)	sɪ 'djus sɪ 'dus
sedulous	SEJ ŏŏ luhs SEJ uh luhs SED yŏŏ luhs	sĕd′ū lŭs § 50(25)	'sɛdʒ ʊ ləs 'sɛdʒ ə ləs 'sɛd jʊ ləs, -jə-
seethe	seeth	sēth	si ð
seigneur	seen YUHR *F.*, *sen* YUHR	sēn yûr′ *F.*, sĕn′yûr′	sin 'jɝ; *ES* -'jɝ(r) *F.*, sɛ 'ɲœːr
Seine	sayn	sān § 24(20)	sen; *F.*, sɛːn
seine	sayn seen	sān sēn § 47(2)	sen sin; *F.*, siːn
seizure	SEE zhuhr	sē′zhēr	'si ʒɚ; *ES* -ʒə(r)
self	self	sĕlf	sɛlf
semester	si MES tuhr	sĕ mĕs′tēr § 49(16)	sɪ 'mɛs tɚ; *ES* -tə(r)
semi–	SEM i–	sĕm′ĭ–	'sɛm ɪ–, 'sɛm ə–
Semite	SEM ait SEE mait § 50(34)	sĕm′īt sē′mīt	'sɛm aɪt 'si maɪt
Semitic	si MIT ik	sĕ mĭt′ĭk	sɪ 'mɪt ɪk
senate	SEN it SEN uht	sĕn′ĭt sĕn′a̤t § 47(1)	'sɛn ɪt 'sɛn ət
seneschal	SEN uh shuhl SEN i shuhl	sĕn′ĕ shăl sĕn′ĭ shăl	'sɛn ə ʃəl 'sɛn ɪ ʃəl
senile	SEE nail SEE nil § 50(34)	sē′nīl sē′nĭl §§ 28(5), 47(3), 50(13)	'si naɪl 'si nɪl
senility	si NIL uh ti si NIL i ti	sĕ nĭl′i̤ tĭ sĕ nĭl′ĭ tĭ § 50(16)	sɪ 'nɪl ə tɪ sɪ 'nɪl ɪ tɪ
senior	SEEN yuhr	sēn′yēr § 47(2)	'sin jɚ; *ES* -jə(r)

	SIMPLIFIED	DIACRITICAL	PHONETIC
sensual	SEN shŏŏ uhl *Not infreq.:* SENS yŏŏ uhl	sĕn′shŏŏ ăl *Not infreq.:* sĕns′ û ăl §§ 40(11), 47(1), 51(8)	'sɛn ʃʊ əl *Not infreq.:* 'sɛns jʊ əl
sensuous	SEN shŏŏ uhs SENS yŏŏ uhs	sĕn′shŏŏ ŭs sĕns′ û ŭs § 40(11)	'sɛn ʃʊ əs 'sɛns jʊ əs
sentence	SEN tuhns	sĕn′tĕns	'sɛn təns
sentences	SEN tuhns iz	sĕn′tĕns ĭz § 48(3)	'sɛn təns ɪz
sententious	sen TEN shuhs	sĕn tĕn′shŭs	sɛn 'tɛn ʃəs
sentience	SEN shi uhns SEN shuhns	sĕn′shĭ ĕns sĕn′shĕns § 28(9)	'sɛn ʃɪ əns 'sɛn ʃəns
sentient	SEN shuhnt SEN shi uhnt	sĕn′shĕnt sĕn′shĭ ĕnt § 47(3)	'sɛn ʃənt, -ʃɛnt, -ʃɪ ənt, -ʃɪ ɛnt
separate (v.)	SEP uh rayt	sĕp′á rāt § 20(8, 9)	'sɛp ə ret, 'sɛp ret
—— (adj., n.)	SEP uh rit	sĕp′á rĭt § 9	'sɛp ə rɪt, 'sɛp rɪt
Septuagint	SEP chŏŏ uh jint SEP tyŏŏ uh jint	sĕp′tŭ á jĭnt § 50(33)	'sɛp tʃʊ ə dʒɪnt 'sɛp tjʊ ə dʒɪnt
sepulcher, sepulchre	SEP uhl kuhr	sĕp′ŭl kẽr	'sɛp əl kɚ; *ES* -kə(r)
sequestration	*see* kwes TRAY shuhn *sek* wes TRAY shuhn	sē′kwĕs trā′shŭn sĕk′wĕs trā′shŭn § 47(3)	ˌsi kwɛs 'trɔ ʃən ˌsɛk wɛs 'tre ʃən
seraglio	si RAL yoh se RAL yoh si RAHL yoh	sĕ răl′yō sĕ răl′yō sĕ räl′yō §§ 26(3), 49(16)	sɪ 'ræl jo sɛ 'ræl jo sɪ 'rɑl jo
seraphic	si RAF ik	sĕ răf′ĭk § 49(16)	sɪ 'ræf ɪk, sɛ-
serenade	*ser* uh NAYD	sĕr′ĕ nād′	ˌsɛr ə 'ned
sergeant, serjeant	SAHR juhnt	sär′jĕnt §§ 24(8), 47(2)	'sɑr dʒənt; *ES* -'sɑ:-, *E also* -'sɑ:-
series	SĬER eez SIR eez SEER eez SĬER iz SIR iz SEER iz SI ri eez SEE ri eez	sẽr′ēz §§ 24(2), 47(3) sēr′ēz sẽr′ĭz sēr′ĭz sē′rĭ ēz sē′rĭ ēz	'sɪər iz, 'sɪr-, 'sir-, -ɪz, 'sɪ rɪ iz, 'si rɪ-; *ES* 'sɪər-
serious	SĬER i uhs SIR i uhs SEER i uhs	sẽr′ĭ ŭs §§ 24(2), 28(9) sēr′ĭ ŭs	'sɪər ɪ əs, 'sɪr-, 'sir-; *ES* 'sɪər-
serpentine (adj., v.)	SUHR puhn teen SUHR puhn taın̑	sûr′pĕn tēn sûr′pĕn tīn § 47(1)	'sɝ pən tin, -taɪn, -tɪn; *ES also* 'sɜ pən-

	SIMPLIFIED	DIACRITICAL	PHONETIC
—— (n.)	SUHR puhn teen	sûr′pĕn tēn	'sɝ pən tin; *ES* also 'sɜ-
serried	SER id	sĕr′ĭd	'sɛr ɪd
serum	SĬER uhm SIR uhm SEER uhm	sēr′ŭm § 24(2) sēr′ŭm	'sɪər əm, 'sɪr-, 'sir-; *ES* 'sɪər-
servant	SUHR vuhnt	sûr′vănt § 20(10)	'sɝ vənt; *ES* also 'sɜ-
servile	SUHR vil	sûr′vĭl	'sɝ vɪl; *ES* also 'sɜ-
	B., SUHR vai͡l § 50(34)	*B.*, sûr′vīl §§ 28(5), 47(3), 51(4)	*B.*, 'sɝ vaɪl; *ES* also 'sɜ-
servitude	SUHR vuh tyood SUHR vuh tood SUHR vi tyood SUHR vi tood	sûr′vĭ tūd sûr′vĭ tūd §§ 48(2), 50(32)	'sɝ və tjud, -tud, -vɪ-; *ES* also 'sɜ-
sesame	SES uh mi	sĕs′a̍ mĕ	'sɛs ə mɪ
settler	SET luhr	sĕt′lĕr	'sɛt lɚ; *ES* -lə(r)
several	SEV uhr uhl	sĕv′ēr ăl § 9	'sɛv ər əl
sewage	SYOO ij SOO ij	sū′ĭj §§ 48(2), 50(32)	'sju ɪdʒ 'su ɪdʒ
sewerage	SYOO uhr ij SOO uhr ij	sū′ēr ĭj §§ 48(2), 50(1, 32)	'sju ər ɪdʒ 'su ər ɪdʒ
shaft	shaft shahft	shȧft § 20(5)	ʃæft; *E also* ʃaft, ʃaft
shampoo	sham POO	shăm po͞o′	ʃæm 'pu
shan't	shahnt shant	shänt shȧnt § 20(5)	ʃant, ʃænt; *E also* ʃant
sheath (See *sheaths*.)	sheeth	shēth § 39(5, 6)	ʃiθ
sheathe	sheeth͟e	shēt͟h	ʃið
sheaths (n. pl. of "*sheath*")	sheet͟hz	shēt͟hz § 39(5)	ʃiðz
sheep	sheep	shēp	ʃip
sheik, sheikh	sheek *B.*, shayk	shēk *B.*, shāk §§ 47(3), 51(4)	ʃik *B.*, ʃek
shellac, shellack	shuh LAK she LAK SHEL ak	shĕ lăk′ shĕ lăk′ shĕl′ăk § 47(3)	ʃə 'læk ʃɛ 'læk 'ʃel æk
shepherd	SHEP uhrd	shĕp′ērd § 27(1)	'ʃep ɚd; *ES* -əd
sherbert	SHUHR buht SHUHR bit	shûr′bĕt shûr′bĭt	'ʃɝ bət, -bɪt; *ES* also 'ʃɜ-
shew (variant of *show*)	shoh	shō § 24(22)	ʃo
shewbread	SHOH *bred*	shō′brĕd′	'ʃo ˌbrɛd
ship	ship	shĭp	ʃɪp

shire	shaîr § 50(34)	shīr § 47(2)	ʃaɪr; *ES* ʃaɪə(r)
–shire (suffix)	–shir –shuhr	–shĭr –shĕr	–ʃɪr, –ʃɚ; *ES* –ʃɪə(r), –ʃə(r)
shone	shohn *B.*, shon	shōn § 47(2) *B.*, shŏn § 51(4)	ʃon *B.*, ʃɒn

short-lived	SHAWRT
	  LAÎVD
	B., SHAWRT
	  LIVD § 50(34)
		shôrt′līvd′
		  § 11
		B., shôrt′lĭvd′
		  § 51(4)
			′ʃɔrt ′laɪvd; *ES*
			  ′ʃɔət-
			B., ′ʃɔrt ′lɪvd; *ES*
			  ′ʃɔət-

shove (*"push"*)	*shuhv*	shŭv § 40(6)	ʃʌv
shrive	shraîv § 50(34)	shrīv	ʃraɪv
shrivel	SHRIV ′l	shrĭv′ ′l	′ʃrɪv l̩
shut	*shuht*	shŭt § 40(6)	ʃʌt
sibyl	SIB il SIB ′l	sĭb′ĭl sĭb′ ′l § 31(3)	′sɪb ɪl ′sɪb l̩
sierra	si ER uh	sĭ ĕr′*à*	sɪ ′ɛr ə
sieve	siv	sĭv	sɪv
sign	saîn § 50(34)	sīn § 25(5)	saɪn

signature	SIG nuh chuhr
	SIG nuh tyuhr
		sĭg′n*à* tûr
		  §§ 40̂(11),
		  50(31)
			′sɪg nə tʃɚ, -tjɚ;
			  ES -tʃə(r),
			  -tjə(r)

significant	sig NIF uh kuhnt sig NIF i kuhnt	sĭg nĭf′*ĭ* kǎnt sĭg nĭf′ĭ kǎnt	sɪg ′nɪf ə kənt sɪg ′nɪf ɪ kənt

signor	SEE nyawr
	SEEN yawr
	SEE nyohr
	SEEN yohr
		sē′nyôr
		
		sē′nyōr
			′si njɔr, -njor; *ES*
			  -njoə(r), *E also*
			  -njoə(r); *It.*
			  sin ′nor

signora	si NYOH rah
	sin YOH rah
	see NYOH rah
	seen YOH rah
		sĕ nyō′rä
		
		sē nyō′rä
			sɪ ′njo rɑ, sɪn ′jo-,
			  si ′njo-, sin ′jo-;
			  It., sin ′no: rɑ

silhouette	*sil* o͞o ET	sĭl′o͞o ĕt′	ˌsɪl ʊ ′ɛt
similar	SIM uh luhr SIM i luhr	sĭm′*ĭ* lĕr sĭm′ɪ lĕr	′sɪm ə lɚ, -ɪ-; *ES* -lə(r)

similarly	SIM uh luhr li
	SIM i luhr li
		sĭm′*ĭ* lĕr lĭ
		sĭm′ɪ lĕr lĭ
		  § 50(20)
			′sɪm ə lɚ lɪ, -ɪ lɚ-;
			  ES -lə lɪ

similitude	si MIL uh tyood si MIL uh tood si MIL i tyood si MIL i tood	sĭ mĭl′*ĭ* tūd sĭ mĭl′ɪ tūd §§ 48(2), 50(32)	sɪ ′mɪl ə tjud sɪ ′mɪl ə tud sɪ ′mɪl ɪ tjud sɪ ′mɪl ɪ tud
simony	SIM uh ni SAÎ muh ni § 50(34)	sĭm′ŏ nĭ sī′mŏ nĭ	′sɪm ə nɪ ′saɪ mə nɪ
simply	SIM pli	sĭm′plĭ § 50(20)	′sɪm plɪ
simulate (v.)	SIM yo͝o layt	sĭm′û lāt	′sɪm jʊ let, -jə-, -ju-

	SIMPLIFIED	DIACRITICAL	PHONETIC
—— (adj.)	SIM yо̅о̅ lit SIM yо̅о̅ layt	sĭm′ṵ lăt § 20(8, 9)	'sɪm jʊ lɪt, -let, -jə-, -ju-
simultaneous	*sai* muhl TAY ni uhs *sim* uhl TAY ni uhs § 50(34)	sī′mŭl tā′nĕ ŭs sĭm′ŭl tā′nĕ ŭs §§ 28(9), 47(3)	ˌsaɪ məl 'te nɪ əs, -ml̩- ˌsɪm əl 'te nɪ əs, ˌsɪm l̩ 'te-
since	sins	sĭns § 39(3)	sɪns
sincere	sin SĬER sin SIR sin SEER	sĭn sēr′ § 24(2) sĭn sēr′	sɪn 'sɪər, -'sɪr, -'sir; *ES* -'sɪə(r)
sincerity	sin SER uh ti sin SER i ti	sĭn sĕr′ĭ̵ tĭ sĭn sĕr′ĭ tĭ § 50(16)	sɪn 'ser ə tɪ sɪn 'ser ɪ tɪ
sinecure	SAI ni kyо̅о̅r SAI ni kyoor SIN i kyо̅о̅r SIN i kyoor	sī′nĕ kūr sĭn′ĕ kūr §§ 34(21), 47(1), 48(2)	'saɪ nɪ kjʊr, 'sɪn ɪ-; *ES* -kjʊə(r)
sinew	SIN yoo	sĭn′ū § 48(2)	'sɪn ju, -u
sinewy	SIN yо̅о̅ i	sĭn′ṵ ĭ	'sɪn jʊ ɪ, -jə-, -ju-, -jə wɪ, 'sɪn ə-
singer (*"one who sings"*)	SING uhr	sĭng′ẽr § 50(24)	'sɪŋ ɚ; *ES* -ə(r)
singer (*"one who singes cloth"*)	SIN juhr	sĭn′jẽr § 51(7)	'sɪn dʒɚ; *ES* -dʒə(r)
singing	SING ing	sĭng′ĭng § 50(24)	'sɪŋ ɪŋ
single	SING g'l	sĭng′g'l § 50(24)	'sɪŋ gl̩
singular	SING gyо̅о̅ luhr	sĭng′gŭ lẽr § 50(24, 32)	'sɪŋ gjʊ lɚ, -gjə-, -gju-; *ES* -lə(r)
sinister	SIN is tuhr	sĭn′ĭs tẽr	'sɪn ɪs tɚ; *ES* -tə(r)
	Former poetry, often: si NIS tuhr	*Former poetry, often:* sĭ nĭs′tẽr § 51(2, 11)	*Former poetry, often:* sɪ 'nɪs tɚ; *ES* -tə(r)
siphon	SAI fon SAI fuhn § 50(34)	sī′fŏn sī′fŭn	'saɪ fɑn, -fɒn, -fən
sirloin	SUHR *loin*	sûr′loin′	'sɝ ˌlɔɪn; *ES also* 'sɜ-
sirrah (arch., dial.)	SIR uh	sĭr′á § 47(2)	'sɪr ə
sirup, syrup	SIR uhp *By sirup-makers, usu.:* SUHR uhp	sĭr′ŭp *By sirup-makers, usu.:* sûr′ŭp §§ 40(7), 51(6)	'sɪr əp *By sirup-makers, usu.:* 'sɝ əp; *ES also* 'sɜ-
sit	sit	sĭt	sɪt
situate (v.)	SICH о̅о̅ ayt SIT yо̅о̅ ayt	sĭt′ṵ āt § 50(33)	'sɪtʃ ʊ et, 'sɪt jʊ-, -ju-

	SIMPLIFIED	DIACRITICAL	PHONETIC
situation	*sich* o͞o AY shuhn *sit* yo͞o AY shuhn	sĭt′û ā′shŭn § 50(30, 33)	ˌsɪtʃ ʊ ˈe ʃən, ˌsɪt jʊ ˈe-, -ju-
six	siks	sĭks	sɪks
skein	skayn	skān	sken
ski	skee *B.*, shee *Nor.*, *Sw.*, shee	skē § 47(1) *B.*, shē § 51(14) *Nor.*, *Sw.*, shē	ski *B.*, ʃi *Nor.*, *Sw.*, ʃi
skillet	SKIL et SKIL it	skĭl′ĕt skĭl′ĭt § 24(5)	ˈskɪl ɛt ˈskɪl ɪt
slain	slayn	slān	slen
slake	slayk *Commonly, esp. when referring to "lime":* slak	slāk *Commonly, esp. when referring to "lime":* slăk § 51(3, 11)	slek *Commonly, esp. when referring to "lime":* slæk
slant	slant slahnt	slȧnt § 20(5)	slænt; *E also* slant, slɑnt
Slav	slahv slav	släv slăv § 47(2)	slɑv slæv
Slavik	SLAHV ik SLAV ik	släv′ĭk slăv′ĭk § 47(1)	ˈslɑv ɪk ˈslæv ɪk
slavish	SLAYV ish	slāv′ĭsh	ˈslev ɪʃ
sleek	sleek	slēk	slik
sleigh	slay	slā § 26(2)	sle
slept	slept	slĕpt	slɛpt
sliver	SLIV uhr	slĭv′ēr § 47(2)	ˈslɪv ɚ; *ES* -ə(r)
sloth	slohth slawth sloth	slōth slôth §§ 34(7), 47(3)	sloθ slɔθ slɒθ
slough (v.)	slow § 50(34)	lou	slaʊ
—— (n.)			
—— "*muddy place; road full of mires; place of hopeless discouragement or moral degradation*"	slow § 50(34)	slou § 51(11)	slaʊ
—— "*wet place; swamp; marshy inlet*"	sloo	slo͞o § 51(11)	slu
slough ("*skin; shed skin*")	*sluhf*	slŭf § 40(6)	slʌf
sluice	sloos	slo͞os §§ 40(4), 48(2)	slus
smooth	smooth	smo͞oth §§ 34(22), 39(4, 6)	smuð

	SIMPLIFIED	DIACRITICAL	PHONETIC
Smyrna	SMUHR nuh	smûr′nȧ	'smɜ nə; *ES also* 'smɜ-
snout	snowt § 50(34)	snout	snaʊt
sobriety	soh BRAI uh ti § 50(34)	sŏ brī′ĕ tĭ	so 'braɪ ə tɪ, sə-
sociable	SOH shuh b'l	sō′shȧ b'l § 47(3)	'so ʃə bl̩
social	SOH shuhl	sō′shăl	'so ʃəl
society	suh SAI uh ti § 50(34)	sŏ sī′ĕ tĭ	sə 'saɪ ə tɪ
sociology	*soh* si OL uh ji	sō′sĭ ŏl′ŏ jĭ	ˌso sɪ 'ɑl ə dʒɪ,
	soh shi OL uh ji	sō′shĭ ŏl′ŏ jĭ § 47(1)	ˌso ʃɪ-; *ES also* -'ɒl-
Socrates	SOK ruh teez	sŏk′rȧ tēz	'sɑk rə tiz; *ES also* 'sɒk-
soft	sawft	sôft	sɔft
	soft	§§ 34(7), 47(2)	sɒft
soften	SAWF uhn	sôf′ĕn	'sɔf ən
	SOF uhn		'sɒf ən
	SAWF 'n	sôf′ 'n §§ 1,	'sɔf n̩
	SOF 'n	34(7), 39(2)	'sɒf n̩
softly	SAWFT li	sôft′lĭ §§ 34(7),	'sɔft lɪ
	SOFT li	50(20)	'sɒft lɪ
soiree,	swah RAY	swä rā′	swɑ 're
soirée	*F.*, swah RAY	*F.*, swä′rā′	*F.*, swa 're
sojourn (v.i.)	soh JUHRN	sŏ jûrn′	so 'dʒɜn,
	SOH *juhrn*	sō′jûrn §§ 40(6), 47(1)	'so dʒɜn; *ES* -'dʒɜn, -dʒɜn
—— (n.)	SOH *juhrn*	sō′jûrn	'so dʒɜn,
	soh JUHRN	sŏ jûrn′ §§ 12, 47(1)	so 'dʒɜn; *ES* -dʒɜn, -'dʒɜn
solace	SOL uhs	sŏl′ĭs	'sal əs, -ɪs; *ES also* 'sɒl-
	SOL is	sŏl′ĭs	
solder	SOD uhr	sŏd′ĕr § 47(3)	'sad ɚ; *ES also* 'sɒd-, *ES* -ə(r)
	Occas.:	*Occas.:*	*Occas.:*
	B., SOL duhr	*B.*, sŏl′dĕr § 51(4)	*B.*, 'sɒl dɚ; *ES* -də(r)
soldier	SOHL juhr	sōl′jẽr §§ 39(1), 40(11)	'sol dʒɚ; *ES* -dʒə(r)
sole	sohl	sōl § 51(7)	sol
solecism	SOL i siz'm	sŏl′ĕ sĭz'm	'sal ɪ sɪzm̩,
	SOL i siz uhm	§§ 47(2), 50(15)	-sɪz əm; *ES also* 'sɒl-
solemn	SOL uhm	sŏl′ĕm §§ 9, 33(1)	'sal əm; *ES also* 'sɒl-
solemnize	SOL uhm naiz § 50(34)	sŏl′ĕm nīz § 33(1)	'sal əm naɪz; *ES also* 'sɒl-

	SIMPLIFIED	DIACRITICAL	PHONETIC
solitaire	*sol* uh TEHR *sol* i TEHR SOL uh tehr SOL i tehr	sŏl′ĭ târ′ sŏl′ĭ târ′ sŏl′ĭ târ sŏl′ĭ târ	ˌsɑl ə ˈtɛr, -ə ˈtær, -ɪ ˈtɛr, -ɪ ˈtær, ˈsɑl ə tɛr, -tær, -ɪ-; *ES* *also* ˌsɒl-, ˈsɒl, *ES* -ˈtæə(r), -tæə(r), *E also* -ˈtɛə(r), -tɛə(r)
solstice	SOL stis	sŏl′stĭs	ˈsɑl stɪs; *ES also* ˈsɒl-
solubility	*sol* yŏŏ BIL uh ti *sol* yŏŏ BIL i ti	sŏl′ū̇ bĭl′ĭ tĭ sŏl′ū̇ bĭl′ĭ tĭ	ˌsɑl jʊ ˈbɪl ə tɪ, -ɪ tɪ, -jə-, -ju-; *ES also* ˌsɒl-
soluble	SOL yŏŏ b'l	sŏl′ū̇ b'l	ˈsɑl jʊ bl̩, -jə-, -ju-; *ES also* ˈsɒl-
somersault	SUHM uhr sawlt	sŭm′ēr sôlt § 20(6)	ˈsʌm ɚ sɔlt; *ES* -ə sɔlt
Somerset	SUHM uhr set	sŭm′ēr sĕt	ˈsʌm ɚ sɛt; *ES* -ə sɛt
something	SUHM thing	sŭm′thĭng § 35(2)	ˈsʌm θɪŋ, ˈsʌmps-
song	sawng song	sŏng §§ 34(7), 47(2)	sɔŋ sɒŋ
sonorous	suh NOH ruhs suh NAW ruhs	sō nō′rŭs § 34(3)	sə ˈno rəs sə ˈnɔ rəs
soot	sŏŏt soot *Arch. or dial.:* *suht*	sŏŏt sŏŏt §§ 34(22), 47(3) *Arch. or dial.:* sŭt §§ 40(6), 51(2)	sʊt sut *Arch. or dial.:* sʌt
sooth (adj., n., adv., interj.)	sooth	sōōth §§ 34(22), 39(6)	suθ
soothe	soothe	sōōth § 34(22)	suð
soothsayer	SOOTH *say* uhr	sōōth′sā′ēr	ˈsuθ ˌse ɚ; *ES* -ə(r)
sophism	SOF iz'm SOF iz uhm	sŏf′ĭz'm § 50(15)	ˈsaf ɪzm̩, -ɪz əm; *ES also* ˈsɒf-
sophistry	SOF is tri	sŏf′ĭs trĭ	ˈsaf ɪs trɪ; *ES also* ˈsɒf-
Sophocles	SOF uh kleez	sŏf′ŏ klēz	ˈsaf ə kliz; *ES also* ˈsɒf-
sophomore	SOF uh mohr SOF uh mawr	sŏf′ŏ mōr § 34(3)	ˈsaf ə mor, -mɔr, ˈsaf m̩-; *ES also* ˈsɒf-, *ES* -moə(r), *E also* -mɔə(r)
soprano	suh PRAH noh suh PRAN oh	sō prä′nō sō prăn′ō	sə ˈprɑ no sə ˈpræn o

sortie ("*sally; sally forth*")	SAWR tee SAWR ti	sôr′tē sôr′tĭ §§ 47(2), 51(7)	′sɔr ti, -tɪ; *ES* ′sɔə-
sought	sawt	sôt	sɔt
sound	sownd § 50(34)	sound § 23(1)	saʊnd
souse	sows § 50(34)	sous	saʊs
souvenir	*soo* vuh NĬER *soo* vuh NIR *soo* vuh NEER SOO vuh nĭer SOO vuh nir SOO vuh neer	soō′vē nēr′ §§ 24(2), 47(3) soō′vē nēr′ soō′vē nēr soō′vē nēr	ˌsu və ′nɪər, -′nɪr, -′nir, -vɪ-, ′su və nɪər, -nɪr, -nir, -vɪ-; *ES* -′nɪə(r), -nɪə(r)
sou'wester	*sow* WES tuhr § 50(34)	sou′wĕs′tēr	ˌsaʊ ′wɛs tɚ; *ES* -tə(r)
sovereign	SOV uhr in SOV rin SUHV rin	sŏv′ēr ĭn sŏv′rĭn sŭv′rĭn §§ 9, 47(3)	′sav ər ɪn, ′sav rɪn, ′sʌv-; *ES also* ′sɒv-
sow ("*scatter seed*")	soh	sō § 51(7, 11)	so
sow ("*female pig*")	sow § 50(34)	sou § 51(7, 11)	saʊ
spa	spah *Occas.:* spaw	spä § 47(2) *Occas.:* spô § 51(8)	spa *Occas.:* spɔ
spangle	SPANG g'l	spăng′g'l § 50(24)	′spæŋ gl̩
spangled	SPANG g'ld	spăng′g'ld § 50(24)	′spæŋ gl̩d
spaniel	SPAN yuhl *Colloq. or dial.:* SPAN 'l	spăn′yĕl *Colloq. or dial.:* spăn′ 'l § 51(2, 3)	′spæn jəl *Colloq. or dial.:* ′spæn l̩
spasmodic	spaz MOD ik	spăz mŏd′ĭk	spæz ′mɑd ɪk; *ES* *also* -′mɒd-
specie	SPEE shi	spē′shĭ	′spi ʃɪ
species (sing. and pl.)	SPEE shiz *Also, esp. in the pl.:* SPEE sheez *In Latin phrases:* SPEE shi eez	spē′shĭz §§ 47(2), 48(3) *Also, esp. in the pl.:* spē′shēz *In Latin phrases:* spē′shĭ ēz § 51(11)	′spi ʃɪz *Also, esp. in the pl.:* ′spi ʃiz *In Latin phrases:* ′spi ʃɪ iz
specious	SPEE shuhs	spē′shŭs § 50(25)	′spi ʃəs
spectator	spek TAY tuhr SPEK tay tuhr	spĕk tā′tēr spĕk′tā tēr	spɛk ′te tɚ, ′spɛk te-; *ES* -tə(r)
sphere	sfier sfir sfeer	sfēr § 24(2) sfēr	sfɪər, sfɪr, sfir; *ES* sfɪə(r)
spherical	SFER i kuhl	sfĕr′ĭ kăl	′sfɛr ɪ kəl, -kl̩

spheroid	SFĬER oid SFIR oid SFEER oid	sfē̆r′oid §§ 24(2), 47(2) sfēr′oid	'sfɪər ɔɪd, 'sfɪr-, 'sfir-; *ES* 'sfɪər-
spinach	SPIN ich SPIN ij	spĭn′ĭch spĭn′ĭj § 22(5)	'spɪn ɪtʃ 'spɪn ɪdʒ
spinet	SPIN et SPIN it spi NET	spĭn′ĕt spĭn′ĭt spĭ nĕt′ §§ 24(5), 47(3)	'spɪn ɛt 'spɪn ɪt spɪ 'nɛt
spirit	SPIR it	spĭr′ĭt	'spɪr ɪt
spiritual	SPIR ich o͝o uhl SPIR it yo͝o uhl	spĭr′ĭt u̇ ăl § 50(33)	'spɪr ɪtʃ ʊ əl 'spɪr ɪt ju əl
splenetic	spli NET ik	splĕ nĕt′ĭk § 47(3)	splɪ 'nɛt ɪk, 'splɛn ɪ tɪk
splenic	SPLEN ik SPLEEN ik	splĕn′ĭk splēn′ĭk § 47(3)	'splɛn ɪk 'splin ɪk
Spokane	spoh KAN	spō kăn′	spo 'kæn
sponge	*spuhnj*	spŭnj §§ 25(4), 40(6)	spʌndʒ
spontaneity	*spon* tuh NEE uh ti *spon* tuh NEE i ti	spŏn′tá nē′ĭ tĭ spŏn′tá nē′ĭ tĭ	ˌspan tə 'ni ə tɪ, -ɪ tɪ; *ES also* ˌspɒn-
spoon	spoon *In compounds, often:* spo͝on	spo͞on § 34(22) *In compounds, often:* spo͝on	spun *In compounds, often:* spʊn
sporadic	spoh RAD ik spaw RAD ik spuh RAD ik	spō răd′ĭk § 34(3)	spo 'ræd ɪk spɔ 'ræd ɪk spə 'ræd ɪk
spouse	spowz *Pop.:* spows	spouz *Pop.:* spous § 51(3)	spaʊz *Pop.:* spaʊs
spurious	SPYO͞O ri uhs SPYOO ri uhs	spū′rĭ ŭs §§ 40(4), 48(2), 50(32)	'spju rɪ əs
squalid	SKWOL id	skwŏl′ĭd	'skwɑl ɪd, 'skwɒl-
squalor	SKWOL uhr *Infreq.:* SKWAY luhr	skwŏl′ĕr § 47(2) *Infreq.:* skwā′lĕr § 51(8)	'skwɑl ɚ, 'skwɒl-; *ES* -ə(r) *Infreq.:* 'skwe lɚ; *ES* -lə(r)
squash	skwosh	skwŏsh §51(7)	skwɑʃ, skwɒʃ
squirrel	SKWUHR uhl *B.,* SKWIR uhl	skwûr′ĕl §§ 40(7), 47(3) *B.,* skwĭr′ĕl § 51(4)	'skwɝ əl; *ES* 'skwɜr-, 'skwʌr- *B.,* 'skwɪr əl; *ES* 'skwɪr-

	SIMPLIFIED	DIACRITICAL	PHONETIC
stabilize	STAY buh lāiz	stā′bĭ līz	'ste bə laɪz
	STAY bi lāiz	stā′bĭ līz	'ste bɪ laɪz
	STAB uh lāiz	stăb′ĭ līz	'stæb ə laɪz
	STAB i lāiz § 50(34)	stăb′ĭ līz § 47(1)	'stæb ɪ laɪz
staff	staf stahf	stàf § 20(5)	stæf; *E also* staf, staf
stallion	STAL yuhn	stăl′yŭn	'stæl jən
stalwart	STAWL wuhrt STOL wuhrt	stôl′wẽrt stŏl′wẽrt § 47(2)	'stɔl wɚt, 'stal-; *E also* 'stɒl-, *ES* -wət
stamen	STAY muhn STAY men	stā′mĕn stā′mĕn	'ste mən 'ste mɛn
stamina	STAM i nuh	stăm′ĭ nȧ	'stæm ɪ nə
stanch (See *staunch*.)	stahnch stanch	stänch stánch §§ 20(5), 51(7)	stantʃ, stæntʃ; *E also* stantʃ
star	stahr	stär	star; *ES* sta:(r), *E also* sta:(r)
starboard	STAHR bohrd STAHR bawrd STAHR buhrd	stär′bōrd stär′bẽrd	'star bord, -bord, -bəd; *ES* 'sta: boəd, -bəd, *E also* 'sta:-, -bəəd
stare	stehr	stâr	stɛr, stær; *ES* stæə(r), *E also* stɛə(r)
started	STAHRT ed STAHRT id	stärt′ĕd stärt′ĭd §§ 24(5), 50(4)	'start ɛd, -ɪd, -əd; *ES* 'sta:t-, *E also* 'sta:t-
static	STAT ik	stăt′ĭk	'stæt ɪk
stationary	STAY shuhn *er* i	stā′shŭn ẽr′ĭ §§ 20(2), 24(9)	'ste ʃən 'ɛr ɪ
	B., STAY shuhn uhr i	*B.*, stā′shŭn ēr ĭ § 51(4)	*B.*, 'ste ʃən ə rɪ
stationery	STAY shuhn *er* i	stā′shŭn ẽr′ĭ §§ 20(2), 24(9)	'ste ʃən ˌɛr ɪ
	B., STAY shuhn uhr i	*B.*, stā′shŭn ēr ĭ § 51(4)	*B.*, 'ste ʃən ə rɪ
statistician	*stat* is TISH uhn	stăt′ĭs tĭsh′ăn	ˌstæt ɪs 'tɪʃ ən
statistics	stuh TIS tiks	stȧ tĭs′tĭks	stə 'tɪs tɪks
statue	STACH oo STAT yoo	stăt′ū § 50(33)	'stætʃ u, -ʊ 'stæt ju, -jʊ
stature	STACH uhr STAT yuhr	stăt′ûr § 50(33)	'stætʃ ɚ, 'stæt jɚ; *ES* -ə(r), -jə(r)
status	STAY tuhs	stā′tŭs	'ste təs, 'stæ-

	SIMPLIFIED	DIACRITICAL	PHONETIC
statute	STACH oot	stăt′ūt	′stætʃ ut, -ʊt
	STAT yoot	§ 50(33)	′stæt jut, -jʊt
staunch (var. of *stanch*)	stawnch	stônch	stɒntʃ
	stahnch	stänch	stɑntʃ, stɒntʃ
stave	stayv	stāv	stev
staves (one pl. of *staff*)	stayvz	stāvz	stevz, stævz; *E*
	stavz	stȧvz §§ 20(5),	*also* stavz,
	stahvz	47(2), 50(6)	stavz
staves (pl. of *stave*)	stayvz	stāvz §§ 48(3),	stevz
		50(6)	
stayed	stayd	stād	sted
steelyard ("*form of balance*")	STEEL yahrd	stēl′yärd	′stil jɑrd; *ES* -jɑːd, *E also* -jɑːd
	Colloq.:	*Colloq.:*	*Colloq.:*
	STIL yuhrd	stĭl′yĕrd §§ 1,	′stɪl jɚd; *ES*
		47(2), 51(3, 7)	-jəd
steerage	STĬER ij	stēr′ĭj	′stɪɚr ɪdʒ, ′stɪr-,
	STIR ij	§ 24(2)	′stir-; *ES*
	STEER ij	stēr′ĭj	′stɪɚr-
stein ("*a mug*")	stain § 50(34)	stīn	staɪn
steppe	step	stĕp	stɛp
stereotype	STER i uh *taip*	stĕr′ĕ ŏ tīp′	′stɛr ɪ ə ˌtaɪp
	STĬER i uh *taip*	stēr′ĕ ŏ tīp′	′stɪɚr ɪ ə ˌtaɪp,
	STIR i uh *taip*	§§ 24(2), 47(3)	′stɪr-, ′stir-; *ES*
	STEER i uh *taip*	stēr′ĕ ŏ tīp′	′stɪɚr-
sterile	STER il	stĕr′ĭl	′stɛr ɪl, -əl
	B., STER ail	*B.,* stĕr′īl	*B.,* ′stɛr aɪl
	§ 50(34)	§§ 28(5), 51(4)	
stevedore	STEE vuh *dohr*	stē′vĕ dōr′	′sti və ˌdor, -ˌdɔr;
	STEE vuh *dawr*	§ 34(3)	*ES* -ˌdoə(r), *E* *also* -ˌdɔə(r)
steward	STYOO uhrd	stū′ĕrd	′stju ɚd, ′stu-,
	STOO uhrd	§§ 48(2), 50(32)	-wɚd; *ES* -əd, -wəd
stipend	STAI pend	stī′pĕnd	′staɪ pɛnd
	§ 50(34)		
stirrup	STIR uhp	stĭr′ŭp	′stɪr əp, ′stɝ əp,
	STUHR uhp	stûr′ŭp	′stʌr-; *ES also*
		§§ 40(7), 47(3)	′stɜr-
stitch	stich	stĭch	stɪtʃ
stocking	STOK ing	stŏk′ĭng § 50(24)	′stak ɪŋ; *ES also* ′stɒk-
Stoicism, stoicism	STOH uh siz′m	stō′ĭ sĭz′m	′sto ə sɪzm̩
	STOH i siz′m	stō′ĭ sĭz′m	′sto ɪ sɪzm̩
	STOH i siz uhm	§ 50(15)	′sto ɪ sɪz əm

	SIMPLIFIED	DIACRITICAL	PHONETIC
stomach	STUHM uhk *Pop.:* STUHM ik	stŭm′ăk *Pop.:* stŭm′ĭk § 51(3)	′stʌm ək *Pop.:* ′stʌm ɪk
stood	stŏŏd	stŏŏd § 34(22)	stʊd
storage	STOHR ij STAWR ij	stōr′ĭj § 34(3)	′stor ɪdʒ ′stɔr ɪdʒ
store	stohr stawr	stōr § 34(3)	stor, stɔr; *ES* stoə(r), *E also* stɔə(r)
story	STOH ri STAW ri	stō′rĭ § 34(3)	′sto rɪ ′stɔ rɪ
stowage	STOH ij	stō′ĭj § 50(1)	′sto ɪdʒ
stowaway	STOH uh *way*	stō′á wā′	′sto ə ˌwe
strata (n. pl. of *stratum*)	STRAY tuh STRAT uh	strā′tá străt′á	′stre tə ′stræt ə
stratagem	STRAT uh juhm	străt′á jĕm	′stræt ə dʒəm
strategic	struh TEE jik struh TEJ ik	strá tē′jĭk strá tĕj′ĭk § 47(3)	strə ′ti dʒɪk strə ′tɛdʒ ɪk
stratum	STRAY tuhm STRAT uhm	strā′tŭm străt′ŭm	′stre təm ′stræt əm
strength	strength strengkth	strĕngth str ngkth §§ 30(1), 33(4), 50(24)	strɛŋθ strɛŋkθ
strengthen	STRENG thuhn STRENGK thuhn	strĕng′thĕn strĕngk′thĕn §§ 33(4), 50(24)	′strɛŋ θən ′strɛŋk θən
strengthened	STRENG thuhnd STRENGK thuhnd	strĕng′thĕnd strĕngk′thĕnd §§ 33(4), 50(24)	′strɛŋ θənd ′strɛŋk θənd
strenuous	STREN yŏŏ uhs	strĕn′û ŭs § 50(25)	′strɛn jʊ əs, -ju-
strew	stroo *Arch.:* stroh	strōō §§ 47(3), 48(2) *Arch.:* strō § 51(2)	stru *Arch.:* stro
stricture	STRIK chuhr STRIK tyuhr	strĭk′tûr § 50(31)	′strɪk tʃɚ, -tjɚ; *ES* -tʃə(r), -tjə(r)
string	string	strĭng § 50(24)	strɪŋ
strong	strawng strong	strông §§ 34(7), 47(2), 50(24)	strɔŋ strɒŋ
stronger	STRAWNG guhr STRONG guhr	strông′gĕr §§ 34(7), 50(24)	′strɔŋ gɚ, ′strɒŋ-; *ES* -gə(r)
strongest	STRAWNG gest STRONG gest STRAWNG gist STRONG gist	strông′gĕst strông′gĭst §§ 24(5), 34(7), 50(9, 24)	′strɔŋ gɛst ′strɒŋ gɛst ′strɔŋ gɪst ′strɒŋ gɪst

	SIMPLIFIED	DIACRITICAL	PHONETIC
strophe	STROH fi *Rarely:* STROF i	strō′fĕ *Rarely:* strŏf′ĭ §§ 47(3), 51(8)	'stro fɪ *Rarely:* 'strɑf ɪ, 'strɒf ɪ
structure	STRUHK chuhr STRUHK tyuhr	strŭk′tûr § 50(31)	'strʌk tʃɚ, -tjɚ; *ES* -tʃə(r), -tjə(r)
strychnine	STRIK nin STRIK neen STRIK nain § 50(34)	strĭk′nĭn strĭk′nēn strĭk′nīn §§ 28(7), 47(3)	'strɪk nɪn 'strɪk nin 'strɪk naɪn
student	STYOO duhnt STOO duhnt	stū′dĕnt §§ 24 (14), 40(4), 48(2), 50(32)	'stju dənt, -ṇt 'stu dənt, -ṇt
studious	STYOO di uhs STOO di uhs	stū′dĭ ŭs §§ 28(9), 48(2), 50(25, 32)	'stju dɪ əs 'stu dɪ əs
study	STUHD i	stŭd′ĭ	'stʌd ɪ
studying	STUHD i ing	stŭd′ĭ ĭng 50(24)	'stʌd ɪ ɪŋ
stupendous	styoo PEN duhs stoo PEN duhs	stŭ pĕn′dŭs §§ 48 (2), 50(25, 32)	stju 'pɛn dəs, stu-, stjʊ-, stʊ-
stupid	STYOO pid STOO pid	stū′pĭd §§ 40(4), 48(2), 50(32)	'stju pɪd 'stu pɪd
Stygian	STIJ i uhn	stĭj′ĭ ăn	'stɪdʒ ɪ ən
Styx	stiks	stĭks	stɪks
suave	swahv swayv	swäv swäv § 47(3)	swɑv swev
suavity	SWAV uh ti SWAV i ti SWAH vuh ti SWAH vi ti	swăv′ĭ tĭ swăv′ĭ tĭ swä′vĭ tĭ swä′vĭ tĭ	'swæv ə tɪ 'swæv ɪ tɪ 'swɑ və tɪ 'swɑ vɪ tɪ
subaltern (n.)	suhb AWL tuhrn	sŭb ôl′tērn	səb 'ɔl tɚn; *ES also* -tən
—— (adj.)	suhb AWL tuhrn SUHB al *tuhrn* SUHB uhl tuhrn	sŭb ôl′tērn sŭb′ăl tûrn′ sŭb′ăl tērn § 47(3)	səb 'ɔl tɚn, 'sʌb æl ˌtɝn, -əl tɚn; *ES* -tən, *ES also* -ˌtɝn
Note: Both n. and adj.	*In logic, esp.:* SUHB al *tuhrn*	*In logic, esp.:* sŭb′ăl tûrn′ § 51(6)	*In logic, esp.:* 'sʌb æl ˌtɝn, 'sʌb ḷ-; *ES also* -ˌtɝn
subdivision	*suhb* duh VIZH uhn *suhb* di VIZH uhn SUHB duh *vizh* uhn	sŭb′dĭ vĭzh′ŭn sŭb′dĭ vĭzh′ŭn sŭb′dĭ vĭzh′ŭn §§ 11, 49(17)	ˌsʌb də 'vɪʒ ən ˌsʌb dɪ 'vɪʒ ən 'sʌb də ˌvɪʒ ən
subdue	suhb DYOO suhb DOO	sŭb dū′ §§ 48(2), 50(32)	səb 'dju səb 'du

subject (adj., n.)	SUHB jekt	sŭb′jĕkt	ˈsʌb dʒɛkt
	SUHB jikt	sŭb′jĭkt § 24(5)	ˈsʌb dʒɪkt
—— (v.t.)	suhb JEKT	sŭb jĕkt′	səb ˈdʒɛkt
subsequent	SUHB si kwuhnt	sŭb′sĕ kwĕnt	ˈsʌb sɪ kwənt
	SUHB si kwent	sŭb′sĕ kwĕnt	ˈsʌb sɪ kwɛnt
subside	suhb SAID § 50(34)	sŭb sīd′ § 49(17)	səb ˈsaɪd
subsidence	suhb SAID uhns § 50(34)	sŭb sīd′ĕns	səb ˈsaɪd əns, sʌb-, -ɛns
	B., SUHB si duhns	B., sŭb′sĭ dĕns §§ 47(1), 51(4)	B., ˈsʌb sɪ dəns, -dɛns
subsidiary	suhb SID i er i	sŭb sĭd′ĭ ĕr′ĭ §§ 20(2), 24(9), 49(17)	səb ˈsɪd ɪ ˌɛr ɪ
	B., suhb SID i uhr i	B., sŭb sĭd′ĭ ēr ĭ §§ 13, 51(4)	B., səb ˈsɪd ɪ ə rɪ
subsist	suhb SIST	sŭb sĭst′ § 49(17)	səb ˈsɪst
subsistence	suhb SIS tuhns	sŭb sĭs′tĕns § 24(14)	səb ˈsɪs təns
substantial	suhb STAN shuhl	sŭb stăn′shăl § 49(17)	səb ˈstæn ʃəl
subterranean	suhb tuh RAY ni uhn	sŭb′tĕ rā′nĕ ăn	ˌsʌb tə ˈre nɪ ən
subtile	SUHB til	sŭb′tĭl	ˈsʌb tɪl
	SUHT ′l	sŭt′ ′l § 47(3)	ˈsʌt l̩
subtle	SUHT ′l	sŭt′ ′l § 21(1)	ˈsʌt l̩
subtlety	SUHT ′l ti	sŭt′ ′l tĭ	ˈsʌt l̩ tɪ
suburb	SUHB uhrb	sŭb′ûrb §§ 40(6), 49(17)	ˈsʌb ɝb; ES also -ɜb
succinct	suhk SINGKT	sŭk sĭngkt′ §§ 26(1), 40(6)	sʌk ˈsɪŋkt
succinctly	suhk SINGKT li	sŭk sĭngkt′lĭ §§ 40(6), 50(20)	sʌk ˈsɪŋkt lɪ
succulent	SUHK yŏŏ luhnt	sŭk′û lĕnt	ˈsʌk ju lənt, -jə-, -ju-
succumb	suh KUHM	sŭ kŭm′	sə ˈkʌm
such	suhch Unstressed: suhch	sŭch Unstressed: sŭch §§ 16, 40(6)	sʌtʃ Unstressed: sətʃ
suède	swayd F., swed	swād F., swĕd	swed F., sɥɛd
suet	SYOO et SOO et SYOO it SOO it	sū′ĕt sū′ĭt §§ 24(5), 48(2), 50(32)	ˈsju ɛt ˈsu ɛt ˈsju ɪt ˈsu ɪt
suffice	suh FAIS suh FAIZ § 50(34)	sŭ fīs′ sŭ fīz′ §§ 22(1), 47(2)	sə ˈfaɪs sə ˈfaɪz
suffrage	SUHF rij	sŭf′rĭj	ˈsʌf rɪdʒ

	SIMPLIFIED	DIACRITICAL	PHONETIC
suffuse	suh FYOOZ	sŭ fūz′ § 48(2)	sə 'fjuz
suggest	suhg JEST	sŭg jĕst′	səg 'dʒɛst
	suh JEST	sŭ jĕst′ §§ 26(1), 47(3)	sə 'dʒɛst
suicidal	*syoo* uh SAID uhl	sū′ĭ sīd′ăl	ˌsju ə 'saɪd əl
	soo uh SAID uhl		ˌsu ə 'saɪd əl
	syoo i SAID uhl	sū′ĭ sīd′ăl	ˌsju ɪ 'saɪd əl
	soo i SAID uhl		ˌsu ɪ 'saɪd əl
	syoo uh SAID 'l	sū′ĭ sīd′ 'l	ˌsju ə 'saɪd l̩
	soo uh SAID 'l	§§ 11, 48(2), 50(32, 34)	ˌsu ə 'saɪd l̩
suicide	SYOO uh said	sū′ĭ sīd	'sju ə saɪd
	SOO uh said		'su ə saɪd
	SYOO i said	sū′ɪ sīd §§ 48(2),	'sju ɪ saɪd
	SOO i said	50(32, 34)	'su ɪ saɪd
suit	syoot	sūt §§ 40(4),	sjut
	soot	48(2), 50(32)	sut
suite ("*personal staff; number of things; musical composition*")	sweet	swēt	swit
—— "*furniture,*" pop.	syoot	sūt §§ 48(2), 50 (32), 51(3, 11)	sjut
	soot		sut
suitor	SYOOT uhr	sūt′ēr	'sjut ɚ, 'sut-; *ES*
	SOOT uhr	§§ 48(2), 50(32)	-ə(r)
sultan	SUHL tuhn	sŭl′tăn	'sʌl tən, -tn̩
	sool TAHN	sōol tän′	sul 'tɑn
sultana	suhl TAN uh	sŭl tăn′ȧ	sʌl 'tæn ə
	suhl TAH nuh	sŭl tä′ nȧ § 47(2)	sʌl 'tɑ nə
sumac, **sumach**	SHOO mak	shōo′măk	'ʃu mæk
	SOO mak	sōo′măk	'su mæk
	SYOO mak	sū′măk	'sju mæk
	In tanning, also:	*In tanning, also:*	*In tanning, also:*
	SHOO mayk	shōo′māk §§ 1, 47(3), 51(6)	'ʃu mek
summarily	SUHM uh ruh li	sŭm′ȧ rĭ lĭ	'sʌm ə rə lɪ
	SUHM uh ri li	sŭm′ȧ rĭ lĭ	'sʌm ə rɪ lɪ
	Emph., also:	*Emph., also:*	*Emph., also:*
	suhm EHR uh li	sŭm âr′ĭ lĭ	sʌm 'ɛr ə lɪ,
	suh MEHR uh li	§§ 40(6), 50(20), 51(11)	sʌ 'mɛr-; *ES* also -'ɛər-, -'mɛər-
summary	SUHM uh ri	sŭm′ȧ rĭ	'sʌm ə rɪ
sundry	SUHN dri	sŭn′drĭ	'sʌn drɪ
superb	syoo PUHRB	sŭ pûrb′	sju 'pɝb, su-, sə-;
	soo PUHRB	§§ 48(2), 50(32)	*ES* also -'pɜb
supercilious	*syoo* puhr SIL i uhs	sū′pĕr sĭl′ɪ ŭs §§ 47(2), 48(2), 50(25, 32)	ˌsju pɚ 'sɪl ɪ əs,
	soo puhr SIL i uhs		ˌsu-; *ES* -pə 'sɪl-

	SIMPLIFIED	DIACRITICAL	PHONETIC
superfluity	_syoo_ puhr FLOO uh ti _soo_ puhr FLOO uh ti _syoo_ puhr FLOO i ti _soo_ puhr FLOO i ti	sū′pēr flōō′ĭ tĭ sū′pēr flōō′ĭ tĭ §§ 40(4), 48(2)	ˌsju pɚ ′flu ə tɪ, ˌsu-, -ɪ tɪ; _ES_ -pə ′flu-
superfluous	syŏŏ PUHR flŏŏ uhs sŏŏ PUHR flŏŏ uhs	sû pûr′flŏŏ ŭs §§ 40(4), 48(2), 50(25, 32)	sjʊ ′pɝ flʊ əs, sʊ-, sə-, sju-, su-; _ES also_ -′pɝ-
superintend	_syoo_ puhr in TEND _soo_ puhr in TEND _syoo_ prin TEND _soo_ prin TEND	sū′pēr ĭn tĕnd′ sū′prĭn tĕnd′ §§ 48(2), 50(32)	ˌsju pər ɪn ′tɛnd ˌsu pər ɪn ′tɛnd ˌsju prɪn ′tɛnd ˌsu prɪn ′tɛnd
superintendent	_syoo_ puhr in TEN duhnt _soo_ puhr in TEN duhnt	sū′pēr ĭn tĕn′dĕnt §§ 48(2), 50(32)	ˌsju pər ɪn ′tɛn dənt ˌsu pər ɪn ′tɛn dənt
superior	syŏŏ PĬER i uhr sŏŏ PĬER i uhr syŏŏ PIR i uhr sŏŏ PIR i uhr syŏŏ PEER i uhr sŏŏ PEER i uhr suh PĬER i uhr suh PIR i uhr suh PEER i uhr	sû pēr′ĭ ēr §§ 24(2), 40(11), 50(32) sû pēr′ĭ ēr sŭ pēr′ĭ ēr sŭ pēr′ĭ ēr	sjʊ ′pɪər ɪ ɚ, sʊ-, -′pɪr-, -′pir-, sə ′pɪər ɪ ɚ, -′pɪr-, -′pir-; _ES_ -′pɪər ɪ ə(r)
supine (adj.)	syoo PAIN soo PAIN	sû pīn′ §§ 11, 48(2), 50(32)	sju ′paɪn su ′paɪn
—— (n.)	SYOO pain SOO pain	sū′pīn §§ 48(2), 50(32, 34)	′sju paɪn ′su paɪn
supple	SUHP ′l	sup′ ′l	′sʌp l̩
suppose	suh POHZ	sŭ pōz′	sə ′poz
supposititious	suh _poz_ i TISH uhs	sŭ pŏz′ĭ tĭsh′ŭs	sə ˌpɒz ɪ ′tɪʃ əs, _ES also_ -ˌpɒz-
sure	shŏŏr	shŏŏr §§ 34(21), 40(4, 11)	ʃʊr; _ES_ ʃʊə(r), ʃoə(r), _E also_ ʃoə(r)
surety	SHŎŎR ti SHŎŎR i ti	shŏŏr′tĭ shŏŏr′ĕ tĭ	′ʃʊr tɪ, ′ʃʊr ɪ tɪ; _ES_ ′ʃʊə tɪ, ′ʃoə-, ′ʃoə, ′ʃʊr ɪ tɪ
surfeit	SUHR fit	sûr′fĭt	′sɝ fɪt; _ES also_ ′sɜ-
surmise (v.)	_suhr_ MAIZ § 50(34)	sûr mīz′	sɝ ′maɪz, sɚ-; _ES also_ sɜ-, _E also_ sə-

	SIMPLIFIED	DIACRITICAL	PHONETIC
—— (n.)	*suhr* MA͞IZ SUHR ma͞iz § 50(34)	sûr mīz′ sûr′mīz §§ 12, 40(7)	sɜ 'maɪz, sə-, 'sɜ maɪz; *ES* *also* sɜ-, 'sɜ-, *E* *also* sə-
surname (n.)	SUHR *naym*	sûr′nām′	'sɜ ˌnem; *ES also* 'sɜ-
—— (v.t.)	SUHR *naym* *suhr* NAYM	sûr′nām′ sûr nām′ §§ 12, 40(6, 7), 47(2)	'sɜ ˌnem, sɜ 'nem, sɚ-; *ES also* 'sɜ-, sɜ-, *ES* sə-
surplus	SUHR *pluhs* SUHR pluhs	sûr′plŭs sûr′plŭs § 40(6)	'sɜ plʌs, -pləs; *E* *also* 'sɜ-
surprise	suhr PRA͞IZ suh PRA͞IZ	sēr prīz′ §§ 9, 24(7), 48(1), 50(34)	sɚ 'praɪz, *by dis-* *similation* sə-; *ES* sə-
surreptitious	*suhr* ep TISH uhs	sûr′ĕp tĭsh′ŭs § 40(7)	ˌsɜ ep 'tɪʃ əs; *ES* *also* ˌsɜr-, ˌsʌr-
surveillance	*suhr* VAYL uhns suhr VAYL uhns *suhr* VAYL yuhns suhr VAYL yuhns suhr VAY luhns	sûr vāl′ăns sēr vāl′ăns sûr vāl′yăns sēr vāl′yăns § 47(3)	sɜ 'vel əns, sə-, -'vel jəns, -'ve ləns; *ES* *also* sɜ 'vel-, *ES* sə 'vel-
survey (v.t.)	suhr VAY	sēr vā′	sɚ 've; *ES* sə-
—— (n.)	SUHR vay suhr VAY	sûr′vā sēr vā′ §§ 12, 47(3)	'sɜ ve, sɚ 've; *ES* *also* 'sɜ-, *ES* sə-
surveying	suhr VAY ing	sēr vā′ĭng § 50(24)	sɚ 've ɪŋ; *ES* sə-
susceptible	suh SEP tuh b'l suh SEP ti b'l	sŭ sĕp′tĭ b'l sŭ sĕp′tĭ b'l	sə 'sep tə b̦l̦ sə 'sep tɪ b̦l̦
suspect (v.)	suhs PEKT	sŭs pĕkt′	səs 'pekt
—— (adj.)	suhs PEKT SUHS pekt	sŭs pĕkt′ sŭs′ pĕkt § 11	səs 'pekt 'sʌs pekt
—— (n.)	SUHS pekt suhs PEKT	sŭs′pĕkt sŭs pĕkt′	'sʌs pekt səs 'pekt
—— "*suspicion*"	suhs PEKT	sŭs pĕkt′	səs 'pekt
sustain	suhs TAYN suh STAYN	sŭs tān′	səs 'ten sə 'sten
sustenance	SUHS ti nuhns	sŭs′tĕ năns	'sʌs tɪ nəns
suzerain	SYOO zuh rayn SYOO zuh rin SOO zuh rayn SOO zuh rin	sū′zĕ răn so͞o′zĕ răn §§ 47(2), 48(2), 50(32)	'sju zə ren 'sju zə rɪn 'su zə ren 'su zə rɪn
swarthy	SWAWR ᵺi SWAWR thi	swôr′ᵺĭ swôr′thĭ § 47(1)	'swɔr ði, -θɪ; *ES* 'swɔə-
swath	swawth swoth	swôth swŏth § 47(3)	swɔθ, swɑθ, swɒθ
swathe	swayᵺ	swāᵺ	sweð
swept	swept	swĕpt	swept

	SIMPLIFIED	DIACRITICAL	PHONETIC
switch	swich	swĭch	swıtʃ
swollen	SWOHL uhn	swōl′ĕn	'swol ən
sword	sohrd sawrd	sōrd §§ 34(3), 42(3)	sord, sɔrd; ES soəd, E also sɔəd
sycamore	SIK uh mohr SIK uh mawr	sĭk′á mōr § 34(3)	'sık ə mor, -mɔr; ES -moə(r), E also -mɔə(r)
sycophant (n., adj.)	SIK uh fuhnt	sĭk′ŏ fănt	'sık ə fənt
—— (v.)	SIK uh fant	sĭk′ŏ fănt	'sık ə fænt
syllabic	si LAB ik	sĭ lăb′ĭk	sı 'læb ık
syllable	SIL uh b'l	sĭl′á b'l	'sıl ə bļ
sylph	silf	sĭlf	sılf
symposium	sim POH zi uhm	sĭm pō′zĭ ŭm	sım 'po zı əm
synonym	SIN uh nim	sĭn′ŏ nĭm	'sın ə nım
synthesis	SIN thi sis	sĭn′thĕ sĭs	'sın θı sıs
syringe	SIR inj *Often:* si RINJ	sĭr′ĭnj *Often:* sĭ rĭnj′ § 51(9)	'sır ındʒ *Often:* sı 'rındʒ
syrup	See *sirup*.		

T

tabernacle	TAB uhr *nak* 'l TAB uhr nuh k'l	tăb′ēr năk′ 'l tăb′ēr nă k'l § 47(3)	'tæb ɚ ˌnæk ļ, -nə kļ; ES 'tæb ə-
tableau	TAB loh *ta* BLOH	tăb′lō tá′blō′ § 47(3)	'tæb lo ˌta 'blo, ˌtæ-
tableaus	TAB lohz	tăb′lōz	'tæb loz
tableaux	TAB lohz *ta* BLOH	tăb′lōz tá′blō′	'tæb loz ˌta 'blo
taboo, tabu	tuh BOO	tă bōō′	tə 'bu, tæ-
—— Polynesian "*tabu*"	TAH boo	tä′bōō	'ta bu
tacit	TAS it	tăs′ĭt	'tæs ıt
taciturn	TAS uh *tuhrn* TAS i *tuhrn*	tăs′ĭ tûrn tăs′ĭ tûrn § 40(6)	'tæs ə tɜn, -ı tɜn; ES also -tɜn
taffeta	TAF i tuh	tăf′ĕ tá	'tæf ı tə

talc	talk § 50(34)	tălk	tælk
talisman	TAL is muhn	tăl′ĭs mŭn	′tæl ɪs mən
	TAL iz muhn	tăl′ĭz mŭn	′tæl ɪz mən
		§§ 47(3), 50(21)	
tambourine	*tam* bŏŏ REEN	tăm′bŏŏ rēn′	ˌtæm bʊ ′rin
	tam buh REEN	tăm′bŭ rēn′	ˌtæm bə ′rin
tangent	TAN juhnt	tăn′jĕnt	′tæn dʒənt
tapestry	TAP es tri	tăp′ĕs trĭ	′tæp ɛs trɪ
	TAP is tri	tăp′ĭs trĭ	′tæp ɪs trɪ
tapioca	*tap* i OH kuh	tăp′ĭ ō′ká	ˌtæp ɪ ′o kə
target	TAHR get	tär′gĕt	′tar gɛt, -gɪt; *ES*
	TAHR git	tär′gĭt § 24(5)	′ta:-; *E also*
			′ta:-
tarpaulin	tahr PAW lin	tär pô′lĭn	tar ′pɔ lɪn; *ES*
			ta:-, *E also* ta:-
task	task	tàsk § 20(5)	tæsk; *E also* task,
	tahsk		tɑsk
tassel	TAS ′l	tăs′ ′l § 9	′tæs l̩
taught	tawt	tôt	tɔt
taunt	tawnt	tônt	tɔnt
	tahnt	tänt § 47(3)	tɑnt
Taurus	TAW ruhs	tô′rŭs	′tɔ rəs
taut	tawt	tôt	tɔt
tavern	TAV uhrn	tăv′ẽrn	′tæv ɚn; *ES* -ən
tawdry	TAW dri	tô′drĭ	′tɔ drɪ
teal	teel	tēl	til
teat	teet	tēt	tit
technic	TEK nik	tĕk′nĭk	′tɛk nɪk
technique	tek NEEK	tĕk nēk′	tɛk ′nik
tedious	TEE di uhs	tē′dĭ ŭs	′ti dɪ əs
	TEED yuhs	tēd′yŭs	′tid jəs
	TEE juhs	tē′jŭs	′ti dʒəs
		§§ 28(9), 47(3)	
tedium	TEE di uhm	tē′dĭ ŭm	′ti dɪ əm
telegram	TEL i gram	tĕl′ĕ grăm	′tɛl ɪ græm
	TEL uh gram	tĕl′ĕ grăm	′tɛl ə græm
telegraph	TEL i graf	tĕl′ĕ grăf	′tɛl ɪ græf, ′tɛl ə-;
	TEL i grahf		*E also* -graf,
	TEL uh graf	tĕl′ĕ grăf	-grɑf
	TEL uh grahf	§ 20(5)	
telegrapher	ti LEG ruh fuhr	tĕ lĕg′rá fẽr	tɪ ′lɛg rə fɚ,
	TEL i *graf* uhr	tĕl′ĕ grăf′ẽr	′tɛl ɪ ˌgræf ɚ,
	TEL i *grahf* uhr		′tɛl ə-; *ES*
	TEL uh *graf* uhr	tĕl′ĕ grăf′ẽr	-fə(r), -ə(r), *E*
	TEL uh *grahf* uhr	§ 20(5)	*also* -ˌgraf-,
			ˌgrɑf-
telepathic	*tel* i PATH ik	tĕl′ĕ păth′ĭk	ˌtɛl ɪ ′pæθ ɪk
	tel uh PATH ik	tĕl′ĕ păth′ĭk	ˌtɛl ə ′pæθ ɪk

telepathy	ti LEP uh thi	tĕ lĕp′*à* thĭ § 47(2)	tɪ ˈlɛp ə θɪ
telephone	TEL i fohn TEL uh fohn	tĕl′ĕ fōn tĕl′ĕ fōn	ˈtɛl ɪ fon ˈtɛl ə fon
telephoning	TEL i *fohn* ing TEL uh *fohn* ing	tĕl′ĕ fōn′ĭng tĕl′ĕ fōn′ĭng	ˈtɛl ɪ ˌfon ɪŋ ˈtɛl ə ˌfon ɪŋ
telephony	ti LEF uh ni TEL i *foh* ni TEL uh *foh* ni	tĕ lĕf′ŏ nĭ tĕl′ĕ fō′nĭ tĕl′ĕ fō′nĭ § 47(2)	tɪ ˈlef ə nɪ ˈtɛl ɪ ˌfo nɪ ˈtɛl ə ˌfo nɪ
telescope	TEL i skohp TEL uh skohp	tĕl′ĕ skōp tĕl′ĕ skōp	ˈtɛl ɪ skop ˈtɛl ə skop

telescopic	*tel* i SKOP ik
	tel uh SKOP ik
		tĕl′ĕ skŏp′ĭk
		tĕl′ĕ skŏp′ĭk
			ˌtɛl ɪ ˈskɑp ɪk,
			  ˌtɛl ə-; *ES also*
			  -ˈskɒp-

telescopy	ti LES kuh pi TEL i *skoh* pi TEL uh *skoh* pi	tĕ lĕs′kŏ pĭ tĕl′ĕ skō′pĭ tĕl′ĕ skō′pĭ	tɪ ˈlɛs kə pɪ ˈtɛl ɪ ˌsko pɪ ˈtɛl ə ˌsko pɪ
temerity	ti MER uh ti ti MER i ti	tĕ mĕr′ĭ tĭ tĕ mĕr′ĭ tĭ	tɪ ˈmɛr ə tɪ tɪ ˈmɛr ɪ tɪ
temperament	TEM puhr uh muhnt	tĕm′pēr *à* mĕnt §§ 9, 50(22)	ˈtɛm pər ə mənt, -prə-
temperature	TEM puhr uh chuhr TEM puhr uh tyuhr	tĕm′pēr *à* tūr §§ 9, 50(3̆1)	ˈtɛm pər ə tʃɚ, -tjɚ, -prə-; *ES* -tʃə(r), -tjə(r)
tempestuous	tem PES choo uhs tem PES tyoo uhs	tĕm pĕs′tŭ ŭs § 50(25, 33)	tɛm ˈpɛs tʃʊ əs tɛm ˈpɛs tjʊ əs
temporal	TEM puh ruhl	tĕm′pŏ răl § 9	ˈtɛm pə rəl, -prəl
temporarily	TEM puh *rer* uh li TEM puh *rer* i li TEM puh ruhr i li *Emph., also:* *tem* puh REHR uh li	tĕm′pŏ rĕr′ĭ lĭ tĕm′pŏ rĕr′ĭ lĭ tĕm′pŏ rĕr ĭ lĭ §§ 20(2), 24(9) *Emph., also:* tĕm′pŏ râr′ĭ lĭ § 51(11)	ˈtɛm pə ˌrɛr ə lɪ ˈtɛm pə ˌrɛr ɪ lɪ ˈtɛm pə rə rɪ lɪ *Emph., also:* ˌtɛm pə ˈrɛr ə lɪ; *ES* -ˈrɛər-
tenable	TEN uh b'l TEE nuh b'l	tĕn′*à* b'l tē′n*à* b'l § 47(1)	ˈtɛn ə bl̩ ˈti nə bl̩
tenacious	ti NAY shuhs	tĕ nā′shŭs	tɪ ˈne ʃəs
tenacity	ti NAS uh ti ti NAS i ti	tĕ năs′ĭ tĭ tĕ năs′ĭ tĭ	tɪ ˈnæs ə tɪ tɪ ˈnæs ɪ tɪ
tenet	TEN et TEN it TEE net TEE nit	tĕn′ĕt tĕn′ĭt tē′nĕt tē′nĭt §§ 24(5), 47(3)	ˈtɛn ɛt ˈtɛn ɪt ˈti nɛt ˈti nɪt
tenure	TEN yuhr	tĕn′ûr	ˈtɛn jɚ; *ES* -jə(r)
tepid	TEP id	tĕp′ĭd	ˈtɛp ɪd

	SIMPLIFIED	DIACRITICAL	PHONETIC
termagant	TUHR muh guhnt	tûr′má gănt	'tɝ mə gənt; *ES also* 'tɜ-
terminate (v.)	TUHR muh nayt TUHR mi nayt	tûr′mĭ nāt tûr′mĭ nāt	'tɝ mə net, -mɪ-; *ES also* 'tɜ-
—— (adj.)	TUHR muh nit TUHR muh nayt	tûr′mĭ năt §§ 20 (8, 9), 50(2)	'tɝ mə nɪt, -net; *ES also* 'tɜ-
terrace	TER is TER uhs	tĕr′ĭs tĕr′ás § 47(1)	'ter ɪs 'ter əs
terrestrial	te RES tri uhl tuh RES tri uhl	tĕ rĕs′trĭ ăl tĕ rĕs′trĭ ăl	tɛ 'rɛs trɪ əl tə 'rɛs trɪ əl
terrible	TER uh b'l TER i b'l	tĕr′ĭ b'l tĕr′ĭ b'l § 47(1)	'ter ə bļ 'ter ɪ bļ
terrific	te RIF ik tuh RIF ik	tĕ rĭf′ĭk tĕ rĭf′ĭk § 47(1)	tɛ 'rɪf ɪk tə 'rɪf ɪk
tertian	TUHR shuhn	tûr′shăn	'tɝ ʃən; *ES also* 'tɜ-
tertiary	TUHR shi er i *B.*, TUHR shuh ri	tûr′shĭ ĕr′ĭ §§ 20(2), 24(9) *B.*, tûr′shá rĭ § 51(4)	'tɝ ʃɪ ˌer ɪ; *ES also* 'tɜ- *B.*, 'tɝ ʃə rɪ; *ES* *also* 'tɜ-
testate (adj., n.)	TES tayt TES tit	tĕs′tāt §§ 20 (8, 9), 50(2)	'tɛs tet 'tɛs tɪt
—— (v.i.)	TES tayt	tĕs′tāt	'tɛs tet
testator	tes TAY tuhr TES tay tuhr	tĕs tā′tēr tĕs′tā tēr	tɛs 'te tɚ, 'tɛs te-; *ES* -tə(r)
testimony	TES tuh *moh* ni TES ti *moh* ni *B.*, TES tuh muhn i	tĕs′tĭ mō′nĭ tĕs′tĭ mō′nĭ *B.*, tĕs′tĭ mŭn ĭ § 51(4)	'tɛs tə ˌmo nɪ 'tɛs tɪ ˌmo nɪ *B.*, 'tɛs tə mən ɪ
tête-à-tête	TAYT uh TAYT *te* tah TEHT *F.*, *tet* ah TEHT	tāt′á tāt′ tĕ′tá tât′ *F.*, tĕt′á tât′ § 47(1)	'tet ə 'tet ˌtɛ ta 'teːt *F.*, tɛt a 'teːt
Teuton	TYOO tuhn TOO tuhn TYOO t'n TOO t'n	tū′tŏn tū′t'n §§ 48(2), 50(32)	'tju tən 'tu tən 'tju tņ 'tu tņ
textile	TEKS til TEKS tail § 50(34)	tĕks′tĭl tĕks′tīl §§ 28(5), 47(2)	'teks tɪl 'teks taɪl
texture	TEKS chuhr TEKS tyuhr	tĕks′tûr § 50(31)	'teks tʃɚ, -tjɚ; *ES* -tʃə(r), -tjə(r)
Thames (**England**)	temz	tĕmz § 1	tɛmz
than (usu. unstressed)	th̶uhn th̶'n 'n -n	th̶ăn th̶'n 'n -n	ðən ðņ ņ n

	SIMPLIFIED	DIACRITICAL	PHONETIC
—— (rarely stressed)	than	thăn § 16	ðæn
thank	thangk	thăngk	θæŋk
thanksgiving	thangks GIV ing THANGKS *giv* ing	thăngks gĭv′ĭng thăngks′gĭv′ĭng § 11	θæŋks ˈgɪv ɪŋ ˈθæŋks ˌgɪv ɪŋ
that (demonstrative)	that	thăt	ðæt
—— (conj., relative)	thuht	thăt §§ 16, 49(18)	ðət
thatch	thach	thăch	θætʃ
the (adj. or definite article)	USUALLY UNSTRESSED *Unaccented before a consonant:* thuh	USUALLY UNSTRESSED *Unaccented before a consonant:* thē §§ 39(5), 49(18)	USUALLY UNSTRESSED *Unaccented before a consonant:* ðə, ð
	Unaccented before a vowel and sometimes before words beginning with y-, hee-, hi-, he-, *and* hay-*:* thi	*Unaccented before a vowel and sometimes before words beginning with* y-, hē-, hĭ-, hĕ-, *and* hā-*:* thĭ	*Unaccented before a vowel and sometimes before words beginning with* j-, hi-, hɪ-, hɛ-, *and* he-*:* ðɪ
	RARELY STRESSED (See "a," page 1.)	RARELY STRESSED (See "a," indefinite article.)	RARELY STRESSED (See comments under "a," page 1.)
	Emph. or alone: thee	*Emph. or alone:* thē § 16	*Emph. or alone:* ði
the (adv.)	thuh thi	thē thĕ	ðə ðɪ
theater, **theatre**	THEE uh tuhr THI uh tuhr	thē′*á* tēr thē̦′*á* tēr §§ 1, 24(2), 39(7)	ˈθi ə tɚ, ˈθɪ-; *ES* -tə(r)
them	them *Unstressed:* thuhm th'm	thĕm *Unstressed:* thĕm th'm §§ 16, 49(18)	ðɛm *Unstressed:* ðəm ðm̩
theology	thi OL uh ji thee OL uh ji	thē ŏl′ō jĭ thē ŏl′ō jĭ § 1	θɪ ˈɑl ə dʒɪ, θi-; *ES also* -ˈɒl-
theorem	THEE uh ruhm	thē′ō rĕm	ˈθi ə rəm
therapeutic	*ther* uh PYOO tik	thĕr′*á* pū′tĭk § 48(2)	ˌθɛr ə ˈpju tɪk
therapeutics	*ther* uh PYOO tiks	thĕr′*á* pū′tĭks §§ 48(2), 50(32)	ˌθɛr ə ˈpju tɪks

there (adv.)	T̶HEHR	t̶hâr §§ 16, 39(5), 49(18)	'ðer, 'ðær, ˌðer, ˌðær; ES 'ðeə(r), 'ðæə(r), ˌðeə(r), ˌðæə(r)
	Lightly stressed: *ther*	*Lightly stressed:* t̶hĕr	*Lightly stressed:* ðer, ðær; ES ðeə(r), ðæə(r)
	Unstressed: t̶huhr	*Unstressed:* t̶hĕr § 16	*Unstressed:* ðɚ, ES ðə(r)
therefor	t̶hehr FAWR	t̶hâr fôr'	ðer 'fɔr, ðær-; ES ðæə 'fɔə(r) E also ðeə-
therefore	T̶HEHR fohr T̶HEHR fawr	t̶hâr'fōr § 34(3)	'ðer for, 'ðær-, -fɔr; ES 'ðæə foə(r), E also 'ðeə-, -fɔə(r)
thereof	t̶hehr OV T̶HEHR ov t̶hehr OF	t̶hâr ŏv' t̶hâr'ŏv t̶hâr ŏf' §§ 11, 47(1)	ðer 'ɑv, -'ɒv, 'ðer ɑv, -'ɒv, ðer 'af, ˌ-ɒf; E also ðeər-, S also ðær-
therewith	t̶hehr WIT̶H t̶hehr WITH	t̶hâr wĭt̶h' t̶hâr wĭth' §§ 39(5), 49(18)	ðer 'wɪð, ðær-, -'wɪθ; ES ðæə-, E also ðeə-
therewithal	*t̶hehr* with AWL	t̶hâr'wĭt̶h ôl' § 11	ˌðer wɪð 'ɔl, ˌðær-; ES ˌðæə-, E also ˌðeə-
thermometer	thuhr MOM i tuhr thuh MOM i tuhr	thĕr mŏm'ĕ tēr §§ 24(7), 48(1)	θɚ 'mɑm ɪ tɚ, (*by dissimilation*) θə-; ES θə-, -tə(r), ES also -'mɒm-
Thetis	THEE tis	thē'tĭs	'θi tɪs
thief	theef	thēf	θif
thieving	THEEV ing	thēv'ĭng § 50(24)	'θiv ɪŋ
thinking	THINGK ing	thĭngk'ĭng § 50(24)	'θɪŋk ɪŋ
third	*thuhrd*	thûrd § 40(6)	θɝd; ES also θɜd
thirty	THUHR ti	thûr'tĭ	'θɝ tɪ; ES also θɜ-
this	t̶his	thĭs §§ 39(5), 49(18)	ðɪs
Thisbe	THIZ bi	thĭz'bĕ	'θɪz bɪ
thistle	THIS 'l	thĭs' 'l	'θɪs l̩
thither	T̶HIT̶H uhr *Often:* THIT̶H uhr	t̶hĭt̶h'ĕr *Often:* thĭt̶h'ĕr §§ 39(5), 49(18), 51(9)	ðɪð ɚ; ES -ə(r) *Often:* θɪð ɚ; ES -ə(r)

Thor	thawr	thôr	θɔr; *ES* θɔə(r)
thought	thawt	thôt	θɔt
thousand	THOW zuhnd THOW z'nd	thou′zănd thou′z'nd	ˈθaʊ zənd, -zn̩d, -zn̩
threat	thret	thrĕt	θrɛt
three	three	thrē	θri
three-pence	THRIP uhns THREP uhns	thrĭp′ĕns thrĕp′ĕns	ˈθrɪp əns ˈθrɛp əns
threshold	THRESH ohld THRESH hohld	thrĕsh′ōld thrĕsh′hōld	ˈθrɛʃ old ˈθrɛʃ hold
throstle	THROS 'l	thrŏs′ 'l	ˈθrɑs l̩; *ES also* ˈθrɒs-
through	throo	thrōō §§ 40(4), 48(2)	θru
Thursday	THUHRZ di	thûrz′dĭ § 20(9)	ˈθɝz dɪ, -de; *ES also* ˈθɜz-
thus (adv.)	*thuhs*	th̶ŭs § 40(6)	ðʌs
thyme	taim § 50(34)	tīm § 39(7)	taɪm
thyroid	THAI roid § 50(34)	thī′roid	ˈθaɪ rɔɪd
tiara	tai EHR uh tai AY ruh ti AH ruh § 50(34)	tī âr′ȧ tĕ ä′rȧ	taɪ ˈɛr ə, -ˈe rə, tɪ ˈɑ rə; *ES also* taɪ ˈɛər ə
Tiber	TAI buhr § 50(34)	tī′bēr	ˈtaɪ bɚ; *ES* bə(r)
ticklish	TIK lish	tĭk′lĭsh	ˈtɪk lɪʃ, -lɪʃ
timbre	TIM buhr TAM buhr *F.,* TAN br'	tĭm′bēr tăm′bēr *F.,* tăɴ′ br' § 20(14)	ˈtɪm bɚ, ˈtæm-; *ES* -bə(r) *F.,* tɛ̃:br [tæ:m br]
time	taim § 50(34)	tīm	taɪm
times	taimz § 50(34)	tīmz § 48(3)	taɪmz
tincture	TINGK chuhr TINGK tyuhr	tĭngk′tŭr §§ 47(1), 50(31)	ˈtɪŋk tʃɚ, -tjɚ; *ES* -tʃə(r), -tjə(r)
tiny	TAI ni § 50(34)	tī′nĭ	ˈtaɪ nɪ
tirade (n.)	TAI rayd ti RAYD § 50(34) *Rarely:* ti RAHD	tī′rād tĭ rād′ *Rarely:* tĭ räd′ §§ 47(3), 51(8)	ˈtaɪ red tɪ ˈred, tə- *Rarely:* tɪ ˈrɑd
—— (v.i.)	ti RAYD TAI rayd § 50(34)	tĭ rād′ tī′rād	tɪ ˈred, tə- ˈtaɪ red
tissue	TISH yoo TISH oo	tĭsh′ū tĭsh′ōō § 47(1)	ˈtɪʃ ju ˈtɪʃ u

	SIMPLIFIED	DIACRITICAL	PHONETIC
tithe	tai͡th § 50(34)	tīth	taɪð
Titian	TISH uhn	tĭsh'ăn	'tɪʃ ən
	TISH i uhn	tĭsh'ĭ ăn	'tɪʃ ɪ ən
tobacco	tuh BAK oh	tŭ băk'ō	tə 'bæk o, -ə
	toh BAK oh	tŏ băk'ō	to 'bæk o
tolerable	TOL uhr uh b'l	tŏl'ēr a b'l § 9	'tal ər ə bḷ; *ES* also 'tɒl-
tolerant	TOL uhr uhnt	tŏl'ēr ănt § 9	'tal ər ənt; *ES* also 'tɒl-
tomato	tuh MAY toh	tŏ mā'tō	tə 'me to, -tə
	tuh MAH toh	tŏ mä'tō	tə 'ma to, -tə
	Occas.:	*Occas.:*	*Occas.:*
	tuh MAT uh	tŏ măt'ŏ §§ 47(3), 51(8)	tə 'mæt ə
tomb	toom	to͡om § 21(1)	tum
tonsillitis	*ton* suh LA͡I tis	tŏn'sĭ li'tĭs	ˌtan sə 'laɪ tɪs, -sɪ-; *ES* also ˌtɒn-
	ton si LA͡I tis	tŏn'sĭ li'tĭs	
took	to͡ok	to͡ok § 34(22)	tʊk
topaz	TOH paz	tō'păz	'to pæz
topography	toh POG ruh fi	tŏ pŏg'ra fĭ	to 'pag rə fɪ, tə-, -'pɒg-
	tuh POG ruh fi		
torment (v.t.)	tawr MENT	tôr měnt'	tər 'mɛnt; *ES* tɔə-
—— (n.)	TAWR ment	tôr'měnt §§ 12, 50(22)	'tɔr mɛnt; *ES* 'tɔə-
tornadic	tawr NAD ik	tôr năd'ĭk	tɔr 'næd ɪk; *ES* tɔə-
tornado	tawr NAY doh	tôr nā'dō	tɔr 'ne do; *ES* tɔə-
torpedo	tawr PEE doh	tôr pē'dō	tɔr 'pi do; *ES* tɔə-
torrid	TOR id	tŏr'ĭd	'tar ɪd, 'tɔr-, 'tɒr-
	TAWR id	tôr'ĭd § 34(7)	
tortoise	TAWR tuhs	tôr'tŭs	'tɔr təs, -tɪs; *ES* 'tɔə-
	TAWR tis	tôr'tĭs § 47(3)	
	Also:	*Also:*	*Also:*
	TAWR toiz	tôr'toiz	'tɔr tɔɪz, -tɔɪs, -tɪz; *ES* 'tɔə-
	TAWR tois	tôr'tois	
	TAWR tiz	tôr'tĭz	
tortuous	TAWR cho͡o uhs	tôr'tŭ ŭs § 50(33)	'tɔr tʃʊ əs, -tjʊ-; *ES* 'tɔə-
	TAWR tyo͡o uhs		
torture	TAWR chuhr	tôr'tûr	'tɔr tʃɚ, -tjɚ; *ES* 'tɔə tʃə(r), -tjə(r)
	TAWR tyuhr	§ 50(31)	
toss	taws	tŏs § 34(7)	tɔs
	tos		tɒs
tour	to͡or	to͡or § 34(21)	tʊr; *ES* tʊə(r)

	SIMPLIFIED	DIACRITICAL	PHONETIC
tournament	TŌŎR nuh muhnt	tŏŏr′na̍ mĕnt	'tʊr nə mənt, 'tɜ-; ES 'tʊə nə-,
	TOOR nuh muhnt	tōōr′na̍ mĕnt	't̯ɜ-
	TUHR nuh muhnt	tûr′na̍ mĕnt § 47(3)	
tourney	TŌŎR ni	tŏŏr′nĭ	'tʊr nɪ, 'tɜ-; ES
	TOOR ni	tōōr′nĭ	'tʊə nɪ, ES also
	TUHR ni	tûr′nĭ §§ 40(4), 47(3)	'tɜ-
tourniquet	TŌŎR nuh ket	tŏŏr′nĭ kĕt	'tʊr nə ket, -nɪ-;
	TŌŎR ni ket	tŏŏr′nĭ kĕt	ES 'tʊə-
	Often:	*Often:*	*Often:*
	TUHR nuh ket	tûr′nĭ kĕt	'tɜ nə ket, -nɪ-,
	TUHR ni ket	tûr′nĭ kĕt	-nɪ ke; ES also
	TUHR ni kay	tûr′nĭ kā § 51(9)	'tɜ-
tout (colloq. or slang)	towt	tout	taʊt
toward (adj., adv.)	TOH uhrd	tō′ĕrd	'to ə·d, tord, tɔrd;
	tohrd	tōrd §§ 34(3),	ES 'to əd, toəd,
	tawrd	42(3), 47(1)	E also tɔəd
—— (prep.)	TOH uhrd	tō′ĕrd	'to ə·d, tord, tɔrd;
	tohrd	tōrd	ES 'to əd, toəd,
	tawrd	§§ 47(1), 51(4)	E also tɔəd
	B., tŏŏ WAWRD tuh WAWRD	B., tŏŏ wôrd′ tŏ wôrd′	B., tʊ 'word, tə-; ES -'woəd
towel	TOW uhl § 50(34)	tou′ĕl § 47(1)	'taʊ əl, -ɛl, taʊl̩
toxin	TOK sin	tŏk′sĭn	'tɑk sɪn; ES also 'tɒk-
trachea	TRAY ki uh	trā′kē a̍	'tre kɪ ə
	truh KEE uh	tra̍ kē′a̍ § 47(3)	trə 'ki ə
tragedian	truh JEE di uhn	tra̍ jē′dĭ ăn	trə 'dʒi dɪ ən
tragedy	TRAJ uh di	trăj′ĕ dĭ	'trædʒ ə dɪ
trance	trans trahns	trȧns § 20(5)	træns; E also trans, trɑns
tranquil	TRANG kwil	trăng′kwĭl	'træŋ kwɪl
	TRAN kwil	trăn′kwĭl §§ 33(4), 47(2)	'træn kwɪl
tranquillity, tranquility	tran KWIL uh ti	trăn kwĭl′ĭ̆ tĭ	træn 'kwɪl ə tɪ
	tran KWIL i ti	trăn kwĭl′ĭ tĭ	træn 'kwɪl ɪ tɪ
	trang KWIL uh ti	trăng kwĭl′ĭ̆ tĭ	træŋ 'kwɪl ə tɪ
	trang KWIL i ti	trăng kwĭl′ĭ tĭ § 47(2)	træŋ 'kwɪl ɪ tɪ
transact	trans AKT	trăns ăkt′	træns 'ækt
	tran ZAKT	trăn zăkt′ §§ 47(1), 49(19)	træn 'zækt

	SIMPLIFIED	DIACRITICAL	PHONETIC
transfer (v.)	trans FUHR	trăns fûr′	træns ˈfɝ; *ES* -ˈfɜ(r)
	Often: TRANS fuhr	*Often:* trăns′fĕr § 51(9)	*Often:* ˈtræns fɚ; *ES* -fə(r)
—— (n., adj.)	TRANS *fuhr* TRANS fuhr	trăns′fûr trăns′fĕr §§ 40(7), 49(19)	ˈtræns fɝ, -fɚ; *ES* -fɜ(r), -fə(r)
transference	trans FUHR uhns TRANS fuhr uhns	trăns fûr′ĕns trăns′fĕr ĕns § 49(19)	træns ˈfɝ əns, ˈtræns fɚ-; *ES also* -ˈfɜr-, -fər-
transient	TRAN shuhnt	trăn′shĕnt § 47(3)	ˈtræn ʃənt
transition	tran ZISH uhn tran SIZH uhn tran SISH uhn	trăn zĭsh′ŭn trăn sĭzh′ŭn trăn sĭsh′ŭn § 47(3)	træn ˈzɪʃ ən træn ˈsɪʒ ən træn ˈsɪʃ ən
translate	trans LAYT *Often:* TRANS layt	trăns lāt′ *Often:* trăns′lāt § 51(9)	træns ˈlet *Often:* ˈtræns let
transmigrate	trans MAI grayt TRANS muh grayt TRANS mi grayt § 50(34)	trăns mī′grāt trăns′mŭ grāt trăns′mĭ grāt § 49(19)	træns ˈmaɪ gret ˈtræns mə gret ˈtræns mɪ gret
transmigration	*trans* mai GRAY shuhn *trans* muh GRAY shuhn *trans* mi GRAY shuhn	trăns′mī grā′shŭn trăns′mŭ grā′shŭn trăns′mĭ grā′shŭn	ˌtræns maɪ ˈgre ʃən ˌtræns mə ˈgre ʃən ˌtræns mɪ ˈgre ʃən
transparent	trans PEHR uhnt	trăns pâr′ĕnt § 20(2)	træns ˈper ənt, -ˈpær-; *E also* -ˈpeər-
transport (v.)	trans POHRT trans PAWRT	trăns pōrt′ § 34(3)	træns ˈport, -ˈpɔrt; *ES* -ˈpoət, *E also* -ˈpɔət
—— (n.)	TRANS pohrt TRANS pawrt	trăns′pōrt §§ 12, 34(3), 49(19)	ˈtræns port, -pɔrt; *ES* -poət, *E also* -pɔət
transverse (v.t., adj.)	trans VUHRS	trăns vûrs′ § 11	træns ˈvɝs; *ES* -ˈvɜs
—— (n., adv.)	trans VUHRS TRANS vuhrs	trăns vûrs′ trăns′vûrs § 49(14)	træns ˈvɝs, ˈtræns vɝs; *ES* -ˈvɜs, -vɜs
travail ("*labor*")	TRAV ayl TRAV 'l	trăv′āl trăv′ 'l § 51(7)	ˈtræv el ˈtræv l̩
traverse (v., n., adj.)	TRAV uhrs TRAV *uhrs*	trăv′ĕrs trăv′ûrs § 40(6, 7)	ˈtræv ɚs, -ɝs; *ES* -əs, *also* -ɜs

—— (adv.)	TRAV uhrs truh VUHRS	trăv′ĕrs tra̍ vûrs′	'træv ɚs, trə 'vɝs; ES -əs, also -'vɜs
traversed (adj.)	TRAV uhrst TRAV *uhrst*	trăv′ĕrst trăv′ûrst §§ 40(6), 50(4)	'træv ɚst, -ɝst; ES -əst, also -ɜst
treason	TREE z'n	trē′z'n	'tri zn̩
treasure	TREZH uhr TREZH ŏŏr	trĕzh′ēr trezh′ŏŏr § 47(1)	'trɛʒ ɚ, -ʊr; ES -ə(r), -ʊə(r)
treasury	TREZH uhr i	trĕzh′ēr ĭ	'trɛʒ ər ɪ
treatise	TREE tis B., TREE tiz	trē′tĭs § 47(2) B., trē′tĭz § 51(4)	'tri tɪs B., 'tri tɪz
tremendous	tri MEN duhs	trĕ mĕn′dŭs	trɪ 'mɛn dəs
tremor	TREM uhr TREE muhr	trĕm′ēr trē′mēr § 47(3)	'trɛm ɚ, 'tri mɚ; ES -ə(r), -mə(r)
trenchant	TREN chuhnt	trĕn′chănt	'trɛn tʃənt
trespass	TRES puhs	trĕs′pa̍s	'trɛs pəs, -pæs; E also -pas, -pɑs
tribunal	trai͡ BYOO nuhl trai͡ BYOO n'l tri BYOO nuhl tri BYOO n'l	trī bū′năl trī bū′n'l trĭ bū′năl trĭ bū′n'l §§ 28(3), 48(2)	traɪ 'bju nəl traɪ 'bju nl̩ trɪ 'bju nəl trɪ 'bju nl̩
tribune (n.)	TRIB yoon *Emph. speech:* TRIB YOON	trĭb′ūn *Emph. speech:* trĭb′ūn′	'trɪb jun *Emph. speech:* 'trɪb 'jun
—— "*an Ameri- can news- paper*," often	tri BYOON	trĭ būn′ §§ 48(2), 51(11)	trɪ 'bjun
tributary	TRIB yŏŏ *tĕr* i	trĭb′ŭ tĕr′ĭ §§ 13, 20(2), 24(9), 47(1), 51(4)	'trɪb jʊ ˌtɛr ɪ, -jə-, -ju-
	B., TRIB yŏŏ tuhr i	B., trĭb′ŭ tĕr ĭ	B., 'trɪb jʊ tə rɪ
tribute	TRIB yoot	trĭb′ūt	'trɪb jut
Trieste	tri EST *It.*, tree ES tay	trĕ ĕst′ *It.*, trĕ ĕs′tå	trɪ 'ɛst *It.*, tri 'ɛs te
trilogy	TRIL uh ji	trĭl′ŏ jĭ	'trɪl ə dʒɪ
trimeter	TRIM i tuhr	trĭm′ĕ tēr	'trɪm ɪ tɚ; ES -tə(r)
Trinidad	TRIN uh *dad* TRIN i dad	trĭn′ĭ dăd′ trĭn′ĭ dăd	'trɪn ə ˌdæd 'trɪn ɪ dæd
trio	TREE oh TRAI͡ oh § 50(34) *In music, usu.:* TREE oh	trē′ō trī′ō *In music, usu.:* trē′ō §§ 47(3), 51(6)	'tri o 'traɪ o *In music, usu.:* 'tri o

	SIMPLIFIED	DIACRITICAL	PHONETIC
tripartite	trī͡ PAHR tā͡it TRIP uhr tā͡it § 50(34)	trī pär′tīt trĭp′ēr tīt § 47(3)	traɪ 'par taɪt, 'trɪp ɚ-; ES -'pa:-, -ə-, E also -'pa:-
triplicate (adj., n.) —— (v.t.)	TRIP luh kit TRIP li kit TRIP luh kayt TRIP li kayt	trĭp′lĭ kât trĭp′lĭ kât trĭp′lĭ kāt trĭp′lĭ kāt § 20(8, 9)	'trɪp lə kɪt 'trɪp lɪ kɪt 'trɪp lə ket 'trɪp lɪ ket
tripod	TRĪ͡ pod § 50(34)	trī′pŏd	'traɪ pad; ES also -pɒd
trivial	TRIV i uhl	trĭv′ĭ ăl §§ 9, 47(2)	'trɪv ɪ əl, 'trɪv jəl
trombone	TROM bohn trom BOHN	trŏm′bōn trŏm bōn′ § 47(2)	'tram bon, tram 'bon; ES also 'trɒm-, trɒm-
troth	trawth troth trohth	trôth §§ 34(7), 47(3) trōth	trɔθ trɒθ troθ
troubadour	TROO buh dōōr TROO buh dawr TROO buh dohr	trōō′bȧ dōōr trōō′bȧ dôr trōō′bȧ dōr § 34(21)	'tru bə dʊr, -dɔr, -dor; ES -dʊə(r), -doə(r), E also -dɔə(r)
troublous	TRUHB luhs	trŭb′lŭs § 50(25)	'trʌb ləs
trough	trawf trof Often (dial.): trawth troth	trôf Often (dial.): trôth §§ 34(7), 51(2)	trɔf trɒf Often (dial.): trɔθ trɒθ
trousers	TROW zuhrz	trou′zērz	'traʊ zɚz; ES -zəs
trousseau	troo SOH TROO soh	trōō′sō′ trōō′sō	ˌtru 'so 'tru so
trow (v.–arch.)	troh	trō	tro, traʊ
truant	TROO uhnt	trōō′ănt § 48(2)	'tru ənt
truculent	TRUHK yŏŏ luhnt TROO kyŏŏ luhnt	trŭk′û lĕnt trōō′kû lĕnt § 47(1)	'trʌk ju lənt, -jə-, -ju-, 'tru kjʊ-, -kjə-
true	troo	trōō §§ 40(4), 48(2)	tru
truffle	TRUHF ′l TROO f′l TRŌŌF ′l	trŭf′ ′l trōō′f′l trōōf′ ′l § 47(3)	'trʌf l̩ 'tru fl̩ 'trʊf l̩
truism	TROO iz′m	trōō′ĭz′m § 48(2)	'tru ɪzm̩, -ɪz əm

	SIMPLIFIED	DIACRITICAL	PHONETIC
truncheon	TRUHN chuhn	trŭn′chŭn §§ 22(6), 47(2)	'trʌn tʃən
truth	trooth	trōōth §§ 40(4), 48(2)	truθ
truths	troothz trooths	trōōthz trōōths §§ 39(5), 48(2, 3), 50(6)	truðz truθs
tryst	trist traist § 50(34)	trĭst trīst § 47(3)	trɪst traɪst
tub	*tuhb*	tŭb § 40(6)	tʌb
tube	tyoob toob	tūb §§ 40(4), 48(2), 50(32)	tjub tub
tubercular	tyoo BUHR kyŏŏ luhr too BUHR kyŏŏ luhr tyŏŏ BUHR kyuh luhr tuh BUHR kyuh luhr	tū bûr′kū lẽr §§ 48(2), 50(32)	tju 'bɝ kjʊ lɚ, tu-, tjʊ-, tə-, -kjə-, -kju-; *ES also* -'bɜ-, *ES* -lə(r)
tuberculosis	tyoo *buhr* kyŏŏ LOH sis too *buhr* kyŏŏ LOH sis tyŏŏ *buhr* kyuh LOH sis tuh *buhr* kyuh LOH sis	tū bûr′kū lō′sĭs §§ 48(2), 50(32)	tju ˌbɝ kjʊ 'lo sɪs, tu-, tjʊ-, tə-, -kjə-, -kju-; *ES also* -ˌbɜ-
Tuesday	TYOOZ di TOOZ di	tūz′dĭ §§ 20(9), 40(4), 48(2), 50(32)	'tjuz dɪ 'tuz dɪ
tulip	TYOO luhp TOO luhp TYOO lip TOO lip	tū′lĭp tū′lĭp §§ 48(2), 50(32)	'tju ləp 'tu ləp 'tju lɪp 'tu lɪp
tumor, tumour	TYOO muhr TOO muhr	tū′mẽr §§ 48(2), 50(32)	'tju mɚ, 'tu-; *ES* -mə(r)
tumult (n.)	TYOO *muhlt* TOO *muhlt* *B.*, TYOO muhlt TOO muhlt	tū′mŭlt *B.*, tū′mŭlt §§ 40(6), 48(2), 50(32), 51(4)	'tju mʌlt 'tu mʌlt *B.*, 'tju məlt 'tu məlt
tumultuous	tyoo MUHL chŏŏ uhs too MUHL tyŏŏ uhs	tū mŭl′tū ŭs §§ 50(25, 32, 33)	tju 'mʌl tʃʊ əs tu 'mʌl tjʊ əs
tune	tyoon toon	tūn §§ 40(4), 48(2), 50(32)	tjun tun
tunic	TYOO nik TOO nik	tū′nĭk §§ 48(2), 50(32)	'tju nɪk 'tu nɪk

	SIMPLIFIED	DIACRITICAL	PHONETIC
tuning	TYOON ing TOON ing	tūn′ĭng §§ 48(2), 50(24, 32)	'tjun ɪŋ 'tun ɪŋ
turbine	TUHR bin TUHR bain § 50(34) *Among engineers, usu.:* TUHR bain	tûr′bĭn tûr′bīn §§ 28(6), 47(1) *Among engineers, usu.:* tûr′bīn § 51(6)	'tɝ bɪn, -baɪn; *ES also* 'tɜ- *Among engineers, usu.:* 'tɝ baɪn; *ES also *'tɜ-
turbulent	TUHR byo͞o luhnt	tûr′bû lĕnt	'tɝ bjʊ lənt, -bjə-, -bju-; *ES also *'tɜ-
turgid	TUHR jid	tûr′jĭd	'tɝ dʒɪd; *ES also *'tɜ-
turn	*tuhrn*	tûrn § 40(6)	tɝn; *ES also* tɜn
turquoise	TUHR koiz TUHR kwoiz tuhr KOIZ	tûr′koiz tûr′kwoiz tēr koiz′ § 47(3)	'tɝ kɔɪz, -kwɔɪz, tɚ 'kɔɪz; *ES also* 'tɜ-, *ES* tə-
Tuscan	TUHS kuhn	tŭs′kăn	'tʌs kən
tutelage	TYOO ti lij TOO ti lij	tū′tĕ lĭj §§ 48(2), 50(1, 32)	'tju tɪ lɪdʒ 'tu tɪ lɪdʒ
tutor	TYOO tuhr TOO tuhr	tū′tēr §§ 40(4), 48(2), 50(32)	'tju tɚ, 'tu-; *ES *-tə(r)
Tuxedo	*tuhk* SEE doh	tŭk sē′dō § 40(6)	tʌk 'si do, -də
twelfth	twelfth	twĕlfth	twɛlfθ
twelfths	twelfths	twĕlfths § 48(3)	twɛlfθs
twenty	TWEN ti	twĕn′tĭ	'twɛn tɪ
two	too	tōō § 42(3)	tu
tympanum	TIM puh nuhm	tĭm′pá năm	'tɪm pə nəm
typhoid	TAI foid § 50(34)	tī′foid § 11	'taɪ fɔɪd
typhoon	tai FOON § 50(34)	tī fōōn′	taɪ 'fun
typhus	TAI fuhs § 50(34)	tī′fŭs	'taɪ fəs
tyrannic	ti RAN ik tai RAN ik § 50(34)	tĭ răn′ĭk tī răn′ĭk	tɪ 'ræn ɪk taɪ 'ræn ɪk
tyrannical	ti RAN i kuhl tai RAN i kuhl § 50(34)	tĭ răn′ĭ kăl tī răn′ĭ kăl	tɪ 'ræn ɪ kəl taɪ 'ræn ɪ kəl
tyrannize	TIR uh naiz § 50(34)	tĭr′ă nīz	'tɪr ə naɪz
tyranny	TIR uh ni	tĭr′ă nĭ	'tɪr ə nɪ
tyrant	TAI ruhnt § 50(34)	tī′rănt	'taɪ rənt
tyro, tiro	TAI roh § 50(34)	tī′rō	'taɪ ro
Tyrol, Tirol	TIR ol ti ROHL *G.,* tee ROHL	tĭr′ŏl tĭ rōl′ *G.,* tē rōl′	'tɪr ɑl, -ɒl, -əl tɪ 'rol *G.,* ti 'rol

U

ubiquitous	yoo BIK wuh tuhs yoo BIK wi tuhs	ū bĭk′wĭ tŭs ū bĭk′wĭ tŭs	ju 'bɪk wə təs ju 'bɪk wɪ təs
ugly	UHG li	ŭg′lĭ	'ʌg lɪ
Ukraine	YOO krayn yoo KRAYN B., yoo KRAIN	ū′krān û krān′ B., û krīn′ §§ 28(5), 51(4)	'ju kren ju 'kren B., ju 'kraɪn
ukelele	yoo kuh LAY li Haw., oo kŏŏ LAY lay	ū′kŭ lā′lĕ Haw., ŏŏ′kŏŏ lā′ lā	ˌju kə 'le lɪ Haw., ˌu kʊ 'le le
ulterior	uhl TIER i uhr uhl TIR i uhr uhl TEER i uhr	ŭl tēr′ĭ ēr § 24(2) ŭl tēr′ĭ er	ʌl 'tɪər ɪ ɚ, -'tɪr-, -'tir-; ES -'tɪər ɪ ə(r)
ultimate (adj., n.)	UHL tuh mit UHL ti mit	ŭl′tĭ mĭt ŭl′tĭ mĭt § 20(8, 9)	'ʌl tə mɪt 'ʌl tɪ mɪt
Ulysses	yŏŏ LIS eez	û lĭs′ēz	ju 'lɪs iz, ju-
umbrage	UHM brij	ŭm′brĭj	'ʌm brɪdʒ
umbrella	uhm BREL uh	ŭm brĕl′a § 40(6)	ʌm 'brel ə, əm-
umpire	UHM païr § 50(34)	ŭm′pīr	'ʌm paɪr; ES -paɪə(r)
unanimous	yŏŏ NAN uh muhs yŏŏ NAN i muhs	û năn′ĭ mŭs û năn′ĭ mŭs	ju 'næn ə məs, -ju-, -ɪ məs
unconscious	uhn KON shuhs	ŭn kŏn′shŭs §§ 40(6), 49(20), 50(25)	ʌn 'kɑn ʃəs; ES also -'kɒn-
unction	UHNGK shuhn	ŭngk′shŭn § 33(4)	'ʌŋk ʃən
unctuous	UHNGK chŏŏ uhs UHNGK tyŏŏ uhs	ungk′tŭ ŭs §§ 50(25, 33)	'ʌŋk tʃʊ əs 'ʌŋk tju əs
understudy	UHN duhr stuhd i	ŭn′dēr stŭd′ĭ § 49(21)	'ʌn dɚ ˌstʌd ɪ; ES -də ˌstʌd ɪ
unduly	uhn DYOO li uhn DOO li	ŭn dū′lĭ §§ 40(6), 48(2), 49(20), 50(32)	ʌn 'dju lɪ ʌn 'du lɪ
unequivocal	uhn i KWIV uh kuhl	ŭn′ĕ kwĭv′ŏ kăl §§ 40(6), 49(20)	ˌʌn ɪ 'kwɪv ə kəl, -kl̩

	SIMPLIFIED	DIACRITICAL	PHONETIC
unfrequent (adj.)	*uhn* FREE kwuhnt	ŭn frē′kwĕnt §§ 40(6), 49(20)	ʌn ′fri kwənt
unfrequented	*uhn* fri KWENT ed	ŭn′frĕ kwĕnt′ĕd	ˌʌn frɪ ′kwɛnt ɛd
	uhn fri KWENT id	ŭn′frĕ kwĕnt′ĭd §§ 24(5), 40(6), 49(20)	ˌʌn frɪ ′kwɛnt ɪd
unguent	UHNG gwuhnt	ŭng′gwĕnt	′ʌŋ gwənt
unison	YOO nuh suhn	ū′nĭ sŭn	′ju nə sən
	YOO ni suhn	ū′nĭ sŭn	′ju nɪ sən
	YOO nuh s'n	ū′nĭ s'n	′ju nə sṇ
	YOO nuh zuhn	ū′nĭ zŭn	′ju nə zən
	YOO ni zuhn	ū′nĭ zŭn	′ju nɪ zən
	YOO nuh z'n	ū′nĭ z'n § 47(3)	′ju nə zṇ
university	*yoo* nuh VUHR suh ti	ū′nĭ vûr′sĭ tĭ	ˌju nə ′vɝ sə tɪ, -nɪ-, -sɪ-; *ES*
	yoo ni VUHR si ti	ū′nĭ vûr′sĭ tĭ	*also* -′vɝ-
unlearned (n., adj.)	uhn LUHR ned	ŭn lûr′nĕd	ʌn ′lɝ nɛd, -nɪd;
	uhn LUHR nid	ŭn lûr′nĭd §§ 24(5), 40(6), 49(20)	*ES also* -′lɝ-
—— (adj. also: "*not gained by study; natural*")	*uhn* LUHRND	ŭn lûrnd′ § 40(6)	ʌn ′lɝnd; *ES also* -′lɝnd
unprecedented	*uhn* PRES i *den* ted	ŭn prĕs′ĕ dĕn′tĕd	ʌn ′prɛs ɪ ˌdɛn tɛd
	uhn PRES i *den* tid	ŭn prĕs′ĕ dĕn′tĭd §§ 24(5), 40(6), 49(20)	ʌn ′prɛs ɪ ˌdɛn tɪd
unsavory, unsavoury	*uhn* SAY vuhr i	ŭn sā′vēr ĭ §§ 40(6), 49(20)	ʌn ′se vər ɪ, -′se vrɪ
unsought	*uhn* SAWT	ŭn sôt′ §§ 40(6), 49(20)	ʌn ′sɔt
until	uhn TIL	ŭn tĭl′	ən ′tɪl
	uhn TIL	ŭn tĭl′ §§ 40(6), 49(20)	ʌn ′tɪl
untoward	*uhn* TOH uhrd	ŭn tō′ĕrd	ʌn ′to ɚd, -′tord,
	uhn TOHRD	ŭn tōrd′	-′tɔrd; *ES* -əd,
	uhn TAWRD	§§ 34(3), 40(6), 49(20)	-′toəd, *E also* -′tɔəd
unusual	*uhn* YOO zhŏŏ uhl	ŭn ū′zhŏŏ ăl §§ 40(6), 49(20)	ʌn ′ju ʒʊ əl
unwary	*un* WEHR i	ŭn wâr′ĭ	ʌn ′wɛr ɪ,
	un WAY ri	§§ 20(2), 40(6), 49(20)	-′wær ɪ, -′we rɪ; *ES also* -′wɛər ɪ
uplift (v.)	*uhp* LIFT	ŭp lĭft′	ʌp ′lɪft
—— (n., adj.)	UHP *lift*	ŭp′lĭft′	′ʌp ˌlɪft
—— "*uplifted*" (adj.–arch.)	*uhp* LIFT	ŭp lĭft′ §§ 40(6), 49(22)	ʌp ′lɪft

	SIMPLIFIED	DIACRITICAL	PHONETIC
uproot	*uhp* ROOT	ŭp rōōt′	ʌp 'rut
	uhp RŎŎT	§§ 34(22), 40(6), 49(22)	ʌp 'rʊt
upset (v.)	*uhp* SET	ŭp sĕt′	ʌp 'sɛt
—— (adj.)	*uhp* SET	ŭp sĕt′ § 11	ʌp 'sɛt
—— (n.)	UHP *set*	ŭp′sĕt′ §§ 11, 12, 40(6), 49(22)	'ʌp ˌsɛt
urbane	*uhr* BAYN	ûr bān′ § 40(6)	ɝ 'ben; *ES also* ɜ-
urbanity	*uhr* BAN uh ti	ûr băn′ĭ tĭ	ɝ 'bæn ə tɪ, -ɪ tɪ;
	uhr BAN i ti	ûr băn′ĭ tĭ § 40(6)	*ES also* ɜ-
urea	yŏŏ REE uh	û rē′á	ˌjʊ 'ri ə, 'jʊ rɪ ə,
	YŌŌ ri uh	ū′rĕ á § 40(4)	'jʊr ɪ ə; *ES also*
	YOO ri uh		'jʊər-
	YŌŌR i uh		
	Among doctors and chemists, usu.:	*Among doctors and chemists, usu.:*	*Among doctors and chemists, usu.:*
	yŏŏ REE uh	û rē′á § 51(6)	jʊ 'ri ə
urn	*uhrn*	ûrn § 40(6)	ɝn; *ES also* ɜn
Uruguay	YOO rŏŏ gway	ū′rŏŏ gwā	'ju rʊ gwe, 'jʊ-,
	YŌŌR ŏŏ gway	ūr′ŏŏ gwā	'jʊr-, -rə-, 'ʊr u-
	YOOR ŏŏ gway		
	Sp., oo roo GWAI	*Sp.,* ōō′rōō gwī′	*Sp.,* ˌu ru 'gwaɪ
usage	YOOS ij	ūs′ĭj	'jus ɪdʒ
	YOOZ ij	ūz′ĭj § 47(3)	'juz ɪdʒ
use (v.)	yooz	ūz	juz
—— (n.)	yoos	ūs § 38(4)	jus
used (adj.)	yoozd	ūzd	juzd
used (to)–past tense of "*use*"	*Before vowels or voiced con-sonants, usu.:*	*Before vowels or voiced con-sonants, usu.:*	*Before vowels or voiced con-sonants, usu.:*
	yoozd	ūzd	juzd
	yooz	ūz	juz
	Also:	*Also:*	*Also:*
	yoost	ūst	just
	yoos	ūs § 47(1)	jus
usually	YOO zhŏŏ uhl i	ū′zhŏŏ ăl ĭ § 50(20)	'ju ʒʊ əl ɪ
usurer	YOO zhŏŏ ruhr	ū′zhŏŏ rēr	'ju ʒʊ rɚ, -ʒɚ-; *ES*
	YOO zhuh ruhr	§ 40(11)	-rə(r)
usurious	yoo ZHŌŌR i uhs	û zhŏŏr′ĭ ŭs §§ 40(6), 47(2)	ju 'ʒʊr ɪ əs
usurp	yoo ZUHRP	û zûrp′ § 40(11)	ju 'zɝp, jʊ-; *ES*
	yŏŏ ZUHRP		*also* -'zɜp
usury	YOO zhŏŏ ri	ū′zhŏŏ rĭ §§ 40(11), 47(1)	'ju ʒʊ rɪ, -ʒə-, -zʊ-
utensil	yoo TEN sil	û tĕn′sĭl	ju 'tɛn sɪl, -jʊ-,
	yoo TEN s'l	û tĕn′s'l §§ 31(3), 40(11)	-sl̩

Utica (N.Y.)	YOO ti kuh	ū′tĭ ká	'ju tɪ kə
utter (v.)	UHT uhr	ŭt′ĕr § 51(7)	'ʌt ɚ; ES -ə(r)

V

vacate	VAY kayt	vā′kāt § 47(3)	've ket, və 'ket, ve-
vacation	vay KAY shuhn	vâ kā′shŭn § 47(3)	ve 'ke ʃən, və-, vɪ-
vaccinate	VAK suh nayt VAK si nayt	văk′sĭ nāt văk′sĭ nāt § 22(2)	'væk sə net, -sɪ-, -sn̩ et
vaccine	VAK seen VAK sin	văk′sēn văk′sĭn § 47(3)	'væk sin 'væk sɪn
vacillate	VAS uh layt VAS i layt	văs′ĭ lāt văs′ĭ lāt	'væs ə let 'væs ɪ let
vacillation	*vas* uh LAY shuhn *vas* i LAY shuhn	văs′ĭ lā′shŭn văs′ĭ lā′shŭn	ˌvæs ə 'le ʃən ˌvæs ɪ 'le ʃən
vacuity	vuh KYOO uh ti va KYOO i ti	vă kū′ĭ tĭ vă kū′ĭ tĭ § 48(2)	və 'kju ə tɪ væ 'kju ɪ tɪ
vacuous	VAK yŏŏ uhs	văk′û ŭs § 50(25)	'væk ju əs
vagaries	vuh GEHR iz vuh GAY riz	vá gâr′ĭz vá gā′rĭz §§ 20(2), 47(1)	və 'gɛr ɪz, -'ge rɪz, ve-; *ES also* -'gɛər-
vagary	vuh GEHR i vuh GAY ri	vá gâr′ĭ vá gā′rĭ §§ 20(2), 47(1)	və 'gɛr ɪ, -'ge rɪ, ve-; *ES also* -'gɛər-
vagrant	VAY gruhnt	vā′grănt	've grənt
vague	vayg	vāg	veg
Valenciennes	*F.,* vah lahN SYEN	vá′läⁿ′syĕn′	*F.,* va lɑ̃ 'sjɛn
	vuh *len* si ENZ *val* uhn si ENZ	vá lĕn′sĭ ĕnz′ văl′ĕn sĭ ĕnz′ §§ 20(14), 47(1)	və ˌlɛn sɪ 'ɛnz ˌvæl ən sɪ 'ɛnz
valet (n., v.)	VAL et VAL it	văl′ĕt văl′ĭt § 24(5)	'væl ɛt 'væl ɪt
—— (noun also: pseudo-French)	VAL ay val AY	văl′â văl ā′ § 47(3)	'væl e væl 'e
valiant	VAL yuhnt	văl′yănt	'væl jənt
valise	vuh LEES *B.,* vuh LEEZ	vá lēs′ § 47(2) *B.,* vá lēz′ § 51(4)	və 'lis *B.,* və 'liz

	SIMPLIFIED	DIACRITICAL	PHONETIC
Valparaiso (Ind.)	*val* puh RAY zoh	văl′pá rā′zō	ˌvæl pə ˈre zo
Valparaiso (Chile)	*val* puh RA͡I soh	văl′pá rĭ′sō	ˌvæl pə ˈraɪ so
	val puh RA͡I zoh	văl′pá rĭ′zō	ˌvæl pə ˈraɪ zo
—— *Sp.,* **Valpa-** raíso	*Sp., vahl* pah rah EE soh	*Sp.,* vähl′pä rä ē′sō	*Sp.,* ˌbɑl pɑ rɑ ˈi so
valuable	VAL yo͝o uh b'l	văl′û á b'l § 9	ˈvæl ju ə b!, -ju b!, -jə-
value	VAL yoo	văl′ū § 34(23)	ˈvæl ju, -ju-
vanilla	vuh NIL uh	vá nĭl′á	və ˈnɪl ə
vanquish	VANG kwish	văng′kwĭsh § 33(4)	ˈvæŋ kwɪʃ
vantage	VAN tij VAHN tij	vȧn′tĭj § 20(5)	ˈvæn tɪdʒ; *E also* ˈvan-, ˈvɑn-
vapid	VAP id	văp′ĭd	ˈvæp ɪd
variable	VEHR i uh b'l VAY ri uh b'l	vâr′ĭ á b'l § 20(2)	ˈver ɪ ə b!, ˈvær-, ˈve rɪ-; *ES also* ˈveər-
variegated	VEHR i uh *gayt* ed VAY ri uh *gayt* ed VEHR i uh *gayt* id VAY ri uh *gayt* id VEHR i *gayt* ed VAY ri *gayt* ed VEHR i *gayt* id VAY ri *gayt* id	vâr′ĭ ĕ gāt′ĕd vâr′ĭ ĕ gāt′ĭd vâr′ĭ gāt′ĕd vâr′ĭ găt′ĭd §§ 20(2), 24(5)	ˈver ɪ ə ˌget ɛd, ˈvær-, ˈve rɪ-, -ɪd, ˈver ɪ ˌget ɛd, ˈvær-, ˈve rɪ-, -ɪd; *ES also* ˈveər-
various	VEHR i uhs VAY ri uhs	vâr′ĭ ŭs § 20(2)	ˈver ɪ əs, ˈvær-, ˈve rɪ-; *ES also* ˈveər-
vase	vays vayz *B.,* vahz vawz	vās vāz § 47(3) *B.,* väz vôz § 51(4)	ves vez *B.,* vɑz vɔz
Vaseline, vaseline	VAS uh leen VAS uh lin	văs′ĕ lēn văs′ĕ lĭn §§ 28(6), 47(1)	ˈvæs ə lin, -lɪn, ˈvæs ! in, -ɪn
vast	vast vahst	vȧst § 20(5)	væst; *E also* vast, vɑst
vaudeville	VOHD vil VAW di vil *B.,* VOH duh vil	vōd′vĭl vô′dĕ vĭl *B.,* vō′dĕ vĭl § 51(4)	ˈvod vɪl ˈvɔ dɪ vɪl *B.,* ˈvo də vɪl
vault	vawlt	vôlt	vɔlt
vaunt	vawnt vahnt	vônt vänt § 47(3)	vɔnt, vant, vɒnt
vegetable	VEJ i tuh b'l	vĕj′ĕ tá b'l § 9	ˈvedʒ ɪ tə b!, ˈvedʒ tə-

	SIMPLIFIED	DIACRITICAL	PHONETIC
vegetarian	*vej* i TEHR i uhn *vej* i TAY ri uhn	vĕj′ĕ târ′ĭ ăn § 20(2)	ˌvedʒ ɪ 'tɛr ɪ ən, -'te rɪ-; *ES also* -'tɛər-
vegetate	VEJ i tayt	vĕj′ĕ tāt	'vedʒ ɪ tet
vehemence	VEE i muhns VEE uh muhns VEE hi muhns	vē′ĕ mĕns vē′ĕ mĕns vē′hĕ mĕns	'vi ɪ məns 'vi ə məns 'vi hɪ məns
vehement	VEE i muhnt VEE uh muhnt VEE hi muhnt	vē′ĕ mĕnt vē′ĕ mĕnt vē′hĕ mĕnt § 27(1)	'vi ɪ mənt 'vi ə mənt 'vi hɪ mənt
vehemently	VEE i muhnt li VEE uh muhnt li VEE hi muhnt li	vē′ĕ mĕnt lĭ vē′ĕ mĕnt lĭ vē′hĕ mĕnt lĭ § 50(20)	'vi ɪ mənt lɪ 'vi ə mənt lɪ 'vi hɪ mənt lɪ
vehicle	VEE uh k'l VEE i k'l VEE huh k'l VEE hi k'l	vē′ĭ k'l vē′ĭ k'l vē′hĭ k'l vē′hĭ k'l §§ 27(1), 47(1)	'vi ə kl̩ 'vi ɪ kl̩ 'vi hə kl̩ 'vi hɪ kl̩
vehicular	vi HIK yŏŏ luhr	vĕ hĭk′ŭ lēr	vɪ 'hɪk ju lɚ, -jə-, -ju-; *ES* -lə(r)
velocipede	vi LOS uh peed vi LOS i peed	vĕ lŏs′ĭ pēd vĕ lŏs′ĭ pēd	vɪ 'las ə pid, -ɪ pid; *ES also* -'lɒs-
venal	VEE nuhl VEE n'l	vē′năl vē′n'l § 33(2)	'vi nəl 'vi nl̩
venerable	VEN uhr uh b'l	vĕn′ēr *a* b'l § 20(2)	'vɛn ər ə bl̩, 'vɛn rə-
Venezuela	*ven* i ZWEE luh *ven* i ZWEE lah *American Spanish* *or Spanish:* *vay* nay SWAY lah *ve* ne SWE lah *ve* ne THWE lah	vĕn′ĕ zwē′l*a* vĕn′ĕ zwē′lä *American Spanish* *or Spanish:* vā′nå swā′lä vĕ′nĕ swĕ′lä vĕ′nĕ thwĕ′lä § 45(3)	ˌvɛn ɪ 'zwi lə ˌvɛn ɪ 'zwi lɑ *American Spanish* *or Spanish:* ˌbe ne 'swe la ˌbɛ nɛ 'swe la ˌbɛ nɛ 'θwe la
venial	VEE ni uhl	vē′nĭ ăl § 28(9)	'vi nɪ əl, 'vin jəl
Venice	VEN is	vĕn′ĭs	'vɛn ɪs
venison	VEN i z'n *B.*, VEN z'n	vĕn′ĭ z'n § 47(3) *B.*, vĕn′z'n § 51(4)	'vɛn ɪ zn̩ *B.*, 'vɛn zn̩
venture	VEN chuhr VEN tyuhr	vĕn′tûr §§ 40(11), 50(31)	'vɛn tʃɚ, -tjɚ; *ES* -tʃə(r), -tjə(r)
Venus	VEE nuhs	vē′nŭs	'vi nəs
veracity	vuh RAS uh ti vi RAS i ti	vĕ răs′ĭ tĭ vĭ răs′ĭ tĭ	və 'ræs ə tɪ vɪ 'ræs ɪ tɪ
verandah	vuh RAN duh	vĕ răn′d*a*	və 'ræn də

	SIMPLIFIED	DIACRITICAL	PHONETIC
verbose	*vuhr* BOHS vuhr BOHS	vûr bōs′ § 40(6, 7)	vɝ 'bos, vɚ-; *ES also* vɜ-, *ES* və-
verbosity	*vuhr* BOS uh ti *vuhr* BOS i ti vuhr BOS uh ti	vûr bŏs′ĭ tĭ vûr bŏs′ĭ tĭ § 40(6, 7)	vɝ 'bɑs ə tɪ, vɚ-, -ɪ tɪ; *ES also* vɜ-, -'bɒs-, *ES* və-
verdure	VUHR juhr VUHR dyuhr VUHR jŏŏr	vûr′dŭr §§ 40(11), 50(33)	'vɝ dʒɚ, -dʒʊr, -djɚ, -djʊr; *ES also* 'vɜ dʒə(r), -dʒʊə(r), -djə(r), -djʊə(r)
veritable	VER uh tuh b'l VER i tuh b'l	vĕr′ĭ ta b'l vĕr′ĭ ta b'l	'vɛr ə tə bl̩ 'vɛr ɪ tə bl̩
Versailles **(France)**	*ver* SAH y′ *Angl.:* vuhr SAYLZ vehr SAI § 50(34)	vĕr′sä′y′ *Angl.:* vēr sālz′ vâr sī′ § 51(1)	*F.,* vɛr 'sɑːj *Angl.:* vɚ 'selz, vɛr 'saɪ; *ES* və-, *also* vɛə-
versatile	VUHR suh til VUHR suh tail § 50(34)	vûr′sa tĭl vûr′sa tīl §§ 28(5), 47(2), 50(13)	'vɝ sə tɪl, -taɪl; *ES also* 'vɜ sə-
verse	*vuhrs*	vûrs § 40(6)	vɝs; *ES also* vɜs
version	VUHR shuhn	vûr′shŭn	'vɝ ʃən; *ES* 'vɜ-
—— *"a translation; a particular account or description,"* popularly	VUHR zhuhn	vûr′zhŭn § 50(28)	'vɝ ʒən; *ES also* 'vɜ-
vertebra	VUHR ti bruh	vûr′tĕ bra	'vɝ tɪ brə; *ES also* 'vɜ-
vertabrae **(one n. pl.)**	VUHR ti bree	vûr′tĕ brē	'vɝ tɪ bri; *ES also* 'vɜ-
vertigo	VUHR ti goh *As Latin, occas.:* vuhr TAI goh vuhr TEE goh	vûr′tĭ gō *As Latin, occas.:* vēr tī′gō vēr tē′gō §§ 47(1), 51(11)	'vɝ tɪ go; *ES also* 'vɜ- *As Latin, occas.:* vɚ 'taɪ go, -'ti-; *ES* və-
very	VER i	vĕr′ĭ	'vɛr ɪ
vestibule	VES tuh byool VES ti byool	vĕs′tĭ būl vĕs′tĭ būl § 48(2)	'vɛs tə bjul 'vɛs tɪ bjul
vestige	VES tij	vĕs′tĭj	'vɛs tɪdʒ
vestigial	ves TIJ i uhl	vĕs tĭj′ĭ ăl	vɛs 'tɪdʒ ɪ əl
veteran	VET uhr uhn	vĕt′ēr ăn § 9	'vɛt ər ən, 'vɛt rən

veterinary	VET uhr uh *ner* i	vĕt′ēr ĭ nĕr′ĭ	'vet ər ə ˌner ɪ
	VET uhr i *ner* i	vĕt′ēr ĭ nĕr′ĭ	'vet ər ɪ ˌner ɪ
	VET uhr i *nay* ri	§§ 20(2), 24(9), 51(4)	'vet ər ɪ ˌne rɪ
	B., VET uhr uh nuhr i	*B.*, vĕt′ēr ĭ nēr ĭ	*B.*, 'vet ər ə nə rɪ
	VET ′n ri § 51(14)	vĕt′ ′n rĭ	'vet n̩ rɪ
via (n., prep.)	V͡AI uh § 50(34)	vī′a͡	'vaɪ ə, 'vi ə
viaduct	V͡AI uh *duhkt* § 50(34)	vī′a͡ dŭkt § 40(6)	'vaɪ ə dʌkt
viand	V͡AI uhnd § 50(34)	vī′a͡nd	'vaɪ ənd
vibration	va͡i BRAY shuhn	vī brā′shŭn	vaɪ 'bre ʃən
vibrative	V͡AI bruh tiv § 50(34)	vī′bra͡ tĭv § 50(3)	'vaɪ brə tɪv
vicar	VIK uhr	vĭk′ēr	'vɪk ɚ; *ES* -ər
viceroy	V͡AIS roi § 50(34)	vīs′roi	'vaɪs rɔɪ
vice versa	V͡AI si VUHR suh	vī′sĕ vûr′sa͡	'vaɪ sɪ 'vɝ sə; *ES also* -'vɜ-
vicissitude	vuh SIS uh tyood	vŭ sĭs′ĭ tūd	və 'sɪs ə tjud
	vuh SIS uh tood		və 'sɪs ə tud
	vi SIS i tyood	vĭ sĭs′ĭ tūd	vɪ 'sɪs ɪ tjud
	vi SIS i tood	§§ 48(2), 50(32)	vɪ 'sɪs ɪ tud
victory	VIK tuh ri	vĭk′tŏ rĭ § 9	'vɪk tə rɪ, -trɪ
victual	VIT ′l	vĭt′ ′l	'vɪt l̩
victuals	VIT ′lz	vĭt′ ′lz § 48(3)	'vɪt l̩z
view	vyoo	vū § 48(2)	vju
viking	V͡AI king	vī′kĭng	'vaɪ kɪŋ
	VEE king	vē′kĭng § 47(1)	'vi kɪŋ
villa	VIL uh	vĭl′a͡	'vɪl ə
villain	VIL uhn	vĭl′ĭn	'vɪl ən
vindictive	vin DIK tiv	vĭn dĭk′tĭv	vɪn 'dɪk tɪv
vine	va͡in § 50(34)	vīn	vaɪn
viol	V͡AI uhl § 50(34)	vī′ŭl	'vaɪ əl, vaɪl
viola (musical instrument)	vi OH luh	vĕ ō′la͡	vɪ 'o lə
	va͡i OH luh	vĭ ō′la͡	vaɪ 'o lə
	V͡AI uh luh	vī′ŏ la͡	'vaɪ ə lə
	It., vee OH lah VYAW lah	*It.*, vē ō′lä vyô′lä § 47(3)	*It.*, vi 'ɔ: la
violet	V͡AI uh let	vī′ŏ lĕt	'vaɪ ə let
	V͡AI uh lit	vī′ŏ lĭt §§ 24(5), 34(12)	'vaɪ ə lɪt

	SIMPLIFIED	DIACRITICAL	PHONETIC
violin	va͡i uh LIN § 50(34) *Used attributively, often:* VA͡I uh *lin*	vī′ô lĭn′ *Used attributively, often:* vī′ô lĭn′ § 11	ˌvaɪ ə ′lɪn *Used attributively, often:* ′vaɪ ə ˌlɪn
violoncello	*vee* uh lon CHEL oh *vee* uh luhn CHEL oh va͡i uh lon CHEL oh va͡i uh luhn CHEL oh va͡i uh lon SEL oh	vē′ô lŏn chĕl′ō vē′ô lŏn chĕl′ō vī′ô lŏn chĕl′ō vī′ô lŏn chĕl′ō vī′ô lŏn sĕl′ō § 47(3)	ˌvi ə lɑn ′tʃɛl o, -lən-, ˌvaɪ ə lɑn ′tʃɛl o -lən-, ˌvaɪ ə lɑn ′sɛl o; *ES also* -lɒn-
virile	VIR il VA͡I ril *B.,* VIR a͡il VA͡I ra͡il § 50(34)	vĭr′ĭl vī′rĭl *B.,* vĭr′īl vī′rīl §§ 28(5), 47(3), 51(4)	′vɪr ɪl ′vaɪ rɪl *B.,* ′vɪr aɪl ′vaɪ raɪl
virility	vi RIL uh ti vi RIL i ti va͡i RIL uh ti	vĭ rĭl′ĭ tĭ vĭ rĭl′ĭ tĭ vī rĭl′ĭ tĭ § 50(16)	vɪ ′rɪl ə tɪ vɪ ′rɪl ɪ tɪ vaɪ ′rɪl ə tɪ
virtue	VUHR choo VUHR cho͝o VUHR tyoo VUHR tyo͝o	vûr′tũ §§ 40(11), 50(33)	′vɝ tʃu, -tʃʊ, -tjṷ, -tjʊ; *ES also* ′vɝ-
virtuoso	*vuhr* cho͝o OH soh *vuhr* tyo͝o OH soh *vir* too OH soh *It., veer* too OH soh	vûr′tũ ō′sō § 50(33) vĭr′tōō ō′sō *It.,* vēr′tōō ō′sō	ˌvɝ tʃʊ ′o so, -tjʊ-, -tʃu-, -tju-; *ES also* ˌvɝ- ˌvɪr tu ′o so *It.,* ˌvir tu ′o: so
virtuous	VUHR cho͝o uhs VUHR tyo͝o uhs	vûr′tũ ŭs §§ 40(11), 50(25, 32)	′vɝ tʃu əs, -tjʊ-; *ES also* ′vɝ-
virulence	VIR yo͝o luhns VIR o͝o luhns	vĭr′ũ lĕns vĭr′o͝o lĕns § 40(11)	′vɪr jʊ ləns, ′vɪr ʊ-, -jə-, ′vɪr ə-
virulent	VIR yo͝o luhnt VIR o͝o luhnt	vĭr′ũ lĕnt vĭr′o͝o lĕnt § 40(11)	′vɪr jʊ lənt, ′vɪr ʊ-, -jə-, ′vɪr ə-
virus	VA͡I ruhs § 50(34)	vī′rŭs	′vaɪ rəs
viscount	VA͡I *kownt* VA͡I kownt § 50(34)	vī′kount′ vī′kount § 38(2)	′vaɪ ˌkaʊnt ′vaɪ kaʊnt
viscous	VIS kuhs	vĭs′kŭs § 50(25)	′vɪs kəs

	SIMPLIFIED	DIACRITICAL	PHONETIC
vise (*"tool"*)	vīs § 50(34)	vīs	vaɪs
visible	VIZ uh b'l VIZ i b'l	vĭz′ĭ b'l vĭz′ĭ b'l	′vɪz ə bļ ′vɪz ɪ bļ
vision	VIZH uhn	vĭzh′ŭn §§ 9, 38(8, 12), 50(28)	′vɪʒ ən
visor, vizor	VIZ uhr VĪ zuhr § 50(34)	vĭz′ĕr vī′zẽr § 47(1)	′vɪz ɚ, ′vaɪ zɚ; *ES* ə(r), -zə(r)
visual	VIZH yŏŏ uhl VIZH ŏŏ uhl	vĭzh′û ăl vĭzh′ŏŏ ăl §§ 40(11), 47(1)	′vɪʒ jʊ əl ′vɪʒ ʊ əl
vitamin	VĪ tuh min VIT uh min § 50(34)	vī′tȧ mĭn vĭt′ȧ mĭn	′vaɪ tə mɪn ′vɪt ə mɪn
vitiate	VISH i ayt	vĭsh′ĭ āt	′vɪʃ ɪ et
vitriol	VIT ri uhl	vĭt′rĭ ŭl	′vɪt rɪ əl
vivacious	vai VAY shuhs vi VAY shuhs § 50(34)	vī vā′shŭs vĭ vā′shŭs § 47(3)	vaɪ ′ve ʃəs vɪ ′ve ʃəs
vivacity	vai VAS uh ti vai VAS i ti vi VAS uh ti vi VAS i ti § 50(34)	vī văs′ĭ tĭ vī văs′ĭ tĭ vĭ văs′ĭ tĭ vĭ văs′ĭ tĭ	vaɪ ′væs ə tɪ vaɪ ′væs ɪ tɪ vɪ ′væs ə tɪ vɪ ′væs ɪ tɪ
vizier	vi ZĒER vi ZIR vi ZEER VIZ yuhr VIZ i uhr	vĭ zēr′ § 24(2) vĭ zēr vĭz′yẽr vĭz′ĭ ẽr § 47(3)	vɪ ′zɪər, -′zɪr, -′zir; *ES* -′zɪə(r) ′vɪz jɚ, ′vɪz ɪ ɚ; *ES* -jə(r), -ə(r)
Vladivostok	*vla* di vos TAWK *vlah* di vos TAWK *vlah* di vos TOK	vlȧ′dĭ vŏs tôk′ vlä′dĭ vŏs tôk′ vlä′dĭ vŏs tŏk′	ˌvlæ dɪ vas ′tɔk ˌvla dɪ vas ′tɔk ˌvla dɪ vas ′tak; *ES also* ˌvlɒ-, -vɒs-, -′tɒk
	Gaining ground: *vla* di VOS tok	*Gaining ground:* vlä′dĭ vŏs′tŏk § 51(5)	*Gaining ground:* ˌvlæ dɪ ′vas tak; *ES also* -′vɒs tɒk
voice	vois	vois	vɔɪs
volatile	VOL uh til VOL uh tail § 50(34)	vŏl′ȧ tĭl vŏl′ȧ tīl §§ 28(5), 47(2)	′val ə tɪl, -taɪl; *ES also* ′vɒl-
Volga	VOL guh *Russ.*, VAWL gah	vŏl′gȧ *Russ.*, vôl′gä	′val gə, ′vɒl- *Russ.*, ′vɒl gɑ
Voltaire	*vawl* TEHR *vol* TEHR vohl TEHR	vôl′târ′ vŏl′târ′ vōl târ′	*F.*, vɒl ′tɛːr, val ′tɛr, vɒl-, -vol-, -′tær; *ES* -′tæə(r), *E also* -′tɛə(r)

	SIMPLIFIED	DIACRITICAL	PHONETIC
volume	VOL yŏŏm	vŏl′ûm § 40(11)	′val jʊm, -jəm, -jum; *ES also* ′vɒl-
voluminous	vuh LOO mi nuhs vuh LYOO mi nuhs	vŏ lū′mĭ nŭs §§ 48(2), 50(25, 32)	və ′lu mɪ nəs və ′lju mɪ nəs
voluntarily	VOL uhn *ter* uh li VOL uhn *ter* i li	vŏl′ŭn tĕr′ĭ lĭ vŏl′ŭn tĕr′ĭ lĭ § 51(4)	′val ən ˌtɛr ə lɪ, -ɪ lɪ; *ES also* ′vɒl-
	Emph., also: *vol* uhn TEHR uh li	*Emph., also:* vŏl′ŭn târ′ĭ lĭ §§ 20(2), 24(9), 51(11)	*Emph., also:* ˌval ən ′tɛr ə lɪ, -′tær-; *ES also* ˌvɒl-, *ES* -′tæər-, *E also* -′tɛər-
voluntary	VOL uhn *ter* i	vŏl′ŭn tĕr′ĭ §§ 20(2), 24(9)	′val ən ˌtɛr ɪ; *ES also* ′vɒl-
	B., VOL uhn tuhr i VOL uhn tri	*B.,* vŏl′ŭn tĕr ĭ vŏl′ŭn trĭ §§ 13, 51(4)	*B.,* ′vɒl ən tə rɪ ′vɒl ən trɪ
voracious	vuh RAY shuhs voh RAY shuhs	vŏ rā′shŭs § 50(25)	və ′re ʃəs vo ′re ʃəs
votary	VOH tuh ri	vō′tȧ rĭ	′vo tə rɪ
vowel	VOW uhl	vou′ĕl	′vaʊ əl, vaʊl
voyage	VOI ij	voi′ĭj § 50(1)	′vɔɪ ɪdʒ
vulnerable	VUHL nuhr uh b'l	vŭl′nẽr ȧ b'l	′vʌl nər ə bl̩
vulture	VUHL chuhr VUHL tyuhr	vŭl′tûr § 50(31)	′vʌl tʃɚ, -tjɚ; *ES* -tʃə(r), -tjə(r)

W

	SIMPLIFIED	DIACRITICAL	PHONETIC
waffle	WOF 'l	wŏf′ 'l	′waf l̩, ′wɒf-, ′wɔf-
waft	waft wahft	wȧft §§ 20(5), 47(1)	wæft, wɑft, waft; *E often* wɑft, waft
Wagner (Richard)	VAHG nuhr	väg′nẽr	′vɑg nɚ; *ES* -nə(r)
wainscot	WAYN skuht WAYN skot	wān′skŭt wān′skŏt § 47(2)	′wen skət ′wen skɑt; *ES also* -skɒt

waistcoat	WAYST *koht*	wāst′kōt′	'west ˌkot
	WAYS *koht*	wās′kōt′	'wes ˌkot
	WES kuht	wĕs′kŭt §§ 1,	'wes kət
		39(2), 47(3)	
walk	wawk	wôk	wɔk
walnut	WAWL *nuht*	wôl′nŭt	'wɔl nʌt
	WAWL nuht	wôl′nŭt §§ 20(6),	'wɔl nət
		40(6)	
walrus	WAWL ruhs	wôl′rŭs	'wɔl rəs, 'wal-,
	WOL ruhs	wŏl′rŭs § 47(3)	'wɒl-
waltz	wawlts	wôlts	wɔlts
	B., wawls	*B.,* wôls §§ 20(6),	*B.,* wɒls
		39(9), 51(4)	
wampum	WOM puhm	wŏm′pŭm	'wam pəm,
	WOM *puhm*	wŏm′pŭm	'wɒm-, 'wɔm-,
	WAWM puhm	wôm′pŭm § 47(1)	'wam pʌm
wan	won	wŏn	wan, wɒn
wander	WON duhr	wŏn′dēr § 34(6)	'wan dɚ, 'wɒn-;
			ES -də(r)
wanderlust	VAHN duhr *lŏŏst*	vän′dēr lŏŏst′	*G.,* 'van dər ˌlʊst
	WON duhr *luhst*	wŏn′dēr lŭst′	'wan dɚ ˌlʌst,
			'wɒn-; *ES* -də-
want	wont	wŏnt	want, wɒnt, wɔnt
	wawnt	wônt	
		§§ 34(6), 47(3)	
wanted	WONT ed	wŏnt′ĕd	'want ɛd, 'wɒnt-,
	WONT id	wŏnt′ĭd	'wɔnt-, -ɪd
	WAWNT ed	wônt′ĕd	
	WAWNT id	wônt′ĭd § 24(5)	
warrior	WOR i uhr	wŏr′ĭ ēr	'war ɪ ɚ, 'wɒr-,
	WAWR i uhr	wôr′ĭ ēr	'wɔr-, 'wɔr jɚ;
	WAWR yuhr	wôr′yēr	*ES* -ə(r), -jə(r)
		§§ 34(7), 47(3)	
Warwick	WOR ik	wŏr′ĭk	'war ɪk, 'wɒr-,
(England)	WAWR ik	wôr′ĭk §§ 1,	'wɔr-; *ES* 'wɒə-
		34(5, 7), 42(3)	
Warwickshire	WOR ik shir	wŏr′ĭk shĭr	'war ɪk ʃɪr,
	WAWR ik shir	wôr′ĭk shĭr	'wɒr-, 'wɔr-,
	WOR ik shuhr	wŏr′ĭk shēr	-ʃɚ; *ES* -ʃɪə(r),
	WAWR ik shuhr	wôr′ĭk shēr	-ʃə(r)
		§ 34(5, 7)	
wary	WEHR i	wâr′ĭ § 20(2)	'wɛr ɪ, 'wær ɪ,
	WAY ri		'we rɪ; *ES also*
			'wɛər ɪ
was	woz	wŏz	waz, wɒz
	Unstressed:	*Unstressed:*	*Unstressed:*
	wuhz	wŭz § 16	wəz
wash	wosh	wŏsh	waʃ, wɒʃ, wɔʃ
	wawsh	wôsh § 34(6)	
wasp	wosp	wŏsp § 34(6)	wasp, wɒsp, wɔsp

	SIMPLIFIED	DIACRITICAL	PHONETIC
wassail	WOS 'l WOS ayl WAS ayl WAS uhl	wŏs′ 'l wŏs′ăl wăs′ăl wăs′ŭl § 47(1)	'wɑs l̩, 'wɒs-, -el, 'wæs el, -əl, -l̩
watch	woch	wŏch § 34(6)	wɑtʃ, wɒtʃ, wɔtʃ
water	WAW tuhr WOT uhr WAH tuhr	wô′tẽr wŏt′ẽr § 20(6)	'wɔ tɚ, 'wɑt ɚ, 'wɒt-; ES -tə(r), -ə(r)
waylay	*way* LAY	wā′lā′ §§ 11, 47(2)	ˌwe 'le
weary	WĪER i WIR i WEER i	wēr′ĭ § 24(2) wēr′ĭ	'wɪər ɪ, 'wɪr-, 'wir-; ES 'wɪər ɪ
weather	WETH uhr	wĕth′ẽr	'wɛð ɚ; ES -ə(r)
Weber (German surname)	VAY buhr	vā′bẽr	G., 'veː bər; Anglicized, 've bɚ; ES -bə(r)
Wednesday	WENZ di	wĕnz′dĭ §§ 20(9), 23(1), 47(1)	'wɛnz dɪ, -de
Weimer (Germany)	VA͡I mahr *Also (pop.):* VA͡I muhr	vī′mär *Also (pop.):* vī′már	G., 'vaɪ mɑr; Anglicized, 'vaɪ mɑr; ES -mɑː(r), E also -mɑː(r)
weird	wĭerd wird weerd	wērd § 24(2) wērd	wɪərd, wɪrd, wird; ES wɪəd
well	wel	wĕl § 51(7)	wɛl
Wellesley	WELZ li	wĕlz′lĭ	'wɛlz lɪ
were	*wuhr* *Old-fashioned American and occas. or esp. British:* wehr *Unstressed:* wuhr	wûr § 40(6) *Old-fashioned American and occas. or esp. British:* wâr § 51(4) *Unstressed:* wẽr §§ 16, 47(3)	wɝ; ES also wɝ(r) *Old-fashioned American and occas. or esp. British:* wɛr, wær; ES wæə(r), E also wɛə(r) *Unstressed:* wɚ; ES wə(r)
western	WES tuhrn	wĕs′tẽrn	'wɛs tɚn; ES -tən
Westminster	WEST *min* stuhr	wĕst′mĭn′stẽr	'wɛst ˌmɪn stɚ; ES -stə(r)
whack	hwak	hwăk § 49(23)	hwæk
whale	hwayl	hwāl §§ 42(4), 47(1), 49(23)	hwel
wharf	hwawrf	hwôrf § 49(23)	hwɔrf; ES hwɔəf
wharfs (one pl. of *wharf*)	hwawrfs	hwôrfs § 49(23)	hwɔrfs; ES hwɔəfs

	SIMPLIFIED	DIACRITICAL	PHONETIC
wharves (one pl. of *wharf*)	hwawrvz	hwôrvz § 49(23)	hwɔrvz; *ES* hwɔəvz
what (pro.)	hwot *Unstressed:* hwuht wuht	hwŏt *Unstressed:* hwŭt wŭt §§ 16, 42(4), 49(23)	hwɑt, hwɒt *Unstressed:* hwət wət
wheedle	HWEE d'l	hwē′d'l § 49(23)	′hwi dḷ
wheel	hweel	hwēl §§ 42(4), 49(23)	hwil
whelk ("*mollusk*")	hwelk wilk	hwĕlk wĭlk §§ 42(4), 49(23)	hwɛlk wɪlk
whelk ("*pimple*")	hwelk	hwĕlk §§ 49(23), 51(7, 11)	hwɛlk
whelp	hwelp	hwĕlp §§ 42(4), 49(23)	hwɛlp
when	hwen	hwĕn §§ 42(4), 49(23)	hwɛn
whence	hwens	hwĕns § 49(23)	hwɛns
where	hwehr	hwâr §§ 42(4), 49(23)	hwɛr, hwær; *ES* hwæə(r), *E also* hwɛə(r)
wherewith	hwehr WITH hwehr WITH	hwâr wĭth′ hwâr wĭth′ §§ 39(5), 49(18)	hwɛr ′wɪð, -′wɪθ, hwær-; *ES* hwæə(r)-, *E* *also* hwɛə(r)-
whet	hwet	hwĕt §§ 42(4), 49(23)	hwɛt
whether	HWETH uhr	hwĕth′ēr § 49(23)	′hwɛð ɚ; *ES* -ə(r)
whey	hway	hwā §§ 42(4), 49(23)	hwe
which	hwich	hwĭch §§ 42(4), 49(23)	hwɪtʃ
whiff	hwif	hwĭf §§ 42(4), 49(23)	hwɪf
whim	hwim	hwĭm §§ 42(4), 49(23)	hwɪm
whimper	HWIM puhr	hwĭm′pēr §§ 42(4), 49(23)	′hwɪm pɚ; *ES* -pə(r)
whining	HWAIN ing § 50(34)	hwīn′ĭng §§ 42(4), 49(23)	′hwaɪn ɪŋ
whinny	HWIN i	hwĭn′ĭ § 49(23)	′hwɪn ɪ
whip	hwip	hwĭp §§ 42(4), 49(23)	hwɪp
whippoorwill	*hwip* pŏŏr WIL *hwip* puhr WIL HWIP uhr *wil*	hwĭp′pŏŏr wĭl′ hwĭp′pēr wĭl′ hwĭp′ēr wɪl′ § 11	ˌhwɪp pʊr ′wɪl, -pɚ-, ′hwɪp ɚ ˌwɪl; *ES* -pʊə-, -pɚ-, -ə-

	SIMPLIFIED	DIACRITICAL	PHONETIC
whir, whirr	*hwuhr*	hwûr §§ 42(4), 49(23)	hwɝ; *ES also* hwɜ(r)
whirl	*hwuhrl*	hwûrl §§ 40(6), 42(4), 49(23)	hwɝl; *ES also* hwɜl
whisk	hwisk	hwĭsk §§ 42(4), 49(23)	hwɪsk
whisker	HWIS kuhr	hwĭs′kẽr §§ 42(4), 49(23)	'hwɪs kɚ; *ES* -kə(r)
whiskers	HWIS kuhrz	hwĭs′kẽrz §§ 42(4), 49(23), 50(6)	'hwɪs kɚz; *ES* -kəz
whisky, whiskey	HWIS ki	hwĭs′kĭ § 49(23)	'hwɪs kɪ
whisper	HWIS puhr	hwĭs′pẽr §§ 42(4), 49(23)	'hwɪs pɚ; *ES* -pə(r)
white	hwai͡t § 50(34)	hwīt §§ 42(4), 49(23)	hwaɪt
whither	HWITH uhr	hwĭth′ẽr §§ 42(4), 49(23)	'hwɪð ɚ; *ES* -ə(r)
whittle (v.)	HWIT 'l	hwĭt′ 'l § 49(23)	'hwɪt l̩
whiz, whizz	hwiz	hwĭz § 49(23)	hwɪz
whole	hohl	hōl	hol
wholesome	HOHL suhm	hōl′sŭm	'hol səm
wholly	HOHL li HOHL i	hōl′lĭ hōl′ĭ	'hol lɪ 'hol ɪ
whoop	hoop hwoop	ho͞op hwo͞op §§ 34(22), 42(3)	hup hwup
whorl	hwuhrl hwawrl	hwûrl hwôrl § 47(3)	hwɝl, hwɔrl; *ES also* hwɜl, *ES* hwɔəl
why	hwai͡ § 50(34)	hwī §§ 42(4), 49(23)	hwaɪ
widow	WID oh	wĭd′ō §§ 34(25), 50(26)	'wɪd o, -ə
width	width	wĭdth § 47(2)	wɪdθ, wɪtθ
widths	widths	wĭdths § 48(3)	wɪdθs, wɪtθs
wife	wai͡f § 50(34)	wīf	waɪf
wigwam	WIG wom WIG wawm	wĭg′wŏm wĭg′wôm § 47(3)	'wɪg wɑm, -wɒm, -wɔm
William	WIL yuhm	wĭl′yăm	'wɪl jəm
wily	WAIL i § 50(34)	wīl′ĭ	'waɪl ɪ
wince	wins	wĭns § 39(3)	wɪns
wind (*"air"*)	wind	wĭnd § 47(2)	wɪnd
	Noun also, poet. or arch.:	*Noun also, poet. or arch.:*	*Noun also, poet. or arch.:*
	wai͡nd § 50(34)	wīnd § 51(11)	waɪnd
wind (*"turn"*)	wai͡nd § 50(34)	wīnd	waɪnd

windmill	WIND *mil* WIN *mil*	wĭnd′mĭl′ wĭn′mĭl′ §§ 23(1), 47(1)	′wɪnd ͵mɪl ′wɪn ͵mɪl
window	WIN doh	wĭn′dō § 34(25)	′wɪn do, -də
wish	wish	wĭsh	wɪʃ
wistful	WIST fŏŏl WIST f'l	wĭst′fŏŏl wĭst′f'l §§ 31(3), 40(13), 50(11)	′wɪst fʊl, -fəl ′wɪst fḷ
witch	wich	wĭch	wɪtʃ
with	with͟ *If accented, or if* *before a voice-* *less consonant,* *often:* with	wĭth͟ *If accented, or if* *before a voice-* *less consonant,* *often:* wĭth §§ 39(4, 5), 49(18)	wɪð *If accented, or if* *before a voice* *less consonant,* *often:* wɪθ
withdraw	with͟ DRAW with DRAW	wĭth͟ drô′ wĭth drô′ §§ 39(5), 49(18)	wɪð ′drɔ wɪθ ′drɔ
withe	with with͟ waith͟	wĭth wĭth͟ wīth͟ § 47(3)	wɪθ wɪð waɪð
wither	WITH͟ uhr	wĭth͟′ĕr	wɪð ɚ; *ES* -ə(r)
withstand	with͟ STAND with STAND	wĭth͟ stănd′ wĭth stănd′ §§ 39(5), 49(18)	wɪð ′stænd wɪθ ′stænd
wives (n. pl. of *wife*)	waivz § 50(34)	wīvz § 48(3)	waɪvz
woman	WŎŎM uhn	wŏŏm′ăn	′wʊm ən
women	WIM en WIM in	wĭm′ĕn wĭm′ĭn § 24(5)	′wɪm ɛn, -ɪn; -ən
wonder	WUHN duhr	wŭn′dĕr	′wʌn dɚ; *ES* -də(r)
wont	*wuhnt* *B.*, wohnt	wŭnt *B.*, wōnt §§ 1, 34(10), 47(3), 51(4)	wʌnt *B.*, wont
won't (*"will not"*)	wohnt *wuhnt*	wōnt wŭnt	wont wʌnt
wood	wŏŏd	wŏŏd § 34(22)	wʊd
woodbine	WŎŎD *bain*	wŏŏd′bīn′	′wʊd ͵baɪn
Worcester	WŎŎS tuhr	wŏŏs′tĕr	′wʊs tɚ; *ES* -tə(r)
word	*wuhrd*	wûrd	wɝd; *ES also* wɜd
Wordsworth (William)	WUHRDZ *wuhrth*	wûrdz′wûrth § 40(6)	′wɝdz wɝθ; *ES* *also* ′wɜdz wɜθ
work	*wuhrk*	wûrk § 40(6)	wɝk; *ES also* wɜk
world	*wuhrld*	wûrld § 40(6)	wɝld; *ES also* wɜld

	SIMPLIFIED	DIACRITICAL	PHONETIC
worship	WUHR ship	wûr′shĭp	′wɝ ʃɪp; *ES also* ′wɜ-
worsted (*"fabric; yarn"*)	WŎŎS ted WŎŎS tid WŎŎR sted WŎŎR stid	wŏŏs′tĕd wŏŏs′tĭd wŏŏr′stĕd wŏŏr′stĭd §§ 24(5), 47(2)	′wʊs ted, -tɪd, ′wʊr sted, -stɪd, ′wɜ-; *ES also* ′wɜ(r)-
would	wŏŏd *Unstressed:* wuhd uhd ′d	wŏŏd *Unstressed:* wŭd ŭd ′d §§ 1, 16	wʊd *Unstressed:* wəd əd d
wound (*"hurt"*)	woond *Arch. or poet., also:* wownd	wōōnd *Arch. or poet., also:* wound § 47(3)	wund *Arch. or poet., also:* waʊnd
wrack	rak	răk	ræk
wraith	rayth	rāth § 39(5)	reθ
wrangle	RANG g′l	răng′g′l § 50(24)	′ræŋ gl̩
wrap	rap	răp	ræp
wrath	rath rahth *B.,* rawth	răth räth *B.,* rôth §§ 20(5), 47(3), 51(4)	ræθ, rɑθ; *E also* rɑθ *B.,* rɔθ
wreak	reek	rēk	rik
wreath (n.)	reeth	rēth § 39(5)	riθ
wreathe (v.)	reeth	rēth § 39(6)	rið
wreaths (pl. of *wreath*)	reethz	rēthz §§ 39(5), 48(3)	riðz
wren	ren	rĕn	rɛn
wrench	rench	rĕnch § 22(6)	rɛntʃ
wrest	rest	rĕst	rɛst
wrestle	RES ′l	rĕs′ ′l	′res l̩
wrestling	RES ling	rĕs′lĭng § 50(24)	′res lɪŋ, -l̩ŋ
wretch	rech	rĕch	retʃ
wriggle	RIG ′l	rĭg′ ′l	′rɪg l̩
wring	ring	rĭng	rɪŋ
wringer	RING uhr	rĭng′ĕr § 50(24)	′rɪŋ ɚ; *ES* -ə(r)
wrist	rist	rĭst	rɪst
wristband	RIST *band* RIST buhnd RIZ buhnd	rĭst′bănd′ rĭst′bănd rĭz′bănd §§ 39(2), 47(1)	′rɪst ˌbænd ′rɪst bənd ′rɪz bənd
writ	rit	rĭt	rɪt
write	rait § 50(34)	rīt § 1	raɪt
writhe	raith § 50(34)	rīth	raɪð
writing	RAIT ing	rīt′ing § 50(24)	′raɪt ɪŋ

	SIMPLIFIED	DIACRITICAL	PHONETIC
wroth	rawth roth *B.*, rohth	rŏth §§ 34(7), 47(1), 51(4) *B.*, rōth	rɔθ rɒθ *B.*, roθ
wrung	*ruhng*	rŭng § 40(6)	rʌŋ
wry	raı͡ § 50(34)	rī	raɪ

X

Xerxes	ZUHRK seez	zûrk′sēz	'zɝk siz; *ES also* 'zɜk-
xylophone	ZAI͡ luh fohn ZIL uh fohn § 50(34)	zī′lŏ fōn zĭl′ŏ fōn	'zaɪ lə fon 'zɪl ə fon
xylophonist	zaı͡ LOF uh nist zi LOF uh nist	zī lŏf′ŏ nĭst zĭ lŏf′ŏ nĭst	zaɪ 'lɑf ə nɪst, zɪ-; *E also* -'lɒf-

Y

yacht	yot	yŏt § 22(9)	jɑt; *ES also* jɒt
yachts	yots	yŏts §§ 48(3), 50(6)	jɑts; *ES also* jɒts
yard	yahrd	yärd	jɑrd; *ES* jɑːd, *E* *also* jɑːd
ye (pro.)	yee *Unstressed:* yĭ	yē *Unstressed:* yĕ § 16	ji *Unstressed:* jɪ
ye (definite article–arch.)	t̶h̶e̶e̶ (See "the," page 290.) *Also, although* *ignorantly* *and wrongly:*	t̶h̶ē̶ *Also, although* *ignorantly* *and wrongly:*	ði, ðɪ, ðə *Also, although* *ignorantly* *c:nd wrongly:*
——humorously	yee	yē §§ 44(4), 51(3)	ji

	SIMPLIFIED	DIACRITICAL	PHONETIC
yea	yay	yā	je
yearling	YĬER ling YIR ling YEER ling YUHR ling	yĕr′lĭng §§ 24(2), 47(1) yẽr′lĭng yûr′lĭng	ˈjɪər lɪŋ, ˈjɪr-, ˈjir-, ˈjɝ-; ES ˈjɪər-, also -ˈjɝ-
yearn	*yuhrn*	yûrn § 40(6)	jɝn; ES also jɜn
yeast	yeest	yēst	jist
yellow	YEL oh	yĕl′ō § 34(25)	ˈjɛl o, -ə
yeomanry	YOH muhn ri	yō′mǎn rĭ	ˈjo mən rɪ
yes	yes	yĕs	jɛs
yesterday	YES tuhr di YES tuhr day	yĕs′tẽr dĭ yĕs′tẽr dā §§ 20(9), 47(1)	ˈjɛs tɚ dɪ, -de; ES -tə-
yet	yet	yĕt	jɛt
yew	yoo	yōō §§ 40(3), 48(2)	ju
yoke	yohk	yōk	jok
yolk	yohk yohlk	yōk yōlk §§ 31(2), 47(2)	jok jolk
yonder	YON duhr	yŏn′dẽr	ˈjɑn dɚ, ˈjɒn-; ES -də(r)
young	*yuhng*	yŭng §§ 40(6), 50(24)	jʌŋ
younger	YUHNG guhr	yŭng′gẽr § 50(24)	ˈjʌŋ gɚ; ES -gə(r)
youngest	YUHNG gest YUHNG gist	yŭng′gĕst yŭng′gĭst §§ 24(5), 50(9, 24)	ˈjʌŋ gɛst ˈjʌŋ gɪst
your (See *yours*.)	yŏŏr yoor	yŏŏr	jʊr; ES jʊə(r), joə(r), E also jɔə(r)
	Unstressed: yŏŏr yuhr	*Unstressed:* yŏŏr [*weaken vowel*] yẽr §§ 16, 34(21)	*Unstressed:* jʊr, jɚ; ES jʊə(r), joə(r), jə(r), E also jɔə(r)
yours	yŏŏrz yohrz yawrz	yŏŏrz yōrz §§ 34(3), 47(1)	jʊrz, jorz, jɔrz; ES jʊəz, joəz, E also jɔəz
youth	yooth	yōōth § 39(5)	juθ
youths	yooths yoothz	yōōths yōōthz §§ 39(5), 48(3)	juθs juðz

Z

zany	ZAY ni	zā′nĭ	ˈze nɪ
zeal	zeel	zēl	zil
zealot	ZEL uht	zĕl′ŭt	ˈzɛl ət
zealous	ZEL uhs	zĕl′ŭs § 50(25)	ˈzɛl əs
zebra	ZEE bruh	zē′bra̍	ˈzi brə
zenith	ZEE nith	zē′nĭth	ˈzi nɪθ
	B., ZEN ith	B., zĕn′ĭth §§ 47(3), 51(4)	B., ˈzɛn ɪθ
zephyr	ZEF uhr	zĕf′ẽr	ˈzɛf ɚ; ES -ə(r)
zero	ZĬER oh	zẹr′ō	ˈzɪər o, ˈzɪr-,
	ZIR oh	§ 24(2)	ˈzir-; ES ˈzɪər o
	ZEER oh	zēr′ō	
Zeus ("a god")	zyoos	zūs	zjus
	zoos	zo͞os §§ 48(2), 50(32)	zus
zinc	zingk	zĭngk	zɪŋk
zodiac	ZOH di ak	zō′dĭ ăk	ˈzo dɪ æk
zodiacal	zoh DAI uh kuhl § 50(34)	zŏ dĭ′a̍ kăl	zo ˈdaɪ ə kəl, -kl̩
zoölogical	*zoh* uh LOJ i kuhl	zō′ŏ lŏj′ĭ kăl	ˌzo ə ˈlɑdʒ ɪ kəl; ES -ˈlɒdʒ-
zoölogist	zoh OL uh jist	zŏ ŏl′ŏ jĭst	zo ˈɑl ə dʒɪst; ES -ˈɒl-
zoölogy	zoh OL uh ji	zŏ ŏl′ŏ jĭ	zo ˈɑl ə dʒɪ; ES -ˈɒl-

INDEX OF TOPICS